ARAB YOUTH

Arab Youth

Social Mobilization in Times of Risk

Edited by
Samir Khalaf and Roseanne Saad Khalaf

SAQI

In Fond Memory of Albert George Khoury (1948–1971)

ISBN 978-0-86356-457-4

First published 2011 by Saqi Books

© Samir Khalaf and Roseanne Saad Khalaf 2011
Copyright for individual texts rests with the authors.

'Reclaiming Youthfulness' first published in
Life as Politics: How Ordinary People Change the Middle East by Asef Bayat
© 2010 by the Board of Trustees of the Leland Stanford Jr. University
All rights reserved.
Used with the permission of Stanford University Press, www.sup.org.

A full CIP record for this book is available from the
British Library.

A full CIP record for this book is available from the
Library of Congress.

Manufactured in Lebanon

SAQI
26 Westbourne Grove, London W2 5RH
www.saqibooks.com

Contents

Introduction

On the Marginalization and Mobilization of Arab Youth

Samir Khalaf and Roseanne Saad Khalaf

Upon submitting our manuscript in early April 2011, startling manifestations of the new "Arab Spring" were unfolding. The sudden mobilization of mass protest, though long overdue, took observers by surprise. Even seasoned and well-informed scholars had become resigned to treating the profound misgivings of the status quo as an inescapable reality in Arab society. This is not unusual given the seeming docility of disenfranchised groups alongside the power of despotic regimes to reproduce their tyranny.

Soon it became apparent that the uprisings could not be dismissed as merely the short-lived protests of embittered and marginalized groups venting their wrath. The days of autocratic regimes seemed to be coming to an end. Already, the Tunisian and Egyptian uprisings, with limited bloodshed, succeeded in dismantling the aggrandizing and corrupt leadership of Hosni Mubarak and Zine El Abidine Ben Ali. Though seemingly leaderless, protestors in both countries revealed remarkable technological savvy and creativity. More significant, the uprisings displayed this generation's unprecedented level of political awareness and activism.

The great philosophers of the Enlightenment would hardly hesitate to endorse the moral consciousness expressed in the postings which flooded cyberspace during the uprisings. Inevitably amateurish and makeshift, they still displayed attributes of moral secularism and civil vibrancy. They were largely informed by the same universal values which have inspired other revolutions: dignity, autonomy, justice, accountability, transparency, tolerance, and solidarity with the weak. In some respects, the uprisings might well represent a nascent "post-ideological generation."

Many of the young who took to the streets displayed at times admirable and contagious recalcitrance and outright defiance. The Iranian Revolt of 1979 and the Islamic movements of the 1980s and 1990s are history. The common concerns which sparked the uprisings in Tunisia, Egypt, Yemen, Bahrain, and Libya were not ideological or religious. Nor did they evince any manifest interest in class consciousness or economic deprivation. Instead, their unifying ethos is the denouncement of poor governance, oppression, and the recklessness and impunity of tyrants. In short, the "kleptocracy" and "graftocracy" of their countries, despised elites and their families. Even regimes considered immune to the mass discontent which gripped the region – that is, Syria, Jordan, and Morocco – are currently witnessing some of the embryonic manifestations of mass unrest.

The case of Morocco stands out because it is markedly different from the experiences of Egypt, Tunisia and Libya. It initiated serious reforms at least a decade earlier by a king (Mohammad VI) generally admired by his people and seen as irreplaceable. He was in support of the liberalization of the press, and women's rights, and fairly open about the years of oppression by his predecessor (King Hassan II). Yet, marginalized youth were still discontented about widespread corruption and human rights violations. Hence, to many of the protesters on February 20, 2011, the problem does not lie with the monarchy but with the political and economic elite who benefit from the status quo and enjoy political impunity. Perhaps this explains why the protest lacked the outburst of rage and anarchy visible elsewhere in the region.

In sharp contrast, the Egyptian and Libyan protestors were explicitly calling for the removal of Mubarak and Gaddafi, lifting the emergency laws, curbing state torture, and holding fair and free elections. Underlying their demands were expectations of the higher order in support of dignity, freedom, and justice. The social media may have helped in inciting the kernel of the protests, which ultimately succeeded in overthrowing Mubarak, yet what mobilized people in the streets were legitimate grievances intrinsic to the misbegotten neo-liberalisms rampant among the Egyptian elite.

It was not though, as sensationalized by the media, a "Twitter" or "Facebook" revolt. Most revealing in this regard are the changing perspectives of once-radicalized Islamists. For example, movements like Libya's Islamic Fighting Group or Egypt's Jamaat Islamiya are now expressing a new-found keenness for peaceful politics; they are keeping their distance from al-Qa'ida and expressing outright opposition to militant and radical strategies.

In Yemen as well, the bloody tug-of-war between civilian protestors and government forces is also exacerbating the pressures on Ali Saleh. The violence beleaguering the country is clearly an expression of the several explosive fault lines deeply entrenched in its tribal structure, along with North-South rivalry. So far, Ali Saleh has refused to step down, vowing to remain in power until January 2012 when parliamentary elections are scheduled.

The case of Syria is very telling and may well disclose the harbingers of more foreboding transformations. The fact that many Syrians bear no personal grudge or animosity towards their president now seems irrelevant. Unfortunately, Bashar al-Assad appears disinclined to heed demands emanating from the uprisings that, after all, reveal one inescapable reality. Once the threshold of popular discontent is reached, regimes become incapable of holding back the tide of outrage. What begins as an expression of ordinary grievances – in the case of Syria, the Baath's monopoly of power, lifting the country's emergency law of 1963, high levels of corruption, and the pervasive climate of fear and intimidation consecrated by its draconic secret agencies – are bound to grow into irrepressible demands for freedom, dignity, and justice. Alas, in his long-awaited speech (March 31, 2011), Assad made only vague promises to introduce reform. Instead, he heaped blame and culpability on "foreign conspiracy and meddling."

It is too early to speculate on the ultimate outcome of the revolutionary uprisings; one auspicious feature, however, stands out. In varying degrees, they all reveal the genesis of a new generation sparked by the desire for civil liberties, advocacy for human rights, and participatory democracy. The chapters in this volume, the outcome of a three-day (April 2009) gathering of involved scholars, intellectuals, and activists in the region, explore some of the antecedents of the upheavals. As well, they anticipate alternative, "softer" venues of resistance that marginalized youth can mobilize to realize their emancipatory expectations.

Long before the current interest, aroused by the surging manifestations of youthful problems associated with the growing disaffection, exclusion and indignation of young adults in the Arab World have recently sparked considerable debate. The concern is both compelling and timely. After all, the region is characterized by a striking and persisting youthful population. This so-called "youthful demographic bulge" is not only markedly higher than patterns observed elsewhere, it is occurring at an impressionable and vulnerable interlude in the lives of the young. It is also taking place in a setting marked by growing risk and uncertainty; a time when the young are grappling with other existential dilemmas, anguishing private angst, and moral turpitude.

Such uncertainties are exacerbated not only by unresolved local, regional, and global transformation but by the changing character of moral entrepreneurs and societal role models. Again, more than other groups, the young have to face situations in which cultural scripts, messages, and codes of the various agencies of socialization are often inconsistent and irreconcilable. Consider some of the disparate and conflicting messages: religious authority, state, national or secular ideologies, family and kinship groups, peer subculture, popular and cyber culture, and, as of late, the seductive global allures of commodified consumerism, virtual images, and life styles.

The young are caught in a poignant and unsettling predicament: the undermining of traditional vectors of stability and loyalty (family and state) as opposed to the modern alternative sources of education, employment, security, public opinion that have proved unable to fill the void. Another dissonant reality intrudes. They are viewed as the hope of the future, yet stigmatized and feared as disruptive, parasitic forces.

To do comparative justice, both conceptually and empirically, the focus of the volume converges on six distinct but related themes. Part one is devoted to a broad consideration of the conceptual and methodological issues associated with youth as a social category. Here the nature of social exclusion, social rupture, delayed marriage, social movements, and other consequences generated by the skewed demographic bulge are explored. Part two examines how the young are forging meaningful collective identities in times of risk and uncertainty, ambivalence, and fear. Issues of deferred adulthood, agency, and resistance, becoming lost in transition, generational conflict, cognitive dissonance, and collective memory assume relevance. In part three, issues regarding the representation and self-perception of the young are examined in an effort to understand the shifting moral politics at home alongside the unsettling forces of globalization. Part four considers, largely through ethnographic and grounded exploration of youth militancy, neighborhood violence and youth gangs in distinct urban and suburban settings. Part five is devoted to the surge of youthful activism in political movements, advocacy groups, and welfare civic associations. Finally, part six explores how disaffected youth seek expressive outlets through popular arts, street music, and popular culture.

YOUTH AS A SOCIAL CATEGORY

Johanna Wyn's particular interest, exploring the impact of education and work on their health and wellbeing, is of immense relevance to the problems and uncertainties currently besetting Arab Youth. Wyn's contribution, taken from her recently published volume, *Youth Health and Welfare: The Cultural Politics of Education and Wellbeing* (2009) is compelling for its fresh empirical findings and conceptual extrapolations. Additionally, she is credited for initiating youth discourse as a social category or construct with different meanings over time and place. Much as gender and class are socially constructed, she sees individuals as linked and shaped by social, political, and economic processes.

Wyn focuses on a generation of Australians born after 1970 who left secondary school around 1990, to assess how policy discourses, interventions, and practices affect the lives of young adults. This particular interlude, marked by the collapse of the conventional labor market in the late 1980s alongside the sharp increase in tertiary and further education, is especially significant. Thus a generation of Australian youth, much like its cohorts in the Arab world, attempts to forge meaningful collective identities during times of rapid social change.

To substantiate how specific policies in three distinctive areas are affecting youth as a social category, she examines educational, health, and labor market policies, identifying their implications on youth as a social category. Wyn's basic premise regarding the nature of human capital is of direct relevance to many subsequent discussions in this volume. The conception of human actor as entrepreneur renders individual choices efforts to maximize human capital, as "investments for the purpose of capitalization of one's own existence."

These entrepreneurial skills are essential when youth is regarded as a "dangerous and risky" social category, with immense vulnerability during a stage of transition to adulthood. They are, as it were, in double jeopardy: personal ambivalence, and anxiety at a time of economic decline, when the state is compelled to reduce public support for them. As such, they are prone to become victims, as Wyn puts it, of the "exclusionary categories of deserving and undeserving youth." As the state withdrew support, a great share of responsibility for resourcing education and health fell on the young and their families. Additionally, the state tightened control through more repressive measures of surveillance and monitoring both the young and the places they frequented.

Another dismaying consequence of such restrictive policies is the increased cost of being young. This is further compounded when the state reduces funding to public and government education, supporting instead non-government schools. It also takes measures to align education more closely with the country's economic goals. Hence, vocational training and technical education became the "centerpiece of youth policies in most Western countries." Much of the same takes place in the area of public health. The universal provision of health is replaced by targeting young people at risk.

More interesting perhaps, is Wyn's ability to place these seemingly disconcerting conditions within a positive context. Drawing on the ideas of Kelly (2006) and Foucault (1988), she suggests that the prevailing youth-at-risk discourse should apply to adults as well. The Entrepreneurial Self which emerges from such settings represents "a desirable set of positive dispositions" which should be extended and cultivated in other segments of society. Essentially, rather than berating and fearing the young as disruptive, parasitic forces, they should be seen as inventive agents for meaningful and plausible change.

The rest of Wyn's chapter considers the specific policies, against this background of unsettling change that the Australian government has introduced in education, health, and the labor market to manage effective and equitable allocation of resources.

Much like Johanna Wyn, Asef Bayat also begins his chapter – "Reclaiming Youthfulness" – by arguing that most of the prevalent perspectives continue to treat youth as an incidental, analytical or displaced category. For example, when the issue of "youth religious radicalism" is addressed, the focus shifts to religion and the young become extraneous as if they just happen to be there. Others assume that youth, as a central category, can and should be the point of departure for any discourse on youth and its interplay with its habitus. Bayat takes a middle position: namely, that as a social category, youth can be subservient agents to repressive state authority or serve as radical agents in bringing about transformative change.

Either way, they are seen as political agents and social transformers, whether for or against Islam. In countries like Egypt, Saudi Arabia, and Morocco, one can witness their direct political mobilization as many of the young are involved in radical Islamist movements. In the Islamic Republic of Iran, however, they have served as recalcitrant agents by defying the moral and political authority of the doctrinal regime.

Bayat employs the concept of a "social movement" to elucidate the nature and outcomes of such youthful ventures. His work is informed by a basic premise: the experience and anxieties of Arab Youth can only be understood within the stringent social controls they are subjected to.

Apart from being associated with surveillance, the Iranian regime sustains a more strenuous doctrinal animosity towards joy and carefree lifestyles, hence the periodic crackdowns on symptoms of "degenerate behavior." The young respond by taking every opportunity to create open and clandestine sub-cultures. Often such defiant reactions assume seemingly benign manifestations like underground pop and rock bands, late night parties, popular fads (such as eccentric fashions, tattoos, smuggled videos) or more aberrant ones (drugs, running away from home, becoming victims of prostitution and other trafficking rings).

Egyptian youth, on the other hand, operate under the constraints of a "passive revolution," opting for a strategy of "accommodating innovation." They attempt to adjust their youthful claims within existing political, economic, and moral precepts. Not being under the same moral and political control as their Saudi Arabian or Iranian counterparts, many of the mainstream young continue prayer, partying, and pornography; faith and fun; the sacred and profane of authoritarian regimes. It is in this sense "the political agency of youth movements, their transformative and democratizing potential, depends on the capacity of the adversaries, the moral and political authorities, to accommodate and contain youthful claims." As such, youth movements in these settings are prone to become efforts of claiming youthfulness.

Clearly the Egyptian regime, despite the repeated claims of Hosni Mubarak, failed to deliver on any of the legitimate demands of discontented youth and ordinary citizens. For over four decades, they have not only been deprived of economic opportunities, and adequate social and educational services, but also denied freedom and justice.

Not surprisingly, in this Iranian context – a regime of surveillance and draconian social controls – youth identity acquires a defiant posture.

What sustained this regime of surveillance for a decade were revolutionary fervor, preoccupation with war, and the repression of dissent. Young men were either on the war front or fleeing the country, preferring the humiliation of exile to "heroic martyrdom" in a "meaningless" battle. Although adolescents sought refuge in schools, often by deliberately failing exams to postpone graduation, they lived in anxiety, gloom, and depression. One out of every three high school students suffered from a behavioral disorder. Girls in particular were more susceptible to stress, fear, and depression.

This is not as contradictory as it may seem. It represents accommodation to realities they cannot totally depart from. The young naturally desire dancing and raving, and having illicit relations. They also need the comfort and solace of religious faith. As one of the law students interviewed by Bayat put it: "I do both good and bad things, the good things erase the bad things." To Bayat this state of liminality, this "creative inbetweenness," demonstrates how the young attempt to redefine and re-imagine their Islam in order to accommodate youthful desires for individuality, change, fun, and "sin" within the existing moral order.

The first two introductory essays view youth as a social category with varied meanings and manifestations in time and place. Both Wyn and Bayat advance another basic premise, one that frames and anticipates many of the substantive contributions: namely, that youth as a social category – much like gender, class, and ethnicity – is socially constructed. It is appropriate, by way of introduction, to consider a striking demographic feature – the so-called "youthful bulge" as another source of disruption and instability in the lives of Arab youth.

Youssef Courbage in "The Demographic Youth Bulge and Social Rapture" explores this phenomenon based on recent statistical evidence of the demographic transition in the Arab world. On the basis of projected evidence, he casts legitimate doubt on this assumed negative relationship between youthfulness of Arab population and sources of instability and political unrest. Indeed, he argues that despite the inevitable risks associated with the demographic transition (such as ageing), altogether its advantages outweigh its drawbacks. The demographic transition – as manifested in increasing literacy (both male and female), fertility decrease, access to contraception, and delayed marriage – is likely, initially, to be a source of social disruption and collective unease. But in the long run, the bulge is bound to diminish and the demographic transition is likely to yield more favorable realities. For example, the projected increase in adults to the ratio of young people will ultimately lead to a proportional increase in the ratio of producers to consumers. Also, the falling birthrate is prone to increase the age groups with a higher propensity to save, thereby narrowing the income distribution gap. More important, the reduction in wealth disparities will generate a fairer distribution of knowledge and provide further impetus for the emergence of a middle class with pluralistic and cosmopolitan predispositions. To Courbage, finally, these are all precursors to a transition towards democracy.

To substantiate his optimistic projections, Courbage focuses first on elucidating the connection between literacy, the darker side of cultural modernization, and the prospects for social rupture and civil violence. Rather than seeking answers in the essentialist qualities inherent in Islam, he persuasively examines changes in mindsets associated with the demographic transition.

His perspective, and the statistical evidence he supplies, depart from certain prevailing assertions, particularly those of Sammel Huntington who advances his contested and widely debated "clash of civilization" between Islam and the West. To Huntington, for example, population growth in Muslim countries, particularly because of the youthful bulge, provides a massive pool of unanchored and embittered masses easily drawn into fundamentalist and insurgency movements or rootless migration. Accordingly disenfranchised groups become a threat to both Muslim and non-Muslim societies alike. Huntington along with many of his disciples assumes that Islam is a static, uniform, and essentialist entity, that demographic behavior is built into their psyche and is unlikely to change. The graphic evidence and projections Courbage provides cast doubt on these premises.

Diane Singerman also views the youthful demographic bulge as a source of considerable social rupture in Arab society and focuses on a vital but largely unanticipated consequence of this socio-cultural reality; namely, delayed marriage. Marriage, virtually a universal reality in the Arab world, exacts on the family some immense financial pressures. Investment in marriage capital requires years to accumulate and has a direct impact on other venues associated with adolescent transitions such as schooling, education, employment, and, above all, identity formation.

The pressures involved in delaying marriage, clearly a byproduct of the growing number of young compelled to remain unmarried and economically dependent on their families, lead to waithood as opposed to adulthood. The implications of this ambivalent, uncertain, and liminal interlude in young lives during a time of hope, opportunity, and youthful exuberance, are grievous. The constraints of negotiating waithood become particularly acute, fraught with added feelings of alienation and exclusion.

Singerman's essay falls in two parts: first, statistical analysis revealing the magnitude of the national cost of marriage in line with salient demographic trends. Second, she provides a graphic account of the social and political consequences of delayed marriage and social exclusion. The repercussions, made poignantly clear by her analysis, cannot be ignored. Not surprisingly, they are reflected in "the rise of new discourses and debates concerning sexuality, morality, youth identity, generational conflict, and the rise of a 'marriage black market' as young people negotiate and attempt to reconcile contradictory public and private norms, values, and expectations."

Her analysis begins by showing how preparing for marriage is so central to the economy and well-being of the Egyptian family.

These costs are negotiated and shared between four parties: the bride, the groom, the bride's family, and the groom's family. The distribution of the shares vary. For example, the bride pays very little of the cost of marriage, the groom pays 40 percent, his family pays slightly less than one-third and the bride's side contributes about one-third. To convey the magnitude of marriage costs, Singerman reveals (based on a national survey she participated in), that for each household the cost amounted to eleven times the annual household expenditure and equal to the entire expenditures of all members of one household over two and a half years.

The second part of Singerman's paper focuses on youthful anxieties alongside the moral and ethical derivatives of such pressures. Foremost is the persisting belief that unmarried men or women are problematic and potentially threatening to religious and normative codes of conduct. An unmarried woman continues to be perceived as a source of *fitna* (literally sedition or sexual chaos). Hence, early marriage allays the anxiety associated with women's presumed promiscuity.

Delayed marriage and its alternative substitutes, the lack of employment opportunities, and continued financial dependence on families compound the frustration of Egyptian youth and force them to pay deference to their families even though they may no longer be relevant to the socio-cultural realities of their lived lives. In this sense, family dependence is both enabling and disabling, a source of gratitude and emotional support but also unease since it traps them in a "double-bind." They no longer conform to accepted social norms, nor can they break away from them. When they do, behavioral departures must be concealed. Singerman makes reference to recent surveys of young unmarried women in Tunisia and Jordan which reveal that the incidence of pre-marital sex (including high-risk sexual practices) is increasing, while the age is decreasing. This surge in sexuality is occurring while young people are both ill-informed and misinformed about sexual diseases, contraception, and reproductive health.

Singerman closes with a probing query: how can young Egyptians, Moroccans, Syrians and Iranians reconcile this new "geography of sex" when parental norms confine sexuality to marriage, and when parents invest huge sums in the marriages and education of their children? The contortions experienced by young people negotiating the risky field of dating and mating puts them in a "no win" situation, living a "don't ask, don't tell" reality.

NEGOTIATING IDENTITY IN TIMES OF RISK

In "Youth at Risk in Two Marginalized Urban Neighborhoods in Amman," Curtis N. Rhodes and his associates assert that increasing numbers of Jordanian youth face profound value conflicts, feelings of uncertainty and unease, largely because of the demographic and socio-cultural transformations in the region. With a fairly high rate of natural increase (about 3.6 percent), Jordan is characterized by a youthful and growing population. Over half of the entire population are under twenty years of age. Economic pressures and high unemployment exacerbate these problems, particularly in low-income urban neighborhoods. The data and extrapolations are extracted from a pilot program conducted by Questscope in Amman to study the impact of neighborhood intervention in two impoverished and marginalized neighborhoods. The intention is to create "prosocial communities" by providing youth with opportunities to develop their talents in a safe environment.

The character of social change in Jordan is first explored to provide background for the case studies. Next, the two neighborhoods are analyzed and finally, five major constraints, which become the basis for fostering strategies for implementing the envisaged program to build prosocial communities, are identified.

The most compelling changes in Jordan today are strikingly interrelated: the youthful demographic bulge, an acute rural exodus, undeveloped social institutions, and the shift away from an authoritarian and patriarchal social system. These, in turn, have sharpened the gap and conflict between generations, becoming a source of discontent among youth. Even more unsettling is the uncertainty of the transition. For although the kinship and communal ties of the young are shrinking, secular and rational city institutions do not, as yet, inspire their allegiance. As elsewhere, exposure to the new global media accentuates these anxieties alongside feelings of restlessness, hesitation, and uncertainty.

For the case studies, two sites were selected to represent different types of low-income communities: first, the typical poor neighborhood, akin to a ghetto, populated by refugees and rural migrants; second, a "quasi-urban neighborhood" near an urban village. In the former, children are not linked through kinship ties or supportive social relations, becoming parasitic sources of annoyance and trouble. Hence, they are alienated from their parents and marginalized from mainstream social institutions. It is little wonder that young boys in such settings seek shelter and comradeship in street gangs which lack autonomy and agency, often falling into violent, delinquent, and anti-social conduct.

In contrast, the urban village is composed of migrant families who maintain their close kin and family ties. They live in close proximity and the extended family networks act as "safety nets". Unlike the boys of the ghetto, they replenish meager financial family resources by selling home-prepared food products. Altogether, and in comparative terms, the neighborhood has a relatively high level of social capital, yet traditional venues and communal supports are no longer adequate to accommodate the needs of the young.

The intervention program, designed by Questscope, used three complementary approaches when building pro-social communities. The first was local development which encourages community members to use their own visions, establish their own priorities and skills to enhance volunteer capabilities. The second entailed establishing collaborative networks with external experts. Finally, the third strategy employed social action to change the social context of the young.

The authors involved in the Questscope program drew some instructive lessons from their Jordanian experience. To begin with, the intervention in the two neighborhoods succeeded largely because a fairly high level of involvement, partnership, and "role enrichment" occurred.

Another concluding inference is also worth noting. The so-called "prosocial" approaches to the young at risk were most effective when adults took the time and effort to understand the views and circumstances of the young. After all, youth at risk remain perceptive and intuitive about the conditions and sources of the alienation and exclusion they endure. Finally, while the pilot program demonstrated the importance of fostering new and enriched roles for both youth and adults at the local level, sustaining such role development depended on institutional responses from actors outside the neighborhoods. Altogether though, issues of negotiating meaningful identities were seen largely as a byproduct of recreating such internal communal solidarities.

Mai Yamani, arguably one of the most noted Saudi scholars when it comes to addressing issues of societal development and the interplay between local and global forces, focuses her analysis on the impact of new technologies of globalization. In her view, Saudi youth today are caught between a vulnerable traditional system of governance struggling to maintain paternalistic and primordial loyalties, alongside the temptations of the new global world order, information technologies, and mass commodification. While the community participation program in Amman, inspired by Questscope, sought to reinforce Jordanian and communal solidarity, the alienated and excluded Saudi youth, by contrast, are seeking a sense of transnational identity, autonomy and freedom outside the Kingdom's borders. Increasingly, it seems, they are finding redemption in global role models, particularly the allures of the internet and cyber space.

The bulk of Yamani's essay explores the circumstances which, she believes, account for the persisting and growing sense of alienation and exclusion of Saudi Youth. The demands of young Saudis are not unusual. They aspire for a more equitable measure of economic and political space, more democratic participation, and freedom to access uncensored transnational sources of popular culture. Five major sources of alienation and exclusion of the young are singled out: fragmentation of state policy, secretive paternalism, Wahhabi inertia, stifling American policies, and the oil temptation.

Despite successive efforts by the regime to establish national integration, Saudi Arabia today remains a distinct and heterogeneous collection of regions, tribes, and sects. The internal pressure for reform and the search for a more coherent and meaningful socio-cultural identity, as articulated by the young and new middle class, remain unrealized. The emergence of this new middle class continues to be mediated by ethnic and culturally based cleavages that serve only to reinforce the prevailing political hierarchy and socio-economic privileges.

Equally disheartening is the proverbial adeptness of the regime to carefully monitor, through divide-and-rule strategies, the struggle between groups. Between the security forces, the *mukhabarat* (intelligence service) and the *mutaw'a* (patrols entrusted with the task of safeguarding virtue and preventing vice on the streets), the Al-Saud have easily enforced the politics of fear, marginalization, and exclusion among the young; specifically those harboring hopes of freedom and transparency.

Another source of alienation is what Yamani labels "secretive paternalism;" the furtive maneuverings of Al-Saud to retain their powers. Since Al-Saud derive their legitimacy from Wahhabi precepts, prospects for democratic reform remain remote, leaving the young more embittered by thwarting legitimate claims to modernize the system of education or limit gender segregation and access to venues of popular culture.

Through oil revenues the royal family maintains a benevolent welfare system that enforces loyalty and subservience. Yet the allure of petro-dollars, as the young are acutely aware, cannot compensate for genuine reform, and the regime's seemingly inflexible alliance with the policies of the United States only compounds their discontent. At the popular level, the resentment of US "hard power" (i.e. security arms and intelligence) is now compounded by the seductive proliferation of "soft power" (i.e. fast food, fashion, and popular entertainment). In closing, Yamani demonstrates how globalization is expanding the space and transnational consciousness of Saudi youth. The advent of satellite television, particularly Al-Jazeera in 1996, played a significant role in revolutionizing Arab media and mobilizing public opinion. Along with the internet, it created unprecedented opportunities for the expression of diverse views and multiple lifestyles, accentuating the dilemmas of ordinary youth.

No wonder that more developed and accessible social media (Facebook and Twitter) played a crucial role in mobilizing upheavals in the early spring of 2011 which dismantled three of the most despotic and tyrannical Arab regimes.

Craig Larkin in "Between Silences and Screams" concentrates on the postwar generation of Lebanese youth caught between the poignant and inconsistent forces of collective memory and collective amnesia. Drawing on Marianne Hirsch's concept of postmemory, Larkin explores how Lebanon's "postmemory generation" reproduce, re-imagine or erase memory traces to identify and locate themselves within contemporary Lebanese society. This is a generation shaped and informed not by direct traumatic events but by the mediated narrative accounts of events preceding their birth. Larkin begins by briefly elucidating the perspective of postmemory before considering how this postmemory generation is situating itself within Lebanon's ambivalent and uncertain future and how emergent identities are shaped by distinct socio-cultural and political settings.

The bulk of his data and inferences are based on extensive field research and qualitative interviews he conducted in 2005–6 with 100 high school and university students. The sample reflected the diversity of educational institutions (i.e., public/private, rural/urban and religious composition). Young people are gripped by a "simultaneous attachment and dislocation to the past, an uneasy oscillation between continuity and rupture." Rami, a village student enrolled at AUB, typifies this new postwar generation: "Those with no lived experience or personal memory of the country's protracted civil war (1975–92), yet with a keen awareness of the lingering pain, suffering and collective loss." For young people like Rami, this dialectical discourse of remembering and forgetting has left his generation "out of time", "out of place" and bereft of a unifying national narrative or a coherent sense of self.

Lebanon's postmemory generation are faced with the task of negotiating relevant and coherent identities through the oral, spatial, and visual relics of the past. Larkin substantiates how "memory scapes" (ruins, scarred and derelict houses, demolished buildings, spatial voids, posters, and memorials to fallen fighters) remain the most vivid and graphic reminders of the country's violent past. War-torn buildings become the "unintentional monuments of war." Likewise, decaying edifices, pockmarked apartment blocks with fire-charred windows and graffiti-strewn walls, and, above all, empty buildings and abandoned neighborhoods evoke and reawaken latent memories and stories. In doing so, they reinforce the sense of estrangement and confusion. Interestingly, Larkin argues that such recollections do not only demarcate earlier battle zones and situate war stories, they also serve to validate themes of continuing crises and contested issues: dispossession, Palestinian presence, Syria's intervention, and the struggle for Christian political leadership.

Dislocated youth become adept storytellers who weave intricate tales to affirm their social identities. One recurrent theme is their overwhelming sense of being helpless victims of circumstances beyond their control. Victimhood is often attributed to a set of recurring causes that converge on the following: Western connivance, Israeli aggression, Palestinian terrorism, Arab backwardness, Maronite expansionism, Sunni greed, Shi'a fanaticism, the rule of warlords, economic injustice, and political corruption.

The beginning of Pardis Mahdavi's compelling chapter on the "Politics of Fun in the Islamic Republic of Iran" is worth paraphrasing:

> Perhaps there is no place in the world where the stakes of "having fun" are higher than in present-day Iran. Drinking (alcohol) and dancing can lead to arrest by the morality police accompanied by up to 70 lashings. Consequences for sex outside of marriage can be even more severe – up to 84 lashes. But even under the threat of such harsh punishment, a youth movement encompassing changing sexual and social behaviors is taking palace. Sex and sexuality have become both a source of freedom and an act of political rebellion for urban young Iranians who are frustrated with the theocratic regime that restricts their sociality. Young people in Iran say, in their own words, that they are enacting a sexual revolution (or *enqelab-i-jensi* in Persian) to speak back to what they view as an overly repressive regime. This sexual revolution, as I observed during fieldwork from 2000–7, is about more than sexuality, it is about changing social mores, carving out new recreational opportunities, and at its very core, bringing back joy, fun, and youth habitus.

This is not a glib or passing assertion but the outcome of extensive qualitative and ethnographic fieldwork Mahdavi conducted for seven years for her recently published book – *Passionate Uprisings: Iran's Sexual Revolution* (2008). Her basic thesis is persuasive and lucidly elaborated; namely that what she perceives as "re-creation of recreation" is a fairly novel form of having fun that stands out as a direct challenge to the moral paradigm of the Islamic republic. It demonstrates that the young, despite the regime's strenuous restrictions, mobilize themselves as an agency to challenge strictures. Getting away with transgressions (e.g. make-up, colorful headscarves, heterosexual encounters), which previously were strictly punished, indicates that the youth movement has already made a dent in the system. Even "wearing lipstick" becomes a defiant expression. As one of Mahdavi's respondents put it, "it's about pissing off them, the morality police, and about me getting satisfaction." "Having fun," Mahdavi argues, is a direct challenge to the moral paradigm of the regime, and a way the young are asserting their agency.

In an Islamic republic, Shari'a law, as interpreted by the clerics in power, stip-ulates explicit rules on comportment, leisure, sociability, and above all, sexual conduct. For example, unmarried men and women cannot be seen together without a chaperon. With regard to veiling, women are expected to be covered in "proper" Islamic dress, typically from head to toe, hiding any body shape. Even in school, they cannot be seen alone and their interactions are limited to conversations.

Over the span of seven years, Mahdavi documented some significant transfor-mations. In her words, "young people have succeeded in carving out new ways and spaces to have fun and engage in behavior which previously would have been punished ... literally, they are re-creating recreational places in order to engage in 'subversive' pleasures, and simultaneously changing sexual and social discourses." The bulk of her chapter explores the character of sexual encounters in a variety of spaces: parks, forests, mountainous areas in the North, semi-private spaces in automobiles, underground parties in private homes, and popular coffee shops.

In short, more young Iranian adults have opportunities today to challenge and depart from the stringent norms of an Islamic republic that has an aversion to fun. These new realities, Mahdavi suggests, are the outcome of certain circumstances: first, increasing difficulty of monitoring large numbers of "subversive" young groups. Second, since their behavioral departures are often unobtrusive and subtle, authorities cannot always ascertain the need to police conduct. Third, the tone of reforms established by Khatami's presidency occurred just as this young genera-tion was coming of age. Hence, the spirit of openness he championed remained with them despite the election of a conservative president like Ahmadinejad. Finally, the growing number of young recruits to the morality police and other positions of power have increased sympathy for the young and for change.

In "Idealistic and Indignant Young Lebanese," Roseanne Saad Khalaf pro-vides a partly autobiographical account of her own experiences as a "returnee" to postwar Lebanon (after an absence of eleven years), alongside the views of her stu-dents who also experienced dislocating encounters upon re-entry to the country. She uses student narratives in creative writing workshops to shed light on how students struggle to forge meaningful identities in a troubled and uncertain political setting. Because workshops allow free and uncensored discussions, ordinary classes are transformed into intense enabling sessions, akin to "charged happenings" or "third spaces" away from the strictures of mainstream gazes.

As a writing-intensive zone, her seminars become a "safe house" where students are encouraged to speak up and out. Hence texts and discourse move beyond narcissistic and restrictive private concerns to address broader socio-cultural and political transformations in society. More than simply defining the views of a new generation, texts insightfully highlight significant youth experiences in a fast-changing postwar society. Since student narratives exist outside the hegemonic influence of public transcripts, something other than the dominant story or accepted biography of a country is being told.

Khalaf collates these views and concerns under the rubric of eight recurring and salient themes. Most striking is the feeling of being trapped and abandoned in a country characterized by a violent past, anxious present, and uncertain future. The bewilderment and anguish of students are all the more acute as they are protracted and reawakened by renewed feelings of fear and helplessness against seemingly insurmountable obstacles. Equally demoralizing in this regard is the way the "Cedar Revolution," which inspired massive mobilization, was derailed by self-serving politicians. The young continue to feel threatened by the ever-increasing exodus of their gifted cohorts and disillusioned by pervasive symptoms of vacuous nostalgia that complicate attempts at formulating strategies to transcend the rigidities of confessional politics. Consequently, hopeful future prospects of a more tolerant, plural, and diverse political culture appear to be quickly evaporating. Altogether, these collective youthful voices, disparate as they may seem, are symptomatic of a longing to participate in efforts to restore trust and dialogue in a country plagued by unresolved conflict and unappeased hostility.

Nicolien Kegels focuses on one seemingly dissonant feature of Lebanon's Janus-like character – nightlife in times of war – to disclose a more probing discourse on national identity. Beirut's national image, particularly in the global and popular media, has perpetually hovered between a battleground and a playground; between a barricaded and hedonistic urban site. Her fieldwork and ethnographic data, supplemented by close interviews and participant observation, are based on the nightlife of a group of upper-class young adults before and during the Israeli war on Lebanon in July 2006.

The Israeli air assault on Lebanon allowed her to explore the interplay between the uncertainties and horrors of war and the way this rather exclusive and unrepresentative group of young adults, transformed the war experience into feelings of belonging and the reassertion of national identity.

Kegel notes that religious identity and sectarian consciousness do not figure prominently in the lives of this group. Instead, they seem sparked by strong class identification most visible in their life-style, leisure, conspicuous consumption, and excessive display of privileges. Other peculiar features of this fairly small and tightly knit group are feelings of insecurity and status anxiety. Despite the ostentatious privileges and life styles they enjoy, their status is not static but an identity that depends largely on seeing and being seen.

Upper-class night clubs in Lebanon, Kegel argues, are "regulated" and "controlled" settings, an antidote to daily chaos. They become "the best place to show off riches because the environment is designed in such a manner as to optimize flaunting wealth and confirming social status." This form of organized beauty allows the upper class to project an image of being secure and in control.

Bars and clubs become much more than entertainment spots, they become the stage on which the upper class performs its ideas about itself and the world around it and reinforces its boundaries. Since nightlife is the place where class boundaries are produced and re-produced, maintaining proper behavior at all times is of vital importance. Kegel suggests that this feature of "serious fun," which allows privileged social groups to indulge but remain civilized, is what distinguishes party scenes in Lebanon from those elsewhere in the world.

MILITANCY AND STREET VIOLENCE

One of the basic premises in this volume is that Arab youth today are not only at risk but also confronting, during a vulnerable and unsettling interlude in their lives, disturbing uncertainties and socio-cultural inconsistencies. Local dislocations, unresolved regional conflicts, and global consumerist incursions have exacerbated the sources of uncertainty, latent trauma, and muffled hostilities. Such unsettling transformations become more problematic due to the peculiar pattern and direction of social change in the Arab world.

As traditional agencies of loyalty and solidarity (family, community, and state) are being undermined, the so-called modern alternative vectors of societal transformation (i.e. education, employment opportunities, new media, political mobilization, and agencies of civil society) have not, as yet, been effective in providing the needed sources of coherence and stability. By and large, different groups of young adults, in difference parts of the Arab world, seek one of three possible modes of resistance or adaptation: resorting to various forms of militancy and street violence, seeking venues of voluntarism and civil society, or finding outlets in popular culture, art, or music.

Julie Peteet's article on the "Rituals of Resistance in the Palestinian *Intifada*" is based on field research carried out in the West Bank (1990), with an added epilogue to update her findings. From the beginning of the Intifada in December 1987 through December 1990, an estimated 106, 600 Palestinians were injured. Her central thesis is based on the premise that "the attainment and enactment of manhood and masculinity" among Palestinian male youths are largely a reflection of the beatings and detention they are constantly subjected to. She goes further to assert that the "beatings (and detentions) are framed as rites of passage that become central in the construction of an adult, gendered (male) self with critical consequences for political consciousness and agency."

The rites of passage and the struggle of young Palestinians to resist the occupation occur in a setting where the military and political authority of an occupying foreign power is overwhelming when pitted against the powerlessness of the Palestinians. As Peteet poignantly reminds, "the juxtaposition of technologies is striking. Offensively and defensively, Palestinians wield stones, one of the earliest forms of weaponry known to humankind. As part of the natural environment and landscape, the stone bears minimal, if any, appellation of human technological skills." Since 1967 successive generations of young Palestinians have known no life other than this discrepant and unequal form of resistance. Yet they have managed to prevent Israel from "normalizing" its power relations with those under its occupation.

The inability of Israel to subdue this form of "primitive" resistance leaves no recourse other than physical and structural violence to quell the uprisings: beatings, detentions, and the latent cruelties of interrogation, torture, and terror have become ordinary forms of the apparatus of domination. The resisting youth, humiliated, tortured, and bloodied, remain unbowed. This alone is testimony that their resistance has paid off. It has also become a way of life. As Peteet explains:

> One quickly discerns that beatings are a common occurrence. The anticipation of an encounter with occupation authorities that might lead to a beating influences the daily mobility of young men. They decline evening social invitations that necessitate driving after dark. Military personnel at roadblocks stop cars and randomly pull out men for beating. Parents hesitate to allow adolescent boys to go downtown unaccompanied, or even on short errands, fearing they might be pulled over for an identity check and in the process roughed up. In the alleys of the camps, children now are more careful to stay close to home because, on their daily patrols, soldiers occasionally chase, manhandle, and detain them for several hours until their parents pay a stiff fine.

She addresses the social meaning of violence, particularly regarding the body, and how young Palestinians transform this treacherous reality into venues for validating their manhood and affirming their cultural and national selves. Arab masculinity (*rujulah*), Peteet tells us, is "acquired, verified, and played out in brave deeds, in risk-taking, and in expressions of fearlessness and assertiveness. It is attained by constant vigilance and willingness to defend honor (*sharaf*), face (*wajh*), kin, and community from external aggression."

Mohammad Abi Samra and Fidel Sbeity, both writers and journalists, are closely connected to the communities and neighborhoods they write about. Their vivid accounts, told from an "insider" perspective, are supplemented by interviews with gang leaders and members in Tripoli and the southern suburbs of Beirut. In "Revenge of the Wretched", Mohammad Abi Samra provides a vivid narrative account of the social roots and changing character of youth violence in an urban neighborhood (*Bab al Tabaneh*) in the northern Lebanese city of Tripoli. While Julie Peteet demonstrates how the involvement of Palestinian youth in acts of resisting Israeli occupation were crucial in asserting their sense of manhood and masculine identity, the violence of the *Bab al Tabaneh* youth was more random and dislocated, largely a byproduct of the destitute, impoverished suburban settings the embittered young live in. Bereft of any stable family support, adequate schooling, re-creative outlets or stable occupational opportunities, pent-up anger and hostility found release in forms of "social banditry." Such settings became breeding grounds for neighborhood organizations (*Meshayakhat Shebab*) led by local leaders. These organizations, which acquired the label of *Munathamat al Ghadab* (literally angry associations), served to channel anger and bitter resentment into forms of civil disobedience, tinged with Arab nationalist sentiments yet targeting the Lebanese state.

Like other forms of social mobilization and collective protest the association sought refuge in the Salafist Islamist movement and, in doing so, the mosque, with its congregation and religious rituals, became an accessible venue for political mobilization and proselytizing activity.

By focusing on the armed organization headed by Khalil Akkawi (Abu Arabi), Abi Samra demonstrates how it became a breeding ground for political mobilization and the *dawa* (proselytizing) movement largely inspired by Khomeini's Islamic revolution in Iran. In no time, these meshayakat shebab acquired the rubric of populist resistance on behalf of the *ummah*. A group of mosque committees from different Tripoli neighborhoods became venues where runaway and derelict kids were recruited in the name of sanctity, honor, purity, and identity of the mosque. As a result, the young men and sheikhs of the neighborhoods were transformed into *abadays* or heroes embodying the spirit of gallantry, honor resistance, and helping the weak and poor.

The account Fidel Sbeity provides of the neighborhoods of Gandour and Masbagha in the southern suburbs of Chiah, the heart of the so-called "Misery Belt," epitomizes all the disheartening symptoms of deprivation and destitution: young boys growing up in places which deprive them of all socio-psychological support, economic security, and political stability. A sheer inventory of such manifestations is menacing and sinister enough: crushing poverty, parental neglect, inadequate schooling, high drop-out rates, total absence of recreational facilities and other integrative outlets. These alone, however, would not have generated all the misbegotten symptoms of gang warfare and criminality had they not been reinforced by the factional and tribal feuds of displaced residents as well as exposure to armed Palestinian resistance groups. The bulk of Sbeity's narrative account is devoted to a graphic elucidation of these circumstances.

Living conditions in both neighborhoods are deplorable. Informants knew not a single family with fewer than ten children, many of whom were not in school and roamed around barefooted and half naked. Bloody confrontations occurred in the empty sand lots adjoining the neighborhoods that served as makeshift playgrounds.

Gangs of street boys, not yet in their teens, were already present in the early 1960s. Yet the gangs of the two communities differed markedly. For example, the *Sharaban* gang of *Masbagha*, who came from Baalbeck and Hermel, were more belligerent and pugnacious, spreading hooliganism, terror, stealing, and murdering, often in cold blood, and brutality, extorting money from residents and shopkeepers. The Ghandour gang, on the other hand, drawn largely from displaced southern families, was better educated. They organized soccer teams and, ultimately, became more predisposed to joining political parties and other non-militant associations.

Sharp divisions between the two neighborhoods, both spatially and socially, increased tension and hostility between the gangs, often instigating blood feuds and turf wars. The growth of these gangs coincided with the early rounds of the 1975–6 Civil War. While members of the Ghandour gang were able to avoid being recruited as fighters, those of *Sharaban* could not resist the temptation. Already, the pre-war setting of Chiah and adjoining suburbs were notorious for their criminality. To many, being a gang member became a coveted status, one which enhanced their access to material goods and social standing, and validated their self-worth, dignity, and brash masculinity. The more boastful they were of their belligerency, particularly when it involved the elimination of other potential rivals in gang leadership, the more acclaimed they became in the eyes of their community. In this respect, the pattern and form of violence which entrapped these young fighters were largely a microcosm of the proxy victimization so salient throughout Lebanon's encounters with collective strife.

VOLUNTARISM AND CIVIL SOCIETY

Lebanon's comparative openness and receptivity to the novelties of foreign and global transformations, give it an advantage over other regional countries in the experimentation with new modes of behavior and institutional arrangements. Consequently, it has acquired the necessary attributes of modernity without breaking away from, or diluting, its traditional ties and loyalties. This is most visible in formal and informal groupings and associations created in times of crises and uncertainty, to cushion individuals and groups against unsettling circumstances. As early as 1860, in the wake of civil unrest in Mount Lebanon and the outflow of rural migrants into Beirut and other coastal cities, dislocated groups employed kinship and village affiliations to form voluntary associations that address welfare and benevolent needs (see Khalaf, 1987: 161-84; Khuri, 1975 for further details).

Reconciling communal sentiments with the secular and impersonal demands of urban life is not always feasible or ameliorative. Indeed, the interplay between such dissonant expectations has often led to some disquieting byproducts. Youth associations are particularly vulnerable to such disruptive forces. Two papers in this section explore how promising and idealistic youth activities, during two different historic interludes, were distorted or aborted. In "Uniform and Salutes", Jennifer Dueck examines how the scout movement in Syria and Lebanon, during the French Mandate, normally an idealistic and consciousness-raising movement, was derailed by the factional rivalries and regional political struggles of the time. Christian Gahre focuses on the spectacle of events surrounding the so-called "Cedar Revolution", the youth uprising of 2005, in the wake of Prime Minister Hariri's assassination.

As early as 1937, groups of Syrian and Lebanese boys were already travelling to Europe to participate in International Scout Jamborees. More relevant, though, is their close association with military and armed forces. During one particular Jamboree, they were hosted by the Hitler Youth and, upon their return home, greeted by national political leaders and reminded that scouting was much like soldiers preparing for battle. In fact, the Prime Minister of Syria at the time, Mardam Bey, affirmed that scouts would become the hard core of any future national army.

Not only did national political leaders in Syria and Lebanon encourage and patronize the movements, but colonizing powers made direct efforts to capitalize on their potential by demonstrating enthusiasm to recruit young students into disciplined para-military associations. In fact, in all foreign schools and educational missions (French, German and Italian), the scouts and other quasi-scout associations became conspicuous hallmarks of success. As noted by Dueck, during the 1930s these youth associations suddenly emerged into political forces of their own, often beyond the control of Mandate authorities or local political elites.

To understand this quasi-military, fascist character of Levantine scout movements and their particular appeal to youth, Dueck focuses on three related dimensions: a brief historical sketch of scouting in its Middle East context; the influence of German and Italian models of youth associations; and the internal rivalries of the Syrian scout movement during the Second World War to substantiate the close association between scouting and fascism. The last part is a case study of scout rivalries in Syria. It illustrates the diversity of scouts and other youth groups and reveals how they were patronized by competing political groups. In the process, Baden-Powell's notion of scouting as a consciousness-raising youth movement was aborted.

The momentous assassination of former Prime Minister Rafik Hariri on February 14, 2005 was epochal for the spectacle of collective events and mass mobilization it unleashed. His poignant funeral procession, the succession of public protests and demonstrations, and ultimately, his makeshift shrine next to the Martyrs' monument, propelled the Bourj (Beirut's historic city center) once again to play host to profound and fateful transformations in the political history of Lebanon. Most impressive was the speed with which the populist uprising (*Intifadah*) or the "Cedar Revolution" came into being. Largely a spontaneous and informal gathering bringing together disparate individuals drawn from varied backgrounds, it was sparked by emotional contagion and a set of common political causes and slogans. The handful of young adults who assumed leadership, cross-confessional solidarity, and a strong sense of urgency were quick to act. Equally remarkable, other than their professional background and a network of contacts with well-placed families, they had absolutely no tangible resources.

Such recalcitrant and entrepreneurial manifestations depart markedly from the prevailing discreditable image of youth. Lebanese youth, in particular, are often berated as a quietist, self-seeking generation in wild pursuit of the ephemeral pleasures and consumerism of the new world order. The Intifadah disproved this image. They articulated a new language of resistance, emerging as the most disparaging voices against the sources undermining the sovereignty, security and well-being of their country. The advocacy and grassroots emancipatory movements they created are in stark contrast to the belligerent overtones of car bombs, suicidal insurgency, and counter-insurgency that continue to beleaguer the political landscape in the region.

Gahre focuses on elucidating the intimate interplay between three vivid dimensions: the core of diehards who assumed leadership in initiating and steering the mobilization; throwing light on the peculiar urban site which played host to the mobilization; and the consequences of such momentous mobilization on reshaping the collective identity of Lebanese youth.

He identifies the five actors – appropriately labeled "identity entrepreneurs" – by virtue of the roles they played as "organizer", "image-builder", "activist", "fundraiser" and "socialist socialite." Despite their diverse background and ideological leanings, involvement in the uprising heightened their national consciousness and the primacy of their Lebanese identity. The emotional impetus, spontaneous circumstances, informal networks, and inchoate mobilization consolidated the main targets of their platform: blaming the Syrians, petitioning the government to resign, and catching the world's attention through the global media. The mass signing of a petition buoyed by a robust creative industry – graphic design, advertising, printing, image-making, event management, and branding – was immensely impressive.

MUSIC AND POPULAR CULTURE

Lara Deeb and Mona Harb, in their ethnographic study of the interplay between piety and pleasure in the southern suburbs of Beirut (al-Dahiya), provide vivid and graphic evidence to demonstrate how youth manage to negotiate sites of leisure without violating sanctioned norms and expectations. More important, their actions are not blind or impulsive. Their work focuses on the generational changes which account for the emergence of a vibrant leisure sector and how a generation of pious youth draw on multiple "authorizing discourses" to arrive at appropriate decisions about how they should behave in emergent leisure sites.

Though reluctant initially, the Shiʿa community, particularly its nascent middle class, became predisposed to the socio-economic incursions, mass consumerism, and forms of public entertainment which, over the past three decades, began to infiltrate the suburbs. As a result, middle-class youth started to demand the same access to leisure outlets that other neighborhoods in Beirut have long enjoyed, yet such activities needed to be consistent with their lifestyle. In the words of Deeb and Harb, "youth in Dahiya participate in a growing global capitalist culture, but a specific one that highlights the construction of particular Muslim identities."

To understand how and why these new forms of "moral leisure" and a generation of "pious youth" emerged in Dahiya, the authors seek answers in the generational shifts away from the moral and cultural scripts of "Islamic vanguards" and imposed "Islamification" heralded by the Islamic Revolution in Iran. Because of such shifts Hizballah is no longer the only voice; the young are now heeding the more progressive views of Sayyid Fadlallah. Hence, they display more flexibility in interpreting situations and texts, flexibility that is becoming visible in outlets of leisure and public entertainment. For example, although dancing music is banned by virtually all sources of moral authority, Fadlallah maintains that it is the content of lyrics which is important. He alerts listeners to distinguish between *shawq* (longing and desire) which is acceptable and *ghara'iz* (sexual instinct) which is not. Views regarding the appropriateness of alcoholic consumption in restaurants and bars are also changing. Tables are appropriately rearranged to provide private and unobtrusive spaces where young couples can meet. Such manifestations have prompted the authors to maintain that "behavior is self-policed and enforced though social convention rather than by the morality police found in Iran or Saudi Arabia."

Deeb and Harb conclude by drawing two instructive inferences regarding the receptivity of "pious youth" in the Dahiya to experiment with various discourses of morality in an attempt to seek leisure outlets and practices. First, the young are driven by a desire to lead a moral life which includes the right to religiously appropriate leisure. Such options are not top-down impositions because the young have opportunities to reformulate choices more consistent with changing local conditions and their own personal relationship with God. Second, the pluralistic and cosmopolitan context of Lebanon, where the young inevitably encounter a multiplicity of cultural scripts, can account for the greater latitude they now have to search for options which reflect their desires and expectations.

Of all Islamized popular cultural expressions music, Miriam Gazzah explains, is the most controversial and contested. This comes as no surprise. A testy relationship between Islam and popular music dates back to the early years of Islamic history when Islamic scholars and popular intellectuals debated the compatibility of Islam with the production and consumption of music. Yet among youth, music has emerged as one of the most compelling sources of leisure and street culture entertainment, an outlet for protest and cultural resistance. Young adults use it to construct coherent identities because of its access to the internet, cyber culture, and transnational and global incursions.

Her main focus is on how second-generation Dutch-Moroccan youth use Islam to give music, fashion, food, style, and cultural imagery an Islamic touch by appropriating particular kinds of music to express a specific kind of identity. By employing deviant styles in dress, fashion, language, and musical preferences, British youth tacitly and subtly express their dissatisfaction with and resistance to dominant middle-class bourgeois values. In this sense, the formation of a youth culture may be regarded as symbolic space where youth freely express their sense of powerlessness and discontent with the status quo without the interference of parents or authorities. Ghazza explores how music consumption is reconciled with faith, as well as the perception of their culture and the importance of popular music in it. To Gazzah these are not ordinary questions. "Popular cultures, including pop music and mass media channels, often serve as important reservoirs of images, expressions, loyalties, and discourses, from which young people draw inspiration to represent, articulate, and express processes of identification."

The ultimate objective of any element of youth culture is the creation of "in-group" or "in-crowd" feelings to establish boundaries between the "us" and "them." In this regard *Shaabi* music, since it evokes a sense of nostalgia and unity, becomes a symbol of authenticity and solidarity. Performances not only take place in private family celebrations, such as weddings, but also in the public sphere. According to Gazzah, "the events represent a space where young people can freely be 'Moroccan', can behave, dance, sing and interact in the way they perceive to be 'Moroccan.' Shaabi plays a significant role in the assertion and preservation of 'Moroccanness' among Moroccan-Dutch youths, some of whom have never even been to Morocco."

In recent years Dutch-Moroccan youth have become visibly active in hip-hop music that incorporates bits and pieces from different sources. Gazzah makes a general distinction between two kinds of hip-hop based on lyrical themes or messages: "materialistic hip-hop" and "message rap." The former celebrates getting rich and all the allures of the good life: fast cars, money, and jewelry; it is also known as "brag and boast rap," implying that one should display one's possessions. The second – message rap – is the antithesis of the former. Rather than being indulgent and narcissistic, the lyrics celebrate political engagement and social awareness. Naturally, this appeals to marginalized and dispossessed minority groups as it evokes local, national, and global themes that connect the problems of local surroundings to global sensibilities and concerns. The lyrics create narratives which invalidate imposed and essentialist images and other stereotypes associated with radical Islamists, terrorists, or homophobic individuals.

While Gazzah shows how shaabi music, particularly rai and other genres of hip-hop, offers Dutch-Moroccan youth expressive outlets to construct meaningful transnational identities, Carolyn Landau focuses on the experience of British-born Moroccans in England. She prefaces her study by noting the singular importance of music as a preferred pastime and its assertive powers in the construction and negotiation of various transnational cultural and religious identities. Her research, based on extensive fieldwork she conducted over four years (October 2006 – May 2009), among three generations of Moroccans, substantiates the role music consumption plays in the lives of a displaced minority, particularly as it relates to their self-perception and feelings of belonging. Landau situates her case study within the current crisis of British identity and the experience of young British Muslims today.

The challenging task of trying to achieve a sense of rootedness, Landau argues, makes the children of migrants feel torn between two cultures. The pressure from parents to conform to Muslim and Moroccan cultural and religious norms conflicts with the desire of young people to find a sense of belonging within mainstream British youth culture. For some British-born Moroccans, forging a religious identity, in contrast to an ethnic one, has led to testy confrontations with parents.

Most interesting is the contested role of music in Islam as evident in the disagreement of scholars and the four main legal schools. Although they all condemn music as *haram* (illegitimate) they differ with regard to their attitudes towards musicians, listeners or patrons. This is where the role of anasheed (traditional songs and recitations performed during religious ceremonies, family celebrations, and on patriotic occasions) is of particular appeal to dislocated youngsters eager to forge a coherent and meaningful identity. As they have acquired a broader lyrical content addressing many contemporary issues as part of an "Islamic Revival" or "Islamic Awakening" (*al-Sahwa al-Islamiyya*), anasheed has surged. In terms of style and presentations, it has been popularized by blending anasheed lyrics with pop and hip-hop.

From vivid ethnographic evidence of personal interviews with second-generation Moroccans, Landau illustrates changes in listening habits which coincide with the questioning of secular music and liberal lifestyles. The advent of satellite television and internet provided greater access to anasheed and other Muslim songs. Hence, they could be connected to a transnational community of Muslims or *ummah*.

Gazzah and Landau show how Dutch-born and British-born Moroccan youth – both in Holland and England – try to blend elements of traditional musical traditions into hip-hop. This hybrid mix of popular music (shaabi and rai in Holland and anasheed in England) were appropriately seen as efforts by displaced and marginalized youth to negotiate cultural identities in order to gain acceptance in their host settings alongside maintaining elements of their local traditions. In Holland, Moroccans transformed hip-hop to celebrate both the good life, mass consumerism of the modern world-along with expressions of social awareness and political mobilization. In England, largely because of the impact of satellite, television, the conversion of Anasheed into hip-hop became embodied in the broader struggle for the invigoration of Islamic *ummah*.

Angie Nassar in "Scratch the Past" turns to hip-hop in Baalbek, Lebanon to demonstrate that youth do not need the alienating settings of diaspora to convert popular music into venues for resisting inherited forms of meaning and exposing them to more viable alternative identity formations. Indeed, in a pluralistic and fragmented country like Lebanon where primordial ties of kinship, community, sect, and neo-feudal affiliations still survive, the freedom to forge unique cultural identities through a blend of hip-hop becomes meaningful on more than one level. By studying the emergence of the Baalbek hip-hop group (*Touffar*), its songs and lyrical themes, Nassar documents how hip-hoppers manage to create hybrid forms of musical expressions. This is largely accomplished by fusing traditional local expressions such as *Atabah* (a form of improvised Arabic poetry) and *Tarab* (an emotional state induced by the ecstasy of the music) with hip-hop. She provides vivid examples of how *Touffar* drew on rich historical diversity, often by employing the local vernacular, to challenge and redefine history and its nebulous social order.

According to Nassar, these new "cultural nomads" are creating a "third space" to give voice to the ruptures and contradictions which beleaguer their everyday lives. Having lived the atrocities of their country's civil war vicariously, they suffer most of its consequences. In this sense, the Lebanese rappers – and *Touffar* is just one group – are not only articulating a new discourse, they are vindicating the absence of any. More important, they do so in stark contrast to the sheer spectacle of decadence and decay, so salient in postwar Lebanon.

Nassar argues that to understand the lyrics of *Touffar* and their project as a hip-hop group, one must understand what Lebanese youth, particularly those entrapped in Baalbek, feel they are up against. The bulk of her chapter is largely devoted to a discursive content analysis of the lyrical themes and rap performances. Overall, songs decry how Lebanon remains in a state of perpetual crises beyond understanding or cure. Nothing is spared, especially the cultural ethos of *wasta*, the obsession with appearance, impression management, conspicuous consumption, the country's sectarian system, and the duplicity of its depraved political elite.

Nassar perceptively suggests that Lebanon should be perceived not only as a landscape but also a "soundscape" where "political spaces can be mapped out in an aural terrain." Hence, the politics of sound, a topic generally overlooked, should invite more serious and deliberate inquiry since verbal cultural artifacts and props are as salient and meaningful as visual symbols of demarcation. Popular music when viewed as part of the cultural capital of Lebanese youth acquires a vital political dimension. It becomes an outlet for creative resistance, representing the struggle to validate damaged self-worth and invent strategies for curtailing oppression and injustice.

Nassar's concluding inference distinguishes between the kind of music produced in the center of Beirut and that emanating from the periphery. It is the youth on the margin, i.e. those in Baalbek, Tripoli, Saida, and the refugee camps who are experimenting with hip-hop to express outrage and conviction in an effort to militate the sources of misery, hardship, and disillusion.

Part 1

Youth as a Social Category

Youth as a Social Category and as a Social Process

Johanna Wyn

I am delighted to have the opportunity to share some ideas about the young people, the idea of youth, and the ways in which individual experiences are formed in social, political, and historical context. I have previously made a case for conceiving of youth as a social construct which has different meanings over time and place (Wyn & White, 1997). I have argued that youth is a social process – a way of defining individuals that is linked to complex social, political, and economic processes, much in the same way as gender and class are also social processes.

In order to elaborate on this idea I focus on one aspect of the context of young people's lives – policy discourses, interventions, and practices. I look at the ways in which these contribute to the meaning and experience of youth and to reflect on the ways in which this impacts on young people's lives. My paper focuses on Australian policies, with a specific focus on the generation that were born just after 1970, and who were leaving secondary school around 1991.

This was an especially significant time for young people in Australia. Much has been written elsewhere about changes that occurred at this time (Wooden, 1998; te Riele & Wyn, 2005; Wyn 2008). For the purposes of this discussion I highlight the collapse of the youth labour market in the late 1980s and the dramatic increase in tertiary and further education in the early 1990s. These and other changes gave particular salience to ideas and theories of social change (Bauman, 2001; Beck and Beck-Gernsheim, 2002; Beck & Lau, 2005). An interest in understanding the impact of social change on youth was widely shared across a number of developed countries (Leccardi & Ruspini, 2006; Furlong and Cartmel, 2007; White and Wyn, 2007a; Henderson et al., 2007). The related processes of individualization, the fragmentation of institutional processes, the significance of biographical 'choice', and requirement to take responsibility for processes that are out of individual control (responsibilization) have arguably had a profound impact on young people at this time. Indeed, as young people were struggling to make sense of their (changing) world, youth researchers and commentators alike began to coin terms to describe this 'new' generation. In the 1990s, concerns about youth transitions began to emerge in policy reports and academic literature, and in the popular press; labels such as *Gen X, Y , Z, Generation Me, Millennials, Baby Boomers, Baby Busters,* and many others came into usage (Twenge, 2006; Sheahan, 1996). Many of these terms are based on market and human resources management research (see for example Jurkiewitz, 2000 and Howe & Strauss, 2007). However, their claim that there are differences between generations based on the context in which they have been born and grown up, and that these differences are not simply age effects, is compelling. Although these terms are simplistic descriptions and sometimes gross stereotypes, they lend weight to the idea of the formation of a social generation. Indeed, there is a surprising convergence of thinking about the time period that each of these cohorts (especially Gen X and Y) represent, based on a consensus about social conditions and their impact on the possibilities and constraints on individuals who are born into and forge their lives through these time periods (Wyn & Woodman, 2006).

These ideas form a backdrop to the main focus of this paper, which is the impact of education, health, and labor market policies on young Australians in the 1990s. In arguing that age is attributed with a particular and relatively unique meaning at every historical period (Mitterauer, 1993; Mizen, 2004), I also make a case for recognizing the role of institutions in the social construction of age and reflect on assumptions about youth that inform policies and programs.

In the following discussion, I provide a brief discussion of the ways in which policy impacts on the idea of youth. I illustrate this through discussions of three distinctive areas of policy and then offer some reflections on the implications of these arguments for youth as a social process:

a. Education policies framing youth;
b. Health discourses naturalizing youth as a stage of life and providing technologies to define and measure youth; and
c. Labor market policies that have unintended outcomes.

POLICY: YOUTH AS A RESOURCE AND A PROBLEM FOR THE FUTURE

Government policies have a powerful impact on the way in which youth is defined and experienced. Although they are not deterministic, government poli-cies, programs, and institutional processes frame possibilities and limits on young people. The institutions of education and health have a broad reach into young people's lives, ensuring a degree of conformity with government directions and defining, creating, and protecting the vulnerable. Employment and labor-market policies too impact directly on the majority of young people. These jurisdictions legitimate ideas, concepts, and narratives that form the foundation on which the construction of youth rests. I agree with Rose (1999) that the objects of political concern are not invented by political thought as such, but are assembled "out of the work of a plethora of practical empiricists" who find "inventive" techniques of government through the development of measurement procedures, classifications of deserving and undeserving, and ways of processing individuals. In other words, policies are not the source of discourses about youth, but they provide an insight into the nature of these discourses and often serve to amplify particular approaches to youth.

Those who work in the youth sector and related areas are likely to be well aware of the differences between education, health, employment, and labor market jurisdictions. Differences in disciplinary background, training, and institutional practices between these areas make inter-sectoral practice and partnership very difficult (Milbourne et al., 2003; Wyn, 2009). However, there are many underlying similarities in their approaches to "youth" – to the concept of this phase of life and its significance – and to the management of young people.

Some of these commonalities are outlined by Rose (1999) in his discussions of the social implications of late modernity. In a powerful critique of Giddens' Third Way politics that dominated Britain's Labor Government in the 1990s, Rose argues that government policies actively shape new ways of becoming. He calls this process of framing human action the "capitalization of citizenship", through the implementation of a wide range of policies across all areas of government that assume that the main source of value and competitive advantage in the modern economy is human and intellectual capital (Rose, 1999: 438). The focus on human capital, Rose argues, is based on the conception of the human actor as an entrepreneur – of his or herself strictly to maximize his or her own human capital by choices which are, as it were, investments for the purpose of the capitalization of one's own existence (Rose, 1999: 438).

The impact of policies on young people's lives is illustrated through a consideration of the shift from policies framed by Keynesian economic approaches to monetarist ones. Mizen's analysis of the impact of these different policy frameworks on the construction of youth by the state is informative (Mizen, 2004). He describes how Keynesian state policies, which informed government policies in the immediate post-war years from 1946 to 1975 in the UK (and it can be argued, also in Australia and New Zealand), established inclusive measures such as support for a welfare state, a commitment to full employment, the expansion of secondary schooling and public hospitals, and the inclusion of youth into civic life.

By 1976, in the face of changing economic conditions, monetarist economic policies began to dominate. These policies made economic goals the primary focus. Under monetarist policies through the late 1970s to the 1990s (in the UK and NZ) and to 2007 in Australia, the state progressively reduced public support for young people, by reducing the scope of the welfare state and developing the exclusionary categories of "deserving and undeserving" youth. In essence, as Mizen (2004) argues, monetarist policies have relied on the category of age as a primary mechanism for narrowing the responsibility of the state for young people's lives while at the same time hugely expanding the reach of monitoring, surveillance, and control over both young people and the institutions in which they spend their time.

A range of monetarist policies has contributed to the increased cost of being young because as the state withdrew support a greater share of the responsibility for resourcing education and health fell to young people and their families. The impact of monetarist policies has been especially significant as Australian (and Western governments) have acted on concerns about global labor market competitiveness. In Australia the reduction of state support included a significant reduction in funding for public education, increases in government funding for non-government schools, and a move to align education more closely with the country's economic goals by focusing on vocational education. The concern about labor market competitiveness has made education and training the centerpiece of youth policies in most Western countries.

Other elements of monetarist policies included the replacement of universal provision of health and education services with targeted and more exclusive approaches, supported by the development of a research industry that can provide the tools to identify young people who are at risk. The policy preoccupation with targeting the health and education dollar has inevitably positioned the period of youth as a time of immense vulnerability and identified youth as a problem for the future of our society. From the 1990s on, policies have positioned youth as primarily a (dangerous and risky) transition to adulthood.

Exploring the relevance of these ideas for youth policies in Australia in the 1990s and 2000s, Kelly (2006) argues that adulthood as a taken-for-granted category should be problematized, and suggests that it should be re-imagined in terms of the Entrepreneurial Self. Drawing on Foucault (1988), he suggests that prevailing discourses about youth-at-risk are truths about what adults *should* become. He argues that the Entrepreneurial Self represents a desirable set of positive dispositions that government policies and programs aimed to achieve in the young population.

This can be seen in the way in which Australian health and education policies position youth as a resource and as potentially a problem for the future. Both provide the foundations of normative expectations of youth by favouring particular types of transitions as the standard and in creating categories of vulnerable, at-risk, and excluded youth. Both of these policy domains also draw primarily on bio-medical discourses about youth, drawing on the loosely related sets of ideas that contribute to the concept of youth as primarily a stage of biological and psychological development and a universal age category, and the use of these ideas as a justification for policies and practices that are enacted on young people.

In the following sections I explore three dimensions of policy and their impact on concepts of youth. Firstly I discuss the impact of educational policies and then I explore discourses of youth that derive from the health sector. Thirdly, I discuss an example of the unintended consequences of policies through a consideration of labor market policies.

EDUCATION: MANAGING YOUTH

Over the last twenty-five years there have been significant changes in education in Australia, some of which are the result of direct policy interventions and others that are related to broader processes of economic, social, and political change. It is now considered normative for young people to complete secondary school, although this only became a reality for the generation born after 1970. In 1976, only 12 per cent of twenty-year olds were participating in some form of education. By 2001, a quarter of all young Australians in their twenties were engaged in education. Secondly, learning is now a life-long process, and it is common for young people to combine study with work during their secondary school years and beyond, until they are well into their thirties (Wyn et al., 2008). Education has become both more significant and more marginal in young people's lives. This is because formal educational credentials have never been more important to labor market security, and yet at the same time, young people are learning from an increasingly wide range of sources, including informal learning. Schools and educational institutions are just one of many sites (including workplaces, leisure activities, the internet, and non-credentialed education and training) where young people engage in learning. Finally, tertiary education has become the new mass education sector. It replaces secondary education (which was the "new" mass education sector in the 1950s) as the desired completion point of an educational career.

Against this backdrop of change, educational policies have contributed to the strong identification of youth with being a student, and have primarily positioned young people as an economic resource and tool for the purposes of ensuring Australia's global economic competitiveness and youth as future workers and citizens.

Youth as Category: Student

Youth in Australia is almost synonymous with student because of the requirement for young people to complete secondary education (Wyn & Woodman, 2006; Cohen & Ainley, 2000). Student is a category based primarily on *age*, underlining the use of age as a management tool (Mizen, 2004). The use of age as mechanism for governing youth ignores the increasing evidence of diversity amongst young people and the increasingly complex relationship between young people's lives and age (Wyn & Woodman, 2006). In Australia, the close alignment between youth and student has recently been strengthened through the announcement of a policy intervention called "Learning or Earning" which compels young

Australians up to the age of eighteen to be in education or employment through the restriction of unemployment benefits.

Policies compelling young people to remain at school are justified by studies that show that higher levels of education are almost universally associated with better pay and job security. However, the ways in which well-educated individuals secure 'good jobs' are diverse and the links between education and employment are complex. A detailed analysis of the long-term outcomes for the post-1970 generation in Australia shows that the promise of labor-market rewards for their investment in education was over-stated and individuals needed to invest enormous energy and effort to negotiate complex, unstable, and unpredictable labor markets during the 2000s (Andres & Wyn, 2010).

Youth as Process: Transition from School to Work
Youth in Australia is widely seen as a period of transition with the emphasis on the process of school-to-work transition (Dusseldorp Skills Forum, 1999; Foundation for Young Australians, 2008). Indeed, Australia's educational policies are primarily designed to align school curricula to the needs of economic development, following the Organisation for Economic Co-operation and Development (OECD)'s calls for the transformation of education systems to meet the needs of knowledge economies. These economies, it is argued, required workers with high levels of post-secondary and increasingly tertiary education who will return regularly to formal education throughout their working lives in order to stay competitive within labor markets that continuously required new sets of skills. This policy preoccupation has had a powerful effect on the way in which youth is conceptualized in Australia, fostering an approach that sees youth as human capital. This policy focus gives the highest priority to academic and vocational outcomes, relegating individual and social well-being to the margins of formal education. Where well-being is admitted, it is generally briefly, framed in terms of individuals' responsibility to ensure they do not compromise their fitness for the workforce, to avoid being "at risk" and to reduce the economic costs of ill health (for example, education about contraception, the harms of drugs including alcohol, and education to instil healthy practices that will counter obesity and smoking) (Wyn, 2009; Wright & Burrows 2004).

Youth as Future: Workers and Citizens
Education policies largely position youth as being of value in the future (when they are adult). Young people's understanding of formal political processes and their sense of belonging to community is a secondary but consistent source of concern and there are many studies that show apparently decreasing levels of understanding by young people about formal politics and their rights and obligations as citizens (Manning & Ryan, 2004). Other work argues that young people find it difficult to relate to formal politics because they feel excluded from this domain, but that young

Australians have a strong sense of association with community and place and relate to a more "everyday" politics (Harris et al., 2007). Despite the increased prominence of the idea of youth participation in Australian state and federal policies in recent times, young people are still positioned as passive recipients of curricula that are determined from afar (i.e. federal government mandates) and have few opportunities to exercise decision-making in educational institutions.

HEALTH: DISCOURSES OF YOUTH

There is a strong association between health and youth discourses that is so taken for granted that it is all but invisible. Health discourses provide the tools that governments use to constitute, govern and manage youth across all jurisdictions (Wyn, 2009). The key component is the linking of youth to a bio-medical phase of development. Health discourses constitute the periods of both youth and childhood as stages of physical and mental development that have a predetermined schedule of progression and that naturally pass with the onset of adulthood. Bio-medical approaches provide a template for this thinking, including ideas about what is normal, and provide a rationale for positioning the period of youth as a formative time that holds serious risks for an individual's future if the correct stages of development are not followed. In the following discussion I identify several strands to the health discourses that frame youth.

Prevention
Regulation, intervention, and control of young people during the 1970s was associated with the metaphor of young people as dangerous or threatening to the established social order and policies tended to identify "problems" of youth in the present (e.g. issues of disengagement and the role of youth subcultures, especially amongst working class youth; Wyn & White, 1997). France argues that in the late 1990s these traditional concerns were overlaid by new policy approaches that aimed to take a preventive role, shifting the focus onto the identification of future problems, and "targeting the youth problem of the future through the children of today" (France, 2008: 2) to achieve more cost-effective outcomes.

France's analysis, like Mizen's, exposes the alignment of policy approaches with political (neo-liberal) agendas. In almost all fields affecting young people, early intervention (meaning childhood as the first point of intervention in a developmental chain leading to adulthood) and prevention (meaning the reduction of risk factors) are the current buzz words. France points out that the prevention approach and the identification of risk factors offer the dual possibility of limiting the "welfarist approaches of the 1980s" and at the same time offering governments the possibility of identifying social problems and finding solutions (France, 2008: 3). Whereas welfarist approaches (linked with the Keynesian economic policies of the years leading up to the 1970s) took a universal approach to supporting health and well-being, the preventive approach limits this by identifying and addressing only groups and individuals who are at risk, moving them from the margins to the mainstream.

The language and ideology of prevention and early intervention have now become almost synonymous with youth policy in many countries, including Australia. According to a recent information paper on key issues relating to children and youth in Australia, "prevention is a key aspect of the main current policies relating to children and youth" and "prevention is a key theme and a cost-effective approach" to Australia's health and well-being (Australian Bureau of Statistics, 2005b). This information paper identifies educational participation and employment as the first two key issues for young people's development.

Drawing the Boundaries that Include and Exclude
A prevention approach only makes sense if there is a mainstream, because prevention strategies are designed to divert faulty processes and transitions into the mainstream. The aim of prevention is to ensure that young people who stray from the mainstream are brought back in through interventions and it is one of the most important concepts legitimating normative assumptions about youth. The bio-medical and developmental psychological underpinning to this provides a "naturalizing" discourse of youth (Lesko, 1996). In other words, constituting youth as simply a bio-medical and developmental stage of life implies that much of what happens to most young people is only natural. The relevance of social conditions to the meaning and experience of youth is seen as being at best an overlay (or, a risk factor) to the more central reality of "normal" adolescent development.

There is a lot of evidence that in reality there is far greater diversity than these models imply, even within the supposed mainstream (Wyn & Dwyer, 2000). However, the most serious problem with prevention approaches is that they are based on a limited understanding of the complexity of social problems that lead young people to fail at school, become homeless, take drugs, experience mental health problems, and experience many other problems (France and Homel, 2006) and are therefore powerless to address these problems seriously.

Many studies of young people who experience marginalizing or exclusionary practices highlight the impact of power relations on young people. Policies have a coercive power which is often ignored and can have unintended outcomes. The actions of young people "on the margins" are often acts of resistance to everyday and chronic experiences of poverty, violence, mental illness, and criminality that run through their lives.

Pseudo-Science and the Idea of at Risk
Scientific measures, evidence-based practise and "hard" data are important tools in the repertoire of policy-makers in late modernity. The risk factor approach is

widely seen as providing a scientific framework for prevention policies, within and across international borders. Even though there are many uncertainties about its usefulness and much remains unknown about its potential stigmatizing qualities, this approach has been embraced and embedded into national and international policy (France and Homel, 2006). Its impact is both to define the problem and to then offer suggestions that shape how the state might respond to youth problems of the future.

Research that is able to assist in allocating resources to the most vulnerable groups is valuable, but there is an emerging consensus that the assumptions underlying research measuring risk and outcomes need to be scrutinised more closely. This is especially the case for research that draws on the positivist assumption that risk factors are social facts – objective, unambiguous, and measurable. It also assumes that values do not play a role in the interpretation of data and that the construction of research questions and the interpretation of data are not themselves a social construct.

One of the difficulties with the "risk factor" approach is that it is not objective. Young people do not interpret risk in the same way that policy-makers do (te Riele, 2006) and the interrelationship between different risk factors in young people's lives is far from clear. Furthermore, there is overwhelming evidence that the project of identifying risk factors is likely to seriously underestimate the complexity of chains of causality and effect (Armstrong, 2004).

Single risk factors are identified from time to time, on the basis of evidence that purports to show that one factor (e.g. literacy or parenting) is the key to solving complex youth problems (France & Homel, 2006). These policies make the individual (parent, young person) the target of intervention strategies. As France (2008) points out, the focus on individual outcomes alone actually undermines the claims about what can be achieved by measuring risks and outcomes because they do not adequately account for the complexity and extent of the issues.

The search for evidence is also very selective. There is a veritable industry in Australia that monitors, measures, and tracks the academic outcomes and the education, training, and employment destinations of individual young people. This information is gathered to inform educational practice in schools and is used to ensure that curricula meet the needs of labour markets. By contrast, very little is known about how schools promote young people's well-being or how communities promote social cohesion. Although well-being is seen as a key element of schooling, education systems do not report on the quality of relationships in schools; understandings of social cohesion and social connection are relatively unsophisticated and very little is known about how "well" young people are when they leave school and beyond (Wyn, 2007b).

LABOUR MARKET POLICIES: UNINTENDED CONSEQUENCES

In this section, I briefly discuss a third dimension of youth as a social process: unintended consequences of policies. It is somewhat contradictory that while Australia's educational policies focussed on essential human capital to feed the new Australian economies, labor market policies positioned young people as disposable and dispensable items in the economic management of workplaces. In Australia in the 1990s changes in educational policies coincided with changes in labor market policies through the introduction (in 1995) of new industrial relations. These achieved the dismantling of collective bargaining, resulting in the replacement of stable full-time work and related benefits with "just in time" employment, short-term contracts and part-time positions (Wyn & Woodman, 2006). The new industrial relations regulations were significant for all Australian workers but had particular implications for young workers. The changes had the effect of reducing the impact of previously negotiated Industrial Relation Awards – that covered multiple employers – to ensure minimum standards for workers across substantial sections of occupations. This was replaced by a regime in which individual employees negotiated their conditions (such as rates of pay, working hours, and conditions) with their employer. This meant that many groups, including young workers, became vulnerable to worsening working conditions.

The unintended consequences of these labor market policies were particularly serious for young people who entered the labor market in the early and mid 1990s. Analysis of the Life-Patterns longitudinal study which tracked the pathways of young Australians between 1991 to the present found that this group bore the personal costs of these policies in the form of delayed marriage and childbearing and elevated rates of mental health problems and concerns about their physical health (Andres & Wyn, 2010). The unfolding story of the Life-Patterns participants has been progressively told over a number of years (see Wyn et al., 2008). From early on (i.e. when they were in their early twenties), the participants struggled to find a balance between the demands of holding one (or often two or more) jobs, studying, and attempting to have a personal life. While the expansion of higher education offered unprecedented opportunities for this group, the restriction of workplace conditions and the uncertain nature of the labor market meant that individuals bore the responsibility of negotiating work, study, and personal life.

By the time they were in their early thirties (in 2004), it appeared that the investment in education had paid off because women with university degrees were the most likely to have secure jobs of any group (Dwyer et al., 2005). However, this group was also the most likely to experience job mobility as they took advantage of opportunities to improve their employment situation (Andres & Wyn, 2010). This group was the least likely to be married or to be a parent.

Women (from higher socio-economic backgrounds) were in one sense the "poster girls" for the educational policies of the 1990s, breaking new ground as they achieved educational credentials at an unprecedented level. In the labor market they have been able to reinvent themselves as necessary, thrive in chaotic and creative disorder, and work regardless of location or relocate as necessary. For many of these, at least for a time, the freedom of flexibility was ideal – as long as they worked full-time and did not attempt to push the notion of flexibility to the point that this involved successfully juggling work, family life, and child-rearing. As educational policies in the 1990s foreshadowed, those who did not invest in education have been restricted to unskilled and semi-skilled positions, especially women, while more of their equally (un)qualified male counterparts have eventually found work in skilled jobs. However, the "success" of the new educated, "flexible", and entrepreneurial elite has come at a considerable personal cost because of "inflexible" and repressive labor market policies.

The study has also revealed an ongoing struggle by the participants to manage their well-being, physically and mentally. Ten years out of secondary school the participants in the Life-Patterns study were also asked to comment specifically on their physical and mental health. A large proportion considered themselves neither physically or mentally well. On average, 57 per cent claimed they were physically "healthy" or "very healthy", and in terms of mental health, 39 per cent described themselves as less than "healthy". It is significant that 50 per cent of these young adults at age twenty-eight did not describe themselves as mentally healthy.

Their concerns about their mental and physical health are backed up by official statistics that show that today one in five young Australians, regardless of their levels of education, experiences mental health problems. The levels of physical and mental health concerns amongst the Australian cohort, and the dissatisfaction felt with their health across all groups, including those who are university-educated, reveal the personal costs of the mis-match of social and economic goals.

CONCLUSION

Perhaps the most interesting conclusion from this discussion is the point that ideas about "youth" as a social category are likely to be at odds with young people's own perceptions and experiences. It is also interesting to reflect that, in the Australian context at least, as the processes of social and economic change have opened up a diversity of ways of learning, new approaches to work and career and have placed pressure on individuals to manage uncertainty, policies pertaining to youth have increased their reliance on technologies and discourses of "certainty". The increasing reliance on age-based policies (and definitions of youth) at a time when the meaning of age is increasingly socially determined (and removed from biological age) is a contradiction.

This contradiction is evident in the mis-match between policies and young people's lives. For example, the instrumentalist educational policies of the 2000s have been described as a journey back to the future in which modernization is modelled on a more deferential time when schooling was made available for the purpose of making young people better able to take their place as workers in an increasingly industrial society. Hence curricula that are designed to build skills and dispositions for contemporary post-industrial economies are often based (paradoxically) on old pedagogies which position students as receivers of knowledge as opposed to constructors of knowledge.

Similarly, the policy trend to regard youth as primarily a phase of life leading to adulthood misses the opportunities there are to recognize the role young people can play in the present, as partners in decision-making (especially about matters that impact directly on their lives). Youth policies instead assume an undifferentiated mainstream that appears at times to be based on assumptions about youth that are derived from a previous era. The idea of a mainstream appears to be increasingly out of touch, especially in the context of an increasing socio-economic and cultural diversity in Australia.

It is important to reflect critically on the often unintended consequences of policies and programs. In a time when significant life transitions are occurring in all phases of life – especially throughout adulthood – it is timely to release conceptions of youth from outmoded models to develop approaches that more effectively address young people's lives.

Reclaiming Youthfulness[*]

Asef Bayat

There seems to be a great deal of both alarm and expectation about the political weight of Muslim youth in the Middle East. While many express anxiety over the seeming desire of the young in the Arab world to act as foot soldiers of radical Islam, others tend to expect youth (as in Iran or Saudi Arabia) to push for democratic transformation in the region (Ash, 2005; Samii, 2005; Shapiro, 2009). Thus, youths are projected to act as political agents, social transformers, whether for or against Islamism. Indeed, the recent history of the region is witness to the political mobilization of the young, as scores of Muslim youth have been involved in radical Islamist movements, from Saudi Arabia to Egypt to Morocco, or have defied the moral and political authority of the doctrinal regimes in the region, such as in the Islamic Republic of Iran. What do these events and involvements tell us about youth politics in general and "youth movements" in particular? Do they point to the necessarily transformative role of the young? Are youth movements revolutionary or ultimately democratizing in orientation? How can the prevalent "social movement theory" help us understand the nature of youth politics broadly, and that of the Muslim Middle East specifically?

While studies on youth-related themes such as AIDS, exclusion, violence, or religious radicalism have flourished in recent years, "youth" as an analytical category appears in them for the most part incidentally. Thus, many studies on "youth religious radicalism," for example, are primarily about religious radicalism per se, where the young people (like others) only *happen* to be involved. This is different from an approach that takes "youth" as the point of departure, as the central category, to examine religious radicalism. On the other hand, youth as a social category has curiously been absent from the prevalent social movement debates. In general, scholarly attempts to conceptualize the meanings and modalities of youth movements remain rare. At best, it is assumed that such conceptual tools as ideology, organization, mobilization, framing, and the like would be adequate to assess youth as a collective body. Consequently, youth activisms, those which do not fall into the frame of classical social movements, have

[*] The chapter was originally published in Asef Bayat *Life as Politics* (Stanford University Press, 2010): 115–136.

fallen into the realm, and are viewed largely from the prism, of "social problems" or subcultures. Whereas historical studies and journalistic accounts do talk about such collectives as youth movements (referring, for instance, to political protests of the 1960s or the subcultures of hippies or punks), they presume *a priori* that youth movements are those in which young people play the central role. Thus, student activism, antiwar mobilization, and counterculture trends of the 1960s in Europe and the United States, or the youth chapters of certain political parties and movements such as Communist youth, are taken to manifest different forms of youth movements (Tse-tung, 1967). My approach differs from these.

I would like to suggest that a discussion of the experience of youth in the Muslim Middle East, where moral and political authority impose a high degree of social control over the young, can offer valuable insight into conceptualiz-ing youth and youth movements. By comparing youth activisms in the Muslim Middle East, I suggest we can productively construct "youth" as a useful analytical category, which can then open the way to understanding the meaning of a youth movement. I propose that rather than being defined in terms of the centrality of the young, youth movements are ultimately about claiming or reclaiming youth-fulness. And "youthfulness" signifies particular habitus or behavioral and cogni-tive dispositions that are associated with the fact of being "young" – that is, a distinct social location between childhood and adulthood, where the youngster in a relative autonomy is neither totally dependent (on adults) nor independent, and is free from being responsible for others. Understood as such, the political agency of youth movements, their transformative and democratizing potential, depends on the capacity of the adversaries, the moral and political authorities, to accommodate and contain youthful claims. Otherwise, youth may remain as conservative as any other social groups. Yet, given the prevalence of the doctrinal religious regimes in the Middle East whose legitimizing ideologies are unable to accommodate the youth habitus, youth movements possess a great transformative and democratizing promise.

Young People, Youth and Youth Movements

The idea of youths as a revolutionary class is not new. The widespread mobiliza-tion of young people in Europe and the United States during the capitalist boom of the 1960s convinced many observers that youths (then active in universities, in antiwar movements, and in producing alternative lifestyles) were the new revolu-tionary force of social transformation in western societies. For Herbert Marcuse in the United States, and Andre Gorz in France, youths and students had taken the place of the proletariat as the major agent of political change (Marcuse, 1969). In this vein, youth movements have often been equated and used interchangeably either with student movements or with youth chapters or branches of this or that political party or movement (Bundy, 1987). Thus, the youth section of the Fascist Party in Germany is described as the German youth movement. Or the youth organization of the Iraqi Ba'th Party is assumed to be the youth movement in Iraq (Laqueur, 1962/1984).

I would suggest that a youth movement is neither the same as student activism nor an appendage of political movements; nor is it necessarily a revolutionary agent. First, movements are defined not simply by the identity of their actors (even though this factor affects very much the character of a movement), but primarily by the nature of their claims and grievances. Although in reality students are usually young, and young people are often students, they represent two different categories. "Student movements" embody the collective struggles of a student body to defend or extend "student rights" – decent education, fair exams, affordable fees, or accountable educational management (Cockburn and Blackburn, 1969). On the other hand, activism of young people in political organizations does not necessarily make them agents of a youth movement. Rather, it indicates youth support for, and their mobilization by, a particular political objective (e.g., democracy, Ba'thism, or fascism). Of course, some youth concerns may be expressed in and merge into certain political movements, as in German fascism, which represented aspects of a German youth movement, or in the current pietism of Muslims in France, which partially reflects the individuality (e.g., through putting on headscarves) of Muslim girls. However, this possibility should not be confused with the situation where young people happen to support a given political organization or movement.

But is the political ideal of the young necessarily revolutionary? By no means. Indeed, the political conservatism of many young people in the West after the 1960s, which compelled Marcuse to retreat from his earlier position, shattered the myth of youths as a revolutionary class. If anything, the political or transformative potential of youth movements is relative to the degree of social control their adversaries impose on them. For instance, a political regime, such as that in present-day Iran or Saudi Arabia that makes it its business to scrutinize individual behavior and lifestyle is likely to face youth dissent. Otherwise, youth movements per se may pose little challenge to authoritarian states unless they think and act politically. Because a youth movement is essentially about *claiming youthfulness*, it embodies the collective challenge whose central goal consists of defending and extending the youth habitus, by which I mean a series of dispositions, ways of being, feeling, and carrying oneself (e.g., a greater tendency for experimentation, adventurism, idealism, autonomy, mobility, and change) that are associated with the sociological fact of "being young." Countering or curtailing this habitus, youthfulness, is likely to generate collective dissent.

But, as the experience of today's Saudi Arabia shows, the mere presence of the young people subject to moral and political discipline does not necessarily render them carriers of a youth movement, because young persons (as age category) are unable to forge a collective challenge to the moral and political authority without first turning into youth as a social category, that is, turning into social actors. When I was growing up in a small village in central Iran during the 1960s, I of course had my friends and peers, with whom I talked, played, cooperated, and fought. However, at that point we were not "youth," strictly speaking; we were simply young persons, just members of an age cohort. In the village, most young people actually had little opportunity to experience "youthfulness," as they rapidly moved from childhood, a period of vulnerability and dependence, to adulthood, the world of work, parenting, and responsibility. Many youngsters never went to school. There was little "relative autonomy," especially for most young girls, who were rapidly transferred from their father's authority to that of the husband and were effectively trained into their roles as housewives long before puberty (that boys were usually exempted from such responsibility indicates how gender intervenes in the formation of youth).

It is partially in this light that Bourdieu has famously contended that youth is "nothing but a word," suggesting that talking about youth as a social unit is itself a manipulation of the young (Bourdieu, 1993). How can we imagine youth as a single category, he argues, when the youngsters of different classes (rich and the poor) have little in common? Indeed, I must add, the differences in the life worlds of male and female youngsters have been even more remarkable. Yet Bourdieu's contention pertains primarily to the pre-schooling situation, when young persons experience radically different lifeworlds. But as he himself acknowledges, in modern times mass schooling has changed all this. It has produced youthfulness on a massive national, as well as global, scale.

Youth as a social category, as collective agents, are an essentially modern, indeed urban, phenomenon. It is in modern cities that "young persons" turn into "youth," by experiencing and developing a particular consciousness about being young, about youthfulness. Schooling, prevalent in urban areas, serves as a key factor in producing and prolonging the period of youth, while it cultivates status, expectations, and, possibly, critical awareness. Cities, as loci of diversity, creativity, and anonymity, present opportunities for young people to explore alternative role models and choices, and they offer venues to express individuality. Mass media, urban spaces, public parks, youth centers, shopping malls, cultural complexes, and local street corners provide arenas for the formation and expression of collective identities. The fragmented mass of young individuals might share common attributes in expressing common anxieties, in demanding individual liberty, and in constructing and asserting subverting identities. Individuals may bond and construct identities through such deliberate associations and networks as schools, street corners, peer groups, and youth magazines. However, identities are formed mostly through "passive networks," the nondeliberate and instantaneous communications among atomized individuals that are established by the tacit recognition of their commonalities and that are mediated directly through the gaze in public space, or indirectly through the mass media (Bayat, 1997, 2010). As present agents in the public space, the young recognize shared identity by noticing (seeing) collective symbols inscribed, for instance, in styles (T-shirts, blue jeans, hairstyle), types of activities (attending particular concerts and music stores, and hanging around shopping malls), and places (stadiums, hiking trails, street corners). When young persons develop a particular consciousness about themselves as youth and begin to defend or extend their youth habitus, their youthfulness in a collective fashion, a youth movement can be said to have developed. Where political repression curtails organized activism, youth may form nonmovements.

Unlike student movements, which require a good degree of organization and strategy building, youth "nonmovements" may augment change by their very public presence. With their central preoccupation with "cultural production" or lifestyles, the young may fashion new social norms, religious practices, cultural codes, and values, without needing structured organization, leadership, or ideologies. This is because youth nonmovements are, I would suggest, characterized less by *what the young do* (networking, organizing, deploying resources, mobilizing) than by *how they are* (in behaviors, outfits, ways of speaking and walking, in private and public spaces). The identity of a youth nonmovement is based not as much on collective *doing* as on collective *being;* and the forms of their expression are less collective protest than *collective presence.* The power of Muslim youth in the Middle East lies precisely in the ability of their atomized agents to challenge the political and moral authorities by the persistence of their merely alternative presence. Even though youth (non)movements are by definition concerned with the claims of youthfulness, nevertheless they can and do act as a harbinger of social change and democratic transformation under those doctrinal regimes whose legitimizing ideologies are too narrow to accommodate youthful claims of the Muslim youth.

In Iran, where moral and political authority converged, draconian social control gave rise to a unique youth identity and collective defiance. Young people both became central to and were further mobilized by the post-Islamist reform movement. The assertion of youthful aspirations, the defense of their habitus, lay at the heart of their conflict with moral and political authority. With the state being the target of their struggles, Iranian youths engendered one of the most remarkable youth nonmovements in the Muslim world. The struggle to reclaim youthfulness melded with the struggle to attain democratic ideals. In contrast, Egyptian youth, operating under the constraints of "passive revolution," opted for the strategy of "accommodating innovation," attempting to adjust their youthful claims within existing political, economic, and moral norms. In the process, they redefined dominant norms and institutions, blended divine and diversion, and engendered more inclusive religious mores. Yet this subculture took shape within, and neither against nor outside, the existing regime of moral and political power. Egyptian youth remained distant from both being a movement and involvement in political activism until the late 2000s, when a new web-based opportunity seemed to offer some venues for a collective mobilization.

Iran's "Third Generation"

The spectacular activism of young people in the Islamic Revolution[1], the war with Iraq, and in the new revolutionary institutions earned them a new, exalted position, altering their image from "young troublemakers" to "heroes and martyrs." This was the image of the "spectacular male youth" drawn sociologically from lower- and middle-class families. At the same time, the young were seen as highly vulnerable to corrupting ideas and therefore needing protection and surveillance. To reproduce an ideal "Muslim man," the Islamic regime launched in 1980 the "cultural revolution" program to Islamize educational culture and curricula. Universities were shut down for two years, Islamic associations were set up in schools, and all public places came under the watchful gaze of morals police and proregime vigilantes.

What sustained this regime of surveillance for a decade were revolutionary fervor, preoccupation with war, and the repression of dissent. Young men were either on the war front or fleeing the country, preferring the humiliation of exile to "heroic martyrdom" in a "meaningless" battle. Although adolescents sought refuge in schools, often by deliberately failing exams to postpone graduation, they lived in anxiety, gloom, and depression. One out of every three high school students suffered from a behavioral disorder. Girls in particular were more susceptible to stress, fear, and depression[2]. The poetic reflections of a young girl talking to herself capture the depth of her inner gloom as she witnesses the gradual erosion of her youth:

My father never recognizes me on the street.
He says "all of you look like mourners."
Yes, we dress in black, head to toe in black.
Sometimes, I get scared by the thought of my father not recognizing me in this
        dark colorlessness ...
I stare at the mirror,
And I see an old woman.
Am I still sleepy?
Oh ... I feel aged and unhappy.
Why should I be so different from other twenty-year-olds?
                They liken my joy to sin,
                They close my eyes to happiness,
They stop me from taking my own steps ...
Oh ... I feel like an old woman ...
No, no, I want to be young,
Want to love,
To dress in white, be joyful, have fun,
And move to fulfill my dreams ...
I look at myself in the mirror.
I look so worn out and aged ...[3]

Few officials noticed this inner despair in youngsters' lives. Blinded by their own constructed image and by their doctrinal animosity toward joy, Islamist leaders failed to read the inner minds and hearts of this rapidly growing segment of the population. The shocking truth emerged only in the postwar years when some officials noticed "strange behavior" among the young. With the war over and postwar reconstruction under way, the young began to publicly express their selfhood, both individually and collectively. The media carried stories about the "degenerate behavior" of Iranian youth. Boys were discovered disguised as women walking on the streets in a southern city. Tomboy girls wore male attire to escape harassment of morals police. College students refused to take religions studies courses[4], and "authorities in an Iranian holy Muslim city launched a crackdown on pop music, arresting dozens of youths for playing loud music on their car stereos" (Daily News, 2005). Other reports spoke of groups of young males dancing in the streets next to self-flagellation ceremonies on the highly charged mourning day of "Ashura". Young drivers had fun by crashing their cars into each other, or by playing a form of the game of "chicken": racing while handcuffed to the steering wheel and trying to escape before flying off a cliff (Qotbi, 2000). Drug addiction soared among schoolchildren. The average age of prostitutes declined from twenty-seven to twenty, expanding the industry by 635 percent in 1998[5].

Yet alongside individual rebellion, the young took every opportunity to assert open and clandestine subcultures, defying the moral and political authority. The severe restriction of music did not deter them. When the reformist mayor of Tehran, Gholam Hussein Karbaschi, established numerous cultural centers in South Tehran, young people comprised 75 percent of those who rushed to fill classical-music classes and concert halls. Smuggled audio and video recordings of exiled Iranian singers filled big-city main streets, while MTV-type music videos found widespread popularity. The young blared loud music from speedy cars, to the dismay of Islamists, while across the capital underground pop and rock bands thrived at covert late-night parties. Teenagers enjoyed not only the music but its subculture and fashion – tight or baggy pants, vulgar English slang, tattoos – acquired through smuggled videos[6]. Rap and heavy metal music in particular became popular. By 1999, music subcultures had become so widespread that the reformist Ministry of Culture was compelled to recognize and even organize the first "concert of pop music" in the Islamic republic. Some teens ran away from home to join rock bands, attracted by a sense of belonging, though many were incarcerated by the morals police.

Indeed, runaway teenagers became a major social problem. In 2000, Tehran was reportedly faced with an "escalating crisis of runaway girls frequently becoming victims of prostitution rings and human trafficking." Between 1997 and 1998 the number of reported runaway teenagers tripled. In Tehran alone 900 girls ran away in 2000, and 4,000 in 2002 when the nationwide number was reportedly 60,000. Assertion of individuality – freedom to have a male partner (42 percent) and freedom from family surveillance – seemed to be the main cause[7]. "I want to leave Iran," lamented a young female who had been arrested for leaving home. "I don't like Iran at all. I feel I am in prison here even when I am sitting in the park."

Although dating openly had become a prime casualty of Islamic moral code, the young devised ways to resist. Well-to-do young boys and girls made contacts not only at private parties and underground music concerts, but also in public parks, shopping malls, and restaurants, often discreetly arranged by cell phone. In such "distanciated dating," girls and boys stood apart but eyed each other from a distance, chatted, flirted, and expressed love through electronic waves. To seek privacy and yet appear legitimate, young couples hired taxis to drive them around the city in anonymity, while they sat back for hours to romance or take delight in their companionship. The popularity of Valentine's Day revealed an abundance of "forbidden love" and relationships in which sex, it seemed, was not excluded. In fact, scattered evidence indicated widespread premarital sex among Iran's Muslim youths, despite the high risk of harsh penalties. An academic claimed that one out of three unmarried girls, and 60 percent in North Tehran, had had sexual relations. Out of 130 cases of AIDS cases reported in hospitals, 90 were unmarried women[8]. An official of Tehran municipality reported "each month at least 10 or 12 aborted fetuses are found in the garbage"[9]. Although public information did not exist, researchers and medical professionals were alarmed by the extent of unwanted pregnancies. Doctors unofficially spoke of the fact that "not one week passes by without at least two or three young girls coming in for abortion"[10]. Reportedly, some 60 percent of patients requesting abortions were unmarried young girls (ibid). The United Nations Population Fund officials in Tehran referred to a survey on "morality" (meaning sexuality) among young people, but the results were so "terrible" that they had to be destroyed (ibid). Attention to self, physical appearance, clothing, fashion, and plastic surgery became widespread trends among young females.

Clearly, sexuality among the young posed a major challenge to the Islamic state, testing the capacity of Islamism to integrate youths, whose sensibilities were inherently subversive to it. In the early 1990s, President Rafsanjani came up with the idea of "temporary marriage" as an "Islamic" solution to the crisis. It meant controlling sexual encounters through fixed short-term (as short as a few hours) relationships called "marriage." Ayatollah Ha'eri Shirazi proposed "legitimate courtship" (without sex), an openly recognized relationship approved by parents or relatives. Others called for some kind of official document confirming the legitimacy of such relationships, meaning something like temporary marriage in which the couple would not live together. And in 2000, conservative Islamists put forward the idea of a Chastity House, where men seeking sex were to "temporarily marry" prostitutes to "legitimize" their encounters.

The desperate cultural politics of young people shattered Islamists' image of them as self-sacrificing individuals devoted to martyrdom and moral codes. By challenging the regime's moral and political authority, the young subverted the production of "Muslim youth." Anxiety over the increasing *bad-hijabi* (laxity in veil wearing) among school and university girls haunted officials. "We are encountering a serious cultural onslaught. What is to be done?" they lamented[11]. Over 85 percent of young people in 1995 spent their leisure time watching television, but only 6 percent of them watched religious programs; of the 58 percent who read books, less than 8 percent were interested in religious literature. A staggering 80 percent of the nation's youth were indifferent or opposed to the clergy, religious obligations, and religious leadership[12], while 86 percent of students refrained from saying their daily prayers[13]. Official surveys confirmed the deep mistrust separating the young from the state and whatever it stood for. The vast majority (80 percent) lacked confidence in politicians[14], and most (over 70 percent) saw the government as being responsible for their problems.

Yet this distrust of the Islamist authorities did not mean that the young abandoned religion. Indeed, they expressed a "high religiosity" in terms of fundamental religious "beliefs" and "feelings" with some 90 percent believing in God and the idea of religion, according to a study (Serajzadeh, 1999). But youth remained largely indifferent to religious practises; religious belief and knowledge seemed to have little impact on their daily lives. God existed but did not prevent them from drinking alcohol or dating the opposite sex. To them, religion was a more philosophical and cultural reality than it was moral and doctrinal. While most refused to attend mosque ceremonies, they flocked to public and private lectures given by the "religious intellectuals," which spread during the mid-1990s. Like their Egyptian counterparts, the globalized Iranian youth reinvented their religiosity, blending the transcendental with the secular, faith with freedom, divine with diversion.

In an ingenious *subversive accommodation,* many youngsters utilized the prevailing norms and institutions, especially religious rituals, to accommodate their youthful claims, but in doing so they creatively redefined and subverted the constraints of those codes and norms. This strategy was best expressed in the way the North Tehrani youths treated the highly charged ritual of Muharrarn, which commemorates the death of Imam Hussein, the grandson of Prophet Muhammad. By inventing "Hussein parties," the young turned this highly austere occasion of mourning into an evening of glamour, fun, and sociability. Boys and girls dressed in their best, strolled through the streets, joined parades of mourners, and used the occasion to stay out until dawn to socialize, flirt, exchange phone numbers, and secretly arrange dates (Yaghmaian, 2002: 61-65). In a similar spirit, they reinvented the "sham-e ghariban" (the eleventh night of the month of Muharram), the most dreary and sorrowful Shi'a ritual in Islamic Iran, as a blissful night of sociability and diversion. Groups of fifty to sixty girls and boys carried candles through the streets to large squares, where they sat on the ground in circles, often leaning on one another in the romantic aura of dim candlelight, and listened to the melancholic *nowhe* (sad religious songs) while chatting, meditating, romancing, or talking politics in hushed tones until dawn[15].

These rituals of resistance did not go unpunished by violent vigilante *baseejies,* or bands of "fundamentalist" youth who attacked the participants and disrupted their assemblies and in so doing turned their "subversive accommodation" *into* political defiance. The cultural became overtly political. In January 1995, 100,000 young spectators of a Tehran soccer match went on a rampage following a disagreement on the result of the competition. Riots destroyed part of the stadium and led to a mass protest of youths chanting: "Death to this barbaric regime"; "Death to the Pasdaran" (*Al-Hayat,* January 22, 1995). In 2004, over 5,000 youths battled with violent vigilante groups in North Tehran; and much earlier, the city of Tabriz had witnessed thousands of young spectators raging against *basiji* bands for objecting to the "improper behavior" of a few individuals in the crowd. Even more than collective grief and violence, collective joy became a medium of subversion. For the mass expression of "happiness" not only defied puritan principles of grief and gloom but circumvented its aura of repression. The success of Iran's national soccer team in Australia in November 1997 and at the World Cup in Paris against the United States in June 1998 sent hordes of young boys and girls into the streets in every major city to cheer, dance, and sound their car horns. For five hours security forces lost control, stood aside, and watched the crowd in its blissful ecstasy (Peterson, 1997). In the city of Karadj, the crowd overwhelmed the *basjies* by chanting, *"Basiji* must dance!" But even defeat was a pretext to show collective defiance. Hours after Iran's team lost to Bahrain in 2001 hundreds of thousands took to the streets, expressing deep-felt anger at the Islamist authorities. In fifty-four different areas of Tehran, young people marched, shouted political slogans, threw rocks and handmade explosives at police, vandalized police cars, broke traffic lights, and lit candles in a sign of mourning for the defeat. Other cities, Karadj, Qom, Shiraz, Kashan, Isfahan, and Islamabad, also witnessed similar protests. Only after 800 arrests did protestors go home. But perhaps nothing was more symbolic about the young's defiance than setting off fireworks to celebrate Nowruz, the coming of the Iranian New Year. The Islamic state had outlawed this ancient Persian tradition. But by setting off millions of firecrackers, youngsters turned urban neighborhoods into explosive battle zones, scorning the official ban on the ritual and the collective joy that went with it[16]. The "mystery of firecrackers," as one daily put it, symbolized outrage against officialdom that the young saw as having forbidden joy and jolliness[17].

The younger generation's defiance deepened the conflict between reformists and conservatives in government. Reformists blamed the youth unrest on the conservatives' overbearing moral pressure and the "suppression of joy." Launching a public debate on the necessity of leisure, the reformists called for tolerance and understanding. In so doing, the reformists supplied the young with a platform, political support, and moral courage. Backed by reformist friends at the top, the young further pushed for their claims, not only through defiance, but also by engagement in civic activism. In 2001, some fifty youth NGOs were registered in Tehran, and 400 in the country. Within two years they reached 1,100, of which 850 participated in the first national congress of youth NGOs in 2003. Still thousands more flourished informally throughout the country, working in cultural, artistic, charity, developmental, and intellectual domains. They organized lectures and concerts, did charity work, and coordinated bazaars, at times with remarkable innovation. On one occasion, a group of youths presented President Khatami with a plan for alternative young cabinet members to form a "government of youths." But reclaiming public space to assert their youthful sensibilities remained the major concern of those whose globalized subcultures (expressed in sexuality, gender roles, and lifestyle) were distancing them even from post-Islamists' commitment to largely traditional moral conventions. Youth's behavior infuriated conservative puritans, who clamored against what they considered a "cultural invasion," "hooliganism," and "anti-Islamic sentiments," blaming them on Khatami's "failure to ameliorate unemployment, poverty and corruption(Nabawi, 2001: 2). Thus, they launched new crackdowns on events, gatherings, places, and behaviors that were seen to cause "immorality," "depravity," and "indecency"; they dispatched special units with groups of uniformed men who carried machine guns and hand grenades to reassert the republic's moral order (Cadiot, 2001; Theodoulou, 2001).

This simultaneous condition of both suppression (of youthfulness by the politico-moral authority) and opportunity (valorization and encouragement of the young) offered these youth a spectacular sense of self and the possibility to act collectively, a status their Egyptian or Saudi counterparts largely lacked. But there was more to the emergence of a national Iranian youth movement than politics. Sweeping social change since the early 1980s had helped form "youth" as a social category. Demographically, by 1996 Iran had experienced a dramatic rise in its number of young people with two-thirds under the age of thirty. Of these, a staggering twenty million, one-third of the population, were students (an increase of 266 percent since 1976). Most lived in cities, exposed to diverse lifestyles with spaces for relative autonomy, extra-kinship identities, and social interactions on a broad scale. In the meantime, as urbanity was permeating the countryside, an "urbanized" generation of rural youth was in the making. The spread of Open University branches throughout the country, for instance, meant that on average every village had two university graduates, a very rare phenomenon in the 1970s. Rural youth began to acquire legitimacy based on competence and merit and became major decision makers, which the dominance of seniority had previously made unthinkable. With sweeping social changes in the countryside and expanding communication technologies that facilitated the flow of young people, ideas, and lifestyles, social barriers separating rural and urban youth began to crumble, giving the country's young a broader, national constituency. Meanwhile, the weakening of parental authority over the young (resulting from the state's valorization of youth) and the reinforcement of child-centeredness in the family (an outcome of rising literacy among women and mothers) contributed to the individuation of the young and their militancy[18].

By the mid-1990s, Iran's postrevolutionary young had become "youth," a social agent. But theirs was not a conventional social movement, an organized and sustained collective challenge with articulated ideology or a recognizable leadership. Rather, theirs was a nonmovement, the "collective conscience" of the non-collective actors, whose principal expression lay in the *politics of presence*, tied closely to the young's everyday cultural struggles and normative subversion. This fragmented mass of individuals and subgroups shared common attributes in expressing common anxieties, in demanding individual liberty, and in constructing and asserting their collective identities. The individual youngsters were tied together not only within dispersed subgroups (youth magazines, NGOs, peer groups, and street-corner associations), but more commonly through "passive networks": those nondeliberate communications formed by the youngsters tacitly recognizing their commonalities through sight and sound in public spaces, by identifying shared symbols displayed in styles (T-shirts, blue jeans, hair), types of activities (attending particular concerts and music stores), and places (sport stadiums, shopping malls, hiking tracks), and by the sound of their music or firecrackers. Thus, the birth of youth as a social category of national scale, operating in uniquely simultaneous conditions of both repression and opportunity, drove the Iranian youths to reclaim their youthfulness in a battle in which the state became the target. Reclaiming youth habitus from state control and moral authority defined Iran's youth nonmovement.

POLITICS OF EGYPTIAN YOUTHS: "ACCOMMODATING INNOVATION"

"Youth" as a social category also developed in Egypt. Quite similar to Iran, in 1996 about half of Egypt's sixty million people were under twenty, and 64 per cent under thirty. Although the total student population in 1996 (11.6 million) was only just over half of Iran's, Egypt had the same number of college students (1.1 million) (Central Agency for Public Mobilization & Statistics, 1999). Similarly, the peculiarity of the Egyptian countryside (with comparatively large villages concentrated along the Nile Valley and Delta and in close proximity to each other and large cities) contributed to their growing urbanity during the 1980s and 1990s. The abundance of electricity; new means of communication; commercialization; the flow of people, goods, and information; and increasing occupational specialization marked the shifting social structure of post-open-door rural settings

(Denis & Bayat, 2001). The spread of mass schooling provided the raw materials to produce educated youth. And urban institutions such as college campuses, coffee shops, shopping malls, concert venues, festivals of saints, and street corners provided spaces for social interaction, active and passive networks, and the construction of youth identities. In brief, the young as social actors had emerged in both Iran and Egypt in a more or less similar pattern.

But the simultaneous processes of urbanization, Islamization, and globalization had fragmented the young generation in Egypt. Alongside actively pious and provincial adolescents had emerged new generations of globalized youths who had been increasingly exposed to the global cultural flows. Clearly, different class and gender experiences had given rise to multiple youth identities. Whereas harsher social control in the Islamic republic had pushed male and female youth to develop similar aspirations, gender distinction in Egypt remained more enunciated; for example, the difference in social aspirations between adolescent boys and girls in Egypt was so pronounced that observers spoke of "more separate male and female cultures than a single youth culture." Especially crucial were male perceptions of women, which seriously threatened their identity as youths' shared habitus. Rarely would men (in Egypt only 4 percent) marry a woman who had premarital sex (Khalifa, 1995). "No one goes out with a girl and marries her. Ninety-nine percent of men would not marry a girl they ever touched," stated a university student in Egypt. And the girls felt this bitter truth. "This is what we hate about the boys; they rarely marry the girl they go out with" (Naguib, 2002).

But in both Iran and Egypt, the mainstream young attempted to assert their habitus, to exert their individuality, aspired for change, and created youth subculture. They did so by recognizing the existing moral and political constraints and trying to make the best out of the existing institutions. However, compared with their Iranian counterparts, Egyptian youth remained demobilized in the political and civic domains. While they showed interest in participating politically, they lacked the means to do so. Unlike in Iran, where ageism was breaking down and youth was remarkably valorized, the elders and political elites in Egypt did not trust the young in the political arena. Egyptian politics, both governmental and oppositional, continued to remain in the grip of very old men, with an average age of seventy-seven in 2002[19]. Meanwhile, the young distrusted party politics, which happened to be the only legitimate channel for activism[20]. A survey by the Ahram Center for Political and Strategic Studies revealed that 67 percent of young people were not registered to vote.

Lack of trust in electoral games pushed the young further away from politics, and restrictions on campus activism put a damper on youth political mobilization. The mobilization of middle- and lower – middle – class youth in the Islamist movement during the 1980s did not repeat itself in other political fields. In the late 1990s political activity on campuses was paltry, as state security intervened to prevent Islamist, leftist, and Nasserist candidates from running for student unions. Only Israel's

reoccupation of the Palestinian Territories in early 2000 galvanized social and political mobilization (Hammond, 1998:7). The remarkable involvement of Egyptian
youths in collecting food and medicine for Palestinians was indeed a watershed in
youth voluntarism, but it was the result of the unique political and moral aura of the
siege of Palestinians by Likud's repressive incursions. Otherwise, the young showed
slight interest in public service or voluntarism. Even the youths of elite families,
whose social and financial resources often make them the prime source of donations, remained indifferent. Of twenty hand-picked students of Egyptian universities, only one had engaged in any volunteer activities (Khalifa, 1995). Genuine youth
initiatives such as Fathi Kheir NGO were exceptions. The prevailing notion was that
the state, not citizens, was to take charge of social provisions.

Clearly, the young were bearing the brunt of Egypt's "passive revolution,"
in which the "secularreligious" state had appropriated the initiative for change
through a remarkable blend of concession and control. Egyptian youth were not
under the same moral and political control as their counterparts in Iran or Saudi
Arabia. Depending on their social and economic capacities, they were able to
listen to their music, follow their fashions, pursue dating games, have affordable
fun, and be part of global trends so long as they recognized their limits, beyond
which their activities would collide with the moral authority and the state. Youths
were to be integrated and guided by the state.

To do so, the state would provide the young with "scientific advancement"
or technical education to catch up and compete in the world, and at the same
time guide them into religious piety in order to withstand both foreign cultural
influences and home-grown political Islam[21]. Indeed, the 1999 presidential decree
to rename the Supreme Council of Youths (established in 1965) the Ministry of
Youths and Sports displayed official anxiety over the "youth problem[22]. Their protection from political and moral ills had become a matter of "national security."
The Ministry of Youth with its control of 4,000 Youth Centers was to help materialize these objectives. Government loans were to enable the young to settle down
and marry by purchasing flats, to provide access to ICT, and to acquire technical
training through NGOs[23]. Meanwhile, the Youth Centers, some kind of state-
controlled NCOs, would organize summer camps, debates, entertainment, training programs, religious education caravans, and sporting events. But the deplorable state of most of these centers, their poor amenities, garbage-infested athletic
fields, poor libraries, and the state's control rendered them inadequate to carry
out this enormous task. Often, only lower-class youngsters, almost all of them
male, attended the centers. Many remained "youth centers without youths," as an
official weekly put it[24]. If the televised annual "dialogue" of the president with
"Egyptian youths" was any indication, a deep distrust separated youths from the
state[25]. The young took solace in nonstate spaces that infringed only marginally on
political and moral authorities. They resorted to the cultural politics of everyday
life, where they could reassert their youthful claims.

For over a decade, young Egyptians were seen in the image of Islamist militants waging guerrilla war, penetrating college campuses, or memorizing the Qur'an in the backstreet mosques of sprawling slums. Moral authorities, parents, and foreign observers expected them to be characteristically pious, strict, and dedicated to the moral discipline of Islam. Yet in their daily lives, the mainstream young defied their constructed image, often shocking moral authorities by expressing defiance openly and directly. "The youth of this country are rebelling against the old traditions," stated a twenty-year-old female student in Cairo, "We are breaking away from your chains; we are not willing to live the lives of the older generations. Women smoking *shisha* is the least shocking form of rebellion going on. Face the changes and embrace our generation; do not treat us as if we are children. Our generation is more exposed than yours, and this is a simple fact"[26].

Reports of "satanic youth" in January 1997 demonstrated not only prevailing moral panic over the alleged vulnerability of youths to global culture, but those youths' emerging self-assertion. Every Thursday night hundreds of well-to-do youngsters gathered in an abandoned building to socialize, have fun, and, above all, dance to heavy metal music. Six weeks of sensational media coverage and the arrest of dozens accused of "satanism" (later released for lack of evidence) proved the existence of underground subcultures that few adults had noticed. The music subculture, however, did not die out after the satanist myth. It reappeared in the form of raving. Egyptian raves began with small bands and small crowds, but after 1998 professional organization and commercialization helped them grow rapidly. They encompassed music genres from around the world, including Egyptian pop, and catered to young elites of "glamour, high fashion and lifestyle". The Egyptian rave was largely sex-free, but it did involve alcohol and (unofficially) drugs (in the form of ecstasy). Indeed, studies indicated that experimentation with alcohol went beyond the well-to-do young. One out of every three students in the cities had drunk alcohol, mainly beer[27]. Although only somewhat more than 5 percent admitted experimenting with drugs (85 percent of whom were cannabis users), the problem became more severe in the early 1990s. Law enforcement professionals warned that the use of ecstasy in particular was on the rise[28].

While in general a "culture of silence" prevailed regarding sexuality, premarital sex seemed to be widespread among Muslim youth, despite normative and religious prohibition. In an approximate but indicative survey of one hundred high school and college girls in various Cairo districts, 8 percent said they had had sexual intercourse, 37 percent had experienced sex without intercourse, 23 percent had kissed, and 20 percent had only held hands. In a survey of 100 school and college male students in Cairo, 73 percent said they would not mind having premarital sex as long as they would not marry their partners (Khalifa, 1995). A more comprehensive study found "substantial rates of premarital sex among university students" (El-Zanaty, 2000: 163). In AIDS education classes, students posed questions about specific sexual practices that surprised health educators.

Although comprehensive surveys did not exist, the use of pornography by males appeared to be quite widespread. Ninety out of one hundred respondents said they masturbated regularly, and 70 percent of those ninety thought they were doing something religiously and physically wrong (Khalifa, 1995). Beyond influences from satellite dishes, illicit videos, and later the internet, the changing structure of households seemed to facilitate youth sexual practices. The father figure, once so important, was changing even in villages. One out of three families was fatherless, resulting from divorce, abandonment, and mostly (20 to 25 percent) fathers working abroad; children might use the home for romance when their mothers went out. Otherwise, lower-class Cairo couples found romantic solace on the benches of inconspicuous metro stations, where they sat and talked or romanced while pretending to wait for trains[29].

Most of these young people were religious. They often prayed, fasted, and expressed fear of God. A few heavy metal "satanists" whom I interviewed considered themselves devout Muslims but also enjoyed rock music, drinking alcohol, and romance. The mainstream young combined prayer, partying, and pornography, faith and fun. Notice how, for instance, a lower-class young man working in Dahab, a tourist resort where many foreign women visit, blended God, women, and police in pursuit of his mundane and spiritual needs: "I used to pray before I came to Dahab. My relationship to God was very strong and very spiritual. Now, my relationship to God is very strange. I always ask him to provide me with a woman, and when I have a partner, I ask him to protect me from the police" (Abdul-Rahman, 2001: 18).

This might sound like a contradiction, but it expresses more a consolation and an accommodation. The young enjoyed dancing, raving, having illicit relationships, and fun but found solace and comfort in their prayers and faith. "I do both good and bad things, not just bad things. The good things erase the bad things," said a law student in Cairo (Naguib, 2002). A twenty-five-year-old religious man who drank alcohol and "tried everything" also smoked "pot in a group sometimes to prove [their] manhood." He prayed regularly, hoping that God forgave his ongoing misdeeds. Such a state of liminality, this "creative inbetweeness," illustrates how the young attempted to redefine and reimagine their Islam in order to accommodate their youthful desires for individuality, change, fun, and "sin" within the existing moral order. Not only did they redefine their religion, they also reinvented notions of youthfulness. "During adolescence," a nineteen-year-old student said, "all young men do the same; there is no *halal* or *haram* [right or wrong] at that age" (ibid). Similarly, many young girls saw themselves as committed Muslims but still uncovered their hair or wore the veil only during Ramadan or only during fasting hours. Many of those who enjoyed showing their hair found consolation in deciding to cover it after marriage, when their youthful stage was over.

To assert their habitus under the prevailing moral and political constraints, Egyptian youths resorted to *accommodating innovation,* a strategy that redefined and reinvented prevailing norms and traditional means to accommodate their youthful claims. Yet the young did not depart radically from the dominant system but made it work for their interests[30]. The relatively widespread practice of *'urfi* (informal) marriage since the late 1990s exemplified this strategy. *'Urfi* marriage is a religiously accepted but unofficial oral contract that requires two witnesses and is carried out in secret. The minister of social affairs spoke of 17 percent of university female students going through *'urfi* marriage, causing a public uproar over this "danger" to "national security." Officials cited declining social authority, absence of fathers, and the employment of mothers as the cause of this "frightening phenomenon." Experts pointed to the lack of housing and especially the absence of a "religious supervision" over youth. But in essence, the young utilized this traditional institution to pursue romance within, but not outside or against, the moral and economic order, to get around the moral constraints on dating and the economic constraints on formal marriage[31]. With the same logic, lower-class youth resorted to, but also modified the meaning of, such religious occasions as Ramadan (the time of fasting), Eid al-Adha (the festival of sacrifice), and the birthdays of saints as occasions of intense sociability and diversion.

Indeed, the phenomenon of Amr Khaled, Egypt's most popular young lay preacher, who since the late 1990s spoke about piety and the moralities of everyday life, should be seen in a similar sense of a reinvention of a new religious style by Egypt's globalizing youth (Bayat, 2002: 23). In a sense, Egyptian cosmopolitan youth fostered a new religious subculture – one that was expressed in a distinctly novel style, taste, language, and message. It resonated in the aversion of these young from patronizing pedagogy and moral authority. These globalizing youth displayed many seemingly contradictory orientations; they were religious believers but distrusted political Islam if they knew anything about it; they swung back and forth from (the pop star) Amr Diab to Amr Khaled, from partying to prayers, and yet they felt the burden of a strong social control by their elders, teachers, and neighbors. As young Egyptians were socialized in a cultural condition and educational tradition that often restrained individuality and novelty, they were compelled to assert them in a "social way," through "fashion." Thus, through the prism of youth, this religious subculture galvanized around the "phenomenon of Amr Khaled" was partly an expression of "fashion" in a Simmelian sense – in the sense of an outlet that accommodates contradictory human tendencies: change and adaptation difference and similarity, individuality and social norms. Resorting to this type of piety permitted the elite young to assert their individuality, undertake change, and yet remain committed to collective norms and social equalization.

Although innovative, these strategies conformed to the prevailing regime of power meaning that Egyptian youth stood largely demobilized within social and political constraints. Egypt's "passive revolution" had ensured this demobilization by offering room to exercise a limited degree of innovation, but only within the political discipline of the "secularreligious" state; it was only toward the end of the first decade of the twenty-first century that Egyptian youth managed to collectively break through the rigid case of the state to mobilize – not in the streets, but on the screens of computers. With the new technological opportunities, e-mail, weblogs, and especially Facebook, some 70,000 educated youths linked up to produce what came to be known as the April 6 Youth Movement. Utilizing such a venue to campaign against political repression, economic stagnation, and nepotism, the young activists augmented a new way of doing politics, a step further than what the Kifaya movement had begun earlier on. For now, we may not be able to judge the political efficacy of such postmodern nonmovements, but they attest to the fact that the subaltern utilize any opportunities to outmaneuver state surveillance and push for change. Yet the point is not to wait for opportunities, but to constantly generate them.

What, then, of youths as a political force in the Muslim Middle East? Do youth non/movements possess the capacity to cause political and democratic transformation? If indeed the youth movements, as I have suggested, are ultimately about claiming and reclaiming youthfulness, then their transformative and democratizing potential would depend on the capacity of the moral and political authorities to accommodate youthful claims. If their youthful claims are accommodated, youth movements would by definition cease to exist, and young people may remain as conservative politically as any other social groups. To act as democratizing agents, the young will need to think and act politically, as the Egyptian April 6 Youth Movement in 2008 illustrates. Yet, because the current doctrinal religious regimes in the Middle East possess limited capacity to contain the increasingly global youth habitus, youth movements retain a considerable transformative and democratizing promise. Thus, Muslim youth, perhaps similar to their non-Muslim counterparts, remain in constant struggle to assert, claim, and reclaim their youthfulness, by taking advantage of available venues, including resorting to religion or subverting it. Negotiating between their youthfulness and Muslimness, mediated through political and economic conditions, marks a central feature of Muslim youth habitus.

NOTES

1   See Ahmad Ashraf and Ali Banuazizi, "The State, Classes, and Modes of Mobilization in the Iranian Revolution," State, Culture and Society, Vol. 1, no. 3 (Spring 1985). Out of a sample of 646 people killed in Tehran in the street clashes during the revolution (from August 23, 1997, to February 19, 1978), the largest group after artisans and shopkeepers (189) was students (149). See Bayat, Street Politics, p. 39.
2   This is according to a national survey reported in Aftab, July 30, 2001, p. 9.
3   Cited in Nowrooz, 24 Shavrivar 1380 (2001).
4   Zahra Rahnavard, in Bahar, 29 Khordad 1379 (2000), p. 2 A one-day symposium was organized to discuss why the youth showed such a disinterest in religious lessons.
5   According to a July 2000 report authored by Muhammad Ali Zam, the director of cultural and

artistic affairs for Tehran. This became a highly controversial survey, as the conservatives disputed its authenticity and negative impact on their image.

6   Drawn on official interviews with youngsters cited in Behzad Yaghmaiyan, *Social Change in Iran*, pp. 65-71.

7   Conducted by psychologist Dawood Jeshan with 120 runaway girls in Tehran, reported in Sina News agency, cited on http://iran-emrooz.net (accessed on June 17, 2004).

8   Reported in Professor Mahmoud Golzari's paper in the workshop "Young Girls and the Challenges of Life," May 2004, cited in *ISNA News Agency*, 22 Ordibehest 1383 (2004), at www.womenin iran.com. On the practise of premarital sex in Iran, see Pardis Mahdavi, *Passionate Uprising: Sexual Revolution in Iran* (Palo Alto, Calif.: Stanford University Press, 2008).

9   In an interview with Siasat-e Rouz, cited in Mozhgan Farahi, "You Cannot Resolve Sexual Misconduct by Exhortation," in *Gozaresh*, no. 148, Tir 1382 (2003).

10 Interview with an anonymous medical anthropologist working on the subject, spring 2001.

11 The contribution of Muhammad Hadi Taskhiri, of the Organization of Islamic Culture and Communication in the Second International Seminar on Hijab, 28 Aban 1376, reported in *Zanan*, no. 26, Meh/Aban 1376, pp. 8-9.

12 This finding was reported by the National Radio and TV, Organization of Islamic Propaganda, and the Organization of the Friday Prayers (Detad-e Namaz), cited by Emad Eddin Baaqui, *Payam-e Emrouz*, no. 39, Ordibehesht 1379, p. 14.

13 From report by the head of Tehran's cultural and artistic affairs July 5, 2000, 5:46 pm, EDT (accessed at www.nandotimes.com; site no longer exists, page was not archived).

14 Ministry of Culture and Islamic Guidance, "An Introduction to Behaviorology of the Youth," Tehran, 1994, cited in *Tahavvolate-e Farhangui dar Iran* (Cultural Developments in Iran), by Abbas Abdi and Mohsen Goudarzi (Tehran: Entisharat-e Ravesh, 1999), pp. 138-39.

15 Interview with Azam, an anonymous participant, June 2002.

16 For some of these reports on confrontation between the youth and the Pasdaran, see *Dowran-e Emrooz*, 25 Esfand 1379 (2001), p.4.

17 This is well illustrated in an editorial of a reformist daily; wee "The Mystery of Firecrackers," *Aftab*, 25 Esfand 1379 (March 15, 2001), p. 4.

18 This seemed to be confirmed by large-scale survey research. See Azadeh Kian-Thiebaut, "Political Impacts of Iranian Youth's Individuation: How Family Matters," paper presented at MESA, Washington, D.C., November 24, 2002.

19 The ages of Egypt's political leaders by their birthdate: President Mubarak, born in 1928; Dia Eddin Dawoud (Nasser Party), 1926; Khalid Mohyeddin (Leader of Tajammo' Party) 1922; Mustafa Mashur (Leader of Muslim Brothers), 1921; Ibrahim Shukri (leader of Labor Party), 1916; Noman Gom'a, the youngest opposition leader of the Wafd Party, 1934.

20 In a survey, only 16 percent of Cairo University students expressed interest in party politics. In addition some 87 percent of elders did not trust the youth to do politics; see Ahmed Tahami Abdel-Hay, "Al-Tawajjohat al-Siyasiyya Lil-Ajyal al-Jadida," *Al-Demokratiya*, no. 6 (spring 2002), pp.117-18.

21 Drawn on the conclusion of a debate in Majlis el-Shura, reported in *Al-Ahram*, July 14, 2000, p.7.

22 This information is based upon my interview with the Minister of Youths and Sports, Dr. Ali Eddin Hilal, November 3, 2001, Cairo.

23 The Ministry of Local Development was to extend some of these loans. See *Al-Ahram*, July 14, 2000, p.7.

24 See Midhat Fuad, "Youth Centers without Youths," *Sawt ul-Azhar*, September 14, 2001, p.2. I have especially relied on Muhammad Shalabi, "Egypt's Youth Centers: Between Ideals and Reality," paper for urbanization class, American University in Cairo, spring 2003.

25 They often presented unsubtle, pre-staged shows where the young attendees were carefully picked, the questions were rehearsed, and the oratory and flattery by which students addressed the president left little genuine interaction.

26 Hoda's statement in response to my question as to "what is it like to be young in today's Egyptian Society?" Spring 2003, Cairo, Egypt.

27 The figure for the country was 22 percent. Based on a survey of 14,656 male high school students

in 1990; see M.I. Soueif et al., "Use of Psychoactive Substances among Male Secondary School Pupils in Egypt: A Study of a Nationwide Representative Sample," *Drug and Alcohol Dependence* 26 (1990), pp. 71-72.

28 Reportedly, the Quantity seized by the police jumped from 2,276 in 2000 to 7,008 in 2001; see *Cairo Times*, March 14-20, 2002, p.16.

29 Ironically, the partially segregated trains made the traditional young women more mobile. Parents would not mind if their daughters took trains (after which they took taxis or public buses), since segregated trains were thought to protect their daughters from male harassment. Seif Nasrawi, "An Ethnography of Cairo's Metro," term paper for Urban Sociology class, Fall 2002, American University in Cairo.

30 Yousef Boutrous Ghali extends this "technique of adaptability" to the Egyptian Psyche in general. "The Egyptian is ingenious and he will manage a problem, weave his way around a crisis and absorb without causing a conflictual situation," cited in *Cairo Times*, May 15-28, 1997, p. 13.

31 CAPMAS report of over 5 million bachelor boys and 3.4 million girls caused uproar in the media about the moral consequences of the state of these unmarried adults. Indeed, the age of marriage reached thirty to forty for men and twenty to thirty for women; see *Al-Wafd*, January 1, 2002, p.3.

The Negotiation of Waithood
The Political Economy of Delayed Marriage in Egypt

Diane Singerman

In order to begin ameliorating youth marginalization in the Middle East, this chapter will encourage conceptualizing the political economy of youth through the lens of the "marriage imperative" because the financial investment in marriage takes years to accumulate and influences other key transitions of adolescence, including schooling, employment, education, and identity formation. Marriage, almost universal in the Middle East, has a tremendous presence and significance in the political economy of Egypt and is a moving target that consumes the relational and financial capital of families for years. After exploring the financial burdens of marriage and variation in the costs of marriage, we can then better understand questions of youth morality, identity, transitions to adulthood, and collective life.

As this paper will show, delayed marriage for women, and particularly for men, leads to "waithood" as opposed to adulthood, where years of adolescence and an ambivalent, liminal social status produces anxieties for both parents and their children. We need to understand how young people (and their parents) negotiate "waithood" as they remain unmarried and financially dependent on their families late into their twenties and thirties. The youth bulge in the region as well as the fertility transition has meant that marriage is increasingly delayed in the region; particularly for men. Age at marriage for women has also increased, which can be seen partially as a result of an intentional policy preference for some decades, to reduce fertility, child and teenage marriage, and to improve health care and education, and the status and labor force participation of women. The median age at marriage for men in Egypt is now 27 and for women. A third of urban men, marry over the age of 30; a quarter of men in our sample married between the 30-40; only one-third of men married before 25; and 17 per cent of women marry over. However, there have been *unintended costs* of these efforts.

While there are more young people than ever in the Middle East, unfortunately many of them are unemployed (slightly more than 25 per cent of youth) (Kabbani and Kothari 2005, 3). In Egypt, about 27 per cent of youth are unemployed or about 1.6 million young people (83 per cent of the total number of unemployed are between the ages of 15-29). Egyptian young women are 3.8 times as likely to be unemployed as young men and the vast majority of females aged 15-29 are inactive since 23 per cent are studying and 39 per cent are out of the labor force (since many of them are housewives) (Amer 2006, 11). Youth unemployment rates elsewhere in the region are also alarmingly high. In 2002, male unemployment rates for the age group 20-29 was 23 per cent and for women it was 46 per cent (Salehi-Isfahani 2005, 142).

Unlike earlier generations, the state is no longer investing its public patrimony in youth, although significant public expenditures in education and health care continue. Most jobs are now to be found in the private sector and the informal sector whereas in previous generations the state employed and trained young people and subsidized everyday living costs.

"Bringing back the economic" to a discussion of demographic trends and delayed marriage broadens our focus on the social exclusion of Middle Eastern youth. While consumption, production, and employment usually are stressed in approaches to social exclusion, it is important to remember its relational aspects and how exclusion "entails distance or isolation, rejection, humiliation, lack of social support networks, and denial of participation," particularly for young people (Silver and Miller 2003, 8). Since marriage equals adulthood in the Middle East, exclusion from marriage or delayed marriage compromise full participation in society.

This chapter begins with a statistical analysis of the national costs of marriage in Egypt, based on the Egyptian Labor Market Sample Survey conducted in 2006 under the auspices of CAPMAS, the Economic Research Forum, and the University of Minnesota, under the direction of Ragui Assaad[1]. It is only in Egypt where this data has begun to be collected for the first time in survey research, which itself is a product of earlier ethnographic research which paid attention to the costs of marriage and their material significance in the larger economy (see Singerman 1995; Hoodfar 1997; Rugh 1984; Mir-Hosseini 1993, 1999; Tapper 1991).[2]

The second part of this chapter discusses some of the social and political consequences of delayed marriage. These repercussions are reflected in the rise of new discourses and debates about sexuality and morality, youth identity, generational conflict, and the rise of a "marriage black market" as young people are negotiating and trying to reconcile contradictory public and private norms, values, and expectations. The media is filled with debates on pre-marital sex, drug abuse, crime, suicide, dating, changing gender norms, and morality in the region yet social scientists have not seriously addressed the economic dimensions of marriage. Without "normalizing" and studying the "marriage imperative" and "waithood" in our general framework about youth transitions we will not be able to recommend or design policy about other complex issues such as youth unemployment, redundant education, political participation, and identity politics for young people. Most importantly, I would suggest that there is a lot more to learn about this subject cross-nationally within the Middle East and it is a wide-open area of research deserving of more attention. It is important however, before delving into the details of a statistical case study of Egypt, to discuss a normative issue about the construction of knowledge and the categories we bring to our analysis. We have to ask why the costs of marriage have been irrelevant to rich debate about young people and their economic problems as well as transitions in their life cycle. Flyvberg's notion of phronetic social sciences as a model of inquiry is quite appropriate to the question of marriage:

> "*Phronesis*, or practical wisdom, concerns values and goes beyond analytical, scientific knowledge (*episteme*) and technical knowledge or know how (*techne*)" ...[to] emphasize values, judgment, and prudence. While *Episteme* [scientific knowledge] concerns universals and the production of knowledge that is *invariable* in time and space and achieved with the aid of analytical rationality, phronetic social science produces context sensitive knowledge which explores what things mean to people (Flyvbjerg 2001, 56).

"Whose youth is it?" Who gets to decide what's important to youth? I am certainly not a "youth" anymore, but why are the obvious economic and social predicaments which young people experience trivialized and satirized in the media too often and ignored by academics and policymakers? Survey research can help; but we have to be more reflexive about the "object" of survey research. Why do we know so much about maternal health, fertility rates, birth control strategies, population growth, the youth bulge, labor force data, unemployment, and economic growth rates, but never consider the sums circulating in the marriage market and the constraints that the cost of marriage place on many other economic decisions and life choices? Who decides what counts as "economic" data while ignoring supposedly "cultural" practices such as marriage from their materialist base? Why does no one seem to recognize systematically the extremely expensive and challenging costs associated with marriage and the ways in this struggle influences other behavior?

Marriage is a contract enforced by the state and shaped by its laws, yet for some reason, we don't see the materiality of marriage – even though most Egyptians will eagerly talk about these financial difficulties. The idea in this chapter is to make marriage costs "legible", if only crudely, as a start. The women's movement has understandably focused on legal change to enhance equality and rights for women and on facilitating female employment and education. But the women's movement has paid less attention to perhaps the single most important economic transaction for many women: their marriage, when families transfer their assets to the next generation of women (as well as to men). Suzanne Rudolph suggests that social science research needs to pursue not universalist comparisons with Western referents but situated knowledge which recognizes time, place, and circumstance; relies on the excavation of meaning; and is committed to the validity and significance of local knowledge, and the way peoples understand their histories, social processes, and worldviews (2005). In some sense, research on the cost of marriage acknowledges "local knowledges, even tacit knowledges, that cannot be taught a priori but which grow[s] from the bottom up, emerging out of practice" (Schram 2004, x).

THE COST OF MARRIAGE IN EGYPT

Marriage "sends off" a couple to start the next phase of their life with all that they need/or is expected that they accumulate. An Egyptian marriage cannot proceed unless everything "needed" for a marriage, which has been previously agreed upon via family negotiations, is in place, quite literally, up to and including new spices in the kitchen, new clothes, and kitchenware. Families insist that a young couple be "prepared" for marriage and the families and the bride and groom are parties to the marriage and commit themselves to specific social and financial responsibilities that while not static, have remained constant over the years, although they may vary by class, region, education, religion, etc.

The six component parts of marriage costs are: housing; furniture and appliances; a gift of expensive jewelry (usually gold bracelets) to the bride from the groom, *shabka*; dower, *mahr* (an "advanced" portion of the dower is paid at the time of the marriage by the groom's family, but a "deferred" dower is stipulated in the event of divorce); celebrations; and the bride's trousseau [*gihaz, kiswa*] including clothing, kitchenware, less expensive furnishings, and smaller household items.

These costs are negotiated and shared between the four parties to the marriage: the bride, the groom, the bride's family, and the groom's family. In short, the bride pays very little of the costs of marriage since female labor force participation is so low, the groom pays 40 percent of the costs, his family pays slightly less than one-third and the bride's side contributes about one-third as well. More generally, the groom's side contributes two-thirds of the cost of marriage and the bride's side, a third.

Our first small national survey and our second much larger sample were quite similar in describing the component costs of marriage. In short, housing costs comprise a third of overall marriage costs; furniture and appliances another third; the trousseau (*gihaz*) 14 per cent; the *shabka* or gift of gold jewelry from the groom to the bride, 9 per cent; the dower or *mahr*, 5 per cent; and finally various celebrations absorbed 6 per cent of the overall costs, although popular media accounts often condemn the supposedly lavish conspicuous consumption spent on the ceremonies and wedding themselves (there can be a few parties involved in a marriage).

To get a sense of what the cost of marriage (COM) meant to each household, our analysis found that it was *eleven* times annual household expenditure per capita (or the market value of all goods and services, including durable products purchased by the household [excluding one's home]) and equal to the entire expenditures of all the members of a household for two and a half years (i.e. the sum of the expenditures of all members of one household). The marriage burden was particularly harsh for those households living *below the poverty line in rural areas whose marriage costs were fifteen times per capita* household expenditures (see Singerman and Ibrahim 2001).

Household Expenditure Per Capita, EIHS/IFPRI 1999

	Total Cost of Marriage for Households			Total Cost of Marriage Relative to Household Expenditures Per Capita		
	Above the Poverty Line	Below the Poverty Line	All Households	Above the Poverty Line	Below the Poverty Line	All Households
Urban	34,012	8,822	24,969	11	9	10
Rural	19,680	11,219	17,373	10	15	12
Total	24,688	9,466	20,194	11	12	11

What does it mean that people living in poverty nevertheless invest so heavily in marriage? How does investing in marriage influence other capital intensive needs, such as health care, education, investments, etc.? Has marriage been bankrupting the parents of couples these days or compromising their future financial status? It is very encouraging that our '99 data is similar to the much richer 1995-1999 cohort data from the 2006 ELMS survey (LE 25,704 in 2006 survey and LE 20, 194 in 1999). We were happy to see that there was only a LE 5,000 discrepancy which suggests our 1999 costs of marriage may have been slightly underestimated. Another way to think about the magnitude of this economic campaign is to estimate the value of marriage costs in the national economy annually.

To try to convince economists and policymakers about the importance of the marriage imperative, we have compared the aggregate cost of marriage to the value of other major economic infusions into the Egyptian economy. Since an estimated one in twenty of all 13 million households in Egypt experienced a marriage each year according to the 1999 survey results, the national cost of all 650,000 marriages equaled LE 13.11 billion or $3.867 billion. This figure, by comparison, dwarfs total economic aid to Egypt from the United States in 1999: $2.1 billion. It also exceeds total foreign remittances ($3 billion) from 1.9 million Egyptians migrants working abroad, and approximately equals tourist revenues ($4 billion) from the five and a half million tourists who visited Egypt in 2000.

Marriage costs vary by region (urban, rural) and by class and, while there is still much rich data analysis ahead, it is very important to explore the relative burden of saving for marriage across income groups. To understand the lion's share of the marriage costs (*the groom and his father*) our data shows that the poorest quartile of wage workers, must save their entire earnings for eighty-eight months, or more than seven years to accumulate the costs of marriage. The next poorest quartile of grooms and their parents dedicates fifty-nine months of 100 per cent of their wages, or just short of five years, to their marriage costs. These are massive sums and represent huge challenges for young couples and their families[3].

Let us assume young men and their fathers cannot save 100 per cent of their monthly earnings. Rather, assume that they only save 50 per cent of their earnings, since a father has to support his household at the same time. In this scenario, it takes the lowest quartile of waged workers almost 15 years to save for COM; the lower middle class, about 10 years; the middle class, 7.6 years; and the highest quartile 5 and a half years!

It is quite difficult to get individual savings rates in Egypt; one source suggested that the personal savings rate in Egypt was 12 per cent and another that official gross domestic savings rate was 17 per cent in 2006. If we take that as an average for Egyptian savings the lowest quartile must now save for 43 years to save for the cost of marriage; the lower middle class, about 28 years; the middle class, 23 years; and the wealthiest quartile, 16 years! It remains a great mystery how people succeed in marrying off the next generation. Let's also remember that one study has argued that about one quarter of Egypt's population is living in poverty and another quarter is on the margins of poverty (Assaad and Rouchdy 1998). If 53 per cent of the population are living on less than $2 a day (World Bank, 2002) how do they accumulate these sums?

A recent study in 2008 received quite a bit of attention in the American media because it demonstrated the increasing burdens of higher education on American families even before the recent financial crisis in late 2008. The lowest quintile of Americans were spending 55 per cent of their incomes on higher education for one child; the lower middle class, 33 per cent of their income. Clearly, a college education is a huge financial challenge for Americans, yet there are many federal programs, and tax initiatives to assist families, particularly those that cannot afford higher education since the education of Americans is clearly a national priority in this increasingly globalized world, where not only low-wage labor, but white collar labor is increasingly lost to emerging economies like India and China. The struggle to afford higher education in the United States is somewhat similar to the struggle and long-range financial planning needed to marry off one's children in Egypt, yet the Egyptian government has only miniscule programs directed toward helping their young people marry.

The burden of paying for college has increased for all families,
but has increased more for middle- and low-income families.

Net College Costs* as a Percent of Median Family Income

At public four-year colleges and universities	1999-00	2007-08	% pts increased
Lowest income quintile	39%	55%	16%
Lower-middle income quintile	23%	33%	10%
Middle income quintile	18%	25%	7%
Upper-middle income quintile	12%	16%	4%
Highest income quintile	7%	9%	3%
At public two-year colleges			
Lowest income quintile	40%	49%	9%
Lower-middle income quintile	22%	29%	7%
Middle income quintile	15%	20%	5%
Upper-middle income quintile	10%	13%	3%
Highest income quintile	6%	7%	2%

* Net college costs equal tuition, room, and board, minus financial aid. The numbers may not add exactly due to rounding. Source: *Measuring Up 2008*

Some governments in the region are paying modest attention to the costs of marriage, but these initiatives largely revolve around identity questions rather than affordability. For example, in the UAE, a Marriage Fund (*sandouq al-zawaj*) provides large grants ($19,000) and free or inexpensive weddings halls to encourage its nationals to marry other nationals. [In labor-importing countries, the propensity of nationals to marry foreigners is seen as a national dilemma]. The Marriage Fund president explained in 1999, "Before our organization existed, 64 per cent of marriages were mixed [married to foreigners]; now we've cut it down to 26 per cent" (Beattie 1999). Other NGOs and private/public partnerships in Egypt, Palestine, and elsewhere fund mass marriages and subsidize or try to control the costs of marriage; yet the target population and beneficiaries are miniscule compared to the need. These initiatives seem closer to publicity stunts to call attention to the charitable giving of leaders and NGOs rather than vehicles to solve public policy dilemmas.

YOUTHFUL ANXIETIES AND MORAL QUANDARIES

Clearly, marriage transactions are financially significant in the national economy and deserve greater policy attention. Due to the value and size of the marriage economy, it is not surprising that there are anxieties about it in society. A recent national adolescent survey confirmed that the burdens of the cost of marriage are at the top of a list of concerns for young people.

Main Problem Facing Youth to Be Married
Adolescent Survey, Population Council, 1997

		Percent
Residence		59
Dowry		4
Furnish house		10
Want everything		1
Can not get work		3
Lack of money		21
Others		2
Total	N+ 6180	100

Source: Ibrahim 2000.

In Egypt, as delayed marriage particularly effects women in higher education, some women are rejecting the "spinster" tag and responding to the family pressures of arranged marriages on blogs and in print[4].

Ghada Abdel Aal, author of the bestselling *Ayza atagawiz* (or "I Want to Marry") is a twenty-nine-year-old pharmacist and blogger ("wanna b a bride-no more") from Mehalla, Egypt. Her new book narrates her many encounters with men that her parents have lined up for her to meet in their living room in the hopes of an arranged match, but she argues against marriage to an unknown suitor. Yet, many marriages are still arranged in Egypt and dating (or chaperoned visits) often begins after the engagement is finalized and publicly announced. Long engagements are one way to "test" a suitable groom, in addition to allowing for the slow accumulation of marriage savings. Now, it is even socially acceptable to break engagements for young women.

Despite social criticism emerging from young people throughout the region, there are still signs that unmarried women and men are problematic and almost potentially threatening to the religious and moral order since sexuality should be housed in marriage, and unmarried young people have no "proper" outlet for their sexuality. One newspaper sensationalized a study that claimed that there were 1.5 million Saudi "spinsters" out of a total national population of 17 million, and this phenomenon has received some national attention in governmental bodies (Al-Zubaydi 2001). Another Egyptian title suggested provocatively, "By a margin of 2 Million ... Egyptian Young Mean are Ahead of Young Women in 'Unoussa" (Spinsterhood). The gendered use of the term 'Unoussa almost mocks Egyptian masculinity, implying that men have been reduced to the status of old maids. Dr. Ahmed El-Magzoub, Professor at the National Council for Social and Criminological Research, complained that Egypt has 9 million people over thirty-five who have never been married – 5.5 million young men and 3.5 million young women ("By a Margin of 2 Million" 2006).

The cultural meaning of adulthood is still defined by marriage – a girl becomes a woman when she is married, whether she is sixteen or sixty. Yet Lebanon, Tunisia, Algeria, and Palestine are witnessing more noticeable trends of what demographers call "female celibacy" or unmarried women between the ages of 35-39 (it is assumed that women exceed the age at which they can marry after thirty-five; Rashad, Osman, and Roudi-Fahimi 2005). How can they be "single" in a society where their legal and social status is linked to their family and they often are legally under the protection of a male guardian from their immediate family if they are unmarried (i.e., they do not have an autonomous legal status as an individual)?

SEXUALITY AND MARRIAGE COSTS

To recap the main points of this analysis: marriage defines adulthood in Egypt and sexual and intimate relations are housed and legitimated by marriage. Thus, to summarize, most crudely, if a young man or woman has insufficient funds, they cannot marry and if they cannot marry they cannot engage in publicly acknowledged intimate relations. Of course, norms are always changing and they are always transgressed as well, but with different risks for young men and women. Furthermore, economists would argue that when a "good" is expensive and demand for that "good", i.e. marriage, is inelastic (universally valued), sub-stitutes appear on the market. In the region, we see evidence of a range of mar-riage substitutes and "social" appearing such as secret common-in-law or 'urfi marriages among young people; misyar "ambient/passerbys" marriage; misyaf "summer" marriages; and revitalized muta'a marriages in Shi'a and even Sunni communities (Abaza 2001). In Egypt, the Sheikh Al-Azhar recently ruled that mut'a marriages or temporary marriages (enacted with a contract for a time period between one hour and ninety-nine years) were valid for Sunni Egypt if a man paid a woman a mahr, dower. The rationale was that the cost of marriage was too high and in a mut'a marriage the man is not legally obligated to support the woman financially.

In the most comprehensive study of *'urfi* marriage, Saher El-Tawila and Zeinab Khadr (2004) estimated that *'urfi* marriages were prevalent among 4 per cent of the total population of youth 18-30, and 6 per cent of university students. It was a much lower figure than popular perception had believed but this recent report, laced with nationalist moralism urged authorities and the media to label *'urfi* "adultery" in the hopes that further social stigmatization will reduce its popularity. In 2000, the Minister of Social Affairs had argued that the incidence of *'urfi* marriage among university students was 17 per cent (Abaza 2001, 20).

In Egypt, common-law or *'urfi* marriages that are secretive (i.e. the couple's family and the larger community is unaware that a marriage has taken place) and unregistered with the government (and largely retained by the husband) are increasingly popular among young people because these types of marriage reduce expenses when couples do not cohabitate but only occasionally meet in hotels, furnished flats or borrowed apartments. Secrecy denies families a role in controlling the financial aspects of the union and the choice of a partner. Estimates of the number of these marriages are crude and range from 20,000 to 30,000 a year (Allam 2000; Shahine 1998; Ezzat 2000).

Other ways to reduce marriage costs are to marry a foreigner (who usually does not insist on the customary financial arrangements or is wealthy enough to forgo them). Marrying a relative or consanguinity is approximately 25 per cent less expensive according to the 2006 ELMS survey. The rate of consanguineous marriages remains at the fairly high level of 31 percent of all marriages, which has varied remarkably little since the early 1960s. Couples that live within an extended family but are not related to each other also reduce their marriage costs although the cost of marriage for extended family living is only slightly lower than nuclear family living – 46 per cent to 54 per cent.

WAITHOOD, POLICY, AND CITIZENSHIP

While young people have invested their energy and hopes in education, high youth unemployment and the informalization of the labor market in Egypt has meant that many of them are frustrated and disappointed. They complain bitterly about the need for patronage, *wasta*, or personal contacts to find jobs and maintain them. At the same time as they age, and continue to live with their families, they often secretly date. Financial dependence is the norm, and it is a largely well-accepted norm that is affirmed by parental discourses of love, caring, and sometimes sacrifice. While not meaning to deny the warmth and caring of families, financial dependence can foster ambivalent feelings among young people: both gratitude and unease. As we all know, dependence can also come with strings attached and when living with one's family, one is also expected to abide by their rules and norms.

Here, I find the work of Roxanne Varzi particularly instructive. In her discussion of Iran, she asks, "how [do] people occupy the same strict ideological space and yet *live in completely different realities*? What happens when young people are forced to try to occupy various realities before they have formed their own?" (Varzi 2006, 12). While the Islamic Republic of Iran may represent the extreme end of the spectrum, young people throughout the Middle East are living different realities when they marry in the *'urfi* style and hide their marriage from their families until perhaps the birth of a child, or date without the knowledge of their families.

In Egypt, youth are also "in a 'double bind' caught between the impossibility of conforming to accepted social norms and denying them" (Tourné 2003, 1). In a recent national study of university youth, the majority of the sample "perceive[d] widespread relationships outside of marriage" and "⅓ of young males and ¼ of females report having had a previous relationship" although the definition of a "relationship" is still somewhat vague (El-Tawila and Khadr 2004, 60-61). In a study of students from four universities conducted by El-Zanaty and Mohamed (1996) 26 per cent of young males and 3 per cent of females report having had sexual intercourse at least once (as quoted by El-Tawila and Khadr 2004, 3). In Tunisia and Jordan, recent surveys of young unmarried women suggest that the incidence of pre-marital sex (including high-risk sexual practices) is increasing and the age is decreasing while young people are ill-informed and misinformed about sexual diseases, contraception methods, and reproductive health (Foster 2002, 2006).

How can young people reconcile this new "geography of sex" in Egypt, Morocco, Syria, or Iran with parental norms that limit sexuality to marriage particularly when parents are investing huge sums in their marriages, and supporting their education? The contortions that young people experience as they negotiate the risky field of dating and mating leave them feeling that no one has won as they live a "don't ask, don't tell" reality. In Iran, "[w]hat is hidden and buried by denial is not yet lost in them but remains just below the surface, a surface that is ready to collapse at any moment" (Varzi 2006, 11).

This paper cannot address the movements and ideological tendencies that have exploited the youth problematique in the Middle East today, but when young people experience social, economic, sexual, and political exclusion at the same time, they cannot be satisfied or productive members of society. Authority figures, the media, and the government need to stop "blaming" youth for their behavior but rather encourage serious pragmatic initiatives that can improve their situation. The questions of dating, intimacy, sexuality, youth employment, and youth activism are extremely sensitive in the region and few voices, outside of the religious sphere, seem willing to begin a public discussion and debate. The women's movement is understandably shy to lead the debate yet might gain a new generation of support if it were able to address some of these problems. Much of the discourse about this complex set of issues has shifted to a virtual world in Iran, Egypt, and elsewhere where young people voice their concerns because of restrictions on civil society, activism, and freedom of speech. By making marriage costs "legible" it is hoped that policymakers will be encouraged to reconceptualize the school-to-work-to-marriage transition for young people and fashion policy interventions which might ameliorate some of the problems of young people.

NOTES

1 I am very grateful for the generosity of Ragui Assaad and the Population Council in providing access to the data and for their collaborative support in designing and conceptualizing the marriage module and its relationship to the larger survey.

2 The first survey research using a "marriage module" was added to a small nationally representative household expenditure survey administered in 1999 (400 HH) asking very basic questions about marriage costs to the female in the household, conducted by the International Food Policy and Research Institute (IFPRI) in conjunction with the Egyptian Ministry of Agriculture and the Ministry of Trade and Supply (See Singerman and Ibrahim 2001).

3 In order to further understand the burden of marriage on parents, we created a proxy for potential fathers of brides and grooms by averaging monthly earnings for male heads of households who are 35 years and older within the earnings quartiles of the waged worker subsample of the total survey sample (N=7,547). Since the cost of marriage module of the survey was only distributed to married females, this approach was necessary because we could not link married females to their fathers (we may be able to do this by looking at households which "split off" from those surveyed in 1998 and resurveyed in 2006). However, the groom's family and bride's family shares of total COM were very similar and thus this approach can be useful.

4 The costs of marriage increase with the education of women, but this pattern could be offset by the older age of educated women which increases the bride's side marriage cost (i.e. the higher the age of women, the more her family has to contribute to marriage costs). In an ordinary least squares regression analysis of women married in 1975 or later (2005LE), we found that for every additional stage of education the bride has completed, the cost of marriage can be expected to *decrease* by LE 2,029, all else equal. Yet, for every additional stage of education the groom has completed, the cost of marriage can be expected to increase by LE 3,349, all else equal.

The Demographic Youth Bulge and Social Rupture

Youssef Courbage

INTRODUCTION

My presentation concerns some Arab countries of the Near East and North Africa, plus two Muslim non-Arab countries: Iran and Turkey. In the first section I will show how the demographic transition, the cycle consisting in increasing male literacy, then female literacy, fertility decrease, contraception, rising age at marriage might be an element of social disruption. In the second section, I will focus on one of the effects of the demographic transition, the youth bulge. I will then show the process of convergence with the developed world, thus inaugurating the era of the end of the youth bulge and the emergence of the aged persons. I will then give a brief enumeration of the advantages of this new demography in the Arab world and the region.

LITERACY AND THE ROAD TO MODERNITY

Higher level of education for males, then females, leads to fertility decline which facilitates economic development. From the era of the Enlightenments to Durkheim, only this positive sequence was considered. As of the end of the 19th century, the dark side of modernization was also emphasized, such as the increase of suicide rate as a by product of urbanization and industrialization, or the world wars, a form of collective suicide. Hence, learning to read and write makes individuals and masses more conscious, but cultural progress might destabilize populations. Concretely, in a society where literacy becomes dominant:

- the son can read and write and not the father who still holds power,
- the daughters become educated as much as their brothers,
- the spread of birth control follows literacy and undermines traditional domination of man on woman.

Thus, universal education might imply a destabilization of relations of authority in the family. These disruptions might disorientate society and contribute to collapse of political authority. The age of literacy and contraception might often be that of the revolution. A typical sequence is provided by the examples of the English, French, Russian, and Chinese revolutions[1] (Courbage & Todd, 2007).

THE CRISES OF MUSLIM TRANSITIONS

In Iran we find similar sequences. Cultural modernization paved the way to the collapse of traditional structures of authority and revolutionary violence. The threshold of 50 per cent literate young men was reached in 1964. The shah's regime collapsed in 1979. The 50 per cent threshold of literate young women was crossed in 1981. In 1985, fertility began to decline due to the widespread use of contraception. The once dominant males tried to react, mainly through symbolic measures such as the obligation to wear the *hijab* and the generalization of Islamic beard. In Algeria, civil strife has ravaged the country since 1992 and is associated with the crossing of the 50 per cent threshold in male literacy in 1964. The 50 per cent literacy threshold was crossed in 1981 for women and fertility decline started in 1985. Terrorism spread when the mental destabilization of the population was at its peak. In Turkey, the crossing of thresholds of literacy came as early as 1932 for young men and 1969 for women. Kemalist revolution preceded by few years the threshold of 50 per cent literacy rate among men. As an effect of increased contraception practices, fertility decline started by 1950. The period of maximal political instability was between 1960 and 2000, with a succession of coups d'état and terrorism of the extreme right. Kurdish question could revive violence, since Kurdistan is culturally and demographically far from a completed demographic transition. In Lebanon war called "civil", inter-and intra-religious, spread over the years 1975-1990. Although perceived by westerners as a form of "regressive barbarism", this period of violence corresponds in fact to the period of acceleration of demographic transition mainly among Lebanese Muslims. They were coping with the Christians, whose fertility transition goes back to the early 1950s. However, violence came much later than the crossing of thresholds of 50 per cent literacy, 1920 for males and 1957 for females.

PROSPECTS FOR SOCIAL RUPTURES

Grasping the dark side of modernization brought by literacy provides the means to understanding the past. It also allows us to interpret the present and to predict the future. We could identify countries led by demographic transition either as zones of risk or countries that have crossed the maximum political risk area. Pakistan, for instance, is a perfect illustration of the first case. It shows signs of fever, Islamist challenge, and rising production of terrorism higher than the average. Indicators of literacy and fertility locate it in the transitional zone of maximum danger. Young female literacy crossed the 50 per cent threshold recently in 2002. In this unstable country fertility decline is very recent, around 1990. Cultural-demographic elements of crisis are at their peak. Hence its transition must be watched with particular vigilance. (Surprisingly, Iran attracts much more attention than Pakistan.) On the contrary, Morocco has benefited of an early drop in fertility (1975) which had the advantage of diluting the spread of phenomena likely to produce ideological disorientation – hence, the results of the 2008 elections and the debacle of the Islamist party (PJD). Morocco is also a good illustration of the fact that demographic transition facilitates relative democratic transition. But there are exceptions hence we should not generalize too hastily. In Tunisia, for instance, literacy reached the 50 per cent threshold in 1960 for men and 1975 for women and led to a sustained fertility decrease. Hence, today's fertility in Tunisia (1.99 children per woman) is lower than in France! Yet, despite cultural and demographic transition, Tunisia has supported an authoritarian regime for the last two decades.

REASONS FOR VIOLENCE IN THE ARAB WORLD

There is no need to account for violence in the Arab and Muslim countries, to speculate on a particular species of Islam. Rather, many of the symptoms of disorientation are more likely to be products of changes in mindsets associated with rising literacy and widespread use of birth control. In a large number of non-Muslims who are crossing the key stages of literacy and birth control, massive political disruption can also be observed, from Rwanda and Kenya to Sri Lanka. The fundamental error made by some Western researchers and most media is to present these crises as a regressive phenomenon, whereas they are only crises of transition during which the modernization process disorients people and destabilize political regimes. Note that the Muslims and Arabs are going through the same routes as Europe under the following sequence: males' literacy, then females' literacy, then spread of contraception and finally fertility decrease. This process, which spread over two centuries in Europe, is now taking place in the Arab and Muslim countries in just three to four decades. This shortening of the process explains the exacerbation of the phenomenon of disorientation and destabilization.

THE VIEW FROM THE DEMOGRAPHIC YOUTH BULGE

The youth bulge is a recent concept coined by G. Heinsohn and later used by American political scientists G. Fuller and J. Goldstone. It is usually measured as the expansion of the 15-24 years age cohort related to the total population (Huntington, 1996). Another measure relates the 15-24 to the mature segment aged 25-64 years (Courbage, 1997). This is a mere mechanical effect of the demographic transition which contributes to the transformation of the age structures. In a first phase, this transformation increases the size and share of the more turbulent segments in the population: the youth.

According to Samuel Huntington: "Population growth in Muslim countries and particularly the expansion of the 15-24 years, provides recruitment for fundamentalism, insurgency, and migration. Economic growth strengthens Asian government, demographic growth threatens Muslim governments and non-Muslim societies" (Huntington, p. 103). There is a direct connection with the increasing level of education: "Islamist activists include a disproportionately large number of the best educated and most intelligent young people in their respective populations, including doctors, lawyers, engineers, scientists...." (Huntington, 1996 p. 113). An excess in young adult male population leads to social unrest, war and terrorism, as the third and fourth sons, that find no prestigious positions in their existing societies rationalize their impetus to compete by religion and political ideology. According to Heinsohn (2006): "most historical periods of social unrest and most genocides can be explained as the result of the demographic youth bulge: European colonialism, fascism, on-going conflicts: Darfour, Afghanistan, Palestine/Israel ..." Hence: "Age composition must be considered as a major coefficient in the incidence of violent behaviour." (Moller, 1968). Looking as far back as ancient Greek wars, they found strong match between frequency of violent outbreaks, from war to terrorism and the ratio of a society's young male population to its more mature segments.

THE LINK BETWEEN YOUTH AND VIOLENCE

One can find a number of explanations to account for why youth are more inclined to violence than more mature persons. The death concept and the wish to die among youth is presumably less developed. This is largely due to an underlying physical basis: brain's prefrontal lobe, which inhibits inappropriate behaviour, does not reach its full development before mature age. Statistically, there are more homicides and crimes against property committed by the youngsters than by the older population. Family demography also plays a role. In larger size families, where there are relatively a larger number of youngsters, violence tends to be higher than in small families. It is therefore easy to jump to the conclusion that terrorism and suicide operations are phenomenon closely associated with youth, and therefore, with the populations where the youngsters are still the predominant group. The "lumpen" youth class, street idlers with nothing to do due to high unemployment rates, are tempted by riots, violence and radicalism. Celibacy and the huge delays in age at marriage, create a sexual frustration in such conservative societies as the Arab and Muslim societies – but not only, as the example of Ireland in the nineteenth to the beginning of twentieth century shows – which might be invested in terrorism (Rushdie, 2006).

CRITIQUE OF THE PARADIGM OF HUNTINGTON

The main problem with Huntington and his followers is that they consider a moving reality as static. Hence they are inclined to attribute this transient phenomenon to civilizational/religion factors. Arab and Muslims are thought as unable to modernize: their demographic behaviour is determined for ever. The youth bulge, the end-result of a high and sometimes increasing fertility rate, is considered as built into their mentality. Their psyche is reluctant to progress. Hence, these authors are unable to acknowledge the profound diversity among Arab societies. The only key to explain their behaviour is the common religion. They are reluctant to accept that these societies are moving forward under the impact of literacy.

A GRAPHICAL ILLUSTRATION OF THE REALITY

On the contrary, the following charts show that there was, there are still, and there will remain in the future, significant differences among Arab and Muslim countries; and that the youth bulge is a temporary phase in the demographic transition. Hence, why not forecast more peaceful societies after the political disruption and the Islamist radicalization?

We consider six Arab countries of the Near East: Egypt, Syria, Lebanon, Palestine, Saudi Arabia, and Yemen, two from the Maghreb: Morocco and Algeria and two Muslim non-Arab countries: Iran and Turkey. Jordan, Iraq and Tunisia are not represented in order not to overcharge the charts. Same for the Emirates of the Persian Gulf: Oman, Kuwait, Qatar, Bahrain, UAE where the charts would be meaningless due to the heavy foreign-born population presence.

Youth Bulge as % of the 15-24 years to total population, 1965-2050
–MORE ADVANCED

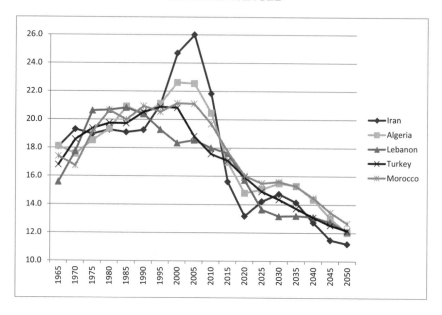

Youth Bulge as % of the 15-24 years to total population, 1965-2050
–LESS ADVANCED

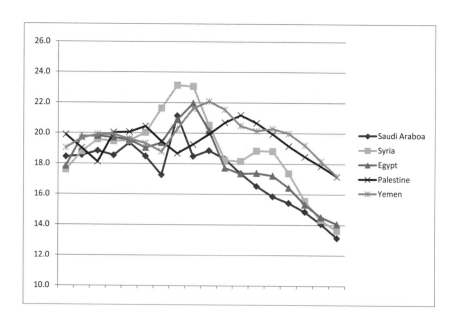

Youth Bulge as % of the 15-24/25-64 years, 1965-2050
–MORE ADVANCED

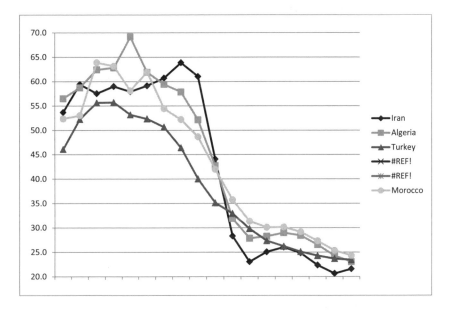

Youth Bulge as % of the 15-24/25-64 years, 1965-2050
–LESS ADVANCED

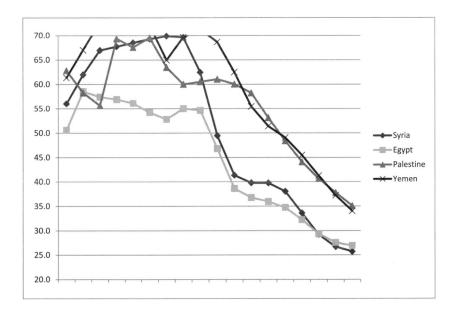

MORE ADVANCED/LESS ADVANCED DEMOGRAPHIC TRANSITIONS

The indicators of the youth bulge are either the share of the 15-24 years to the total population or the share of the 15-24 years of age to the mature adult population 25-64 years.

Two groups of countries are distinguished: the more advanced: Lebanon, Morocco, Algeria, Iran, and Turkey; and the less advanced: Syria, Egypt, Palestine, Yemen, and, not represented in the charts, Jordan and Iraq whose situation is similar to Syria or Egypt. The classification between more advanced and less advanced is based on the proportion of youth at the horizon of the projections, 2050.

Four decades only are required to reach the convergence with the developed world. In 2050, the situation of the more advanced Arab/Muslim countries will be similar to that of the developed regions: Europe, North America, Australia... with 12.8 per cent aged 15-24 years and a ratio of the 15-24/25-64 of 23.4 per cent. This will be the case of Lebanon, Morocco, Algeria, and Turkey. Iran will be even more advanced. Yet, these countries have been through severe youth bulges.

REASONS FOR OPTIMISM: THE END OF THE YOUTH BULGE

Youth bulge belongs to what we can call the dark side of the demographic transition. It is an indisputable reality. Yet, the error of the followers of Bernard Lewis, the first author to have created the concept of clash of civilizations (Lewis, 1990), is to consider a historical phase as determined for ever due to the very essence of the Arabs or Muslims, to the essence of their religious faith. Yet, these charts show that after these difficult phases the worst is behind.

The peak of the youth bulge belongs to the past in most of these countries. The only exceptions are Palestine (2020) and Yemen (2010).

- Lebanon (1985)
- Morocco, Algeria and Saudi Arabia (2000)
- Turkey (1995)
- Iran, Egypt and Syria (2005)
- Yemen (2010)
- Palestine (2020)
- Average (2002.5)

We are therefore at the end of the youth bulge. We are in the middle of a universal process of modernization, a long cycle in which literacy, secularization, then declining fertility accentuate at first the differences between areas, then lead to a convergence (as presented in the charts). The Arab and Muslim world is currently at the heart of the transition to modernity. Some countries have already joined Europe's low fertility levels: Lebanon, Tunisia, Iran, Morocco … Others have just started their fertility decline: Yemen, Palestine. But all will have converged within a very short time span with the levels of the developed regions.

EMERGING RISKS

If the Arab and Muslim countries are likely to resemble the developed countries in a not too distant future, this should concern also the phenomenon of ageing and its disastrous effects. Indeed, the demographic image as presented in this chart looks quite gloomy.

Emerging risks: ageing rather than youth bulge (% 65 years and over)

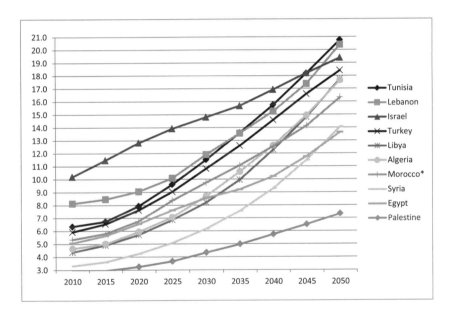

CONCLUDING REMARKS

All in all, demographic transition implies a certain amount of risks, ageing being one of them. Yet, there are no reasons for pessimism, since its advantages clearly outweigh its drawbacks:

a. Increase in labor productivity with shift from quantity to quality.
b. Each member of the labor force will be able to transfer more in cash or kind to his parents, thus limiting the impact of ageing.

c. The slowdown of demographic investments, compared to economic investments; the more directly production-related, job-creating sectors.

d. The increase in adults to young people ratio, thus the ratio of producers to consumers.

e. The falling birth-rate will produce an expansion of the age-groups with higher propensity to save, thus increasing the national saving rate.

f. The narrowing income distribution gap.

g. Reduced wealth disparities, a fairer distribution of knowledge, might give fresh impetus to the middle classes and favour pluralism.

h. Therefore, it is not exaggerated to correlate the on-going demographic transition to democratic transition.

NOTES

1   The father of this law linking literacy and revolution is the British historian Lawrence Stone in *Literacy and Education in England, 1640-1800*. His book was published one year after the May Revolution of 1968. It postulates that the threshold of 50 per cent literacy among young males means the start of political troubles.

Part 2

Negotiating Identity
in Times of Risk

Social Learning and Community Participation

Youth at Risk in Two Marginalized Urban Neighborhoods in Amman, Jordan*

Curtis N. Rhodes, Jr., Haytham A. Mihyar, and Ghada Abu El-Rous

Increasing numbers of Jordanian youth face growing value conflict and restlessness, partly as a result of profound social and demographic changes that have refashioned the urban landscape. Since the mid-1970s, the ratio of urban to rural population shifted from 20:80 to 80:20. With a rate of natural increase of 3.6 per cent, Jordan's youth population is growing rapidly, and over half of all persons are currently under twenty years of age. Economic pressures stemming from inflation, declining purchasing power, and high unemployment have imposed hardships on all families, but especially those living in low-income urban neighborhoods. Parents now confront situations that were unprecedented in their past experience raising children, particularly if they moved from rural to urban areas during the period of rapid social change.

In this chapter, I review the promise and pitfalls of neighborhood interventions planned and implemented with at-risk youth that were based on a pilot program conducted in Amman, Jordan. The program involved youth in devising and implementing strategies for neighborhood improvements in two economically and socially marginalized urban communities. The neighborhood is the central locus within which youth develop relationships with adults and adult-mediated structures and events.

In what follows I elaborate the character of social change in Jordan, describe the two sites in which the intervention was implemented, and draw systematic comparisons between the two neighborhoods as contexts for prosocial youth development. Subsequently, I describe the intervention to transform the two sites and create prosocial communities by providing youth with opportunities to develop their talents in a safe environment. The final section draws lessons from the experience and summarizes the key findings.

---

* First published in: *Youth and Cities: A Cross National Perspective*, Eds: Marta Tienda and William Julius Wilson (Cambridge University Press, 2002): 191-214.

SOCIAL CONTEXT OF JORDANIAN YOUTH

Jordan has witnessed a rapid pace of social and economic change as it develops into a modern, urbanized society. The most striking changes include a large youth population, an unprecedented movement from rural to urban settings, under-developed social institutions, and a shift away from an authoritarian, patriarchal social system that has created a generation gap between youth and their elders.

Movement from rural areas to towns began during the 1950s and continued through the 1960s as farm families sought to enter a wage-based economy, and as traditionally nomadic people settled into stationary communities. The pace of migration quickened by the 1980s, such that 80 per cent of the population resided in urban areas in the 1990s as compared to 20 per cent in the 1960s. Furthermore, a population growth rate of 3.6 per cent has resulted in a youthful society: Fifty-five percent of Jordanians are under the age of twenty, and at least 43 per cent are under the age of fifteen.

The return-migration of Jordanians (particularly after the Gulf War of 1991) decreased outside remittances to families whose members once provided income from jobs abroad. Jordan's economy was not prepared to absorb large numbers of employable individuals; consequently, living costs increased and incomes stagnated for large segments of the population during the 1990s.

By international standards, Jordan is a patriarchal society. Authority lies in the hands of the head of an institution, whether it is the family or a formally constituted social organization, and relationships among people are authoritarian in nature (Hasan, 1997). In families, the father is the seat of authority and sons assume family responsibility and make decisions. In the tribal structure of this society, men with status make decisions for larger groups of related individuals.

Until the relatively recent rapid urbanization of Jordanian society, communities of extended families and clans existed in a context of localized trust, one in which actions were based on shared knowledge and experience.

These communities were *facework* communities, in which relations of trust were sustained by or expressed in social connections established in the presence of all significant persons (Giddens, 1990). These communities stabilized social relations over time through kinship. Major community activities took place within familiar sites and were organized by using local resources. Meaning was rooted in tradition.

Despite these stabilizing forces, urban youth confront different circumstances. In the modern city of Amman, institutions play more active roles than do parents in raising children. A child may spend more time in school, on public transport, and in street play than in the family home. Because the institutions in this rapidly urbanizing city are overwhelmed with demands for services while the roles of parents and local communities are shrinking, the social supports needed for normative youth development are eroding.

Young Jordanians who have been exposed through modern mass media to different models of life – sexuality and gender relations, child-parent relations, student-teacher relations, and citizen-bureaucracy relations – find that modern viewpoints often conflict with local models. In their socialization process, young Jordanians are also exposed to conflicting influences: traditionalism versus modernism, tribalism versus nationalism, authoritarianism versus freedom. These tensions place stress on them as they seek to build their value systems and form new cultural expectations.

Adjustment to change is accompanied by conflict between the new and the old values and life perceptions. Moreover, in settings that are rapidly changing, it is difficult for the elder generation to provide the young with meaningful guidance. Therefore, young people look for their life paths alone in untried, uncertain directions. Internal and external value conflicts lead to feelings of restlessness, hesitation, dependency, and failure (Hasan, 1997).

BACKGROUND FOR CASE STUDIES

In 1994, two types of urban neighborhoods were selected as learning sites within which to discover capabilities of at-risk youth and to encourage actions for improving their living circumstances. Selection of youth was based on their history, their social characteristics, and the various attributes that isolated them from productive social relationships within the community and with external agencies. In both communities youth were alienated from adults and socially isolated from the urban mainstream. Youth perceived adults as unsympathetic, threatening, and unwilling to understand their viewpoints; adults viewed children's behaviors as problems. Neighborhood residents viewed municipal authorities and social agencies as unresponsive and unaware of their problems, and municipal authorities viewed the poor neighborhoods as intransigent obstacles to urban improvement. In turn, alienation produced antagonism and estrangement between children and adults and also between adults and municipal authorities and representatives of social agencies.

The Questscope social learning project sought to understand the consequences for children and youth living in distressed neighborhoods. The intervention project described here was designed to assess and improve the situation of youth by transforming their neighborhoods to make them child-friendly (prosocial). Special emphasis was placed on male youth aged 6-14, who were followed for four years while the project was active. To accomplish this goal, neighborhood residents were involved in identifying factors that supported or undermined their children's development and subsequently taking action to alter those circumstances that prohibited children's participation as valuable members of their community.

TWO TYPES OF URBAN NEIGHBORHOODS

Two sites were selected to represent different types of low-income under-served communities in the social landscape of Jordan: a typical poor urban neighborhood and a "quasi-urban neighborhood." The former functions much as do urban ghettos throughout the world, whereas the latter is a type of urban village, where gemeinschaft-like relations maintain the rural character of the original communities. For convenience and for differentiating between them, hereafter we refer to the conventional urban neighborhood as a *ghetto,* and the quasi-urban site as an *urban village.*

Residents in the ghetto are not linked through social relations or kinship ties, and their children are an obvious source of annoyance and often in trouble with legal and institutional authorities. Residents in the urban village are closely bound by kinship ties, clan loyalty, and traditional social practices. Parents discourage children from interacting with individuals and institutions outside their geographical boundaries, thereby reinforcing social isolation while perpetuating rural traditions. Both sites are densely populated with large low-income families and weak social institutions. In both sites, youth experienced a high risk of neglect and abuse (Questscope, 1995).

The Ghetto. The urban ghetto is populated by refugees (established after the "1967 War") and rural migrants. When the project began, youth were alienated from their parents and other adults and there was little cooperation among families. Residents were marginalized from mainstream social institutions, and consequently also from the benefits enjoyed by mainstream society, such as employment, income security, and social participation. Many poor families were trapped there and unable to move.

Despite these problems, several factors made the site attractive to families. Low rental and construction costs allowed low-income families to build or rent a house. The proximity of the neighborhood to work and public transportation reduced time and travel costs. There were job opportunities for nonskilled work in a busy nearby commercial area, including parts of the city where young boys (ages 10 to 17) collected cans, glass, and scrap iron from the trash.[1] An underground economy (related to drugs and prostitution) operated in and around the area, and some individuals had life-styles that benefited from the anonymity afforded by the crowded neighborhood.

Although a strong entrepreneurial spirit existed among neighborhood residents, the lack of capital and appropriate skills (including vocational training, personal life skills, and small-business acumen) prevented them from actualizing their economic potential. Low-wage unskilled labor provided the main income source, but many children supplemented family income when they worked for daily wages or collected materials for resale from the trash. Several small grocery stores and service shops (tailors, etc.) also provided day-to-day income for some families. Most adult breadwinners were unable to compete for jobs that required moderate or high skills. Public assistance to alleviate poverty was not available. Externally, this neighborhood was considered an offensive urban problem that was best "cleaned up." All residents were aware of the neighborhood's problems, but there were no mediating structures to help them envision that they belonged to something worth improving. Therefore, to manage these circumstances, families adopted one of two strategies: to protect youth from the problems of the streets, many isolated their children indoors; others simply allowed youth to grow up in the streets.

Children living in the poor urban neighborhood lacked the basic necessities for normative development. "Family" meant a place to sleep and serious problems, such as adult unemployment, alcoholism, and mental illness. By the age of six, many children shouldered the responsibility of increasing family income by collecting aluminum cans, selling chewing gum in the streets, cleaning car windshields, or begging at traffic lights. Young men aged 10 to 18 typically assumed parental responsibilities that ranged from breadwinning to making important family decisions. Many children suffered abuse from intoxicated fathers who spent meager earnings on alcohol and gambling, leaving little or nothing for the family. Most mothers were uneducated, and their main concern was providing food for their children. Because many mothers had to work to make ends meet, they often did not know where their children were during the day (or night) or what they were doing.

Young boys searched for affection, protection, and security in gangs of other children with similar needs. But belonging to a gang meant a loss of autonomy and agency. When the gang collected cans throughout the night, all members had to do so as well. When the gang sold the cans, everyone had to sell to the same vendor. When gang members sniffed paint thinner or glue or drank alcohol, all members participated. They stole together, and they shared affection and sex with each other. Their fights were each other's fights. In return, the gang was "family" for each member. Each "family" had a leader who gave orders; to disobey was to risk physical beating.

Youth from the ghetto easily differentiated between patronizing behavior and serious concern for them as individuals. Feeling rejected by their community, they resorted to aggression and violence as a way to establish their presence within the neighborhood. Many carried switchblades and concealed razors to defend themselves. As one of the adult volunteers mentioned during the initial community assessment, "Violence is our language."

The Urban Village. This neighborhood in Amman is an urban "village" that comprises families who migrated over a period of more than forty years from a single rural village in the south of Jordan. They have maintained their clan and kinship structures, traditions, and values almost intact. Because their site was established before land ownership issues were settled, the entire neighborhood (around 12,000 residents) was considered a "special case." The municipal authorities were in a difficult position because provision of services to this community would represent "de facto" recognition of ownership of land that was legally owned by other parties.

These residents maintained their "subsociety" by kin living in close proximity to each other. Their strategy involved building more and more dwelling units (sons' apartments atop fathers' houses) within the same neighborhood (about 1 km^2). This practice reached its limits, as there is now little space (either vertical or horizontal) in which to expand. Because the houses were small and families large (averaging seven to nine children), many children lived on the streets during the daytime.

Residents earned relatively low wages through public sector employment as teachers or civil servants and in army service. In the past, these jobs provided relatively adequate incomes for living in a low-cost neighborhood (because land was not purchased and houses were built adjoining relatives' houses). However, the rising cost of living and contraction of public-sector employment created a crisis in the viability of this strategy.

Extensive clan obligations had created a highly integrated "social safety net" for residents. In the past, marriages, deaths, religious events, and holidays were accompanied by the exchange of money and goods. As incomes fell, the base for this internal support system did not keep pace with the demands made on this social network. Youth assisted their families by selling home-prepared sweets, tea, and so on, in public squares near the neighborhood. Although the young were not alienated from their neighborhood, the traditional strategies for keeping the community intact had reached the limit of their ability to accommodate the needs of youth.

Nevertheless, there was a relatively high level of social capital in this neighborhood. Every family participated in a variety of social networks, which were usually of a religious or traditional nature. Although the presence of these networks represented a potential for concerted community action, in practice there were few relationships with national organizations that could assist them with their growing problems. In part, this resulted because the internal solidarity of this community had created an isolated (and sometimes alienating) stance toward the larger city and its institutions.

In the urban village, practically all the children attended school, including those who were obligated to augment family income. Male youth lived in two worlds: the traditional and authoritarian world of their fathers and adult male relatives, and the modern world of the larger city that required a different set of personal competencies. They could not be like their fathers because the life-style their parents knew no longer existed. They also were not prepared to meet the demands imposed by city life.

Inside the neighborhood behavior was carefully regulated. Adult males controlled the social environment. The only space for children was the street, where they developed their own games and activities to fill time. The most remarkable difference between the urban village and the ghetto is that the street was considered safe for youth and the peer groups were largely made up of relatives and cousins. Relationships within the household were warm and nurturing but conformed to traditional lines of authority: boys did not interrupt their fathers when they were speaking or even talk in the presence of fathers or uncles. A male child could go where he wanted only after informing his father. Girls did not leave the house without an accompanying male relative (husband, brother, or father) except to attend school. (Most of the girls were enrolled in school.) Community norms also accepted women working as teachers and in some types of public sector employment.

All the institutions to which youth might relate were located outside the neighborhood, including schools. When youth were obligated to leave the neighborhood, they were keenly aware that external conditions were different. Both adults and children considered school attendance dangerous because it put them at risk in the city. Therefore, boys who ventured into the city in groups developed an elaborate system of whistles and "call signs" that allowed them to be located and surrounded by their peers whenever they perceived danger. Furthermore, all of the male children carried switchblades, concealed razors, or sharpened objects.

CREATING PROSOCIAL COMMUNITIES

The goal of the Questscope program is to develop prosocial communities that reinforce prosocial behavior among children and youth by developing positive attitudes and practices within the community (Tyler, 1997). However, given the lack of effective institutions to provide assistance to the community, it was necessary to emphasize residents' roles in guiding its direction. Awareness that troublesome children could change their behavior provided an incentive to collaborate with external resource providers. Once the prosocial behavior of individual children and youth was observed and understood, the neighborhood was positioned to create a healthy environment for normative youth development.

Participatory interaction within the community fostered discussion about social issues down to the grass-roots level. Neighborhood residents discussed social issues and problems, identified priorities, and subsequently took action to improve conditions. In turn, these outcomes provided a strong base for building informed, self-directed volunteerism, which proved vital in rapidly growing urban centers where the voices of poor, young citizens were seldom heard or even sought.

The intervention used three complementary approaches to building prosocial communities. Together they have a cohesive prosocial effect because they create collaborative and enhanced roles for everyone (Tyler, 1997). The first approach was locality development. Consensus among neighborhood members grew as they identified common concerns and planned collective solutions. Community members were trained in the use of social assessment tools to create their own vision of their community, establish their own priorities, and develop a plan for action. They used their skills and resources to work with providers of external resources to strengthen volunteer capabilities within the community.

The second approach to building prosocial communities entailed building collaborative linkages, such as involving local experts to assist in problem solving by jointly designing and implementing interventions. External experts treated community members as active collaborators rather than as passive clients (Tyler, 1997). Expert providers were able to suggest and implement programs that suited the community environment as they became aware of the community's constraints. Accordingly, they tailored their roles to reshape the social environment and to develop competencies that suited youth's needs.

Social action was the third strategy used to change the local social context in which youth are reared. Mainly, this entailed attracting the attention of urban leaders and managers who could modify policies that created hardships and prevented cooperation between the community and broader urban structures. Since marginalized communities have traditionally been invisible to policymakers, the project began to capture their attention.

COMPONENTS OF THE QUESTSCOPE PROGRAM

Program staff identified five important constraints operating on or within the two marginalized urban neighborhoods. These served as arenas for implementing the program to build prosocial communities. The five constraints were (1) frustrated aspirations, (2) changed family relations, (3) neighborhood deterioration, (4) truncated roles of youth, and (5) ineffective institutions (Szanton Blanc, 1994). Emergent strategies were developed to address improvements in each of these areas, and the strategies were oriented around locality development, establishment of linkages, and social action.

(1) Frustrated Aspirations. Frustrated aspirations (the results of psychological and subjective causes) reflect bleak futures and a protracted inability to satisfy material longings. In the world of the information highway and satellite superchannels, everyone is cultivated as a market for consumption through beautiful advertisements by beautiful people for beautiful products.[2] The media make youth aware of what others have and the limited possibilities to acquire what is advertised, thereby creating frustrations. Children in both neighborhoods were made aware of material deprivation through television and through proximity to an affluent urban environment just beyond their neighborhoods.

In the ghetto, a high percentage of male children abandoned school between the ages of nine and twelve, thereby exposing themselves to a future of limited employability and social marginalization as adults. In the urban village, the high value placed on education by adults did not motivate the youth to remain in school because they understood all too well that a high school certificate (the *tawjihi*) no longer guaranteed a job that would pay enough to survive in the city. Not even college completion could ensure a living wage. Moreover, economic demands of their families drove many youth from marginalized urban neighborhoods to engage in petty informal activity, like collecting cans for resale. This responsibility did not, however, gain them a respected role in their local neighborhood and in the broader society. Rather, the inability of parents to fulfill basic needs led children to seek support in peer-group structures that encouraged alienating behaviors, such as substance abuse and early unprotected sexual experiences.

The initial approach to address the problem of frustrated aspirations involved identifying the risk factors that were present in young people's lives (substance abuse, early unprotected sexuality, truancy and dropout from school, gang behavior, etc.) by involving neighborhood volunteers in participatory community assessments (Questscope, 1995). The goal was to create more child-friendly atmospheres by creating activities that were beneficial to children and youth. Such activities were based on young people's expressed desires and were designed to reduce the sense of "not belonging." Once youth were involved in constructive activities such as studying or reading in a library, working in a computer lab, or participating in sports programs, a foundation was established from which to cultivate positive links with the rest of the neighborhood.

In the ghetto, provision of new activities increased the time spent in the social center by "troublesome" boys. Initially, this led to new problems because the problem youth carried their aggressive behaviors into the center. Adult staff and volunteers in the center were initially unprepared to handle these problems because they had been selected to operate narrowly defined programs (preschool day care, embroidery and sewing classes, etc.), and their main recourse was to hold lectures in the center on topics they selected.

At this point in the Questscope program, staff established ties with a researcher and two graduate students affiliated with a university counseling center. They took counseling roles in a 1997 summer camp for "troublesome" young men (ages 10-17) designed to help them understand what motivated their positive and negative behaviors. This counseling camp enabled adults to understand their roles in creating an environment that provided positive reinforcement for alienated youth. The young men themselves gained an understanding of options for relating to others apart from violence and aggression.

The staff of the camp were drawn from individuals who lived in the site and who worked in the local center, from Questscope staff, from the counseling center, and from two cooperating government agencies, namely, the Juvenile Department of the Ministry of Social Development and the Housing Organization. Everyone was surprised at the ability of the troublesome young men to adjust their behavior to the structure required in the camp (regular schedule, physical activities, kitchen and clean-up duties, community service projects, etc.). Although the young men were aggressive toward each other, they never expressed aggression toward adults who interacted with them in the camp or later in the neighborhood.

At the end of the camp, everyone was surprised that the young men considered themselves partners with the staff. Upon their return to the neighborhood, the young men organized themselves and arranged to meet for coffee with the juvenile authorities and to talk over their problems. In the past, their only relationship with authorities was related to juvenile justice and detention. This loose self-organization has continued because the gang leaders identified a new direction in which to lead their protégés, which involves more constructive relationships with adults and adult-mediated structures. This activity allowed them to cultivate identities and social roles that are recognized and respected.

The urban village was isolated from the surrounding city partly because of the residents' desire to keep their own identity and traditions alive. In fact, every weekend (Friday, the day for Muslim worship), most of the residents departed to their home village. It was in the village where young women enacted social roles that matched expected behavior that allowed them a measure of freedom of movement and association that was not possible in the city. For residents, maintenance of their village atmosphere in the city had the cost of social isolation, but isolation by choice (Caincar and Abunimah, 1998).

(2) Changed Family Relations. Shifting relationships within and beyond the family can create an emotional poverty that is devastating for children. Social relations, particularly within the family, represent both the cause of and a potential remedy for a great many disturbances affecting young people. Focusing on these relationships highlights the importance of the loving capacities developed in the child-adult relationship and identifies problems that transcend those of poverty.

Urban living is wage-dependent because city dwellers do not grow their own food and have few noncash resources to fall back on in case of unexpected demands. Increased cost of housing in a growing city means smaller homes and more crowding, and less opportunity for extended family members to live together. As urbanization accelerated the shift from patriarchy to less authoritative families, parents had to provide increased resources of time, money, energy, patience, and institutional linkages on behalf of youth while also exercising less traditional control over them.

Few institutions were prepared, either with mandates for programs or with experience in communities, to assist families in accommodating to the dramatic social transformation brought about by rapid urbanization. Parental responsibilities – even the understanding of what constitutes good parenting – also became more difficult to comprehend. As parents proved unable to provide their children with an adequate livelihood, there was growing pressure on youth to shoulder family responsibilities. In the ghetto, fathers with traditional expectations encouraged their sons to leave school and contribute to family support. One father refused his son entrance to the house if he failed to meet his daily income target (approximately US $4.25). The fourteen-year-old son slept on the doorstep of the house. These pressures, coupled with a densely crowded urban environment and little or no support from national institutions, led ultimately to a crisis for children.

Therefore, the Questscope intervention program placed a very strong emphasis on establishing volunteer committees for children's issues from the outset. Organizers assumed that the presence of motivated community members who were oriented to action to improve the neighborhood environment for their children was a key component of a strategy for change. After the initial community-based assessments in each site, the volunteer committees began to establish priorities for activities for their children.

In the ghetto, women volunteers observed the benefits of personal and group counseling for male children. The counseling team was aware that many of the boys' problems could not be addressed unless parents provided information about the specific backgrounds of their children. Women volunteers willingly met with the counselors to discuss the problems youth faced. When it became apparent that youth's interpersonal relationships within families were beyond the scope of the project, group sessions on family issues were gradually discontinued.

In the urban village, family issues were not discussed with "outsiders;" therefore, the process of involving women and girls in participatory assessments was much slower. Allowing women and girls to join in open discussions and to think of activities for both boys and girls was possible only after a social center was established for children. Residents observed that something significant beyond "just talk" was possible.

A first step involved assisting adults to listen to young people, but progress in responding to children's concerns slowed when adults demanded immediate tangible results. Two lessons stem from observing children's responses to building (or rebuilding) healthy relationships with adults (parents or others). One is that a person-to-person relationship with a caring adult can bring about a remarkable shift in the attitudes and behaviors of these children. The other is that all caring, concerned adults can have positive, encouraging relationships with young people if they take the time to understand the individual child. An adult's role as a mentor can be vital, particularly if there is a program to support that relationship. If caring adults are from the young person's neighborhood, the impact of the supportive relationship not only enhances the youth's development, but also augments adult competencies needed to cope with the consequences of poverty. As a result of these observations, Questscope developed a program to train volunteers to acquire mentoring capacities and implemented it in a subsequent project.

(3) Deteriorated Urban Neighborhoods. Cities are not designed with children in mind. The physical environment – pollution, traffic, noise, poor housing, insufficient social spaces outside the homes and off the streets, and insufficient green areas – contributes to the social isolation of children. The organizational environment of inadequate, unresponsive, or inaccessible social services contributes to this social isolation and creates myriad hardships.

Deterioration of urban neighborhoods is a difficult problem for an intervention to address. When youth from the ghetto were asked about changes they would like to see in their neighborhood, staff assumed that their first priority would be a playground. Instead they indicated that a playground would only make life more dangerous for them. They felt that problems associated with gang-related fights and being hurt by razors, and so on, had to be solved first, before making any changes to the physical space. The school setting was equally inhospitable because the institutions were unable to cope with the large numbers of youth entering the system. Many of the children from the poor urban ghetto were unwelcome in school – a learning environment critical for normative development.

The urban village witnessed another type of neighborhood decay, namely, overcrowding. Three or four generations of families had built apartments composed of sons' homes atop fathers' houses, until no vertical or horizontal space remained. Yet, the 12,000 members of this closely knit community bound by kinship and clan linkages did not wish to live elsewhere. The collective strategy for raising children entailed keeping them in the neighborhood (bounded by three streets, about 1 km^2) to protect them from the corrupting influences of the wider city. Because of the rapid demographic growth, the sheer numbers of children – composing 60 per cent of the community – created a crisis of space and resources, which strained families' ability to cope with the growing pressures of urban life.

Nevertheless, when approached by Questscope, community leaders were willing to focus attention and resources on their children and were very active in the initial appraisal of young people's needs. The crucial issue for them was maintaining leadership and involvement in community change. The establishment of a community center and the development of a plan for action through a local committee were turning points in their ability to manage the deteriorating environment. First, a group of adults with experience in assisting their own children served as community leaders. Subsequently they took the initiative to increase linkages to and cooperation with national providers of services and assistance. This represented a major behavioral change for a community that had become culturally isolated by design.

Neighborhood physical quality was a major concern for residents of both sites involved in this project. In the ghetto, no organization was responsive to these concerns, partly because of ambiguous land ownership and the legality of housing construction. The owner of the land (upon which squatters had settled) was often not the owner of the house. Furthermore, the owner of the house was often not the tenant in the rented house. Consequently, the neighborhood lacked legitimacy in presenting its concerns.

During the period of the Questscope project, municipal authorities flattened about a third of the buildings in the neighborhood to complete a long-planned highway. Displaced families received only minimal compensation for the destruction of their houses. Even more devastating was the challenge that displaced residents faced in rebuilding a new life in a resource-poor environment. Destruction of homes placed particular stress on those young men who were involved in the neighborhood programs designed to give them new roles, respect, and a hope for the future.

In the urban village, project staff focused attention on microimprovements, such as building a wall around the social center to make it safe for children. The library and computer learning lab were attractive facilities in an otherwise resource-scarce center. Other activities, such as sports and camping, helped to alleviate some of the pressures on children anticipating loss of their homes and to enrich their lives devastated through prosocial experiences. Once the bulldozers arrived to complete the building of the highway, more emphasis was placed on programs to strengthen young men's involvement in community service, sports, and camping.

In the urban village, a social center to sponsor activities and to gain the support of the community was established first. This was essential to address the priorities expressed in the initial participatory assessment. The social center was a novelty in this community, and its presence drew attention to the need and ability of the community to organize itself for social goals. The leaders of the voluntary action committee for children capitalized on this opportunity to interest the municipal authorities in considering a larger multipurpose building that could be used for broader social goals and activities. Project staff developed programs to assist residents to engage in community improvement.

The ability to attract the attention of a government agency to act on needs and priorities of the urban village was due largely to its success in improving the social environment for children. This illustrates a successful relationship for social action fostered by residents engaged in a deliberate path of change. The process was fragile, because it depended on the motivation and patience of local residents, as well as the political will of outsiders to recognize their enabling roles in opening up opportunities for positive change.

(4) Truncated Roles of Children – Growing Up Marginalized. The alienation and isolation of children living in marginalized urban communities are exacerbated when children shoulder adult responsibilities without the requisite capabilities. When the project began, staff emphasized understanding the attributes and circumstances of children at risk (markers of violent behavior, substance abuse, neglect, etc). As the project evolved into building prosocial communities oriented

toward promoting normative development, children's roles took on greater importance. Therefore, the project design was continually adjusted to allow the roles of youth to be clarified and strengthened as more was learned about them and the circumstances in which they lived.

Jordanian youth also face conflicting viewpoints on how they should direct their lives as their society wrestles with changes in authoritarian roles. This tension was reflected, for example, in public discussions about the rights of a child or an adult other than the father to report child abuse. Children's premature assumption of adult roles also affected their social development and eventually lowered their educational aspirations. Therefore, the challenge for project staff was to make space for children, allowing them to try out many roles during the school years so they could grow into well-balanced adults. Given the limited geographic mobility of residents of poor urban neighborhoods, it was especially important to treat youth as participants in a community of practice, where they learned how to become competent, respected adolescents (and later adults).

In the ghetto, it was impossible to relate to boys on a totally individual basis. Gang behavior meant that controlling the boys' violence and aggression required reliance on their leaders. In one sense these boys were not integrated in their neighborhood because they lived on the street as part of a special subculture, and adults took great pains to ensure that their children avoided them. Adults also excluded them from activities in the social center because of their antisocial behavior. To resolve this impasse, Questscope planned a summer camp to provide an environment outside the neighborhood where adults responded to children in a civil and responsible manner – for example, no drunkenness, no physical danger from angry adults, no cursing. The camp was based on the simple idea that if adults provided a safe atmosphere, the boys could be "children": able to take instruction, follow rules, control their anger, learn new things, and enjoy new activities.

As a result of this experience, the troubled boys began to behave as partners within the program – a change that lasted after camp was concluded. Thereafter, the camp participants took an interest in what their community offered, and they were aware of being treated as equals in planning activities. Quite simply, they had opinions that they wanted heard and taken seriously. This new form of participation was very different from their customary approach, whereby the loudest shout or the quickest fist was the means to draw attention.

Another significant outcome from the camp experience was cooperation with a national program for youth (14-25 years of age). A member of this organization provided challenging physical activities in the camp program and became interested in how the national program could be adapted to suit disadvantaged street children. He designed novel ways to incorporate the ideas of community service, vocational development, and sports participation into the lives of marginalized youth. The activities that resulted from this initiative have provided young men from the urban neighborhood with a chance to be accepted in a broader circle of relationships, thus increasing their role and importance.

One of the community service activities that had a strong rehabilitative effect on the boys involved visiting handicapped children in local institutions. Through individual relationships with these children, the troublesome boys found someone who needed them and to whom they could offer encouragement and help. Increasing their roles as caregivers to others in this way had a significant impact on their own emotional development.

(5) Ineffective Community Institutions. The final aspect of youth's social environment the Questscope project addressed was the problem of ineffective community institutions. Because rapid urbanization and a fast-growing youth population created unprecedented social conditions in Jordan, most social development institutions were neither prepared for nor responsive to this change. Furthermore, the viewpoints of "young" urban neighborhoods were not represented in the design and implementation of solutions to emergent social and economic problems.

Before the Questscope project, institutional practices focused on children as offenders. This focus led to growing pressure to increase the capacity of detention facilities. However, because new institutional approaches view children as victims, they respond by establishing shelters for abused youth. The majority of at-risk urban youth were neither offenders (suitable for detention), nor victims (requiring sheltering). Rather, they existed in a continuum between these two publicly identified types. The implication is that children living in marginalized urban neighborhoods had to be seen as important clients whose cooperation was indispensable to help transform their communities into prosocial environments. Otherwise, the numbers of offenders and victims could potentially increase. In short, youth needed to be viewed as the solution rather than the problem.

Residents offered great strengths to build on in developing prosocial community involvement. The traditional relations of trust sustained in social connections are an important aspect of Jordanian sociocultural history that could be bolstered as problems and issues were addressed. Residents realized that creating safe, prosocial environments for youth would require collaborative relationships with "outsiders" – namely, professional experts and institutions that provide assistance and respond to marginalized communities as clients.

Questscope staff assumed that listening to youth would encourage adults to modify their relations with young people. Therefore, project staff anticipated that instead of plans, lectures, and activities based on the authoritarian, adult-centered approaches, the viewpoints and struggles of young people would serve as the starting point to develop solutions. Staff also assumed that organizations were receptive to collaborative approaches that drew on the wealth of professional knowledge and of neighborhood self-knowledge and experience. Thus, professionals, experts, and municipal authorities could build on a solid base of neighborhood experience, with marginalized residents as partners and not just beneficiaries.

In the ghetto, the housing organization was the logical unit to initiate a collaborative process: the social center belonged to them, and the center's staff were community residents. Center staff and neighborhood volunteers had, after all, cooperated successfully during the initial participatory appraisal in 1994–5 and in creation of a safe place for children equipped with resources for learning (library and computer learning equipment). However, once these physical issues were resolved, the deeper issues of the children's roles (the "troublemakers") in the center remained problematic. Responsible adults in the center were not prepared to recognize the new roles of children, which eventually led to separation of children's activities from the center. In fact, center staff considered that the existing activities (day care, lectures, beauty-salon training, weaving, and embroidery) mandated exclusion of the very youth for whom the new activities were designed.

That adult and youth agendas could not be reconciled in a single facility using a regular staff and volunteers led to an impasse, and activities for troublesome children were excluded from the center. The housing organization, which had previously decentralized its control over the center staff, could exert little influence on the dilemma. And the center staff were determined to maintain their control and compensation as employees. Because of its emphasis on developing an emergent strategy, Questscope itself may also have contributed to misunderstandings by not clarifying for center staff the potential benefits of changed roles for all parties. The impasse triggered relocation of activities for preadolescent youth from the center to individual homes and other nearby locations. This exodus of young people had the positive effect of increasing residents' commitment to constructing a supportive neighborhood environment for its youth that allowed them to enact newly emergent roles.

By 1998, Questscope had catalyzed a collaborative relationship between young men in the urban village and a national youth organization with more than fifteen years of experience with Jordanian youth. The youth organization was committed to adjusting the principles of the national program to the special needs of troublesome youth from marginalized urban communities. Therefore, the youth program focused on self-reliance, leadership skills, personal development (ranging from literacy to crafts to vocational counseling and training), as well as sports and community service. It included a "wilderness camping" activity to provide challenging experiences that required building trust in others and teamwork. Each of these endeavors was fraught with difficulties, as both youth and providers struggled to learn how to cooperate. However, the program provided a robust model for involving marginalized young people in an existing institution/program in which they worked to build their life skills. The involvement of counselors from a university counseling center in the Questscope pilot sites was another major learning experience for the project because the experts had to modify their approaches to be responsive to the problems faced by marginalized urban youth.

A Vocational Training Center (one of a network of twelve government centers) that participated in the intervention also modified its curriculum for nine boys who were functionally illiterate and accustomed to controlling relationships through violence. Vocational center staff cooperated patiently with Questscope staff to integrate the "troublesome" boys into a special training program in automotive electrical systems. At the end of the three-month course, the boys graduated with new skills. But more importantly, the center director learned how to adjust institutional policies and practices to serve disadvantaged young people.

In the urban village, residents maintained their identity and traditional rural practices by insulating themselves from external institutions. Engaging community cooperation required sufficient trust of Questscope to conduct a participatory appraisal their children with community volunteers (Questscope, 1995). Once the community volunteers heard their own youth articulate the hardships and obstacles they faced, they mobilized to establish a small social center for children. Two outcomes resulted from this small initial step. First, the community became confident of its ability to act on behalf of young people. This willingness to improve the condition of youth eventually included cooperation with units outside their bounded neighborhood. Second, in reaching out to external institutions, the local municipal authority acknowledged neighborhood capacity and began to cooperate in providing better facilities and support to the community.

LESSONS FROM THE QUESTSCOPE PROGRAM

There were several strengths and limitations of the Questscope program that focused on changing the social environments of poor, socially isolated neighborhoods in the interest of promoting normative youth development. The two-site comparison affords an opportunity to observe similarities in the developmental needs of youth and the diverse strategies devised in the ghetto and the urban village. In the following I describe four main lessons derived from the intervention, with a focus on the implications for youth.

First, new and enriched roles for children and adults were necessary to promote collective participation in choosing and making improvements in their local neighborhoods.

The Questscope program succeeded in achieving a high level of involvement, partnership, and role enrichment within the sites. Particularly among young males (10–18 years), the capacity for self-organization was directed to building positive roles and neighborhood acceptance. "New" lessons learned in the neighborhoods must be incorporated into "old" authority structures in order to be maximally effective. Institutionally, this was most easily facilitated through high-level managers who worked with their middle managers and staff to enhance institutional effectiveness.

However, it is unclear whether the outcomes of this pilot project signal institutional behavior change (policy and procedure). In general, units external to the community did not perceive changes in the roles of the neighborhoods as constituencies whose viewpoints required modifications to institutional policies and practices. The two exceptions to this were the national youth program's intent to adjust their practices to accommodate children from marginalized neighborhoods and the Vocational Training Center's willingness to restructure their programs for uneducated boys. Redirecting resources and refocusing institutional agendas to accommodate the needs of marginalized youth require changes within the institutional culture of organizations. The Questscope pilot project did not address this need because their top priority involved learning from young people to develop a strategy for changing their proximate environment.

That programs for female children were delayed represents a third limitation of the Questscope intervention to promote healthy youth development. Staff and neighborhood members assumed involving young girls in programs that took them out of strictly familial relationships would introduce unnecessary complexity to the project. In retrospect, this assumption appears misguided. However, it appeared reasonable on the basis of neighborhood sensitivities that encouraged a focus on boys and young adolescent males in this early pilot phase of the work. In subsequent interventions, the issues of adolescent girls have been successfully approached through centers that serve only female clients.

A few words of explanation from us about the previous paragraph: because no organization had worked with these kinds of "at risk" children at the community level, no one knew what to expect as the interventions took place. It was only possible to reach community consensus on approaching children's problems of substance abuse, sexuality, truancy, and so forth, if the work was initiated with males. Once it became clear to everyone involved (local community members, cooperating institutions and their staff, and Questscope staff) that interventions were not disruptive in a basically conservative social environment, then the lessons learned and the success demonstrated could be (and have been) applied to girls. But to start with girls would have led to the immediate closure of the project. The social environment was not ready for work with "at risk" female children. Now such projects with female clients are viable and making progress, but it took a long time and lots of effort to build trust to make this possible. The pilot project with male children provided us with the lessons and "track record" to initiate work with female clients. We do not want to include much detail about this in the chapter, because the focus of the project was on male youth and because we do not want to imply any criticism of the socially conservative nature of the community.

Second, there were characteristics common to both marginalized urban neighbor-hoods though both sites differed in their strategies to regulate the behavior of young people.

The use of emergent strategy, participatory methodology, and social learning theory created a rich picture of each community, including relations with children and with outside service providers. However, the approach used to learn about the two neighborhoods did not focus on their myriad commonalities. Similarities lend themselves to deriving standard principles that, in turn, can simplify such interventions in the future. Furthermore, the emphasis on participatory learn-ing should be complemented with a broader network of institutional resources to address the needs of several marginalized urban communities simultaneously. The pilot program design did not concentrate on building this broader perspec-tive. Had such a perspective been established, the meaning of community-specific characteristics would have been greatly enhanced.

Third, neighborhood linkages with national providers proved vital to the success of the pilot.

The pilot program established at least four important linkages. First, experts in psychological counseling took seriously the severity of problems in these margin-alized neighborhoods. Second, a national program for youth adjusted its operat-ing principles to accommodate the special needs of disadvantaged youth. Third, a national vocational counseling and training center amended its procedures to incor-porate children at risk into its programs. And finally, organizations for handicapped persons created opportunities for troublesome boys to volunteer that proved pivotal in helping them discover how to assist other individuals also in need.

Establishment of linkages with individuals who shared ideas for prosocial approaches was relatively straightforward, but such persons were seldom policy makers and decision makers in their institutions. There was always a risk that after a period of successful project work the institutions themselves would curtail the support, or the representative assigned to the project would become overworked as a result of assuming additional responsibilities. Moreover, not all institutions are receptive to allowing youth participation in agenda setting. In only one case – the national youth program – did the organization make it an institutional priority to develop a program responsive to at-risk youth of marginalized urban neighborhoods.

As community members began to trust experts from external organizations, institutional consistency was expected. Once new paradigms involving external organizations were envisioned and new relationships were established, organiza-tional political will and financial resources should have matched the initiatives of residents who were at the forefront of community change. Unfortunately, the organizations involved in linkage relationships often lacked the resources (or did not earmark resources) needed to maintain such consistency. The focus on developing collaborative linkages proved to be a time- and resource-intensive process, and the design of the pilot did not include a strategy to maintain institutional consistency.

Fourth, building prosocial communities through fostering vision, capacity, and experience in local neighborhoods; through establishing effective resource collaboration with national providers/experts; and through calling decision makers' attention to their role in eliminating policies and procedures that exclude marginalized youth is crucial to change the landscape and the "peoplescape" of poor urban areas.

Nongovernment organizations (NGOs) and private volunteer agencies (PVAs) have important roles, along with government organizations, in building prosocial communities. The design of the Questscope pilot capitalized on the ability of an NGO/PVA to be reflective and reflexive in improvements, understanding the developmental needs of children reared in deprived urban settings during a period of rapid social change. The ideal role for NGOs/PVAs involves taking risks and exploring novel ways to deal with emerging problems. Developing prosocial communities requires building a broad base of consensus at multiple levels in a variety of institutions. But it was more satisfactory in the public eye to reduce the visibility of "problems" by increasing the capacity of detention and reform centers. It was also more socially captivating to individualize problems of "poor youth" by providing shelters and services for abused children, for whom the general public had sympathy and compassion, as long as they were victims. The design of the pilot program did not take into account the necessary options for public and institutional education that would have created public awareness of the variety of prosocial roles marginalized youth can assume. It also did not consider how funding could be obtained and maintained for preventive prosocial initiatives with the majority of disadvantaged urban youth who could not be classified either as offenders or as victims.

SUMMARY AND CONCLUSIONS

Prosocial approaches to at-risk children were most successful when adults took the time and effort to understand the points of view offered by children about their own circumstances. After all, at-risk youth are the "experts" at succeeding in their neighborhoods. Their behaviors made perfect sense to them, given the pressures they endured.

Adults were responsible for refashioning environments that reinforced children's proactive roles and behaviors. This was accomplished at the neighborhood level as adults responded positively to new roles enacted by their youth. It was accomplished at institutional levels when directors and staff comprehended the needs of young boys to be respected and rewarded for prosocial behavior.

Experts involved in the program were able to suggest interventions that improved the capacities of adults, institutions, and children to cooperate effectively. The emphasis on emergent strategy allowed all parties to observe the effects of "small steps" and to make adjustments that facilitated positive interactions between youths' roles and "outsider" roles.

Neighborhoods required assistance to provide physical facilities and to design and implement activities that reinforced new, positive behaviors of both children and adults. Neighborhood members wanted to understand how to help and encourage their children when they experienced positive responses. As they became more comfortable with their new skills, much volunteer energy was released in both sites. Whereas the pilot program demonstrated the importance of fostering new and enriched roles for both adults and children at the neighborhood level, sustaining role development depended on appropriate institutional responses from actors external to the neighborhood. Although the emergent strategy approach addressed circumstances unique to each community (efficient coverage), it became evident that strategies must also address issues common to all marginalized urban communities (effective coverage).

Another important lesson is that providers external to the neighborhood must strive for both institutional and individual learning. Municipal authorities and government agencies were assisted in establishing relationships that were responsive to children's priorities articulated to cooperating adults. Prosocial community building must ultimately be supported by the highest municipal authorities in order to incorporate local initiatives into policy and practice to alter the urban environment. In the pilot project, such governing agencies became facilitators of local initiatives that originated with children. This was a change from the usual paradigm of agencies' designing urban plans "for" rather than "by" residents of marginalized neighborhoods.

The most encouraging outcome of the Questscope program design and implementation was the emergence of a shared community consciousness in both neighborhoods: that what could be accomplished with children was important and that such efforts would be supported by experts and national agencies. The key to success was returning to the viewpoints and expectations of children as they learned and enacted new roles in their personal lives and in the life of their neighborhood.

NOTES

1   The underground economy provided income, but only to certain types of families, and the amount and nature of this income were outside the scope of the study.
2   The proliferation of the means of information dissemination (satellite dishes) as part of the modernization of Jordan ensures media coverage throughout the kingdom. The delivery of the same message to a vast and varied number of people is one aspect of globalization that enhances urbanization and is enhanced by it.

Saudi Youth

Initiative and Inertia

Mai Yamani

This is a story of youth and alienation like so many stories of youth. But this is a story of a country that is systematically alienating its youth and, like many other parents with estranged children, they neither know what causes this distance and disobedience nor what to do about it. Instead they keep laying down the law and imposing the old punishments. The country is Saudi Arabia where the *uli al amr*, the royal family, always know best. But the children to whom they give their name Saudi are gradually losing their innocence and subservience. Through internet seductions, many youth are looking outside their country for role models.

Across the Kingdom of Saudi Arabia, civil society is struggling to be born. The state is doing its best to keep it under its control, as the tensions inherent in any social transformation are perceived to be a threat to the stability of the regime. The challenges the authorities face are immense: a diverse population, a traditional patrimonial model that is increasingly vulnerable to the inherent uncertainty implied by dependence on oil revenues, and a population explosion that has heightened the need to reduce unemployment. Indeed, over one third of the Kingdom's population of more than 24 million (of which 18 million are nationals) is now under fourteen years old[1].

With the new generation demanding economic and political space, the entire system of governance, based on the idea of *uli al amr* (those with authority as the benevolent fathers of the nation) and designed not to be challenged by its subjects, is now problematic and under pressure. Exposure to the outside world and communication with their peers in the region through travel, satellite TV, and the Internet has increased the new generation's demand for social and political rights. Foremost, they aspire for democratic representation that state paternalism has historically denied. The more they are suppressed by their state, the more Saudi youth rely on the technologies of globalization to create a sense of transnational identity and to search for "freedom" beyond the Kingdom's borders.

The proliferation of new media has exposed the realities on the ground to public view. Official programs of control and containment are being challenged, since they do not meet the new generation's worldviews and needs. Alternative media such as digital video cameras bear witness when the Saudi *mutawa'a* (religious police) brutalise Shi'a pilgrims in the Great Mosque of Mecca and of Medina. Indeed, videos of Saudi prison guards beating juvenile detainees – and even depictions of frustration with the ban on women drivers – have become easily accessible on YouTube, while Saudi youth have embraced virtual social networks such as Facebook. A Google generation is rising and cannot be contained unless electricity is cut off. Studies show that in 2009 more than 97 per cent of internet users in the Kingdom rely on Google (*Al Riyadh*, March 7, 2009). Currently, there are 7.7 million internet users and 1.3 million internet users have broadband connections. Internet use shows phenomenal growth. Since 2004, there have been over 5 million new internet users (Ministry of Economy and Planning).

The electronic news media pose a serious challenge to the authoritarian state. The challenge is not only a reflection of their overwhelming and fast-moving images, but also because the internet, in particular, has ushered in a new political culture. The internet creates a space for convergence, bursting open national jurisdictions of content regulation (Hargreaves, 2003: 19). Hundreds of Saudi websites defiantly expose the secrets that protect the illusion of stability and harmony within the Kingdom. The Al-Saud cannot hope to bar, ban, and block all of these avenues of publicity. Although the government's Internet Services Unit attempts to filter "subversive" and "disruptive" internet content, the task is too daunting (Zittrain & Edelman, 2009). The nature of the new media and the vulnerability of the official narrative underlying the regime make such an attempt impossible (Yamani, 2008). The theme of exclusion and alienation as perceived by the youth stems from fragmentation of state policy, secretive paternalism, Wahhabi inertia, stifling American policies, and the oil temptation.

FRAGMENTATION AS STATE POLICY

The Al-Saud, who gave their name to the country in 1932, aspired to strong identification with their subjects, creating an image of themselves as the benevolent "fathers of the nation" ruling over a conservative society. However, that image masks a reality of diversity and even schism. Saudi Arabia's regions, tribes, and sects have preserved their cultural distinctiveness, which the regime has refused to recognize. Instead the regime has launched successive failed attempts at national integration (Yamani, 2004).

Systematic exclusion of significant sections of society has fuelled persistent internal pressures for reform and a search for complementary identity. Often, this is inspired by the wider Arab world and Islamic *umma* (the global community of Muslims). However, the regime is split over how to respond to the new voices within and how to contain their outside connections.

Yet socio-cultural heterogeneity is central to the self-understanding of Saudi Arabia's new generation. Heterogeneity is compounded by the failure thus far of the appearance of a cohesive middle class. For example, the regime's reliance on oil revenue has contributed to the creation of a middle class that, in some ways, has become another key source of reformist pressure. However, as a historical and sociological phenomenon, the emergence of a Saudi middle class is not entirely comparable to its significance for political development elsewhere. On the contrary, it is more relevant to speak of "middle classes" whose concomitant rise continues to be mediated by ethno culturally-based cleavages which reinforce the prevailing political hierarchy and its socioeconomic privileges.

Within this hierarchy, the Najdis, who are native to the Al-Saud's base in the central region of the Kingdom, maintain privileged status, while the Hijazis of Mecca and Medina are partly included, and the Shi'a in the Eastern Province and the southern tribes of Asir – especially the Ismailis – are practically shunned. Given these divergent interests and loyalties, middle-class members do not present a united stance against the regime. Indeed, such cleavages, reflected in recent expressions by the young, reveal that class identities, even the "nation" – with its connotation of a shared past and a shared destiny – is problematic in describing Saudi Arabia.

As a result, the emergence of an economically empowered middle class, in combination with continuing discrimination and repression of minorities and other politically marginalized groups, could very well lead to fragmentation. The Shi'a, who constitute 75 per cent of the population in the Eastern Province, the Kingdom's main oil-producing region, currently pose the gravest challenge to the state, especially given their new generation's strengthening political affiliation to Iraqi, Bahraini, Kuwaiti, and other Shi'a groups in the region. Saudi Shi'a websites such as *Khalas*, salvation, aim at mobilising young Shi'a in their search for separation from the state. Interestingly, their ultimate goal is cessation and inclusion or unification to the "Republic of Hajr" within a Greater Bahrain (Yamani, 2009).

So far, however, King Abdullah has shown no sign of creating a policy of inclusion aimed at the country's minorities. At the same time, he has been unable to promote the rise of an empowered new middle class. Instead, Abdullah's strategy is one of political decompression: offering just enough concessions to appease Saudi Arabia's subordinate and alienated peoples and thus relieve pressure for more radical reforms. To this end, he appears to be constructing a centrist political alliance equipped to compromise between demands for recognition of diversity and official repression in the name of homogeneity and national unity (Yamani, 2009).

The Al-Saud's divide-and-rule policy ensures that people are unable to develop a national opposition. The Al-Saud have proven adept at controlling the degree of hostility between the Salafis (Wahhabis), the Shi'a, the Hijazis, and the Ismailis, as well as between the conservatives and the liberals. Indeed, such strategies have limited the degree of conflict and competition to what is necessary for their survival and never allowing it to reach the point of tipping the country into civil war. The regime carefully monitors the struggle between groups and maintains a dynamic tension, pouring water or fuel on the fire, as the circumstances require. The security forces and the *mukhabarat* (the intelligence services) enforce the politics of fear.

An official National Dialogue was initiated by then Crown Prince Abdullah in 2004, as an acknowledgement of pluralism and diversity. Different religious sects gathered for the first time: Wahhabis, Sufis, Shi'a, and Ismailis. But, since the discussions within the National Dialogue meetings have not been legitimized by the religious authorities, nothing has changed in everyday life. The Shi'a still cannot practice their religious rituals, be witnesses in court, or even work as butchers, because the Wahhabis, closely allied with the Al-Saud, consider them heretics and apostates. The hope of the youth that "the dialogue" will provide freedoms and transparency was followed by a sense of marginalization and exclusion (Yamani, 2005).

Not surprisingly, as the "King Abdul Aziz Centre for National Dialogue" has become divorced from domestic reality, it has turned into a center for propaganda, whose participants believe that they are part of the state's message to the outside world. At home however, the road to change is closed. Indeed, the National Dialogue has been transformed by officials into an "intellectual encounter". One meeting, held in Dhahran in December 2004, entitled "Encounter with Youth: Reality and Aspirations", consisted in a procession of grand speeches by the authorities, who tried to convince the 665 young Saudis in attendance that conditions in the country were ideal. The young men and women are expected to listen to "those with authority", the fathers of the nation and never question their wisdom[2].

SECRETIVE PATERNALISM

Another source of alienation from the regime Saudi youth feel is the secretive royal manouverings for authority. The rule of succession is ambiguous, and the next in line is uncertain, as the increasing size of the Al-Saud (currently 22,000 members) has fuelled an increasing clash of factions and potential claimants. Indeed, the octogenarian line of successors to the aged King Abdullah recalls the final years of the Soviet Union, when one infirm leader after another assumed power, making for brief and ineffective rule.

King Abdullah announced an initiative that made the situation more obscure and uncertain than ever. In 2005, Abdullah's authority was insufficient to appoint the "Second Deputy" in line of succession, which had been the tradition since the Kingdom's founder, Ibn Saud, and which had given the process a degree of predictability. King Abdullah embarked on an innovation to the succession process in 2007 in the form of the "Allegiance Council", but then reversed course in 2009 and appointing a "Second Deputy". Although a number of younger princes such as Al Walid bin Talal and Bandar bin Sultan have publicly expressed their hope to rule, this is unlikely – not only because of sheer numbers of competitors, but also because of unwritten rules of seniority.

From the point of view of Saudi youth, the problem of succession is not so much the uncertainty regarding who will rule, but the policy of the next ruler, and that nothing – neither institutional rules nor informal norms – can guarantee his effectiveness. Moreover, details concerning the succession battle within the Al-Saud can no longer be kept behind closed doors. The internet has opened a window on all the family plots and ambitions.

Many young Saudis are concerned about and discuss this pattern of continuous uncertainty regarding succession. This concern is legitimate given the gap between old rulers and a young population becoming increasingly pronounced in cultural, as well as generational, terms. The discourse of the old rulers has little influence or relevance for the country's youth. The political components of this form of monarchy are distinctive from others such as the Bahraini or the Kuwaiti that allow for modern political forums. Within the current Saudi system of rule, there are no tools, methods or programs that create interactions with the youth. Political participation is constrained by the idea that "those with authority" know better. The state has the right to determine the interest of the people and knows the capabilities of its offspring. Hence, the *shura* (consultative council) is appointed by the King and will remain unelected for the foreseeable future. Crown Prince Sultan confirmed that decision in 2005 in order to end a debate, initiated by liberal reformers, about the possibility of an elected *shura*, arguing "Saudi Arabia is not ready to have an elected parliament because voters might elect illiterate and unqualified candidates" (*Al-Riyad*, 2005).

WAHHABI INERTIA

The Al-Saud base their legitimacy on custodianship of Islam's holiest sites, and claim to be the special representatives and defenders of the faith. To be sure, the fact that the regime derives its religious authority from Wahhabism, a narrow, austere Sunni sect, limits its popular legitimacy among a diverse and young population that does not subscribe to the Wahhabi doctrine. However, the Kingdom's leaders believe that control of Mecca and Medina is sufficient justification for authoritarian rule, and that there is no need for popular representation or democracy in any form. The regime comments favorably on the democratic upheavals in Iran and supports and funds Lebanese democratic elections but at home the concept remains taboo. This stark irony is quite apparent to Saudi youth.

The Wahhabi religious establishment who are the co-rulers of the Saudi state have severely circumscribed the process of political modernization (Abdullah, 2004). There is a deep-seated antagonism between Wahhabism and democracy, which is rooted in the ideology itself. Saudi Wahhabi clerics stand *in principle* against democratic reform. This is largely a reflection of their belief in both the infallibility and immutability of Wahhabi interpretations of Islamic texts and *bai'a*, unquestioning political allegiance to the ruler.

In the absence of free, fair, and genuinely competitive elections, the Wahhabis' share of power as co-rulers of the Saudi monarchy remains highly disproportionate to their share of Saudi Arabia's diverse population. Wahhabism is a minority sect, both in Saudi Arabia and in the Muslim world as a whole. Democracy, on the other hand, implies the distribution of power through institutional arrangements – particularly universal enfranchisement and elections – that ensure some form of majority rule.

This does not mean that the Wahhabi system is incapable of adopting forms of democratic rule. In order not to appear to be lagging behind other Arab states, municipal elections were held in 2005, but were only partial and heavily managed, reflecting the regime's tendency to manipulate electoral reforms in order to strengthen its hold on power (Al-Hassan, 2006). The entire female population was excluded, and a quarter of the male population was appointed. This exclusion from the vote was particularly questioned by young Saudi women on the internet who compared their state with that of other Muslim countries. This debate came to a halt as the *uli al amr* cancelled municipal elections scheduled for 2009.

The Wahhabi religious establishment controls some of the most important levers of state power. Within the region, only in Saudi Arabia do the *mutawa'a* (official employees of the Committee for the Propagation of Virtue and Prevention of Vice) represent the "hand of God" and remain above the law. The *mutawa'a* patrol the Kingdom's streets in their government cars searching for sinful youth. In May 2007, the *mutawa'a* launched an aggressive offensive, raiding houses and locking up individuals for days, with some tortured and others beaten to death. To the new generation, the authorities appear to be unable or unwilling to stop this violent intrusion into their lives, and criticism of the *mutawa'a*'s brutal practices, which also impact business and tourism negatively, is a leading indicator of the pressures for reform[3].

The state, however, continues to present and use Islam as an obstacle to reform. The strategy is to impress on the Saudi young population that other countries in the region that have embarked on democratic reform are fundamentally different, because they do not bear custodianship over Mecca and Medina. Hence, from this perspective, Saudi reform must be carefully calibrated and engineered to meet the unique situation of a country blessed with this awesome responsibility.

The most pertinent question for the new generation is education, which is also the central mechanism of reproducing the Saudi state. It is through the expanded educational system that the vast majority of the population was intended to be socialized into a specifically Saudi national identity. The educational system therefore embodies the tensions at the heart of the Saudi state, which are rooted in the symbiotic relationship between the religious and the political establishment. The empowerment and constraints of the alliance run through the whole national curriculum. The *ulema* (religious scholars) control the religious curriculum, which comprises six subjects revolving around the official Wahhabi doctrine – Qur'an, *tafsir* (interpretation), *tawhid* (unification), *hadith* (sayings of the Prophet), *tajwid* (recitation), and *fiqh* (jurisprudence). These subjects make up nearly half of the total national curriculum, while the country languishes under a huge skills gap. As a result, despite Saudization programs, the Kingdom does not possess enough indigenous expertise to staff the economy, much less take it forward into the twenty-first century. Many youth believe that this religious heavy dose is an obstacle to their intellectual and financial capabilities, and weakens their future opportunities.

For the state, defending Islam precludes modernizing the educational system and establishing social amenities like cinemas and youth clubs. But demands for educational reform are voiced by young Saudis, including young members of the royal family. In a recent television interview, Prince Muhammad Abdullah Al Faisal strongly criticized the Saudi curriculum, saying that it "produces terrorists" and is totally unsuitable (http://wasatonline.com). Likewise, the educational system's sectarianism was criticized during a session of the National Dialogue and in local newspapers. Ismailis and Shi'a in particular have voiced criticism of the intensive religious education and the negative impact on the Shari'a colleges on the labor market (Okaz, 2009). Mohammad Al Hayazi', the director of Jazan University (located in a predominantly Southern Ismaili city) explained that "we do not want to increase unemployment through more religious specialisations." Likewise, Khalid Al Hammudi, the director of Qasim University (a Shi'a populated city) encourages the closing of places for such education in the light for the need to focus on scientific studies (Okaz, 2009). In addition to the compulsory religious studies at secondary school level, there are thousands of religious schools and universities such as Imam Muhammad bin Saud Islamic University which has another 124 affiliate institutes and the Islamic University of Medina, which has five affiliated institutes[4]. The religious establishment reacted to calls for minimizing the religious education, by increasing the spending on the Imam Mohammad Bin Saud University's religious website by 200 million Sr [53 million dollars] on top of the annual budget of 1.5 million Sr [400,000 dollars]. Although the late Sheikh Abdul Aziz bin Baz issued a fatwa permitting the studies of science such as engineering, he stressed that this should only be after pervasive religious education and obedience to *uli al amr* (Bin Baz, 1993: 302). In fact, the use of educational reform is officially rejected by the Saudi state, which instead uses terms such as educational development (Al-Isa, 2009: 78-80).

Wahhabi rule creates a kind of medieval guild-like structure in the economy. Puritanism prevents economic diversification particularly in the service sector, advertising industries, restaurants, and shops. Gender segregation is strictly imposed in all public spheres including in shops that cater to only half the population and at universities where teaching for women is through closed-circuit television (Yamani, 1996). Many among the new generation perceive the system to be inefficient and stunted.

THE OIL TEMPTATION

The state's traditional strategy for maintaining domestic legitimacy has depended on patrimony, which in turn is based on oil revenue, with the royal family providing a very generous welfare system. In exchange for loyalty and subservience, the state would pay for everything and avoid taxing the population.

The regime clings to this strategy still. Saudi Arabia is the world's largest oil producer with the largest spare capacity. But oil prices fluctuate creating feelings of insecurity among the new generation. Oil prices quadrupled between 2002 and 2008, enabling King Abdullah to build the world's largest petrochemical plant in record time as part of his $500 billion initiative to build new cities, create jobs and diversify the economy (Muawwad, 2008).

But, while oil can buy popular subservience and delay political demands, it cannot compensate for genuine reform. In fact, the money spent so far has not improved public services for the vast majority of people, with water, sewage, electricity, education, and health facilities remaining abysmal. According to Abdullah Bin Mahfooz, Deputy Director of the Jeddah Chamber of Commerce, around 65 per cent of Saudis do not own houses (City Skype conference, 2009). Housing loans applications could take twenty-five years to be delivered (Okaz, 2009). Moreover, the distribution of wealth has been uneven due to a policy of discrimination based on sect, region, tribe, and gender.

Most importantly, intermittent periods of high oil prices, which have been unstable since the mid-1980s, cannot solve the unemployment problem. Unemployment has risen by 2 per cent from the first half to the second half of 2007 (Ministry of Economy & Statistics–Census Data, 1999). In light of the Kingdom's excess demand for labor, owing to mismatches between the educational system and the needs of the national economy, reliance on foreign workers is a major factor in unemployment among Saudi nationals (UNDP, 2003). The traditional patrimonial model is, therefore, increasingly vulnerable to the inherent uncertainty implied by dependence on oil revenues, as well as to rapid population growth and falling per capita income. In an unprecedented act a number of young male university graduates gathered outside King Abdullah's palace in Riyadh demanding jobs (Sabq website). For others with less hope of employment within the Kingdom, neighboring Gulf countries offer some opportunities. Since 2007 the Saudi state gave permission to its nationals to work in Gulf Cooperation Council (GCC) countries. Young Saudis are mainly working in the educational sectors in Kuwait and the UAE. The Emirate of Sharjah is favoured by young Salafi Wahhabi Saudis, while the openness of Dubai appeals to the more liberally inclined.

For the new Saudi generation, there is the additional burden of increasingly direct competition with the royal sphere, which is expanding rapidly. With the ratio of royals to commoners at one to a thousand, the new generation is acutely aware of the growing princely privileges, salaries, and demand for jobs. For example, royal perks include lifetime sinecures and domination of the civil service, which enables the princes to award contracts and receive commissions on top of their salaries. Princes, especially important ones, also compete against indigenous merchants for contracts.

The private sector is concentrated in the oil sector and is deeply connected with the royals. The distinction between private and public treasury is murky at best. Business and government are family affairs. In Saudi Arabia economic success requires close connections with the rulers. The practice of *wasta*, economic benefits through family connections, is widely criticized by young Saudis[5].

The rise in oil prices between 2002 and 2008 prolonged the Saudi rulers' reliance on their traditional means of appeasing the Kingdom's young population. But, as the subsequent price reversal suggests, a workable formula for long-term stability cannot be based on the yo-yo of the world oil market, which can snap suddenly, leading to a violent reaction that could have truly global significance. That is certainly not the desire of most Saudi youth, who have ordinary concerns as national and world citizens. What they want is a state that responds to these concerns by establishing more mature democratic ties between rulers and ruled, and that can assume a more progressive place in the community of nations.

STIFLED BY AMERICA

Youth discontent and alienation are compounded by the regime's alliance with the United States. The external backing provided by the US makes the Saudi state appear weak, with the regime staking its survival and authority on international necessity, rather than domestic legitimacy. The perception is that Saudi Arabia's extraordinarily abundant wealth is put to work through investments in the US and phenomenal arms purchases. Riyadh's willingness to invest its revenue in US-supported causes, and to increase oil production to advance US interests, while this might have earned it considerable favour in Washington, has brought it criticism by young Saudis, who feel deprived and disaffected.

Many young Saudis believe that the strategic relationship with the US does not serve their country's long-term national interests, as it diverts resources from internal investment, particularly in efforts aimed at promoting economic diversification. Most young Saudis have no objection to US protection of the Saudi regime, but seek to break the link between the defense of international sovereignty and domestic repression in the name of "fighting terrorism" – a mission that has ignored abuses of justice in the name of security. Moreover, official repression has been enabled by a myopic perception of Saudi Arabia as a homogeneous society rather than a mosaic of significant but little-known communities that demand recognition.

At the popular level, resentment of US "hard" power – security, arms, and intelligence – is in considerable tension with attraction to its abundant resources of "soft" power. Thus, anti-American sentiments coexist uneasily with the ubiquity of American fast food and clothes, and a universal desire among ordinary Saudis for American brands (Yamani, 2000).

While the longstanding US-Saudi alliance has served as a bulwark against a broad array of external challenges – from the Arab nationalism and communism of the past to the continuing Shiʻa Islamism exported by Iran and the Sunni "terrorism" of today – the US also provides a cover for repressive domestic policies. The justification for keeping interference in domestic affairs to a minimum is the idea that Saudi Arabia is a special case where reform must move slowly because of Islamic duties. To the new generation, this sharp contrast with other Muslim countries, such as Iraq, Syria, and Iran, where US policy during the Bush administration was to support regime change and far-reaching reforms, appears hypocritical – a policy based on the view that domestic security, not democracy, remains the key to regional stability. Obama's policies appear to young Saudis as ambiguous and even as a continuation and confirmation of those of previous administrations.

However, while Saudi rulers are acutely aware of US criticism of their human rights record and their deviation from international norms, they have been largely able to fend off foreign pressure. As a result, US influence over domestic policy remains negligible, and the link between security and reform has been increasingly ignored. To be sure, for a short period after 9/11 and the mutual shock that the majority of the hijackers were Saudi, the US stressed the need to reform the Saudi educational system, especially Wahhabi teachings of exclusion and intolerance. The Saudi authorities introduced minor, cosmetic changes to textbooks, which proved sufficient to move Saudi Arabia to the top of the class of "moderate" states in the region.

This contradiction has, in fact, encouraged the view that the US's talk about democracy is merely a cover to legitimize its occupation of Iraq and its interference in the Middle East. It is quite likely that this might have given rise to many young Saudis' obsession with conspiracy theories, which are often discussed on the internet. Even among those who spurn such theories, US policy has been viewed as one of selective support for authoritarian regimes that serve its interests, with Saudi Arabia being the prime beneficiary. As a result, the US is criticized for its lack of concern about resolving the real problems of the region's people, and is considered an obstacle to reform.

GLOBALIZATION AND THE ILLUSION OF FREEDOM

Globalization is expanding the space for Saudi youth, posing a highly complex challenge for the regime. The advent of satellite television, especially *Al Jazeera* in 1996, has created a new stage, a new public sphere for intellectual debate with frank political discussions highlighting the extent of domestic censorship. Indeed, the *"Al Jazeera* syndrome" has revolutionized Arab media, mobilizing popular opinion and threatening government control as a subsequent wave of copycat satellite television stations, together with the internet, has created unprecedented opportunities for expression of heterodox views.

But the breakthrough represented by *Al Jazeera* has not transformed the theatre of discussion among Saudi youth, nor paved the way for democratic reform, because, while globalization is expanding the public space, the Saudi government is attempting simultaneously to shrink it. The Kingdom's rulers continue to use their power and influence to regulate the domestic cultural and political field in order to impose limits on public debate and controversy, taming the effects of globalization by embracing its communications technologies wherever the regime can then set the rules.

The Saudi government has shown an ability to use a variety of means, including regulatory and technological measures, to control the availability of information and restrict both the scope of issues subject to public debate and the language that may be used. Restrictions are enforced both by direct ownership of media by royal princes and, perhaps more importantly, by less direct control of newspapers and journalists. In particular, young Saudi academics and journalists are keenly aware of where the lines of what is permissible are drawn, and of when it is safe to cross them. Because most intellectuals receive their wages directly from the state, their livelihood and future depend on their ability to maneuver within the guidelines.

For young people, crossing the lines of censorship often results in a late-night call, from appointed members of *uli al amr*, to "advise" the youth or their guardian about misjudgments in the analysis and in the ideas expressed. The youth are aware of the custodial rule and paternalistic rule of their state. For those rebellious few who ignore the system of *al munasaha* (advice), harsher means are employed, such as sacking, flogging, and/or imprisonment.

The state has also used the media as a lever of "soft power". The Saudi rulers own satellite television stations in many Arab countries, as well as large shares in the Arab press published outside the Arab world. These include *Al Mawarid*, owned by the Middle East Broadcasting Corporation (MBC) group, founded in 1991 and now based in Dubai, which has six entertainment television channels and two radio channels. In 2003, the *Al Arabiya* news channel was added to MBC's portfolio in an effort to counter the influence of *Al Jazeera*.

Likewise, the Saudi Press Agency (SPA), the state news agency, owns major publishing companies, such as Saudi Research and Marketing (SRM), which distributes private pan-Arab newspapers such as *al-Hayat* and *al-Sharq al-Awsat*, both based in London. Saudi princes also own television channels, including *IRT*, *Orbit* (in partnership with LBC International in Lebanon), *Al Mustaqbal* and the Rotana Group in Lebanon.

Almost all the Saudi satellite television channels present a paradox. A viewer of Saudi satellite TV can watch an old blind cleric in obvious pain holding forth about potential carnal sin or answering questions about menstruation and male versus female body hair. The viewer can then switch to another Saudi-owned channel and watch Lebanese and Egyptian girls dancing and enacting provocative scenes that surpass the most risqué of Western videos. This seemingly polarized concoction of dogmatic preaching and visual provocation uses the globalization of communications to fuse religion and hyper-consumerism.

In fact, however, sermonizing and tantalizing go hand-in-hand to serve a clear purpose: distracting the young generation's attention from real debate and attention to socio-economic realities. Both modes of communication represent distorted pictures of reality, offering fantasies that present a one-sided version of adulthood. Sermonizing projects a strident sense of responsibility and an ascetic form of self-control, whereas tantalizing presents a libertine form of irresponsibility and abandonment. The one relates to the individual's position vis-à-vis the state and its repressive apparatus, and the other to his status vis-à-vis the market. The space in the middle, of maturity, judgment, solidarity, and citizenship, is simply missing.

Nevertheless, an obedient, docile population, amenable to the orders of the state, is a thing of the past. Failures of representation, politics, and economics, as well as the need for jobs and education for a youthful population, are real problems that cannot be solved by clerics threatening viewers with the fires of hell or by dancing women beckoning to them before the cameras. The Al Saud's monopoly of mass-media ownership has effectively constrained new ideas and perspectives, but their investments in suppressing debate, criticism, and diversity have merely bred myopia and a delusion of control.

External challengers, ranging from satellite television to YouTube to Facebook, expose the limitations of the totalitarian rule. As young people are denied recreational opportunities such as cinema, clubs, and concerts, and must conform to strict gender segregation in all public spaces, television and computer screens become their main attraction. But, as one might expect with any medium of free expression, their fascination with what amounts to privatized public participation takes varied forms.

Such outlets find a broad audience among Saudi Arabia's new generation, which, given its members' disconnection from domestic affairs and the fact that demonstrations are illegal, looks outward to regional affairs. This affords them an opportunity to participate as either spectators or followers of forces such as Hamas or Hezbollah, and express their dissatisfaction and anger either passively in front of the television screens or in anonymous debates on the internet. Reflecting the regime's strategies for minimizing political debate and controversy, as well as the absence of civil organizations to safeguard and monitor the rule of law, human rights, education, and sectarian and ethnic diversity, the new generation's response embodies a combination of ambition and fear, together with initiative and inertia.

One of the most widespread forms of communication reflects the consequences of the state's denial and control of religious pluralism, which drove dissent underground, but now threatens the regime in a new guise: Islam on-line. After years of attempting to establish a monopoly for its theological decrees, the Saudi state faces thousands of websites that defy, challenge, and compete with established dogma, confronting the regime with aggressive and distorted versions of its own religious guidance. New technology contributed to the creation of a transnational Islamic political movement in which some Saudi youth, indoctrinated in traditional Wahhabi thought, were exposed to Salafi and other Sunni movements outside the Kingdom, some of which adhere to the inflammatory rhetoric of the regional and global *jihadis* and Al Qaeda. As a result, the interior ministry established *al lajnah al munasihah* (the Committee of Advice) in 2003 to monitor all websites (numbering roughly 20,000) associated with jihadis.

Shi'a media pose yet another religious-political threat, including satellite TV channels such as Hezbollah's *Al Manar* in Lebanon, *Al Furat* in Iraq, and Iran's *Al Alam* and *Al Kawsar*, which broadcast in Arabic from Tehran and focus on promoting the Palestinian cause. In addition Shi'a religious discourse is broadcast on *Al Zahra*, *Ahl Al Beit*, *Al Anwar*, and other outlets. Aggressive 24-hour Shi'a TV channels attract Saudi Shi'a and other alienated youth. Moreover, a proliferation of Shi'a websites emerged after the Iraq war, including Abdul Aziz al Hakim's Iraqi Islamic Council website *"Buratha"*. This regional new media attracts young Saudi Shi'a who perceived themselves as politically and economically marginalized. They are increasingly creating a transnational identity.

THE FUTURE: INCLUSION OR DIVISION?

Most Saudi youth, whether liberal, conservative, or radical, believe that the Wahhabi religious establishment must be reformed. Many believe this possible in view of democratic experiments in other Gulf countries, particularly Qatar, the only other Wahhabi state on the Arabian Peninsula. These examples provide a telling counterpoint, which suggest that Saudi Wahhabism will be forced to change its guiding attitudes and principles. Indeed, in Kuwait and Bahrain, Salafis (a wider fundamentalist group whose members' beliefs are closely linked to the Wahhabis') have become more moderate as a result of their participation in those countries' parliaments. It is noteworthy that the Salafis in Bahrain and Kuwait entered Parliament only after receiving permission from the highest Wahhabi authority, Sheikh Abdul Aziz Bin Baz, and later from his successor, Sheikh Abdul Aziz Al Sheikh. The permission indicates that Saudi Wahhabis object to democracy only at home, where they fear – probably correctly – that a pragmatic approach to political reform would weaken their power. The democratic experiments in the Gulf Cooperation Council (GCC) countries are particularly inspiring and encouraging for the Saudi youth. The similarities in tribal and religious traditions make the transnational identity more real for the new generation of Saudis irrespective of their sect or tribe.

But the domestic stance includes defending Saudi Arabia's strict methods of censorship against demands for more freedom of expression. By supplementing direct and indirect ownership with strict administrative measures, Saudi Arabia continues to have the region's most controlled media, which are overseen by a censorship committee, comprising representatives from various government ministries, that monitors all local and foreign publications (Amin, 2001: 27). From the perspective of the Al Saud, public amenability to the orders of the state remains what most characterizes their relationship with their subjects, to whom they give their name.

However, Saudi youth have expectations and demands for a new political narrative. The reigning narrative's dominance exhibits inflexibility and thus fragility. It is both stuck in time and unable to modify and innovate in response to the ever-changing present. Thus, the relationship of the Al Saud with their young subjects may not be as enduring as it appears. Any sudden and sustained exposure of the gap between appearance and reality may cause deeper feelings of alienation, thereby forcing the youth to seek solidarity and a sense of security from transnational belonging.

Thus, there are two possible directions for the regime: a Wahhabi veto on reform, or acceptance of a more diverse Islam and a more inclusive Saudi Arabia. The latter approach would mean sidelining the Wahhabis. A revised conception of both Islam and Saudi Arabia, endowing each with a plural identity, would require greater flexibility. At the least, it will generate a measure of give-and-take, and a willingness to engage in genuine dialogue with the voices of the new generation.

Saudi youth, whether liberal, conservative or radical, are increasingly contesting the traditional concept of *uli al amr*, a system that demands complete submission to political authority. Yet serious political change could be undertaken with the preservation of royal traditions in mind. King Abdullah could vigorously pursue a policy of political liberalization, thereby trusting the Saudi population with greater freedom of expression and influence over government. The needs of the young, which are now at the crossroads of a new, challenging unity, subnational loyalties, and increased solidarities beyond the borders, must be recognized and addressed.

At such a crossroad, young Saudis will move forward according to their social experiences. They could find a meeting place a potential for integration of the country on a basis of equality and tolerance, or they may opt for divisions within the country; divisions based on regional and sectarian belonging and align with fellow sectarians.

NOTES

1   Ministry of Economy and Planning. Kingdom of Saudi Arabia Economy in Figures. Available from: http://www.mep.gov.sa/index.jsp;jsessionid [Accessed July 18, 2009].

2   See: Fourth National Meeting. King AbdulAziz Center for National Dialogue. Available from: http://www.kacnd.org/eng/fourth_meeting.asp (Accessed May 22, 2009).

3   In April 2007, *Al Watan* reported twenty-one incidents in the past year of confrontations between the mutaw'a and Saudi nationals involving firearms and knives. See also, *al Quds al Arabi*, July 7, 2007. and *Time*, 2007. Vice Squad: The Power of Saudi Arabia's Morality Police is being challenged amid Allegations of Abuse and Violence, August 6.

4   See: Ministry of Education: the Centre for Statistics, 2006. and also see Al 'Isa, A., 2009. *islah al ta'lib fi al saudia: bain ghiab al ru'ya al siasiyya wa tawajjus al thaqafah al diniyya.* Beirut: Dar Al Saqi, 24–25

5   The term "wastah", which literally connotes an intermediary, refers generally to "influence", which may be along familial lines in the case of nepotism or tribal

Between Silences and Screams

The Lebanese Postmemory Experience*

Craig Larkin

Memory of the war I don't know if I can even talk about it – I mean if there is something in society that helps you to think about it but everything encourages us to escape. Nothing encourages you to deal with it, to face it, nothing! They don't even talk about it anymore and even if they do it's from different perspectives: a theory and idea – not specific facts. I mean it's very dangerous to awaken something that is not yet ready to be awakened ... It's not easy to remember and it's such a blessing to forget sometimes; but if you want to remember and you want to deal with it, and I hope each one of us will want to face something, and when he is ready, then it will help.

Rola, 22, Lebanese University student[1]

Despite the recent cracks to emerge in Lebanon's wall of public silence concerning the civil war – whether due to activist calls for disclosure and healing, politicians championing the search for historic truth (Haugbolle, 2007), or academics concerned with post-war nostalgia and historic imaginings (see, for example, Khalaf, 2006; Makdisi, 2006) – little attention has yet to be given as to how Lebanese youth are negotiating both the silences and screams of their nation's bloody past. This paper, drawing on Marianne Hirsch's concept of *Postmemory* (Hirsch, 1997 & 2008) seeks to explore the memory of a generation who have grown up dominated not by traumatic events but by narrative accounts of events which preceded their birth. This is an inherited form of memory, which carries and connects with the "Pain of Others" (Sontag, 2003), transfusing temporal frames and liminal positions. The complex and

* Author's note: A previous version of this paper was first presented at a Middle East Studies Association (MESA) Conference: Montréal, Nov. 2007 and then at a conference "Marginalization and Mobilization of Arab Youth", American University of Beirut, Center for Behavioural Research, May 29–31, 2009. A longer version of this article has been published as "Beyond the War? The Lebanese Postmemory Experience", *International Journal of Middle East Studies*, Vol.42, Issue 4, (Nov. 2010): 615-635. This research and writing were undertaken as part of the "Conflict in Cities and the Contested State", project funded by the Economic and Social and Research Council (RES-060-25-0015).

ambivalent position of Lebanese youth, caught between the contradictory forces of collective remembrance and social forgetting, is demonstrated in Rola's entreaty to face the past but fear of rousing "something that is not yet ready to be awakened". This chapter seeks to examine how the Lebanese Postmemory generation reproduce, re-imagine or erase memory traces to locate, identify and position themselves within contemporary Lebanese society. I will address this dynamic process by initially situating this theory within Lebanon's post-war context. Secondly, I will explore how student memories, shaped by social settings and political circumstances, are mediated and negotiated through the agency of visual landscape (sites and spaces) and oral narrative. In each setting memory takes different forms, is subject to various pressures, and performs contrasting functions.

To best examine these themes, I will draw on a variety of case studies which emerged from extensive research and qualitative interviews among 100 Lebanese high school and university students, from ten different educational institutes during a one-year period: the summer of 2005 to the summer of 2006[2]. My sample attempted to reflect Lebanon's diverse religious composition (26 per cent of students interviewed were from a Shi'a confessional background, 24 per cent Sunni, 13 per cent Druze, and 33 per cent Christian), its continuing socio-economic divides (the schools and universities chosen were both public/private, secular/religious and rural/urban), and its demographic spread (interviewees were from Beirut, Tripoli, the South, the Beqaa, the Shouf, and Metn Mountains). Access to schools and students was obtained through personal contacts with teachers and headmasters, and with the help of conflict resolution centers and local civil activists[3].

Student interviews were semi-structured and open-ended; allowing themes and stories to emerge naturally. Arabic and English was used interchangeably depending on the context and fluency of the student[4]. High school students were interviewed on school grounds, while university students were given freedom to choose a place that they felt most comfortable with. The individually selected interview locations provided interesting social and political backdrops to frame family memories, historic events, and political positions. The timing of the research, conducted in the aftermath of the Syrian military withdrawal and the March 14 (*al-Muwalaa* – Loyalist) and March 8 (*al-Mu'arada* – Opposition) popular mobilizations[5], offers an intriguing insight into how Lebanese students are negotiating newly emerging memory discourses – from the civil campaigns which seek memory as a remedy for an unresolved past, to political movements which project memory recovery as national issue connected to "freedom, truth and independence" (Safa, 2006).

LOCATING A POSTMEMORY GENERATION

Postmemory is perhaps best defined as a residual type of memory, a recollection of an event not personally experienced but socially felt; a traumatic rupture which indelibly scars a nation, religious group, community, or family. Marianne Hirsch posits the concept in regard to the overwhelming weight of Holocaust memory and its discursive power, particularly through photographs and visual images, to fix and shape Jewish historical consciousness and remembrance. For Hirsch postmemory exists as "a powerful and very particular form of memory precisely because its connection to its object or source is mediated, not through recollection but through an imaginative investment and creation" (Hirsch, 1997: 2). Such memory often simultaneously works to connect yet distance subsequent generations to their collective pasts: helping to provide mnemonic frames and schemata for affirming social identities, communal traditions and temporal continuity, while imprisoning them within historical discourses which have "silenced us verbally" and which "neither can be understood nor recreated" (Hirsch, 1997: 24, 22).

This postmemory dialectic, of simultaneous attachment and dislocation to the past or "uneasy oscillation between continuity and rupture" (Hirsch, 2008: 106), is clearly observed in the lives of many Lebanese youth. An interview with Rami, a twenty-year-old student from Kaflek enrolled at the American University of Beirut (AUB) captures the essence of such trans-generational trauma. He begins tentatively: "It's hard to hide the effects of war. I think the war greatly affected our family from the stories I heard and every family has stories. So my family has difficult stories from the war, maybe no-one died, but it still lives in you, somewhere and haunts you." For Rami, the effects of civil war cannot be easily buried; like ghostly spectres family stories continue to haunt his private world, disturbing his perceptions and attitudes. Rami's response typifies a new generation of Lebanese: those with no "lived experience" or personal memory of Lebanon's fifteen years of protracted civil conflict (1975–92), yet with a keen awareness of the lingering pain, suffering, and collective loss. The Lebanese war claimed around 170,000 lives, with twice as many inhabitants injured and wounded, and two-thirds of the population displaced or uprooted from their homes[6]. The residual effects remain stark with 28.5 per cent of the populace continuing to live below the poverty line[7], one in four having war-related mental disorders (Karam et al, 2008), and the occurrence of high levels of adolescent violence and weapon carrying (Sibai et al, 2009). Despite attempts to forge national recovery around a "state sponsored amnesia"[8] – a culmination of censorship laws, a general war amnesty, truncated history syllabuses and the absence of criminal tribunals, compensation schemes, or truth and reconciliation committees – unresolved social ills and private internalized wounds still threaten to destabilize Lebanon's fragile co-existence.

Amongst Lebanese youth war memory exists in paradox: forgotten and remembered, incomprehensible yet the source of discussion, finished yet very much alive. As Rami elucidates, lack of memory does not hinder debate, but fear of what that memory actually holds encourages amnesia, repression, and oblivion:

The war is talked about all the time – the war is always on people's tongue even though we have no memory of what happened ... Taboo – yes in class it is just known as the *Ahdās* (the events). After the "events", during the "events", the "events" are a big void, a nebulous concept, what's inside you don't know, but you know it's black! You know it's there, it's ominous, but you don't know what's inside. (Interview, November 2, 2005)

He continues, "The war may have ended in 1990, but we were left in 'a timeless existence' – they tried to make us forget what happened, when it happened and why it happened! We lost ourselves in this process." For Rami the overwhelming discourse of forgetfulness and erasure has left his generation dangerously "out of time" and "out of place"; bereft of a unifying national narrative and a cogent sense of self. This dislocation is perhaps best captured in the abstract and vacuous use of the term *Ahdath* or "the events", to refer to the fifteen years civil conflict. It seems the Lebanese may be also "out of words" when it comes to articulating the unspeakable past.

Despite Rami's sense of temporal disorientation he remains ambivalent in his attitude to the bloody conflict; distancing and disavowing himself of the collective guilt and responsibility "it was not my war"; yet reluctantly acknowledging its lasting social legacy of fear, mistrust, and prejudice. This tension is clearly demonstrated in his ironic exclamation, "We are beyond the war – it's not very fashionable anymore – but do you have wrong perceptions of the other – the formal rhetoric is that we all lost together: no winners, no losers; but if you go to the individual communities they believe they lost more ..."

Rami's cynical swipe at the "unfashionability" of war can be interpreted on many levels. Firstly it can be understood as a social criticism of a hedonistic, self-absorbed, consumer generation more concerned with designer brands and latest trends, then by a re-evaluation of the past. Such detached trivialization of the war is reflected in macabre Lebanese T-shirts, for sale in trendy shopping malls, which read "Lebanese war 1975–1990. Game over." Secondly and perhaps more importantly it may be read as a condemnation of the enforced public silence, which has created a lacuna between an imagined post-war recovery and the reality of simmering sectarian resentments and communal grievances. For Rami the "formal rhetoric" which underpins the official war discourse of *lā ghalib lā maghlūb* (no victor, no vanquished) or "no winners, no losers" stands in stark contrast to the private sectarian discourses of suffering and victimization.

For Rami, this failure to confront and reconcile competing memory discourses is most apparent within the setting of the Lebanese school, where war memory "remains an untouchable topic". Schools mirror the country's post-war stasis, with conflict managed through censoring public debate rather than addressed through open dialogue. Contentious topics such as local politics, religious diversity, and the civil war are therefore considered *Mamnu'a* (forbidden) and simply banned from teaching syllabuses and classroom discussions. In Rami's mind this is further confounded by the continued national failure to produce a standardized history textbook (Bashshur, 2003); in his words "people are still growing up with prejudice due to the absence of a common story." By denying students the opportunity of balanced and objective teaching on contemporary history and by neglecting to provide safe forums and settings for cross-communal discussion, students are left ill equipped to process or critically engage with the past. In abdicating this educational right to interpret or explain the war, memory has been relegated almost exclusively to the private realms of the family, home, and local community. As Rami pessimistically concludes, "grudges die hard, traditional misconceptions die hard. It's difficult to move forward from this old petrified mentality and the perception of the 'other'. There is a difference between integration and interaction, there is not much merging." Although Rami's interview successfully sketches some recurring themes and tensions evident in Lebanon's postmemory generation, it is the dynamic engagement and mediation of memory through visual and oral frames that offers a more nuanced understanding of how the past is being negotiated.

MEMORYSCAPES: RUINS, ABSENCES, AND (RE)IMAGININGS

Lebanon's urban landscape, still scarred by derelict houses, bullet-pocked walls, posters and memorials to fallen fighters, demolished buildings and spatial voids, remains one of the most enduring reminders of the country's violent past. For Alain, a sixteen-year-old student from Dekwaneh, these physical remnants of war are infused with mnemonic power and meaning, evoking images, narratives, and emotions which bring the past to life. He recalls, "I was born 1990 when it all ended, but I hear all the stories ... I have pictures of the war and I have memories of the buildings and what happened there. Sometimes when we drive through an area, I am reminded of the past, the violence, and destruction, it still shouts out to you." Yet historic traces cannot be merely limited to what can be seen, for Alain they are also to be found in the silences, empty spaces, and voids, that dominate Beirut's downtown and still punctuate the *khutut at-tammas* (line of fire) or "Green line", delineating East and West. These sites of displacement are just as salient as the physical remnants of the war, and indeed offer more creative space for forms of emplacement (Flynn, 1997), in which Lebanese can redefine themselves and their relationships to others. Both tangible sites and spaces of absence help establish a dynamic memory landscape of multi-layered social histories and personal (re)imaginings. While space is notoriously difficult to delimit, I want to turn my attention firstly to the particular case of war-torn buildings, or what historian Robert Bevan (2006) terms the "unintentional monuments of war"; and then secondly the broader use of visual landscapes to evoke wider interpretations of the conflict.

IF THE WALLS COULD TALK (*al-Ḥitān Btiḥki*)

Although many students share a common heritage of war memory embedded in Lebanon's decaying edifices, they are selective about the buildings they recount, often fitting them within sectarian narratives of the war which emphasize personal suffering or communal victimization. Mona focuses on her family's commercial property destroyed by militia fighting in central Beirut. The buildings she recalls is part of a lost past, a site of displacement, demolished and rebuilt by Solidère[9], yet perpetually existing in her mind as a ruined shell, with fire-charred windows, graffiti-strewn walls and collapsed floors. Alain speaks of apartment blocks close to his home in Dekwaneh pockmarked through attacks by Palestinian fighters from the former camp of Tel al-Za'tar[10]. Finally Bashir recalls buildings in the Ashrafieh suburbs devastated by Syrian shelling in 1978 and then subject to Christian in-fighting between General Aoun and Samir Geagea's Lebanese Forces. Interestingly these students select buildings not only to demarcate former battle-lines and situate war stories, but also to validate continuing emotive themes: dispossession, the Palestinian presence, Syrian military involvement, and the struggle for Christian political leadership.

Other students recall destroyed homes as part of nostalgic narratives which seek to recover or make sense of rupture and exile. Indeed, many of the students I interviewed talked of the pain and dislocation of leaving a village, a family home, a beautiful landscape, despite having no personal recollection of the traumatic events. Their postmemory remembrances balance stories of collective suffering and expulsion alongside tales of communal harmony and local belonging, both grounded and imagined through physical sites. Ghassan, a university student from Bhamdoun, recalls his own sense of estrangement and confusion, as his family would return every summer to visit the ruins of their former home: "I remember picnics in an empty building ... Why did we do that? I don't know ... But when you are in Beirut and your church is in the village, living in Beirut cuts you off from your community, you know nothing." Although Ghassan struggles to understand the reason behind the picnic trips, evidently his attachment to his village church and local community has been formed through such physical returns to the land, accompanied by narratives of daily life and relationships. For other students such as sixteen-year-old Jamela, her home and village in the South of Lebanon remain banished to the realm of her imagination. She recounts vividly the desecration of her house by "violent forces" that destroyed "everything my family ever owned in this world." Dispossession for Jamela is keenly felt through her parents' loss, which causes her to forcefully vow never to return to the site of familial suffering. For both Ghassan and Jamela, images of destroyed homes, both real and imagined, represent not only loss of a perceived community, but also the shrinking of negotiable Lebanese space.

Youth living in areas of former confrontation (Beirut's 'Green line', the Occupied zone in the South of Lebanon) and scenes of horrific massacre (Hanf

& Salam, 2003) (Karantina, Damour, Chekka, Tel al-Za'tar), often draw on their visual built environment to justify memories of besiegement, abuse, and fear. This was very evident in personal interviews and keenly observed during a project, carried out by a Lebanese NGO "Umam Documentation and Research" (April 3–24, 2005) working on memory of war amongst Lebanese teenagers. "Our Sunday back then" marking the thirtieth anniversary of the outbreak of war, drew together twenty-six students from diverse social and religious backgrounds, giving them tape recorders and disposable cameras to capture the sounds, images, and testimonies of their parents, families, and communities, concerning the past "events".

Unsurprisingly one of the most controversial group activities involved the display and explanation of the students' photographs, which were dominated by images of damaged buildings, and war-scarred homes. Students gravitated towards religious corners, seeking comfort in like-minded clusters. Maronite Christian youth from Ain al-Rummaneh offered pictures of churches, crosses and religious statues, reminding the audience of the initial attack on Pierre Gamayel in a Maronite chapel which sparked the conflict in April 1975, while suggesting a continuation of localized religious intimidation and confrontation. In the words of sixteen-year-old Lisa,

> We still have these problems with the other side, just last month. Who are they and who are us, I'll explain. We are my community, the Christians of course and they are the Muslims, the other community ... Some youth guys from "them" come over into our territory, to "us" and drank beer at the Statue of the Virgin Mary and showed disrespect and caused problems.

Lisa in her recollection of war memory seamlessly integrates past conflict between the Maronite Kata'ib and Palestinians, into present-day disputes between Christian and Muslim youth. The Ain al-Rummaneh church is replaced by the Virgin Mary statue, as a symbol that has been religiously defiled and publicly shamed. Territorial and spatial boundaries have been infringed and disregarded, inevitably leading to intensified hostilities and disputes.

A Palestinian group of students presented mostly images of Sabra and Shatila; haunting snapshots of graves, families huddled in small rooms, ragged and scarred camp walls, and shacks disfigured by gunfire. For Muhammad, the massacre of September 1982, which resulted in an estimated 3,500 deaths, remains the landmark event that subsumes all else, it is the starting point for any discussion or explanation of the war. In his words these photographs represent an unforgettable and ingrained past, "its part of our history, from family, friends, neighbors, and the camp. You learn it from when you are very young." Although this informal group contained students from Ain el Helwe Palestinian camp in Saida, the images and narratives of Sabra and Shatila became the collective symbol to project

Palestinian suffering and abandonment, while linking it to contemporary fears of being "victims of renewed ethnic cleansing – sanctioned by the international community."

This commemorative project again underscores how Lebanon's post-war remnants, whether physical sites or mental images, can be used to justify and legitimate memories of besiegement and fear, and historical traditions of perceived injustices and communal mistrust. However, Lebanon's dynamic memoryscape is also utilized by Lebanese youth to challenge sectarian boundaries and war narratives. During the course of my research a number of university students chose to convene their interviews in places of symbolic importance, which enabled a dramatic reframing or (re)imagining of the past. This may be delineated along a number of themes: resistance, dislocation, and rebirth.

FRAMING AND TAMING THE PAST

For some students the setting chosen celebrated specific historic events or political themes. For Ahmad, coffee at one of Lebanon's most famous hotels, "The Bristol" in Verdun, was not merely a tribute to the recent birth of the Lebanese opposition movement (Dec 2004 – "The Bristol Declaration"[11]) but a celebration of the hotel's rich legacy of harbouring exiles, rebels, and war correspondents: "This is the best place to discuss Lebanon's past – history has been observed, reported and made in this hotel." (Interview, November 2, 2005)

For Zeina, the legendary Wimpy sandwich bar on Hamra Street, badly lit, uncomfortable, and sporting Formica tables, remains a site of legendary resistance. One afternoon in 1982, so the story goes, Khalid Alwan, an SSNP militiaman, was disturbed by the arrogance of an occupying Israeli officer who was insisting on paying his bill in shekels. Nonchalantly Khalid strolled across the road, shot the officer and his two accompanying soldiers, and then calmly walked home. Thus began a national response against the Israeli occupation. The mythical power of this act, while commemorated by a small plaque and sign on the pavement outside the Wimpy restaurant, lives more intimately in Zeina's imagination. The story functions as both a metaphoric lens for her reinterpretation of the war, courage and defiance offsetting shame and oppression, and simultaneously a contemporary symbol of hope in Lebanon's struggle against foreign intervention and the ever-present threat of Israel.

Pierre, a medical undergraduate, prefers the familiarity of his native town in Lebanon's northern hills to add authenticity to our discussion. His memory is intrinsically tied to his local identity and the soil of Zgharta: "Togetherness flows from a common history – my family name – it dates from one of the oldest families in Ehden. It was before Christ, in this part of the north of Lebanon, my family dates 5,000 or 6,000 years ... I'm very rooted here." Zgharta[12] derives from the

Aramaic word *zaghar* or fortress, and is well named, perched high amidst snow-capped mountains (in winter) and surrounded by olive groves and natural springs. During the war it was also a strategic stronghold for the Christian frontline, particularly former President Suleiman Franjieh's Marada forces against Muslim and PLO militias in Tripoli. Despite an infamous and bloody past, involving Christian infighting and assassinations[13], Pierre remarkably claims that his town remained distant from the war; a safe haven and refuge from the storm. Zgharta exists in Pierre's mind romanticized and idyllic, "a city that could not let go of its village characteristics, everybody knows everybody." The Lebanon he is most at ease with is similarly hazy, forgetful, and selective.

For Tony, a Christian Maronite from a small village in the Kisrawan Mountains, Beirut's reconstructed centre was the most fitting stage for our interview. In an elegant Western-style café, pop music vied with the call of a nearby *muezzin* as Tony recounted his escape from his "sectarian cocoon" and emancipation in Lebanon's 'only neutral space':

> When I worked in my restaurant *al-Balad*, this was my real opportunity. I got to meet Muslim Arabs and people from the Gulf. I worked there for three years and will never forget the experience ... Downtown Beirut is more cosmopolitan. You cannot identify the religion of the shop owners. It's a business area and Lebanese meet on business; they can join together on business.

Beirut's center-ville represents, for Tony, not just a spatial symbol of Lebanese unity (albeit centered upon a capitalist vision) but a place of actual liberation and awakening. It is a refuge from the restrictions and narrow confessionalism that the war enforced, and an opportunity to make Muslim friends, experience life, and lose himself amidst the anonymity of a cosmopolitan crowd. Lebanon's memory landscape offers an eclectic array of visual prompts, spaces, and absences which help sustain a multiplicity of historical discourses and narratives, which enables youth to relive, subvert or (re)imagine the conflict, depending on presentist demands, needs, and changing social contexts.

POSTMEMORY NARRATIVES: TELLING STORIES, SITUATING SELF

The post-war tension surrounding the impulse to recover or resemble the past and the individual's capacity to recreate it is embodied in Lebanese author Elias Khoury's character of the 'Storyteller' in his novel *Mamlakat al-Ghurabā'* (The Kingdom of Strangers). The Storyteller, who weaves and reworks the lives of others through disjointed narratives which "transform the past into the present", in an attempt "to impose order on a land in which all order has been smashed to pieces", also must acknowledge that he has become complicit in the process: "You are the storyteller, she said. No. I am the Story." The challenge of distinguishing teller from tale; truth (*al-ḥaqīqa*) from story (*al-ḥikāya*); distorted memory from actual experience, while a recurrent theme of contemporary Lebanese literature[14], is reflective of Lebanon's postmemory condition. Like Khoury's Storyteller, Lebanese youth often become entwined in the narrative process itself – transfusing family stories and local histories to affirm social identities, political discourses, and temporal continuities. This act of narrative emplotment[15], a grasping together of discordant events, actors, and interactions into an ordered coherent story, perhaps can be understood as a way of providing historic meaning and purpose for the lived present. Inevitably these mnemonic strategies also reflect broader social traditions of remembering, as well as dominant political and religious discourses. To illustrate this process I want to draw on two dominant narrative themes or plots: recurrence and redemption.

RECURRENCE: THE VISIBLE INVISIBLE WAR

Mark Twain once claimed history doesn't repeat itself but it rhymes. In Lebanon those rhythmic patterns are at times difficult to distinguish from the sheer volume of historic precedence. Irresistible temporal cycles seem to throw together all too familiar protagonists (family clans, *zuʿamā*, religious leaders, politicians, foreign interests) into all too familiar struggles (land reforms, economics, political power, and regional balance) with all too predictable outcomes (civil conflict: 1820, 1860, 1958, 1975-1990). The consequence is both the evocation of a feeling of déjà-vu, and a fatalistic acceptance amongst Lebanese that the past is never truly past. Pamela, a seventeen-year-old student from Zahle, typifies this nonlinear approach to time, as her narrative splices past and present realms, fusing them together in a "recurrence" theme. Her particular remembrance focuses on a contemporary image, which is then explained retrospectively. The impression created is one of stagnancy, moral intransigence, and the ever-corrupting influence of the war. In her own words:

> Nothing has changed. Those leaders during the war are now politicians. I had seen recently after Geagea's release, young kids queuing up to see him in the mountains, standing with flags and political t-shirts. What do they know? It is being passed on from their parents, the hatred, the prejudices, and the sectarian feeling. Even small kids in this school, they chant the names of political leaders and wear symbols, but they don't know what they are talking about. Look! Before the war we had the same parties. During the war we had the same parties. After the war we still have the same parties. What has changed? People who are with Geagea during the war remain with him now. They stick to the same person.

For Pamela the continued presence, popularity, and rule of war-time militia leaders, now posing as national politicians, undermine the very idea of a break with the Lebanese past. How can all the same "old gangsters" ever usher in a new era of reconciliation, she inquires indignantly. Her ire is particularly kindled by the adulation and support afforded former leader of the Lebanese Forces Samir Geagea, upon his release from prison, after serving only eleven years of his life sentence for war crimes and political assassinations[16]. Amongst Lebanon's Christian communities Geagea remains a highly controversial figure even by Lebanese standards, radically polarizing loyalties and opinions. His notoriety, gained through his violent struggle for power within the Lebanese Forces, his fierce militia rule, and his bloody confrontation with former Army General Michel Aoun in the "War of Elimination" in 1990, was further consolidated through years of solitary confinement, as Lebanon's only tried war combatant. His release from Yarze prison on the July 26, 2005 triggered both fireworks and curses; for Pamela it was like petrol on a smouldering flame. Past bitterness, tension, and hatred were once again reawakened and invoked through stories, flags, and rallies.

While recalling the passion and fervour of young kids waiting in the Christian mountains in anticipation of their returning hero, Pamela transposes this to her personal world and Luwayzeh's junior playground where children chant political slogans and their allegiance to "Nasrallah, Aoun, Geagea, Berri, Jumblatt, and Hariri". Despite their ignorance, these sectarian cries and prejudices represent echoes of the war, reverberating around contemporary school walls. Similarly Pamela imagines Samir Geagea's gaunt and haggard face, as the physical embodiment of a past long imprisoned but sadly not forgotten.

The same recurrence theme features in the narratives of students across religious, political, and class divides. Fouad, a twenty-one-year-old student from the Shi'a suburbs of Dahiyya, connects current political tensions with previous antagonisms and struggles. His narrative begins with a militia battle in 1985 and returns to the increasing violence occurring in the Beirut suburbs of Chiyah and Ain al-Rummaneh. He reflects:

> In 1985 Jumblatt tried to change the colour of the Lebanese flag. They tried to combine the *al-Ishtirākiyya* (Progressive Socialist Party) flag with the Lebanese flag and they tried to take over Lebanon and change the whole presidency to Druze. Now they want it back. The Druze are playing a game, Geagea is playing a game, Aoun is playing a game, Hizb' Allah wants to rule, Berri wants to rule. Everyone wants to sit on this chair, to rule and make money, not to unite Lebanon, to help their pocket (interview, December 19, 2005).

Fouad's cynical reading of Lebanese history reduces all to a political "game": a no-holds barred competition, spanning decades, contested by the same rapacious autocrats, for the exclusive right to rule and plunder Lebanon. His stinging criticism of Walid Jumblatt, the Druze leader and head of the *Ishtirākiyya* party (PSP), perhaps derives from his deep-seated mistrust of this guarded community whom he labels, "untrustworthy" and "always scheming". Yet his reference to Jumblatt's drive in 1985 to assimilate the Lebanese tricolor and the PSP flag, as part of greater designs for a Druze realignment of constitutional power, reveals both the power and fluidity of oral historical tradition.

Fouad's recollection most likely alludes to the so-called "Flag War" of November 1985, which saw PSP militiamen and the Shi'a Amal forces battle for control of West Beirut. The climax of six month of hostilities, witnessed PSP militiamen replace Cedar flags flown for Lebanese National Day with *Ishtirākiyya* flags on all public buildings. This act of rebellion remains embedded in local memory, as does the ferocity of the ensuing violence, which claimed 65 lives in one day, with 400 abducted, shocking both sides into a temporary cease-fire (Hanf, 1993:305). In Fouad's mind, the story of the Lebanese flag and the attempts to change, transform, or replace it, is a perfect lens for observing the contemporary power struggles within Lebanese society. Although the emotive recollection is vague on specific details, Fouad uses it to substantiate his present suspicions that sectarian leaders are once again pulling Lebanon apart.

Fouad's narrative then becomes more personal as he shares his own fears for "another bad war", his reluctance to visit certain districts of Beirut like Dora where "they will beat you up" for saying you're a Muslim, and finally his disgust at annual street confrontations when "Lebanese Forces fight Shi'a and Palestinians" to commemorate the beginning of the civil war in April 1976. He continues, "There is a lot of fighting these days between young people, many people are carrying weapons, sixteen year olds are carrying knives. If you are a Muslim going into a Christian area you should be careful and the same vice-versa ... This whole issue is going to affect civilians in Lebanon. I think people want war, those who follow Geagea want war." For Fouad, communal violence is not just confined to the pages of history, or the stories of his parents, but it is experienced as an everyday reality, in the tensions of the Beirut street. His present concerns that another war may be imminent, help shape his remembrances of the past, causing him to emplot recurrence scenarios and to predict aggressive intent, "I think people want war". Such pessimism derives not merely from a growing fear of conflict, but a frustration and rejection of his life in Dahiyya, and a consuming desire to escape to the West. Typical of many disenchanted Lebanese youth, Fouad feels imprisoned and confined by the lack of job opportunities, religious freedom, and social progress in post-Ta'if Lebanon. Consequently his nihilistic vision of future bloodshed is as much a judgment or condemnation of Lebanon, as it is a realistic expectation.

REDEMPTION: FROM SUFFERING VICTIM TO RESILIENT HERO

Faced by the horrors and shame of an incomprehensible past Lebanon's postmemory generation often seek refuge and redemption in the status of the helpless victim. Oral tradition tends to focus on the losses, killings and atrocities committed by the adversary, while romanticizing their own tragic struggle for freedom, independence, or just the right to exist. In this, they are similar to the Northern Irish context, where both Protestant and Catholic communities perceive themselves as victims, invoking images of famine, imperialism, and subjugation or remembrances of bombs, shootings, and terrorism. In Lebanon however, the permeations are endless, students recall their victimhood at the hands of Western connivance; Israeli aggression; Palestinian terrorism; Arab backwardness; Maronite expansionism; Sunni greed; Shi'a fanaticism; the rule of warlords; economic injustice; and political corruption. Perhaps such attitudes are a means of absolving blame, escaping guilt or merely the collective heritage of parents and grandparents still unwilling and ill-prepared to deal with ambiguities of history. Yet this self-assigned status of victim is not always an indication of weakness; rather, it is often an occasion for reactionary narratives of defiance, resistance, and heroism.

For Yasser his sense of belonging is inextricably tied to a sense of struggle. In a dimly lit student bar, over beer and carrot sticks, he unpacks his past. Born to a Lebanese mother and a Palestinian father, Yasser's very birth ushered him into life "complex" and full of "ambiguities." His Marxist upbringing, attendance at both Islamic and Christian schools, and experience of "living all over Lebanon" furthered his feeling of social detachment and disillusionment with what he terms "a racist country." Although vague on specific memories of the war, Yasser is more definite in his conclusions: "... the war needed to happen to some degree ... This war is like many of the Lebanese civil wars, an uprising of the poor and then the revolution was shifted into civil conflict." His socialist critique of Lebanon's class struggle, extends further to a need for a new form of nationalism: "put the Lebanese flag in every classroom" and a justice system, capable of bringing "judgment against all the war criminals in power. Anyone who did massacres cannot be considered in ten or fifteen years as a war hero." As Yasser turns his attention to narrating his personal experience of the violence he begins with his internal battles of identity and belonging:

> Firstly I identify myself as Yasser – identity is an ever-changing concept, I don't have a conflict of belonging. I feel like I belong, but my identity is much to do with my rights ... in some way it is reactionary. If I was born in a place that didn't have conflict, I don't know if I would have the same sense of belonging.
>
> I belong to all Palestinian communities ... I discovered I have a kind of nostalgia for Palestine because of all the songs and stories I listened to as a kid, I

have this feeling ... I do believe that Palestine is my homeland ... also I do believe that Lebanon is my homeland ... particularly since my rights are raped here, this is my defensive status, I want to defend it these days, therefore in Palestine and Lebanon I feel a sense of belonging to the land (interview, December 11, 2005).

Perhaps what is most striking about this narrative is that it is both abstract and self-absorbed. War and conflict remain faceless, generic forces which have caused Yasser to carve out an identity and an attachment to the land. The analytical and self-reflective style of his response is matched by a coolness of tone, which accentuates his distance from the subject matter. Perhaps this is a conversation so familiar and engrained; so dissected, stretched, and refined in the mind that it appears to lack the passion of the heart.

While Yasser admits a nostalgic longing for a Palestinian homeland, birthed from parents' stories, folktales, and songs, it is the denial and violation of his present rights that connect him firmly to the Lebanese soil. His sense of injustice as a dispossessed Palestinian and as a second-class Lebanese citizen, fuels in him a desire to assert his hybrid identity and to fight for both national causes. This tension of belonging is reconciled through a resistance discourse that becomes a reactionary way of life. Like many third-generation Palestinian exiles, Yasser's sense of belonging "to all Palestinian communities" is simultaneously consuming yet vague, everything and nothing. The Palestinian cause may reverberate through-out the interview, but Yasser fails to ground his thoughts in any physical reality, such as his experience in the camps, his father's land, relatives, and memories of life before 1948. For Yasser, Palestine exists as a rallying cry, an inspirational goal to motivate and encourage resistance, an idea rather than a place. Unlike many war narratives, Yasser shows little attempt to explain the nature, source, and cause of the violence, rather he is more concerned with how it has shaped him.

For Khalid some war memories are so intense, they almost feel as if they have been personally lived. Sitting in an aging Hamra flat, this first-year economics student from Tripoli recounts tales from 1975, the Palestinian cause, the battles for Tripoli, Syria, and Israel's intervention. Despite the obligatory apolitical precursor, "I'm not into parties but I have my own political views," Khalid soon feels at ease to share his "contempt for the Lebanese Forces", his "admiration for Hassan Nasrallah's (Secretary General of the Shi'a Islamist Hizballah) integrity" and his belief in the need for "Chinese-style population restrictions for Palestinians." The cynicism and disaffection, hinted at by his Ché Guevara T-shirt, are further revealed in an ironic dismissal of Lebanese honesty: "Off the record you must be aware that you can't really trust what people tell you. They will always give you different answers depending on their environments." The tension between what is said and what is known is a Lebanese trait almost exclusively observed in others. Khalid's detached, informed, and balanced understanding of the war is accredited to his reading of foreign correspondents and researchers: "I learnt about the war mostly from Robert Fisk, this is the irony about it. That's why I feel I got an objective view[17]."

Khalid's most vivid postmemory recollection draws on a resistance theme, which turns the tragedy and brutality of war into an occasion for heroism and defiance:

> Personal memories I have none, I was born in 1988 – but I have my parents' memory. I have heard lots of tales, like they were always running from bombs, but I have this one memory that I can really feel that I lived it, for it's pretty intense and my dad told it to me. He wasn't linked to any parties or anything, but he was getting blood for people and he was in a car, with a microphone shouting, "We need blood, just donate!" And he sees a car coming and there is a guy tied to that car and he was being dragged alive, through the streets. And the Party was the Syrian Party called *Tishrīn* (the name of the newspaper), an important party. And he lost it and just started screaming, "Don't drag people. No for dragging people, No for doing this!" He was really in danger but he couldn't hold himself, and most of my uncles and aunts worked in hospitals to help people (interview, February 11, 2006).

This story, like many post-war narratives, is a family tale, handed down from a father to his son, infused with intensity and emotional attachment. The image is powerful and symbolic; Khalid's father seeking to save lives through finding blood donors, while Syrian Party militia-men attempt to destroy lives through brutal forms of torture. The juxtaposition of mindless barbarism and compassionate humanity is stark and graphic. Khalid's father emerges as both a shining hero and a defiant voice amidst the prevailing darkness and depravity of the Lebanese war period. For Khalid the story functions on many levels. Firstly, it confirms his family's virtue and selfless desire "to help people", even at risk to their own lives. In this sense it inverts the normal war themes of death, suffering and victimization, by focusing instead on redeeming qualities such as communality, empathy, and sacrificial service. Secondly, it is a story that inspires and celebrates resistance in the face of overwhelming social violence and oppression. The unwillingness of Khalid's father to passively acquiesce to the horrors of torture on the war-torn streets of Tripoli provides a contemporary symbol of hope and courage in the midst of troubled times. For Khalid this postmemory image is easily transposed onto Lebanon's current political impasse, in which "extremism and random violence, such as car bombs and the Ashrafieh riots" confront ordinary citizens and in which "Syria has now become our enemy." Khalid connects not merely with the intensity of this memory, but importantly with the values it embodies and the daring it represents. His feeling of having really "lived it", suggests a longing to replicate his father's courage and to carry on the legacy of resisting coercive power.

Finally the story serves as an important bridge to other narratives; fusing disparate time frames, and explaining contemporary events. As Khalid concludes:

Despite the things my dad experienced, forgiveness is possible. I saw this in the recent elections when my dad voted for someone directly involved with killing people from Tripoli. His name was Antoine Kharat, but his nickname was Antoine *Barbar*, because he killed people on the *Barbar*, "the Army spot." But my father still voted for him. He said, "*khalās* (enough), it's time to forgive ..." My mum couldn't, for example. She said, "I forgive him but I don't have to vote for him." But my dad said, "No, let's have reconciliation." (Interview, February 11, 2006)

Khalid seamlessly moves from his father's act of bravery amidst the depravity of war to his more recent magnanimity in forgiving a notorious war criminal. Somehow both virtuous gestures are intertwined or explained consequently. The postmemory narrative sets the scene for, or is the prelude to, the most recent display of courage; the decision to forgive former enemies. Similarly Khalid seeks to demonstrate his own willingness to move beyond traumatic family memories and embrace the spirit of reconciliation. His imaginative investment in his father's story allows him to courageously reach out beyond divides and accommodate a new inclusive vision of Lebanon:

Two years ago I would say I'm Arab, but now I'd say Lebanese. Why the change? I discovered that there is no such thing as the Arab nation. I was really into Abdul Nasser and everything, I still admire the guy but I don't really believe in that, especially when I'm talking to friends and they refuse to consider Israel as an enemy ... So I'm looking for another way to approach these people, I'm talking about the Lebanese Forces, they don't understand Arabism, but if I say I'm Lebanese and Israel is attacking Lebanese territory, maybe they will understand. (Interview, February 11, 2006)

Khalid and Yasser's narratives both reflect this journey from victimized to resilient hero. For Yasser, the war is inextricably linked to his struggle to reclaim his Palestinian heritage and identity; for Khalid it is the social backdrop for his father's act of defiance, and his inspiration for resisting social oppression and injustice. These personal stories are less concerned with assigning blame or guilt, but redeeming broken images of loss, pain, and suffering and constructing new narratives of hope out of them.

CONCLUSION

These case studies serve as mere snapshots of the complexity and fluidity that invariably surround Lebanese postmemory. While many of the respondents sought forgetfulness as an antidote to future conflict, few demonstrated an ability to free themselves from the haunting power of a scarred, fragmented landscape and the painful legacy of oral traditions. Public silence and evasion of the historical memory of the Lebanese war (political amnesty; media censorship; history curriculum) have arguably exacerbated and internalized private trauma, pain, and sectarian resentment; failing to provide space for critical engagement, contestation, and interaction. Despite the postmemory generation's attempts to distance and anathematize themselves from a destructive past, suppression is not redemption, just as forgetting does not necessarily lead to forgiving. This goes beyond Lebanon's perpetual identity crisis or continuing political crisis; it marks a generation trapped between silences that provide no historic context and screams that preclude any future hope. They are left bereft of meaningful narratives to explain their personal experiences or Lebanon's post war realities. In the words of Tony, a twenty-two-year-old student from the Metn, reconciliation must begin with the desire "to reconcile with our history. We don't just want a single version of history ... it's irrational or unscientific. The problem is we didn't reconcile our past in order to live for our future."

NOTES

1 This quote is from a personal interview transcript, part of a series of interviews conducted with Lebanese youth over the period of one year (June 2005-June 2006). The interview took place on 2 March 2006 in a "Bliss Street" cafe in the Hamra district of Beirut.

2 Although the interviews were carried out during a one-year period, many of contacts, observations and ethnographic insights come from having spent five years living in the region.

3 These included activists involved with the Center for Conflict Resolution and Peace-building (CCRP) based in *Hamra* and "Umam Documentation and Research" based in *Haret Hrayek*.

4 Interviews were conducted in Lebanese dialect Arabic, English and a mixture of both, a common trait amongst urban youth. Phrases such as '*Ya'nī ana ktīr* tired' or 'Sorry would you like *mūsā'da schwaī*' are not unfamiliar hybrid terms used in Beiruti streets, shops and campuses.

5 Various titles have been given to the political period between February 2005 and May 2005 in which protest, euphoria, and popular mobilization followed the assassination of former Prime Minister Rafik Hariri. In Lebanon, among supporters of the emerging loyalist coalition, led by Saad Hariri (Future Movement), Samir Geagea (Lebanese Forces) and Walid Jumblatt (Progressive Socialist Party) it was commonly known as the Independence *Intifāda* or Uprising (*intifādat al-istiqlāl)*, in the West it became dubbed the "Cedar Revolution" or the "Beirut Spring."

6 These statistics vary according to sources I am relying on from my analysis of the post-war consequences in, *Civil and uncivil violence: a history of the internationalization of communal conflict in Lebanon*. (New York; Chichester: Columbia University Press, 2002), 3-4.

7 See 'Poverty, growth and Income Distribution in Lebanon', Country study, International Poverty Centre (IPC), United Nations Development Programme, No. 13 January 2008. Available online: http://www.undp-povertycentre.org/pub/IPCCountryStudy13.pdf (first accessed July 1, 2009). For deeper statistical analysis see Lebanese Republic's Central Administration for Statistics http://www.cas.gov.lb

8 This phrase was first coined by Lebanese journalist, historian and civil activist Samir Kassir in "*Ahwal al-dhakirah fi lubnan*" (The Situation of Memory in Lebanon) in Amal Makarem's *Memory for the Future* (2002):195-200.

9   Solidère is a Lebanese development company founded by Rafik Hariri in 1994 and in charge of planning and redeveloping Beirut's Center-ville after the devastation of war. Its thirty-year Master Plan (1994-2024) focuses on reconstructing Beirut as a global tourist commercial centre, replete with beautifully restored churches and mosques, gardens and Roman ruins. For more details see the website: http://www.solidere.com.lb (first accessed May 1, 2005). For critiques of Solidère's reconstruction plans see Saree Makdisi, "Laying Claim to Beirut: Urban Narrative and Spatial Identity in the Age of Solidere," *Critical Inquiry,* 23(1997): 661-705; Jens-Peter Hanssen and Daniel Genberg (2002) "Beirut in Memoriam: A Kaleidoscopic Space out of Focus," in *Crisis and Memory: Dimensions of their Relationship in Islam and adjacent Cultures,* ed. Angelika Neuwirth and Andreas Pflitsch (Beirut: Orient Institut, 2002); Caroline Nagel, "Reconstruction space, re-creating memory: sectarian politics and urban development in post-war Beirut," *Political Geography,* 21 (2002): 717-725 and "Ethnic Conflict and Urban Redevelopment in Downtown Beirut," *Growth and Change,* 31(2000): 211-234; and Adrienne Fricke, "Forever Nearing the Finish Line: Heritage Policy and the Problem of Memory in Postwar Beirut," *International Journal of Cultural Property,* 12(2005): 163-181.

10 Alain's selective remembrances of the battle surrounding Tel al-Za'tar is instructive. While he reflects on the legacy of conflict in the urban disfigurement of his own neighborhood, he fails to acknowledge the seven-month siege on the camp by Christian militias (the Tanzim and the Maron Khoury group) and the subsequent massacre of 2,000-3,000 Palestinians. Alain's omission may be put down to sectarian prejudice, historical ignorance, or willful forgetfulness. For more details on Tel al-Za'tar see Helena Cobban, *The Palestinian Liberation Organisation: People, Power, and Politics* (Cambridge: Cambridge University Press, 1984) p.73 and William Harris, *Faces of Lebanon. Sects, Wars, and Global Extensions* (Princeton: Markus Wiener Publishers, 1996) p.165.

11 The political manifesto, of the Lebanese opposition (*al- Mu'ārada*) was first delivered at the Bristol Hotel in December 2004 and later published as the "Beirut declaration." For more details see the website http://www.beirutletter.com (first accessed July 4, 2006). It proclaims: "We have a common responsibility, Christians and Moslems, for the war which devastated our country; we believe that recognizing this responsibility is the essential condition for learning the lessons of the war so we will not be condemned indefinitely to repeating our past errors ... We, Lebanese of all confessions and all regions, are convinced that change is now possible because we are stronger today than in the past. We are stronger because we have decided to take our destiny in our own hands and become self-reliant; because we refuse any discrimination amongst us; because we are convinced that what unites us is much more important than what divides us; because we understand that only respect for the law ensures that our differences are not perceived any longer as a factor of division, but as a source of richness; because we know now that we can live together, different but equal."

12 The name Zgharta is thought to have come either from the Aramaic root *Zaghar* which means fortress or the Syraic word *Zeghartay* meaning the barricades. The town has its own website detailing its unique history, culture, and heritage. It also acts as a forum for local news, providing social networking through a Zgharta Chat Room, as well as a database of Zghartawen living across the world. See http://www.zgharta.com (first accessed January 1, 2007).

13 The most notable incident being the violent confrontation between Bashir Gemayel's Kata'ib and Suleiman Franjieh's *Marada* militia and, which resulted in the death of Franjieh's eldest son Tony and his family in the summer resort of Ehden, just above Zgharta (June 14, 1978). As a consequence the Christians in the Northern Mountains broke permanently with the Lebanese Front and a family feud developed between the Franjieh and Gemayel clans. For a more detailed account see Theodor Hanf, *Coexistence in Wartime Lebanon: Decline of a state and rise of a Nation* (London: Centre for Lebanese Studies in association with IB Tauris, 1993): 235-237.

14 These themes which illustrate the complex internalization of war, and illusive search for truth, meaning, and ultimately self are to be found in the writings of Lebanese authors, such as Jad el-Hage, Rabih Alameddine, Rashid al-Daif, Nada Awar Jarrar, Ghada Samman, and Patricia Sarrafian Ward.

15 Hayden White's literary concept of "Emplotment" explains the transforming power of narrative

to give meaning, completion, and a sense of purpose to a sequence of events, by establishing chronological progression and "followability" of a story which directs it towards a conclusive ending. In Paul Ricoeur's words in *Time and Narrative* (Chicago: University of Chicago Press, 1984), 67-68, emplotment provides an inversion of the natural order of time: "In reading the ending in the beginning and the beginning in the ending, we also learn to read time backwards, as the recapitulation of the initial conditions of a course of action in its terminal consequence"

16 Geagea was arrested in April 1994 and subsequently convicted on charges of instigating acts of violence and assassinating former Prime Minister Rashid Karami and National Liberal Party leader Danny Chamoun. He served eleven years in solitary confinement before his sudden release in July 2005.

17 Robert Fisk, the ubiquitous war correspondent and Beirut-based journalist, who has devoted much of his life to covering politics and violence in the region.

Part 3

Representation
and Self-Perception

The Politics of Fun in the Islamic Republic of Iran

Re-creation of Recreation

Pardis Mahdavi

"The Islamic Revolution is a Revolution of Values and is not about Fun. In fact there is no Fun to be had in the Islamic Republic."

Khomeini

Perhaps there is no place in the world where the stakes of "having fun" are higher than in present-day Iran. Drinking (alcohol) and dancing can lead to arrest by the morality police accompanied by up to seventy lashings. Consequences for sex outside of marriage can be even more severe – up to eighty-four lashes. But even under the threat of such harsh punishment, a youth movement encompassing changing sexual and social behaviors is taking place. Sex and sexuality have become both a source of freedom and an act of political rebellion for young urban Iranians who are frustrated with a theocratic regime that restricts their sociality. Young people[1] in Iran say, in their own words, that they are enacting a sexual revolution (or *enqelab-i-jensi* in Persian) to respond to what they view as an overly repressive regime. This sexual revolution, as I observed during fieldwork from 2000-2007[2], is about more than sexuality; it is about changing social mores, carving out new recreational opportunities, and at its very core, bringing back joy, fun, and youth habitus.

This re-creation of recreation, and new emphasis on "having fun," I argue, is a direct challenge to the moral paradigm of the regime, and a way for young people to assert their agency in the face of a regime that has sought to restrict it. The fact that young people are able to get away with previously punishable behaviors (such as make-up, colorful headscarves, or heterosocializing), is evidence that this youth movement is changing the sociopolitical atmosphere of post-revolutionary Iran, and presenting the clerical members of the regime with their biggest challenge yet.

The self-termed sexual revolution, led by the educated, restless youth, is changing sexual and social discourses and re-defining pleasure and recreation. Having fun, and carving out spaces for recreation are politicized by Islamists in power (For an excellent discussion see Bayat, 2002) who seek to regulate social activities and cleanse the public sphere of "morally questionable" behavior[3]. Young people in an attempt to subvert the fabric of morality woven by the Islamic regime in power in post-revolutionary Iran, are attacking that fabric of morality by embodying their resistance, using their bodies and social behaviors to subvert the power of the regime. Today, 70 per cent of Iran's population is under the age of thirty. Literally, children of the revolution, many of these young people were born during or right after the 1978–79 Iranian revolution which led to the theocratic Islamic Republic of Iran. Urban young adults who comprise almost two-thirds of Iran's population (Esposito and Ramazani, 2001) are highly mobile, highly educated (84 per cent of young Tehranis are currently enrolled in university or are university graduates with 65 per cent of these graduates being women) (Joseph, 2005) and underemployed (there is a 35 per cent unemployment rate amongst this age group)[4]. Many are also highly dissatisfied with the current regime, and using their social behaviours and comportment (such as sexual behaviours and drug use)[5], a major battleground between them and the regime, to speak back to what they view as a repressive government. In the past twelve months we have seen many of these young people take to the streets and engage in the Green (*Sabze*) movement supporting presidential hopeful Mir-Hossein Moussavi. For some young people, involvement in the sexual revolution paved the way for their involvement in this civil rights type movement that we are witnessing on the streets of Tehran today. (For a full discussion, see Mahdavi, forthcoming.)

It is important to note that what may seem to us on the outside to be flippant or casual behaviours (such as wearing make-up, attending underground parties or gatherings, and driving around in cars playing illegal music), these actions have an intellectual architecture behind them for many young people in Tehran. "Me wearing lipstick," noted Mahnaz a twenty-year-old beautician, "is more than just looking good, it's about pissing off them, the morality police, and about me getting satisfaction." Another young man talked about the meaning of resistance to him, "Look, this regime, the one in power, they are all about taking away fun," explained Ali Reza, a twenty-two-year-old student from Tehran University. "They are so focused on what we do, they made recreation (*tafree*) political, so we use our fun, we use our day-to-day looks, fashions, and fun times to tell them we don't care what they think. This is us resisting," he added. Another young woman commented on the regime's focus on make-up and expressed her confusion. "What I'm trying to understand is why can't I do *namaz* (prayer) wearing nail polish or make-up? Why do I have to wipe those things off for doing *namaz?* Why can't I present myself to God the way I want to? The way I present myself to my friends? I have so many questions, the regime is full of contradictions, and then they wonder why we don't want to follow," she lamented. Her boyfriend Saasha, a twenty-one-year-old religious studies major, took her sentiments one step further. "They sit for hours and tell us, when you want to enter into the bathroom, enter with the right foot. If you sit on the floor, cross this foot over this one. Ay, *Khoda* (God)! We are really out of it, this regime is really out of it. This is what they want to teach us. They want to focus on going to the bathroom, and when and where to have sex. There are more important things like dealing with our huge unemployment or traffic problems, but they have chosen these things to focus on, so this is how we fight back, by focusing our attentions on social, sexual, and cultural relations (*ravabet*)."

The Islamic Republic of Iran (IRI) is governed by Islamic Law (or the *Shari'a*)[6]. *Shari'a* law, as interpreted by the clerics in power, contains strict rules on comportment, leisure, sociality (specifically heterosociality), and sexuality. *Shari'a* mandates among other things that women and men should interact minimally before marriage (this, in effect, means that an unmarried young man and woman seen in the company of one another without a chaperone could technically be arrested and punished. Likewise, young men and women are not to spend time alone with one another, and should limit their interactions to conversations at school, in groups, or with the presence of family members). With regard to veiling, *Shari'a* also dictates that women should be covered in "proper" Islamic dress (ideally a cloak from head to toe, hiding any bodily shape). Islamic law as interpreted by the morality police also mandates a somber habitus, and devotion to higher powers as the main source of pleasure and recreation.

HISTORICAL AND THEORETICAL BACKGROUND

In his piece "Islamism and the Politics of Fun," Asef Bayat astutely explores the reasons behind many Islamists' "aversion to fun." (Bayat, 2007) He notes that "anti fun-damentalism is a historical matter, one that has to do significantly with the preservation of power" and argues that "the adversaries' (Islamists') fear of fun revolves ultimately around the fear of exit from the paradigm that frames their mastery; it is about anxiety over loss of their 'paradigm power.'"(ibid: 435).

In this important article, Bayat chronicles the history of Islamist (and other religious) resistance to fun, especially the type of activities enjoyed by young people that venture into the realm of the chaotic, erotic, and morally questionable. It is important to understand how and why Islamists throughout history and in various Muslim majority countries (Bayat presents us with case studies from Saudi Arabia, Egypt, Afghanistan, and Syria in addition to Iran) feel threatened by certain types of recreation and seek to regulate it. As scholar Michael Cook elaborates (2003), many Islamists see "fun" as an antidote to Islam. Bayat extends this further by pointing out that "fun presupposed a powerful paradigm, a set of presumptions about the self, society, and life that might compete with and undermine the legitimizing ideology of religion." (Bayat, 2002: 455).

Young Iranians, in an attempt to explore and express their selfhood both individually and collectively, are now using this alternative paradigm brought forth by their youth culture to step out of the paradigm approved by members of the regime in power. The alternative paradigm presented and embodied by many young people in Tehran is at one and the same time destabilizing the regime (by questioning their paradigm), and strengthening young people's sense of selfhood and identity.

It is important to note that the desire for and importance of leisure are not a new phenomenon following the revolution, but have historical roots, most significantly in the years leading up to the revolution. As notable Iranian scholar Nikki Keddie has noted, "people in Iran in the late 1950s, 1960s and 1970s were definitely having fun, attending parties, and had the latest fashion. In fact, when I first visited Iran in 1959, I was surprised to see that only a few months after Yves Saint Laurent designed skirts above the knee in Paris, people in Tehran were wearing these skirts! And they had their hair done in beehives to reflect the fashion of the times and were attending parties."(Keddie, 2007). There is a strong cultural memory of leisure, especially in the years immediately leading up to the revolution (the 1970s) whereby many people were interested in the joys of fashion, parties, relaxing at the beach (near the Caspian), skiing, and going to cafes, discos, and social clubs. (For more details, see Hourcade and Habibi, 2007). In fact, many young people were so interested in globalized fun and fashion, that this became a point of criticism during the years leading up to the revolution, and many were accused of being "westoxicated" or "struck with the west," which was considered to be a betrayal of Iranian culture (Al-Ahmad, 1962).

Immediately after the revolution, the period of Islamification began, which included tight controls on forms of recreation including the closure of cafés, discos, and movie theaters, and the regulation of the public sphere by the morality police. Under the rule of Ayatollah Khomeini, non-government approved cinema, radio, and television were condemned as "corrupting the youth." (Naficy, 1995).

During the 1990s and after the death of Khomeini and the end of the Iran-Iraq war, young people began to engage in recreational activities, and started publicly expressing their desires for fun. They began taking to the streets with alternative styles of Islamic dress, young women began wearing more make-up, young men and women were arrested for playing loud music in their cars or in public areas, and unmarried couples began dating outside their homes and were found intermittently in parks, cars, or in the few cafés that began opening their doors. As Bayat notes, "by challenging the regime's moral and political authority, the young subverted the production of 'Muslim youth' (while) anxiety over the increasing *bad-hijabi* (laxity in veil wearing) among schoolgirls and female university students haunted officials." (Bayat, 2002: 440).

The recreation wars had officially begun in the 1990s, but took root and became a force after the election of Reformist President Khatami in 1997.

While it is difficult to identify whether the urban young Iranians who are the focus of my study are constructing a new sexual and social culture or are a part of a subculture within Iran, it is useful to look at literature describing the creation of subcultures as well as frameworks for understanding and describing emerging sexual cultures. The idea of subculture has been defined as:

A set of people with a distinct set of behaviors and beliefs from a larger culture of which they are a part. The subculture may be distinctive because of the age of its members, or by their race, ethnicity, class and/or gender, and the qualities that determine a subculture as distinct may be aesthetic, religious, political, sexual or a combination of these factors. Subcultures are often defined via their opposition to the values of the larger culture to which they belong, although this definition is not universally agreed on by theorists."(Hebdige, 1979 & 1991: 76).

Literatures on subcultures and ways in which they use style and comportment provide some tools with which to analyze the emerging shift in sexual discourse amongst this particular population of Iranian young adults.

Dick Hebdige (1991) and Stuart Hall (1993), both originally written in the 1970s, analyze ways that countercultures and subcultures form and shape themselves as unique and distinct to the dominant culture through style of dress, music, and demeanor. Hebdige, Hall, and Genet all explore the status and meaning of revolt within youth subcultures, the idea of style as a form of refusal, and the elevation of "crime" into art. Hebdige notes that within some subcultures (punks, mods, rockers, hippies, beats, and teddy boys in England during the 1960s and 1970s), the core values of the "straight world" – for example sobriety, ambition, conformity, etc. – are replaced by their opposites such as hedonism, defiance of authority, and the quest for "kicks" (Hebdige, 1979 & 1991: 76).

He notes that the young people (similar to young Iranians) are trying to elicit an outraged response from their parents, teachers, and employers. Many young Iranians appear to be experimenting with some of the characteristics that defined various subcultures in the West in the 1960s and 1970s – specifically characteristics of rebellion, resistance, and the desire to be separated from the Islamic ideology that members of the regime have sought to inject into society. Hebdige also discusses ways in which style becomes intentional communication. Many young urban Iranians are also seeking to make social and political statements through their style. Choosing to wear Islamic dress in defiant ways (for women: head scarves pushed back to reveal dyed hair, high-heeled shoes, shorter pants that reveal ankles, and open-toed shoes during summer; for men: hair grease and long locks, smoothly shaven faces, tight pants, and chunky jewelry), they are using their style both to make a public statement and to communicate. Their style becomes a code and a means of communication in much the same way as in many of the subcultures studied by the Birmingham School.

Dick Hebdige suggests that counter-cultures and subcultures form and make themselves unique and distinct by their style of dress and demeanor. Tehrani young adults involved in this social movement feel that they use their clothes and styles as codes to one another and as ways to express identity. Leila, a twenty-year-old urban planning student at Azad University in Tehran, told me, "young people in Iran are undergoing an identity crisis, we know we are changing, but we are not sure who we are or how to tell the world who we are. Some, like me and my friends, express this identity in our style. We wear colorful headscarves and tight coats; it is our way of expressing how we are changing." Though these changes and silent statements may not receive acknowledgement from members of the Iranian diaspora, or consumers of Western media, the state in the Islamic Republic does see the changes and is struggling to new youth social movements.

Any violation of Islamic dress code was previously grounds for punishment. Today, things have changed. For example, during the first decade and a half after Islamification, young women wearing tighter coats or open-toed shoes were harassed, physically threatened, and often jailed for not adhering to Islamic dress codes. Women who wore lipstick might have their lips slashed with razors by men and women who sought to promote Islamic ideology, and women who wore nail polish were punished by lashings. Today, young women wear make-up, tight-fitting Islamic dress and nail polish without punishment and limited harassment (if any). These changes reflect a shift in the state apparatus that now have been forced to be more tolerant of the new styles embraced by young adults.

Many of my interlocutors were quick to point out that transformations in various styles have ultimately led to new responses by the morality police. "Now young people don't have big problems any more, we can put on style the way we want to," explained Morteza, a young student living in the Western part of Tehran referred to as *Shahrak-i-Gharb*. Morteza is a twenty-year-old university student who had his eyebrow, nose and lip pierced with a faux *mohawk*, wearing baggy jeans, and a tight white t-shirt over which he wore three large silver chains. "It's not just our government that is changing, it's our culture, our parents," he emphasized. Another young man who was strolling around the shopping mall with Morteza added to this idea that the change in parents' attitudes has become an important indicator of culture change that is beyond government change. "Yeah, you know, five years ago, if I walked around with this nose ring, my hair all done up and these fashionable clothes, my mother and father would have given me a hit on the bottom (*mizadan dar-e-koonam*) and kicked me out of the house. Now, I still live with them, they see how I walk around and they don't say anything. That means something," he told me as other young "hipsters" walked past us at the mall. These transformations were part of what my interlocutors called the social and sexual revolution. Leila emphasized that for her group of friends, having altered the response of the morality police to the point where the youth now have some control and choice in what they wear was an important milestone in their social revolution. It was also of no small significance that many of their parents seemed to accept their new styles, and they saw all of this as an indicator of changes in culture, not just government. It seemed that for many of my interlocutors, issues of agency and citizenship manifested themselves in having a say over what they could and should wear and how they should look.

PUBLIC USES OF PRIVATE SPACE:
HAVING FUN IN THE ISLAMIC REPUBLIC

Daily experiences with "fun" and recreation reflect the changes taking place in the Islamic Republic. Ten years ago, young people were not dating in the parks, mating online, partying in the mountains, or having elaborate underground parties with as much ease as they are today. Recently, though there have been irregular crackdowns on young people in the streets of Tehran, the amount of heterosocialization, and sexual socialization has actually been increasing, and young people are getting away with private uses of public space. As I describe below, young people are re-shaping public spaces, and are getting away with what would have previously been punishable behaviors deemed immoral by members of the regime. Today, however, the morality police is unable to punish the large numbers of young people engaging in these behaviors, and thus has had to adjust its standards.

Indeed, both the state and many of the young people themselves view changes in sexual and social behavior and discourse as an integral part of de-legitimizing the power of the regime over social behaviors, a regime which claims to have brought moral values to the Islamic Republic. It is also important to note that the legitimacy of the regime is being shaken and questioned by the young people making clear that the regime has not won the hearts and minds of a large portion of its population (for example, in a survey conducted in 2000, it was found that "some 80 per cent of the nation's youth were indifferent or opposed to the clergy, religious obligations and religious leadership while 86 per cent of students refrained from saying their daily prayers.") (Bayat, 2007: 441). Additionally, it is of importance that the regime is not able to control the "revolutionary behavior" of young adults. Young people's social behaviors (such as gathering in cafés or listening to "un-Islamic" music and dancing in their cars) are also difficult to police because of the large scale on which they are occurring (thousands of youth in cafés, millions in cars). Iran's demographic shift in favor of large numbers of educated, unemployed youth, present the dwindling numbers of morality police with their greatest challenge yet: being outnumbered by youth and supporters of young adults. Also, some of the behavior is so subtle (such as colorful headscarves) that the state is unsure about the need to police it, and some of the behavior does still occur in private (such as the drinking and sexual encounters), regardless of occasional harassment by members of the morality police. "It's difficult to know exactly what to arrest people for," indicated one morality policeman with whom I spoke in 2004 while he was off duty. He lamented the fact that young people were increasingly "behaving badly and without morals", but said that it was often difficult to arrest young people "because the rules keep changing. I don' t know if make-up is ok now, or if beige *montows* (Islamic outer coats for women) are ok or no. So do I arrest someone who is suspicious, or would that mean I would have to arrest thousands? It is getting difficult these days."

Perhaps it is this inability to police large numbers of people that has prompted the state to reconsider its moral standards, or, and quite likely, the young have succeeded in installing a discourse shift. Either way, young people interact with the state and members of the morality police in a different way today from how they did twenty years earlier. Today, young people in Tehran are seen talking back to members of the morality police who are trying to arrest them. Passersby come to their aid, sometimes physically assaulting members of the morality police and telling them to leave the youth alone. When I ask my informants as to why this has happened, they invariably point to a shift in discourse that their sexual revolution has brought about. They describe the majority of Tehran's population as either restless youth or sympathetic "adults" who are all tired of the regime's repression. They are ready to respond and stand up for their rights. "Everyone knows that they (the regime) can't go on making us live like this," said Soraya, a nineteen-year-old student at Azad University. "We will find ways of lashing out, we will drive around in our cars and blast rock and roll, we will have sex, do drugs, we will continue to do what we want, and as long as our parents and many of the adults are on our side, we will keep winning, and that will have an impact," she added.

CARS: PRIVATE BUBBLES MOVING IN THE PUBLIC SPHERE

Driving around in cars was a form of extracurricular activity for many of the young people (both men and women) who viewed driving as a skill and a fun way to pass the time. Everyone in Tehran spends much time in a car (sitting in traffic, trying to get from one place to another, or deliberately spending time cruising particular streets in town to show off a car or meet other young people in a car), and perhaps because the numbers of young people who have cars have increased, many young people have made a deliberate attempt to make driving a recreation and a sport. Weaving through cars on crowded streets (*mār bāzi* or playing like a snake or snaking through cars) was thought of as an admirable talent. Also, competition to see who drives the best, gets to their destination the fastest, and does the nicest job of driving a nice car, was also a large part of making driving a form of recreation. Women, especially, took pride in racing and beating young men on the streets of Tehran, and in fact, one of the most prominent and successful race car drivers in Iran is a woman (Laleh TKTK). While it was interesting to spend hours in a car, watching young people pass phone numbers between open windows, or even purchase and sell drugs or black market movies and music, there were many occasions where I (the American side of me) was terrified by the driving style, feeling that at any moment an accident would occur, and many people would be hurt. It should be noted in this regard that Iran has one of the highest car accident fatality rates in the world.

The car has also become a somewhat portable private bubble that can be used in the public sphere. In their cars, young people can play illegal music, heteroso-cialize, engage in sexual behavior, and consume illegal substances. Though they are moving through the public sphere, the car gives them a sense of agency, a sense of control over their own bubble, or a segment of their lives. Many of them also felt that cars brought about independence, as they felt secure in the knowledge that they could speed away from angry parents or morality police in a difficult situa-tion. The car, for these young people, has become a sacred space, perhaps one of the only spaces in which they feel that they have full autonomy.

"I love my car because it's my space," explained Sahand, a twenty-five-year-old taxi driver from the southern part of Tehran. "I had many of my major life experi-ences in cars. I lost my virginity in my car, tried opium for the first time in my car, and had my first drink [of alcohol] in my car. It's my world," he noted. Another young man, Shahab, a twenty-two-year-old butcher from the center of town, echoed Sahand's sentiments. "Cars are a big source of freedom here. We listen to our music in cars, pick up girls in cars, and sometimes party in cars. It's like our own moving disco," he told me. Indeed, it did seem that many young people spent significant amounts of time in cars, either driving around, listening to music, or engaging in sexual behaviors. Over fifty of my informants told me that they had had sexual experiences in cars, and twenty informants indicated that they had engaged in some form of substance use in their cars. What is interesting to note, is that these experiences are taking place in the private space of the car as it moves through the public city streets.

CAFÉ CULTURE

Internet cafés, coffee shops, tea houses and *hookah* (water tobacco pipe) cafés are among the most popular venues frequented by the majority of my inform-ants in Tehran. Most of the young people with whom I spoke indicated that they spent at least five hours a week at an internet café or coffee shop, meeting other young people, going on or searching for dates, or spending time online engaging in cybersex or looking at pornography. Because these cafés facilitate moral trans-gression of Islamic boundaries (by providing venues where young people can het-erosocialize and sit closely with one another, listen to music deemed "immoral" by the authorities, and participate in potential online "debauchery") their very existence is a threat to the moral order of the Islamic Republic. The fact that many of these cafés have not only not been closed down, but have opened up additional cafés and become chain cafés, is significant in assessing the re-creation of recreation, the political significance of recreation in these spaces, and the public spatial takeover of this new youth paradigm. Rather than spend hours in mosques or in devotion to prayer (as the authorities would wish), they spend their time in these public cafés in open defiance of the Islamists preferred paradigm.

As noted earlier, prior to the revolution, and especially in the years leading immediately up to the revolution, there was a strong leisure culture which encompassed a café culture, especially in Tehran and Shiraz. Many "traditional" coffeehouses (*ghaveh khani e sonnati*) had been popular at that time, as well as more modernizing cafes. However, these were all closed down during the period of Islamification in the 1980s, as they were deemed to be "dens of immorality" (TKTK). In the 1990s, after the death of Khomeini, and then increasingly after the election of Reformist president Mohammad Khatami in 1997, cafés and tea houses began once again to open their doors. When I first began my fieldwork in 2000, there were only a few coffee shops, and one or two internet cafés in Tehran, and these few cafés were rarely crowded, let alone overflowing with stylish groups of young people, couples, and individuals surfing the net. Today, there are entire books filled with names and descriptions of popular cafés, and most neighborhoods in Tehran play host to dozens of these cafés which are all quite crowded. On more than one occasion, I drove around with a group of informants for an hour in order to find a café that was not only to their liking, but which could accommodate a group of more than two. Many of these cafés are small, dimly lit, and packed with young people sipping cappuccinos, mochas, and milkshakes. In terms of style, these cafés can compete with the best cafés in France, New York, or San Francisco, and cater to young Tehranis' changing tastes. One popular café, on Valiasr Avenue, offers non-*mojaz* (Islamic approved) music, free internet, and a delicious menu of what young Tehranis refer to as "junk food" (using the English term to refer to pizza, chips, hamburgers, and French fries). This café also has a stylish décor with exposed adobe brick inside, comfortable velvet couches set next to a fireplace, terracotta tiles and copper chairs and tables, creating a welcoming, yet stylish and sophisticated atmosphere for its young Tehrani client base. "It's my favorite café," Moji told me in the summer of 2004. "I come here at least three times a week!" she added.

At these cafés, young couples sit very close to one another, whispering into each other's ears as they share coffee drinks. Certain cafés play host to gatherings of young activists who come to the café to organize and strategize political movements. At other cafés one might find groups of artists or scholars. Some gather in groups to socialize, drink tea, or smoke the *hookah*. Others come to cafés in search of computers and internet, where they can surf the net, play online games, chat with potential cyberlovers, or download pornographic photos and films. These cafés are emerging as major public recreational venues, where young people spend a large portion of their free time, meet and interact with other young people, organize, philosophize, and relax.

By not responding to Islamic laws (of dress, comportment, modesty, and lack of heterosociality), young people are rejecting the notion of being Islamic subjects and making their choices public. This public defiance and re-appropriation of space results in an important spatial takeover, where the streets of Tehran increasingly belong to the youth as opposed to the morality police who (in the 1990s) used to use the streets for public arrests and flogging. Policymakers in Iran are increasingly trying to find ways of inspiring belief in Islamic ideology, especially among the youth. Their efforts thus far, however, have been met only with failure.

THE POLITICS OF HAVING FUN IN THE ISLAMIC REPUBLIC

As mentioned earlier, there is perhaps no place in the world where the stakes of having fun are so high. Technically, young people who are heterosocializing in parks, cars, or cafés could be arrested, detained, and whipped. But they aren't; they continue to engage in these recreational activities in increasing numbers, while fewer young people are arrested for immoral behaviors. Cafés which provide venues for moral transgressions could be closed at any moment. They are not. In fact the numbers of internet cafés and coffee shops have actually increased in recent years. Given Islamists' aversion to fun (Bayat, 2007), it seems that young people are stepping out of the Islamically approved paradigm, and into their own. This is a threat to the regime, and young people and members of the regime alike are aware of this.

How is this possible? Why is this new behavior permitted? The answers are not exactly clear, though it may be a combination of the factors that I have described thus far. Namely: 1) it is difficult to police such large numbers of "subversive" youth as their numbers multiply annually, 2) the behavior is subtle and thus morality police are not always certain regarding the need to police it, 3) perhaps the climate of reform as set by the tone of Khatami's presidency was well-timed just as this generation of young people were coming of age, and thus the spirit of openness he promoted has stayed with the youth despite the election of conservative President Ahmadinejad, and/or 4) the numbers of young people in the morality police, in government, and in positions of power are increasing while many mature adults are increasingly sympathizing with the youth and frustrated with the Islamist regime, leading to an increase in the number of sympathizers in general. The youth movement has resulted in a spatial takeover that challenges the intellectual apparatus of the state and potentially may lead to a change in the regime or at least in the regime's ability to operationalize its power.

Harassment and crackdowns have occurred in the past few months (especially since the election and fraudulent re-election of President Ahmadinejad).

There have been periods of time when morality police attempted to close down cafés where young people meet, arrest youth who are congregating in parks and mountain side areas, and ban internet sites rumored to hold immoral content. The fact that these measures are taken is further evidence that the existence of these new types of recreation are a threat to the moral order and power of the regime. However, the fact that cafés remain open, that youth continue to take to the streets, that the Green Movement hasn't been silenced, that young people continue to date and mate in cars, parks, and mountains, and cybersex and the online porn industry continues to flourish are a clear signal that the youth, and their efforts to re-create spaces of recreation often in the public sphere, are succeeding at chipping away at the fabric of morality woven by the clerics, the cement of the regime. Members of the regime are not able to police the increasing numbers of youth who participate in what they deem "un-Islamic" behaviors, and are not able to patrol the hundreds of cafés, thousands of parties, or millions of young people in cars listening to "un-Islamic" music, or behaving in ways which threaten the moral order of the state. In the words of my interlocutors, "our quiet revolution is triumphing."

CONCLUDING THOUGHTS

Young people from all socioeconomic backgrounds are increasingly seeking to carve out recreational spaces for themselves against the backdrop of a repressive regime. Their unending efforts to create these spaces despite harassment and punishment from the morality police, speak to a strong resistance to Islamic ideology. My interlocutors repeatedly told me that they were embodying the changes in sexual and social culture that they would like to see enacted through their lifestyles. They reminded me that their sexual and social revolution was not about momentary acts, but rather a way of life which included social gatherings and social behavior that could be viewed as hedonistic (such as gatherings which focused on unprotected group sex, or parties with drugs and alcohol which had a likelihood of being raided by the morality police). These acts are a necessary part of constructing a world over which they had control, rather than the world of the Islamists who would have them stay home and obey. Much of their discourse, many of their utterings on their way to school, to group gatherings, or to an illegal dance class focused on resistance and enacting changes in social, sexual, and political discourse. Though much of this paper has focused on recreational and social activities of young people, I want to be clear that most of my interlocutors also had political consciousness and were not solely focused on "fun." Rather, the goal in presenting their social lives is to point to a shift in behavior and a transformation of discourse. Their lifestyle choices could be seen as evidence that thoughts and discussions about a sexual revolution are not fleeting. Two decades ago, young people were not frequently attending elaborate parties (and the few who did, did so with trepidation and recalled that they could never "let loose" and "dance the night away"). Today, young people go to parties on the eve of Islamic anniversaries which previously used to be cause for staying at home out of fear of being caught by the morality police and accused of being un-Islamic for not grieving the loss of a particular martyr or Islamic ideologue. They are less afraid, which is an indication of the ways in which the state has shifted in order to accommodate its youth in certain ways. This suggests an important interactive process in the dialogue between the youth and the state, which could change the future of Iran. To see evidence of this, we only need to look to the streets of Tehran today, which have been taken over by the Green Movement and are seriously de-stabilizing the current regime.

NOTES

1   I do not wish to perpetuate artificial dichotomies of young versus old or secular versus austere, and I recognize that the generational divide is not always along political lines. However, during my field-work I found that the majority of people engaged in what they termed a "sexual revolution" were young people (indeed the majority of the population are youth under the age of thirty), so in this paper I will refer to them as the youth, though I recognize that there are young people who do not identify with this movement and mature adults who do identify with the movement.

2   The ethnographic research for this project was conducted between 2002-2007. During this time I made several extended trips to Iran, engaged in participant observation, and conducted in-depth qualitative interviews with 350 young people and 110 parents, teachers, and health care providers. I received Human Subjects Approval to conduct the study from the Columbia University International review Board. The full exploration of the project can be found in my book, *Passionate Uprisings: Iran's Sexual Revolution*, Stanford University Press 2008.

3   Behavior deemed "morally questionable" is based on interpretation and can be as small as wearing excessive make-up or bright colors, to public displays of affection, drug use, or sex work.

4   As scholars such as Jahangir Amuzegar have noted, however, "statistics on Iran's employment and unemployment are the flimsiest, least reliable and most contested of all basic indicators" (Amuzegar 2004). I believe that many of the statistical figures on Iran including those on health, marriage status, population, and family planning are also flawed, which makes it difficult to provide exact baseline statistics for the reader given that, "the principal sources of data are either out of reach, limited or largely conjectural. Iran's total population itself is based on conflicting *estimates*. And estimated figures for any given year vary between those of the UN Secretariat, Iran's Statistics Center, other local authorities, and foreign organizations – often with a 10% margin of difference" (Amuzegar 2004). Also see K. Basmanji, *Tehran Blues: Youth Culture in Iran* (Tehran: Saqi Books, 2006) & J. Amuzegar, "Iran's Unemployment Crisis," *Middle East Economic Survey, 2004.*

5   Note that while drug use is a significant issue amongst young people in Iran, many of whom couple most recreational activities with some form of substance use, a thorough discussion of drug use and its implications is beyond the scope of this paper. For a further discussion of the impact of drug use on young people please see Mahdavi, P. (2009) "Who Will Catch Me if I Fall?" in *Contemporary Iran.*

6   The many meanings of *Sharia* or Islamic law are complex and vary depending on who is inter-preting the laws. In this article I refer to Islamic law as it has been interpreted by members of the clerical regime in power in Iran since the revolution, though I acknowledge that this is just one set of interpretations of Islamic law.

Idealistic and Indignant Young Lebanese

Roseanne Saad Khalaf

In most societies, the insecurities and fears of young people are associated with the inevitable process of becoming an adult, particularly in postmodern settings where fluidity and uncertainty have replaced structure and tradition. For Lebanese youth, roughly half the country's population, living in the shadow of the Civil War, with no rule of law or true democracy, the tensions and savage realities of their country are alarming. So far they have witnessed a succession of horrific political assassinations, massive public protests, a devastating war between Hezbollah and Israel (2006), a long-running power struggle between Hariri's supporters and Hezbollah that exploded into violent street clashes in Beirut (May 2008), and, most recently, threats of a new wave of destruction stemming from the Netherlands-based tribunal's attempt to uncover and prosecute the killers of former Prime Minister Rafik Hariri. Not surprisingly, the vast majority of young people suffer from postwar stress, yet little is known about their views, inner thoughts, and feelings. My paper focuses on the dominant discourses and themes of creative writing students at the American University of Beirut (AUB) in an attempt to better understand how they navigate the threatening circumstances that influence and shape their young lives in a disturbing postwar society. On another level, the paper is a reflexive account on the importance of relocating lived experiences to writing workshops in order to create *third spaces* where deep and open accounts of what it means to be living in Lebanon today can be meaningfully explored.

CREATIVE WRITING IN A POSTWAR SOCIETY

Having survived a grueling decade of violence during the Lebanese Civil War, I left Beirut in 1984 with my husband and two young children for what we thought would be a year's research leave. Over the next eleven years, our life in the quiet university town of Princeton was in stark contrast to the ugly battleground of Beirut. Yet I constantly longed to go back home. Upon my return in 1995, I launched the first creative writing workshops at the American University of Beirut (AUB). The relevance of such courses to the lives of numerous students, particularly returnees, who took refuge in writing as a redemptive pastime, seemed indisputable.

In addition to developing and refining creative potential, it addressed the need for significant literary production in a difficult postwar moment and a discourse around it.

Almost immediately, concerns began to echo similar themes and when drafts and manuscripts were presented, my academic world took on new meaning. Workshopping texts and sharing ideas instigated an ongoing conversation where "real experiences" became intuitive venues for text creation and shared discourse, for reflexivity and multiple encounters with the self and the outside world. Locations are never neutral (Kamler, 2001), especially in Lebanon, a country where violence always lurks in the shadows, erupting sporadically, often after periods of relative calm. In such a volatile postwar setting, exploring issues that deeply matter to young people sets into motion a complex interaction between biographies, society, politics, and history, thus shedding light on broader societal transformations. In addition to defining the views of a new generation, narratives become an integral element in highlighting experiences in a troubling, fast-changing postwar society

Though writing like other creative ventures is essentially an individual endeavor, it is nurtured and enriched in an interactive group setting. Collaborative work-shops are based on shared commitment. The classroom is a writing-intensive zone but also a *safe house* where students are encouraged to take risks. Goffman's (1971) distinction between front-stage and back-stage situations is particularly apt here. Students are granted rare artistic license as well as freedom of expression, both unavailable outside our safe house. Eventually, they move beyond the explora-tion of mere personal views to thinking through dominant Lebanese discourses. Precisely because their narratives exist outside the hegemonic influence of public transcripts, something other than the dominant story or the accepted biography of Lebanon can be told.

POSTWAR LEBANON

Postwar Lebanon was optimistically perceived as a period when the violence that had pervaded almost two decades of civil war could finally be tucked away leaving the Lebanese to focus, at last, on reconciliation, reconstruction, and revamping a decaying political system and economy. Instead, Lebanese continue to live in a vol-atile climate where clashes can quickly spiral out of control at any given moment. Currently tensions are running high. The country seems on the edge of a new wave of destruction as deep feuds between Western-backed parties and Hezbollah worsen over the UN tribunal's task to uncover and prosecute Hariri's killers.

Lebanon plays host to eighteen different religious communities and an archaic sectarian political system constructed to represent and protect them. Sadly, during the postwar years, little has been done to reform the underlying structural problems inherent in Lebanon's defunct confessional system of governance and increasingly fragmented political system. Crucial questions regarding inter-communal conflict, accountability for wartime atrocities, and nation-building in a crumbling country have all been conveniently ignored. Furthermore, on the national level, there is the inability to "render the war years coherent and meaningful, and to ritually enact a national drama of forgiveness and reconciliation," (Seidman, 2009); while on the individual level, Lebanese seem to have agreed to a conspiracy of silence and denial (Khalaf, 1993b) that prevents any unifying national narrative necessary for postwar recovery. Sadly, the avoidance of responsibility seems to be the only commonality between the different narratives.

In such a precarious postwar setting, Lebanese youth are particularly vulnerable. They, perhaps more than any other group, remain traumatized by the growing confusion and despair resulting from the harsh realization that having scarcely recovered from an extraordinarily violent civil war, Lebanon is again in the throes of becoming a failed state. Worse still, the collective enthusiasm generated by the Cedar Revolution uprising did not materialize in any of the fundamental, progressive, or transforming ways initially anticipated by the youthful groups who organized and participated in the successive waves of massive demonstrations. Young people are painfully aware that the problems which instigated and sustained the Civil War remain unaddressed, leaving feelings of hate and hostility to simmer between sectarian groups. In the absence of reconciliation, there can be no sustainable or meaningful postwar recovery; conflict seems inevitable, the war far from over. It cannot be conveniently forgotten or delegated to the past. Consequently, Lebanese youth are trapped in a violent, unresolved past, unstable present, and uncertain future. Their life narratives and personal stories offer a deep and moving account of what it means to be young and living in a threatening postwar terrain. Narrative excerpts reveal a growing demoralizing dissonance between expectations and actual lived realities – a dissonance that continuously disrupts their lives, informs their narratives and plays a crucial role in the way they view themselves and the society they live in.

EIGHT THEMATIC CATEGORIES

I have organized my paper around eight recurring and salient themes in the reflexive life narratives of fifty creative writing students at AUB between the ages of eighteen and twenty-one and given each an appropriate title: *A Dangerous Political Climate, Disenchanted Youth, The Brain Drain, A Culture of Nostalgia, The Problem of Identity, A Different Political Language, Resentment of Foreign Interference* and *Youth Adrift*. None of the categories are mutually exclusive; all inevitably contain overlapping material.

After a brief analysis of each thematic grouping, excerpts that capture the voices of students are incorporated. Daring to openly explore complex, volatile issues and voice deep inner feelings and opinions can be a daunting experience. Yet moving ideas into a collective space of public discourse and critical debate is the first crucial step in the process of empowering students to shift from imagining to articulating and eventually constructing strategies that will assist in actualizing a new and transformed Lebanese terrain.

A Dangerous Political Climate
The tragic and seemingly unsolvable circumstances gripping the country have taken a toll on the daily lives of young people. They feel anxious and abandoned in a country that offers no promising prospects for the future, where violence is always waiting and ready to be unleashed by insidious political exploiters forever eager to incite political unrest, and where parties gain political capital through acts of violence.

My village was never occupied but it was next to villages that were constantly under attack. I remember the terror I felt, the fear of being caught up in the chain of violence and destruction that I watched daily on the news. I remember being hurt when I saw TV presenters talking coldly about the bombings in South Lebanon or when politicians pretended they understood our pain, fear, and suffering when in reality they knew and continue to know nothing except how to line their pockets and stay in powerful positions. (Fatima)

In 2006 a war took place in my country. Most people may think it was scary but for me it's customary. Bombs here and there, hundreds of innocent dead or displaced. The usual suffering: devastated homes and shattered lives. This country is all about loss. We have even lost our dreams of hope, hope for a better tomorrow. (Oussama)

I come from a torn country, a country that has always been destroyed and fought upon. Lebanon has killed my sense of belonging and stolen my hope. It's a land of occupation and devastation, car bombs and assassinations, a land torn apart by confessionalism and fractured national identity. (Leila)

No matter how hard one tries to deny the political danger and instability in Lebanon, the tight security measures are a grim reminder of all the repressed emotions waiting to explode. (Suha)

Today Lebanon echoes turmoil, political instability and conflict of interests. Today my country is still bleeding from confessionalism, corruption, and occupation. (Dalal)

Disenchanted Youth
There are many reasons for the renewal of pervasive fear. Reawakened confessional and sectarian loyalties persistently define most aspects of life, leaving no rational way forward. Since the Civil War officially ended in 1992, there have been few serious, if any, encouraging attempts, and certainly none that have gained momentum, to address the initial causes that have plagued the country for generations. Civil society and committed individuals of all ages, as well as active organizations, have remained incapable, so far, of altering Lebanon's feudal and corrupt system of politics and wasted national potential. Even potentially relevant movements like the Cedar Revolution quickly became ineffective despite initial demands to address and reshape Lebanon's decaying political system. As a result, young people, trapped in rising political tensions alongside fears of renewed sectarian strife, continuously witness the degradation of their society and lives.

In a deeply divided country, my students move in a landscape of bleakness and despair.

My society is full of contradictions: a society that dissolves the identity of the individual into the identity of the group, a society that is afraid of change, a society that praises freedom of expression but ultimately suppresses it. One learns to remain silent, to become a coward, to accept reality regardless of the discrepancies. One is taught that things in Lebanon will remain the way they are no matter how hard one tries to bring about change. There is no logic in our society. We must live up to the expectations of the family, the community, our religious sect, and political party but I have no intention of doing so. (Yasmine)

We are brought up to worship corrupt and inept politicians who only pocket money and remain unaccountable. Being different is not a blessing in Lebanon. A person is forced to keep quiet, to accept what is outdated and illogical and to simply go with the flow. (Zahi)

I am from a country where nobody is allowed to love the rainbow because every color belongs to a certain faction. In my country hypocrisy rules because everyone hates the other from the moment they are born because of their religion but they hide it behind a fake smile. My country is still fighting past wars instead of looking to the future. My country is a nightmare. (Sahar)

I feel ashamed to be Lebanese because Lebanon is a country that lives on lies covered with more lies. Everything is wrong about the government and I see nothing here that encourages me to cling to even a shred of hope. Lebanon is as dead as a rotting corpse. (Salah)

Understandably, many express feelings of exhaustion, disenchantment, and a longing to disengage from escalating political tensions.

> Life here is exhausting. It forces me to re-examine what Lebanon means to me. The future will never be bright. But right now, I am tired, tired of being asked why I refuse to join in the demonstrations, or why I choose not to watch political events on television for twenty-four hours a day, or even why I look at the sea of Lebanese flags with a vacant, unmoved expression. (Mariana)

Immediately following Rafik Hariri's assassination, when many students joined the active opposition group that took a strong stand against Syria and the Syrian-backed Lebanese government, it seemed a time of unprecedented opportunity for youth mobilization. A serious youth political culture, one that might change or, at least, disrupt the status quo, was forming. Youth-led activism seemed suddenly capable of playing a significant role in instigating broad social and political change. Young people felt empowered to demand a more democratic, transparent, freer, united Lebanon. Sadly, the optimism was short lived. Today politics is back to the semi-feudal divisions of power and Lebanon's onetime warlords and militia leaders are, once again, in control. Even the politicians who, five years ago, supported the massive public protests have decided it's more advantageous to share the spoils rather than risk losing their privileged positions. By maintaining the weakness of the state, creating sporadic crises, and reinforcing deep divisions, the leaders justify their positions of power. Understandably, students feel betrayed by the March 14 politicians who as Omar explained, "simply used us to regain power and reclaim their seats in the government and parliament." The role and results of activism now appear futile and completely incapable of radically challenging or reshaping Lebanon's defunct political system.

> All our dreams are just delusions because politicians in Lebanon used us to achieve their own ends. It's true that we accomplished a certain level of national unity after Hariri was killed, but that's not enough. His assassination has been followed by one tragic event after another and the opposition and pro-government politicians are all back in office. They have forgotten about their promises to our generation and to the people of Lebanon. What kind of Lebanon are they creating for us, the future generation? Day after day people are leaving the country to pursue a better life. I don't want to sound so pessimistic but only a miracle can alter our miserable situation. All our angry protests and hard work have proved useless! (Maher)

The Brain Drain

The exodus of young Lebanese during the postwar years has reached dramatic proportions exacerbating the country's proverbial "brain drain." Growing concerns about the stability of the country alongside limited job prospects have led students to seek greener pastures elsewhere.

> At this stage in my life, building a successful career is my main objective. So, I have decided to continue studying for my MA in Canada. I don't believe I will ever work in Lebanon or even live here in the future. I have no hope that stability will return and job opportunities open up. In my opinion, lasting peace is impossible because regional politics are a mess and corrupt politicians resist change. I don't want to waste my time believing in a bright future that will never happen. (Ahmad)

One overshadowing concern is Lebanon's historical legacy of unresolved conflict. For many, there seems no impending end to this shockingly turbulent postwar era and no alternative to emigration.

> I am the child of a country wounded by fifteen years of civil war followed by fifteen years of foreign occupation. Our economy bears the burden of thirty-eight billion dollars of public debt. Our youth are victims of high unemployment and crippling uncertainty. As far as I'm concerned, leaving is the only logical alternative. (Huda)

> Lebanon is drowning. Every time my country attempts to reach the surface to gasp for air, it is violently pulled under again, left to sink deeper into stagnant waters. Won't this deadly suffocation end? I can't even remember what it's like to breathe freely. It's time for me to leave. (George)

Students are acutely aware that religion, and not qualifications, acts as a filter from which they are viewed by the Lebanese government as well as most other employers. As a result, many job opportunities remain largely unavailable to college graduates.

> When I graduate I intend to look for a job abroad so my qualifications will count for something. If I stay here, religion will be the determining factor and certainly not my qualifications. (Adnan)

> I think it so unfair that my confessional and religious identity will determine what job I'm able to get. When I graduate, I'll seek employment in a foreign company where my qualifications are what count. (Hala)

> In my country I am identified as a Moslem, Christian or Druze. I am merely a member of a certain family and a particular political party. My profession, my ideas, my convictions, and my dreams are all irrelevant. (Naji)

Against a Culture of Nostalgia

To a significant group of students, Lebanon has always been exactly what they are now witnessing: a country on the verge of disintegration and therefore in drastic need, of neither nostalgic daydreams nor collective amnesia, but of immediate, pragmatic solutions.

> The Lebanon I kept with me for so long was a beautiful place. Its soil was the color of terracotta, its wooded hills towered towards a clear blue sky: while the sea stretched along a welcoming shore. Its villages were full of little stone houses, with heaps of fruit put out on blanketed roofs to dry in the sun. Somewhere in the background, Fairuz sings. It was a perfect place, but it simply didn't exist. The real Lebanon is a country torn apart by war, religion, and ignorance. The truth is that most Lebanese, including my parents, refuse to face the ugly facts. (Mariana)

They see their parents as prisoners of selective memory, blindly subscribing to a culture of nostalgia or the "feel good narrative." In contrast, students consider the act of remembering a way to uncover the truth so it can serve as a necessary resource for present revision and renewal.

> My parents don't talk about the war. They never discuss the causes or admit to the hatred that still exists. I guess it's too painful. They prefer to live in denial. It was a real shock to grow up and see my country for what it really is. If "Oriental Switzerland" ever truly existed it has disappeared forever. (Chadia)

> Lebanon is a country in the eye of a hurricane, lost in an endless sea of blood and conflict, anguish and torment. This storm will not end until the people of Lebanon come together and solve the conflicts that started the war. But how can this happen when the country is composed of fractured groups held together by blind and fictitious dreams of past glory? (Imad)

The Problem of Identity

The youth-led Cedar Revolution brought, across the confessional divide, hundreds of thousands of angry Lebanese to Martyrs' Square in the aftermath of Hariri's assassination, demanding to know who was behind the heinous crime, calling for Syrian withdrawal, and a more democratic, secular, and united Lebanon. Young and educated, this group of postwar activists envisioned citizenship based on democratic rights and responsibilities rather than privilege and entitlement. My students, many of whom participated in the massive public protests, fiercely reject the notion of individuals defined according to a fixed, inherited, confining identity based on religion, ethnicity, or tribe.

I used to be very politically active. In fact, I belonged to a prominent political party that drew its members from one religion. But after Hariri was assassinated, I changed and started to question my earlier affiliation to one political party and one way of thinking. For a short time, I was actively involved in the Cedar Revolution. I am now a spectator and critic. I no longer want to take sides. I want people to come together and create a viable nation based on a workable unified national identity. (Elie)

Narratives are a prism into the larger sociopolitical and religious story of Lebanon that students would like to eradicate.

Unlike most people in Lebanon, I respect and value the friendship of X or Y because I like them. For me a name is just a name. I never look at a name to determine a person's religion, background, political affiliation, and entire history. (Celine)

Imposed local identities prevent individuals from seeking a more meaningful and broader national identity.

Lebanese people have strong ties to their communities, religion, and feudal political parties because their national identity is nonexistent. Or perhaps it's the other way around. (Hala)

In pushing for secularism and questioning fixed identities, students are attempting to construct identities and subjectivities infinitely more significant than those determined along sectarian lines alone. They aim to inter the dialogue in far more complex ways, to transcend the stagnation of confessional politics and replace it with pluralism, tolerance, and responsible citizenship.

In the eyes of others in Lebanon, I am merely a person who belongs to a certain family, sect, and religion and I must act accordingly. Well, I resent such labels and so do my friends. I am first and foremost a Lebanese and all the other things are irrelevant. I am part of a younger generation that intends to eradicate such archaic barriers. (Salim)

A Different Political Language
Students are overwhelmingly of the view that the political elite do not address the needs or concerns of the citizens they claim to represent, let alone the younger generation. More striking is their alarm and rejection of the language of *retriabilization* used by politicians, primarily because it leaves no room for political tolerance and honest dialogue. Instead of being reform-minded, political leaders resort to language that upholds a dysfunctional political system

reinforced and safeguarded by religious and sectarian allegiances. They have no intention of reversing ineffective practices, improving state institutions, or creating a stable, just, and forward-looking society by speaking to a larger political discourse.

Politicians in Lebanon underestimate the swift changes that have occurred. They talk endlessly but in actual fact, they say nothing and they think we will listen forever to their empty words. We want modern and progressive leaders who have vision and who can reform our worthless system. We need to move ahead and become part of the modern world. (Hala)

Those in government must learn to address the concerns of the Lebanese in simple words they can live up to. If they cannot reform our system they must exit and allow others who are more qualified to take over. (Raneem)

Politicians are masterminds at deception and clever words that poison the minds of their blind followers. (Siham)

We need a secular system that allows the most qualified persons to seek political positions. No one should be elected because of their religion or family. (Dina)

Lebanese who belong to different religions hate each other. They say things like, "Let's not talk to this person because he's Christian or because he's Muslim." This mentality is what started the war and we as Lebanese can't continue to talk this way. We can't continue to let politicians deceive and manipulate us. (Ibrahim)

In the Lebanon of the future, religion must belong to the church and to the mosque and we must all live together bound by our national identity. Confessionalism must no longer breed divisions and impede national progress. Difference and diversity must become opportunities and not sources of conflict and violence. (Imad)

Blogging is becoming increasingly popular among students who are aware of how powerful web-based information can be.

Lebanon now has bloggers who are calling for a revolution. They think it's the only way to change the political system. I know one of them whose radical ideas are making more and more sense to me. Maybe he is right. A revolution might be the only way to achieve change. (Saeb)

Lebanon, according to one student blogger, has been hijacked by destructive feudal forces.

I have become a blogger to express all the ideas and feelings that are driving me mad. I need to reach people and urge them to unite. We must put an end to the dangerous feudal system that is strangling our country. (Samia)

Resentment of Foreign Interference

Though students are keen on establishing the democratic practices of transparency, accountability, and secular reform, they harbor strong misgivings when it comes to the intentions and role of Western countries, particularly the U.S. Many express resentment that Lebanon is a puppet in the hands of foreign powers. The Iraq War has fuelled anti-Americanism sentiments. Even those who strongly supported the March 14 coalition dismiss the legitimacy and credibility of US interference, arguing that Lebanon is regarded as nothing more than a key front-line state in the Western battle for regional influence.

> How can we trust the US when we see the destruction they brought to so many countries in the name of democracy? I do not believe any of the reasons they give for going to war. The most recent example is Iraq that is now in chaos and on the verge of civil war thanks to US interference. The US does nothing unless it is beneficial to them. If they continue to interfere in Lebanon what is to prevent them from establishing military bases and instigating another civil war? Even Obama cannot change their foreign policy. (Nassib)

> I wish the US would leave us alone. To begin with, if they insist on becoming internally involved, it will be the kiss of death. Hezbollah will start to kidnap and kill foreigners as they did during the last civil war. (Munira)

> I think all foreign powers should leave our country. The Syrians have exploited us and now the US, along with their Western friends, are doing the same thing. I took part in the Cedar Revolution because I wanted to help create a new Lebanon that is independent and free of all Western and Arab interference. (Katia)

Students attribute the problems of Lebanon to the imperial determination of Western powers to enforce policies that satisfy their own agendas rather than the needs and rights of Lebanese.

> The US has no interest in helping Lebanon achieve the kind of democracy that is beneficial to us. They do only what is good for them. So basically I do not see a bright future. I see a "Cold" civil war, an extension of what we have had since the official end of the Civil War but with much more deceit and corruption from our beloved politicians and their Western accomplices. (Hussein)

Yet the anger directed at US foreign policy does not deter students from developing an ever-increasing appetite for popular culture, particularly infotainment and fast food.

> I know the US is an imperialist power but I still enjoy the products they import. (Said)

> I have many American friends that feel the way I do. They are angered by the arrogance and violence of US foreign policy but I don't see why this should stop me from enjoying all the good things that the US has to offer like music, movies, technology, clothes, and junk food. (Hiba)

The West is paradoxically conceived as a dominating power politically yet an emancipating power when it comes to individual freedom.

> I hear people criticize younger generations for adopting a Western way of life. But they do not understand that westerners got it right; they are not uncouth or uncultured, they are individualistic. Individualism is really all that one yearns for; freedom to express, freedom to move, freedom to speak freely. (Asma)

Youth Adrift
Restoring trust, dialogue, and hope among the young in a country of growing political instability and constant oscillation between periods of relative normalcy and chaos is extraordinarily difficult. The past has not served as a foundation to revision and a renewed commitment to the present, to "making a world where all people can live fully and well, where everyone can belong" (Hooks, 2009). The present is characterized by impending doom resulting from a constant fear that fresh episodes of violence can easily erupt; the future promises only repetition of a turbulent past. While returnee students complain of having no sense of homecoming, of being forced to exist on the margins of a country that is supposedly home (Khalaf, 2009), other students also suffer from strong feelings of disconnectedness, disappointment, even hostility. All struggle with the bitterness of the postwar Lebanese experience which leaves them bewildered and bereft of direction or meaning.

> I am not religious. I do not believe in Allah but if He truly does exist, then I can say with human certainty that He has forsaken this country a long time ago. (Yasmine)

> My country has beautiful scenery, perfect weather, and wonderful food. It should be the ideal place to live but it's not. It is sad and dangerous. I opened my eyes to the final phase of a war that I never understood: a war that I consider

to be useless, pointless, and hopeless. And now I am still terrified because I have witnessed more wars and more violence and more bloodshed. How can I feel I belong to a country that has caused me so much pain? (Leila)

Life in postwar Lebanon is full of absurdities. Resilience, in particular, is not an attribute most students appreciate.

What is so awesome about being able to forget the bloodshed and not understanding why the conflict happened in the first place? We need to know the causes and find workable solutions. If we ignore these questions, how can we fix a faulty system that keeps breaking down? Most Lebanese want to have crazy fun and avoid difficult questions and solutions. (Maher)

My parents have the extraordinary ability to be patient about things that will never change here. I believe this acquired patience has slowly rid us of our humanity. We become desensitized and blasé about things that are shocking to others. Apathy becomes the key to survival and resilience an acceptable and conditioned way to live. (Tala)

These are just a few of the reasons why I reject my country and the Lebanese way of thinking: in order to survive we must accept the fact that our government, when not too busy going for each other's throats, does not care about Lebanese citizens. Understand that religion, whether one is religious, agnostic, or atheist governs our lives. Accept threats of war from militias we are raised to admire or despise depending on our religion. And realize that our violent history will continue to repeat itself. (Ghassan)

SOME CLOSING REMARKS

Patricia Ewick and Susan Silbey (1995) believe the voices of the least powerful in society reflect the social and structural influences impacting and shaping individual lives. Clearly, the texts of my students form a "collective narrative" which relates a much larger journey highlighting the underlying conditions and tensions experienced in a disturbing postwar society. Narratives reveal that, at least among a small group of young Lebanese, rapidly expanding expectations are outdistancing the pace of change in political institutions and national discourse. My students are part of an emerging dynamic public sphere where the young are demanding a politics of greater secularism, modern workable institutions, democratic practices, and transparency. Even in the absence of secular transcending associations, students are distancing themselves from outdated parochial groupings. They want tolerance, less rigidity, and strong national loyalties to replace local identities.

Their scripts, grounded in lived experiences, call for the urgent negotiation of public and private in ways that transcend and move far beyond what is actually happening on the ground.

Relocating lived experience to the creative writing classroom is a minor first step in understanding the role young people are beginning to play in challenging the constraints that have silenced them during a difficult postwar period. Spaces where serious concerns are explored outside the hegemonic influence of public transcripts permit them to think through and beyond sociopolitical realities and envision innovative scripts that challenge the silencing representations and the degradation the political system has on their lives. Their role as agents of change is crucial for Lebanon. Writing workshops are a vital step in moving youthful ideas from the realm of imagining to that of realizing and eventually creating the momentum for change (Scarry, 1985). At the moment, student discourse is moving between the tensions of disheartening realities and hoped-for expectations. Unless incorporated into the wider public sphere, it will inevitably turn into despair and bitterness. Now, more than ever, there is a need for young people to establish a credible presence, to speak out against the negative forces that mold and determine their lives. Their views and the role they will hopefully play in shaping public experience discursively, are essential in redefining a postwar society urgently in need of real change.

In Good Times or Bad?

Discourse on the National Identity of Lebanese Upper Class Youth

Nicolien Kegels

INTRODUCTION

In 2005, when Rue Monot was still the glitziest and most popular street in Beiruti nightlife, there was a bar on one of its corners called "1975." This was not the usual cigar-and-champagne kind of location prevalent in the rest of the neighborhood – quite the contrary. Where the other bars and clubs were home to the shiniest little lights, the most modern furniture, and the reflections of innumerable mirrors, this bar was furnished with sandbags and decorated with bullet holes, graffiti war-time slogans, and pieces of shrapnel. Drinks were served by a waiter in camouflage gear with a parachute on his back, and the *nrguilehs* (waterpipes, also known as *shishas* or *hookahs*) were made from old rocket-parts. The music was also in sharp contrast with the mix of Western and Arabic pop songs played in the other bars and nightclubs around it: on the DJ's list were songs from the 1970s and 1980s only, songs lamenting the broken city and the divided country as well as songs urging the true patriots to fight and defend.

It was not entirely clear which clientele this bar was meant to attract; such a grim place in the street that gives Beirut its reputation of a city with glamorous, extravagant nightlife. Was it a place for foreigners, to show them another side of Lebanon – a side much less luxurious and lighthearted than the one visible in the neighborhood around them or to make them experience a safe version of the war so inextricably linked to the image of Lebanon? Was the place meant to take the Lebanese clubbers back to "the good old times," to their childhood, even if that childhood was spent in times many would rather forget? Or was it a way to remind the upper-class youth of the history of their country by integrating it into their lifestyle? Whatever its goal, the friends I was with – all upper-class Lebanese who had grown up during the civil war – were having a good time. They reminisced about time spent in the shelter playing games, not going to school, and got excited when the DJ played a song they had not heard since those days.

That summer of 2005 was the time of my first visit to Lebanon, and "1975" was the first indicator of the ambiguous role that war plays in the lives of all Lebanese, but specifically in the lives of the upper-class youth. When I came back in April 2006 to further research this issue with "1975" as a starting point, however, the bar no longer existed. In its stead was a futuristic-looking lounge with the name "1975-2015: 40 years later," furnished entirely in white without so much as a hint to the previous "1975" decoration. When I asked around for the reason of the change in theme – was it not as successful as it seemed at the time? – my friends answered that any bar in Beirut will have to change at least once a year if it wants to retain its clientele. Those who had visited the bar further added that the decoration simply wasn't well done "and besides – those sandbags were really uncomfortable."

Within a few months, however, I found myself again in a combination of nightlife and war: the fighting between Israel and Hezbollah was taken to new extremes in July 2006, just as the country (and specifically its upper class) was expecting the most peaceful and prosperous summer in decades. Far from coming to a complete standstill, however, society – and also the glamorous Beiruti night-life – adapted and continued. It became clear to me that just like in times of peace when the upper class identified with and through nightlife, so did they in times of war – the resulting discourse of national identity, however, being in sharp contrast with their peace-time narratives.

What follows is a description of the Lebanese upper-class youth in peace and in war times, with a close-up of their nightly lifestyles, through which I will be tracing their narrative of national identity and belonging and the change it undergoes from one situation (peace) to another (war).

"WE ARE ALL THE SAME" – THE LEBANESE UPPER CLASS

Although they hardly make up more than 5 per cent of the population, the Lebanese upper class and its lifestyle are very visible in society and in Lebanon's reputation abroad. I chose to focus my research on the upper-class youth for practical reasons of language and accessibility of informants on one hand, but mainly because I think anthropology too often takes society's elites for granted, assuming a shared understanding of their motives and reasoning that completely overlooks the differences in what being "upper class" means across societies.

I did not have a hard and fast definition of who exactly belongs to the upper class and who doesn't. To determine my research population, I looked at family background, living situation, education, employment, income, and my inform-ants' social circle, although the last one usually follows from the first four. These criteria also reflect the idea that there are many aspects to 'class' beyond income – as Bourdieu stresses, social stratification depends on *and* is expressed by "eco-nomic capital (in its different forms), cultural capital, social capital, and symbolic capital, which is the form that the various species of capital assume when they are perceived and recognized as legitimate." (1989:17)

It follows that my interviewees, men and women in their twenties or early thirties, the sons and daughters of fathers who were businessmen, university professors, or generals in the army and of mothers who were teachers, businesswomen, or housewives, were not part of the more than 95 per cent of the Lebanese population for whom the chaos, the weak economy, and the failing state mean a lack of even the most basic necessities such as electricity and running water. They are not part of the majority of the population that has to live on a minimum wage of $250 a month; of people who on average sustain a family of five with a monthly salary of no more than $500. Instead, they lived with their parents in apartments in well-maintained buildings where running water is available at all times and electricity comes from a private generator, with a janitor to take care of the common areas and wash the cars, and a live-in maid to cook and clean. They usually had their own car, sometimes shared with a sibling, so public transport was hardly used. They had all gone to prominent private universities, such as AUB (American University of Beirut) or LAU (Lebanese American University), or universities in France, the United States, or Canada. Most of them were now working for banks or international firms, their salaries as high as four or five times the average income of a whole Lebanese family. They were internationally oriented and had often traveled outside of the region or gained work-experience in Europe, North America, or (most commonly) one of the Gulf countries.

Religious identity did not feature prominently in their lives, whether they were active believers or not, side-stepping the prevalent political rhetoric of sectarian differences, and displaying instead a strong class identification. This is nothing new among the Lebanese elite according to Peleikis: under Ottoman rule, social boundaries were status-based and drawn between powerful elite families. These families were interdependent, despite their diverse religious backgrounds, and they shared the same code of conduct, distinctive dress, and similar responsibilities and privileges (2001:402-3). As Joelle, one of my interviewees, said about my research population: "We are from the same environment, we have all been to the same schools, we have been to the same universities, we have all done the same majors. [...] You know, we have all followed the same path, there is no variety." In fact, most of the people I interviewed felt they had nothing in common with the poor part of the population. Their cosmopolitan, wealthy lifestyle set them apart from the rest of society, they deemed.

The difference between my research population of upper-class youth and the rest of society was indeed most visible in their lifestyle, particularly in how they would spend their free time away from their family. In sharp contrast to the everyday disorder of daily life in Lebanon with its power-cuts, tumultuous traffic, dust, and noise, they would go to places that were luxurious, organized, and sparkling clean. Instead of getting their clothes from the crowded, grimy markets, they would go to shopping malls with branches of Western stores such as Virgin and Vero Moda and luxurious Lebanese brands such as Aishti; instead of picking up a *manquoushe* (round, flat pizza-like bread covered with thyme, sesame-seeds, and oil or white cheese) at the old, dark bakery on the corner, they would eat fast-food at diners decorated in 1950s American style – their favorite hangouts were not only in appearance but also in prices far removed from the average Lebanese customer.

The same applied to their choice of entertainment in summer: they would make small road-trips to restaurants throughout the country, or go to one of the many private beach-clubs along the coast that charge a $10 admission fee and where the brand of one's car determines how close it will be parked to the entrance. Inside these clubs, one still has to pay for the lounging chairs and tip the waiter, because bringing one's own food and drinks inside is out of the question. And it's not just the staggering costs (compared to the average salary in the country) that would keep the "common wo/man" outside clubs like these; inside, status is everything and nothing escapes the critical eyes of the other visitors, so the wrong brand of sunscreen, or earrings that don't match one's bikini can do serious social harm.

Because the Lebanese upper class is such a small part of an already small population, it often seems like everybody knows everybody – or at least knows someone who knows someone who knows you. For many upper-class youth, this determines to a large extent the behavior they will display. Belonging to the upper class is an insecure status, because it is not static, it is not a "given" identity that one can claim for oneself solely by meeting certain requirements. It is an identity that depends largely on seeing and being seen (especially of the "group" I describe in Lebanon) and thus as being "accepted" by others as such – these others not being automatically part of it either; in- and exclusion are very much a product of group processes following unwritten rules that change with the people and the times. The social status of the people in my research population is a precarious position, one can say, that is carefully maintained through lifestyle (in one's own hands) and gossip (in others'). Wanting to belong to the upper class means that there is a limit to what one can do, and the cultural norms and ideals that govern in- and exclusion of this specific "group" of the Lebanese upper class, and to what extent transgression of these rules can be disregarded or ignored, are nowhere more visible than in nightlife.

"NOTHING SHINES AS BRIGHT AS A BEIRUT NIGHT" – LEBANESE UPPER CLASS NIGHTLIFE

Where daily life in Lebanon can best be described as "chaotic," the most apt adjective for its nightly counterpart would be "regulated," especially when it comes to the upper-class venues. Unwritten rules guide the behavior of visitors of the glamorous venues that since long ago have earned the city its epithet "Paris of the Middle East." This regulated-ness starts even before entering a club: the classier the venue, the more one is expected to make reservations and dress up according to strict dress codes. Like in the previously mentioned beach-clubs, people are seen in nothing but the costliest designer clothes, sporting brand-names from head (sunglasses) to toe (shoes and handbags). The girls' make-up looks as if they are going on stage – eyes outlined with black kohl, lashes heavy with mascara, eyelids covered in sparkling colors varying from bright blue to gold, lips full of lipstick, earrings and necklaces glittering in the spotlights. The men are no less groomed, every hair held in the right place by hairspray that makes it all look glued together. Expensive watches, the latest model phones – everything gleams and shines like gold and diamonds.

From the moment of arrival everything is subjected to rigid order and procedures: the valet-parking will put the cars in order of status – the most expensive vehicle is put closest to the entrance; the hostess will make sure everyone gets seated at the right (VIP-)table; and the waiters are all dressed in similar attire, often a shirt and a tie. On a summer night at a club like "Crystal" in Rue Monot, a famous night-life area, one could spend the whole evening admiring the large variety of Ferraris, Lamborghinis, Porsches, and big and shiny SUVs of the club's customers. If you show up in anything less fancy, car- or fashion-wise, you will need connections with the owner or a very wealthy customer to be allowed to enter.

As said before, this nightlife, at least the visible part, is to be an area of organized beauty, an antidote to the dirt and chaos of the day. The nightclub is the best place to show off riches because the environment is designed in such a manner as to optimize flaunting wealth and confirming social status. Thus, the walls of the nightclub are covered in mirrors and disco-balls reflect the moving spotlights, breaking the beams of light into thousands of tiny spots that mingle with the guests' glittering jewelry. The music is too loud to engage in conversation, but the popular songs from all over the world are perfect for dancing. Some girls get on the bar – lifted by strong men – to have a better view of the crowd, sensually moving their hips. When a wealthy guy orders a bottle of champagne with a price-tag of a staggering $1750, however, all attention is redirected to the accompanying spectacle – the bottle is delivered to the client accompanied by the DJ's drum-roll and followed by a spotlight, from the bar all the way to his table, for the rest of the club to see.

All of this enables the visitors to project an image of being secure and in control. Being able to afford spending literally hundreds of dollars on alcohol in a single night, maybe even several nights a week, means they are not bothered about life in the way so many others in the country are. On the contrary – here they can treat their friends to an expensive bottle of whisky, and another one and another one and then one more, and act as if the city is theirs when they tip the valet-parking guy and leave the club in their expensive cars, drunk but always able to drive.

Like Van de Port, who focused on the so-called "gypsy bars" in Serbia to understand the war-torn society of the Balkans in the early 1990s, I turn to Victor Turner, according to whom "cultural 'performances' [in the broad sense of the word] are eyes by which a culture sees itself and a drawing board on which creative actors sketch out what they believe to be more apt or interesting 'designs for living.'" (Van de Port 1998:5) This leads Van de Port to ask exactly "what sort of design for living is sketched in these venues" (ibid), a question that is very relevant in the Lebanese situation as well. If I am understanding correctly the "cultural performance" of the Lebanese upper class (particularly in nightlife) and the symbolic actions and representations of its aesthetics, what I see is a meticulously painted image of a people that is well off, secure and in control, with not a single worry in the world; a people that remains civilized even when the opportunity presents itself to be the opposite.

Nightlife is *par excellence* the place where class boundaries are produced and reproduced; where those who are unable to project this materialistic image of well-being (or image of materialistic well-being?) are excluded from those who can show how civilized they are by the way they entertain themselves. Although incomparable in terms of aesthetics, Sharryn Kasmir's study about the formation of Basque identity among the youth in Mondragón (Spain) through shared hangouts (punk bars) is of value here. She notes the importance of bars as a "stable and dependable milieu for collective experience" as well as a place where the youth experimented with or even adopted the Basque identity, an identity that, according to her, did not depend so much on heritage as it did on a certain lifestyle (Kasmir, 2002). It is not a big stretch to apply her argument to the Beiruti nightlife-scene when it comes to the formation or rather reinforcement of "class": the rather exclusive character of many bars and clubs (if only because of the cost of the drinks) makes it that only a selective group of people (the upper class) visits these places over and over again, enjoying the same drinks and the same atmosphere, thus creating shared experiences. In order to belong to this crowd or social group, then, it becomes essential to be seen in exactly these bars and clubs, or in the magazines that publish the pictures from the events in these venues. This is an example of what Bourdieu calls a "social space [that] tends to function as [a] symbolic space, as [a] space of lifestyles and status groups characterized by different lifestyles." (1989:20) Bars and clubs become much more than places to entertain oneself or drown one's sorrow in alcohol; they become the "stage" on which the upper-class acts "performs" its ideas about itself and the world around it (as mentioned in the introduction) and reinforces its boundaries. As my interviewee Ahmad said: "Nightlife is a big part of the country. People relate to each other through nightlife. They meet each other through nightlife. [...] In the end, with us, different ideas, but at the end of the day, it's a drink that we share."

From the interviews it became very clear how much the nightlife as they know it put my interviewees apart from the rest of the population: "The other Lebanese people are ... not different but they have another life-style. We are a little bit like Europeans, and we want to be like Europeans and we want to live like them, but Lebanese people are not like this. They are more conservative, more religious ... They don't go out like this," Sabine said. The explanation offered usually had the argument of religion lurking in the background, but the main reasoning was most often something like Sandra's: "People who go out on the Corniche are really people who cannot afford ... they bring their arguileh with them, and this is their weekly outing – it doesn't cost much. Going into bars, it costs money!" To my interviewees, these were two types of people who definitely don't mix.

"SERIOUS FUN" – MORE LEBANESE UPPER-CLASS NIGHTLIFE

As I mentioned before, the most important feature of upper-class nightlife in Lebanon is not its glamorousness or luxuriousness, but how well regulated it is. It is set up to maximize appearance and showing off, both of wealth and of being in control, and this creates a lot of social pressure. Sandra, a well-dressed young woman who I have never seen without make-up, put it this way: "It's a country of appearances. [...] You cannot wear the same clothes twice, at least not for an outing. I think it's because you just need to prove yourself. And we have very high standards." Because nightlife is the place where class boundaries are produced and re-produced, it is important to make sure to maintain proper behavior at all times, even when drinking and dancing.

Although most interviewees stressed that they would go out to have fun and get away from the concerns of daily life, and Lebanese nightlife may *appear* to be all about unlimited extravagance, its regulated-ness and the accompanying social control make it incomparable to almost any other anthropological explanation of fun and nightlife. For example, even though people might end up dancing on the table, this is in no way similar to the bar clientele as described by Van de Port, who "launch their attack on etiquette and abandon themselves to an orgiastic violation of their everyday endeavours" (1998:9) – dancing on the table is a way to show off one's dancing skills and expensive outfit, not a funny act performed in a drunken frenzy that would be unthinkable being sober, and definitely not a way to experience one's inner passions or taste the "wilder pleasures of life." The "fun" that Samir and Ahmad referred to when they told me: "We are an active people. We enjoy life to the max, life is too short," and: "The Lebanese people, they like to enjoy their time. It's something that's in the people; they like to go out, they like to have fun," is almost the complete opposite of Bayat's definition of it in his study of the politics of fun in Iran: "[fun is] an array of ad hoc, nonroutine, and joyful conducts [...] – where individuals break free temporarily from the disciplined constraints of daily life, normative obligations and organized power. 'Fun' is a metaphor for the expression of individuality, spontaneity, and lightness, in which joy is the central element' (2007:434), definitely so when it comes to upper-class nightlife. A case in point is the attitude towards alcohol consumption."

In the fancy bars and clubs of Beirut, hardly anyone orders a simple beer; mix-drinks with hard liquor such as vodka and whisky are very popular, and so are cocktails and champagne. Alcohol consumption in Beiruti nightlife is very high and my interviewees made sure to tell me so, but they were also very adamant in telling me that "Lebanese can handle their alcohol very well," that they know how to hold their liquor. Wondering why they drink so much, I was given the same reasons as to why people go out in the first place and why they are so concerned with looks and status: it is a way to fight of the feeling of insecurity that comes with living in Lebanon, a way to forget the troubles and concerns of daily life. As Myrna said: "Lebanese people drink too much. They are very oppressed, and they need something to release it. They are very stressed, and if they are not stressed they stress themselves somehow. They're always on the run. The way they work, the way they talk to each other. That's why they need a lot of alcohol, to wash it out."

So far, it may sound like the stereotypical images that come to mind when thinking of groups of people going out and drinking excessively: drunken groups rolling around in the street fighting, crawling across the bar and vomiting in public. But my interviewees assured me that Lebanese people are not like that. Samir compared the Lebanese with the English: "In Cyprus, for example, there is a bar for English people, so we don't go to it because they are trouble-makers. When they get drunk, they act roughly. Even the Germans ... We don't have this! We are nice people." To which Yves added: "Lebanese are friendly, they always stay friendly." Sandra said people don't even get drunk at all; "we drink a lot, but we don't get drunk, very few people get really drunk. We just go out to have fun and forget and laugh and ... see people, meet people, talk about them ..." Interestingly enough, it happened to most of them once or twice – they got insanely drunk and spilled their dinner all over the table, or had a one-night stand and cheated on their girlfriend – but never in Lebanon. These things always happened when they were living abroad and hanging out with non-Lebanese. Even when talking about those moments, they carefully picked their language not to make it sound too harsh. Like Lila, who told me: "There was never any alcohol restriction for me, nor education. I was in control of myself. Once I wasn't, on a trip with the basketball team in the Ukraine. I hugged the toilet-seat, so to speak ... [laughs]. But never again, ever!"

Only once did I see a girl who had had one drink too many, throwing up in the bathroom in "Asia", a rooftop bar in the posh downtown area of Beirut. All the other girls waiting in line carefully looked away and only the hostess was there to hand her a glass of water when she was done. The girl fixed her skirt and her hair and then returned to her friends, who pretended everything was fine and they hadn't seen the state she was in when she left the table. All in all it was only the excess of alcohol that was best kept secret; drinking alcohol seemed to be widely accepted. My friends and interviewees were very clear about why this was the case: social pressure. Wissam thought he would never get completely drunk and out of control because "it wouldn't look that nice. [...] You don't want to give a bad image of yourself, it wouldn't look good." Beirut is tiny and everybody knows everybody – especially in the nightly scene – so one misstep can ruin a reputation. According to Myrna people do get staggering drunk, but "it doesn't show because they are conscious of others, they care about what others say, how they look at them ... Oh, if they meet someone they know, that's total disaster. Because the community of people who go out is very small, and chances of you getting to see people you know are very high. So they wouldn't really go crazy, it's not a big country where nobody knows you and you can do whatever you want. You might be talked about the next day and you'd regret it ..."

To some, this almost inescapable form of social control – always having to stay in control and bearing the responsibility to uphold the reputation of not only yourself but also the people around you such as your friends and your family – felt like a burden. To others, this distinguished Lebanese nightlife from the party-scene everywhere else in the world; it made it fun and civilized, and hence a very nice place to be. Either way, it should be clear that the "serious fun" of Lebanese upper-class nightlife is in stark contrast with definitions of fun like Bakhtin's, who sees fun as almost equal to laughter, which means "the defeat of power ... of all that suppresses and restricts" (in Bayat 2007:453). It is not meant to "defy normal hierarchies" or "rebel against authority" (ibid.), rather it is a way of having fun controlled and delineated by the unwritten rules of social control.

In many ways, night-time can be considered the opposite of day. It is dark, and in many societies there are different rules at night – things that are frowned upon during the day are considered acceptable at night. For many people in other countries in the world, night is the time that they can let go of the responsibilities they have during the day, they can forget about work, they can dress differently and behave differently, especially after a few glasses of alcohol. It seems as if the Lebanese upper class trades one kind of worries for another one: instead of having to deal with the insecurities of living in a politically tumultuous region, they have to worry about their hair, their clothes, their make-up, and most of all their behavior. Of course they also have to think about their reputation during the day, but with no alcohol, drugs, and seductive men and women dancing and parading around that is probably a lot less hard. It is at night-time that they are most aware of their social status, and of how they have to follow the unwritten rules that mark the boundaries of their social "group" in order to reinforce that status.

The performance of "serious fun" of the glamorous yet regulated nightlife of Lebanon not only defines the boundaries of the upper-class, it also determines their place in society (and, by extension, the rest of the world); they are often seen as outsiders. The much more "apt" and "interesting" designs for living (see Van de Port, earlier) that are sketched out by the Lebanese upper class are in such sharp contrast with the realities of daily life of the majority of the population that they are often labeled superficial, and their luxury lifestyle is often considered to be "fake", by others as well as amongst themselves. They are often seen as not being part of the country due to their international lifestyle – theirs is considered a "typical" Lebanese-ness, not a "real" one, as they would say. And this is a distinction that, as we will see, can only be bridged by war.

A DEFINING EXPERIENCE? – LEBANESE SOCIETY AND WAR

Considering the fact that almost half of its independent years have been spent at war – with itself or with others – it is no surprise that the Lebanese population has developed a discourse of national identity in which war plays a big role. That war against a foreign power can serve to unify a population seems only natural (us against them), but due to the intricacies of Lebanese society and the divisions and alliances among its people and the contacts with outside forces, it is rare for the whole country to rally behind one cause even during war and as such it does not play its obvious role. Instead, it gives Lebanese people an opportunity to feel united over something more personal and hence less controversial: their supposed resilience. "We lived in it and we somehow accepted it as normal life. It lasted 15 years, so everyone in Beirut who got married during the war, or had children during the war, will tell you that life continued. That is why it is very important to show war not as an exotic thing, but just as one way of living life. When I was a kid I used to think this was normal, that the whole world lived in war. I didn't know what peace was. We are human beings and we accept and adapt" (in Jaafar, 2004). With these words, Director Danielle Arbid not only states that war can be normal, "just another way of living life"; she also reasserts the humanity of the Lebanese exactly because they "accept and adapt" and live life as if war is how it is meant to be.

It was mostly the older people I met or interviewed, those who had been teenagers or young adults at the time, who assured me of the "normalness" of life during war, or rather, how normal war is in Lebanese life. "Our social life during the war was very normal – going to school and back unless there was 'some war,'" said Alexandre. "You get used to it, we don't pay attention until it's right on top of us. It was normal for us. Sometimes we would be afraid of getting hit by a stray bullet, but mainly we were just used to it – it was normal." Many times they drew comparisons with the current war in Iraq, and expressed their contempt for those "barbarians" who let go of all civilized behavior and completely lost control, raiding and ransacking stores and public buildings, looting and plundering museums and banks. In their eyes, it's one thing to have a war, but it's another thing to misbehave in such a way. Proudly they proclaimed that I should go and take a look in the National Museum in Beirut, where no item in the whole collection had been damaged during the entire war – conveniently forgetting about the fact that almost all sculptures had been encased in thick concrete covers at the beginning of the war, this protection only to be patiently and painstakingly removed quite a while after the mayhem was over. "Mind you," they would tell me, as Hassan did, "nothing criminal happened in Lebanon during the war. Other than the killing and the snipers and these war-things, there was no 'crime,' it was still 'safe'. It was a 'clean' war. No one took advantage of the situation. They stayed with their sects and followed their leaders." Or as Arlette Tawil Jreissati, judge and president of Lebanon's Labor Court, says:

> "... Look at what happened in New York when you had a blackout ten years ago. People went on a rampage. They vandalized stores and private property. In Lebanon, we have lived not only with a blackout for seventeen years, but with no government, nothing – only militiamen and outlaws everywhere. How many crimes did we have during this period? Well, as a percentage, we had almost nothing compared to other very civilized countries with a government, a police force, and a strong army" (in Lateef 1997:183).

This is in complete contradiction to what Samir Khalaf, professor at the American University of Beirut, notices during the war: that "violence has not been confined to the warring factions involved in the political struggle. It has spilled over into other segments of society." He goes on to say that "a significant portion of the society has been living unlawfully" (1982:57-8), naming crimes such as vandalism, looting, and pirating of public utilities, amongst others. If the people who told me their "clean" stories of the war were trying to find a place in the collective memory to deal with this less-than-presentable part of their past, they had found the ultimate one: by blatantly denying the unlawful behavior of their compatriots and instead depicting them as ultimately civilized, war can be seen not only as a normal state of being, it is also something that the Lebanese are better at than any other country or population! Elias Khoury, a Lebanese intellectual, believes that this is "the most tragic thing about the Lebanese civil war": "that it is not a tragedy in the consciousness of the Lebanese" (in Haugbolle 2005:197).

As with any nationalistic quality, the famous "resilience" has a starting point in history, but it is claimed to be timeless – or at least going back further than anyone could possibly remember. "It is this ability to go on leading our lives that has enabled us to survive seventeen years of war," said Bahia Hariri, a member of parliament and chair of the Parliamentary Committee on Education, in an interview; "the Lebanese people live for the moment; they don't think about tomorrow. This is not a new attitude; this has always been the mentality of the Lebanese people from way back" (in Lateef 1997:175). When Lebanese talk about their incredible ability to continue living, to continue their lives during war, they go back through "decades" of war and "centuries" of invasions, battles, and occupations.

This shared narrative of resilience may exist to be able to cope with the situation (without causing friction within the population as a whole), it may serve to not feel completely helpless and powerless in the face of overwhelming adversity, but at the same time, it can be seen as a statement, a message for the outside world as much as for the Lebanese themselves. In Novi Sad, according to Van de Port, a popular explanation for the outbreak of the war was 'after all, these are the Balkans' – hinting at the inevitableness of the use of violence in a region with 'uncivilized' people. My research population in Beirut turned this way of reasoning upside down: it's not that there is war *because* we are, after all, in Lebanon (although this often seemed to be what was being said); no, we are Lebanon *because* there is a war. The war is what makes Lebanon Lebanon.

When presenting themselves to the world outside of Lebanon, mainly to the West, the war is the ultimate stage on which the upper class can enact its civilized-ness: contrary to what one may expect during a war, there is said to be no crime and no chaos; instead it is a model for organized-ness and self-regulation. War is often considered to be the ultimate breakdown of civilization, yet the Lebanese upper class projects an image of being almost more civilized in war-time than in "normal" times.

DISCOURSE VS. REAL LIFE – LEBANESE UPPER-CLASS YOUTH DURING THE JULY 2006 WAR

It was barely three months into my research when the war between Israel and Hezbollah/Lebanon broke out in July 2006. Israel bombed the airport, the southern suburbs of Beirut, villages in the South and the Bekaa valley, and some of the border crossings with Syria. Embassies scrambled to evacuate their visiting citizens and Lebanese with double nationalities. Public life came to a standstill – for a while. After an initial period of trying to assess the gravity and direct danger of the situation, in many parts of the country and its capital, people who had not left slowly began to pick up (parts of) their daily routine.

The fact that many of my research population had not left was not always their own choice. They cited work, no visa for any other country, and the closed airport and roads as reasons. Some stayed in Lebanon simply because they wanted to. When I asked Carla why she did not leave the country, she said: "Because it's home! I have my job, my friends here. I am sure that if I were younger, my parents would have left the country, like my sister did now [with her daughter]. But I'm established here. Maybe if the war had lasted longer ... but it's home – as much as it sucks, it's still home!" Sandra expressed the same feeling, albeit less articulate: Although her dad proposed that she and her brother leave several times, she told me she just couldn't get herself to leave. Others gave even more passionate reasons for staying. "I could have gone to

Canada, I could have gone to France, half of my family was there begging me to come. I could have gone to Dubai because I was opening some business in the Gulf, but … I don't know. I don't want to sound corny, but a lot of people said 'khalas, we're going to stay and see what … see it through, you know. I'm not better than the next Lebanese just because I have a [foreign] passport. We have to be here […]' So I couldn't, I couldn't just leave" were Ramzi's words. He was not the only one who expressed this opinion. Many people shared his feeling that they would not let someone else decide for them when they should leave the country. Especially those who had been away for part or all of the 1975-1990 war were determined to stick it out this time.

Since, as I described before, war was seen as inherent to life in Lebanon, I was not surprised to see the come-back of a type of reasoning that I recognized from the stories about the 1975-1990 war: the unwavering belief in the Lebanese resilience and toughness. Once again the Lebanese I spoke to boasted of how strong they were as a people; how daily life continued like normal; and how their resilience kept the country going despite all the destruction. However, this time around, I had seen and experienced it myself: I had seen the panicked people in the supermarket, buying enough food for months. I had seen how quickly the city became deserted and how scared people were to go out at night. And I had also seen how slowly and hesitantly parts of life were picked up – maybe the normal things were getting done, but they were mainly the essentials; the absence of traffic and the empty services (a shared taxi, a popular way of semi-public transport) were a clear indication that definitely not *everyone* was as war-resistant as a Lebanese was supposed to be.

"GOING OUT WHEN THE BOMBS ARE FALLING" – NIGHTLIFE DURING THE WAR

It was not all only a matter of words, though. Rue Monot may have been deserted and without a sign of its pre-war glamour, but those upper-class youth who wanted to go out to drink and dance still could – and did. Several bars in the more low-key areas of Hamra and Gemmayzeh stayed open. So did the clubs in the cities in the North (such as Jbeil and Batroun) and in the mountain areas (such as Faraya and Broumana). Some Beiruti venues even opened up branches in those areas to serve their customers who had fled there from the capital. There was, though, a marked difference in the atmosphere in the different areas. Hamra and Gemmayzeh were generally quieter, with a disproportional number of foreign journalists and photographers recovering from a "day of war." I only passed through the Northern cities, but I did spend a weekend in Faraya, and one could easily believe there was nothing strange going on in the country: the cars, the clothes, the jewelry, it was all as glitzy as ever. A large part of the clientele there was from the area. For them it may have been as if nothing was happening, but many of the clubbers had fled other areas of the country that were under Israeli fire.

Whatever the background and motives of those who kept on going at night, for some people the thought of going out was enough to send them through the roof. "Going for a drink with friends, yes, I could do that. But going out to a nightclub? No way. Not during a war. There are people dying!" exclaimed Faysal. Others, such as Najib, held a completely opposite view: "All my friends say I'm crazy, because I only go out more now that there is war. Hell, if I'm going to die, I want to make the most out of my days!" Yet for most, going to a bar for a drink (or two) was a way to blow off steam, to physically get away from it all: no TV meant no news to worry about. Those who went out tried to get a feeling of "normalness", as Ramzi expressed it, it was an attempt to forget everything that was happening. Going to a bar or club was seen as a "breathing space", a break, a way to deal with the stress and horrifying realities of the war. It was the same argument I had heard for the abundance of nightlife before the war: a place to forget about the worries of daily life, to wash away your sorrows with alcohol if you like. As in Ramzi's story:

> "We used to have a few drinks ... everybody was drinking so much. My parents, during the last war, the civil war, everybody was on valium and taking some pills to relax. This time, everybody, all my friends, me and my wife, everybody was drinking every night, And then the MK [an Israeli reconnaissance plane] ... you know the MK, you're Lebanese now ... so the MK would come zzzzzz and we would moon them after a few drinks, fuck off you know!"

It was not just Ramzi and his friends who needed a drink to get them through tough times. Many others admitted to having resorted to alcohol and other (illegal and legal) drugs to deal with the situation. Although willing to be understanding of people who turned to nightlife and all its vices, other people disdainfully told me that they "had no trouble sleeping through the bombings." They "did not need any outside remedies."

It was not only the alcohol that sparked a controversy. Although "acting like normal" and "continuing life as if nothing was happening" were the proud slogans of many Lebanese, nightlife seemed to be another issue altogether. Looking back upon the atmosphere in the clubs up in the mountains, different people gave me very different accounts: some said it was as if nothing was happening, people were dancing and making merry like they always did. Others were convinced everyone was stressed out and only pretending to be happy. Some expressed their discontent with the party-crowd who continued their routine by focusing on the practical side: how can it be alright in someone's eyes to spend $100 on a bottle of vodka while the country is being destroyed and will have to be rebuilt, when so many refugees finding shelter in schools and parking garages need to be fed and clothed?

Those who objected, however, took the moral high road: how can somebody dance and drink when there are people, fellow Lebanese, getting wounded or dying from bombings?

The sensitivity of the issue is obvious in the words of the owner of "Asia" who reopened his club in Broumana:

> "We told the people that Mondays, half the bill goes to charity. But then I gave all the profits to charity, to help. [...] A lot of magazines came, foreign and local, to do interviews; and TV stations, but I didn't let anyone in because I didn't want anybody to twist it that the Lebanese people are partying and having fun while other people are dying, which was exactly the total opposite. It was more quiet than here [in his bar in Beirut at the time of the interview], it was more of a restaurant-lounge, but we had music and people were ... not dancing but enjoying, getting their stress out, you know, just seeing each other, feeling a bit of normalcy again. Basically that's it."

He added that this was "the Lebanese resilience, you know." To Sonya, going out was indeed a marker of Lebanese resilience. Going clubbing in Broumana did not feel right to her. She knew people in other parts of the country were having a tough time. But out of conviction she went to some of the bars in Gemmayzeh, "to show people that we are still alive ... that Lebanon is still going out." Imad also had no problem in giving me arguments for his "extrovert" behavior during the war. Partly, he took pride in the Lebanese resiliency: "I don't think Europeans would have behaved the same, I don't think so. I don't think someone whose city is getting hit would go to Broumana and have a drink and be relaxed and everything." Yet interestingly, he also claimed he could go out for a drink so often only because he identified it with something bigger than Lebanon. From my conversation with him, I could tell, that not unlike a few of his peers, he was very universal, a true cosmopolitan. Hence, he saw no big difference between children dying in the war in Iraq or in Lebanon when it came to his conscience. He would not allow others to "destroy his life" – or rather, his way of living. Ironically, this way of reasoning is similar to that of the Israeli youth who refused to stay home after a series of suicide-bombings had hit cafés and restaurants, writes Rebecca Stein in an article on Israeli leisure and "Palestinian terror". She calls this a "narrative of defiance through consumerism, whereby the abnegation of normal consumptive patterns was deemed a victory for 'terrorists'." She continues: "Consumption, itself, became an act of defiance, and the constant consumer the defiant citizen-soldier" (Stein, 2002). According to her, this discourse borrowed heavily from the post-September 11 narratives in the Western media and was quickly picked up by the Israeli press. This did not happen with the press in Lebanon, leaving the narrative of consumerism as a private discourse of the consumers. It was up to the Lebanese clubbers themselves to explain their behavior in terms of "true Lebanese resilience," even if part of it was just keeping up appearances, as I understood from a conversation with Pamela and Maya shortly after the war:

Pamela: Where shall we go? Downtown is packed now!
Me: Yeah, why wasn't it during the war?
Maya: They were scared! You never know where bombs might fall.
Pamela: No! They don't care. But you can't party when other people are dying.
Me: Well they were partying up in Faraya and they had no problem with that ...
Pamela: Ah, but don't forget where you are. Here [in Beirut], you can't do that, it's too close, you know, people will see you.
Maya: Exactly. I mean, it's not like people stop dying when others party.

It is clear that the "continuing nightlife as normal" was not as easily accepted as Lebanese resilience as were the arguileh-smoking ways of the refugees from the Southern villages and suburbs. All these were taken as signs of defiance, a proud statement against Israel. It seemed that, once again, "real Lebanese" was tied up with suffering and hardship, almost impossible to achieve for the upper class. Yet even though the continued clubbing of the Beiruti party-crowd was seen by many as "un-Lebanese", their own application of the discourse of resilience indicates otherwise.

"FAKE" OR "REAL" – THE DISCOURSE OF NATIONAL IDENTITY OF THE LEBANESE UPPER-CLASS YOUTH

It is as if the "real" Lebanese identity of war and the "fake" (superficial) upper-class identity of nightlife are mutually exclusive. Yet the adherence of the people from the upper class to the stories of resilience and civilized behavior during war show their attempts at bridging the gap between war and their lifestyles. These stories show that they want to belong to their country, including their lifestyle.

Although seemingly having the same meaning, "typical" and "real" were used by my respondents to denote two very different things. Typical is the lifestyle of the upper class – rich, cosmopolitan, glamorous, superficial – representing, or rather *appearing* to be Lebanese. Real is the rest of society, those who are poor and suffer. Real is war. War, because this is when society shows what is hiding beneath the surface. "[W]ar serves as a moment of truth, a moment when individuals – be they soldiers or civilians – have to define their deeply held priorities and act on them" (Faust, 2004:377). It is no surprise, then, that many from the Lebanese upper class – modern, and nation-wide understood to be superficial, "fake", and thus outside of the rest of society – take the war as an opportunity to assert their "real-ness" through a discourse that stresses their similarity with the rest of the Lebanese population and includes them in the narrative creation of a national unity of sorts. By continuing throughout war to live according to their regular lifestyles (which includes going to the beach, shopping and, most of all, going to expensive bars and clubs almost every night), they show the same resilience as those refugees who fled the South and were now sitting on the *corniche* (the sea-shore boulevard in Beirut that runs from Ein Mreisse to Ramlet el Bayda) smoking their arguileh. This attitude, of going on as normal – as if nothing is happening (whether this attitude exists mainly verbally or also in practice) – bridges the gap between the different social classes in Lebanon. It is, as they say themselves, what makes the Lebanese Lebanese, and Lebanon Lebanon.

War was somehow seen as "the real thing". It meant that everything had come down to "the basics of life and death," as Charif said when I called him at his house in Saida, and he continued: "as long as someone picks up the phone, they're alive, and that's all that matters." Some others said it brought them back to a state of survival; all they cared about was the safety of their family. A sense of urgency was prevalent among many people – the awareness that really, every day could be the last. I chatted with my friend Reina, a Lebanese girl living in New York City, on the first day of the war, and she told me: "There is a rush, a blood rush, of having lived this before. Something VERY familiar. We've lived in war more than we lived in peace, and frankly, being at war makes you feel very alive." In her eyes, war was more real than anything else: "The Lebanese have been dead in the past 15 years ... becoming superficial, caring only about cars and cell phones, to forget ... not to think. Now they are alive again."

From a story to cope with the hardships and traumatic experiences of war, the narrative of resilience has turned into a discourse that shapes the national identity. And it is no wonder that the Lebanese cling to this story so dearly; it is one of the few that does not invoke the existing or imagined differences between the many political and religious groups in the country, as so many other war-discourses do. One can imagine that this is another reason why this discourse appeals to the upper class despite the fact that their living conditions are, even during war, so much better than those for whom resilience literally means survival: they do not *want* to turn to the war-narratives of their religious compatriots, because that is not how they usually identify either. In their lives, class is a much more distinctive feature than religion.

War thus becomes the defining element of Lebanese-ness, for Lebanese of *any* class or group. I heard it from so many of my friends, I read it on blogs and in books: war is "real". These are the moments that count, that make the blood rush through the veins, the important events that go down in the annals of history. As such, they are in sharp contrast with the superficial, "fake" (night)life of the upper class in peacetime. Yet through the above-described narrative, a period of war gives the upper class the chance to shake off their "outsider status" even when they continue to live the luxurious life: after all, it is due to their much-praised resilience that they are still partying despite the bombs that are falling. From "typically Lebanese" as is going out in peace-time, it becomes "real Lebanese": continuing the pre-war lifestyle is an act of resistance and thus the ultimate sign of Lebanese-ness. And should it be that one can't go out and party, even if this is only because of a feared lack of fuel due to a blockade, then one suffers like all the other Lebanese. As Nidal said: "all we share in this country is suffering." Thus, their discourse about the war and about their own actions during the war (whether their words were a truthful account of their behavior or not) help to ensure both their cultural identity/class *and* their national identity – it includes them in the upper class at the same time as it makes them part of the wider Lebanese population and hence "guarantees" their belonging to the country. To be able to keep up this narrative of resilience, war becomes a necessity: true Lebanese-ness can only be proven in times of war. The war tells the Lebanese people: you belong here; at the same time destroying exactly that which they belong to.

The way I see it is that the war-narrative of my respondents is an exercise in belonging. It is impossible to let go, just as it is impossible to belong to a country that constantly "mistreats" you. There is a sense of longing for belonging that resounds in every word these young, wealthy people speak about their country, whether it is about Lebanon in peace or in war. The over-enthusiastic ways they speak about their country, waxing poetically about its beautiful features – they are an antidote to the perpetual awareness of the country's troubled state of existence, aimed as much at luring in a potential visitor as at convincing the speaker him- or herself. Their narrative of resilience is a frank rejection of the destruction of their country, showing that they will not give up now that they finally belong; and most of all, their stories show that war is at the core of the Lebanese identity, in past, present, and personal.

Part 4

Militancy and Street Violence

Male Gender and Rituals of Resistance in Palestinian Intifada

A Cultural Politics of Violence

Julie Peteet

This paper examines the attainment and enactment of manhood and masculinity among Palestinian male youths in relation to ritualized beatings and detention in the occupied West Bank. The beatings (and detention) are framed as rites of passages now central in the construction of an adult, gendered (male) self with critical consequences for political consciousness and agency. While central to discussions of bodily violence, a Foucaultian analysis does little to focus attention on the way in which the subaltern interprets the practices of violence and power. In shifting the discussion to the recipients of violent practices, the focus is on the symbolic role of active agency in the interplay of power and transformation. As a methodological strategy to approach the terrain of cultural resistance to domination, I examine ritual performances that, in effect, inscribe power on the body and their subsequent construal as a rite of passage by one set of performers – those who are beaten or imprisoned – as an instance of the social construction of a male gender and resistant subjectivity. The beating is cast as performance in the sense that interaction between participants and audience (Schieffelin, 1985:710) is critical to the meaning and efficiency of the ritual in a social rather than simply cognitive sense. Brenneis calls our attention to audiences as "not solely targets for rhetorical strategies; they are, rather, active interpreters, critics and respondents" (1987:237).

To illustrate the points elaborated above, I examine the Israeli policy and practice of beating and imprisoning young Palestinian males in the Occupied Territories during the intifada (uprising) (1987) as constitutive of gender and power. I will argue that a Palestinian construal of the practice of violence as a rite of passage into manhood that galvanizes political consciousness and agency is a creative and dynamic act of resistance; a trick, if you will. After a brief discussion of inscriptions of power on the body, I turn to an ethnographic account of applications of violence. The article concludes with a discussion of ritualized physical violence as a transformative experience that galvanizes one set of participants to unsettle power arrangements. At the same time, it both reaffirms and transforms internal Palestinian forms of power. As such, this text involves the intersection of several themes: ritual performance and political agency, bodily inscriptions of power and the construction of manhood in the Middle East, and the transformation and reproduction of relations of domination.

RITUAL, OPPOSED MEANINGS, AND REVERSAL

The anthropological literature increasingly displays less hesitancy to view symbols and rituals from the perspective of empowerment and the establishment of authority (Aronoff 1982; Kertzer 1988). The anthropology of ritual often assumed a generalized continuity of cultural categories and meaning for the participants in ritual performances, given that the ethnography on rituals was, by and large, conducted on single-cultural groups, without, however, assuming an essentializing homogeneity. As I shall argue, and as Schieffelin suggests, participants in ritual may not all experience the same significance or efficacy.

> Indeed, unless there is some kind of exegetical supervision of both performance and interpretation by guardians of orthodoxy, the performance is bound to mean different things to different people. In the absence of any exegetical canon one might even argue that there was no single "correct" or "right" meaning for a ritual at all (1985:722).

Kertzer calls attention to the multivocal quality of symbols in ritual to refer to their capacity to embody a variety of meanings (1988:11). Given the absence of a canon and the contingent, multivocal nature of rituals and symbols, I will show that, where power relations are vastly asymmetrical between ethnically and nationally distinct groups, ritual may have opposed rather than simply different meanings and may lead to a practice designed to overthrow the ritual itself and its political context. According to Schieffelin, the efficacy of a ritual, what it does and how it does it, is to be located less in the text and its cultural categories of meaning and more in the "emerging relation between the performer and the other participants (and the participants among themselves) while the performance is in progress" (1985:722).

I would like to take Schieffelin's argument about ritual performances meaning different things to different people in a novel direction, to a situation where people stand in rather starkly opposed positions of power and powerlessness as a consequence of belonging to different and opposed national and cultural groups. I would suggest, however, that if ritual performances take place in a highly charged atmosphere of domination and crisis and are then cast as relations of power, they may inform a political agency designed to overthrow the domination of one set of performers. Thus ritual, while certainly a system of meaning and its communication can simultaneously foreground a human agency with consequences for the power of its performers. In short, the consequences of ritual can be manifested in attempts to reverse the social order of hierarchies and relations of domination.

If we acknowledge that the cultural meaning of symbols can be construed in diametrically opposed ways for the participants in a ritual who themselves stand in hierarchical opposition to one another, what does this mean then for the question of agency? The potential for agential empowerment arising from ritual has been noted by anthropologists who study ritual in the context of politics. Kertzer argues that rituals do more than simply maintain and reaffirm the status quo; they can be galvanized to accomplish things. They overturn political orders, and opposition politics can be expressed in "rites of delegitimation" (1988:2). Incidentally, The Rites of Ashura, a ritual commemoration of the death of the Prophet's grandson Hussein, engaged in by the Shi'a of the Middle East (Iraq, Southern Lebanon, and Iran), is such an example. The playing of specific roles in the play reflects the power structure of a society at a particular moment, and the ritual itself has opposed meanings for its participants. In Hegland's analysis of Ashura rituals during the Iranian Revolution of the late 1980s, she confirms that participation in a ritual "does not necessarily indicate that all participants share the same mindset or ideology or even that they all consider themselves to be or wish to be members of the same social or political group" (1983:90). In representing a reversal of the social order, Ashura rituals in revolutionary Iran were crucial symbolic and real agents of the "complete overthrow of the political, economic, and social order" (1983:96). Gilsenan indicates that the drama of Hussein, while seemingly a fixed, immutable religious ritual central to Shi'a belief and practice, is socially produced in specific social historical contexts. In both turn-of-the-century Iran and Lebanon, it gave dramatic expression and enactment to relations of powerlessness/powerfulness while also presenting, in the case of Iran, an image of the world that reverses the social order. In Southern Lebanon, the drama confirmed the existing social order when the "learned families," the sheikhs, were losing power and prestige to an emergent peasant-trader group (1982:55-74).

BODIES

As the most personal and intimate realm of the self, bodies are the most striking sites for the inscription of power (Outram 1989) and the encoding of culture (Combs-Schilling 1991). Foucault eloquently captures the body/politics equation when he writes, "the body is also directly involved in a political field; power relations have an immediate hold upon it; they invest it, mark it, train it, torture it, force it to carry out tasks, to perform ceremonies, to emit signs" (1979:25). Combs-Schilling persuasively argues that "durable systems of domination are often ones in which the structures of power are so embedded within the body of self that the self cannot be easily abstracted from them" (1991:658). The daily inscription of power on the unwilling bodies of Palestinians, almost a routine occurrence, is an attempt to embed power in them as a means of fashioning a domesticated subject whose terrorized silence would confirm the mythical Zionist landscape of an empty Palestine. Through bodily violence, the occupier desires not just to fashion a laborer but equally to assure a quiescent population, one sufficiently terrorized so as not to engage in acts of rebellion. For example, in the drive to create a state in 1948, Israel did not seek to win Palestinian consent to the Zionist project or ideology, only to ensure either flight or nonrebellion (by those who stayed). But, unlike the Moroccan situation of which Combs-Schilling writes, it gives rise instead to an oppositional political agency.

Foucault's view of the body as text, as a site of inscription and exhibition by dominant forces, shows little concern with people's responses to having their bodies appropriated and designated as sites of inscription. In short, he does not concern himself much with the individual's consciousness of himself or herself in the historical process. English historian E. P. Thompson's (1978:79) call for restoring the subject to the history-making process dovetails neatly with anthropology's contemporary concern with integrating history, culture, and the individual. One can do this by approaching the body from the standpoint of its owners, who are always more than inscriptive sites, as they creatively respond by challenging the prevalent political order (Outram 1989). Outram argues in her discussion of the French Revolution that "bodies are active creators of new power relations and sustain individuals in their confrontations with and against systems of power" (1989:23). E. Martin astutely shows how an alternative discourse and conception of the body exists that challenges the legitimacy of the hegemonic medico-scientific discourse that constitutes knowledge of, and thus a crucial basis for control over, women's physiological processes from menstruation and childbirth to menopause. She also asserts that "Because their bodily processes go with them everywhere, forcing them to juxtapose biology and culture, women glimpse every day a conception of another sort of social order" (1987:200).

The occupation is, similarly, a daily accompanying presence governing one's physical state of being. Mobility, safety, and daily routine are out of the control of Palestinians under occupation. Occupation is a daily shared experience that is subject to continuous questioning and widespread rejection. A prominent mode of embedding the power of the dominant group is to beat, daily and publicly, Palestinian male bodies. Like monarchal spectacles of public torture, the public beating, widespread during the intifada, is a representation of the power of the occupier, encoding and conveying a message about the consequences of oppositional expressions and practices.

The body, however, does not merely represent. Bodies also signify contradictions in everyday experiences (Comaroff 1985:8). The Palestinian interpretation and organization of this experience is strikingly at odds with the meaning underlying Israeli actions. With these measures, Israel intended to control, humiliate, and punish; the ultimate, publicly recognized, and reiterated aim was to quell resistance. In other words, public spectacles of violence serve as a means of encoding and reproducing the Palestinians as Israel's acquiescent, though not consenting, "other." The intent was not to normalize social life under occupation but to rule through what Taussig called in the Latin American context the "strategic art of abnormalizing" (1990:219). Public violence was not meant to fashion homeostasis but to give rise to a continuous situation of crisis and instability as a way of putting obstacles in the way of Palestinian political organizing.

But the Palestinians made of the signs something radically different. These were experiences of transformation and empowerment, not humiliation and pacification. These experiences have been construed as rites of passage into manhood, with its attendant status and responsibilities, and concomitantly as vehicles of entry and, to a large extent, initiation into underground political leadership. For the community under occupation, the signs inscribed on the individual bodies were read as a collective assault and a commentary on suffering (see Keesing 1985, and Peteet 1987). I set these opposed interpretations into a dialogic frame whereby meaning is created in the process of engagement between, in this case, two asymmetrical forces. The meaning of the beating and its construal as a rite of passage into manhood, with its attendant agential imperatives, has resonance throughout the occupied territories, upsetting established hierarchies of generation, nationality, and class yet reproducing and reaffirming other hierarchies such as gender.

MANHOOD AND RITES OF PASSAGE IN THE MIDDLE EAST

Masculinity is neither natural nor given. Like femininity, it is a social construct. Herzfeld argues that, in a Cretan village, there is more stress on how rather than on what men do – what counts is "performative excellence" (1985:16). Gilmore notes that a "critical threshold" is passed by various forms of tests and ordeals (1990:11). While cautious of the perils of essentializing the category of gender, male or female, it is fairly safe to say, on a reading of the anthropological literature on masculinity in the Arab world[1] and its conflation with the deed, that this conflation conforms to Gilmore's criterion of being "something almost generic ... a ubiquity rather than a universality" (1990:2-3).

Arab masculinity (*rujulah*) is acquired, verified, and played out in the brave deed, in risk-taking, and in expressions of fearlessness and assertiveness. It is attained by constant vigilance and willingness to defend honor (*sharaf*), face (*wajh*), kin, and community from external aggression and to uphold and protect cultural definitions of gender-specific propriety. Unlike masculinity in the Mediterranean, especially Spain, public displays of lust and sexual bravado are not explicit components of Arab manhood. Indeed self-mastery of lust and romantic emotions is crucial to the construction and maintenance of Arab manhood (see Abu-Lughod 1986; Gilmore 1990:40). In Muslim thought, unregulated sexuality can lead to *fitna* (social chaos).

The occupation has seriously diminished those realms of practice that allow one to engage in, display, and affirm masculinity in autonomous actions. Frequent witnesses to their fathers' beatings by soldiers or settlers, children are acutely aware of their fathers' inability to protect themselves and their children. In a study of the dreams of Palestinian children, Bilu (1991) noted that in nightmares of violent encounters between their families and Israeli soldiers or settlers, parents are unable to protect children from violence, whereas in Israeli children's nightmares or violence emanating from Arabs, salvation arrives in the form of fathers, families, and the army. In one case the nightmare is resolved, in the other it is simply a nightmare from which the child can find no escape. A study discussed by Peretz had a similar conclusion. In a study of children's dreams, a prominent theme was the presence of soldiers in their homes, smashing furniture and beating parents. Peretz commented that a major conclusion was that these children regard themselves as victims of violence initiated by armed men and that the family no longer provides security. The father almost never figures in these dreams; according to the analysis, he has lost his authority (1990:116). His source is Amos Lavav "Jewish-Arab Psychoanalysis" *Sof-Shavooa*, weekly supplement to *Maariv International Edition* 12-23-88.

Manliness is also closely intertwined with virility and paternity, and with paternity's attendant sacrifices. Denying one's own needs while providing for others is such a signifier. The consequence of resistance to occupation is a category of sacrifice with long-term implications for the autonomy and security of the community and larger national collectivity (Peteet, 1987: 105-7).

Several anthropologists have referred to the concept of honor as a defining frame for masculinity. Among North Yemeni tribesmen, Caton (1985) argues that honorable deeds can be expressed in oral form. While not explicitly concerned with masculinity, his study of poetic performance and the acquisition of honor are gendered in that he is dealing with a performative genre exclusive to men, at least in public occasions. To best one's opponent in games of oral poetry is to perform an honorable deed. In another instance, Caton (1987) foregrounds power in language. The ability to persuade using verbal skills is central in establishing and displaying power and masculinity, I would contend, rather than fighting skills and achievements as is usually assumed.

Abu-Lughod explicitly uses honor as a point of departure. Among the Egyptian Bedouin, the notion of control is crucial in signifying "real men." Control is the lack of "fear of anyone or anything," for to exhibit such fear "implies that it has control over one" (1986:88). "Real men" are able to exact respect and command obedience from others while they themselves resist submitting to others' control (Abu-Lughod 1986:88-90). Among the Berbers of Algeria, Bourdieu locates the man of honor in the context of challenge and riposte. A challenge confers honor upon a man, because it is a cultural assumption that the "challenge, as such, requires a riposte and therefore is addressed to a man deemed capable of playing the game of honor" (Bourdieu 1977:11). The challenge provides an opportunity for males to prove their belonging to the world of men. A point to which I shall return later concerns Bourdieu's contention that challenges directed to men who are unable to take them up dishonors the challenger.

Elaborate, well-defined rites of passage to mark transitions from boyhood to adolescence to manhood are difficult to discern in Arab culture (Ammar, 1954). Manhood is always more than the culmination of a series of biological transformations. The transformations, and their markings by a loose set of rites, must be accompanied by performative deeds to convince and win public approval. Like honor, with which it is inextricably bound, manhood is easily lost if one is not vigilant about its display and protection.

Assumption of the tasks, authority, and status associated with masculinity is a gradual process of becoming a member of the world of adult men and acquiring 'aql (reason) or social common sense (Rosen, 1984). 'Aql has been described as the "faculty of understanding, rationality, judiciousness, prudence, and wisdom" (Altorki 1986:51). Males begin to acquire 'aql around the age of twenty. While acquisition of this quality has no definable starting date, it does grow with marriage, and most men attain it fully "no earlier than forty, or mature adulthood, when men are perceived to have achieved sufficient capacity to deal with the complex problems of social existence" (Altorki 1986:52). Milestones along this path to adulthood are circumcision, educational achievements, marriage, income earning, the birth of children, and the acquisition of wisdom that comes from knowledge of one's society and its customs (Granqvist, 1931, 1935, 1947). Each of these points further reaffirms, in time, masculinity and belonging to the world of men. None of these milestones is violent, except perhaps circumcision. Having briefly discussed the Middle East literature on masculinity, manhood, and rites of passage, we will return to the question of constructing masculinity and rites of passage after an ethnographic discussion of inscriptions of violence on the Palestinian male body.

BACKGROUND TO BEATINGS AND IMPRISONMENT

Around 40 percent (approximately 2,100,000) of Palestinians live under Israeli rule, either in Israel proper (around 645,000), in the West Bank and East Jerusalem (around 938,000), or in the Gaza Strip (around 525,000) (Hajjar & Beinen 1988). From the beginning of the intifada in December 1987 through December 1990, an estimated 106,600 Palestinians were injured mostly by plastic bullets, rubber bullets, metal marbles and tear gas. Beatings are not isolated in these statistics, so it is impossible to calculate with any certainty the numbers beaten[2].

One would be hard pressed to find a young male Palestinian under occupation who has not been beaten or who does not personally know someone who has been. Under the political and military authority of a foreign power Palestinians possess few, if any, political rights, nor do they possess or have access to technologies of domination. Their powerlessness is all the more pronounced given their occupation by a major military power. The juxtaposition of technologies is striking. Offensively and defensively, Palestinians wield stones, one of the earliest forms of weaponry known to humankind. As part of the natural environment and landscape, the stone bears minimal, if any, application of human technological skills.

The occupying authority continuously displays the potential for and the actuality of violence to stem opposition and to imprint upon the subject population its lack of autonomy. In spite of more than two decades of occupation and a generation of youths who have known no other way of life, Israel has not been able to "normalize" its power relations with those under occupation. Since the beginning of the occupation (1967), resistance has been common (Aronson, 1987). The inability to establish a "naturalness" to occupation has meant a continued recourse to physical violence along with the standard forms of structural violence.

One quickly discerns that beatings are a common occurrence. The anticipation of an encounter with occupation authorities that might lead to a beating influences the daily mobility of young men. They decline evening social invitations that necessitate driving after dark. Military personnel at roadblocks stop cars and randomly pull out men for beating. Parents hesitate to allow adolescent boys to go downtown unaccompanied, or even on short errands, fearing they might be pulled over for an identity check and in the process roughed up. In the alleys of the camps, children now are more careful to stay close to home because on their daily patrols, soldiers occasionally chase and rough up children and detain them for several hours until their parents pay a stiff fine.

Beatings have been a part of the apparatus of domination since the beginning of the occupation, both in public and as an integral part of the interrogation process that leads to the question of how pre-intifada and intifada beatings differ. While framing beatings in the context of time periods, one must not draw too distinct a boundary. In the first weeks of fieldwork in a refugee camp in the West Bank, I would pose many of my questions in terms of a distinct set of time frames—"pre-intifada" and "intifada." Finally, one woman kindly, but with some exasperation, told me: "Look, we've been having an intifada here for forty years, since 1948! The difference now is the rest of the population of the occupied territories is involved, and the continuity of resistance is being sustained! Though this word *intifada* is new to us, we've been resisting for forty years."

Before the intifada, beatings were less public, usually taking place while in custody. Their actual numbers are somewhat harder to estimate because, with the intifada, human rights organizations began making a concerted attempt to keep monthly and annual figures on human rights violations, breaking them down into distinct categories. They were an integral part of an interrogation procedure, designed to break the will of prisoners and to extract confessions as to their alleged deeds and those of their acquaintances and to possible externally based political backing and material support for resistance against the occupation[3].

Soon after the launching of the intifada in December 1987, beatings became an explicit policy of the occupation authorities. On January 19, 1988, Defense Minister Yitzhak Rabin announced a new policy of "might, power, and beatings" to quell the uprising. The international witnessing of the public beatings and bone-breaking evoked widespread alarm among Israel's supporters, particularly in the United States. Subsequently, Likud ministers barred the media from the territories. Until the ban (spring 1988), the beatings were featured prominently on the nightly news in this country. In diminishing the external witnessing of the infliction of pain, the occupying authorities were attempting to create a fictitious reality of nonviolent techniques of riot control for external consumption.

For the Israelis, the beatings were an encoded medium intended to convey a message regarding the consequences of opposition. The young male is a metonym for Palestinian opposition and struggle against domination, the idea and symbols of which must be rooted out and silenced: the Palestinian population must be made acquiescent to the colonizing project. Israeli violence proceeds on the assumption of collective guilt and responsibility among Palestinians. In the occupied territories, violence is directed at individual bodies as representations of a collective transgressive other. Zionist fictionalizing, and I would add, fear of collective Arab sentiment and action, go far in explaining why the shooting of an Israeli diplomat in London could be presented as justification for the 1982 invasion of Lebanon and yet why Israel has usually insisted on bilateral negotiations with Arab states. This collective other, however, is denied a national identity. The pregiven defining power of the collective Palestinian body, which requires a violently negating intervention, lies precisely in its assertive national identity, which in its very existence denies the mythical Zionist landscape of Palestine. Taussig draws our attention to torture and terror as "ritualized art forms" that "far from being spontaneous, sui generis, and an abandonment of what are often called the values of civilization ... have a deep history deriving power and meaning from those very values" (1987:133). Unbowed males signified an assertive resistance to the colonial project and a Zionist self-identity.

The walking embodiment of power, the Israeli soldier, totes the modern technology of violence – automatic rifle, pistol, grenade, hand-cuffs, tear-gas canisters, and batons. Anthropologist and Israeli army captain Ben-Ari remarked that some soldiers, given their training for warfare, were very uneasy with their tasks of policing heavily civilian areas (1989:376). This unease, he suggests, should be understood against the images soldiers had of the uprising. The mass media presentation was one of "mass demonstrations, concentrated rock throwing and tire burning, and the constant use of Molotov cocktails." Ben-Ari frames the behavior of soldiers in the territories in terms of the metaphor of masks and disguises. He suggests "that for the limited period of *milium* (reserve duty) the reservists cease to be the normally identified, circumscribed, constrained members of Israeli society who must be concerned with how they are regarded by themselves and by others" (1989:378).

Donning masks and disguises facilitates construction of "highly delimited – spatially as well as temporally – episodes during which they become an-other person" (Ben-Ari 1989:378-379). Rather than "donning masks" and becoming "another," I would cast their behavior as more analogous to what Taussig referred to as "colonial mirroring," where "the terror and tortures they devised mirrored the horror of the savagery they both feared and fictionalized" (1987:133).

Tolerance of physical abuse of Palestinians was underwritten by a regime of knowledge that cast them as lawless and socially primitive and violent – terrorists, threats to law and order, bands, gangs – and thus as amenable to violent extrajudicial measures. Beyond the pale, Palestinians were cast as possessing a fundamentally different set of morals and knowledge – commonly stated as "they only understand force." Their human status does not correspond to that of others. Israeli military announcements do not use the Hebrew word for "child" when reporting injuries or deaths of Palestinian children in confrontations with the military. The Israeli Palestinian writer Anton Shammas commented that "for twenty years now officially there has been no childhood in the West Bank and Gaza Strip. ... [A] ten year-old boy shot by military forces is reported to be a 'young man of ten'" (1988:10). Military discourse bypasses childhood, collapsing male Palestinian life-cycle categories. This regime of knowledge, together with a widespread ideology of the rights of the occupiers to Palestinian land and resources, constitutive of a claim to an Israeli national identity, and a judicial system that tolerated systematic human rights violations, if not indeed encouraged them as Amnesty International (1991) argues, fostered an atmosphere where inflictions of bodily violence flourished.

Whether pre-intifada or intifada the intent behind the beating was to re-constitute the Palestinian male as a nonresistant, though certainly not consenting subject of colonization. Stone throwing, tire burning, demonstrating, or displaying symbols of Palestine, such as the flag or its colors, could bring a swift and violent response. But rather than being mute repositories or sites on which the occupier exhibited and constructed power and affirmed its civilization and identity, the meaning of the beating has been appropriated by the subject in a dialectical and agential manner.

ETHNOGRAPHY AND BEATINGS

The bodies of those under occupation are continuously called forth to present themselves to outsiders. Visits to families are punctuated by the display of bodies with the marks of bullets and beatings and are social settings for the telling of beatings, shootings, verbal exchanges with settlers and soldiers, and prison stories. After several visits to Um Fadi, I noticed that her children were always in the house or in the walled garden around the house with the gate locked. Once when I had to knock very loudly several times for the children to open, she rushed to open and explained that she no longer leaves the gate open or allows her children to play in the alleys of the camp. After we were seated in the house and drinking tea, she quietly motioned her eleven-year-old son and thirteen-year-old daughter to come stand in front of us. With the reluctance of children their age, they silently did so. In a subdued and controlled tone, she related how they once were caught by soldiers while playing in the alley. Soldiers regularly patrol the streets and alleys of the camp, and occasionally groups of children throw stones at them. Four soldiers claimed they had been stoned by children in the vicinity and accused Um Fadi's son and daughter. Both were beaten with batons and rifle butts directed to the kidneys, arms, and face. When he got up to run, the boy was shot in the side. She asked him to raise his t-shirt to show me the scar. During this telling, several neighbor women were present as well as friends of her children. There was hushed silence as she told the story. The older women would periodically interject, almost inaudibly: "In the name of God – how can they do this to children!", "What can we do?", "What kind of people are these!" The act of telling lends dramatic narrative form to a dialogic process. For the listener, a sense of community is evoked through empathy. Many families have experienced such pain, and, for those who have not, the possibility looms large.

The physical marks of beatings, rubber bullets, and live ammunition constitute crucial elements in dialogue with others, particularly Americans whose near official silence on the matter of Palestinian human rights violations by the occupying authorities is seen as a form of complicity. Given the levels and continuity of US financial support for the occupying power, they consider it all the more appropriate to display the physical signs of their suffering to Westerners. The battered body is a representation fashioned by the Israelis but presented by Palestinians to the West. To the Palestinians, the battered body, with its bruises and broken limbs, is the symbolic embodiment of a twentieth-century history of subordination and powerlessness – of "what we have to endure" – but also of their determination to resist and to struggle for national independence.

A representation created with the intent of humiliating has been reversed into one of honor, manhood, and moral superiority. But bodies do more than represent. Torture and beatings are ordeals one undergoes as sacrifices for the struggle (*qadiyyah*). It should be firmly stated that this argument in no way is meant to imply that Palestinians make light of physical violence. It is rather to try to understand how culturally they make sense of it. Displaying physical marks of violence stands as a "commentary on suffering" (Keesing 1985; Peteet 1987) but also, I would suggest, as a commentary on sacrifice. As such they are poignant communicative devices. These displays are powerful statements belying claims of a benign occupation and resonate with the honor that comes from unmasking and resisting.

BECOMING MEN

One sign of things to come – amidst the jokes and nervous laughter there were signs of genuine excitement by some soldiers at the prospect of "teaching them not to raise their heads" (Israeli soldier in the occupied territories, quoted in Peretz 1990:122).

I first had an inkling of the meaning of the beating and imprisonment as rites of passage when Hussein, twenty-four years old and resident in Jalazon refugee camp, remarked casually and with a hint of resignation that, on his first evening home from a nine-month stint in prison, a neighbor had come to ask his help in mediating a dispute he was involved in with another neighbor. Hussein pleaded fatigue and the crush of visitors to avoid assuming this mantle of community responsibility, a responsibility that carries with it substantial moral authority. To be a mediator is a position and task usually the preserve of well-respected, older men known for their sagacity and even temperament. Such men have achieved 'aql. Hussein did handle the matter the next day, talking to both parties, eventually hammering out a compromise solution. Like many young men of his generation and experience, he suddenly found himself with the responsibility for community affairs, mainly such tasks as mediation in disputes and participating in popular tribunals to try suspected collaborators (McDowell, 1982; Peretz, 1990; Peteet, 1987).

During visits to Hussein's family, I began to notice the deference paid him by his father, an unusual state of affairs in Arab family relations where sons are usually deferential to their fathers. Much about hierarchy and submission can be read in seemingly mundane, everyday gestures. Seating patterns in Arab culture are spatial statements of hierarchy. Those who stand or sit closest to the door are usually subordinate, younger males, while those farthest from the door, and centrally positioned, are older, respected men who are able to command obedience. The spatial arrangement of visitors and family members when congregating at Hussein's home did not conform to the traditional pattern. Indeed, Hussein often was centrally positioned with his father clearly on the periphery. During conversations where his father was present, along with other family members and friends, his father deferred to Hussein in speech, allowing his son to interrupt him. Hussein's father listened attentively as his son talked for lengthy periods of time before interjecting himself. In short, he gave Hussein the floor. When Hussein would describe his prolonged torture at the hands of the interrogators, his father was quiet, only to occasionally interject "Prison is a school, a university" and "Prison is for men."

In observing resistance activities in camps, villages, and urban neighborhoods, it was clear the older men played little, if any role. It was the preserve of the young (under twenty-five years of age), and as such they embodied the prestige and respect that come from, and yet give one access to, leadership positions. It did not take long to realize that Hussein was a member of the local underground leadership. He had spent nineteen months in jail on charges of organizing local forms of escalation, such as stone throwing and barricade building. Chased and publicly beaten in the camp's alleyways before being thrown into a jeep, he was then taken to prison and subjected to eighteen days of interrogation. Naked, deprived of food, water, and sanitation facilities for the first three days, he was subjected to beatings with fists, pipes, and rifle butts, which alternated with questioning over an eighteen-day period.

Once interrogation procedures are completed, prisoners join their fellow inmates in daily prison routine. Palestinian political prisoners are highly organized. Classes are conducted daily in a variety of subjects ranging from foreign languages to math, science, and history. Classes in political theory and practice are the high points in this educational project. For this reason, it is commonplace in contemporary Palestinian discourse to hear the comment "prison is a university." A leadership hierarchy emerges, and as young men are released they take up the leadership mantle of those who are newly detained. In this way, young men circulate between prison and leadership positions. This circulation of young men ensures a leadership in spite of the campaign of massive arrests and detention of young males.

Upon his release, Hussein returned home to several days of visitors – kin, friends, and neighbors – and new responsibilities in the camp leadership. Within the prisons, recruitment to political organizations flourishes, and leaders of each political faction emerge to lead their followers. From the prison they can have some voice in the daily actions and policies of the intifada as they confer instructions and ideas on prisoners about to be released. Upon returning to their communities, young men like Hussein have acquired the stature to lead. They have withstood interrogation and not given away information or become collaborators. More importantly however, they return "educated men." Hussein, and other released detainees, spoke of prison as a place where they learned not only academic subjects, but also about power and how to resist.

Another young man I became acquainted with in the West Bank was Ali. Ali's experience of bodily inflictions of violence began substantially before the intifada. Within a five-year period, he had been detained seventeen times. Politically inactive before he was taken away from home in the middle of the night during his last year of high school, the soldiers assured his frightened parents that they would just ask him a few questions and let him go. Handcuffed and blindfolded, he was placed on the floor of a jeep where he was repeatedly kicked and hit with rifle butts. He recalls that the jeep stopped and picked up someone else. Once they started beating the other fellow, and he screamed, Ali realized it was his friend Sami. Sami told him: "Don't cry or shout. Don't let them know it hurts." He told me:

> At first, of course, I was scared to death and then once you're in that room and they slap your face and start hitting you – that's it, it goes away and you start being a different person. All of a sudden you have a power inside you – a power to resist – you want to resist. You can't help it; you feel very strong, you even want to challenge them though basically I had nothing to tell them since I had done nothing.

After his release several days later, he returned home. Two weeks later, soldiers appeared again and detained him, this time for about two weeks. Upon his release, he decided to join the underground resistance movement and after several months was active in the local-level leadership. He now had stature in the community as a result of the beatings, arrests, and interrogations. He was effective in mobilizing others to join in demonstrations, national celebrations, and the resistance movement on the university campus he later attended.

Physical violence can be construed by its recipients as "bridge-burning" activity (Gerlach and Hines 1970). One often hears comments such as "I've nothing left to lose" and "I've already paid the price, I might as well be active." Palestinian males need not necessarily do violence to become political agents as Fanon (1969) argued for the Algerian revolution. As its recipients, they acquire masculine and revolutionary credentials. Marks on the body signal a resistant, masculine subjectivity and agency. The pervasiveness of beatings/detention, their organizational format, and their construal by recipients as entry into the world of masculinity make possible their casting as a rite of passage.

In his classic study of rites of passage, Van Gennep (1961) identified three characteristic stages: separation, marginality, and aggregation. Logic of sequences is apparent in the transformative process of physical violence. In the initial phase, the individual is physically detached from the group. He is either taken from his home and family to the jeep and then the interrogation room, or he is detached from the crowd in public and held by soldiers or settlers who try to keep at a distance those who would intervene. The second, or liminal, stage is a state of marginality and ambiguity and is one fraught with dangers. The young novice exists outside of social time, space, and the categories of the life cycle. Social rules and norms are suspended. Interrogation, with its applications of physical violence, is such a liminal stage during which social hierarchies of age and class are diluted. Oppositions between normal social life and liminality (Turner 1977) can be applied to the one being beaten, especially those in custody who are frequently naked, in a state of humility and without rank or status, and who silently undergo pain and suffering. Imprisonment is also a liminal period because communitas is achieved and expressed in the emergence of new hierarchies that rest on an ability to withstand physical violation and pain, political affiliation and rank, and ability to lead in the prison community.

The final sequence, aggregation or the postliminal reentry into normal social life, is verified and enacted by the family and the community at large. The return home is marked by a fairly well-defined celebratory etiquette. Relatives, friends, and neighbors visit for several weeks to show respect to the released detainee and his family. Special foods, usually more expensive meat dishes, are prepared by the women of the household both to strengthen the detainees' often poor health as well as to show appreciation and respect for his endurance. New clothes are bought to mark reentry into the community. The respect shown by deferential gestures to the former prisoner or beaten youth all mark his reentry into society with a new status of respect and manhood.

In emerging from the beating unbowed and remaining committed to resistance activities, young men exhibit generosity to the point of sacrifice that asserts and validates a masculine self. The infliction of pain reveals, in the most intimate and brutal way, the nature of occupation and strengthens them, they contend, to confront it.

Endowed with the qualities of adulthood, honor, and manhood, emergence from the ordeal dovetails with access to power and authority. In a reversal of meaning, the beating empowers the serf and informs an agency of resistance. Palestinians, as participants in and as audience to the public spectacle of beatings, have consciously and creatively taken a coherent set of signs and practices of domination and construed them to buttress an agency designed to overthrow political hierarchies.

THE INTIFADA: TREMORS IN THE CONSTRUCTION OF MASCULINITY

The term *intifada* comes from the Arabic root n-f-d, which indicates a shaking, as in shaking the dust from (Harlow 1989:32). It implies a shaking off of foreign occupation and ties of economic and administrative linkage. While its eruption was fairly spontaneous, the intifada was the culmination of years of accumulated frustrations and outrage. A decade of grass-roots political and social organizing undergirded its direction and ability to sustain itself (Hiltermann 1991). The intifada brought to the forefront of international diplomacy an internally based Palestinian leadership. Equally, it signaled a generational shake-up. The young, armed only with stones and facing death and pain, were to sweep away the older generation in terms of political relevance and actual leadership. Shaking off also implicates forms of internal domination embodied in age, class, and gender hierarchies. The continuity created by life-cycle transitions such as marriage, employment, and reaching the state of *'aql* were destabilized by the actions of young boys.

The assertion that the male under occupation is reconstituted via violence implies that the creation of meaning is a matter of Palestinian control. The transformative power of the ritual lies in the individual who consciously commits himself to political action and in the community's ability to confer adult status. Ritual mediates between relations of violence and domination and political agency by subordinates in such a way as to defy any notion of directional unilineality between oppression and resistance. As Feldman argued in his discussion of political violence in Northern Ireland, "Political agency is not given but achieved on the basis of practices that alter the subject." (1991:1) Yet it is political practices by boys, many undertaken willingly and often spontaneously rather than given, that lead to further political agency via ritual.

As rites of passage, beatings and imprisonment are procedures that are not controlled or overseen by the family or kin group. It is an individual experience within a collectivity of young men. Thus a critical rite of passage into adulthood, with its corresponding privileges of power/authority/respect, is now accomplished earlier and is initially out of the bounds of the kin group. Indeed, it underscores the powerlessness of the kin group to protect its youth.

To return to Bourdieu's mapping of the relationship between masculinity and honor, we can now pose the question, what happens to the cultural categories and concepts around which honor is organized and expressed when challenge and riposte take place not between members of the same social group, but between a colonial entity, and its apparatus of force, and a subjugated, indigenous population? A man dishonors himself when he challenges a man considered incapable of "taking up the challenge" (Bourdieu 1977:11). When Israelis pursue and engage Palestinian youths, the cultural interpretation available to Palestinians is to consider the Israelis as lacking in the emotional and moral qualities of manhood. Only men of little honor and thus dubious masculinity would beat unarmed youths while they themselves are armed with and trained in the use of modern implements of warfare. Because little or no effective riposte is possible at the instant, there is no challenge – and the encounter degenerates into mere aggression (Bourdieu 1977:12). Such aggression deprives its practitioners of claims to honor and morality.

Palestinians construe these aggressions as cowardly and immoral, rather than a challenge. But what has all this to do with manhood? Palestinians have changed the cultural categories of the encounter so that manhood comes from a "riposte" not to a challenge but to what Bourdieu distinguished as "mere aggression." And thus is constituted the national backdrop against which Palestinians are re-constructing defining elements of their culture and society. This will take on more meaning when read against the following scene.

MORAL SUPERIORITY: AFFIRMING CULTURAL AND NATIONAL SELVES

On my way to an office in East Jerusalem, I was rushing to avoid the 1:00 p.m. closure of all commercial activity in the Palestinian sector of the city in observance of the general strike. Children were returning home from school, and shop shutters were hastily rolling down. As I rounded the corner, I saw two jeeps and about six or seven heavily armed soldiers. They had a ten-year-old mentally handicapped boy pressed against the stone wall, slapping him in the face, shaking him, and yelling in broken Arabic for him to admit throwing a stone at them. Being mentally handicapped, the boy could only whimper and cry – he was incapable of talking. I ran into our office to tell the others that they were beating the boy who lived across the alley. By this time several neighborhood women, by and large middle-class Jerusalemites, had also appeared. One of these women fluent in English, calmly walked up to the group which had now expanded to four jeeps and about fifteen soldiers. She politely asked why they were bothering this boy who was retarded and could not barely speak. She kept repeating to the soldiers that the boy could not understand and speak like a normal child. By now, she had a slight mocking smile on her face and appealed to the soldiers with a kind of sarcasm: "Can't you see he's retarded!? It takes all of you soldiers and four jeeps to question a retarded boy!?" The other women were smirking and exchanging comments on what possesses these people to beat retarded children. Several of the soldiers were clearly embarrassed and physically distanced themselves, turning their backs on the boy and the two soldiers roughing him up. They smiled sheepishly to the women gathered there and shrugged their shoulders as if to say "What can we do?"

An audience of women defused a potential escalation of violence through mockery and joking. The imbalance of forces is so patently absurd that Palestinians find an almost comic relief in watching soldiers engage in such morally revealing behavior. In imposing interpretation and meaning on the violence of the occupiers, Palestinians are (re)-constituting themselves in a moral sense. Violent encounters where Palestinians are both participants and audiences are public scenes where their moral qualities are dramatically juxtaposed with the occupiers'.

The re-constitution of a moral self via violence involves both men and women. To some extent, however, a gendered distinction appears in the practice of violence. While women have been active in all arenas, a task assigned to them early in the intifada, and one in tune with cultural notions of female propriety and "natural" concerns and mobility constraints, was to intervene in violent encounters. In other words, women were to witness and defuse rites of violence. A leaflet (bayan) distributed on March 8, 1988, and signed "Palestinian Women in the Occupied Territories" said, "Mothers, in camps, villages, and cities, continue confronting soldiers and settlers. Let each woman consider the wounded and imprisoned her own children." It should be noted that leaflets are printed several times a month by the underground leadership of the intifada. They contain a listing of the strike days and days of confrontation, and additionally exhort people to boycott Israeli goods, to actively participate in popular committees – in general, to support the uprising.

Despite a gendered division of roles, the moral reconstruction consequent to violent acts does indeed permeate gender boundaries. The re-constituting moral self, whether male or female, is a cultural category, in this case one with a national content, constructed as it currently is vis-à-vis a foreign other. As the witnessing audience, women provide a running commentary intended to shame soldiers to cease a beating or to stop an arrest. "Don't you people have children?!" "Has God abandoned you?" While women's moral self is enacted and affirmed publicly in this act of witnessing, the male being beaten or arrested is also positioned performatively to place himself against another. But how are nonparticipants positioned such that they also ultimately are enabled to construct a moral self? I would argue that the "telling," punctuated by moral and evaluative judgments that circulate throughout Palestinian society as people visit one another in the course of daily life, is one such event in which a moral constitution of the self unfolds.

Israeli behavior is considered rude and boorish. Palestinian discussions are punctuated by surprise at their bad manners. "These are supposedly educated peoples – why do they behave so obnoxiously?" They are regarded as lacking in ethics and morality. Most significantly, they are seen as deficient in empathy with the suffering of others. Jewish theologian Mark Ellis suggests that "Holocaust theology" – emergent since the creation of Israel in 1948 – is a self-absorbed phenomenon based on a joining of religious heritage with loyalty to Israel. Such self-absorption diminishes Jewish capacity for empathy with Palestinian suffering (Neimark 1992:21; see also Mark Lewis 1990). In contemporary constitutions of self vis-à-vis their occupiers, Palestinians have recourse to a "poetics of contrast" (Comaroff and Comaroff 1987:205). Clear and defining distinctions are drawn between their behavior and the occupiers'. Palestinians consider themselves polite to others and reserved in public, personal qualities that are central to a Palestinian etiquette. Images of contrast are rhetorical devices that lend meaning to the occupiers' behavior. The moral nature of these images provides Palestinians with the stuff of which they construct a collective self-image in a situation of subordination and an absence of autonomy.

TRANSFORMING HIERARCHIES: CLASS AND GENERATION

In the historical encounter, sociocultural systems are simultaneously transformed and reproduced (Sahlins 1981). Inscriptions of bodily violence and their construal as rites of passage both transform and reproduce certain structural, relational, and cultural features of Palestinian society. The intifada has had profound implications for class and generational structures and relations in the occupied territories. While the intifada is a popular uprising, those in the forefront of resistance to occupation are subaltern male youths from the refugee camps, villages, and urban popular quarters who are usually under twenty years of age and can be as young as ten.

The power and status of the older generation were eclipsed. Young males took over the tasks previously the preserve of more mature, often notable men. For example, disputes were mediated in new judicial tribunals organized and staffed by the underground leadership. A common lament was that the young were out of control, displaying little or no respect for their parents. It reached such a pitch that several leaflets in 1990 called for parents to reassert control and for youth to heed the voices of their parents and teachers.

The older generation (those over the age of thirty-five), played little, if any, visible role in the daily activities of the intifada. A telling incident occurred one day in a *service* (shared taxi) ride from Jerusalem to Ramallah. There were six passengers, myself included. As we approached a roadblock manned by soldiers, we could see several other cars stopped with young male passengers being searched and questioned. No one in our car seemed particularly worried or concerned. Our car came to a halt and the soldiers peered in, gave each of us a searching glance, and then motioned the driver to proceed. My husband commented to the rest of the passengers, "Why didn't they ask to see our identity cards or search us?" The other men in the car, none of whom appeared to be younger than thirty or thirty-five, turned around in their seats and looked at him with incredulity. One of them said, "You think you're a boy! They aren't interested in men our age!"

Bodily inscriptions of violence are more prevalent in camps and villages and thus are somewhat class bound. The politically active urban elite, often from notable families, who have traditionally striven for leadership, are not usually exposed to bodily inscriptions of violence though they may well undergo periods of administrative detention. Indeed, they can be subject to derision for assuming a mantle of leadership when they have not been credentialized by violence. Um Kamel is a forty-year-old mother and activist in a refugee camp. Her husband is in jail serving a ten-year sentence on the grounds of organizing anti-occupation activities. One son has spent considerable periods of time in prison, and a sixteen-year-old son had been shot twice in the stomach. Twice she has had homes demolished, with only a few hours notice, because of allegations of her sons' political activism. She commented sarcastically of the urban-based leaders: "What do they know of suffering? Who are they to lead? They and their sons aren't beaten and they rarely go to jail. Their sons study here and abroad while our sons are beaten, shot and imprisoned!"

REPRODUCING HIERARCHIES: GENDER

Contemporary rites of initiation into manhood articulate with and set in dramatic relief the social reproduction of asymmetrical gender arrangements, while a hierarchical male identity and notions of selfhood and political position are reaffirmed in these rites of passage.

Given the casting of the beating as a zone of prestige for young men, what does it mean for women? The number of women beaten, arrested, and detained is small, and their status afterwards is more ambiguous than heroic. The number does not index women's level of involvement in the uprising, which has been extensive. It does indicate, however, their less visible role, and the tendency of the Israeli Defense Forces to go for males first. Ambiguity devolves for the women from the shame of having bodily contact with strange men, a stark transgression of the code of modesty and shame. Foremost on everyone's mind is the question of sexual violation. Women who violate the modesty code by engaging in illicit sexual activities (i.e., pre-marital sexual relations or adultery after marriage) risk incurring reprisals by kinsmen. But when the violator is a common enemy in whose face one's kinsmen hold no power and few means of recourse, ambiguity sets in. Ambiguity arises from the notion of will and intent. Arab women are seen as possessed of an active sexuality. When transgressions of the sexual code occur, the women can be held responsible. Yet, if a woman's nationalist activity set in motion a series of events that culminated in a beating and detention, and an interrogation procedure that included sexual torture, it is difficult to cast her as having violated the modesty code. The nationalist, patriotic cast of her intent and actions precludes the usual cultural interpretation. By the time of the intifada, ambiguity was giving way to a cautious respect for the woman detainee.

While femininity is no more natural than masculinity, physical violence is not as central to its construction. It does not reproduce or affirm aspects of female identity, nor does it constitute a rite of passage into adult female status. Women frame their physical violation as evidence of their equality with men and wield it to press their claims – "We suffer like men, we should have the same rights," quipped one former prisoner who had undergone a lengthy detention and was tortured during interrogation. While the violence visited upon males credentializes masculinity, that visited upon women indicates a potential equality of citizenship. (Peteet, 1991)

Women experience the phenomena of beating from a multiplicity of subject positions. The "mother" saving boys from soldiers' blows is one of the most widespread and enduring images to emerge in the intifada. Mothers of the subaltern are extolled as the "mothers of all Palestinians." Known in the camp as "a mother of all youths," Um Kamel explained her actions in intervening in public beatings: "I feel each and every one of those boys is my son. If it was my son, I would want other mothers to try to protect him." The mothers intervene during beatings, at once screaming for the soldiers to stop and pleading with them to show mercy. They hurl insults that highlight the soldiers' denial of the humanity of others: "Have you no compassion and pity?" "Aren't we human beings, too?" "Don't you have mothers and sons – how would your mother feel if you were treated this way; would you like to see your sons beaten like this?" "What kind of a people takes the land of another and then beats them when they protest?" This protective action of middle-aged mothers accomplishes several things: It can create a diversion that allows boys to escape. The noise and confusion it generates can quickly mobilize large groups of passersby and nearby residents to surround soldiers and try to intervene. But above all, it casts shame on soldiers by scrutinizing their moral qualities in a dramatic, public narrative. Women as mothers of all are a collective moral representation of a community testifying to the abusive nature of occupation.

Thus women are not silent witnesses to everyday violence. Witnessing is itself a form of political activism. When the occasional foreign journalist enters a camp, a delegation comes from abroad, or the anthropologist such as myself comes, the "mothers," those who risked their own safety to protect others, are called forth. Much like the vaunted position of the "mothers of the martyrs" in areas where Palestinian resistance takes the form of armed struggle (Peteet 1991), they are called upon to tell their stories, to assume the position of communal witnesses and tellers of suffering. The experience of a beating may not affirm a feminine identity and selfhood, yet it does evoke some female traits – stoicism and silence to protect the community.

While beatings reproduce a masculine identity, they also reproduce men's authority and physical domination in the family. Asymmetrical gender relations may be reaffirmed as a result of a young man's assumption of adult tasks and authority that in this case are assumed through violent rites of passage. Young wives and sisters complained that their husbands and brothers returned from interrogation and detention with a new authoritarianism expressed in attempts to assert control over their mobility. Style of dress was another arena of conflict, as women were pressured to wear head scarves. Domestic violence, wives and social workers claimed, was on the rise. Some men who were subjected to beatings and torture return home and inflict violence upon women.

CONCLUSION

The meaning of the beating is central to new conceptions of manhood and ultimately access to leadership positions. Violence has almost diametrically opposed meanings. For one, it is an index of a fictionalized fear and image of inferiority of a subject population and is intended to control and dishonor; for the others, it is constitutive of a resistant subjectivity that signals heroism, manhood, and access to leadership and authority. Practices that intimately situate Israelis and Palestinians are construed by Palestinians as transformative and agential. How did the experience of physical violence become construed as a rite of passage into manhood with its associated practices? In other words, can we identify a dynamic interplay between meaning and agency? The categories of experience, meaning, and agency should not be arranged in a unilinear manner so as to identify a direction of transformation. A more fruitful line of inquiry would cast these categories as existing in a relationship of mutual constitutiveness.

While beatings, bodies, and rite of passage are texts and structures of meaning, they are also historically grounded social constructions derived from particular signs and practices that galvanize a community to action. The call to action derives less from the actual structure of the ritual and more from its performative essence, in which the audience plays a crucial role in reversing the meaning intended by the dominant performers. The intifada abruptly and violently signaled an end to what Scott has referred to as the "public transcript. . . the open interaction between subordinates and those who dominate" (1990:2). Israel's public performances to exact submission are no longer efficacious.

The act of incorporating beatings and imprisonment into a cultural criterion of manhood and assigning them status as a rite of passage is a "trick," if you will, that reverses the social order of meaning and leads to political agency. To let bodily violence stand as constitutive of an inferior and submitting social position and subjectivity without interpretation and challenge would be to submit to the dominant performers' meaning. For the anthropologist, to interpret it otherwise would leave it as a textual rather than an agential problematic.

The occupying authorities, with constant attention directed to detecting ripples of change in Palestinian cultural categories and social relations, have by now caught on to the way applications of bodily violence and imprisonment have empowered a generation committed to resistance. A new element of knowledge seems to be emerging in their regime of pseudo knowledge of the subject population. Interrogation procedures now contain a sexual practice designed to thwart the meaning and agency of physical violence as rites of passage to masculinity and manhood. Rape during interrogation is now being more widely discussed among some released prisoners, as is fondling by interrogators with photographs taken of these incidents. Sexual forms of interrogation deprive young men of claims to manhood and masculinity. One cannot return from prison and describe forms of torture that violate the most intimate realm of gendered selfhood. If knowledge of such sexual tortures circulates widely, violence and detention will be diluted of their power to contribute to a gendered sense of self informing political agency.

NOTES

1   Literature devoted explicitly to masculinity in the Arab world is rare, but the topic surfaces in a variety of works, not exclusively but largely based on ethnography in North Africa (Abu-Lughod 1986; Caton 1985, 1987; Davis and Davis 1989).

2   The Palestine Human Rights and Information Committee (PHRIQ) cautions that the figure of 106,600 should probably be doubled, especially the beatings. They receive their information from hospitals and clinics, and many people do not seek medical care. Moreover, they do not receive

figures on beating cases treated in emergency rooms, in local or private clinics, or by the medical communities. The figures from the Gaza Strip for the month of December 1990 indicate 273 reported beatings (66 were of women, 45 of children) (Palestine Human Rights and Information Campaign 1990).

3   Amnesty International (1991) states that in the occupied territories, Palestinian detainees are "typically subjected to forms of torture or ill-treatment, with the aim of obtaining information as well as a confession ... Torture or ill-treatment seem to be virtually institutionalized during the arrest and interrogation procedures ... The practices relating in particular to interrogation procedures have been officially endorsed or are generally condoned, and therefore effectively encouraged, by the authorities" (p. 45). Amnesty's report also questions the "fairness of military court trials" because of the prominent role of confessions and "the apparent reluctance by judges to investigate claims of coerced statements" (p. 49). The report states that "the substantial evidence available indicates the existence of a clear pattern of systematic psychological and physical ill-treatment, constituting torture or other forms of cruel, inhuman, or degrading treatment, which is being inflicted on detainees during the course of interrogation" (p. 58).

Revenge of the Wretched

Islam and Violence in the Bab al Tabaneh Neighborhood of Tripoli

Mohammad Abi Samra

This partial study on the structure of local, urban violence and aggression among the youth of Bab al Tabaneh, a neighborhood in the northern Lebanese city of Tripoli, is based on the following premises: First: Overcrowded, haphazardly built residential neighborhoods emerged on the outskirts of the cities to house a mix of transplants from rural areas that could not be absorbed into the fabric of the modern city. Later, these people were incapable of integrating on a social, economic, and cultural level into the urban environment, leading to the emergence of ad hoc ghettos of poverty, unemployment, misery, and violence. Second: The armed violence in these areas was populist and local in nature, and spread with the outbreak of the Lebanese Civil War in 1975. The causes of this violence, its evolution, and its many faces and consequences are many an varied. This is what Samir Khalaf addresses in his book *Civil and Uncivil Violence in Lebanon* (2002). Third: The stockpiling of weapons and the presence of armed Palestinian groups in Lebanon after they were driven out of Jordan in 1973, is the primary cause behind the explosion and spread of violence that overwhelmed civilian life in Lebanon. The armed Palestinian organizations were intent on mobilizing and recruiting and hiding behind Lebanese fighters, and in so doing benefitting from their weak allegiance to the political system and the Lebanese state, as well as their inability to integrate into the Lebanese political, social, economic, and cultural structures of the cities and the surrounding suburbs.

This study relies on sociological methodology in order to reveal the social roots of violence in Bab al Tabaneh in Tripoli and how it is utilized by local organizations, first and foremost the armed *Meshyakhat Shebab* which took local anxiety and used it as a bulwark for recurring vengeful uprisings against the state and its authority, against the city, and against other neighborhoods.

THE NEW SAVAGES

In an article published in the second edition of *Esprit* (2008) in a portion of which was quoted by Hayat's World Press section (March 5, 2008), the French thinker Jean Monnot recounts how forty years earlier in the late 1960s he had published the first book in French about the youth gangs of the Parisian suburbs. He wrote the book after reading a piece by the famed anthropologist Claude Lévi Strauss in which he said that when he used to stroll the Champs Elysees and see the young men in their black jackets, he felt as though he was walking amidst a tribe as exotic as the tribes of the Amazon he had studied up close.

Monnot's article notes the presence of groups in industrial societies that are "descended" from "primitive" societies, as opposed to the popular notion in the social sciences that all the societies of the world are headed towards homogeneity and the differences between and within them will be erased.

Monnot called the youth of the 1960s in Paris suburbs the "new savages", asking himself: what right do I have to be among you as long as I do not share your view of the self, life, and the world? This question drove him to adopt a new outlook towards this age group and its culture, which was considered to be radically different from that of the adults by virtue of it being "a mix of imagination and reality" which drove the youth to "found their own community far from the gaze of their families and society at large." This attitude resulted in a misunderstanding that was among the causes behind the emergence of the gangs and their self-segregation and marginalization from the society in which they lived.

Monnot concludes that the relationship among the youth of the suburban gangs was governed by "a popular masculinity" that Monnot himself cannot avoid experiencing. He goes on to note three features that determine the internal relationships of the gang:

a. "Belonging" or inclusion in a special group
b. A special language for communication and expression
c. A latent homosexuality that binds the members of the gang together.

THE ARAB UPRISINGS

In Arab societies after World War I and what has been called the "shock of contact with the west and modernity," and in the mirror of Jean Monnot's theory, an image became emblematic in the popular imagination and memory of a history built on recurring revolutions and uprisings that combined countless factors and manifested in countless ways. But none of these revolutions and uprisings, according to Waddah Sharara (2007), succeeded in changing modern Arab politics in any meaningful way. Sharara discusses some instances of killing, assassination, and uprising and the place of these acts within Arab societies. He places all this "chaos, civil and military strife in the Mamluk and Ottoman cities and later in the mandate and independence era" in the same category. Despite the fact that these Arab revolutions and uprisings were undertaken by mostly civil, dissident factional groups, including neighborhood parties, gangs, and *abadays* and angry mobs, as well as local armed organizations that were constantly splintering and killing each other, there were also secret suicide groups, *mujahideen* working on behalf of God or the sultan. Despite all this, all those who undertook these uprisings did so on behalf of either "the nation" or "the people", not to mention God and the "holy cause." In all these instances, the target of the uprising was really just a ghost, according to Hazem Saghiyeh (1995).

MESHYAKHAT SHEBAB

This is exactly the situation of the families of the Bab al Tabaneh neighborhood in the northern Lebanese city of Tripoli, who, since the end of the 1950s, have periodically undertaken armed uprisings. Bab al Tabaneh, which lies on the outskirts of the city, is the most densely populated area in all of Lebanon. According to voting registration, over 55,000 people live there in just 8,800 rundown housing units.

One United Nations agency classified Bab al Tabaneh as a natural and social disaster area. The population lives well below the poverty line. Illiteracy and unemployment rates are high and broken families are common, as is early marriage and random divorce and pregnancy. This poor neighborhood has become an environment of instability, violence, and broken homes, a breeding ground for street gangs of unemployed and drug-addicted youth who get into pointless bloody fights on a daily basis.

The French researcher Michel Sura, who lived in Lebanon during the 1980s before he was abducted by a group of Islamists from the Khomeini movement in Lebanon and died in captivity, wrote an academic study of the social world of the *meshyakhat shebab* [neighborhood organizations led by a local leader, or sheikh] since their emergence in Baba la Tabaneh following the time of Ali Akkawi's *meshaykha* and the founding of *munathamat al ghadhab* [the organization of anger] in the 1960s. This organization was comprised of young men from Bab al Tabaneh who turned their "anger" into a form of civic disobedience tinged with Arab nationalism that targeted the Lebanese state. "Death for the sake of the people" became their rallying cry. The "people," in the imagination of the *meshyakhat shebab*, were the residents of the neighborhood. It is their anger, presented as the anger of the entire people and the nation, that inspires *meshyakhat shebab*. It is in their name that *munathamat al ghadhab* fought the Qadisha electricity company every time it tried to collect bills from the people.

"Social banditry" was a form of resistance, of venting socio-economic and popular resentment. It was also a source of funding for the groups in the neighborhood. This strategy led to the bombing and plundering of the bank, the robbing of a pharmacy and grocers, and the participation in organized uprisings that were finally made official with the declaration of October 15, 1971 to be "a day for the people's anger." According to Khalil Akkawi, who was quoted in Michel Sura's biography of his older brother Ali Akkawi, these acts were vital to keeping the group's high morale and their spirits inflamed with resentment. Such pent-up anger and hostility would have exploded in some form or another even without the flood of armed Palestinian factions into Lebanon in 1968. These groups and their networks spread throughout the working-class Muslim neighborhoods of Lebanon's cities and suburbs, where they served as an example of "Arab revolution", providing a source of arms and organizations, including *munathamat al ghadhab*, which the Lebanese security forces were able to root out in the early 1970s.

Ali Akkawi, "*Sheikh ash-Shebab*," was sent to prison where he died in 1972. His younger brother Khalil inherited the *meshyakha*. His "revolutionary path" led him to join the armed Palestinian organization Fatah. He was full of vengeful anger and determined to take revenge against the two parties he considered responsible for his brother's death: the Lebanese state and Hafez al Assad's Baathist regime in Syria.

During the Israeli military campaign against the armed Palestinian groups in Lebanon in the summer of 1982, one news report claimed that thousands of people from Tripoli had gathered in front of the Tawba Mosque to pledge allegiance to the mosque's Imam, Sheikh Said Shaaban, as their Salafist "emir." The Emir-Sheikh stood at the mosque's entrance accepting the allegiance from those who shook his hand, one by one. Soon after, armed men appeared on the street of the city, which was controlled by the Lebanese Army. And this is how the *Harakat al Tawheed al Islami* [Islamic Unity Movement] was started in Tripoli.

Khalil Akkawi and his armed organization in Bab al Tabaneh joined this Salafist Islamist movement, making the mosque with its congregation and religious rituals into a breeding ground for "political," organizational, and *dawa* [proselytizing] activity, influenced by the Khomeini's Islamic revolution in Iran.

A group of mosque committees from different Tripoli neighborhoods, committees that had pushed disobedient youth towards the "sanctity", "honor", "purity", and "identity" of the mosques from which they extended their power, created an Islamic *Ummah*, which had been an Arab *Ummah* in the days when *meshyakhat shebab* were a "populist resistance" whose goal, according to a man quoted by Michel Sura, was "to be able to hold our heads high in our neighborhood."

Thus the "*ummah*", whether Islamic or Arab, is nothing but the neighborhood, and the youth are its "heroes" or "*abadays*". Each of them represents a face of the "unemployed youth" in a society at its low point in Bab al Tabaneh. The

Meshyakhat Shebab in Bab al Tabaneh is just a piece of the history of this "rebellious" city, an image of itself. The *Meshyakhat* are a local, social expression and "political tool" of that latent rebellion that lies hidden, delayed, waiting to become an uprising. The young men and *sheikhs* of the neighborhood saw themselves as a product of the nation or *ummah*, an embodiment of its spirit, its roots, its purity, and its original identity.

Thus the *abadays* of the neighborhoods along with their gangs of unemployed young men, those who lacked familial support or any other kind of social bonds had fallen to the lowest social level of the city; a place of misery, violence, and decay. Yet despite, perhaps because of their low social standing, they were transformed into "heroes of the people." The "neighborhood-nation" rallied around them, and they wore haloes of "gallantry", "honor", "resistance", and "aid to the weak and the poor."

THE PEOPLE'S EPIC AND ITS HERO

Today, more than two decades since the assassination of Khalil Akkawi (Abu Arabi) in 1986, and after the bloody end of his armed "people's *emirate*" in Bab al Tabaneh, this emirate and its emir still live in the memories and collective imagination of the "neighborhood-nation," those acts of bravery and kindness suspended in a time that is both past and present.

"If I had lived in the time of Abu Arabi, I would have been one of his followers," said Abdullah, who was not older than twenty-one. Abdullah was born in Bab al Tabaneh the same year Khalil Akkawi was assassinated (1986). His father's nickname in the movement was "Mao" and he was a soldier of the armed people's emirate, which was always in a state of uprising against "tyranny". They made it their mission to spread "brotherly love" and provide "assistance" to the people, their ultimate goal being to eradicate poverty and unify them, according to Abdullah's veteran father.

In the popular imagination, Abu Arabi the *sheikh shebab* is remembered as a "leader" who protects the neighborhood, a source of "gallantry," "fortitude," and "brotherly love" to his men who, by their arms and their guns, "liberated" the people and created the emirate. He was an example of "honor, purity, honesty, reliability, and sincerity" until the day he died. He was mourned in the neighborhood as a departed hero by every man, woman, child, and remaining member of his emirate.

They have elevated him to the status of legendary, popular hero who rose out of the broken social fabric of the ghetto-neighborhood and its common, miserable, disintegrating culture.

PATRONAGE AND LOYALTY

If one were to ask the residents of Bab al Tabaneh today (2008) about the distribution of local loyalties among the various political leaders and personalities of Tripoli, the answer will always be "whoever pays more." After speaking with many residents, one will be quick to discover that the system of financial support for loyalty is based on fierce competition among inner circles of local leaders, their clients, and their representatives in the local elections. This group is comprised of middle men between the local leaders and the people, who shift their allegiances between one *zaim* and another, depending on the conditions and the ability of each to pay either with money, gifts, or social services, including health care, hospitalization, school tuition, gifts, sponsorships, and other forms of material assistance.

This clientelistic system where one pledges his loyalty in return for basic services is essentially a series of networks that move and adjust to cover the gaping holes in the social fabric, sometimes overtly and other times more subtly. The most obvious manifestations of these networks, both explicit and implied, are the pictures of political figures covering the crumbling walls of Bab al Tabaneh, like a mural of human misery and deprivation.

Many of the middlemen and leaders within this system are former soldiers of Abu Arabi's People's Emirate, especially the organizers and fighters, those who experienced the civil war and maintained those connections from their youth in the "neighborhood-nation" before the Syrian regime wiped out the emirate. Many were thrown in jail, and could not be released except through the intervention of Tripoli politicians who were loyal to Assad's regime and his security policies in Lebanon.

This was one of many factors that exacerbated the misery and deprivation of Bab al Tabaneh in the period of Syrian control. Hundreds of soldiers of the People's Emirate died in the regional and Lebanese civil wars that were supported by Assad's own security apparatus, along with the Palestinian military apparatus under Yasser Arafat. Hundreds more were killed in the battle to suppress the emirate, and many more were thrown into notorious Syrian prisons.

Thus many of the youth of Bab al Tabaneh were raised in broken homes with high birth rates. Those children were essentially orphans, their futures bleak, condemned to a desolate, violent life on the streets. If they did not find ways to take out their verbal and physical violence on each and outsiders, they would take it out on themselves, because violence was their only means of expression. Their early childhoods were spent among street gangs and cliques, with neither education nor parents to give support and act as role models.

When they grew up, the only work they could find was temporary and hard jobs in mechanic or chop shops taking apart damaged cars. They married quickly, randomly, and young, having only a room or part of a room in their parents' house where other members of the extended family were always dropping in. In these shared, overcrowded houses, many children were conceived. Many of those who married and had children also divorced and remarried quickly, sometimes two or three times, all the while having more and more children. The children of these successive marriages were raised in overcrowded, violent homes which they eventually left, preferring the hard life of the streets to being neglected and abandoned by their families.

BOYS OF MISERY AND EMPTINESS

If we combined the bloody legacy of the Islamic Unity Movement after it took military control of Tripoli from 1983 to 1986 with the legacy of the security and military organizations that preceded it, it would tell the story of the emergence of "dark" security networks and other secret movements based on Salafist Jihadi Islam which sent *mujahideen* to Afghanistan, Bosnia, and Iraq.

"Despite the abundance of firearms in our neighborhood, knives and razors and other sharp objects are preferred over firearms in the daily fights that occur here," said a man I met in Bab al Tabaneh. "But the people tell the security forces and Lebanese Army *ahlan wa sahlan* and welcome, come into the neighborhood, so they come in after the bloody affrays, but they leave soon after. They are tired of these fights, and of always having to come in and out of the neighborhood."

More often than not these fights break out in the vegetable market between the *abaday* gang leaders. Each *abaday* of a gang controls one or two or even three areas for emptying, loading, and display in the market. If one of them tries to extend his control to another area, the two will begin to harass each other, first verbally, then cursing, which inevitably leads to a fight between the opposing gang members. If one of them is carrying a razor or a gun, he will brandish it threateningly while yelling the worst curses he can think of. Then the fight escalates until shots are fired and someone is killed or wounded, sparking even more feuds and battles between the gangs and their *abadays*.

They are boys of misery and emptiness. Misery surrounds them, and they are enveloped by the sound of the *muezzin* from the Harba Mosque; the biggest which receive worshippers and listeners for the Friday sermons in Bab al Tabaneh. Bissan al Sheikh, in the story he wrote (*al-Hayat*, September 25, 2006), depicts scenes from the family and personal lives of the boys living in that ghetto of misery, violence, and self-destruction, including one named Abu Bakr who worked as a porter in the vegetable market and who prayed every day in the Harba Mosque.

Before he became known as Abu Bakr in 2005 when he joined the Islamic group *ash-Shebab al Mu'min* [The Believers], Abu Bakr, who was born in the early 1980s, was named Amer, his original name given to him by his father. Today, Abu Bakr is a model of an entire generation of orphaned children in Bab al Tabaneh, orphaned by the era of Syrian security apparatus in Tripoli, which widowed many mothers in their youth after an early marriage, their futures bleak with no real means of providing for their children who grew up steeped in "resentment" for their slain fathers and relatives who were soldiers in Khalil Akkawi's emirate, which was the backbone of the Islamic Unity Movement. In his report, Bissan al Sheikh reveals that about a thousand of the fighters from this movement and their military leaders and organizers, especially in Bab al Tabaneh, were killed in the war during the first half of the 1980s in Tripoli.

Since the violent end of the Islamic Unity Movement Emirate and Khalil Akkawi's tenure as *Meshyakha Shebab* in 1986, a culture of poverty and armed anger has arisen as a reaction to the concealed resentment simmering in Bab al Tabaneh, especially among the children of the conscripts of the lost emirate and *Meshyakha*. Not finding an outlet for their repressed anger, one can understand how movements like *ash-Shebab al Mu'min* would have special appeal to groups of orphaned youngsters who had nothing to look forward to but a life of delinquency, cruelty, and violence.

A life in the streets was awaiting them. Most of them ran away and became delinquents early amid the violence and hustle of the streets. Their teachers did not notice their absence, or ask for a reason. Amer, like his peers, was kicked out of his home and ended up on the streets before the age of ten. There was no room for them in those small, crowded houses, which were the exclusive preserve of women, their mothers, sisters, and grandmothers. Alaa's house, for example, "at one point held fifteen people between children, wives, husbands and grandchildren" and "the only bedroom was given to the most recently married of the children". One bride decorated the walls with "pictures of Nancy Ajram and Amrou Diab next to *ayaas* from the Quran." Some of these female-centered houses were extremely clean and tidy, despite signs of extreme poverty in the furniture and walls, the decaying chairs, the peeling paint, the worn windows. But "the smell of homemade soap (a traditional product of Tripoli) and incense to ward off jealousy and the evil eye and flies" wafted and mixed with the light scent of women's perfume.

THE ISLAMIC REPENTANCE

Amer, who lived in one of these homes that did not welcome unmarried boys, had become accustomed before he was ten years old to leaving in the morning to earn a hard living in a mechanic's shop. On the threshold of these houses leading into the street, the ground was soft and sticky due to small, grassy streams that ran between the piles of garbage. The stench of wastewater was so strong it burned the nose. In the shop that took him in as a child, Amer was introduced to another boy who was addicted to sniffing the paint thinner used on the cars. Breathing the fumes had the same dizzying effect as drugs or alcohol. In his interview with

Bissan al Sheikh, Amer known as Abu Bakr after his Islamic repentance, admitted that he was twelve when he emptied an entire bottle of wine in one go to impress his friends. This enhanced his self-regard among them, and this prestige soon grew until he had a reputation as a *futuwa* in the neighborhood. This is what led him to persist in intimidating shopkeepers and collecting protection money from them until he was being arrested and jailed on a weekly basis. But with each imprisonment he only became more violent and criminal, and with each release he had to prove along with his peers that he was crueler and more ruthless than ever before.

Before "repenting", Amer was addicted to thinner fumes, like other boys of the street and the shops who used various substances to calm their nerves. This was called "*hebhebeh*" addiction to depressant "pills" that, like drugs, caused dizziness. They say that "Khodr Lettuce", as he was called because he sold lettuce in the market, was one of the biggest users. His mother used an anti-depressant, so he began stealing her pills and mixing them with liquor, and then he became addicted. Amer tried it for the first time in prison when he went into a rage and began banging his head against the wall and screaming. One of the guards gave him one pill and then a second, and a third until he calmed down. When he left prison, he immediately bought a bottle of 100 Benzhexol pills for less than 5,000 Lebanese liras.

THE GANGS OF SELF-DESTRUCTION

After following Amer on his journey from being addicted to a number of substances, from thinner to anti-depressants and alcohol, we arrive at the stage of mutilation, when he harmed his body using sharp objects to cut himself until he bled. When Abu Bakr tells stories of the scars and burns on his body, he refers to the period before he repented. Sometimes he speaks about a girl in the neighborhood whose family did not let him court her. He also talks about his friend who was imprisoned after a fight when he fired an unlicensed gun, and about the long weeks sitting in the street with no work or food. Often he would come across a gang of young men like himself who, under the influence of pills or alcohol, would take their mutilation to another level, cutting and burning their faces and chests, using razors, lit cigarettes, and hot iron skewers.

Romantic songs by Kathim Sahir or Hani Shaker were often the soundtrack to these group rituals of self-inflicted pain and suffering. One of the boys of the gang would begin to mutilate his chest, announcing that he was wounding himself "for the sake of" whomever as an expression of his painful, forbidden love for a particular girl, or in memory of an imprisoned friend. Others in the gang followed his example, taking up the instruments of pain until the blood ran from their wounds, which would remain on their skin as scars or marks. Abu Bakr told how one night as his family slept he was overcome with boredom. So he went to the kitchen and got a hot iron skewer and burned his leg to stave off the boredom. When his mother was awakened by the smell of burning flesh and saw what he had done, she became so furious she fainted.

In his narrative account, Bissan al Sheikh reveals that the young often identify themselves as "sons of the same *dawaa*" or calling, noting that they did not use the word *dawaa* in its religious sense, but rather to mean a "solid friendship". They belonged to an internal order based on addiction to drugs and alcohol and self-mutilation, which strengthened their feeling of belonging and solidarity. These gang rituals of mutilation and scarring from cuts and burns, which left marks on the skin, were important rites of passage for young men. They mark their transition from childhood to adolescence. This initiation is similar to the sense of "belonging" which Jean Monnot spoke of in his book on youth gangs in the suburbs of Paris in the 1960s. It is one of three features that distinguished youth gangs in that area. The second feature Monnot speaks of, the "special language," is also found among the gang members of Bab al Tabaneh, one of whom has shared some of his life story with us.

Belal is not yet twenty years old, but he belongs to one of the gangs that engages in drug use and mutilation in the ghetto with its culture of poverty. In this state, he mixes reality with fantasy and hallucinations that are dreamlike in their metaphors and symbolism. In this language, the boy begins to recount his life story:

"I don't sleep before four in the morning. Before laying down on the bed or the sofa at home, I usually watch porn on DVD and masturbate. I wake up between twelve-thirty and one on the afternoon, wash my face, brush my hair and put on a tie [here he is being sarcastic]. I go out into the street where I eat one or two *manouche* for breakfast. When I'm full I take two pills. I take the pills, and then I go and pick a fight or make trouble. I see someone walking in the street, maybe a friend from the neighborhood, and I stop him and say: 'give me 1,000 LL.' Then I slap him if he doesn't give it to me. I get on my motorcycle and me and a bunch of the other guys from the gang who have motorcycles go to the street where all the Syrian workers gather and we take some of their money. In the evening we take the money we've gathered and buy a liter or two of whiskey and some beer, then we sit on a corner under some window where we know there are pretty girls. I haven't had sex with a girl for three years. Here there are only boys available."

This last statement by Belal brings us back to the third feature of suburban gangs identified by Jean Monnot, who called it "latent homosexuality." Belal continues:

"I am tortured and desperate. The option of going to Iraq as a fighter is no longer available as it was before, and I was too late to enlist and go. When the war broke out between Hezbollah and Israel in July 2006, I was invited to go to the south but I didn't find a way. I thought once about leaving by myself and just wandering; anything to get out of this misery.

A few months ago I met a girl at my sister's engagement party, my sister-in-law's sister. We talked and I fell in love with her. Her house is by the port, so I started going there every day to see her. We smile at each other and trade looks. One time she came down and we went for a walk along the sea. She told me we were meant for each other, and she convinced me to stay out of trouble and stop cutting my face and chest, and I felt I was in love like in a movie or a novel. But when I went to see her after that, I fought with her brother near her house and I stopped going. A month later I learned she became engaged to someone else and married him, so I cut my face three times.

I can't stand the religious Islamists that grow out their beards and wear religious clothing. They all talk to you about religion and God and supporting Islam and Muslims, but they are liars and frauds."

When Belal concluded his story, he turned to me and said: "Take me, take me to Beirut and find me some work there. Take me."

FATHERS OF REPENTANCE AND FINDING THE RIGHTEOUS PATH

Is there a link between Belal's last cry and his frustrated desire for a jihadist Salafist Islamist network to take him to kill and die a martyr in Iraq, or his lost opportunity to fight in Hezbollah's Shiite jihadist war (the honest promise and divine victory–2006) in southern Lebanon?

Despite the differences and contradiction between the different ways he has considered getting out of Bab al Tabaneh, Belal's cry and his desires are all a product of his yearning for a promise of salvation, something quick and unexpected, that he hopes will take him away from a life that has been doomed from birth: orphaned, deprived of family support, ending up lost, drifting through a life on the streets among gangs of young men addicted to drugs, mutilation, and rituals of self-destruction. These rituals are based on a need for performance to validate the sense of masculinity and power of enduring pain in order to cleanse themselves of the pain of life and at the same time banish feelings of guilt, failure, and humiliation.

Belal's desire for some salvation also touches on his feeling that he has no way of achieving his aspirations of a "normal" life, except to wait for a coincidence. He is waiting for someone to come and take him and find him work somewhere, or to be conscripted in some militant network or sent on Jihad. But Belal's desire to be saved by one of these networks, even if it means committing suicide, could also be a reflection of his desire to be part of a trend. Over the last twenty years, militant networks have come to occupy a place in the local and global imagination and media. This fad is part of the wave of populist, Salafist Islam, sometimes jihadist as well, that Belal hopes will carry him away from the ghetto of Bab al Tabaneh and its culture of poverty, hardship and violence. It is revealing that Belal could still consider such venues despite his aversion to Islamist manifestations in his own environment in the form of religious men who grow their beards and dress in Islamic garb, the same sheikhs he considers "frauds."

It was one month since the end of the 2006 July War between Hezbollah and Israel and two months after the World Cup when the sound of the *muezzin* rose from Harba Mosque in Bab al Tabaneh, calling worshippers to the evening prayer that day in September. Abu Bakr chose to pray in the Harba Mosque in order to listen to the "convincing and enthusiastic sermon" of one of the sheikhs. Abu Bakr said that he and his "other religious friends" had taken the "advice" of this sheikh when he gave a sermon during the World Cup two months earlier calling for "the replacement of infidel flags (any team flag of a World Cup team) with flags of the Messenger of God. The religious young men busied themselves distributing black flags with the phrase 'there is no God but God' which they raised over the houses" where the people who lived there had placed flags for the World Cup team they supported. Abu Baker recounted how the young men of Bab al Tabaneh did not share in their joy when the team they were rooting for won. But he felt "happy that the Iranian team lost to Mexico" because he held a grudge against the young men from the Alawi neighborhood of Baal Muhsin who had fired "celebratory gunfire" for the death of Sheikh Abu Masaab al Zarqawi in Iraq. Baal Muhsin is located next to Bab al Tabaneh, which is Sunni. The two neighborhoods have been waging war since the 1970s, and the anger and the feuds are renewed by general events in the country.

Abu Bakr considers his new religious commitments to be "a noble mission worthy of sacrifice." The religious commitment represented in Bab al Tabaneh by the *dawa* and the sheikhs "is a project to reform the minds of the young men," according to Sheikh Amer, one of those from the *Dinniyeh* group who was arrested and imprisoned following the bloody events of 2000 and released in 2005. This sheikh, who is no older than twenty-eight, believes that his call to religion is "the only salvation for these young men from the cycle of delinquency, drifting, life on the streets, and self-destruction." The boys see their absent fathers in their *meshyakh* and the religious leaders, who became the role models they never had during their lost, orphaned, or homeless childhood, nor in their harsh adolescence.

Thus, some of the young men who are addicted to rituals of self-inflicted violence began to listen to and obey Sheikh Amer as an "older brother" or father, and he discouraged them from doing *haram*, or forbidden acts. He told them their bodies are not their own, but belong to God or the Creator. The young men, according to Abu Bakr, feel guilty for what they did before they repented and converted, but they were encouraged by the thought that at one time Abu Masaab al Zarqawi had been like them.

THE BOYS OF THE SALAFIST INSTITUTES

On the corner of Harba Mosque in Bab al Tabaneh, I drew near to three adolescents wearing Islamic dress in the Afghani style. Their coarse, dark clothes stood out amidst the chaos of the surroundings, making them appear organized, like military recruits from another time, the Soviet era or perhaps Stalin's. The oldest among them, who was seventeen and also the sturdiest, said they were students in the Imam Bukhari Institute for *Sharia* and *Faqih* in Wadi Jammous near Tripoli. Their clothes were their school uniforms, but were also religious and military.

It was almost three in the afternoon. The youngest boy who was fourteen said they had just returned from the institute, arriving by a special bus that picks up students living in Bab al Tabaneh every day at six in the morning and drops them off at two in the afternoon for 30,000 LL per month per student. I asked them to meet me some place, and the middle one who was fifteen said they were on their way home but that they would meet me after they had eaten lunch and prayed.

Based on what the three boys from the Imam Bukhari religious institute said about their daily lives with the other students on the "straight path" as well as their lives at home and in the neighborhood, it is clear that the mosques and prayer halls of Bab al Tabaneh were a sort of "safe haven" for them in a society plagued by a culture of poverty, begging, violence, delinquency, and even self-destruction of the kind favored by street gangs, which we discussed earlier.

The three boys share similar life stories in two aspects:

They all attended mosque and prayers in Bab al Tabaneh and registered in the religious institute after dropping out of public schools which they considered to be a breeding ground for delinquency and "corruption." They were united by their opinion that these destructive forces were reason enough to distance themselves from the "corrupt environment" of their neighborhood and schools. According to the older, chubby boy, the prevalence of *dawat* [proselytizers] and sheikhs whose positions they admired was the greatest contributing factor in their choice to begin their religious studies back before they enrolled in the Imam Bukhari Institute when they were still attending the schools of "chaos and corruption" in Bab al Tabaneh. Many of these sheikhs and *dawat*, like Abu Bakr, were repentant gang members who had given up violence, crime, and addiction. "Today, we try to call people to goodness," the chubby boy said, adding without hesitation, one of three refrains: *"Inshallah azza wa jel"*, which they said automatically after the conclusion of each statement.

And if we add the other two refrains, *"Salla Allah alayhi wa Sallam,"* and *"Alayhi as-Sallah wa as-Salaam"* which they said every time they mentioned the Prophet Mohammad, and in specific instances the adjective *karim* as well, we have the pillars of their unreflective linguistic structures, and the memorized expressions with which they adorned their simple speech and which gave their words an echo that amplified the illusion of their strength, depth, and timelessness. But these linguistic artifacts were not able to hide the hollowness of their words, or the emptiness of their poor, mute lives.

The boys of the Imam Bukhari Institute spoke to me about their daily lives for more than two hours in the Harba Mosque. What became clear from their words, which otherwise did not hold up without those repeated refrains, was that the institute was their "safe haven" from a society of ruin, a mental barrier that protected them from the violence and harshness of their society. It was a means of keeping them together, granting them security and the tranquility of engaging with an imaginary nation or group, which derives its presence and strength from the power of words that transcend time and language.

These words fill the language and daily lives of the boys, in the institute from six in the morning until two in the afternoon, and in their daily meetings at the mosques and prayer halls after they return from class. Usually between "prayers and dinner" they meet up with each other in one of the nearby mosques. They hold sessions for reading and discussing the Qur'an and perform their prayer duties. They often do their homework from the institute in the mosque before heading home where they watch the evening news before going to bed around nine. Even during their days off on Thursday and Friday, they attend Friday prayers and sermons at the different mosques they frequent. They also visit the small prayer halls that dot the neighborhood in order to "benefit and learn from" the religious sessions that they attended. The middle boy explained that they vary the mosques and prayer halls they attend because they draw no distinction between one Friday sermon or another, one orator or another: "they are all good and bring blessings, *biznallah*."

THE TRUE MUSLIM

"The last Friday sermon we attended," said the chubby one, "was about supporting the Prophet Mohammad *Salla Allah alayhi wa Sallam* against Denmark. The orator called for a boycott against Denmark and Danish products because of the drawing insulting the great Prophet."

Finally, after the chubby one had finished recounting a few excerpts from the sermon, he concluded, "when we grow up, we want to live, get married, and have a home and children. We want to have families." This is what he had taken away from the sermon: get married, have children and start a family, as if breeding is the goal and weapon of the nation, the source of its power, which is threatened by other nations. Another sermon the three boys had attended previously in the Harba Mosque focused on "piety," the middle boy said. Piety is an obligation for an individual to be "a true Muslim," a Muslim who enjoins good and prohibits evil so as not to burn in hell. "Evil" is to "disobey orders" dictated by "piety" so that one may enter heaven.

SALVATION FROM "CORRUPTION"

After performing their daily religious obligations, the three boys return to their homes where they "don't watch a single movie or program that isn't religious or news," said the youngest one. The middle one added: "why waste our time on corrupting things?" The older chubby one said that there was a television in his house but because his family wanted it, not him. "When we grow up and start our own families" there will be no television in "our house," he said proudly. "We don't mix" with other boys from the neighborhood unless they are "like us, religious," the middle one said, using the word "corruption" yet again. The environment of Bab al Tabaneh was "corrupt and corrupting" because of the "lack of religious learning." But, the youngest added, virtuous and wicked people could both be found in the area. By "wicked" he meant the delinquents in the streets, those who were running away from the same schools the boys had described as "corrupt," and from which they themselves had escaped by joining the religious institute. After finishing his primary education in a public school, the middle boy had spent two years as a student in a vocational school studying nursing. Of those two years, he says the atmosphere of the school was incredibly "corrupt": "there was no learning, just smoking on the playground, gangs of thugs, and making fun of teachers." It was rare that a student would actually want to learn in the institute, which was coeducational. The boys harassed the girls and when asked about this harassment, the boy repeated words from the religious lexicon that he had later learned at the Imam Bukhari Institute.

The youngest of the three boys had enrolled in the religious school a year ago. Before that, he had been a student for five years at the *Dar al Kitab al Karim* religious primary school. The school's administration and curriculum were tied to the Imam Bukhari Institute and students were required to wear Islamic dress.

The oldest boy had been enrolled at the Bukhari Institute for four years. He had completed his primary and half of his middle school education in Bab al Tabaneh public schools, where he "didn't learn a thing," so his family gave him the option of continuing or transferring to a religious school. "Even though I was lost and on the wrong path and saw others pray while I did not, God guided me to a religious session in one of the prayer halls, then I listened to sermons on tape and I found the true faith, thank God. I wanted to study *Sharia* in the institute in order to save myself and others from hell and show them the right way. *Biznallah* I am on the straight path that will lead me to heaven with the believers, *inshallah*."

ROBOTIC LANGUAGE

The three students of the Imam Bukhari Institute emphasized that their teachers at the institute were licensed sheikhs from the Islamic *Awqaaf,* which also approves the diplomas bestowed upon students when they officially graduate. The entire period of study in the institute was for seven years, divided into two parts: the intermediate level lasted for four years and the advanced, for three. All 200 students wear Islamic garb that they buy from the market. Almost all stores sell these clothes, *jalbab* for men and *abayas* for women. Some of the graduates of the institutes continue their *sharia* studies in Islamic universities. The best of these colleges are in Saudi Arabia, said the oldest boy, adding that he would like to study there someday like many of his peers, because there is more work there and "we can work and study at the same time." If he does not get the opportunity to travel to Saudi Arabia, there is Jinan Islamic University in the Abu Samra neighborhood of Tripoli.

I asked the oldest one to tell me what happened to him and what he saw during his days off. He did not speak from the language, imagination, and memories that had been swallowed by the impersonal expressions, ready-made linguistic structure that he and his friends had been taught in the religious meetings at the mosques and prayer halls and in the religious institute. Rather the expressions and words come from a sacred and elevated lineage, passed down orally through repetition and memorization. These words, which were already perfect, come from the venerable forefathers. They exist outside time, life, and experience, and they are repeated by those who seek knowledge and passed on as "popular Salafist culture" that becomes a comforting and safe haven from "culture of destruction" in Bab al Tabaneh.

It is interesting to note that when one of the three boys was accounting for why they felt as "strangers" on the street in Bab al Tabaneh, he denied that the cause of this alienation of salvation is a personal preference or inclination, or that it is based on personal experience. "There is a hadith that says: Islam began strange and it will return strange. Therefore we feel that we are strangers in this world. Our habits and our dress make us stand out amidst thugs who have no religion." It is a "Salafist *ghurba*" [alienation] whose legitimacy and tranquility are derived from the holy words of the forefathers. If the three boys and those like them had not found the true faith, they would never have left the society of destruction that they live in.

But this Salafist means of salvation grants its adherents the strength and ability not only to accept and live with their "alienation," but to take pride in it, imagining they belong to a special group that is being guided down the straight path, the path of righteousness and light that will lead them to heaven. The others, those who have not found the light, belong to the "misguided" who are corrupt and corrupting on the face of the earth. Their corruption will only lead to miserable fates and the fires of hell. The "alienation" of salvation, which is adopted and even pursued by adherents of the popular Salafist model, is the alienation of those whose vocal strength and echoes become a complete language of their own that excludes the dialect of the neighborhood and community, as well as normal narrative and news, anything directly relating to the sensual world and its experiences.

Neighborhood Violence among Youth Gangs in the Southern Suburbs of Beirut (Chiah)

Fidel Sbeity

The neighborhoods of Ghandour and Masbagha are located in the area of Chiah to the west of Ain al-Ramaneh and the east of Shatila and the Rawdat al-Shahedeen cemetery. Behind them lie the neighborhoods of Tarik al-Jadeeda and Sabra and Shatila. The two neighborhoods are divided by Asaad Asaad street, which started as just a few buildings in the 1940s and 1950s and was later completely paved over by the mid-1960s.

The first residents of Ghandour were displaced villagers from southern Lebanon who came to Beirut and settled behind the Ghandour sweets factory on the old Sidon road. They worked either in the factory or at the port, or else as vegetable sellers or garbage collectors for the Ghbayreh municipality. They hailed mostly from Kfarseer and Khiam. In the mid-1950s, the population of Ghandour swelled with southern families from the so-called "misery belt" which emerged in the 1920s and stretched from Furn al-Shubek to Ashrefieh, Nebaa and Dikwaneh, as well as new arrivals from the South. The displaced residents built their homes room by room, sometimes on top of each other, with relatives continuing to build onto the same house until the neighborhood came to resemble a large communal housing project.

Also beginning in the mid-1950s, villagers from Baalbek began to settle in Masbagha along with a few southerners. The neighborhood is located between Asaad Asaad street and Abdel Karim al Khalil Street, from Hirsh Beirut to the houses belonging to the Kazma and Kanj families that extend all the way to the old Sidon road. The development of Masbagha, like Ghandour, was somewhat haphazard, poor, and miserable. Most of the residents worked the same jobs, in addition to a large number of horse grooms drawn from Baalbek and Hermel after the hippodrome was built in the 1930s.

The two neighborhoods are surrounded by a stretch of empty sand dunes dotted with cacti. A number of horse stables were built at the edge of the district, as well as free private schools that the government allowed to be built. The intention was to compensate for the shortage of schools serving the displaced families that flooded into the district and who had, on average, no less than ten children.

Most of the children from families in the Bekaa Valley did not study in those schools, while the majority of children from southern families studied in the free primary schools located in Masbagha or Ghandour, the middle school, and in *Kulia al-Amiliyah,* the vocational high school in Nebaa for those who made it that far.

There were many factors that contributed to the rise of gangs of boys in the streets of these neighborhoods: poverty, hardship, high dropout rates, neglectful parents who were too busy trying to eke out a living. In addition, one must consider the limitations of their station and the creation of a world based on the neighborhood and its gangs, along with the culture of blood feuds in which they were raised. All these factors led to the emergence of gangs where the use of theft and violence became their way to secure a daily income and consolidate their power over the streets.

Based on interviews I conducted with informants who grew up in the neighborhood[1], one can conclude that these gangs of street boys were formed in the early 1960s and eventually became a reservoir of fighters for the militias that flourished towards the end of that decade. This coincided with the spread of Palestinian arms and the advancement of the Palestinian cause. Members of the Shahraban gang of Masbagha were feared militia fighters who became infamous for spreading terror and violence, hooliganism, and murdering in cold blood during the early years of the war. The Ghandour gang, on the other hand, joined political and ideological parties, paving the way for them to spread throughout Chiah.

Naji Jamal, one of my informants, knew the members of the Shahraban gang, which emerged in the mid-1960s in Masbagha. In the beginning it was made up of the sons and cousins of a family from Baalbek with strong clan ties. They used violence and brutality to extort money from shopkeepers and residents in the neighborhood, and banned outsiders from their territory. Soon after, another gang of boys from Ghandour formed a soccer team. At that time it should be noted, none of the boys from either gang was older than thirteen.

The two gangs financed their activities by collecting iron and copper scrap metal, as well as robbing, pick pocketing, and running small-time gambling operations. The two neighborhoods' geographical and social divisions contributed to creating tensions between the gangs, which fought in Asaad Asaad street using sticks, knives, pipes, and other kinds of sharp objects. They also took their rivalry to the soccer field, where games often ended in violence. These altercations sometimes escalated into a blood feud between members of the two gangs.

As fate would have it, the two gangs were growing up just as the war in Lebanon started. Starting in 1968, some members of both gangs underwent weapon training with some of the Palestinian factions. While the fate of the Shahraban gang turned out to be bloody and war-torn, the boys of Ghandour were able to avoid this fate because of their educational opportunities, and by not being drawn into the war and its bloody consequences.

WARS OF STREET BOYS IN PREPARATION FOR WAR:
FIGHTERS IN MASBAGHA

Waves of displaced families from southern Lebanon arrived in Beirut and its suburbs following the declaration of the state of Greater Lebanon in the early 1920s and the French administration's construction of the port of Beirut, the hippodrome, and the new tram in the new capital.

Naama Sbeity was twenty years old when he left his native village of Kfarseer in southern Lebanon for Beirut. It was the 1920s, and Naama joined thousands like him who came to the capital to seeking work at the port, or as vegetable sellers or porters in Martyrs' Square. Naama rented a room in Ashrefieh, where the houses were surrounded by gardens and orchards and the owners rented out to new arrivals who came to the capital from other areas of Lebanon. Sbeity moved to the neighborhood of Rahal, an empty area between Furn al-Shubek and the Sioufi side of the Ashrefieh hill. The neighborhood is one of the oldest belts of tin and wooden houses built by displaced villagers arriving in Beirut.

Life in Beirut was better for a young man than life in the village. Naama had left behind the destitution and hardship of village life with its family feuds over tiny pieces of land that could barely provide a subsistence living. Upon arriving in Ashrefieh, Naama began to work cultivating the land that surrounded the few scattered houses. Later, he became a porter at the port of Beirut, transporting goods from the port to the surrounding areas. He was able to save a bit of money and buy a vehicle that he used to sell vegetables, chestnuts, or corn cobs, according to the season, in Martyrs' Square and around the city. This was one of the best jobs for a displaced young man from the South, especially compared to working as a porter, garbage collector, or shoe shiner.

When he was thirty-two, Naama got a job as an office boy at the Ministry of Education with the help of Ahmed Bek Asaad. He kept the job until he retired. The Sbeity family and others like it from the village of Kfarseer were beholden to the feudal Shiite strongman Ahmad Asaad. Like other feudal chiefs, he had to contend with challengers from the Ouseiran and the Zein families in Nabatiyeh and the Khalil family in Tyre, all of them competing to employ the people of the South on their lands.

After one year of working as an office boy, one of his friends arranged for Sbeity to marry his niece after her father died and her mother remarried. The girl was just twelve years old, so Sbeity married her to save her from being an orphan and relieve her uncle from having to raise her, and to have someone to look after him later. Most of his life until then had been free of the worries of marriage and children.

Sbeity took his young wife to live in Rahal, where all the houses were made of tin and most of the residents were displaced Shiites from two neighboring villages in the South and made up four or five large families. All were somehow related by blood. His wife bore him seven children in their single-room with a kitchen consisting of nothing but a kerosene stove and some pots and pans. The bathroom was an outdoor hut shared between the neighbors.

THE NEIGHBORHOOD OF GHANDOUR

Since the 1930s, the Ghandour factory on the old Sidon road in Chiah attracted workers from south Lebanon, many of whom lived in small concrete rooms that began to proliferate and expand to accommodate new arrivals. Gradually buildings of one or two floors began to appear and form small neighborhoods whose residents worked in the factory or the nearby orchards. Naama Sbeity moved to one of these neighborhoods, known as Ghandour, following some of his relatives and friends from the village who had settled there.

In their new rented cement home, his wife bore seven more children, making Sbeity a father of fourteen, although three died from sickness or neglect: one from sun stroke, another was poisoned when he accidentally drank kerosene he thought was water, and the third was suffocated by his mother's breast while she fed him. The children who were born after the ones who died carried the same names, as if the souls of the departed children could live again in the new children.

One of those children, Ahmed, born in 1952, remembers images from his childhood growing up in Ghandour, including the incidents of 1958, which remain foggy in his memory. Suddenly weapons were distributed among some of the young men, roadblocks were erected in nearby Asaad Asaad street, tires were burned, and bullets flew in the neighboring districts, including Ain al Ramaneh. Ahmed also remembers the "revolutionary" bomb that went off near the Ghandour plant, although it had been intended for a different target. As a child, Ahmed was not fully aware of what was happening, nor did he know that just fifteen years later he would be a participant in an even bloodier and more violent war, the first rumblings of which began in Chiah in 1975.

IN THE FREE SCHOOLS

Another son of a southern family from Khiam living in Ghandour recounts how his family and others like his were very keen to educate their sons (not their daughters). This set them apart from the families from Hermel and Baalbek, who did not put their children in school or pay them much attention. Those children, he said, spent most of their days barefoot and half-naked in the orchards that surrounded their neighborhood.

Ahmed Sbeity remembers how in the mid-1950s he used to walk from his family's house in Ghandour to Muhathi Street every morning with a small group of friends in order to attend the Rihani School, which was free. The school was founded by Qassem Rihan from the southern village of Kfarseer. The school was comprised of two rooms that were used by a bakery before dawn and became two classes for students of different ages from morning until noon. The school's desks at which Ahmed sat for the first years of his schooling were made from the wooden panels on which the bread dough was placed at dawn. The school merely put stones beneath them to convert them to seats. The first class was comprised of students from preschool to fifth grade, and the second was for middle-school students. Their teacher was an old woman who taught all the subjects. During the breaks she sold them chocolate and *manouche*. After the school day was over she cleaned the two rooms and prepared the school to become a bakery again the next day.

Beginning in the mid-1950s, free schools began to proliferate in the face of a shortage of public schools serving the large numbers of new students from displaced families. Successive Lebanese governments opened free schools as a quick solution to the problem of the immediate and growing demand for education. The government gave out licenses to charities to open these schools. Effectively, this allowed anyone to open a school, especially if they had the support of a politician. The government gave grants to the owners of the school and in exchange the school offered heavily subsidized education with the families paying a small fee of 3 lira per month. Many of the teachers, known as *murabeen*, maintained close ties with Shiite politicians who grew rich off the schools in just a few years. The Sbeity family and Qassem Rihan, both of them from Kfarseer, were able to get a license to open a free school because half of Ghandour came from the same village and because they had strong connections to the Shiite leadership there.

After two years in the bakery, Qassem Rehan was able build a two-story building in a neighborhood close to Asaad Asaad street. He formally named the new school the Rihani School, combining his name with that of the famous Lebanese writer Amin Rihani.

But Ahmed Sbeity, after a year of studying at the Rihani school, moved to the National Culture School, which was also free, in Masbagha, the neighborhood located between Asaad Asaad street and Abdel Karim Khalil Street in Chiah. The National Culture School was founded by Hassan Shamsiddine. Free schools cropped up all over Chiah. The Scientific Renaissance School was founded by the Sbeity family in Ghandour. When the family partners split, one of them went on to found the Modern Redemption School, while another founded the Modern Education School in the same neighborhood. Ahmed Sbeity moved between these schools for most of his primary education until he was twelve. He remembers that in the early 1960s students of these schools were already organizing themselves into small gangs, some of whom skipped school and took refuge in the surrounding streets where they fought and collected iron, aluminum, and copper metal from the streets and buildings under construction to sell to scrap metal dealers.

MASBAGHA AND THE SHAHRABAN GANG

By enrolling in the National Culture School in nearby Masbagha, Ahmed Sbeity came to know some of the boys in the Shahraban gang, after hearing much about their aggressiveness and ill treatment of strangers in the street. These boys were not more than thirteen years old, and all of them were from displaced families from Baalbek and Hermel that had carried their clan rivalries with them.

Naji Jamal from Masbagha, who joined the Labor Party in 1973, recounted how the Shahraban gang was named after the mother of the group's core members, who were from the Mubarak family. Shahraban was a woman from Baalbek famous for her sharp tongue, strong personality, and power. The residents of the neighborhood would go out of their way to avoid Shahraban and her children because she would personally defend them if they were attacked or someone started a fight with them. Whenever there was a fight between two children of Masbagha, it would soon become a feud between the two families.

Naji Jamal recounted how one of Shahraban's boys worked as a groom for Henri Pharaoun, who favored the boy and took him to Paris at the outbreak of the civil war when the hippodrome closed. After that, people's imaginations were set loose and some imagined they strolled the streets of Paris dressed in fur while in reality the children ran half naked and barefoot through the neighborhood, which extended to the wood, which later became a cemetery called Rawdat al Shahedeen.

According to multiple sources, the neighborhood of Masbagha was divided into two areas: families from Baalbek and the Bekaa, including Shahraban and her family, lived in the southern half next to Abdel Karim Khalil street, while Shiites from the south resided in the northern half near Asaad Asaad street. The population of both districts swelled in the early 1950s with new displaced from the southern villages and the "misery belt" that extended along the edge of Ashrefieh, Nebaa, and Bourj Hammoud. Of the people from Baalbek, one group had arrived in Chiah and Ghbayreh earlier than the other, and this group worked mostly as grooms at the hippodrome. Regardless of the rumors and legends surrounding Shahraban, it is clear that she pushed her children to take revenge on the children who attacked or fought with them. But she also incited them to create controversies and quarrels with the children of the neighborhood. And so, her children became a small feared gang and expanded their gang to include cousins and other children of Baalbeki families from the neighborhood, especially those who shared a tribal pride. None of them went to school. Rather they spent their time fighting in the street, harassing and robbing strangers and beating up the children coming and going from school, until the residents became cautious of them. Some people assigned them small tasks to avoid offending them, while others used them for protection. The owner of the National Culture School pleaded with them not to bother his school. On occasion, he used them to prevent the demonstrators who wanted the school to join the strike. He also relied on them to help him keep track of truant or troublesome students. Some of the storeowners asked them to protect the shops in exchange for money paid to one of them to avoid trouble with the others.

AIN AL-RAMENEH

When he started middle school in 1964, Ahmed Sbeity moved to the Dagher Public Middle School in Ain al Rameneh. Most of the other students were Christians and the school curriculum was far more rigorous than in the free schools he had attended in Chiah. The students at Dagher Middle School were monitored strictly by the teachers and their success was the administration's top priority. Sbeity met new friends as well, including Samir Geagea, who was the most courageous and unyielding of his peers. The young men of the school feared Geagea, who was slender with long hair, for his ferocity and toughness. Weaker students or those without tribal or regional connections would often ask him for protection. Samir Geagea lived in a small house of two rooms that showed signs of poverty despite the elegance of the furniture and its arrangement. It was clear that his mother was keen to secure a minimum of well-being for her sons. The family was observant, their faith evident in the images of the Virgin Mary and the saints found throughout the house. The father was a policeman and rarely home.

Ahmed and Samir became friends and often visited each other at home. Their mutual friends were Gabriel Usta and others from the Haydamous family who later entered the Lebanese Army and rose within the intelligence wing. In Ain Al Rameneh, Sbeity also met a young man named Ramz Minovitch and his brother Nasif, the cousins of Ali Manovitch, who lived with his family in Masbagha and was active in the Shahraban gang. During his time at the Dagher School, Ahmed Sbeity never experienced sectarian prejudice except for a few occasions when he fought with one of the Christian boys who had made fun of the Prophet Muhammad for forbidding pork because he once buried wine in the dirt and when he came back he found a pig had already dug it up and drank it.

After leaving the Dagher School in Ain al Rameneh, Ahmed Sbeity returned in 1968 to visit his old friends and see how they were doing. It was dusk when he came to Ain ar-Rameneh's main street and saw some of his old friends dressed in khaki military garb, chanting slogans, and training with weapons in the street under a Kataeb Party banner. Rather than greeting them, he turned and headed back to his neighborhood, avoiding the many checkpoints. This was his last visit to Ain al-Ramaneh.

BETWEEN GHANDOUR AND MASBAGHA

The neighborhood of Ghandour sprung up behind the factory of the same name, on land that was farmland before it became barren. There were water wheels and scattered houses belonging to the "original" inhabitants of Chiah from the Kazma, Kanj, Khalil and Chahine families, who owned the land along with some old Christian families. In the 1950s, the houses of the "original" inhabitants were divided by large sandy stretches dotted with cacti. In the later 1950s when the neighborhood of Ghandour first began to emerge, Ahmed Sbeity remembers these large, sandy spaces were wide open and came all the way to the edge of the *Hirsh* (pine grove). Then the new houses that started as single rooms became to resemble housing projects for the new arrivals who came from Jebel Amel to work in the Ghandour sweets factory on the old Sidon road. In the 1930s, after the hippodrome was built near Hirsh Beirut next to Pine Palace, workers came from Baalbek to Chiah-Ghbayreh to work as grooms for the racehorses, eventually bringing their families with them, some of whom settled in Masbagha. Most of those who came from the South worked as porters in the port or performed other menial labor. Some of the residents of Ghandour moved there from Rahal or Housh at the bottom of the Ashrefieh hill on the Sioufi side on the border with Furn al-Shubek. The horse stables had sprung up throughout the area between Ghandour and Masbagha.

The families of Sbeity, Qamhiyyeh, Mshaymish, Awada, Noureddine, and Mihyeddine arrived in Ghandour from the villages of Kfarseer, Taybeh, and Khiam. The first arrivals from those villages bought a small plot of land from the original owners from the Kazma and Kanj families. Without any kind of plan or layout, they began to build small houses consisting of one room and a bathroom. As time passed, they built new rooms next to those rooms to make a two-room house. The first arrival would host his brother or relative in his home for a few months until they built another room next to the old one or on top of it. By the beginning of the 1960s, the neighborhood had become a like a housing project for villagers.

According to one of the first residents of Ghandour, the neighborhood split into two parts: *al-Fuqani* and *al-Tahtani* [the ones above and the ones below], names that were inspired by the pattern of building in the residents' home villages. The people of the two neighborhoods were bound by familial bonds that weakened over time as the children intermarried and lived in their families' houses or on the outskirts of the neighborhood in buildings erected by Ruweida Ruweida in the mid-1960s. Families expanded and the original clan connections that bound the first generation of displaced villagers weakened.

Masbagha, which sits across from Ghandour on the other side of Asaad Asaad street, evolved in a similar manner. It also attracted families that had been displaced from the South, including the Qamhiyyeh, Mshaymish, Hassawi,

Damashq, Hamdan, Tahan, Jamal, and Atwi families. They settled alongside two other groups who had come earlier from Baalbek and Hermel and who included the Moussawi, Mubarak, and Saqr families, in addition to the grooms from the stables. One side of Hirsh Beirut was near Masbagha before it became the Rawdat al Shehedeen cemetery when the war started in 1975. There was also the Itani orchard, which stretched from the cemetery to what is now Msharefiyyeh Square, on that side, as well as stables mostly belonging to Henri Pharaoun. The residents of Masbagha were from Baalbek and the South. The southerners made up most of the western and northern half on the side of Asaad Asaad street facing the Hirsh facing the street that would later become the Hadi Nasrallah highway. This area became known as Haramieh, directly facing the mosque built by Sheikh Muhammad Mehdi Shemsaddine. The inhabitants originally from Baalbek lived in the eastern side next to Abdel Karim Khalil street in two lanes lined with two- and three-story buildings.

All the land of Masbagha was owned by the Salim and Kazma families. Every building that went up in the early 1950s is named for members of these two families. Just as in Ghandour, the first displaced families to arrive in Masbagha bought a small plot of land from the original owners and built rooms close together, some of which became housing complexes with courtyards as the rooms multiplied and new relatives arrived. The neighborhood remains unruly even today. Naji Jamal, who grew up in Masbagha, says that when his father first came to Beirut he rented a room in the neighborhood and would host relatives who worked with him removing tiles. Twenty to thirty people from the same family lived in that room temporarily and paid rent until moving to work somewhere else. The houses during that period, at the beginning of the migration were shared, with everyone sharing food and a single toilet and tap to wash their utensils and clothing. Things had not changed significantly when his father decided to move to a modern apartment in the same neighborhood where he lived with two other families, one in each room, with a shared kitchen and bathroom for more than twenty people.

This is how the neighborhoods that make up the so-called "misery belt" in Beirut's southern suburbs came about. The neighborhoods of Ghandour and Masbagha in Chiah-Ghbayreh were the first seeds of those suburbs, south of the hippodrome and the Ghandour factory. These two areas exploded like popcorn, creating the other neighborhoods of the southern suburbs. Both neighborhoods were created by rural displacement and founded on tribal bonds transferred from the villages of origin. Buildings piled on top of each other, rising higher and higher without ever expanding out.

The average number of children for the families from these neighborhoods was not less than seven. Ahmed Sbeity recalls not knowing a single family that had less than ten children. Some of those children were born after their families moved to the city, while some were born in the village or in the misery belt surrounding

Ashrefieh, in Housh Rahal, Nebaa, or Bourj Hammoud. Most of the children from southern families studied in the National Culture School owned by Hassan Shemsiddine from Arabsalim. Most of them, however, dropped out by the fifth grade to take menial jobs or work as craftsmen with their fathers. Not many made it to middle school, and Jamal remembers that just one or two would go on to high school over the course of several years. For the most part, the children from Baalbek did not go to school and became street children who learned violence and extortion instead.

STREET GANGS AND THEIR ACTIVITIES

In the early 1960s, the Shahraban gang was famous in the Masbagha and through-out surrounding neighborhoods for the violent acts and theft committed by its members. Ahmed Sbeity says that the leaders were Oqab Saqr, his brother Ali, their friend Rida Aoun, and his brothers Suhail and Zuhair. There were also Khodr, Mohammad and Hussein Halabawi, and Ibrahim Halabi. Oqab Saqr was the most vicious and violent of them all, although none of them were older than thirteen. This is what made him the most famous in the group and their undis-puted leader. If someone from the gang stole something from neighborhood or outside he had to split his spoils with Oqab.

H.T., who has lived in Masbagha his whole life and joined the Amal Movement in the early 1980s, describes Oqab Saqr as being short with dark skin and short hair, his face scarred from knife fights. His eyes were never still and rather than look at whoever was talking to him, he surveyed the surrounding area as if prepar-ing a counter-attack. One had to remain on guard in Oqab's presence, watching his hands, which could at any moment fly out of his pockets grasping a razor or knife to slash whoever was speaking if he said the wrong thing. His brother Ali, on the other hand, was handsome and tall with sleek hair and he was always well dressed. If we can describe Oqab as a thug, then his brother Ali was an *abaday* in the original sense of the word: he did not initiate the attack, but would defend himself and those around him who asked for his help.

Naji Jamal, the university professor who lived in the neighborhood, belonged to a street gang before he went to France to do his doctorate. He remembers that once Ali Saqr saw a small boy crying in Asaad street and asked him why. The boy told him that a boy had hit him and stolen his money. Ali walked into the café where the boy was sitting and beat him before anyone had a chance to defend him. Ali was also strengthened by his brother Oqab, who was widely feared in the streets of the neighborhood. This description could also be applied to Rida Aoun and his brother Suhail, the first considered a bully and the second an abaday. Despite that fact that the core group consisted of those four, Rida Aoun was always with Oqab while Suhail and Ali were inseparable.

In the early 1960s, the number of members of the Shahraban gang did not exceed ten thirteen-year-old boys from two or three families connected through Baalbeki clans. But after a year or two, the gang grew to more than twenty boys from different families in the neighborhood, including some from southern Lebanon, like Fayez Atwi, Ali Minovitch, and a dark-skinned boy named Santo whose mother was African and father was Lebanese. The gang's activities ranged from extorting money from the shopkeepers in return for protection to petty theft of children's games left on the ground-floor balconies and copper wires and pipes from construction sites, which were everywhere at that time. The gang claimed a small patch of land from the nearby *Hirsh* [woods] and hung out there most of the time. The *Hirsh* became off-limits to strangers, who, if they happened to wander in, would be stopped and robbed blind by the boys. Oqab Saqr was always accompanied by Rida Aoun and Ali Manovitch. Oqab and his friends insisted on harassing any boy who appeared shy and well-dressed, the "mama's boys" who in their view deserved a beating. Students and children would avoid passing through areas where they knew Oqab would be waiting with his friends Aoun and Minovitch.

Another one of the gang's activities was to force the neighborhood children to play soccer with them. During the game, which was held on an empty lot, the Shahraban gang would attack the other players and take their ball, especially if the Shahraban had lost the game. Ahmed Sbeity narrated how the Shahraban gang once challenged a team from Ghandour to a game. There were more than fifty boys from the Shahraban gang and their fans carrying what looked like wooden swords. They surrounded the field during the match, which the Ghandour team won. Oqab refused to acknowledge their victory and asked for overtime twice, until the boys from the Ghandour team decided to lose on purpose for fear of being attacked by the Shahraban gang and their fans. The match ended and the Shahraban gang collected the half lira reward, but not before they had stolen the other team's ball, which they had saved up for a week to buy.

Naji Jamal says that there were gang fights at least once a day, and not a single boy emerged without a cut or punch to his face, or a *bouna* to his shoulder [a *bouna* is a piece of metal that fits around the knuckle and has nails sticking out]. The neighborhood boys were always challenging boys from the surrounding area, and they would pelt each other's heads with stones. Some of the boys from the South did not enjoy the protection of the Shahraban gang, so they formed their own soccer team, which included boys from the Hayek, Faour, Damashq, Jemel, and Aisi families, as well as one boy from Baalbek named Ali Moussawi.

IDENTIFICATION AND PROTECTION

After the Shahraban consolidated their power and their reputation spread throughout the suburbs, other gangs began to appear, some of which were allies of the Shahraban and some enemies. These gangs were not as tight-knit or powerful as the Shahraban gang.

In the mid-1960s, a group of boys from the South and some from Baalbek living in Ghandour formed their own gang. Most of them attended the same school, and they decided on a meeting place in the neighborhood square and rarely strayed outside it. They ranged in age from twelve to fourteen. But the families of Ghandour were determined to educate their children and save them from a life on the streets, while none of the Shahraban gang went to school or were subject to any supervision by their families. The boys of Ghandour began to imitate the Shahraban gang and so they also formed a soccer team, and when some of their members carried knives or razors, they did so too. In fact, in some ways they were more like the Shahraban gang more than the Shahraban gang itself.

The most prominent members of the Ghandour gang were Ahmed Sbeity, Ghazi Fran, Kamel Qamiha, and Moustafa Nouraddine, Hussein Shami, and Youssef, Lutfi and Wajih Sbeity. The leader, Ali "The Upholsterer" Abdel Khaliq was called so because his father worked as an upholsterer in the neighborhood. He was the oldest and going to school did not distract him from leading the gang. He was also the largest and most brutal of his peers. "Natural selection" had endowed the boys with gifts that allowed them to distinguish themselves by assuming leadership. Every now and then, violent fights took place among members of the same gang in order to accede to leadership. Eventually though they would all acknowledge the leadership of the strongest. But the Ghandour gang was nothing more than a group of boys who met after school. They were never very powerful players in the violent, tough life of the streets. Nonetheless, the group did afford them some protection from the brutal Shahraban gang.

The empty sand lots surrounding the neighborhood were a haven for the Ghandour boys whose small houses were cramped and overflowing with brothers and sisters, mothers and fathers, and relatives arriving from the village. Even at the age of twelve, their world was limited to the neighborhood, the port, Asaad Asaad street, and the neighborhood of Masbagha on the other side. Those of them who attended school went to one located in one of the two neighborhoods, and all their relatives lived in the same area so there was no reason to leave. Only the fathers left in the morning to go to their menial jobs and did not return until sundown. Women and girls were confined to the house all day and the boys were at school or in the street. The gang used to meet on one of the floors of an unfinished building in Asaad Asaad street to prepare for soccer games or fight with another group of boys, often the Shahraban. The challenges were not limited to soccer, but extended into fights in Asaad Asaad street where the boys of the two gangs would brawl using rocks and sticks and even knives.

The times and places for these battles were decided upon by both sides, or groups from both. Usually Asaad Asaad street, which divided Musbagha from Ghandour, became the stage for these fights that involved knives, wooden sticks,

metal pipes, and razors. Sometimes, the fights reached theatrical heights of a spectacle. One of the boys would wave a flag to start the fight, and the boys would run
towards each other as fast as they could and clash, the air ringing with screams
of pain and attack. After a short time, each boy would pair off with an opponent
and they would exchange blows in the middle of the fray as their friends fought
around them. Wood and iron cracked against skulls and bones, blood and sweat
flowed, and breath became ragged as the boys played out a scene resembling something out of Martin Scorsese's "Gangs of New York". The fighting would continue
until one of the neighbors called internal security and the boys would run and
disappear into the back alleyways. The tight alleyways, formed by ad hoc and overcrowded construction, made excellent escape routes for the boys who knew every
inch of the neighborhood.

THE DEATH OF OQAB SAQR

In one of these fierce battles, Ali "The Upholsterer," the leader of the Ghandour
gang, struck Oqab Saqr, leader of the Shahraban, over the head and wounded
him. Saqr decided to take revenge on Ali personally. Saqr recruited two of his
companions and set an ambush for Ali in Ghandour. When he passed by, the
three attacked him, beating and kicking him to the ground. When he was able
to get free from them he ran home and called to his cousin Zuhair Abdul Khaliq
for help. Zuhair ran down carrying a bar towards the three attackers and fell on
them, wounding one in the head before they ran away. But the feud did not end
there. It simmered and grew between the two families from Baalbek so that any
time they met on the street they would exchange curses, and, more often than not,
blows as well.

Years later, after the Civil War had already begun in 1975, Zuhair Abdul Khaliq
joined one of the Palestinian parties that had sprung up, spreading their weapons
throughout the neighborhoods of the displaced Shiites in Beirut's southern
suburbs. Oqab Saqr's gang had split up, with each of the former members finally
leaving the familiar streets and pursuing his own activity, some with links to the
drug trade, prostitution, gambling, and extortion in the heart of old Beirut, especially in the red light district near Martyrs' Square.

Ahmed Sbeity tells how one afternoon after 1975, Zuhair Abdul Khaliq came
to Oqab Saqr's house in Musbagha. He called him out by name, and his sister
came out on the balcony. Zuhair asked to speak to her brother, who came out
on the balcony with a towel over one shoulder as if he were preparing to shave or
bathe. Before Oqab could say a word, Zuhair shot and killed him. Afterwards,
Zuhair Abdel Khaliq disappeared, and his fate during the war is unknown.

On the other hand, Naji Jamal, who grew up in Masbagha and was a small boy
when Oqab was killed, says that no one knows the motive behind the crime or the

perpetrator, notwithstanding that all the rumors tie the killing to a rivalry over a woman, or the drug trade, or the mafia-like activities of Oqab Saqr, which had expanded before the war to tourist resorts in the mountains and Beirut. These illicit businesses generally revolved around prostitution, gambling and drugs. Oqab's small mafia empire grew swiftly. He went from controlling just the local neighborhoods to having a hand in the far districts of Beirut and the mountain resorts. In the early 1970s, Oqab had been able to extend his power beyond his own neighborhood to the nearby Asaad Asaad street, which was undergoing a construction boom during this period and was full of new money exchangers, real estate offices, building materials, and gambling tables. Oqab would collect money from all of them in exchange for protecting their businesses from his gang.

THE CITY AND THE GANGS

Ahmed Sbeity, Naji Jamal, and H.T. recount how these gangs of boys, after they had grown, needed money in order to visit the city center or go to the cinema and partake in the amusements there. They started selling what they stole from construction sites in Asaad street. They took iron, water pipes, copper bars, and used electrical equipment and sold it to scrap dealers in exchange for money they could use to buy tickets to the movies, especially after a cinema opened nearby in Asaad street. But collecting and selling scrap materials was not limited to the gangs. It was something all the boys did at the time, so much so that some of them transformed it as a regular job. Groups of brothers or friends would collect cans, iron, and copper wire from distant neighborhoods and load them into vehicles until they had enough to sell to scrap dealers for a bit of money for themselves and their families.

The boys of the street invented other sources of income; some started their own black market, especially the Ghandour gang. The educated ones would buy movie tickets for Saturday and Sunday mornings, so that when people arrived and found the shows were sold out they were forced to buy tickets from the boys who scalped them at the entrance. They bought the tickets in the morning for sixty pennies and sell them in the afternoon for a lira. In those days the cinema was very popular considering it was still new and had spread throughout Beirut, especially in Martyrs' Square.

Selling retail cigarettes was another source of money, in addition to petty gambling with packets of cigarettes in the city center. One of them carried a wooden box, on top of which he would place a number of Lucky cigarette packets, and ask passers-by to make bets, which were, or course, fixed. This would go on until the police came by and the vendor would take his wooden box and escape into the crowd.

Another way of making money was smuggling people into wrestling and soccer matches in the Sports City. The smuggling was done in coordination with the guards stationed at the rear door of Sports City on the side facing Sabra. The price was tickets ranged between three and five liras, but the smugglers took half a lira or a lira, which they split with the guards. After they had finished smuggling around the second or third round of wrestling, the boys would sneak in and sit on the bleachers and cheer with the other spectators. During soccer matches they would also get involved in fights between opposing fans. These fights often took place between fans of the Nejma Team and those of the Hometown Armenian Team, the two teams that were most competitive among the Lebanese teams. And when the guards prevented them from sitting in the stands with the spectators on the Hometown, knowing they were not fans, the boys would throw empty bottles at the fans in order to start a fight.

But all these enterprises, selling stolen goods, smuggling spectators into Sports City, and selling scrap metal and movie tickets on the black market, were not only gang activities. All the boys of the suburbs partook in them, without belonging to s specific gang.

THE BEGINNINGS OF POLITICAL ACTION

In the late 1960s, five of the boys from the Ghandour gang went on to middle school in Nebaa at another free school owned by someone from the Sbeity family. They walked from Chiah to Bourj Hammoud in order to save their transportation money, which they saved until the end of the week when they would buy movie tickets to sell on the black market, or else go to the market in Martyrs' Square. While moving about the city they encountered student demonstrations and sometimes joined in. These included demonstrations after defeat of the Arab armies in 1967 and the death of Gemal Abdel Nasser in 1970. Others were student, labor, or political protests, most of which were associated with the Palestinian cause.

But even if the boys participated in those events, they did not do so as principled or committed partisans. Rather, they used it as an opportunity to express their outrage and vandalize property. At that time, weapons were spreading throughout the Palestinian camps close to Nebaa, including Bourj al Barajneh. Some of them had links to the political parties in the southern suburbs. Hence many of the boys participated in weapons training in the camps with the Democratic Front for the Liberation of Palestine three times a week. At first, the goal was not political or ideological so much as to spark enthusiasm among young people to bear arms.

Ahmed Sbeity was attracted to these training sessions and political culture after reading the popular Marxist books of the time and soon became a member of the central committee in the Abu Nidal Palestinian group. This was before joining the ranks of the Organization for Communist Action, which was born out of the Arab Socialist Movement and the Lebanese Socialists' Movement.

After a short period, Ahmed Itani, who was a year older, distinguished himself from the other boys and joined the Arab Nationalist Movement, which was influenced by Marxism. In 1968, Itani was assigned by the movement to recruit young men from the neighborhood and push them towards weapons training in the camps with the Democratic Front for the Liberation of Palestine. Many of them did go train with weapons, which gave them a sense of power after growing up amid feuding street gangs. The party members used to impose themselves on their communities through their ideas or by carrying the banner of the Palestinian cause at a time when weapons from the Palestinian organizations were plentiful and widespread. The training started in the Bourj al Barajneh camp and then moved to Arqoub or "Fatah Land" after the Cairo agreement of 1969.

In every neighborhood there were one or two young men who were active in some movement or political party. They would gather the boys and recruit them by holding social gatherings where politics was mixed in with the normal youthful discourse that took place among the young men who attended. This was how the Arab Nationalists attracted young men to their meetings. They made an effort not to dwell too much on heavy intellectual topics like politics and culture, but by mixing these ideas in with normal conversation or issues that affected the boys' daily lives in the neighborhood and their relationship with each other and their community. The young activists in that movement were able to recruit a large number of boys from the neighborhoods in this way. In Ghandour alone, they were able to convince more than twenty young men, most of them from the old gang. The young men were attracted by the discussions, which moved them to join one party or another.

Ahmed Itani, a vegetable seller who never learned to read or write, was able to ignite the spirit of determination and struggle in the hearts of his young listeners and convince them that their problems could be blamed on the Lebanese political system, and that the Arab nation could only be liberated by taking back the occupied Palestinian lands.

The young men were impressed by Itani, who taught them about Marxist culture and boosted their self-confidence and pushed them to use their physical and intellectual abilities in the political class struggle. They began to feel that they could be more than members of a childish neighborhood clique. They were swept away by slogans that were somehow bigger than their tiny neighborhood, and they took up the banner of the major issues, first and foremost among them the Palestinian cause, the resistance, and the end of class struggle. After completing their intermediate education (*brevet*) in Bourj Hammoud, the friends from the old Ghandour gang went on to high school at the *Kulia al Amiliah,* the vocational school in Ras al Nebaa. There, they began working with the student action committee of the Organization for Communist Action.

As recalled by Ahmed Sbeity, during their first year at the school, the boys began to re-examine their lives, and their view of their social status began to change. Ahmed himself became more aware of his poverty and the difficulty of his situation compared with the other students. His pants had holes, and the money his family gave him was not even enough to buy a sandwich in the big cafeteria where the students sat to eat lunch and socialize. The other students were from the new Shia middle class that began to emerge at that time. Most of the students arrived at school in the morning by bus or their parents drove them by car, while he and his friends came by foot no matter how bad the weather. The only solution to their feelings of inferiority and dispossession was to cut school and hang out in Martyrs' Square or on the rocks by the sea in Ain al Mreisseh where they gambled with the little money they had. When one of them lost everything he had, the winner would give him ten pennies so he could get home and the winners would go to the cinema in Martyrs' Square to watch back to back movies, which started at nine in the morning and finished at four in the afternoon. Meanwhile, they were being drawn in to the political struggle by talking to Palestinians who came to Lebanon from Jordan, attending political education meetings, and performing "party" tasks in the neighborhood. They participated in the demonstrations organized at their school, and during the summer vacation they went with members of the Democratic Front for the Liberation of Palestine to train in Arqoub.

THE FATE OF THE SHAHRABAN GANG BOYS IN WAR

Rida Aoun was killed. After the death of Oqab Saqr at the beginning of the civil war, his friend Rida Aoun joined one of the armed militias that had become active by the early 1970s. His influence grew with that of the militias and the parties and the spread of weapons in the neighborhoods. Aoun began working for the General Command of the Popular Front [for the Liberation of Palestine] then the Organization for Syrian Commandos and then in the early 1980s he joined the Amal Movement.

Ahmed Sbeity, who joined the Organization for Communist Action, moved to Nabatiyeh to attend the teachers college there. He took his political and military activities with him to southern Lebanon. At the start of the war in 1975, he was appointed an official in the Popular Security movement in his town and the surrounding villages. The Popular Security was an umbrella faction for a group of parties belonging to the National Movement and was responsible for security in the towns and villages of southern Lebanon.

By the late 1970s, something happened in one of those towns that invoked images from the feud between the two gangs of street boys in Chiah. Ahmed Sbeity, who was an official in the Popular Security, received information on a group of individuals pushing hashish in the nearby town of Zibdeen outside Nabatiyeh.

A military contingent from Public Security searched one of the houses in Zibdeen and it turned out that Rida Aoun, one of Oqab Saqr's old friends from the Masbagha gang, was in the house. It seemed as though the feud between the two gangs had moved from the streets and games of their adolescence to the backdrop of the civil war. Ahmed Sbeity and his group arrested Aoun and imprisoned him in the Popular Security's prison in Nabatiyeh. After ten days, Aoun cut himself with a razor and bled so much that he was released because his captors feared for his life. After his release, Aoun followed members of the Popular Security who had arrested him and attempted to take revenge.

In 1984, Rida Aoun was moving between a number of Palestinian factions and became an official in General Command, which had consolidated its strength in Chiah after the Syrian Army entered Lebanon in 1976. But Aoun was also counting on the Amal Movement, which had grown in strength after the Israeli invasion on 1982 and the February 6 Intifadah in 1984. The group had extended its influence in the Shiite neighborhoods of Beirut, including Ghandour, Masbagha, and Asaad street.

One day that year Rida Aoun was managing the pumps at one of the gas stations in Asaad street, deciding who could go and who couldn't, and controlling the sale of fuel, despite the fact that the station belonged to someone from a different party that did not control the street and neighboring districts. A young man arrived and wanted to fill his tank, and Rida Aoun refused. The two began to argue, and Aoun slapped the young man, who left the station and returned minutes later carrying a Kalashnikov, shot Aoun thirty times and ran. It is said that the young man did not know who Rida Aoun was until after he shot him. It is also said that he committed the crime in a rage after Aoun slapped him. In any case, it was the end of the era of Rida Aoun and his influence in Chiah.

Before his death, Aoun had started stealing houses in Masbagha and the surrounding area after their owners left during the Israeli invasion of Beirut in 1982. His accomplice in this was a girl named Kawkab who directed him to the houses that had been abandoned by their owners so that he could steal them. These thefts were well known among the residents of the neighborhood, but no one could stop him. Rida Aoun did one other thing before he died: he killed an old friend of his. Someone told Rida that Ibrahim Hourani, his old friend, had shot at his brother Ahmed Aoun. Rida went looking for Hourani, who, as the story goes, had shot at Ahmed's feet by mistake while they were playing with a Kalashnikov. Rida chased down his old friend, who ran in front of him begging forgiveness, but the chase ended at the gates of *Hirsh* next to Rawdat al Shehedeen with Aoun shooting and killing Hourani.

Ibrahim al-Hourani had been a member of the Shahraban gang and was famous for his viciousness. It is said that one summer afternoon he lured a small child into the Dunia Cinema in Asaad street and sexually assaulted the child, covering his mouth to silence his screaming until he died of asphyxiation. He was jailed for the crime but escaped at the outbreak of the civil war and returned to his old stomping grounds.

After Rida was killed at the gas station a young man named Akif Rmeity was charged with his murder. This man had disappeared after the killing, but Rida's older brother Suhail wanted revenge, so he went looking for Rmeity's relatives and found that a woman and her children who were relatives of Rmeity lived in a house in Shiyeh. He went to the house and killed the woman and her children in cold blood and fled away.

MINOVITCH THE BUTCHER AND HALABAWI

Ali Minovitch was a friend of Oqab Saqr and a member of the Shahraban in Masabagha. His mother was Lebanese from Kfarseer and his father was originally from Yugoslavia and fought with the Allies during World War I, and was given citizenship after moving to Lebanon. Ali Minovitch, Rida Aoun, and Oqab Saqr made up the core of the Shahraban gang. During his youth in the early 1970s, Minovitch joined the General Command in order to gain access to weapons and protect his community. At that point the activities of the gang appeared "childish" compared with the rise of the resistance and its parties. Most of the members of the gang had joined General Command before joining the Organization of Commandos, and from there some of them went on to the Amal Movement. Moving between warring parties was just a way to join the strongest party that had managed to consolidate its power in the neighborhood.

But Ali Minovitch was headed towards the same fate as his two murdered friends. He distinguished himself among the gang even before the civil war by his courage and daring in battle. Thanks to this courage, he was chosen for the "internal operations" wing, the military operations General Command carried out inside Israel. This gave him more power and authority than any of his friends from the Shahraban gang who had become militiamen.

Minovitch had ties to different parties, as well as to Syrian intelligence and the Commandos, despite the fact that officially his loyalty lay with General Command. His actions also indicate he was cultivating political alliances between his party and others, but would sabotage them if he was dissatisfied. He would even start armed clashes between the two parties. Often these agreements and truces occurred between warring Palestinian factions that were split between those that followed Syria and those that were affiliated with Fatah under Yasser Arafat.

When his brother Mohammad was kidnapped in one of the rounds of street fighting that broke out between the factions in 1975, Ali accused the Communist Party of being behind his brother's disappearance. The same night, his younger brother Osama was killed in Kfarseer, the southern village where most of the boys from the old Ghandour gang were from. Ali set his sights on the communists of that town and chased them down. Once again, coincidence or fate pitted the members of the two old gangs against each other in a bloody conflict in the midst of a war.

Minovitch gathered an armed gang from among his friends and followers and led them to the town of Kfarseer where most of the young men were members of the "Organization for Communist Action" and the Communist Party. In fact, it was sometimes called *Kfarmoscow* because it was home to so many communists.

Ali entered the town and fell upon every communist he saw, firing on many of them, wounding and killing at random. Ahmed Sbayteh himself was nearly killed and Minovitch shot both his brothers in the legs in the town square. The communists could not stop Minovitch due to his ferocity, military training, and the flanks of Palestinian fighters protecting him, most of whom were allies of Syria. But the attack on the communists was too vicious to be explained away by the death and disappearance of Minovitch's brothers, especially since the communists' role in either was uncertain, and the assault was extraordinarily secure and tightly orchestrated. Later, it was revealed that Minovitch had ties to the National Liberal Party through his cousin Ramz Minovitch, who grew up in Ain al-Ramaneh where he was a member of the gang led by Samir Geagea before the war, according to Ahmed Sbeity. After his death, the National Liberal Party eulogized Minovitch with the tribute that he "died to give life to Lebanon." H.T., who grew up in Masbagha, says that he remembers Ali Minovitch and some of his friends used to come to Ain al Ramaneh during the two-year war (1975-1976) and after, despite the fact that there were constant battles between Ain al-Ramaneh and Chiah, and the road dividing the two districts was one of the most dangerous fault lines in Lebanon. Ali's cousin Ramz had joined the Lebanese Army and rose in the ranks until he became an officer. His father was a retired soldier like Ali's and his mother was from the Abdullah family in Khiam. After the Lebanese Army split and the Southern Lebanese Army was created under the leadership of Saad Haddad, who was working with Israel, Ramz led an attack on behalf of Haddad on Khiam, where he and his forces massacred civilians and demolished a large number of homes. These ambiguous party relations were no secret from the armed parties to which Minovitch belonged and which also·tended to fall under the Syrian sphere of influence. But the confusing nature of the battles and the shifting alliances were well served by a person like Ali Minovitch, who made things even more convoluted and sparked new battles day after day between the factions that were constantly breaking or entering into alliances. This phase became infamous even more than the period of 1976 when the Syrian Army entered Lebanon.

After just two years of war, Minovitch had already demonstrated his power and influence in the area of Nabatiyeh and the neighborhood of Masbagha and the surrounding districts. One day near the end of 1976, he was standing with a friend named Khodr Halabawi, who had also been a core member of the Shahraban gang and later joined the same parties as his friend Minovitch, General Command and the Commandos. They were loitering next to a girls' high school in Ghbayreh on the border of Musbagha next to the Hirsh with the intention of harassing girls.

According to Ahmed Sbeity, Minovitch harassed a girl who was friends with a young man named Ali Khreis, a student at the nearby high school. Khreis was also a member of the Socialist Labor Party, which was loyal to the Popular Front for the Liberation of Palestine. He was there when Minovitch and Halabawi started harassing the girl. Khreis approached Minovitch and slapped him. Minovitch drew his gun, but before he could shoot, Khreis pushed him and the gun fired into the air. Khodr Halabawi drew his own pistol in the face of the young man, who had dodged the first bullet and who rushed to put Minovitch between himself and the gun. Halabawi fired three bullets and took the life of his friend Minovitch before firing another three and killing the young Khreis.

Some people, including H.T. and Naji Jamal, maintain that Halabawi intended to kill his friend, and that the murder was tied to Syrian intelligence. Others say that the same parties that had facilitated his rise to power wanted to get rid of him after his excesses and independent streak became a burden on them.

Ali Khreis, the youth who was killed, had been a member of the Labor Party and the PFLP. He was also well trained. Halabawi hid in his home in Masbagha for a while fearing he would be hunted down by the young man's friends from the Labor Party. Months later, a friend came to Halabawi's home and convinced him to come with him to visit another friend in Barbir hospital. At first, Halabawi refused to leave the house but then his friend convinced him, telling him there was no problem and no one would know. As they reached the Barbir bridge, a group of some twenty men emerged from the crowd and opened fire into the air, terrifying the drivers and shoppers that crowded the market. They used this time to load Halabawi and his friend into a car and took them to an unknown location. Halabawi was never heard from again, but his friend reappeared shortly after only to leave his house in Musbagha and move somewhere else after it became known that it had been a trap.

Hussein Halabawi, Khodr's brother, was killed during a robbery of a clinic in Asaad street after he exchanged fire with the doctor and members of the doctor's family. Halabawi's other brother, Mohammed, was killed in Maroun street off Abdul Karim Khalil by the Shaban family. His death is widely thought to be tied to the drug trade, although some say it was because he kept switching parties and knew too many military secrets.

ALI ABU QASIM AND THE HUSSEIN SUICIDE FORCES

After the two-year war (1975-1976), armed Palestinian factions and their Lebanese allies spread throughout most of Beirut and Lebanon. It was also then that the Amal Movement emerged and began consolidating its power in the Shiite neighborhoods of the southern suburbs and Nebaa; another armed faction was founded in Masbagha by a man named Ali Abu Qassim Moussawi, who called his new group the Hussein Suicide Forces. When these forces were founded, Ali (Abu Qassim) Moussawi was in his forties and still living in Masbagha where he had grown up. When the war started, all the boys from the Shahraban gang joined this group except for Oqab Saqr, Ali Minovitch, and Khodr Halabawi, who were killed before the Hussein Suicide Forces were founded. Rida Aoun, who was still alive, did not join because he was busy stealing, extorting, and terrorizing.

The fighters of the Hussein Suicide Forces, who numbered more than fifty from the neighborhood, armed themselves and went out to collect donations to finance the movement. Shopkeepers, trade establishments, and everyone else were forced to donate or pay protection money so that their shop would not be attacked and closed.

The forces only controlled the neighborhood, and were really just the wartime militia face of the gangs, including the Shahraban. Just a few months after its inception, the leader of the Hussein Suicide Forces, Ali Abu Qasim, was walking with a handful of supporters on the west side of the neighborhood where the Hadi Nasrallah highway would later be built. At that time the road was still a dirt alleyway lined with illegal mechanics and vegetables sellers that disappeared when Amin Gemayel became president and authority returned to those neighborhoods. During his walk a car full of armed men drove by and riddled him with bullets and fled. Within a short while it was said that his brother Abdullah Moussawi (Abu Haidar) took revenge by killing Riad Taha in Raouche. It was clear that the killings were related to a blood feud between the Taha and Moussawi families, both of them from Hermel. Another young man from the Atwi family who was nicknamed Gharo also took part in the assassination of Taha. He emigrated to the United States but died of cancer, so his body was brought back to Lebanon to be buried in his village in the south, according to H.T. Abu Haidar, meanwhile, is hiding to this day in the town of Nabisheet and will not leave out of fear he will be arrested. After taking revenge for the murder of his brother, Abdullah Moussawi took over leadership of the Hussein Suicide Forces and was able to turn it into a local mafia that engaged in organized robberies and murders, and terrorized the people of the neighborhood and neighboring districts.

In early 1980, the Amal Movement decided to eliminate the Hussein Suicide Forces. Following what appeared to be an internal agreement between the leadership of both groups, the Forces surrendered quickly and handed over their weapons so that there were no casualties on either side. Amal carried out a swift raid on the houses of members of the Suicide Forces and confiscated their weapons and forbade them from carrying arms again. And so ended the era of the Hussein Suicide Forces, which its first leader, Ali Abu Qassim, had aspired to turn into a political Islamist group that took direction from the Syrian intelligence apparatus.

His untimely death shattered that dream, especially after his brother killed Riad Taha, a member of the Press Syndicate, without realizing the syndicate was connected to that apparatus and benefitted from its relations with it. Moreover, the emergent Amal Movement was tightening its iron grip on the Shiite neighborhoods and would never allow another armed faction to operate and expand in the territories under their control.

Two brothers from the Damashq family known as Abu Aghdab [the father of anger] and Abu Thilam [the father of darkness], formerly of the Shahraban gang, were particularly close to the leader of the Hussein Suicide Forces. Their other brother, known as Abu Khishbeh [the father of wood], is the current head of security for Parliamentary Speaker and Amal party leader Nabih Berri. Abu Kheshbeh won Berri's favor when he stood by him in a violent battle against an offshoot branch calling itself the Islamist Amal Movement headed by Moustafa Dirani, which eventually led to Berri signing the tripartite agreement with Walid Jumblatt and Elie Hobeika

Another young man to distinguish himself among the Suicide Forces was Mahmoud Ramadan who was also known as Abu Khiwaraq [the father of miracles] and struck fear into the hearts of everyone in Musbagha because of his brutality, opening fire on anyone who made him angry. After passing through a filtering process carried out by the Amal Movement, the Father of Miracles moved to Jneh next to Ouzai where he lives to this day as the neighborhood strongman and the leader of the young men, according to H.T., who says that everyone in Jneh knows Abu Mazen, as he is now called after having a son named Mazen.

Abu Jemajem [the father of skulls], who was a member of the Arab Liberation Front that was tied to Iraq, was famous for the skull and crossbones he painted on the walls of Musbagha, the neighboring areas and along the front lines along with the words "Abu Jemajem was here." After the raid, he moved first to Sabra and later to Musaytbeh. Today, he sits on a street corner in Musaytbeh being unable to work after his leg was amputated due to diabetes-induced gangrene.

DIFFERENT DESTINIES

The boys of the Ghandour gang did not suffer the same tragic fate as their peers from Masbagha during the war. Thanks largely to their pursuit of education and their early induction into political parties, specifically those with Marxist and nationalist ideologies, many of them were able to chart a life for themselves beyond the world of street gangs. They joined military political organizations during the two-year war before moving on to the worlds of business and higher education, with a number of them going on to study education and join the military and security institutions. Others emmigrated to foreign countries and either stayed there or returned to Lebanon having made their fortunes.

The differences in the fates of the members of the two gangs mirrors the differences in the fates of the children of families from Baalbek and those from southern Lebanon. The former did not push their children to study, but rather burdened them with the same clan feuds they had brought with them from their villages of origin. The families from the South, meanwhile, were keen to improve their living conditions and educate their children so that they might find better jobs when they finished school.

A number of the boys of Ghandour turned out to be first division soccer players and played for teams such as Nejme and Ansar. Others formed a *debke* and dance troupe and opened a school in Asaad street. Most of them, however, have been in politics since the late sixties without leading to the loss and murder that destroyed the lives of the Shahraban gang.

NOTES

1   I wish to single out Ahmed Sbayteh, a public school teacher who grew up in Ghandour and was a member of a gang; university professor Naji Jamal, who was born and raised in Musbagha in the late 1960s; and another individual from Masbagha who declined to be identified except by his initials, H.T.

Part 5

Voluntarism and Civil Society

Uniforms and Salutes

Fascism and Youth Politics in Syria and Lebanon under French Rule[*]

Jennifer Dueck

A group of Syrian boy scouts excitedly travelled through Europe in the autumn of 1937. This was the first international jamboree in which a Syrian boy scout troop had ever participated. It was a thrilling moment[1]. The boys had visited many cities and were welcomed in Paris as proud representatives of their nation. Returning home, they stopped off in Beirut, where they paraded waving high the Syrian flag, and leaving riots in their wake between proponents and opponents of Lebanese unification with Syria. Once in Damascus, Prime Minister Jamil Mardam Bey greeted them with a speech in their honour, lauding their self-sacrifice as scouts and their patriotism as Syrians[2]. Mardam Bey had some important messages for the scouts in his message. Most important, the boys had a duty to build their nation, and Mardam likened their task to soldiers preparing for battle. This last statement was not simply metaphorical: in the next breath he evoked the future national army of which the scouts would be the core[3].

For those familiar with scouting, one might wonder how far this overlap between scouting and the military would go and what it might mean. Hearing about the scouts' intended military role, one might also look back over the boy scouts' trip and notice that, amid their smorgasbord of activity, they were hosted for tea by the Hitler Youth. This begs the question of how historians should understand the creation and evolution of organized youth groups such as the scouts in Syria and Lebanon during the time of the French Mandate. Scouting was, in fact, a prominent socio-political phenomenon throughout the Middle East at this time. Not only did various Syrian and Lebanese leaders encourage scouting, but foreign governments and organizations also tried to capitalize on its potential. The attempt to gather school children and young people into disciplined organizations was a conspicuous component of the French educational

---

[*] Material for this article is taken from chapters 3, 7, and 8 of the author's book *The Claims of Culture at Empire's End: Syria and Lebanon under French Rule* (Oxford: Oxford University Press, 2010).

missions, as well as a cornerstone of the German and Italian propaganda. Almost all foreign schools had scout troops, which were complemented by a host of scout and quasi-scout associations in the local schools. The presence of an active scout troop in a school was even seen as a hallmark of the establishment's success and its capacity to compete with its rivals[4].

One reason why scouting attracted such enthusiastic attention is the political symbolism with which it quickly became associated. Although not all scouting was politicized, many troops emerged as a political force in Syria and Lebanon. Frequently accompanied by one flag or another on their outings, scout groups associated themselves with particular political visions for the region, whether Lebanese, Syrian, or pan-Arab. In the anecdote cited above, after the scouts' passage through Lebanon, one commentator even called their use of the Syrian flag an "emblem of sedition."[5]

Relatively little has been written on the scout enterprise in the Middle East, and particularly on its role in the birth of political parties and paramilitary associations. Recent work on the Young Egypt organization, the Iraqi Futuwwa, and the Lebanese Secret Arab Movement suggests that the importance of scouting in political development has been underestimated by historians. This is an especially significant gap given that during the 1930s scout and youth groups grew into a political force which both the foreign authorities and local elites had difficulty controlling (Watenpaugh, 2006: chap. 9). The lacuna is particularly evident for Lebanon, a nation which was the springboard from which scouting spread throughout the Middle East[6]. In order to begin to grapple with nature of fascist impact on the Levantine scout movement, this paper will first look briefly at the history of scouting in the Middle Eastern context. Following on from that it will be possible to examine the influence of Italian and German models of youth organization, with particular emphasis on the militarism manifested in scout practices and rhetoric. Finally, the article will draw on the case study of internal rivalries within the Syrian scout movement during World War II to suggest some interpretations of the intermingling of fascism with scouting.

THE EARLY DEVELOPMENT OF SCOUTING IN SYRIA AND LEBANON

Scouting was first introduced to the Middle East by two Indian brothers who learned of Baden-Powell's ideas in Britain. They founded a troop called the Ottoman Scouts at their school, Dār al-ʿUlūm, in 1912. In 1914 the Ottoman government formally recognized their association, whose statutes acknowledged the Caliph as its Supreme Leader. Although this group became a casualty of World War I, in 1920 a Beirut Sunni named Muhi al-Din al-Nuṣūli founded another group called the Muslim Scouts of Syria (al-Kashshāf al-Muslim)[7]. Nuṣūli, dubbed the "jewel of the Beirut youth" by the Syrian scoutmaster Ali

Dandashi, led scout delegations around Europe and Arab world, and would figure prominently in scout circles for the next two decades. Nuṣūli found his first scout recruits among the children at the AUB school, but the largest Muslim troops were soon located at the Islamic College (al-Kullīya al-Islāmīya), and the schools of the Maqasid Islamic Charitable Association. The Abbasiya troop (al-Firqa al-'Abbāsīya) at the Islamic College numbered eighty in 1928, and the four troops at the Maqāṣid schools boasted 300 members in 1936. Photos currently displayed at the office of the Association of Muslim Scouts in Lebanon show large groups of boys recruited at the Maqasid schools, and a sizeable troop called the Fayṣal Troop (Fawj Faysal) which laid the foundation stone of a new Maqasid theatre constructed during the interwar years (Naqqash & Khalifa, 1927: 21-3).

The Muslim Scouts of Syria were recognized by the International Scout Federation in 1922, and the organization grew to embrace troops from Damascus and Aleppo. Poorly organized in the 1920s, the Syrian scout troops were disbanded during the Great Revolt of 1925-27. Subsequently, however, Syrian scouting flourished under the able direction of Rushdi Jabi and his side-kick Dandashi. By 1931 the Muslim Scouts of Syria and Lebanon federated, and the movement was organized into proper chapters, each with its own leader. Nuṣūli remained at the helm in Lebanon, as did Jabi in Syria. In 1933 the Syro-Lebanese federation comprised forty-five troops with 3000 scouts, and built up sufficient momentum to send a delegation to the international scout jamboree in Hungary[8]. Booklets produced by the Association of Muslim Scouts in Lebanon note that the first attempt to set up Girl Guides (*murshidāt*) did not take place until 1937. However, a 1936 history of scouting in the Middle East by Shafiq Naqqāsh and 'Alī Khalīfa cite the existence of girls' troops in the south, and a 1927 issue of the Beirut scout journal *Al-Kashshāf* devotes a column to them (Naqqash & Khalifa, 1927).

In 1934 the federated Muslim Scouts of Syria suffered a setback following a scout rally in Damascus at which youngsters exalted Syro-Lebanese unity. Many Lebanese scout troops were present, and the Maqasid's Fayṣal troop even wore special badges to indicate that they had the largest contingent (Naqqash & Khalifa, 1927). Although the High Commission had approved the federation in 1931, French trepidation mounted that the scouts would become a compelling force for Syro-Lebanese unity[9]. Opposing tooth and nail any hint of Syro-Lebanese unity, the French High Commission passed a decree in July 1934 forbidding any joint Syro-Lebanese youth associations. As a result of this measure, Nuṣūli and Jabi went their separate ways, but neither renounced his interest in scouting. Nuṣūli reconstituted his association in Lebanon as the Muslim Scouts while Jabi's cohort became the Scouts of Syria. Neither branch was ever recognized by the International Scout Federation[10]. From this point forward, scouting in the two countries developed independently.

MILITARISM IN SCOUTING:
TRACING THE GERMAN AND ITALIAN INFLUENCES

Foreign influences on scouting in Syria and Lebanon included not only French and Anglo-Saxon sources, but also Italian and German models. The promotion of youth organization was no less institutionally important for the Italians than for the French. The Italian Consulate used Italian schools and community centres to recruit children into troops organized along the lines of the fascist youth groups in Italy. The French took careful note of which schools had such units, such as the Carmelite schools in Tripoli (Nordbruch, 2009). Youth organization in the Italian missionary schools was influenced by pedagogical trends in Italy, just as scouting in French schools reflected prevailing practices and beliefs in the Hexagone. While the Scouts de France perpetuated an emphasis on play and imagination, Italian clubs in Syria and Lebanon were drawn ever more into the sphere of fascist social governance. All youth associations in Italy were dissolved in the late 1920s and youth leisure became the prerogative of the Opera Nazionale Balilla which fell to the Ministry of National Education in 1929. In 1937 the Balilla were incorporated into the fascist party's Gioventù Italiana del Littorio, responsible for youth between the ages of six and twenty-one, and in 1939 Bottai's famous School Charter harmonized youth groups and schools into a single and homogenizing unit. These measures extended to the Italian Catholic schools on the Levantine shores of the Mediterranean. By 1937 youth clubs in the Italian schools of Syria and Lebanon bore the name Balilla and school-children donned the uniform prescribed in Italy (Koon, 1985: 87-100). Italian Catholic schools in Syria and Lebanon enforced the use of fascist uniforms owing either to financial inducement or to sincere conviction. Ostensibly universal in their Catholic persuasion, the schools nevertheless incorporated these powerful national symbols into their para-scholastic activities.

Ideologically and methodologically the Balilla of the late 1930s bore little resemblance to British and French scouting. Fascist youth organizations emphasized athletic training in preparation for military service and the subjugation of individualism to collective patriotic ends. Much of these organizations' appeal in the Middle East lay in the use of uniforms and participation in parades (Koon, 1985: 95-6; Kater, 2004; Lewis, 2000). That said, one might be forgiven for hearing echoes of *Scouting for Boys* in fascist youth programmes, particularly with regard to Baden-Powell's patriotism and readiness to defend the Empire in war. Mussolini and Hitler had both been attracted by Baden-Powell's ideas and the great scoutmaster himself sought to establish ties with the Hitler Youth in the early 1930s (Jeal, 1999: 543-53; Rosenthal, 1986: chap. 6.). The insistence on athletic fitness was certainly a feature shared by the scouts and the Balilla, as well as many other organizations devoted to sport in child and adolescent development throughout Europe at this time. A variety of sports clubs had been founded in

Italy before the state clamp-down and one of these, the National Corps of Young Explorers, had been organized according to Baden-Powell's directives (Minio-Paluello, 1964:32). That said, the commonalities between Balilla and boy scouts should not be exaggerated. The parallels just outlined are not intended to suggest an intimate relationship between scouting and fascist youth leagues, but rather to help explain the mixture of these models in the Levantine context.

One particularly controversial component of the Balilla in Syria and Lebanon was the significance accorded to parades and uniforms. When the Italian Consul visited Italian schools or attended other official events, troops of schoolchildren dressed in fascist garb were invariably present to honour him. These same children wore their uniforms for school expeditions, ceremonies, funerals, commemorations, and even film screenings. In May 1937 the Italian schools organized an expedition to the Krak des Chevaliers for which all the participants sported their Balilla uniforms, and when Levantine students returned from free trips to Italy, the French authorities were distressed to learn that they had been given their own fascist outfits[11]. To be sure, the public function and visual impact of uniforms in Italy were very different from those in Syria and Lebanon. In Italy the sight of youths in identical dress performing synchronized exercises enforced a sense of homogeneity and unity (Koon, 1985: 99). In the Levant no such dominance could be claimed by any group. Uniforms were no less fundamental as socio-political tools but, given the variety of youth organizations and their attendant apparel, clothing likely heightened a sense of competition and diversity in the region.

The German government, unlike the Italian and French leadership, did not have institutional intermediaries, such as schools, through which to organize youth groups. Thus the Germans could not impose state-sponsored activities on educational establishments in the Levant as the Italians did. However, German agents targeted Muslim young people and encouraged indigenous groups to found their own youth organizations. In 1937 Baldur von Schirach, leader of the German youth movement, personally visited Iraq, and in 1938 Arab youth leaders attended a Nazi rally at Nuremberg where they were formally welcomed by Hitler. In 1939 Schirach visited Damascus and met the youth leaders of the Arab Club, animated by the bona fide Axis agent Sai'd Imam. The French were equally convinced that other agents, such as Fritz Grobba, were working to create cells of Nazi youth. Nevertheless, Nazism as an ideology had limited success in the Middle East, and while youth associations adopted certain fascist practices, there is little to suggest sustained support for National Socialism (Nordbruch, 2009: 15-16).

Where clearly fascism did genuinely appeal was in its example as a means to national revival and regeneration through the youth, particularly apparent in the scouts' tendency toward militarism, and a predilection for fascist salutes, slogans, and uniforms. Historians have classified many of the Arab youth associations, which became a prominent feature of political life in the Middle East in the late 1930s, as paramilitary leagues. These include regional groups such as Antun Sa'ada's Syrian Social National Party and the Armenian Tachnag, as well as more localized ventures such as the White Badge and the Steel Shirts in Syria, the Phalanges, the Najjāda and the White Shirts in Lebanon, or the Blue Shirts and Green Shirts in Egypt. The fact that such movements gathered true momentum in the 1930s supports the argument that they were of Axis inspiration; and it is hard to miss the fascist influence in many of their names which echoed the names of Mussolinian and Hitlerian youth factions. Such impressions are compounded by their adoption of salutes, logos, and slogans similar to those used by fascist leagues in Europe (O'Zoux, 1948). Pierre Gemayel, founder of the Phalanges, was influenced by his vision of the fascist youth organizations which he witnessed on his trip to the Berlin Olympics in 1936. Husayn Sij'an, president of the Najjāda after 1943, was on the same trip and returned similarly impressed by the collective discipline of these formations (Nantet, 1986: 33-35). The Germans were interested in wooing the Arab youth, and many Arab nationalists saw Germany as an ally in their struggle against British and French imperialists. Even French right-wing groups had a place in the rumour-mill: Arab nationalists accused the White Badge in Aleppo, a Christian youth league, of being allied with Colonel de la Rocque, leader of the right-wing Croix de Feu in France (National Archives and Records Administration, 1936).

Much of the Syrian and Lebanese interest in the fascist leagues derived from the conviction that youth organization represented an ideal means to national revival after defeat, for which the German example of the 1930s provided particularly compelling evidence in Arab eyes (Nordbruch, 2009: 58-9). This was especially so after 1936, when heightened local aspirations for independence led many Syrians and Lebanese to think of forming a proper national army. Prestigious nationalist leaders such as Sati' al-Ḥusrī believed that an army and education were the two most critical institutions for building a strong nation, and in 1945 students and school children staged demonstrations calling for a national army in towns and cities across Syria (al-Husri, 1944; Public Record Office, 1946). According to French sources, in 1944 the Syrian political leadership paid for scouts from all over the country to attend a general assembly in Damascus which was meant to provoke popular demonstrations for the establishment of a national army[12]. In 1939 one of the Syrian government's chief motives in nationalizing the scout movement and integrating it into the state school system was to provide early military training for children. The Syrian desire for an army became all the more pressing in the face of French unwillingness to withdraw from the region and transfer control of the Syrian and Lebanese military units to the local leadership (El-Solh, 2004: 243-5). In Lebanon, the Muslim scouts saw themselves as the core of the envisaged Lebanese military and enlisted the support of the Maronite Phalanges, thereby demonstrating an acceptance of Lebanese national institutions that included the most ardent defenders of a Christian Lebanon. The Lebanese government reputedly claimed that the new national army would be made up of members from the scouts, the Najjāda, and the Phalanges[13].

French observers found the conflation of militarism and scouting deplorable, especially since they intended scouting to promote a pacific cultural attachment to France (Grandjouan, 1936: 111). This militarism was all the more threatening to the French when applied toward political ends. One official remarked, in a fashion quite representative of more general French feelings:

It seems that the oriental temperament cannot adapt to an outdoor life that is active and energetic, as recommended by scout law. Above all it seems that the scout mystique does not hold the attention of youths seeking immediate profit. What interests them in scouting is the uniform, the military exercises, and the possibilities for political action[14].

Most historians now argue that the ideological impact of fascism was superficial, and that the appropriation of Nazi slogans was tactical, rather than symptomatic of coherent support for a Nazi agenda (Hirszowicz, L., 1966: 18-19; Jankowski, J., 1975: 58-60; Nicosia, F., 1980: 356; Wild, S., 1985). The Najjāda, for example, in supporting the German-backed coup by Rashid Kaylani in Iraq, did so primarily to express their resentment against British violations of the Anglo-Iraqi treaty and their pride in the Arab nation.

Although the French believed that political and military activism had no place in a true scout's activities, militarism was in fact a leitmotif of Baden-Powell's directives instructing boys to be "citizen-soldiers" and prescribing that even foot-ballers or cricketers should not be admired unless they could shoot and drill. Moreover, even French scout troops used military détachés sent to them by the French government as trainers, and after the start of the war the Scouts de France emphasized the importance of scouting in preparing useful soldiers. In March 1941 the Beirut journal *Action Catholique* printed an article about the benefits of scouting as pre-military training, evoking the origins of scouting in the colonial army. The "good" French scout troop at the Alliance israélite universelle in Aleppo also encouraged a military ethos. One teacher integrated various military trappings into his vision of scouting, making a great fuss over the military braid on the uniforms and the military-style exercises. He proudly wrote that the parents were seduced by, among other things, the scouts' serious attitude like "miniature soldiers." Militarism was thus a multi-faceted phenomenon and its various manifestations within youth organizations belie reductionist interpretation.

A CASE STUDY: SYRIAN SCOUT RIVALRIES

In looking at how scouting and fascism intermingled in inter-war years Levant, it is helpful to see how a series of scout rivalries that played out in Syria during the French Mandate period. In fact, the different scout and youth groups that emerged in Syria aligned themselves quite neatly with local political rivalries. The principal Syrian scout leaders, 'Ali Dandashi and Rushdi Jabi were both associated with the "opposition" League of National Action, which served as an underdog rival to the dominant ruling National Bloc coalition. This younger political opposition tended to embrace a pan-Arab vision of nationalism and disliked the National Bloc's pragmatic cooperation with the French authorities to advance the narrower goal of Syrian independence. Dandashi and Jabi established a the Ghuta scout troop in 1927, and this group refused to affiliate itself with the Nationalist Youth, a National Bloc initiative under the charismatic youth leader Fakhri Barudi. Barudi, whom one American observer called "the popular demi-god,"[15] responded by sponsoring a troop called the Umayyad scouts, in 1929, as a rival to Jabi and Dandashi's Ghuta troop. Although competitors, both organizations were affiliated with the joint pre-1934 Syro-Lebanese Muslim Scouts of Syria; however, in 1931 Barudi's Umayyad troop lost members to the Ghuta, and disbanded. Simultaneously, the Ghuta troop was instrumental in pushing for formal federation and recognition by the International Scout Federation under the direction of Jabi and Dandashi.

As noted earlier, the joint Syro-Lebanese scout movement was forbidden by the French Mandate authorities in 1934, at which point Syrian and Lebanese scouting developed along separate trajectories. As the Syrian scout movement reconstituted itself after 1934, Jabi and Dandashi lost some support owing, in part, to their abstention from militant political activism and also to renewed efforts by dominant National Bloc leaders to lure in the educated youth. Jamil Mardam recruited former Umayyad troopers to lead the Nationalist Youth, and one founding member of the Umayyad troop established a new group called the Maysalun scouts in 1934. Although the French soon disbanded the Maysalun troop for inciting unrest, it was absorbed into the Nationalist Youth and retained its cohesion there. Indeed, the continuity in the membership of the Umayyad and Maysalun troops who participated in the Nationalist Youth is significant for the post-1936 period because the Maysalun troop subsequently formed the core of the Damascus branch of the Steel Shirts. This paramilitary association, founded in 1936, even adopted the anthem used by the defunct Maysalun scouts. The rivalry born in the late 1920s between Jabi and Dandashi on the one hand, and Barudi and the Steel Shirts on the other, persisted throughout the 1930s and into the 1940s. Historian Philip Khoury has argued that in 1936 the League of National Action lost much of its force as a political opposition because the National Bloc successfully incorporated key members into its fold (Khoury, 1983: 971-6). This interpretation is born out by the history of Syrian scouting during the late 1930s and early 1940s.

Although the National Bloc did succeed in coopting members of opposition youth associations, more research is still needed to determine the degree of friendliness between the Syrian scouts and the Steel Shirts across the country. Watenpaugh has suggested that in Aleppo the Steel Shirts were unable to draw in the bourgeois families, who generally preferred the scouts or the youth wing of the League of National Action. However, in Hama the head of the Scouts of Syria also participated in leading the newly formed Steel Shirts unit. What is clear is that the scouts and the Steel Shirts often appeared together at public events and demonstrations where violent clashes with the police occurred (Watenpaugh, 2002: 328). In February 1937, a series of skirmishes broke out between the French military and the Steel Shirts in Aleppo and then in Latakia. In each case, the violence occurred in the context of a scout parade. The Steel Shirts in Aleppo had been marching ahead of the scouts when the incident took place. In Latakia, the violence broke out when the Steel Shirts assembled to meet a group of scouts sent from Damascus, Tartus, and Homs. In the aftermath of these events the National Bloc and the French High Commission curbed the violence among the youth: the High Commission issued injunctions against wearing uniforms and a number of participants were charged in military tribunals, although the sentences were subsequently revoked owing to popular protest. Politicians such as Quwatli expressed a desire to conquer the "poor frame of mind of the young people and their apparent taste for violence."[16]

Jabi, having ceased to be a formal member of the League of National Action in the late 1930s, continued his work with scouts and was the official president of the Scouts of Syria during World War II. After 1938 Dandashi took on a role at the Ministry of Information, but his main focus remained the scout movement (Dandashi, 1996: 36). Although Jabi was absorbed into the government administration of scouting, pre-war rivalries persisted and government leaders continued to try to exploit fascist rhetoric and scouting for political purposes.

This ongoing rivalry is best illustrated by a series of mid-war events that were sparked off when Jabi unexpectedly closed the scout office in March 1942. When questioned by the Syrian president, Shaykh Taj al-Din al-Hasani, he confided that he and his members feared arrest in light of the recent claims that they were Nazi supporters. Hasani personally asked Jabi to resume his activities, and when Jabi requested guarantees for their safety, Hasani promised to send his own son to join a scout group. Hasani took a keen interest in scouts, and a month later, offered his patronage for a scout camp in Damascus which the Hama scouts had been invited to attend. In May of the same year, scouts from all over Syria went to Damascus for a general inspection at which time Hasani awarded them with a national medal of honour. After the brief disruption with Jabi, scouting returned to normal, and the prestige of scouts increased owing to the special attention from Hasani. At the end of June top police officers attended a play put on by the scouts at a new camp site at Kassioum[17].

However, in early July 1942 Jabi's administrative committee was dissolved by Munir 'Ajlani, the Syrian Minister of Propaganda and founder of the Aleppo Steel Shirts, who suddenly established a new executive body for the Scouts of Syria. 'Ajlani came from an old Damascene religious family which was at the "summit of the Damascus political elite" (Khoury, 1983: 31-2). Jabi and his cohorts organized numerous meetings to attempt to disrupt the work of the new committee, and 'Ajlani himself went to the scout headquarters with police agents to stop the former committee members from entering. At the end of July, 'Ajlani presided over several ceremonies with speeches by his newly appointed committee members, and was presented with flowers by the girl guides at one such event[18].

These gatherings seemed to suggest business as usual, but 'Ajlani, with the approval of Hasani, had essentially declared war on the leadership of the Scouts of Syria. In spite of this, Hasani's earlier promises to Jabi did not fall completely by the wayside. At the end of July, Hasani attempted to reconcile 'Ajlani and Jabi. The latter agreed to submit to the new committee and successfully applied for permission to establish a new scout troop.

Although 'Ajlani won the initial battles, he was not to win the scout war, which lasted for approximately six months. Scout groups across the country refused to recognize the legitimacy of the new committee, and opposition was particularly strong in Aleppo, where scout groups clearly delineated themselves from 'Ajlani's Steel Shirts. Nationally only four troops, with a total of 150 scouts, were loyal to 'Ajlani, while Jabi's supporters in Damascus numbered 700 scouts in fourteen independent troops and 1,200 scouts in school troops, in addition to 4,720 scouts in Homs, Hama, Aleppo, Dayr al-Zur, and Latakia.

The scouts raised two main points against 'Ajlani. The first was that the government had no business mixing scouting with politics. Jabi declared at a meeting in September:

The scouts were born free and will remain free. They cannot be subjugated to a Ministry or to a political party. The recent measures taken against them will only be a passing cloud which will be obliterated[19].

Although President Hasani renewed his efforts to reconcile the two committees in October, the effort foundered on the insistence by Jabi's scouts that scouting was an autonomous international movement which could not swear allegiance to any particular government.

More significantly than the charge of mixing scouting with politics, the accusation of Nazi sympathies or activism was also used by each side to try to discredit the other. The accusation is interesting because it demonstrates the tactical motives of Syrian groups using pro-Axis rhetoric. Supporters of 'Ajlani and Jabi accused each other of harboring Nazi sympathies as a means to discredit one or the other. One member of the League of National Action declared:

If Mounir Ajlani thinks that the Scout Association has nazi tendencies, I can say that he is the one who introduced the microbe of nazism into the country by organizing in his way the Steel Shirts, and by instituting the fascist salute[20].

An anonymous scout in Aleppo made opposite allegations, alleging to the police that the Scouts of Syria were pro-Nazi and that Jabi was inciting them to revolt against the Allies. He further claimed that Jabi and his committee refused to accept 'Ajlani's measures because the replacement committee members were not sufficiently Nazi. Thus, Nazism became a charge which different groups levelled against each other in an attempt to undermine their opponent's credibility. This suggests not only that previous manifestations of pro-Axis support were superficial, but also that the language of the European battles pitting fascist dictatorships against democratic regimes was appropriated into the struggle for power over the scout movement in Syria.

The French were on the whole duped by these tactics, and saw fascist enemies everywhere. French allegations in 1942 described Dandashi and Jabi as infamous francophobes keeping regular contact with the Nazi propagandists in Damascus, which contradicts the authorities' earlier endorsement of the two scout leaders in 1935-6. In 1944 a French official characterized the nationalization of the scout movement during the late 1930s as a "pro-fascist" step and hyperbolically claimed that the scouts had accepted government involvement because it assured them of national honour and power.

To be sure, the French perception of fascist influence among the Scouts of Syria was augmented by the latter's association with the student committees in national high schools. These committees adopted various fascist practices, including a daily salute to the Syrian flag which was variously described as fascist, Hitlerian, and Communist. The confusion between scouting and fascist paramilitarism was further compounded by the genesis of the Steel Shirts, whose Damascus branch, as noted earlier, was built on the foundation laid by the defunct Umayyad and Maysalun troops. The Steel Shirt movement as a whole was strongly influenced by 'Ajlani, who had inspired Fakhrī Barūdī and Jamil Mardam as early as 1934 with a new vision of youth activism based on fascist youth leagues in Europe as the model of disciplined and dedicated organization. Like Pierre Gemayel and Husayn Sij'an of the Phalanges and the Najjāda respectively, 'Ajlani had travelled in Europe and witnessed at first hand the European associations. He incorporated their fascist salute and slogans, and the uniform for the leading cadres mirrored the European monochrome shirt and belt combination.

Nevertheless, the only established youth group for which there is evidence of sustained ties with Germany is the Arab Club of Damascus, led by Sa'id Imam. There were of course individuals involved in both the Scouts of Syria and the Arab Club, such as Zuhayr Dalati, a leader of the Club and brother of the Minister of Public Instruction and Scouting in 1941. In spite of such cross-overs between the Arab Club, the Steel Shirts and the scout movement, the true ideological attachment of their members to fascism is doubtful (Watenpaugh, 2002: 325-6). Even the occasional French contemporary observer made similar remarks. When the Syrian Scouts were hosted for tea by the Hitler Youth during their trip to an international scout jamboree, one French commentator argued that such occurrences were normal in peace-time, and did not indicate a commitment to Nazism. He went on the lay the blame for this influence on the French:

> These ideas [sc. Nazi ideas], if they really do exist, have never been fought with a deft propaganda on our part[21].

Another French report noted that the Muslim Youth of Syria had made a tactical decision in July 1941 to divide into two camps, one of which would cultivate a relationship with the Allies, while the other would remain passively reliant on Germany.

The British seem to have been more adept than the French at understanding the strategic nature of Syrian pro-Axis rhetoric. Early in the war, the British had requested that the French repress Jabi's activities on the grounds of their apparent fascist sympathies, but this soon changed and they increasingly sought to befriend the so-called "fascists". When Jabi protested to Catroux and Spears in 1942, calling on them to intervene with the Syrian government to restore the original scout leadership, he easily won British support, while the French prevaricated. The French adviser to the Syrian Ministry of Public Instruction finally proposed to act as a mediator between the two scout factions, owing mainly to the risk of security breaches given the overwhelming scout support for Jabi against 'Ajlani. In October 1942 Jabi accepted the offer, but 'Ajlani refused, which helped swing French opinion further in Jabi's direction. In November a scuffle broke out between pro-and anti-'Ajlani scouts in which the latter threw firecrackers at a group led by Dandashi which was parading towards the Tajhiz school in Damascus. Shaykh Taj al-Din al-Hasani became afraid that such unrest would spread beyond the scout movement and threaten public order. Consequently in early December he ordered 'Ajlani to reconfirm Jabi as head of the Scouts of Syria.

Looking back to Jamil Mardam's speech when he welcomed home the troop of Syrian boy scouts from their trip to attend the international scout jamboree, one clearly sees how the scout movement in Syria and Lebanon was nourished by a conglomeration of local and imported philosophical and ideological threads. Taken together, these threads are full of contradictions and ambiguities. This cross-fertilization included French revolutionary rhetoric, apparent in Mardam's appeal for equality among citizens, an unsurprising tack given the speaker's education in France and his stint at the École des Sciences Politiques in Paris. No less important were Baden-Powell's ideas, imported directly from Anglo-Saxon sources or indirectly through the French scouting model, as well as the practices of European fascist youth leagues. Many youth groups in the Middle East adopted the militaristic practices of the fascist leagues that were sprouting in Europe, such as salutes, slogans, and uniforms. As a result of this cross-pollination with right-wing leagues in Europe, scout and youth movements were often seen by the Mandate authorities as a primary conduit of fascism in the Middle East. However, the fascism that worked its way into the Syrian and Lebanese youth politics should not be seen as anything like its homogenizing European cousin. French, Syrian and Lebanese government discourse about scouting betrayed a perpetual tension between the will to capitalize on its popularity for political gain and the fear that, once unleashed, it might prove uncontrollable. Little surprise then that the national scout movement in Syria became a pawn in power struggles between different coalitions of political leaders vying for influence. The charge of fascism became one more tactical tool used within that rivalry. But as a tool, it was quickly used, and quickly forgotten when it no longer served local political objectives. The reliability of scouting as a vehicle for fascist, or any other foreign, political, or cultural influence was, at best, tenuous. The wide appeal of scouting in so many different cultures effectively ensured that no one ideology or government could effectively monopolize it.

NOTES

1   Alliance israélite universelle [henceforth AIU], Syrie/II.E/Bob.6, Baruk to AIU, 5 Sept. 1937.
2   Ministère des Affaires Étrangères, Nantes [henceforth MAE.N], Beyrouth/Cabinet Politique/459, speech by Jamil Mardam Bey, 1937.
3   Ibid.; Archives Historiques de la Compagnie de Jésus [henceforth AHCJ], Fonds Louis Jalabert [henceforth FLJ]/1.2-L, press review, 16-22 Sept. 1937.
4   MAE.N, Beyrouth/Cabinet Politique/804, Haddour to Tisserand, 1941.
5   Quote from *L'Orient* in AHCJ, FLJ/1.2-L, press review, 16-22 Sept. 1937.
6   *Jam'iyat qudāmā al-Kashshāf al-Muslim fi Lubnān* (The Association of Former Muslim Scouts in Lebanon), *Alī Dandashī: bā'ith al-nahda al-kashfiya al-'arabīya (Alī Dandashī: The Man Who Spread the Arab Scout Renaissance)* (Beirut: Dār al-Sirāj li-l-tibā'a wa-l-nashr):11–12. Henceforth cited as "Dandashī".
7   This account appears in several booklets published by the *Jam'iyat al-Kashshāf al-Muslim fi Lubnān* (Muslim Scout Association in Lebanon). My thanks to 'Isām Mukakhkhal at the Muslim Scout Association in Lebanon for showing me the premises and providing me with booklets published by the association.
8   The Archives of the Scout Association Headquarters have only one photograph relating to Syrian scouts in their photographic supplement to the January 1931 issue of the publication *Jamboree*. The photo is listed as "Syrian scouts in camp at Lebanon". I thank Patricia Styles at the World Scout Organization for her assistance in finding this information.
9   Booklets of the Muslim Scouts include the letter from the High Commission in 1921 authorizing the association; a framed copy of the document also hangs on the wall at the Muslim Scout Association in Lebanon.
10 MAE.N, Beyrouth/Sûreté générale [henceforth SG]/102, Pierre Bart to Beynet , 'Note sur le scoutisme au Liban', 25 March 1944. Khoury, *Syria*, 407-08.
11 Service historique de l'armée de terre, Guerre/1939-45/7N/4190, dossier 3, note by the administrative councillor in Tripoli, sent by Huntziger to EMA (Section Outre-Mer), 13 April 1938; MAE.N, Beyrouth/SG/2, SG (Aleppo), Info., 14 Oct. 1936.
12 MAE.N, Beyrouth/SG/102, SG (Kamchlié), Info., 17 Feb. 1944; SG (Damascus), Info., 13 April 1944.
13 The Muslim Scouts organized meetings in 1944 to discuss for military service. MAE.N, Beyrouth/SG/102, SG (Beirut), Info., 22 Jan. 1944.
14 MAE.N, Correspondance Politique et Commerciale/E-Levant/495, unsigned report "Scoutisme",

undated (likely 1936-1937). MAE.N, Beyrouth/SG/102, Pierre Bart to Beynet , "Note sur le scoutisme au Liban", March 25, 1944. Bart compares the local scouts to the Polish and Czech "Sokols", the French "Bataillons scolaires", and the British Cadets.

15 American University of Beirut Archives, RB/NECA/AA7, 3, unsigned (AUB) to Albert Staub (NY), 5 Feb., 1937.

16 MAE.N, Beyrouth/ Cabinet Politique /492, SG (Damascus), Info., 17 Feb. 1937.

17 MAE.N, Beyrouth/SG/ 102, SG (Damascus), Info., 31 March 1942, 26 June 1942; SG (Beirut), Info., 29 April 1942, 9 May 1942, and 11 May 1942.

18 MAE.N, Beyrouth/SG/102, SG (Beirut), Info., 6 July 1942, 21 July 1942; SG (Damascus), Info., 4 July 1942, 25 July 1942, 24 Aug. 1942.

19 MAE.N, Beyrouth/SG/102, SG (Damascus), Info., 1 Sept. 1942.

20 MAE.N, Beyrouth/SG/102, SG (Damascus), Info., 1 Sept. 1942.

21 MAE.N, Beyrouth/SG/102, SG (Damascus), Info., 12 Oct. 1942. AIU, Syrie/I.C/Bob.3, Baruk to AIU, "Impressions sur le Judaisme durant mon voyage en Europe", Dec. 1937.

Youth Networks, Space, and Political Mobilization

Lebanon's Independence Intifada

Christian Gahre

INTRODUCTION

The killing of former Prime Minister Rafik Hariri on February 14, 2005 was followed by a massive political mobilization that peaked on March 14. The "Independence Intifada" rallied Christians and Muslims under the Lebanese flag in Martyrs' Square, Beirut, proclaiming "national unity". The predominantly Shia Muslim counter-mobilization on March 8 had a different political agenda, but gathered under the same flag, in an adjacent square, and similarly claimed to represent Lebanon.

How did the Independence Intifada produce a Lebanese we-story of "national unity" and what were the reaches and limitations of this particular staging of a Lebanese nation?

The momentous days of the Independence Intifada saw very large numbers of people gathered in a particular space waving the Lebanese flag. Walking around during these events, I became curious about the dynamics of mobilization; the uses and meanings of the sites of mobilization; and projections of national identity. Mobilization, space, and identity became the dimensions of the present inquiry. I believe they are intimately interlinked. From the outset, I suspected that patterns of mobilization and uses and meanings of space fed into a particular Lebanese we-story.

Young people were prominent among the individuals I have called identity entrepreneurs who produced much of the colour, shape, form, and content of the Independence Intifada. These key players were a collection of informally networked organizers, mobilizers, and communicators. The identity entrepreneurs were all, according to one of them, "members of a lucky sperm club," a figurative way of saying they were born into a high social class. They were highly educated in prestigious institutions, and often abroad. For the most part they were successful, young professionals, predominantly in the fields of media and communication.

Their families had occupied privileged strata for generations. At their level in society, confessional cleavages, as most of them admitted, were less important than social divisions. Even if, for the most part, the identity entrepreneurs held no political positions, nor saw themselves as part of the political establishment, all had access to and familiarity with leading politicians through family, social, or professional connections.

Despite their privileged backgrounds, the identity entrepreneurs emerged from a sense of marginalization, as anti-Syrian leanings had either been violently censored or subdued in complacent docility. The euphoric experience of making Christians and Muslims cooperate in a common project gave the identity entrepreneurs a strong feeling of legitimacy.

The national imaginings of the Independence Intifada represented a contradiction whereby "national unity" was professed *against* domestic political adversaries whose supposed aspirations for Lebanon were cast as essentially problematic. I argue that nationalist practices of the Independence Intifada, ostensibly intended to unite Lebanon, were supported by and promoted ideas of a domestic other which was presumed to hold a vision for Lebanon which was irreconcilable with that projected by the Independence Intifada.

The chapter, extracted from the extensive personal interviews I was privileged to conduct, supplemented by non-participant observation and repeated visits to the site of the Intifada, explores five related dimensions. All five are naturally efforts to shed light on the interplay between youth networks, access to public space and political mobilization, employing the notion of "identity entrepreneurs." I explore first the role of five such actors under the rubric of "organizer", "image-builder", "artist", "fundraiser", and "socialite." I then consider the initial stages of the uprising to elucidate how the five emergent identity entrepreneurs experienced and began to identify central issues, platforms, and forms of mobilization. Third and perhaps most significant, I expose the spontaneous and largely informal networks which sparked the mobilization, and defined its agenda and courses of action. Fourth, albeit briefly, I amplify how the spectacle of the Intifada was hosted in the evocative historic setting of Martyrs' Square. Finally, I conclude by recapturing the connection between networks of mobilization, the social construction of space and identity-making.

THE IDENTITY ENTREPRENEURS

The first striking feature of the Intifada was the speed with which a spontaneous and informal gathering brought together disparate individuals, drawn from different backgrounds yet sparked by emotional contagion and a set of common political causes, beliefs, and slogans. Despite the pervasive feelings of shock, disbelief, and fear prevalent at the time, they did not become complacent. Other than their professional background and a network of contacts with well-placed families, they had no tangible resources to deploy. Yet they evinced a strong sense of agency reinforced by cross-confessional solidarity, a strident belief in the agencies of civil society and collective mobilization. In this way, they served as key actors and identity entrepreneurs.

Organizer: Asma Andraos
"It was so, so violent I have never heard anything like it. I felt it from beneath, you know, as if something was coming up from the ground" (Andraos, 11/17/06).

Asma Andraos, a woman in her early thirties exuding an air of no-nonsense ambition, almost stood up from her chair. It had taken me weeks to get the appointment with her, but after our meeting, what was before a barren, fleeting landscape of loose ends and transient informants positively flourished and solidified. Asma was my gateway to what she called inter-connected "spider-webs" of organizers, sloganeers, printers, advertisers, and media people who engineered the March 14 mobilisation (ibid).

We were seated in the office of her event management company. She was behind her wide desk strewn with glossy magazines and a jumble of documents, "Independence 05" pamphlets, and assorted memorabilia of the Beirut Spring. Slightly left of centre there stood a plaque carrying the insignia of *Time Magazine* with a grand, though somewhat puzzling, text reading "European Hero 2005". As the only non-European that year, Asma received the award for her efforts during the Independence Intifada. Reflecting on why she got this recognition, she said:

> Because I speak languages and because I'm quite articulate, I became sort of a favourite of the international media. The *Time Magazine* editor for the Middle East, Scott McLeod, who was close friends with Gibran [Tueni],[1] was telling Gibran, "I want to meet people from the camp [which constituted the sit-in in Martyrs' Square]." And Gibran said, "I have just the person for you." Gibran calls me up ... and introduced me to Scott. One thing led to another (ibid).

Her second-nature facility with three languages and ability to entertain the foreign media were fostered through private international schooling. "I was French-educated in Lebanon, very British-educated in England. The boarding school I went to was a very, very British boarding school, with a quota on foreigners. I was the first Arab ever to be allowed in. It was the Eton for girls." She also studied political science and international relations in English at Concordia University, Canada. Asma Andraos, whose father is Greek Orthodox and mother a Maronite Christian, is from a fairly wealthy family who could afford to send their children to prestigious educational institutions around the world. Her family are also well connected politically, though not directly engaged in politics.[2] Before 2005, Asma Andraos was not politically involved, though she said she was a politicized person, "you know, with a political conscience, but not belonging to a political party. I guess what you would call civil society" (ibid).

She partly blamed her political inaction on the Syrian presence, during which critical political activism was met with intimidation and violence. Meanwhile she was doing well for herself in the event management business, setting up her own company in 1999 (ibid). "I was very dormant. [Lebanon] was a Syrian stronghold. I just went into a bubble, and I was living my life happily" (ibid).

On February 14, 2005, she was in her office as the bomb that killed Rafik Hariri went off. A couple of kilometers away from the bombsite, the huge blast shook her building and the windows were blown open. Asma was devastated, but out of devastation grew a will to act:

> When my assistant told me it was Hariri, I got so nervous I threw something at her, and I'm not a violent person. It was an ashtray. I said, "you don't dare say that!" I started crying hysterically. I was sad, I was angry. I just thought "f... the Syrians, f... everyone, f... everything, we're going to be in such trouble now. Who's going to look after us? Who's going to make it?" Of course, slowly but surely, we realized it was pointless to go on working. So, we went to my house, a lot of friends joined, we started watching the news, and we decided well before they decided about a public funeral that we have to start mobilizing everyone for this funeral (ibid).

Image-Builder: Eli Khoury
Atop the Quantum Tower, a glitzy and futuristic office building in one of Beirut's most coveted quarters, for businesses and residents alike, I found the jovial and burly Eli Khoury, a soaring media and advertising executive with operations extending throughout the region. "I was in this office, actually. I immediately started watching the news. It reminded me of Bashir Gemayel [the Phalangist president-elect who was assassinated in September 1982]."[3] He was in his early twenties at the time, and a keen observer of politics. Already as a sixteen year-old he was a political cartoonist[4]. In the thirty years since, Eli Khoury said, he has been an activist. "I've always waited for that moment where all the Lebanese unite to say one thing, 'Lebanon comes first'. I've always waited for that. I lived in the States for ten years. I came back and now I run a group of companies, all in the field of communications."[5] To Eli Khoury and his associates, Hariri's death was an opening:

> My mind went back all the way to Bashir [Gemayel], when everybody thought he was alive, and then a few hours later we knew he was dead. So, I had the same feeling. We called each other, we met at my place. Samir Franjieh, Samir Kassir and a couple of others from March-14-to-be. We knew that it was make-it-or-break-it time. If this event doesn't mobilize people, nothing is going to mobilize people (Khoury, 11/28/07).

Already in late 2004, Eli Khoury and a small entourage, including historian-cum-journalist-cum-activist Samir Kassir, who commanded a particularly strong following among students and was himself assassinated on June 2, 2005, and Samir Franjieh, a prominent anti-Syrian politician associated with the Qornet Shehwan Gathering, had been contemplating how to rouse the Lebanese populace to shake off what they viewed as a Syrian occupation:

> The little, unknown fact in this was that what was later called the Cedar Revolution was started before the killing of Hariri. We discussed the fact that people are actually ready to make a peaceful movement. And we were aiming at doing this right before the elections [which, before Hariri's killing, were slated for early spring 2005]. I told them, "listen, if you're serious, people will come down [to demonstrate]. If you're not serious, people won't. And in order to make the people see that this is serious, I think we have to put a date to it." That's why I first came up with "05", telling people this is the year of change (ibid).

When Hariri was killed, Eli Khoury wanted to seize the moment of opportunity. Himself a Maronite Christian comfortable with his perception of Lebanon as an aspiring nation-unto-itself, he banked on the assumption that after the 1989 Taef Agreement, Lebanon's Muslims had been given more of a share in the country so that they "had finally realized that this country had something different, some-thing special, and that it concerned them as well as much as [it did] the Christians. It was a bet. I had the theory, and everybody was saying, 'are you sure?' I said, 'well, do we have the time?'"(ibid) Eli Khoury got his way, and his ideas would perme-ate the mobilization that ensued:

> The symbol was "Independence 05". The line was "*kulluna lil watan*", which is the national anthem, which means all of us [for the nation], and we all wore red and white, because these are the colours of the country, the flag. And it caught up like fire. We wanted a civilized message. We wanted to show the world that we are civilized, peaceful people (ibid).

Activist: Nabil Abou-Charaf
With his beak-like nose, a piercing, yet relaxed gaze and an unbent posture, Nabil Abou-Charaf cut an aristocratic figure. A lawyer-in-training, he studied at Université St. Joseph, the leading French-language University in Lebanon. "I have been a political activist since I entered university in 1998. And as such I've been arrested, jailed, kidnapped and tortured many times by the Syrian and Lebanese secret security services." (Abou-Charaf, 11/25/06). His tone of voice was level and matter-of-fact. "St. Joseph's University was known to be the only place in Lebanon that was opposed to the Syrian occupation. So we were, you can say, five persons

who were always being tortured, electrocuted, all kinds of torture you might see in a movie."

Nabil Abou-Charaf's university is run by the Jesuits, and before Hariri's death, the anti-Syrian activists tended to be Christian, often Maronites like himself. According to him, this worked against them. "We used to be treated as Christian isolationists, as if we didn't represent the whole country. Although we had some Muslims with us, we were not accepted as a national resistance."

Though having been a political activist for years and even if his grandfather was a founding member of the Kataeb Party, he had never been a member of a political party. He felt that with the current political culture, Lebanese political parties "are more fitted to people than ideas. I mean, it's the truth in Lebanon. Today, the Socialist Party is not a socialist party; it's Walid Jumblatt's party. The National Liberal Party is not a national liberal party; it's Chamoun's party. The Kataeb Party is not a Phalangist party; it's the Gemayels' party. The National Bloc is Eddé's party. Aoun's party is for Michel Aoun." Nabil was very critical of the political elite, to whom he had access regularly through his family connections and background as a student activist[6]. "I had a lot of meetings with them. Well, before the assassination of Hariri, we used ... I used to meet with them to tell them that they are losers. They don't do anything for their country" (ibid).

Nabil was in Paris at the time of Hariri's assassination and returned to Beirut immediately, cutting his trip short by one week. "Before he was assassinated, I was always saying that something would happen in this country that would send all the people to the streets. All the Lebanese people on the streets against Syria." (ibid)

Nabil and his activist friends were experienced organizers of demonstrations and instantly leapt into action after the killing of the former Prime Minister:

We were immediately down. We were ready for that. Let me tell you, the political class was very hesitant. I mean, after the assassination of a guy like Rafik Hariri, they really didn't know what to do, or how to react. So, what happened was that the street, and the youth on the street, led them (ibid).

Fundraiser: Farid Fakhreddine

"When they made this song in Arabic, I don't know if you know it, 'Beirut is crying and even the stones of the city are crying about the guy who built it.' I felt that was true." (Fakhreddine, 11/25/06). Farid Fakhreddine bent over the coffee table from a deep, leather-clad armchair in an up-market restaurant in downtown Beirut. The killing of Rafik Hariri had obviously profoundly shaken him. Farid, whose Druze family was originally from the Shuf Mountains though residing in the western part of Beirut, said he had always been politically conscious, ever since his days at the American University of Beirut in the early 1980s. Back in 1982, in reaction to the Israeli invasion, he led a university association that championed the Arab cause and decried the plight of the Palestinians. His group participated in demonstrations but remained unaffiliated with any particular political party (ibid). However, in recent years, his Abu Dhabi-based business and his family had been taking most of his time.

"I developed in different phases in my political thinking during my life. I lived in the western part of Beirut during the war but we ran away during the [Israeli] invasion. And my political thinking was always towards the Arab conflict, the Arab-Israeli conflict, how to support the Palestinians" (ibid). With the onset of normalization between Israel and Jordan, against the backdrop of positive prospects for Palestinians and Israelis created by the Oslo process, and seeing the end of Israeli occupation of southern Lebanon, Farid started to believe Lebanon also needed to move towards establishing peaceful relations with its southern neighbor. He rejected the continuation of the resistance against Israel for the sake of the disputed territories of the Shebaa Farms. "I couldn't understand why we needed to keep the country in turmoil because of a small area which is really not inhabited by people. I felt that my kids needed to live in peace. I didn't want my kids to live what I lived: War, risk, shortage, rejection"(ibid).

In the autumn of 2004, he began to feel it had gone too far. "The thing started when they had agreed to extend the era of Emile Lahoud. I felt that the Syrians, along with the others who are in this camp, they don't know the culture of life. They know the culture of death" (ibid).

When Rafik Hariri was killed, Farid was in Cairo on a business trip. He flew back to Beirut the following day. An old schoolmate, Basil Fuleihan, a former Minister of Economy and Trade, was badly hurt in the explosion, and later died of his injuries. Farid paid his condolences at the Hariris' Beirut residence and participated at the funeral with his family:

The next day we went where they had buried him and a guy came with a poster and he wrote "resign" on it [asking for the resignation of the government]. And we started coming and signing ... "resign, resign, resign, resign" ... and through a common friend I met Asma [Andraos]. We started working, and then the camp started: The Freedom Camp (ibid).

The common friend was Karim Hamade, the son of Marwan Hamade, Walid Jumblatt's long-time right-hand-man and Minister of Telecommunications, who narrowly survived an assassination attempt in October 2004. Once involved, Farid was able to mobilize significant resources:

I contributed financially personally. I got donations, funds from every single friend I know in the world. I even put my office here to work on fundraising. It happened I had connections in restaurants because I sell water filtration equipment to restaurants. So I have a database of them, and the staff in the office started working with me on that. We called everybody and started getting donations from people we know and people we don't know. We started getting more and more and more funds. And I have good contacts in the Gulf, so I started contacting them, and they started sending us funds in different ways (http:/i-lovelife.com).

Socialist Socialite: Nora Jumblatt

"I was right here in this office. I was here with other ladies who work with the festival, and I was actually calling London. And my phone goes dead. My cell-phone goes dead. So, I call out to my secretary to give me London again by landline. And while I was speaking, the whole place, these whole windows broke through. A huge explosion! And the first I thought of was immediately to try to call my husband, because he had gone out that morning. And we knew already that he was in danger, and so was Hariri. So, there were only two options. This explosion was Walid Jumblatt or Rafik Hariri" (N. Jumblatt, 12/07/06).

The lanky and striking Nora Jumblatt told me this as we were sitting in her office where she runs the Beiteddine Festival, one of the most prestigious music festivals in the Middle East. Her husband is Walid Jumblatt, the pre-eminent Druze politician in the country and the head of the Progressive Socialist Party (PSP).

From the very outset, Nora Jumblatt got involved. On Tuesday February 15, 2005, the Hariri family decided that Rafik Hariri would be buried next to the huge Mohammad Al-Amin mosque on Martyrs' Square (which he had built) the following day, a decision that was crucial in directing public attention to this particular site in central Beirut. Nora Jumblatt was at the Hariris' that day, and together with a few other ladies she organised for five thousand white roses to be handed out to mourners from Martyrs' Square on the day of the funeral. As she was leaving the Hariris' on Tuesday night, she made a detour on her way home to have a look at the place where Rafik Hariri had been assassinated. There, she came upon Tima Khalil, a young film producer and civil society activist, who had initiated a candle-light vigil calling for the truth about Hariri's killing. "Tima asked me, 'would you care to sign a petition to ask for an international tribunal?' I said, 'yes, for sure.'" (ibid) Nora Jumblatt used her contacts to help Tima Khalil get newspaper coverage of this initiative. She provided metal structure on-site and large-scale printing of the petition. The space between the Intercontinental Phoenicia and the St. Georges Marina, which was where Hariri was killed, thus became a focal point for the early days of public action. Tima Khalil's "Citizens 4 Lebanon" was the first civil society action to take place after the bomb, and it was explicitly non-partisan. It asked for an international investigation to uncover the truth about the "hidden hands" which were behind the killing of Hariri and twenty-one others, who were either travelling in Hariri's motorcade or simply bystanders[7]. In an interview with the author, Tima Khalil expressed gratitude for the support offered by

Nora Jumblatt, but she also voiced regret that what they had started as a non-partisan call for "truth and justice" quickly became a contentious and politically exploited issue in an increasingly polarised political landscape (Khalil, 11/30/06). On Thursday February 17, 2005, Nora Jumblatt got a call from Asma Andraos, whom at the time she did not know, though she knew her parents well. (Jumblatt, op.cit). Asma Andraos was in charge of a petition at Martyrs' Square that was expressly political. It called for the resignation of the government. In this case, too, Nora Jumblatt assisted in getting the press to cover what had started as a spontaneous initiative on the eve of Hariri's burial the day before. Nora Jumblatt reflected on the impulsive beginnings of the post-Hariri mobilization:

> So, it was two different things, done by two different entities. Tima Khalil and Asma Andraos. Tima Khalil and her group had started to demand an international tribunal down at the St. Georges, and Asma and her friends had started after the funeral the signing of a petition for the resignation of the government. It's very strange how these things came out randomly and spontaneously (ibid).·

> Thursday night, Nora Jumblatt went down to the venue she had helped set up near St. Georges Marina and together with a group of around 150 people she walked to Martyrs' Square, via the Parliament. "That was the first march. I remember talking to Brent Sadler [CNN's Beirut bureau chief]. He asked me, 'do you think this is gonna fizzle out like everything else in Lebanon?' And I said, 'no, this is not gonna fizzle out.' He didn't believe me at the time, I suppose" (ibid).

As the first demonstration had taken place, discussions were on in the political circles of the opposition about how to proceed:

> There were a lot of discussions about the Bristol Meeting and the opposition, and the discussion of colors was in the air. Different people were discussing it. At the time I had not linked up with Samir Kassir. We were closely working together, but on different things, such as catalogues for the Beiteddine Festival. He was a friend, but we had not linked up. We had not linked up to any of these random things at the time (ibid).

Nora Jumblatt talked to PSP MP Wael Abou Faour about the choice of colors, which at the time was white. She disagreed as that gave the impression of a funeral. Green was considered "too Islamic", and red was "too socialist". "How about ... we just came up with white and red. And it was random like that."(ibid)

On Friday February 18, Samir Kassir called Nora Jumblatt and suggested they get together and discuss slogans. Thus, the next day she joined Samir Kassir, Eli

Khoury, and their group for a brainstorming session, where the final decision on the colors red and white was taken. (Khoury, 11/28/06) It was a pregnant choice that would, throughout the Independence Intifada, color all manner of paraphernalia, artefacts, and merchandising, from scarves to wristbands, banners, and buttons.

SETTING THE STAGE: EXPLORING IDENTITY, NETWORKS, AND SPACE

The first week after Hariri's assassination was one of fluidity and contingency. The country was in shock and disbelief. There was also a sense of fear. Whoever had taken Rafik Hariri's life had taken the country a large step into the unknown. Shock, disbelief, and fear could perhaps be expected to lead to paralysis. However, there is a compelling sense of agency evinced by the glimpses presented above of how some key figures – emergent identity entrepreneurs – experienced this initial period. Furthermore, we may already glean some interesting issues pertaining to the present exploration of identity, mobilization and space.

Firstly, as far as mobilization is concerned, there was an emotional impetus and recognition of a moment of opportunity; the actors drew on considerable human and financial resources; there were spontaneous actions that were quickly linked through informal networks; and civil society rather than the political establishment took the initiative. Secondly, in the early days, two distinctly different urban public spaces served as focal points for the mobilization. Thirdly, in terms of identity, there was the issue of whether national sentiments were no longer predominantly held by Christians; and a vision of a "united" and "civilized" Lebanon was being articulated against an imagined other construed as antithetical to this vision.

Blaming Syria and Catching the World's Attention
The night of February 14, 2005, Asma Andraos gathered a group of friends at her house. They decided to make a statement at the funeral about who was behind Hariri's killing, but they were afraid to go too far. (Andraos, 11/17/2006).

Laying the blame squarely on Syria or elements of the Lebanese authorities was considered dangerous, as these powers were still in charge in the country (ibid).

Asked by the BBC who was behind his father's death, Saad Hariri, the eldest son and political heir, provided an answer that was at once unequivocal and ambiguous: "it's obvious, no?" This line, implying Syria and its Lebanese allies were to blame, became the first "slogan" of the then inchoate March 14 mobilization (ibid). Two big banners brandished at Hariri's public funeral, deliberately carrying this slogan in English, caught the attention of the ambient international media. According to Asma Andraos, "[t]hat's how it started. Cameras stopped.

Crews stopped. And suddenly we started talking. CNN said, 'what do you mean?' And at first I was saying, 'well, you know ...' And then I said, 'you know what, Bashar al-Assad did it.'" (ibid).

Petition for the Government to Resign
It could have ended with the funeral. Ideas were brewing here and there, as I have sought to illustrate, but these spontaneous and sparse actions had yet to coalesce. And, unless one believed firmly in preordination, it was not at all given that they would. Asma Andraos remembered waking up the day after the funeral thinking that had been it.

She refused the thought, and when she got an sms text message summoning people to gather at Hariri's burial site, she was quick to get there (ibid). Her friend Nicole Fayad received the same sms, and when she arrived at the *darih* [grave], there were only fifteen people present. "Gucci people," she told me, almost apologetically, meaning they were of the similarly narrow socio-economic extraction as her (Fayad, 11/24/06).

Nicole Fayad remembered how, suddenly, a sheet of the canvas covering the *darih* was taken down and, with her lipstick, they wrote "demission!" on it (ibid).

Written in French, the imperative of "resign" expressed in no unclear terms what they demanded of the Lebanese government. Though it had not been intended thus, Nicole Fayad recalled, "a Hariri guy came and signed it, and then we all did" (ibid).

There was an immediate ripple effect, as people paying their respects to the deceased also signed what had consequently become a petition asking for the government's resignation. This included political personalities, such as Walid Jumblatt and Fuad Siniora, who at the time was a prominent politician and adviser in Hariri's Future Movement and would become prime minister in summer 2005. Gibran Tueni apparently added the plural "s", incongruously rendering the inscription "demission!s", which was an unmistakable extension of the call for resignation to include President Emile Lahoud alongside the government (ibid).

The canvas was soon filled, and Asma Andraos called up a friend, Jad Khoury, the owner of a printing house, who promptly delivered several hundred meters of plastic-coated paper that was then laid out on Martyrs' Square. It was quickly filled by thousands of signatures, drawings, and remarks. (Khoury, 11/27/06)

A Civil Society Platform for Politics
Asma Andraos and her friends were on a roll. They saw they could have an impact. Mostly, these people came from creative fields, such as media and advertising, printing and publishing, and were all enterprising young professionals. Together, they could pool tremendous experience in event management, branding, fundraising, and public relations. And, almost equally important, they were well connected. Asma Andraos put it bluntly: "Lebanon is very stratified in class ... so this

is one world. Because we're part of the lucky sperm club, let's put it that way, we knew people" (Andraos, op.cit). On Saturday, two days into the petition campaign to demand the government's resignation, Asma Andraos and eleven of her friends meeting in her house decided to venture further. They completed and signed a one-page document they had entitled *Ideas of crisis management brainstorming session dated 19.02.2005* (ibid). In effect, the document outlined a communication and mobilization platform.

The main objectives listed in the document concerned streamlining and coordination of message and image. The message was suggested to be "Independence", the Lebanese flag being the proposed unifying image. The document urges coordination with leaders of student groups, movements and parties to make sure the message and image be unified, presumably to avoid excessive display of particularistic symbols. The stated reason for adopting the national flag was "in order to show one single sense of belonging vs. disparate entities" (ibid). In the first week of public action, political party flags and slogans were prevalent. This was the case at the funeral procession, which gathered mourners in the tens of thousands.

The insistence on a unified message and image was certainly a reflection of a professional approach to communication. However, it was also an expression of an ambition to actually build bridges across the many cleavages, or "disparate entities", with which Lebanon is so proverbially beset. This altruistic aspiration, which went hand in hand with the precepts of effective mass communication, was made plain in the many interviews I conducted with key organizers.

In a similarly philanthropic vein, the document urged the mobilization to "drive the message to stop harassing Syrian people/workers; encourage all to dissociate the Syrian regime from its people."

Attuned to global trends in political mobilization, the document impelled the employment of "multilingual banners for international media coverage" and to "make optimal use of FTV [Future Television, owned by the Hariri family] coverage and propaganda."

The second part of the document was a more practical section, entitled "logistics". It proposed the establishment of cells and committees for core areas of responsibility, such as communication, press liaison, logistics, and finance. A range of communication tools and avenues were recommended, e.g. red and white scarves, arm bands, pins, stickers, t-shirts, caps; sms, print media, posters, flyers, websites; Lebanese opinion leaders and trend-setters, artists, businesspeople, athletes, and professional associations.

The document made a significant distinction between "the opposition", or "opposition leaders", and "the street", or "the people", and a gap was assumed to exist between the two. This gap was to be avoided by "mak[ing] sure to have leaders of the opposition appearing and speaking at every one of these meetings, to keep momentum and motivation." This distinction also opened up the conceptual space – a lack of clear definitions notwithstanding – in which Asma Andraos and her group would later establish themselves under the name "*al-mujtama al-madani*", meaning civil society.

The leaders of cells and committees were exhorted to liaise with the (then, anti-Syrian) opposition. One ought to presume that "opposition leaders" referred to the leaders of the political opposition. Interviews with signatories of the document attest to their identification with the street and their non-identification with the political establishment (ibid). Nevertheless, the document urged close coordination with the politicians of the opposition, effectively giving them the leadership, while offering to do the mobilization and communication groundwork.

The distribution of the document is noteworthy in this regard. Thanks to the professional, social, and family networks of the document's authors it quickly reached around twenty of the top opposition politicians, including Walid Jumblatt, Samir Franjieh, Nassib Lahoud, Nayla Moawad, Amin and Pierre Gemayel, and Gibran Tueni (ibid). The reception of the document was very positive. This somewhat surprised its authors, as they had imagined the politicians might already have clearer ideas of their own. In fact, Asma Andraos said, "the reaction to this document made us realize that we were needed. And so we thought, 'ok, we're in.' *Khalas*. There was no turning back. I was in. I was involved."[8]

NETWORKS OF POLITICAL MOBILISATION

A characteristic aspect of the Independence Intifada mobilization was how quickly spontaneous and separate initiatives were brought together under a common political umbrella of causes, slogans, and colours. Yet, most initiatives were not undertakings of the political establishment. Another striking feature was how the mobilization took off and was perpetuated by actions of individuals who were driven by charged emotional experiences. In the following, I analyse these two facets against the roles of *informal networks* and *emotions* as suggested in mobilization literature.

The Role of Informal Networks
I have chosen to call identity entrepreneurs a host of individuals who made significant and sometimes crucial contributions to the political mobilization called the Independence Intifada. I have thus grouped people who had quite different functions, but they shared in making the uprising predominantly through informal ties to one another. Several of them did not even know each other before February 14, 2005, and nevertheless they quickly entrusted one another with various tasks. This is remarkable. According to a 2002 survey conducted by Theodor Hanf, only 52 per cent of the Lebanese trusted their friends (2003: 199), not to mention strangers[9].

There were many shared structural factors in the backgrounds of the identity entrepreneurs that represented opportunities for cooperative resource mobilizátion. In particular, they were especially well placed to influence the fields where they seem to have had the largest impact, namely communication and logistics.

To understand how these opportunities for cooperative resource mobilization were realized, we may first recall another of Asma Andraos' assessments: The mobilization was carried out by inter-connected "spider-webs" of people whose aspirations and interests intersected on a set of common objectives. Informal networks of people were informally connected with other networks, which in turn could be both informal and formal (such as political parties). Second, as far as realization in the cognitive sense is concerned, we may take as an example the change from guarded apprehension to bold assertiveness when Asma Andraos dared tell the international media out loud that "Bashar al-Assad did it," that she thought the President of Syria was responsible for Hariri's death. Participation in the mobilization with the co-presence of masses of people in an evocative urban public space stirred emotions, moved cognitive horizons, and shaped aspirations.

The first week after Hariri's killing was particularly telling as far as mobilisation in interconnected informal networks is concerned. Eli Khoury assembled Samir Franjieh, Samir Kassir, and a couple of other associates at his home to discuss slogans and colours; Nora Jumblatt was discussing colours with a representative of PSP; and Asma Andraos gathered her friends at home several evenings in a row, organised various initiatives, and suggested a communication and logistics platform for the mobilization; and the extraordinary thing was how quite similar ideas developed in various settings only to be funnelled together in a matter of very little time indeed. In several cases, people who previously did not know each other personally, got in touch over the phone and quickly began cooperating and trusting one another. Eli Khoury gave a compelling sense of this atmosphere:

> For some reason, people were all coordinating with each other without knowing who's who. The spontaneous cooperation was remarkable, really. That's it, you know, "Eli is doing the message, it means Eli is gonna give me the message, I'm not gonna argue. I'm gonna do the sandwiches, that means X is gonna do the sandwiches." So, everybody just took charge of something, and the others let him. (Khoury, 11/28/07).

Yet, "everybody" was not just anybody. For example, even if Asma Andraos did not know Nora Jumblatt personally, she certainly knew *of* her – Mrs Jumblatt being one of the country's most well-known public figures. Asma Andraos already knew they were on the same side on the crucial political issue of Syria and frequented circles, which made it easier to quite forthrightly solicit the help of a figure such as Nora Jumblatt. This is suggestive of Mario Diani's (2000) network theory of social movements that builds on Georg Simmel's concept of intersecting social circles and Stein Rokkan's idea of political cleavages.

However, we should note the role of action and initiative. For the most part, there were not pre-established networks, in a static sense, which organized the mobilization; highly characteristic was the ongoing *networking*. The use of gerund here is a way of emphasizing linking up as an ongoing activity through which the mobilization was produced, in a situation of contingency, fluidity, and uncertainty. Samir Franjieh remembered sitting on the plane, hurrying home to Beirut after receiving the news of Hariri's death, running scenarios in his head for what might happen – and this was a man, we should remember, who had been working for a long time on the "Independence 05" project – but he was unable to foretell what would happen: "All the scenarios were wrong." (Frangieh, 13/03/07).

Furthermore, Diani takes a rather static concept of "shared identities" as a basis for his theory, and this, as well, needs revision and nuance in the case of the identity entrepreneurs. I shall argue below that a network analysis of the Independence Intifada requires an understanding of identity based on the dynamics of self-making in history-making and that this was a process which drew on and promoted a kind of governmental belonging to Lebanon as a nation.

The Role of Emotions
Networking by resourceful people made the Independence Intifada possible, but emotions made it happen. All of my interviewees spoke of, and laid bare, strong emotions when recounting what had come to pass after Hariri's assassination. It would usually be enough to ask "Where were you when he was killed, and how did you feel?" I was impressed by the level of detail, sometimes down to an hour-by-hour narrative, and moved by the evocations of shock, disbelief, fear, anger, resolve.

Eli Khoury and Nabil Abou-Charaf, who had been involved in political strategising in the past, both recalled feeling at the hour of Hariri's death that it was going to present them with an opening, an opportunity to gather many Lebanese around a political project indexed by ending the Syrian interference in Lebanon. For people with fewer political investments, such as Asma Andraos, Nicole Fayad, and Farid Fakhreddine, the first reaction was shock and disbelief. They saw Hariri's death as an attack against their safe and prosperous lives that they had precariously constructed in post-civil war Lebanon. Hariri, despite allegations of mixing business and politics, and criticisms for a slanted, debt-ridden reconstruction process, had been part of the hope in a future in Lebanon on which these identity entrepreneurs had based their stay in the country.

One of the earliest emotional reactions among the identity entrepreneurs was to seek out friends and spend time together digesting the situation. Several of the interviewees were abroad when Hariri was killed, and all told me how desperately they needed to get back and connect with their friends and loved ones in order to understand what was going on, but also, and through this, to seek emotional comfort. Given their resources and opportunities, they might as well have gone or stayed abroad. However, seeing their way of life in Lebanon threatened, they felt they could no longer be complacent or politically docile.

Taking part in the successes in mobilizing large numbers of people, even for the earliest events; experiencing the exhilaration of being together from across traditional lines of division; seeing people overcoming long-held fears; feeling the popular excitement which was present in Martyrs' Square and magnified by the constant press and television coverage of media houses involved in or sympathetic to the mobilization; all combined to conferring onto the identity entrepreneurs a heady sensation of historical agency. Cognitive horizons moved, aspirations developed, and they felt their vision of Lebanon could win the day.

The repercussions were also strong on the individual level. Asma Andraos confessed to having been changed for life through her work in the Independence Intifada. She felt she could never return to her complacency; she now felt she had a role to play in shaping Lebanon's future.

There was among most of the identity entrepreneurs I interviewed a feeling that their vision of Lebanon, amounting to a way of life, was at once on the verge of being realized *and* about to be resoundingly quashed. The intensely emotional terms whereby the struggle was perceived, already from the outset, fed back into a whirlwind of existential sentiments that polarized the political landscape.

This study shows how focussing on emotions can be a fruitful way of making sense of political mobilisations and therefore supports claims to this effect made by some theorists (e.g. Jasper 1997; Goodwin, Jasper and Polletta 2001, 2004; Goodwin and Jasper 2004; Aminzade and McAdam 2001). Through an ethnographic approach, combining intensive semi-structured interviews with participant observation, while reviewing documents, slogans and visual aspects, "the emotional repertoire of protest" appears (Goodwin, Jasper and Polletta 2004). We may appreciate how emotions are a crucial aspect of agency: Without the emotional reaction to Hariri's death, all the resources of the identity entrepreneurs would have been left idle. Also, we may observe how emotions followed action so that, *in practice*, emotions moved cognitive horizons and shaped aspirations.

SOCIAL CONSTRUCTION OF SPACE

Beirut is song. Beirut is bullet holes. Living in Beirut and walking its streets attuned me to the thought that space is at once produced and productive (Soja 1989, 1996). The spectacle of the Independence Intifada took place in a splendidly evocative setting. In turn, being thus staged, Martyrs' Square exuded a celebratory vision of Lebanon based on coexistence. However, the sizeable counter-mobilization in an adjacent space showed that this vision and its stage were intensely at stake.

Many histories of the formations of Lebanon resonate in Martyrs' Square and its immediate surroundings of Downtown Beirut (Kassir 2003; Khalaf 2006; Khalaf and Khoury 1993; Rowe and Sarkis 1998). It got its name from the public execution there of Lebanese nationalists in 1915; it was a meeting point, transportation hub, commercial and leisure centre in happier times; it was an image of Lebanon in national histories which portrayed it as a modern trading city with cosmopolitan flair; heavy street-fighting pitting Christian against Muslim desecrated its famed conviviality and left a wasteland cut across by weeds and shrubbery making for the notorious Green Line; and Hariri was the largest investor, financially and politically, in a contentious attempt at resurrecting it after the civil war. But for many Lebanese it remained distant, both because of its identification with atavistic violence and because its reconstruction provided spaces mainly for the rich.

The identity entrepreneurs were acutely aware of this. Indeed, a character such as Samir Kassir had for years contributed significantly to a current understanding of Beirut through his scholarship and journalism. Eli Khoury said the communication strategy of the Independence Intifada aimed at recreating a sense of the Beirut that was lost during the civil war and by the prevailing encroachments on Lebanese sovereignty and independence, which he and the identity entrepreneurs saw represented first and foremost by Syria, and increasingly also by Hizbullah. This revival, to the identity entrepreneurs, was a Beirut both convivial and symbolic of Lebanese self-determination.

In terms borrowed from Ghassan Hage (2000), we may say that historical Beirut was both the *ideal* and the *spatial referent* of the Lebanese nation being staged in its present central square. Strengthening such an analysis is the insistence of Gisele Khoury, a prominent journalist and widow after Samir Kassir, that the Independence Intifada was a triumph of the "city mentality" over the "village mentality". (Khoury, Gisele 03/16/07).

To Samir Kassir, March 14 embodied a "city mentality" (ibid). Samir Kassir dedicated his book on the history of Beirut to his wife, Gisele Khoury, whom he gave the honorific characterisation "*Beyrouthine extra-muros*". "Samir always had big problems with people coming from the village to the city, people coming with the mentality of the village. I'm from a village in the mountains; I'm Maronite," said Gisele Khoury, "but I have the mentality of the city" (ibid). She said that while March 14 was an expression of a city mentality, March 8 represented the mentality of the village. People with a city mentality, according to her, love their city – Beirut, not any city – and take pride in it being an open and tolerant place, accepting all religions and nationalities. The people with a "village mentality", she said, "refuse anyone who's not Lebanese, not from the village with a confession very clear. They are not tolerant. They are not modern." (ibid) While telling me about the differences between city and village mentalities, Gisele Khoury remembered that when she spoke with her husband in the month before he was killed, he repeatedly had told her that "I won't forgive them what they did with the Western hostages; I won't forgive them what they did to Michel Seurat [French sociologist captured and killed by a Shia militia, a forerunner of Hizbullah]."[10]

There is, in other words, identification – part implied, part explicit – between "village mentality", Hizbullah, and intolerant, anti-Western, un-modern attitudes, altogether amounting to a threat to Beirut and its ways. The image of this menacing other leaves no room for any appreciation of their self-perception – whereas a recent ethnographic study shows that Shia Muslims in support of Hizbullah may "consider themselves simultaneously deeply modern, cosmopolitan, and pious" (Deeb 2006).

Thus, Gisele Khoury provides further leads to our understanding of Martyrs' Square, and by implication, Beirut, as a stage for the forging of a Lebanese nation. While acknowledging her village ancestry she emphasizes she is a Maronite from the *mountain*. (Khoury, Gisele, 03/16/07). This, we may infer from her claim, has aided in her assimilation into city life. In a sense, she embodies the very socio-geographic principle on which Lebanon was construed as a nation and constructed as a state, according to the narratives of leading Lebanese historians, namely a marriage between City and Mountain (Hourani 1988; Salibi 1988).

In droves, village folk descended on Martyrs' Square on March 14, 2005. Indeed, the phrase most commonly used by my interviewees to express "going to Martyrs' Square" was simply "going down". By Lebanese standards, huge distances were crossed, even on foot, and more symbolically, they were shrunk through encounters between middle-class Beiruti identity entrepreneurs and lower-class aspiring activists from faraway regions, such as Akkar. March 14 thus adds physicality in the sense of bodies in space to Benedict Anderson's (1991) famous notion of "imagined community" with a quarter of this nation's population gathered in one place. Here, what for Anderson was imagined primarily through the print media became realized in presence; to the identity entrepreneurs, a national community (or body politic) was there[11].

The socially constructed geography of Lebanon embedded in the way the identity entrepreneurs spoke of City, Mountain and Village reproduced national narratives which located the country's essence in a marriage of City and Mountain. By the same token, the explicit and implicit identification of most Shia Muslims with the Village represented their marginalization by socially constructing peripheries and essentializing their inhabitants.

PRACTICES OF LEBANESE NATIONAL IDENTITY-MAKING

Studies of networks of mobilisation (e.g. White 1992; Emirbayer and Goodwin 1994: 1436-1447; Diani 2000) and social construction of space (e.g. Keith and Pile 1993; Gupta and Ferguson 1997) are copiously invoking and probing issues of identity. In both fields, the interest in identity was inspired by the cultural turn in social theory (Harvey 1989; Jameson 1998). In the literatures on mobilization and space, identity has consequently been construed in terms of discursive frameworks (Emirbayer and Goodwin 1994: 1439) or processes (Gupta and Ferguson

1997; Mische 2003). These tend to be discursive approaches in a rather limited sense of meaning and textuality.

Two extraordinarily engaging volumes, *Identity and Agency in Cultural Worlds* (Holland et al. 1998) and *History in Person* (Holland and Lave 2001), invite us to conceive of identity as a process that connects intimate and public venues through social practice. In particular, Holland et al. (1998) argue, enduring struggles and contentious practice are situations in which social practice intensely interlocks self-making and history-making.

Hage (2000) employs a similar notion of social practice in the context of our overriding concern with national identity. He shows how situating identity in social practice offsets shortcomings in the kind of discursive approaches that focus on meaning and textuality. He fuses a focus on representation, as seen in his concept of the ideal nation (ibid: 38-42), with a focus on practice, in Bourdieu's sense of active, bodily experience (ibid: 44-45). Moreover, to Hage, nationalist practices should be understood as ways of effectively seeking to manage a national space (ibid: 47).

The Independence Intifada is an evocative instance of how enduring struggles and contentious practices directed at managing a national territory climaxed in nationalist fervour through flourishing networks of mobilization in a charged urban public space.

History-Making and Self-Making

For the identity entrepreneurs, the Independence Intifada was a formative event. They made history, and at the same time they remade themselves. Certainly, the history-making and the self-making did not occur in a vacuum but rather in a multi-layered historical and biographic context with both enabling and disabling features (Jasper 1997).

In Lebanon there is an enduring struggle over state sovereignty and national identity. The modern history of Lebanon shows that allegiances to different conceptions of national community (Lebanese, Syrian, Arab, Islamic, etc.) have vied for supremacy. The main domestic actors of this struggle have tended to be religio-political communities and their monopolizing helmsmen, by implication of the confessional political system. Each conception of national community has its separate set of politico-territorial ramifications, both in terms of where state borders are ideally to be drawn, and in terms of the solicitation of foreign sponsors to gain domestic ground. Certainly, these foreign sponsors have also had interests of their own in gaining influence in Lebanon. Indeed, this struggle has been utterly devastating in times when state power has been weak and the interests of foreign powers predatory (Hanf 1993; Khazen 2000). At each critical turn in this tumultuous history, the struggle over state sovereignty has simultaneously been a struggle over the question of the identity of the state (Picard 2002). This was the struggle into which the identity entrepreneurs threw themselves. They made their mark on it, and it made its mark on them.

The identity entrepreneurs saw themselves as a different breed of actor than those of the political establishment that dominated the struggle. The way they painstakingly construed and projected themselves as youthful members of "civil society" attested to this. Their understanding and representation of self rested on perceived boundaries between "the street" and "the politicians". An important element in the distinctions being made was that the identity entrepreneurs saw themselves as authentic and sincere embracers of cross-confessional solidarity while they considered the political leaders to be espousing a more instrumental approach to building alliances.

However, the perceived lines of distinction did not remain stable. As the identity entrepreneurs engaged in the struggle, their perceptions and representations of self changed. In the majority of cases, the largest mutation happened when they went from being politically docile and complacent to seeing themselves as influential actors. This occurred rather spontaneously, was triggered by emotions, yet rested on a structural potentiality represented by these individuals' resources, including political connections, social ties, and professional liaisons. A combination of familiarity with political leaders and their circles and the attitude that to get things done, politicians needed to be on board, made the budding identity entrepreneurs offer their services to the leaders of the political opposition at the time.

Some of the identity entrepreneurs had been working with figures in the political elite since a long time before the killing of Hariri. In the case of Eli Khoury, he already had an established working relationship with several political figures of the opposition, but maintained the same rationale for his involvement: He did not see himself as a politician; though very little of a romantic, he had no doubts politicians were needed to get things done and he would offer his help "when it matters" (Khoury, Eli 11/28/06). With a background as student activist, Nabil Abou-Charaf had a long-standing belief that he needed to work with the political establishment to pursue the Lebanon he envisaged, but he kept a critical distance – which appeared to have widened with the Independence Intifada and its aftermath – in the way that he dealt with and spoke of the country's leading politicians (Abou-Charaf, 11/25/06).

As certain political figures, in particular Samir Kassir and Gibran Tueni, who were previously marginal for their lack of confessional followings, took centre stage in the Independence Intifada, the identity entrepreneurs were mindful that they had had a large hand in setting that stage. Inspired by these two leading figures, who appeared to the identity entrepreneurs as authentic representatives of wider political change and transcending solidarities, the identity entrepreneurs began to relax the distinctions they had drawn between themselves and the political establishment. The Independence Intifada appeared to have the promise of not only reaching a common set of goals, such as the government's resignation, Syria's withdrawal, an international investigation into Hariri's killing, and the resignation of key officers of the security apparatus. At its peak on March 14, it represented to the identity entrepreneurs an opportunity for politics to be done according to new rules whereby they would have a significant say, whether as representatives of "the youth", "civil society" or of a "modern, secular Lebanon".

The subsequent assassinations of Samir Kassir, Gibran Tueni and other promising and prominent political figures of the Independence Intifada coupled with the atmosphere of compromise and instrumental electoral alliances between traditional elites across the March 14-March 8 divide caused resounding disappointment among the identity entrepreneurs. Asma Andraos said that many people left her group demoralized, realizing "what we really wanted was going to take ten years of work" (Andraos, Asma, op. cit).

Nicole Fayad was among those who stayed on: "Many people left us. Only ten–fifteen stayed. Why? They were disappointed by all the political figures and felt there was nothing to do. They don't want to take sides and preferred to get out of politics. We said we're doing politics – doing our thing – from the inside of March 14" (Fayad, Nicole, op.cit). Even those who stayed active, thus confirming their new-found identity as socio-political actors, developed or reverted to a much more critical understanding of who they were in distinction to the political elites.

The identity entrepreneurs' senses of self evolved with their involvement in organizing historical political events in the context of an enduring struggle over state sovereignty and national identity.

Governmental Belonging

Governmental belonging is the term used by Hage to describe a person's sense of ownership of the nation, even if this only entails the belief in having a legitimate opinion of its internal and external politics (2000: 45-46). He contrasts this against passive belonging denoting the sense a person may have that "I belong to the nation" (ibid.). The work done by the identity entrepreneurs to organize the Independence Intifada showed a very active sense of ownership of the Lebanese nation. They had visions for Lebanon that were developed and sharpened through the mobilization, and even if they might emphasize different nuances, they had no doubts about their right to their opinion and to trying to realize their vision of the ideal nation on Lebanese soil.

As I have argued elsewhere (Gahre, 2007), from the late nineteenth century onwards, a governmental belonging to Lebanon developed most strongly among the elites of Mount Lebanon and Beirut. The Maronites were the leading group in this respect, while the urban Sunni Muslim and Greek Orthodox elites were also prominent.

Classical narratives of modern Lebanon nostalgically locate its national identity in the marriage between Mountain and City and thus reproduce relations of power that lay at the foundation of Lebanon as a state.

The struggle over state sovereignty and national identity endured, and the marriage between Mountain and City was strained, indeed severed. During the civil war, the mansions of the City and the Mountain were sites of war; Christians and Druze fought each other in the mountains, and Christians and Muslims in the cities. In the context of pan-Arabism, Nasserism and the Cold War, the question of Israel and Palestine, and the Syrian hegemony after the civil war, Lebanese nationalism seemed increasingly an exclusively Christian pursuit.

Meanwhile, the Shia Muslims, who were marginal, both at the establishment of Lebanon and in the leading national narratives, mobilized politically, socially, and militarily under a religious banner, supported by Iran, acquiesced to by Syria and in reaction to the Israeli occupation.

The killing of Hariri and the Independence Intifada brought the Druze and Sunni Muslims firmly into the anti-Syrian camp. We may therefore understand the euphoric attractiveness of the Independence Intifada by recognizing that it felt like a "nationalist homecoming". As far as the identity entrepreneurs were concerned, whose understanding of Lebanese history tended to repeat leading national narratives, it was as if the nostalgic dream of a re-marriage of Mountain and City had come true. With the Independence Intifada, Christians, Sunni Muslims, and Druze appeared to share a view of how to end the struggle over state sovereignty and national identity. The identity entrepreneurs and the political leaders of Mountain and City thus demonstrated a reasserted governmental belonging to Lebanon.

Nabil Abou-Charaf told me how the anti-Syrian struggle he partook of in the late 1990s and early 2000s as a student activist was discredited as Christian isolationism. For him, who believed in Lebanon as a pluralistic society, those were disheartening times. He was elated and deeply moved when he saw the Independence Intifada gather hundreds of thousands of Sunni Muslims, Druze, and Christians behind the cause for which he and his student friends had earlier been able to summon merely a couple of hundred people, predominantly Christians. (Abu-Charaf, op.cit).

The identity entrepreneurs hailed mostly from the elite strata of City and Mountain. I would argue this was a significant reason why they took quite naturally to managing a nationalist mobilization once the killing of Hariri had profoundly stirred them. Fear was quickly converted to resolve. Criticism of representing a Gucci Revolution did not bite. The identity entrepreneurs' governmental belonging to Lebanon was in no small measure the result of structural conditions.

Unity and Othering
The nationalist practices of the Independence Intifada were ostensibly a celebration of national "unity" but rested on explicit and implicit notions of a domestic other which would be interchangeably indexed as "Hizbullah", "Shia Muslims", "pro-Syrians", "backward people", "religious extremists", proxies of Iran and/or Syria, "villagers", "people who do not value life like we do", etc.

This other, and what was perceived as its vision of Lebanon, tended to be objectified, essentialized and construed as threatening.

Due to historical marginalization, the Shia Muslims had a limited share of state power from the outset and, consequently, they had been given a trifling role in the narratives that construed Lebanon's identity as the marriage between City and Mountain. Lebanon's independence in 1943 saw the country's Maronites and Sunni Muslims in the front seat, and the Shia Muslims' minor role was reconfirmed (Norton 1987, 2007). Ever since the Shia Muslims began their reassertion on the Lebanese scene, beginning in the 1960s with the mobilization led by Imam Musa Al-Sadr (ibid.), there had been no City and Mountain alliance, as Christians and Muslims were torn over issues of state and nation. Meanwhile, the Shia Muslim parties of Amal and Hizbullah gained political and economic inroads through political manoeuvres and resistance struggle against the Israeli occupiers of southern Lebanon.

The mobilization on March 8, 2005, of predominantly Shia Muslims led by Hizbullah, was met by trepidation among the young Independence Intifada supporters camping on Martyrs' Square. Some of the dwellers in Martyrs' Square feared an assault or provocation by the demonstrators in Riad al-Solh. Yet, the demonstration on March 8 was in fact peaceful and seemingly well organized.

However, to some people, including key mobilizers in Martyrs' Square, there was not only the fear of violence, but also that of a different vision of Lebanon taking hold.

Serge Yared, a young man who participated in the demonstrations in Martyrs' Square, reflected to me that when he looked at the masses of people gathered in Riad al-Solh Square he thought it would "never [be] possible to build a country with two such radically different views" (Yared, 11/01/06). Asma Andraos told me that the March 8 demonstration represented a threat of "another vision, another Lebanon, another Teheran" (Andraos, op. cit).

To the identity entrepreneurs the Independence Intifada represented a blissful reunification of Lebanon's foundational alliance of City and Mountain. However, in the narratives propagating the marriage of City and Mountain as the source of Lebanon's unique identity there is limited space for the country's Shia Muslims, and the Independence Intifada reproduced such narratives. This proved particularly polarizing it happened on the back of forty years of mobilization of the Shia Muslim community.

The identity entrepreneurs' governmental belonging to Lebanon made them insensitive to the historic-political ramifications of their success on March 14 that appeared to reunite the City and Mountain alliance.

CONCLUSION

The Independence Intifada was produced by spontaneous and separate initiatives that were quickly brought together around a common line in political communication. Networking by identity entrepreneurs – young, resourceful, politically connected people who considered themselves outside of the political establishment, yet espousing a governmental belonging to Lebanon – made the Independence Intifada possible, but emotions made it happen. Correspondingly, the Independence Intifada was a formative event for the identity entrepreneurs. The Independence Intifada was a nostalgic attempt at creating a sense of a Beirut both convivial and symbolic of Lebanese self-determination. The socially constructed – and thereby polarized – geography of Lebanon embedded in the way identity entrepreneurs spoke of City, Mountain, and Village reproduced national narratives which located the country's essence in a marriage of City and Mountain.

By the same token, the explicit and implicit identification of most Shia Muslims with the Village represented and reproduced their marginalization by socially constructing peripheries and essentializing their inhabitants.

NOTES

1   Gibran Tueni was editor and publisher of the *An-Nahar* newspaper until he was assassinated December 12, 2005, and a family friend of Asma Andraos.

2   Asma Andraos' father is a close friend of the Tuenis, a prominent Greek Orthodox family straddling for generations the worlds of politics and journalism; her mother hails from the Gemayels, one of the most important Maronite Christian political families in Lebanon.

3   Bashir Gemayel was the brother of Amin Gemayel and the son of Pierre Gemayel who founded the Kataeb Party in 1936 (originally a youth movement) which was the leading Christian party in the civil war; the Gemayels were a Maronite family of notables from northern Mount Lebanon who settled in Bekfaya in the region of Kisrawan in the mountains to the north of Beirut in 1545; they came to political prominence through the Kataeb Party. Salibi 1988: 14; available from http://en.wikipedia.org/wiki/ Pierre_Gemayel, Internet; accessed May 5, 2007.

4   Ibid.

5   Eli Khoury is the CEO of Quantum, the mother media company of Saatchi & Saatchi Levant, of which he is CEO and COO.

6   Nabil Abou-Charaf's godfather is Ghassan Tueni, an octogenarian newspaper publisher, journalist, and statesman currently replacing his son, Gibran, in Parliament after the latter was assassinated in December 2005; Nabil's godmother is Nayla Moawad, currently Minister for Social Affairs and the widow of former President René Moawad. Nabil Abou-Charaf, interview with the author December 13, 2006, Beirut.

7   Letter from "Citizens 4 Lebanon" dated March 9, 2005, to then Secretary-General of the UN, Kofi Annan. http://www.alhaqiqa.net/pdf/UN%20letter.pdf. At the time, the number of deaths resulting from the blast was nineteen. Later, two additional people would die from injuries.

8   *"Khallas"* is Lebanese colloquial Arabic for "enough", but in this context it means "no question".

9   According to Hanf's 2002 survey (with numbers from 1987, i.e. wartime, survey in parentheses), 52 (59)% trust friends; 76 (67)% close relatives; 24 (20)% colleagues; 24 (10)% superiors; 17% fellow villagers; 16% neighbors; 8% "all Lebanese" (Hanf 2003: 199).

10 Ibid. More information on Michel Seurat's story is found on http://fr.wikipedia.org/wiki/ Michel_Seurat.

11 The image of the Lebanese nation which the identity entrepreneurs saw embodied in the million on Martyrs' Square was a celebration of a unity of difference which became a manifestation of unity *over* difference, in other words a master image of a cosmopolitan body politic which, to borrow from Sennett, cast March 14 as Athens, a city "open to the world", and March 8 as Sparta, whose citizens "blindly and stupidly follow orders" ([1994] 2002: 23-26, *32*).

Part 6

Popular Culture and Music

Sanctioned Pleasures

Youth Negotiations of Leisure Sites and Morality in al-Dahiya[1]

Lara Deeb and Mona Harb

Beirut is known internationally for a youthful jet set that likes to be identified with the world clubbing circuit, including such stops as B018, an underground nocturnal haunt reminiscent of a coffin built by Lebanese architect Bernard Khoury upon the remains of a war crime. Images of these cosmopolitan young people – particularly the women among them – have been highlighted in media coverage of Lebanese political protests since 2005, whether waving the Lebanese flag or unexpectedly combining Hizbullah bandannas with bare midriffs. Such representations of Lebanese youth fit the "Paris of the Middle East" stereotype that comforts Westerners and also comports with the desires of many in Lebanon. It is this Beirut that topped the *New York Times'* list of "44 Places to Go in 2009," a designation almost immediately cited in the Facebook status updates of Lebanese youth across the globe.

Beirut – or rather, certain areas of Beirut – is also known internationally as the home of Hizbullah, the party once described by a US official as the "A-team of terrorists." Residents of this Beirut are pictured as somber, bearded young men toting Kalashnikovs and alternately timid and fiercely outspoken young women dressed uniformly and completely in black. It is this Beirut that dominated CNN and other mainstream US media images of the July 2006 war, not in terms of the damage and destruction, but rather, as aggressors to be feared, and representative of the "them" in the former administration's good-evil binaries.

A polarization similar to the one between these two Beiruts also exists in much of the scholarship on youth. Ted Swedenburg (2007) has cautioned against falling into this polarization which frequently gets caught between a reliance, on the one hand, on overly Western models of youth as fun, transgressive, or shallow consumers, and, on the other hand, on an image of youth in constant danger of being coopted by Islamic movements. Recent work on Iranian youth has tended towards the "youth as transgressive" model, casting young people as actively resisting the Islamic regime through their practices of fun, sexuality, and "breaking the rules" (Khosravi 2008, Mahdavi 2009, Varzi 2006). The latter image of youth coopted by militant movements tends to dominate US media depictions of Muslim youth[2].

This pair of polar opposite images and approaches leaves out many – perhaps most strikingly, the thousands of more-or-less pious young people who want to have fun, and who strive to differing extents to follow religiously sanctioned norms in their recreation. Just as Christian youth groups in the United States organize dances along with devotional study groups and ski trips along with evangelical work, young people in the pious Shiʿa community in the southern suburb of Beirut seek out spaces for social interaction that accord with the norms of morality and appropriate behavior defined by their religious tenets. Yet they do not do so blindly; rather, in those spaces, young people often redefine those tenets as well, interpreting injunctions in ways that may open moral codes to broader definition or limit them more stridently. In what follows, we highlight the ways in which pious youth in the southern suburb of Beirut – al-Dahia – challenge notions of youth as necessarily transgressive or defiant. Taking choices made with regard to leisure sites as our focus, we suggest that youth practices and discourses of morality are flexible in their deployments, perhaps especially when it comes to ideas about leisure.

In the process of navigating and rewriting the boundaries of moral comportment in relation to leisure, pious Shiʿa youth are contributing to the (re)production and (re)construction of an Islamic milieu in the city that also extends to other regions of the country. We have been collaboratively researching several elements of this "Islamic milieu" for the past few years[3]. Although the Shiʿa Islamic milieu in Lebanon has no geographic borders, it is possible to imagine it as centered in the southern suburb of Beirut. Over the past ten years it has grown both spatially and in terms of popularity, and has proliferated into ever-more arenas of life, most recently into the realm of leisure and entertainment. In our larger project and in other venues, we discuss the production and contestation of the Islamic milieu, spatialization and spatial practices in relation to the vibrant leisure and consumer sector in Dahia, the history and political-economy of the new leisure sector and the role of capital and international investments in its development, and shifting ideas about taste in relation to class mobility in Dahia (See Deeb and Harb, 2010; Harb & Deeb, 2009).

In this chapter, we focus instead on two aspects of the youth component of our project: first, on the notion of generational change as one factor in the emergence of a vibrant leisure sector in Dahia, and second, on the ways that pious youth draw on multiple authorizing discourses, including their own, in order to make decisions about appropriate behavior and/in leisure sites.

WHY NOW?

Why have youth debates about places of leisure proliferated in the early years of this century? Several factors are important here. The first is sheer political contingency, with 2000 and 2006 marking significant dates in recent Lebanese history. The liberation of South Lebanon in May 2000 marked a moment when, in the words of one of our interlocutors, "We could breathe again." She continued, "People wanted to go out again, especially youth. People wanted to be out and about. It's natural, because we could breathe."

These consumer desires were reflected in and encouraged private capital investment in the entertainment sector. Several entrepreneurs, often Shi'a expatriates returning to Lebanon, told us that they felt confident about investing in the leisure sector after 2000. This confidence was partly related to the general atmosphere of renewal that accompanied Liberation, but also related to the successes of two large-scale entertainment projects in al-Dahiya that launched the area's leisure sector: Fantasy World and al-Saha Traditional Village. Initiated in 1999 by a private contracting firm close to Hizbullah (al-Inmaa' Group), Fantasy World provides "family entertainment" in its theme park, restaurants, and cafés. Al-Saha Traditional Village was inaugurated in 2001 by al-Mabarrat, the philanthropic organization affiliated with Sayyid Muhammad Hussein Fadlallah, and includes restaurants, cafés, wedding halls, a motel, and a museum (Harb 2005). In addition to establishing the existence of a market for leisure in al-Dahiya (and contributing to the production of that market), both places formally legitimized new forms of social and spatial practices in the area.

While one might expect that the war of July 2006 and its political aftermath in Lebanon would reconfigure community priorities once again to the detriment of leisure, the opposite seems to have taken place, with its development continuing at an even more rapid pace. The political polarization in Lebanon that followed the July war fortified territorial enclaves, limited mobility and consolidated sectarian-based practices. At the same time, Hizbullah's political alliance with a key Christian opposition figure, General Michel Aoun, brought people – especially youth – from different sectarian communities together in new ways. As people, especially youth, began to go out closer to home and as young Shi'a Muslims began to spend more time with Aounist youth, often in cafés in al-Dahiya, entrepreneurs responded to these new market pressures. And indeed, in our summer 2008 survey of half the cafés and restaurants in al-Dahiya, 64 per cent had originally opened between 2006-2008[4].

Another important factor has been the socio-economic transformation of the Lebanese Shi'a community over the past thirty years and especially the growth of middle-class Shi'a consumerism. Indeed, the 1990s saw the consolidation of an urban Shi'a middle class in Lebanon, the result of greater educational and sectarian institutional support in the community, as well as remittances and high rates of return emigration. New market demand for leisure compatible with moral norms based on specific forms of Islam is also related to the growth of a transnational Muslim public sphere (Eickelmen and Anderson 1999, Salvatore and Le Vine 2005) and growing markets for pious fashion (Balasescu 2007, Moors and Tarlo 2007), faith-based travel and pilgrimage (Pinto 2007), and religious commodities and commemorative practices (Starrett 1995, Schielke 2006).

In Dahiya, pious middle-class youth have begun to demand the same access to leisure that other neighborhoods of Beirut have long enjoyed, but with the caveat that the leisure activities remain consistent with their lifestyle. In this way, youth in Dahiya participate in a growing global capitalist culture, but a specific one that highlights the construction of particular Muslim identities. However, political and economic factors do not sufficiently explain the growth of a leisure sector that meets particular moral criteria. Nor, as we detail below, can we point to formal Hizbullah censorship as a satisfactory explanation for the development of this "moral leisure" sector. Instead, we suggest that a complete understanding of why new sites and ideas about leisure have recently emerged in Dahiya must take into consideration the generational shifts that have occurred in the area.

A GENERATION OF "MORE-OR-LESS" PIOUS YOUTH

The extension of the Shi'a Islamic milieu in Lebanon into leisure represents the continuation of a trajectory that began with a Shi'a Islamic mobilization in Lebanon in the late 1960s and 1970s (for more on the history, see Deeb 2006, Harb in press, Norton 1987 and 2007). This mobilization or movement initially resulted in two changes that are significant to understanding the contemporary context. The first change is that there are today numerous Shi'a social and political institutions that emerged from this movement in the 1970s, including the political party Hizbullah and the *marja 'iyya* and institutions of Sayyid Muhammad Husayn Fadlallah[5]. This ensures the existence of multiple sources of moral authority in the community, the significance of which we return to below.

The other major change, equally if not more crucial to our argument, is that a particular sort of pious and moral lifestyle based on specific religious ideas and practices has become both a part of commonsense knowledge and desires for many in al-Dahiya, and a social norm to which people are often expected to conform. This sits in sharp contrast to the imposed "Islamification" (Mahdavi 2009) that followed the Islamic Revolution in Iran[6], where Islamic "practice was emphasized over inner faith" and assumed to lead to the creation of Islamic subjects (Varzi 2006:146), and where "a state of imposed normality makes transgression a norm." (Varzi 2006:124). In al-Dahiya we instead see a significant proportion – indeed a critical mass – of young people who strive to live moral lives. We suggest that this critical mass of youth and their genuine concern for their souls reflects one of the major successes of the grassroots Islamic mobilization efforts in Lebanon, and attests to the *different* success of the Lebanese Shi'a mobilization and the ways in which Iran's revolution was eventually looked to for inspiration rather than a blueprint. Indeed, we argue that the emergence of this generation of pious youth provides the missing explanatory link for understanding why new practices and ideas of leisure are currently proliferating in the southern suburb of Beirut.

The power of generational shifts in producing social change has been widely discussed and theorized from a number of perspectives. Perhaps one of the best known is the Birmingham School of Cultural Studies, which popularized a notion of youth as actively constructing subcultures, particularly through commodity forms (Hebdige 1979, Hall and Jefferson 1993, others). Several anthropologists have recently noted that the consequences of the subsequent focus on "youth culture" as a universally applicable concept has been a fetishization of both youth as a category and of resistance, divorcing both youth and their actions from their political-economic, historical, and relational contexts (Cole 2007, Christiansen et al 2006).

Recent works that have emerged from this critique (Borneman 1992, Cole and Durham 2007, Christiansen et al 2006, Vigh 2006) often re-center Karl Mannheim's classic essay, "The Problem of Generations," and his discussion of a generation as a group of people sharing "a common location in the social and historical process" (1952:291) and participating "in the common destiny of this historical and social unit" (303). Generation here is produced and defined both through shared experiences and understandings of particular historical and cultural events, and through specific responses to those experiences and events (Borneman 1992, Christiansen et al 2006). Cole and Durham (2007) additionally emphasize that although youth are often crucial to social change and its imagination, youth as both category and actors have to be understood in conversation with both older generations and state structures[7]. To this conversational context, we would add shifting moral norms and sources of moral authority.

In concert with these approaches, we understand generational categories to emerge in relation to specific cultural and political-economic contexts and through social processes. Returning to the specific case of al-Dahiya, today's pious youth represent a significant generational shift away from the previous generation: the "Islamic vanguard" generation. The vanguard generation are those whose efforts in the 1960s, 1970s, and 1980s led to the Lebanese Shi'a Islamic movement and its institutionalization in Lebanon. That generation often had to fight against their own parents' notions of morality – cast by the rebelling Islamic vanguard generation as "traditional" – in order to be able to enact their new understandings of both religious and political commitment.

This contrasts sharply with the experiences of young people in al-Dahiya today, who were born and raised in the 1980s, after the key struggles of the vanguard generation had taken place, may have attended schools affiliated with either Fadlallah or Hizbullah, and came of age in an environment where particular norms of public piety were taken for granted and where Hizbullah was already a popular and powerful political party. Hajjeh Um Ja'far, a woman in her early fifties, described her perceptions of the difference in the experiences of her generation as compared to today's youth: "When I became committed [to Islam] there was a lot of talk about us. Even within my family there was talk, you know, 'What is this commitment?'

While today, it is normal, a girl can put on the headscarf and she doesn't have a problem."

At the same time, mothers who are part of the vanguard generation have expressed concern that their daughters were not adequately pious, and some suggested that this may have been related to the extent to which the community as a whole had reached a point where particular forms of pious comportment were a hegemonic norm (see Deeb 2006). In other words, they were concerned because pious practice for youth had become normative and perhaps routinized in new ways, and because it was *not* constructed in opposition to the norms of their environment (ironically echoing expectations of youth as defiant). Many parents feared that this very normativity would provoke an abandonment or insincerity of piety in their children.

And indeed, these fears may not be entirely unfounded. We suggest that these parental concerns point to the ways that Shi'a youth in the southern suburb of Beirut have begun to question moral boundaries related to ideas and practices of leisure, by engaging with multiple sources of moral authority, including their own interpretations. While religious faith is certainly important to many young people in al-Dahiya today, and many do embrace a pious lifestyle, their definitions of that lifestyle differ from those of the vanguard generation. Specifically, it is the details of practice that are consistently debated and redefined.

MULTIPLE MORAL AUTHORITIES

The diversity of youth opinion and interpretation, especially on matters of leisure, cannot be underestimated, and is itself facilitated by the existence of multiple sources of moral authority in the Shi'a community in Lebanon today. While young pious Shi'a Muslims often hold expectations that the spaces and behavior of people around them will conform to certain moral standards, they are also well versed in the interpretations of multiple religious scholars and authorities, and tend to view moral standards with a greater flexibility than did the vanguard generation[8]. It is through this flexibility that this new critical mass of "more-or-less" pious youth has contributed to a new market for particular sorts of leisure sites.

Hizbullah is a key voice in defining the boundaries of moral behavior with regard to both leisure sites and appropriate behavior in them. Obviously not everyone in the southern suburb supports Hizbullah, not everyone is religiously committed, and not everyone is Shi'a. Yet the fact remains that the party has the support of the majority of the population of al-Dahiya, even of many who do not agree with all of its positions, whether political or moral. While the party does not formally enforce many religion-based moral norms, there are certain moral limits in the southern suburb that differ from other parts of Beirut – the most obvious of these is that cafés and restaurants in this area do not serve alcohol. Hizbullah will exert pressure on a restaurant that tries to serve alcohol and may resort to threatening its owner. However, situations rarely escalate to that extent because the broader community will usually first exert social and economic pressure that would put any establishment that tried to serve alcohol out of business. Other limits and boundaries are far more flexible, and despite Hizbullah's popularity, the party is only one source of moral authority in the community and it struggles constantly to negotiate the boundary between political power and the promotion of particular social norms.

Another key voice in defining the boundaries of moral behavior is a high-ranking and very popular religious scholar named Sayyid Muhammad Husayn Fadlallah. Since the 1990s, Fadlallah has been a *marja' al-taqlid,* which translates as "source of emulation," and refers to Fadlallah's role in a Shi'a-specific institution of hierarchical religious knowledge, the *marja 'iyya.* Practicing Shi'a Muslims are to choose a religious scholar who has attained the rank of *marja'* and follow that person's interpretations on religious matters. This is sometimes assumed to involve blind emulation, but emulation itself is something that practicing Shi'a negotiate from situation to situation, frequently changing their *marja'* to suit the contingencies of the moment. Notably, disagreement among these religious scholars is common.

Fadlallah is the most popular *marja'* in Lebanon, followed by Ayatollah Khamenei and the Iraqi Sayyid Sistani, both of whom have representatives in al-Dahiya who provide guidance and advice to their followers[9]. Fadlallah's popularity is due in part to his clarity of language and pragmatism in his books and sermons. He is also popular because he believes in the need for Islam to adapt to the contemporary world and thinks that interpretation should work to facilitate young people's lifestyles whenever possible within the limitations of Islam. This is especially important in the pluralist context of Lebanon, where Fadlallah is appreciated as a *Lebanese marja'* in particular. As a result, he tends to be viewed as more progressive than others on a wide variety of issues[10].

Fadlallah also consistently encourages his followers to use their judgment and interpret situations and sometimes religious texts for themselves, a practice and call that some view as existing in constant tension with the practice of following a *marja'* to begin with. As his son and representative Sayyid Ja'far explained to us, Fadlallah is concerned with advising people on what is *haram* and *halal,* and things like proscriptions on alcohol and adultery fall into this realm. But, he continued:

There is another level that is related to life in general, and that is the level/ *mustawa* of *akhlaq* or *qiyam,* morals or values. And this level rests on the choice of the individual himself, meaning that he chooses to participate or not participate, [yankharit bi or la yankharit bi], depending on his mood, depending on his environment, on his culture, depending on his perspective on his role in life. There are people who, maybe don't like to go to certain places and people who don't like to go there at all, and other people no ... and as long as a person doesn't do anything forbidden/*muharram* in these places, then there is no problem with him going there.

While here Sayyid Ja'far is speaking specifically about cafés, the point is a more general one about Fadlallah's approach to the implementation of particular rules, values, and morals in society. At another point in our interview, he explained, "It falls to the religious side to make a person aware of his *takleef*/charge/responsibility/duty and tell him the *shar'i* conditions/limits ... however, their implementation/application/*tatbiq* rests in the first place, on him (the person)."

This emphasis on individual responsibility is crucial to the emergence of today's pious youth as a generation that is gently pushing the boundaries of moral behavior. Furthermore, while the vanguard generation generally keeps their personal interpretation within the frameworks set by Fadlallah and Hizbullah and looks regularly to them for guidance, more recently young people have been using personal interpretation to push the boundaries set by those formal authorities and to prompt broader discussions that touch on different areas of life. These youth are educated, literate, expectant, and media-savvy, and, as a result, feel entitled and able to engage in debates about moral norms. For this reason, we describe them as "more-or-less pious." Their commitment to religion is by no means uniform. Instead, many have taken Fadlallah's teachings about individual moral responsibility to heart and believe religiosity is something to be developed by the individual. That notion is then extended into their discussions and debates about leisure sites and practices.

LEISURE SITES, "APPROPRIATE" CAFÉS AND RESTAURANTS

Since 2000, young people living in the southern suburb have been enjoying their free time in new places that have been multiplying throughout *Dahiya's* neighborhoods. There are at least seventy-five new cafés and restaurants in the area, bustling with smartly dressed customers smoking *argileh,* drinking cocktail juices, eating *saj manaqish,* chatting and gazing, enjoying the privacy of a space hidden behind a column, or being part of the spectacle. Cafés operate also as catwalks: young women, whether muhajjaba or not, go to cafés made up and very well dressed, exhibiting their bodies. Young men show off brand names and other external signs of distinction – sometimes in relation to faith or politics. For example, they may wear large single-stoned rings that contain a protective "hijab" (a slip of paper with a Qur'anic verse written on it) or they may set their mobile phone ring tones to a speech by Sayyid Nasrallah or a party anthem – both signs associated in Lebanon specifically with Hizbullah. One young woman related to us that such signs of association with the Resistance are perceived quite positively by young women, despite their awareness that young men may be exaggerating their relationship to the party just to score points with them.

Most of these new sites are intent on providing their predominantly young customers with modern stylized decor, high-quality food, coffee, *hookahs* and wireless internet access. In this sense, hangouts in the southern suburb compare to those in other parts of Beirut. Consider for example an internet café in a prime location in the southern suburb. Waitstaff dressed stylishly in all black serve Illy brand Italian coffee along with French and Arabic pastries and *hookahs*. The café is colorfully designed, with chairs and tables fitting into each other to form red, black, and white cubes, and shiny reflective floors and walls that produce a sleek, polished effect. Many young people expressed their appreciation for the high-end services and aesthetic provided by this café and others like it. In describing these places, they highlighted how the recreational sites previously on offer in their neighborhoods were not up to "quality standards," while those available in Beirut proper were (and are) not respectful enough of the religious norms to which they strive to conform. New leisure sites in the southern suburb combine both of these requirements: aesthetic and service qualities with what many called a "conservative atmosphere." Indeed, what distinguishes these places from others in Beirut, and marks them as "moral" spaces in particular, is their facilitation or accommodation of a particular Muslim lifestyle.

These cafés and restaurants have one particularity: they are described as *'shar 'V* (licit) or conservative *(muhafiziri)* – or often simply "appropriate" *(munasib)* – by both their clientele and their owners. At its most basic, this means that they do not offer alcohol or non-*halal* meat. It also sometimes means that they do not play dance music or allow intimate interactions between sexes, though these latter restrictions are far more debatable and are among the moral norms being contested by today's youth. Elsewhere, we have discussed the ways in which these new leisure places themselves contribute to the reshaping of conventional boundaries and lifestyles by introducing new social practices and providing spaces where the varied tastes and desires of their young clientele can unravel (Harb and Deeb 2009). Here our focus is on the ways youth are shaping these spaces through their negotiations of moral norms and their simultaneous desires for both fun and faith.

Again, these negotiations are taking place in conversation with the formal sources of moral authority in al-Dahiya. Fadlallah and other *maraji'* weigh in informally about the appropriateness of various sites, suggesting standards of behavior rather than assessing specific sites. In keeping with his views on individual responsibility, Fadlallah emphasizes that beyond the clear rules on what is *halal* and *haram* – into which fall things like alcohol, *halal* meat, and physical intimacy between unmarried people – everything else falls into the realm of personal interpretation and has more to do with societal values than religious law.

More critically, Hizbullah itself is both directly and indirectly involved in defining the relationship between play and morality. Party-run municipalities provide support to specific establishments and discourage others – by facilitating legal permits for the former and exerting pressure on the latter to redefine their business to fit within the party's ideas about moral standards. One café owner whose establishment has Italian soda syrups lined up on a wall behind a coffee bar reported a visit by guys who "looked like Hizbullah" who seemed to be inspecting the contents of those bottles. Apparently he passed the test, as his business has been doing quite well since. This speaks also to the indirect censorship – led by committees resembling "neighborhood watch" groups – that takes place via unofficial boycotts of local cafés that do not fit the party's ideas about moral standards. This enmeshment was highlighted by a woman who is a prominent party member, who explained that such cooperation between "society" and the party was "natural," saying, "Our society is helping a great deal with this. So today, you see that there are *shar'i* swimming pools, for example, and you find, as you mentioned, cafés, and these things are increasing a lot. And it is under our control, I mean, it's not outside our control. Even many of the owners of these projects make sure that we are in support of the project, because we have our organizations and centers, and people ask us, 'Can we go to this place? Is there a problem with going to so-and-so's place?' It's not Hizbullah that's doing it. I'm saying that society, people are demanding these projects, and are also asking our opinion of these projects." Hizbullah's leaders may also legitimize establishments through their patronage, though their visits can also be interpreted as attempted co-optation.

Of course, how one feels about Hizbullah's involvement in this process depends in large part on the extent to which one identifies with and supports not only the party, but the specific understandings of piety and morality that it promotes. Some people – including some who support many of Hizbullah's political platforms – feel stifled by the party's involvement and view this enmeshment as an unwelcome form of moral regulation or policing – but that is a topic for another paper. For us, the key question is the extent to which the party is in fact able to influence the ideas of pious youth about particular places or how much of this influence is wishful thinking on the part of party officials.

Our conversations with youth suggest it may be more the latter. For example, music conducive to dancing is understood by most youth to be forbidden by Fadlallah, Hizbullah, and many in the vanguard generation. In the last decade, official opinions on music have shifted, so that today Hizbullah utilizes a wide variety of musical instruments in its compositions, including electric guitar and drums, and Fadlallah emphasizes that the content of lyrics is what is important, and suggests that listeners be alert to the difference between *shawq* (longing or desire), which is acceptable, and *ghara 'iz* (sexual instincts), which are unacceptable, in love songs. Yet in the absence of official regulation of music in Lebanon, acceptability is interpreted widely by youth, as well as by the managers and owners of the establishments that they frequent.

What constitutes inappropriate music changes depending on the time of year and on the clientele of an establishment at any given moment. One café owner told us that she turns the MTV channel on if the clientele appears to her like they would enjoy that type of music, but that she would then change the channel if other customers who look more "religious" came in. On an individual level, some young people refuse to listen to all forms of pop music entirely, others determine appropriateness based on the specific lyrics of songs, some emphasize context and conduct over type of music, and still others publicly shun pop music but listen to it secretly on their MP3 players. Similar differences emerge in relation to whether one would enter an establishment that serves alcohol or not. Time of year is also relevant here, and during Ramadan or Ashura, for instance, people who might frequent restaurants with alcohol on the menu during other months cease to do so temporarily[11].

With regard to both norms around the presence of alcohol and certain forms of music, what is perhaps most striking is the diversity of opinion among youth and their acceptance of that diversity of opinion among their friends and peers. For example, in one of our focus groups, young men disagreed with one another on whether or not it was appropriate to go to restaurants that play pop music. One felt strongly that it doesn't matter what music is playing and noted that his cell phone rang to the tune of a popular song. Another commented that he recently stopped listening to popular music because in his opinion religion tells him not to, but then said, "but it's only me personally, I can't restrict other people from listening. Everyone should change what's in him," again reflecting Fadlallah's views on individual responsibility. A third young man shifted the conversation to the topic of alcohol, and expressed a view similar to that of the first, noting "if restaurants sell alcohol I have no control over that and I have nothing to do with it, I'm not going to drink." In contrast, the young man who recently stopped listening to popular music tries not to enter restaurants with alcohol, but occasional does when family is visiting from outside Lebanon. For others, it comes down to how blatant a violation of moral standards appears to be. In another interview, twenty-year-old Firas explained, "It is one thing if there is a table with a few people drinking beer sitting there, but it is another thing when it is a bar, and there are only people drinking and dressed like that and dancing on the chairs."

With the exception of the red-line violation of actually drinking alcohol, youth are willing to admit their differing standards, opinions, and behaviors to one another. Again and again in our focus groups, young people admitted to listening to pop music or going to cafés that serve alcohol (without drinking themselves) in front of friends, peers, spouses, and strangers. And while certainly some do feel pressure to conform, many reported that the prevailing understanding is that faith is something that every individual develops in his or her own way and own time. As long as the absolute red-lines are not crossed, there remains space for negotiation, movement, moods, and even day-to-day changes in activities and comportment without accusations of hypocrisy or immorality.

Another crucial aspect of defining particular places as conservative, moral, or appropriate are the social interactions that take place within them. The ideal moral standard of conservative behavior means that unrelated men and women do not touch or sit too closely to one another, though unlike some conservative Sunni contexts, there is no enforced segregation between "family" and "shabab" sections of most restaurants and cafés in Dahiya[12].

On the one hand, it is difficult to overemphasize the importance of the social component in establishing whether a site is "appropriate" or not. Put bluntly, "the kind of people who go there" are a primary criterion by which people generally judge places. In this regard, cafés and restaurants in al-Dahiya also incorporate a sense of *entre-soi* – the security, comfort, and validation that come from being among one's peers and community. On the other hand, ideas about moral behavior may serve to mask other concerns. Given the ways that sectarian divisions have continued to be spatially entrenched in Beirut, "the kind of people who go there" may also reflect recent polarized sectarian discourses in contemporary Lebanese politics. Yet it is important also not to overstate the sectarian dimension to the detriment of sheer moral flexibility. As one young woman, Hawra', put it, "You go to places that fit with your values. You can tell immediately, from the place, the setting, you can just tell. And when you are living somewhere, you know about the places." And as evidenced by the diversity of opinion on the specifics of what constitutes a zone of comfort, this space of *entre-soi* – is relative to each person's history and experiences.

It's crucial to emphasize that behavior is self-policed and enforced through social convention, rather than a "morality police" such as those found in Iran or Saudi Arabia. In cafés and restaurants, "appropriate" behavior appears to be regulated through a combination of self-disciplining and enforcement by wait-staff, with significant room here for flexibility of interpretation and practice. Café owners declared that "parents feel safe about their children coming here; because they know we make sure the ambiance stays controlled (*madbuta*); even if a girl is with a guy, parents know that they are in a place where morals rule (*fi akhlaq*) and nobody here will allow anything immoral (*ghayr akhlaqi*) to happen, because this girl is like our daughter." Yet during our visits to cafés across Dahiya, we saw a good deal of mixed sex interaction that this café owner, and the parents to whom he refers, would no doubt find immoral. Most cafés have organized the layout of their tables to provide several intimate spaces for their customers, with dedicated floors for tables of two, private rooms, and various corners where young couples can spend time with one another relatively out of sight. We witnessed numerous couples sitting in very close proximity to one another and sometimes making out in the not-quite-private nooks and crannies of these cafés. It is also not uncommon for young couples to arrive and depart from cafés separately, highlighting their use of the space as a place to meet away from the eyes of their families and society.

Not only have cafés and restaurants have provided new public spaces where young people can hang out with one another, whether as friends or more intimately, but they have also provided new spaces where young people can meet new acquaintances, friends, lovers, and partners. Flirtation is an inevitable part of the café experience: young people check each other out, ask each other out, and even use Bluetooth technology to pass their phone numbers around. One young man we interviewed met his girlfriend by "accidentally" sending her an image on her cellphone via Bluetooth while they were sitting at nearby tables in a café. He then approached her, and, after she initially brushed off his advance, he followed her down the stairs, apologized for accidentally sending the image, and explained to her that she now had his phone number from the Bluetooth interaction and said that he'd like to "talk with her" – a euphemism for dating. While she had at first pretended not to notice the Bluetooth message, she later miscalled him, so that he would be the one to call her first, and they are now in a dating relationship using the rules of temporary marriage[13].

CONCLUSIONS AND CONTINUING QUESTIONS

We have used this example of youth debating appropriate leisure in order to argue that a complete understanding of the recent emergence of leisure as a key part of the Islamic milieu in al-Dahiya requires an understanding of the flexible ways in which pious Shi'a youth deploy multiple discourses of morality in relation to ideas about leisure spaces and practices. Two key points must be underscored in relation to this argument. First, it is important to keep in mind that pious youth in Dahiya express a strong desire to live a moral life that includes the right to *religiously appropriate* leisure. This is not a top-down imposition, but a ground-up desire to rework the terms of morality to begin with in ways that make sense both socially and for their own personal relationships with God. Through their choices in relation to leisure, a generation of young Shi'a Muslims in al-Dahiya is striving to formulate norms of behavior that are commensurate with *all* their desires, including desires for both pleasure and piety. In the process, they are also contributing to changes within their community as their ideas and practices contribute to the reshaping of moral norms, including the emergence of a vibrant leisure sector.

The second point we wish to emphasize is the importance of a context where the existence of *multiple* moral authorities is the norm and where pious youth live in close proximity to and interact regularly with youth who live very different lifestyles. Pluralist Lebanon is a context in which youth encounter a wide variety of views in various settings, including in universities, workplaces and leisure sites, and among friends, colleagues, and family members. Even from Hizbullah's perspective, one official explained that the party understands that their circle of supporters has grown over the years, and that this growth "naturally" leads to blurrier boundaries between the pious and the nonpious. Unlike in Iran, where the moral disciplining of bodies and spaces is viewed as a prerequisite to an Islamic nation-state, in Dahiya, Fadlallah's views on individual moral responsibility are more common. The existence of these differing perspectives and of the flexibility to choose from multiple interpretations and authorities allows youth today to search for interpretations and opinions that most closely reflect their own desires and ideas.

To these three major sources of moral authority – political party, religious leader, and self – we can potentially add peers and possibly, a transnational context where Islamic consumerism has become more common as well. Interestingly, family is rarely mentioned by youth as a major factor in their deliberations, perhaps because one of the effects of the growing Islamic milieu in Dahiya has been an emphasis on the community as a space where moral norms are shaped as much as, if not more than, within the family. For example, Fadlallah emphasizes balance in relationships between parents and children, and Hizbullah has deliberately worked to reduce the power of large families in Lebanon by asserting a sectarian identification over a familial one. This is one area for further thinking and research.

Another question we continue to consider is that of the potential consequences of ideas about individual moral intention in this context. For youth, faith and religious commitment are understood to exist in varying degrees, and to change over one's lifetime and even from month to month. Diversity of opinion is the norm, and our focus groups have been lively forums for debate and argument, ranging from whether or not it is appropriate for a "religious" person to mock another person, to discussing which verse from the Qur'an supports a particular argument. Having an opinion, and ideally, being able to ground the opinion in a story from religious history, a parable, a hadith or verse, or an example, locates youth within the sphere of the more-or-less pious.

On the one hand, this diversity and flexibility facilitates a certain amount of leniency on the part of many young people with regard to their own choices as well as those of their friends. Importantly, young people often cautioned against judging others' piety, and frequently warned one another against judging others in the focus groups and emphasized the importance of being tolerant and open to others' perspectives and lifestyles. Yet on the other hand, this flexibility may also open new spaces for moral censure and sanction. Belief in the mutability of faith and religious commitment should not be mistaken for moral relativism, as such belief works in relation to the interpretations of religious scholars, one's personal trajectory, shifting community norms, and Hizbullah-related censorship. In considering the ways that youth are pushing the boundaries of morality with regard to leisure in al-Dahiya, it is important not to discount any of these multiple sources of authoritative interpretation. Indeed, it is this multiplicity itself that creates the conditions of possibility within which people striving to live pious lives are able to enact various expectations and desires for a moral life. It remains to be seen how the Islamic milieu may be influenced by the ideas and decisions of today's educated pious Shiʻa youth, and potentially shaped by their concerns about moral boundaries in relation to leisure. What is clear is that this is a generation that is bringing its own interpretations, tastes, and desires to the Islamic milieu.

We'd like to let our interlocutors have the last word. As one young man put it, "We don't complicate things, we just want to be normal. I try to get more religiously educated, but that doesn't mean that I become isolated and separated from people. I don't have to become paranoid about every little thing. I just stay normal." His friend added, "I got engaged last year and people think I'm very religious because my fiancée dresses according to the shar'ia. But I just pray. And if someone opens a religious topic, I will engage with them, but I will not be the one who opens it. And if the topic is non-religious I also engage it. So what? Yan'ni, I'm not going to lie, sometimes we talk about Haifa Wehbe."

NOTES

1   Portions of this manuscript were published as Deeb, Lara and Mona Harb, 2007. "Sanctioned Pleasures: Youth, Piety and Leisure in Beirut," *Middle East Report* 37(4): 12-19. A shorter version of this piece is forthcoming as Deeb, Lara and Mona Harb, 2010, "Piety and Pleasure: Youth Negotiations of Moral Authority and New Leisure Sites in al-Dahiya", *Bahithat: Cultural Practices of Youth in the Arab World,* 14. This research is based on collaborative fieldwork funded by the Wenner-Gren Foundation and the American Council of Learned Societies. We would like to thank Pardis Mahdavi and participants at the "Marginalization and Mobilization of Youth" conference at the American University of Beirut in May 2009 for their comments.

2   For example, in a recent *New York Times* article by Robert Worth titled "Hezbollah Seeks to Marshall the Piety of the Young."

3   We use the phrase "Islamic milieu" as a gloss for term *hala islamiyya,* commonly used in al-Dahia. *Hala* literally means "state of being" or "condition," and together with the adjective *islamiyya,* the phrase translates as "Islamic state of being." The use of *hala* also connotes both the physical spaces where pious Shiʻa Muslims in Lebanon live or enact this "state of being" and the public sphere where its norms and values are debated. Pious Shiʻa Muslims thus are always participating in defining what the Islamic milieu is, and where it boundaries lie. For more, see Deeb 2008.

4   The majority of these cafes have been opened by local small businessmen, many of whom invest in a cafe or restaurant along with a few friends or family members. For more on these cafes and restaurants in al-Dahiya, see Harb and Deeb 2009.

5   Another key political party that emerged from this mobilization is of course Haraket Amal. However, Amal is the group least involved in the construction of the *hala islamiyya* we are discussing, and its relationship to faith is much less pronounced than that of Hizbullah or Fadlallah.

6   It also provides a rather different picture than that depicted by Asef Bayat in his discussion of the way in which Islamists in post-revolutionary Iran "are so distinctly apprehensive of the expression of 'fun'" (2007:433).

7   Cole and Durham posit the concept of "regeneration" to describe this "mutually constitutive interplay between intergenerational relations and wider historical and social processes" (2007:17).

8   One of the reasons for this is greater ease of access to *marjaʻ* opinions, facilitated by the plethora of print and audio-visual media utilized by *marjaʻ iyya* offices. Sermons, decisions, and

recommendations are published and distributed in books, pamphlets, audiotapes, and CDs, and are broadcast on television and radio. Youth also seek and obtain knowledge about religious interpretations through private meetings and discussions with sheikhs, or through telephone call-in consultations.

9   Although he is often described by some scholars, and recently in the *New York Times*, as "the spiritual leader" of Hizbullah, this is not the case, and in fact, the conflation of these two sources of authority has the effect of hiding the diversity of official opinion that exists within the Islamic milieu. As a political party, Hizbullah officially follows Khamenei, but individual party members are free to emulate anyone they choose. Furthermore, Fadlallah and Hizbullah have often differed, most critically in their views about the relationship between spiritual and political authority.

10   An example of this can be seen in the stark contrast between ideas about women's sexuality presented to us in interviews we did with representatives of the *marja'iyyas* of Khamenei and Fadlallah's in Lebanon. The shaykh representing Khamenei provided a long, gendered litany of active and passive conjugations of Arabic verbs, along the lines of "the man desires, the woman is desired." Fadlallah representative, his son Sayyid Ja'far, instead stated simply: "It is clear that human beings need sex, men and women."

11   For an eloquent analysis of the ways in which Ramadan is a time of "exceptional morality" and the effects of this exceptionalism, see Schielke 2009.

12   Fadlallah, for example, does not believe in enforcing sex segregation in social or work spaces. With the exception of schools and his library, though the rationale he uses here is not "morality" but rather, "distraction" – akin to the arguments used for single-sex education in the US.

13   Temporary marriage (*zawaj mu 'aqqat* or *zawaj mut 'a* in Arabic, *sigheh* in Persian) is a contracted relationship between a man and a woman, without any witnesses, limited to a specified period of time and in accordance with a specified dowry, either symbolic or substantial, provided for the woman at the end of the contract. For more on the practice in Iran, see Haeri 2004. For more on the practice among Lebanese youth today, see Deeb and Harb 2007.

European Muslim Youth

Towards a Cool Islam?

Miriam Gazzah

INTRODUCTION

This article focuses on the role of music (in the broadest sense of the word) in Dutch-Moroccan youth culture. It explores the way Dutch-Moroccan Muslim youth appropriate particular kinds of music in order to express a specific kind of identity. How do they bring music consumption and conviction together – or not – and why? For Dutch-Moroccan youth Islam is an important element in their lives, but other factors, like ethnicity, are equally important. Before going into detail on the Muslim youth culture in the Netherlands, I will give a short outline of what youth culture is and the importance of (popular) music in it. Then, I turn my view to the specific case of the Netherlands and in particular to Dutch-Moroccan youth.

Youth culture is nothing new. From early on in the twentieth century until more recent times, youth culture in Western-Europe and the Western world has received much media and academic attention from sociological, anthropological, and psychological perspectives. However, youth cultures evolving among European youth with non-European ethnic backgrounds and especially among European Muslim youth have not yet reached a level of study as have the "traditional" youth cultures like the punks, the Mods, or the Ravers.

European Muslim youth are the children and grandchildren of immigrants and guest workers who moved to Europe in the 1960s, 1970s, and 1980s. These workers came from Turkey and Northern Africa to Germany, France, Belgium, and the Netherlands to work. Even though most of them dreamed of returning to their home countries, the majority of them stayed. In due time, they brought their wives and children over. These families form the base of most of the Muslim communities in Western Europe. Their different ethnic background and their religion, Islam, or in short their "otherness", provided considerable mistrust and caution among the Europeans. At present, the second and third generation offspring of the very first Muslim immigrants is aged between eighteen and thirty and these young people are born, raised, and educated in Europe. They are living in a post-migration situation; the myth of return is long gone. A great number of them (not all) have few or no skills in speaking Turkish, Arabic, or Berber, but are fluent in Dutch, French, German and English. Above all, they master the language of youth culture as good as well as any other youths.

Popular culture, including pop music and mass media channels, often serve as important reservoirs of images, expressions, loyalties, and discourses, from which young people draw inspiration in the way they present, represent, articulate, and express processes of identification. Popular culture and youth culture are intrinsically linked. Islam is often seen as standing in a tense relation to many aspects of popular culture such as arts, music, popular entertainment, or as some say in one word: fun. In the last decade we have witnessed the emergence of forms of artistic and popular entertainment and consumption culture that find their inspiration in Islam. In particular after 9/11/2001, Muslim youth in Europe as well as in the US have become more involved in creating their own niches and markets, be it in music, fashion, food, leisure time activities (nightlife and dating events), humour, literature, and a range of commodity goods. In Europe, styles and fashion are often inspired by American aesthetic standards or a simply a copy of them (Boubekeur 2005: 12).[1]

Some examples: In the fall of 2007, the Dutch daily newspaper *Spits* published a story in 2007 on the first "Muslim singles-night event" in the Netherlands. This first-ever dating-event organized especially for Muslims who are in search of a life-partner was, according to the reporter, a big success. Another Dutch daily newspaper *De Volkskrant* reported on "a Muslim comedy tour", talking about the debut performance of three American-Muslim comedians in the Netherlands (Henfling 2007). The same newspaper that same day also contained a short item on "the production of an Islamic car", about a Malaysian car-factory that wants to produce an Islamic car, including a compass to find the direction of Mecca and special filing compartments for the Qur'an and headscarves.

Already in 2005 the Islamic cell phone was introduced in the Netherlands. Invented and produced in the Middle East, this mobile phone has several applications for Muslims: it reminds you of the call to prayer five times a day, it automatically points you in the direction of Mecca (*qibla*), it contains an English translation of the text of the Qur'an, and during Ramadan it presents a special calendar which reminds you of the times for breaking the fast.

A Dutch company called Little Muslim recently introduced "Fulla", a play doll for girls: the answer to Barbie, according to the website[2]. Fulla likes to shop, play, cook, and pray. Underneath her clothes Fulla always wears a bathing suit, so that she'll never be completely naked. Fulla stimulates little Muslim girls to learn "Muslim" values and norms, such as modesty, decent dress, respect for the elderly, but also stimulates little girls to become a teacher, doctor, lawyer, or a dentist.

On the level of popular culture, Islamized consumer commodities slowly but steadily become more and more common on the Dutch market. Besides commodity goods, in the past years "Islamic" music or Islamically inspired music is also gradually surfacing. Islamic music is not completely new. Islamic hip-hop has already conquered a place in the American and British hip-hop scene and industry, but appears to be still in its infancy in the Netherlands and has not yet reached the level of popularity it has in the UK and the United States. Islamic American hip-hop artists Native Deen, Soul Salah Crew, the British-Asian band Fun-da-mental, the British rap-band Mecca II Medina, and the French rap-crew Médine have become known as Islamic hip-hop acts (Popp 2004; Swedenburg 2001; Solomon 2005; 2006; Abdul Khabeer 2007). Other examples of Islamic popular music acts are the contemporary Islamic pop singers Sami Yusuf, with roots in Azerbeidjan, born and raised in London, and Cat Stevens, who converted to Islam in 1978 and changed his name to Yusuf Islam. They both have been active for several years in creating *anasheed* music in pop style that is popular among Muslim youth in Europe and the Arab world. Traditionally, *anasheed* music is performed with a limited number of instruments or *a cappella*, because of the assumed prohibition of certain musical instruments in Islam. *Anasheed* is usually performed with a choir that is made up of either male or female performers. Pop idols such as Sami Yusuf and Yusuf Islam, however, perform with bands that use (Western) instruments and who are the sole performers around which a fan-culture has emerged. In the United Kingdom, the all-girl band Pearls of Islam make music (rap, *anasheed*, poetry, and spoken word) with percussion instruments and vocals. Their lyrics often praise Islam and the prophet Muhammad. Islamic music is also popular in Indonesia. A vibrant popular music culture of bands inspired by the success of Western boybands à la Backstreet Boys and Take That has emerged there. Barendregt reports on the superstar status of anasheed bands in Indonesia and Malaysia such as S'Nada, Raihan, and Rabbani (Barendregt 2006: 10). A kind of (female) fan-culture familiar in the West, idolizing boy bands like Take That, has also arisen around the Southeast-Asian Muslim boy bands, which has resulted in heated public debates. Many considered the bands too commercial and found that they focused their performance too much on the visuals (the good looks of the singers), rather than on the music and the vocals.

Of all Islamized popular culture, music is one of the most controversial. The tense relationship between Islam and music dates back to the early years of Islamic history. Ever since, Islamic scholars and laymen have been discussing the compatibility of Islam and music (i.e. the production or consumption of music). The combination of music and Islam is not accepted and appreciated by all Muslims. Yet, in youth culture music is often a driving force. This has several reasons, the most important being that music and its related social activities are probably the primary form of leisure for most young people worldwide. Besides, since music is a relatively democratic cultural phenomenon, it is easily accessible to youth and it is far-reaching; it is widely available and accessible through radio, television, and the internet. (Bennett 2000: 1; Huq 2006: 4, 42; Carrington and Wilson 2004: 65).

Moreover, music, as a cultural practice, is very open to influences from outside. It is easily mixed with new and/or other cultural practices, and is consequently able to innovate and thus to articulate new identities, which is at the heart of most youth cultures (Baily and Collyer 2006: 174).

Since the 1970s, the study of pop music was often incorporated into research on youth, youth culture, and identity from a wide range of scholarly perspectives. A noteworthy idea that stands out in many of these studies is how strongly pop music and identity are interconnected. Many ideas and theories within the study of youth culture, music, and identity derive from the famous work *Resistance through Rituals. Youth Subcultures in Post-War Britain* (1976). Sociologists Stuart Hall and Tony Jefferson of the Centre for Contemporary Cultural Studies (CCCS) in Birmingham indicated that there is a connection between certain music styles and youth (sub-) cultures. Their pioneering study explained how British youth subcultures constructed and expressed their identity by means of clothing, lifestyle, and music. The post-war period brought about a destruction of traditional social structures of British society: changes in the leisure-time structures of youth and modernization and industrialization processes, which resulted in unequal socio-economic developments, caused a large discrepancy between the different social classes and between different generations (youth and their parents). The CCCS regarded youth subcultures as "magic solutions" for the economic and social contradictions experienced by British middle and lower working-class youth.

Hall and Jefferson's "resistance through rituals" is, in my view, not the most appropriate term for the new youth culture(s) emerging among European Muslim youth. In their case, it may be better to speak of "resistance through consumption", or "distinction through consumption."

THE STUDY OF MUSIC AND YOUTH CULTURE IN EUROPE

During the 1970s and 1980s, the studies and ideas of the CCCS on youth cultures dominated the field. Style, including fashion, behaviour, language use, and music and the mixing and matching of all of these elements were seen as a form of resistance to the hegemonic ideology of British society. This ideology consisted of the promotion of the nuclear family, as opposed to the extended family that was part of the lower and middle working-class ideology and the imposition of media and school systems ruled by the bourgeoisie. By means of deviant styles (in dress, language, behavior, and musical preferences) British youth tacitly and subtly expressed a dissatisfaction with and resistance to the dominant middle-class ideology. The establishment of a youth culture was regarded as a claim to symbolic space in which the youths could freely express their powerlessness and discontent with the status quo, without the interference of parents or authorities. However, due to an exaggerated concentration on these hidden ideologies behind style, the

CCCS did not go into the reasons why certain groups used certain kinds of style, fashion, language, or music to express this resistance (Bennett and Kahn-Harris 2004: 4-6).

In due course, the CCCS's concept of youth subculture was used as an all-encompassing term for whatever social aspects in the lives of youths were related in one way or another to some kind of music, style, and fashion (ibid.: 1). Critics accused the CCCS of assuming that behind each youth subculture there were latent ideologies of resistance towards the hegemony of British bourgeoisie (Huq 2006: 14). In addition, the CCCS's supposition that youth subcultures comprise a fixed group of people was criticized because it overlooked the possibility of fluidity and turnover of membership (Martin 2004: 30-31). Finally, the CCCS was criticized for attributing too much value to the role of class, and neglecting the role of gender and ethnicity, in the formation of youth subcultures (Huq 2006: 10-13).

After a spate of publications in the 1980s and 1990s on youth and subcultures and the role of style and bricolage, still following for a large part the CCCS's track (Hebdige 1979; Thornton 1995; McRobbie 1999), a new wave of studies dealing with the meaning and social significance of pop music entered the debate. The ongoing critique of the CCCS eventually resulted in the emergence of new perspectives on youth (sub-) cultures, the use of the term subculture gradually being replaced by new terms and concepts. Instigated, among other things, by flows of migrants into Europe and by the increasing popularity of African-American and Caribbean music genres – such as reggae and hip-hop – in Europe and the US during the 1990s there surfaced new interests in the role of ethnicity, race, and music in youth culture (Carrington and Wilson 2004: 71; Huq 2006: 12, 24, 33-38).

In sum, during the 1980s and 1990s, there occured a shift in the methodology of youth culture studies. The focus shifted from an "outsider's perspective" that analyzed youth cultures from the outside, presupposing a resistance to political and socio-economic circumstances, with little attention given to the discourse by youth themselves about the reasons why they do the things they do, to an "insider's perspective" that focuses more on the discourses of youth culture participants and their motivations, with an eye for external influences and changing circumstances. This renewed insight resulted in interesting studies in France, the United Kingdom, and Germany on the role of ethnicity and the impact of post-migration situations on the emergence of youth culture among North African, Asian, and Turkish youth.

In France, since the 1990s, studies on the second-generation North Africans (in France often called *beurs*) have appeared regularly. For example, Gabriele Marranci's articles (2000; 2000a; 2003) shows how raï music and its corresponding youth culture are significant in the identity construction processes of second-generation North African immigrants. Raï music is an Algerian genre that is known for its rebellious, taboo-breaking lyrics in Algerian dialect and its fusion of Arab and Western music. Its most famous exponent is (cheb) Khaled (born in 1960, Oran).

According to Marranci, raï music offers *beurs* the opportunity to construct and express identities that are distinctly different from the identities of their parents and other ethnic youth in France. Other scholars contributing to this field are Bouziane Daoudi and Hadj Miliani. They wrote one of the first studies on Algerian raï music (Daoudi and Miliani 1996) and they recently wrote on North African influences in French culture (ibid: 2002). Anthropologist Ted Swedenburg (2001; 2001a; 2003) has also published on raï music and Arab music in general with varying focuses, ranging from an analysis of raï music in France to an examination of the link between hip-hop and Islam in Europe. His work often deals with ethnic youth in post-migration situations and music in European contexts. France and its North African youth have frequently been studied in relation to raï music and more recently in relation to hip-hop.

A great deal of these studies describe how, through the use and production of these types of music, youth try to escape their marginal position by striving for more acceptance in overall French society, but all the while maintaining and giving expression to their "otherness". This becomes particularly clear in Marranci's analysis of the case of singer Faudel, born 1979 in France (Mantes-la-Jolie, near Paris) from Algerian parents. He is a successful singer who makes modern raï music, including North African rhythms and melodies, but who increasingly sings his lyrics in French and also adds French translations of his Arabic lyrics in his CD-booklets, in order to reach a wider audience and get more airplay on French radio and television (Marranci 2000: 11). Faudel's 2006 album *Mundial Corrida* is predominantly sung in French.

In Germany, Turkish youth are widely researched, the focus often being the vibrant German-Turkish hip-hop scene (Kaya 2002; Soysal 2001; El-Taybeb 2004; Çağlar 1998). Andy Bennett (2000; 2001), for instance, did work on hip-hop in Frankfurt-am-Main and included the views and roles of ethnic youth within the German hip-hop scene in his study. Bennett's work demonstrates how American hip-hop is not simply imitated, but is applied to a local context, Frankfurt in this case. Hip-hop made by German-Turks in Frankfurt, mostly deals with racism and citizenship. Bennett describes how hip-hop for German-Turkish youth is a very local expression; through rapping about local experiences and sensibilities and performing them in "the right way", the rapper offers a credible expression of a social connection to this local environment. Besides, hip-hop has become a tool for German-Turkish youth to act out their "coolness", i.e. it becomes a way to express a certain authentic identity and to set oneself apart from others who are "not cool" (Bennett 2000: 149–150). Authenticity and "coolness" are important elements in all youth cultures around the world.

DUTCH-MOROCCAN YOUTH CULTURE: RELIGION, ETHNICITY AND POLITICS

Being true to oneself is important for many young people. Credibility is often a synonym for authenticity; this means to be true to oneself and to put up a credible performance of this authentic identity. For young people who find themselves in a post-migration situation it is often not all that easy to know who you are. Terms like "living in two cultures", "living in-between cultures", "hybrid identities", "multiple identities" and so on have been used to describe their often complex situation. For Dutch-Moroccan youth, music is an important tool used to express themselves to express their multitude of identities and to articulate to what worlds they feel connected.

Islam is an important aspect in the lives of Dutch-Moroccan youth. They often use it as a frame of reference around which they build up their identities (De Koning 2008). But Islam is not their *only* point of reference. This becomes particularly clear in the music genres that are prominent in Dutch-Moroccan youth culture. Besides Islam, ethnic background, socio-cultural imagery, and the Dutch political situation affect the nature and content of the Dutch-Moroccan musical youth culture.

A trend of privatization of Islam among young Dutch Muslims has been detected, meaning that although the participation in religious rituals and mosques is decreasing among second-generation Turks and Moroccans, their identification with Islam remains (Phalet and Ter Wal 2004: 39).

Ethnic background also remains an important frame of reference in the identity construction processes of Dutch-Moroccan youth. Many attribute great value to the preservation of what they perceive as *Moroccan* cultural traditions. This is reflected, for example, in the way they organize and celebrate weddings and religious holidays. The desire to conserve what they perceive as Moroccan traditions, requiring Moroccan food, dress, music, and art, has triggered the establishment of a Dutch-Moroccan retail-circuit in many Dutch cities. This circuit includes shops owned by Dutch-Moroccans selling fruit, vegetables, and halal meat, but also businesses that sell Moroccan art, hand craft and furniture, Moroccan traditional dresses, and fashion. There are also several music shops in the larger Dutch cities, like Utrecht, Amsterdam, and Rotterdam, selling Moroccan and Arab music.

The way Dutch-Moroccans present themselves to the outside world is also influenced by the way they are perceived by others. The way migrants in the Netherlands have been labelled has changed considerably in the past thirty years. Whereas during the 1980s, the country of origin was considered the most important marker, and immigrants were simply labelled as guest workers from Morocco or Turkey, or as an ethnic minority on a more abstract level, nowadays religion has become one of the most important identity markers. The immigrants themselves also activated an increased self-identification based on religion: while the first generation of immigrants often did not emphasize their religious identity, second-generation Moroccans and Turks gradually started to present themselves more as Muslims, rather than Turks or Moroccans. In fact, the rising visibility of Muslims in the Netherlands is the result of two trends taking place simultaneously. On the one hand, large numbers of second-generation immigrants prioritize their Muslim identity over their cultural or ethnic background. On the other hand, government policies and public debates in the media on the position of Muslims and Islam in the Netherlands also triggered this inclination to present oneself as Muslim. Overall, Dutch-Moroccan youth consider themselves Muslims, although variation exists in the way Islam is practiced in daily life. In youth culture of Dutch-Moroccan, Islam is used to give music, fashion, food, style or cultural imagery in general an Islamic touch.

HISTORY OF THE DUTCH-MOROCCAN COMMUNITY

Dutch-Moroccans have been part of Dutch society for over thirty years. The first generation of Moroccans arrived in the 1960s and 1970s as guest workers with the intention to make their stay in the Netherlands only temporary. However, in the 1980s it became clear that their return to Morocco would not take place. Today, the Moroccan community consists of approximately 335,000 people, which is around 2 per cent of the total Dutch population. The Moroccan community is the third largest minority community in the Netherlands after the Turkish and the Surinam population. Currently, the second generation of Moroccan immigrants consists of approximately 168,000 people included in the 335,000 (Dutch Central Bureau of Statistics, 2009). They were born and raised in the Netherlands, often only having Dutch nationality. In public opinion they remain nevertheless "foreigners"[3], a term that is also frequently associated with being Muslim and they are often considered a problem group.

Dutch society has gone through some major changes in the last decades due to national and international political developments. Before 9/11, the Dutch political and media debate mainly focused on the disadvantaged position of the Dutch-Moroccan community. The worries expressed concentrated on the supposed oppression of women, the increasing crime rates among boys and high drop-out rates. All in all, it was feared that the integration of the Moroccan community into Dutch society had become a total failure. However, after 9/11 the focus of the debate shifted to Islam and the Muslim community in the Netherlands, and especially to the fear of Islamic radicalism among Dutch-Moroccan youth. In due time, and especially since 9/11/2001 a trend has developed in the media to lump Muslims, may they be of Moroccan, Turkish, Iranian, Dutch, or whatever descent, together under one label; that of being a Muslim.

In addition, several local Dutch events, of which the murder of Dutch TV director Theo van Gogh by a young second-generation Dutch-Moroccan was the most important, have transformed the debate on the position of Muslims in the Netherlands into a debate on the position of the Dutch-Moroccan community. Young Dutch-Moroccans have received much bad press in Dutch politics and media. Many face racism and stereotyping, not only because of their often difficult economic, social, and cultural position, but also because of the rising global fear of Islamic terrorism. However, these obstacles have not prevented them from expressing themselves creatively and musically. Often excluded from public debate, parts of Dutch-Moroccan youth have created their own cultural and musical spaces, in which a subgroup of young Dutch-Moroccans actively participates. These musical spaces and places reveal a vibrant Moroccan musical culture in which Dutch-Moroccan youth are active both as producers and as consumers.

DUTCH-MOROCCAN MUSICAL YOUTH CULTURE

Today's Dutch-Moroccan musical youth culture is built on the foundations of a musical circuit that goes back to the late 1980s when some small organizations started to organize musical festivals and other activities dedicated to Moroccan (and Berber) music (Bousetta 1996: 186). In the early 1990s, raï music was becoming increasingly popular internationally, due to the success of the Algerian raï singer Khaled, and gradually spread from the Maghreb to Europe. In the Netherlands, raï music first and foremost found a fan base among the Dutch-Moroccan community. This resulted in the creation of several raï music bands and acts, some of which eventually became very successful in the Netherlands, such as Raïland, Noujoum Raï, and Cheb Ashraf. It was at this time that the so-called raï parties, often day-time parties, became very popular and were organized all over the Netherlands.

However, from the late 1990s, the international hype around raï music settled down and gradually disappeared, while other musical genres came to the foreground. Inspired by the success of the raï-parties, some organizations started out producing one or two events yearly targeted at Dutch-Moroccan youth. Gradually this grew to several events per year and resulted in the creation of different kinds of events, ranging from mega-concerts to small lounge events, from concerts to festivals, from student parties to women-only parties.

The Dutch-Moroccan musical scene does not only consist of concert and party organizers, but is also supported by a retail trade of Moroccan and Arab music. The four major Dutch cities, Rotterdam, Amsterdam, Utrecht, and The Hague, have music shops specializing in Arab and/or Moroccan music. Undoubtedly, the internet has also enlarged the possibilities for buying and downloading music from all over the world and gives people the opportunity to search for very particular music goods on a global scale. The continuity of the Dutch-Moroccan musical youth culture is also supported by numerous websites enabling users to download, share, and provide music and video clips. Peer-to-peer programs such as Kazaa and LimeWire provide the opportunity to share and exchange music and Dutch-Moroccans intensively make use of these kinds of networks. Other sites such as www.marokko.nl have several forums where music and events are central topics.

Additionally, sites such as www.soundclick.com offer (amateur) artists the possibility to make their music accessible on-line and available for others to download onto their computer (after registration). Today, internet-users have the opportunity to create a "web space" (Myspace), where users can build up a profile and add all kinds of personal information including music. These web spaces are often ideal promotion opportunities for starting new artists. Finally, the YouTube website has become very popular worldwide and serves both as a resource for watching music videos and a platform for amateur artists to put on view their musical qualities. The internet is thus a major factor in the permanence of an on-line Dutch-Moroccan musical world, which also contributes to the expansion and development of the real, off-line Dutch-Moroccan scene.

The Dutch-Moroccan musical scene consists of events targeted at a young Dutch-Moroccan audience. Through providing the opportunity to listen and dance to Arab and Moroccan music, these events have become excellent meeting places for Dutch-Moroccan youth and offer them the opportunity to express and construct a Dutch-Moroccan identity, by means of dancing, clothing, and socializing with other Dutch-Moroccans. At these events one can often literally taste the Moroccan atmosphere: Moroccan tea and food is served, and sometimes there are stands that sell books on Morocco or music, handcraft, or jewellery. By their visiting these events, Dutch-Moroccan youth can clearly distinguish themselves from Dutch peers, since the average Dutchman does not visit these events.

Often no alcohol is served during these events and, in this sense, the events comply with an Islamic norm. Also the scheduling of the events is different from regular Dutch events. The events often start in the late afternoon. This gives more girls the chance to attend, because a large number of Moroccan girls cannot or does not want to go out late at night. By starting and ending parties "early", Dutch-Moroccan girls can conform to socio-cultural norms set by the Dutch-Moroccan community. Recently, the women-only events have become increasingly popular. These women-only parties offer girls the chance to go out and have fun without the presence or interference of men; something that many Dutch-Moroccan girls love. Going out without having to be bothered by the looks of unknown, intrusive, or intimidating boys, or chaperoned by brothers, neighbors, or cousins, is much appreciated.

This musical youth culture thrives on the desire to spend leisure time with peers and like-minded people, without the interference of parents. It has an eye for Dutch-Moroccan youth's ethnic, socio-cultural, and religious identities, by focussing on music through which they celebrate their Moroccan roots, and complying with certain Islamic and Moroccan social norms, such as the absence of alcohol, early starting and ending times, and sometimes gender segregation.

Two musical genres play a prominent role in the musical youth culture of Dutch-Moroccan youth. *Shaabi* (popular Moroccan folk music) and hip-hop are both important in the creation of an in-group or in-crowd feeling among Dutch-Moroccan youth. In the end, youth culture is all about setting boundaries between the "in-crowd" and the outsiders. Both these genres are used to draw up boundaries in specific ways. *Shaabi* music is a symbol for Morocco and Moroccan tradition and culture and serves therefore as a tool to evoke a sense of nostalgia, solidarity, and unity among Dutch-Moroccans. During *shaabi* events the central focus is on defining an in-group feeling and being recognized as a young Dutch-Moroccan. Hip-hop music is also used to differentiate between "us" and "them", although the significance of the genre and the identities associated with it are much more open to individual interpretations. Whereas *shaabi* is predominantly a genre that is consumed rather than actively produced by Dutch-Moroccan youth, the Dutch hip-hop scene is a scene where many rappers, producers and DJs with a Moroccan background play a prominent role.

SHAABI: A FEELING OF DUTCH-MOROCCANNESS

Shaabi music is for many Moroccans the ultimate way to create a "Moroccan" atmosphere and is a symbol of authentic Moroccan music. *Shaabi* is a central genre in Moroccan family celebrations, such as weddings, but it has conquered a central place in more public events. The word *shaabi* is the Arabic for "of the people"; when used to describe music, it refers to popular music. In the specific context of Morocco, *shaabi* represents a category of music consisting of different genres from different regions including for instance *reggada* music from Oujda and Berkane and *rewaffa* music from the Rif. Moroccan musicologist Aydoun writes about a contemporary Moroccan urban genre ("la chanson populaire cita-dine") characterized by its festive character; fast, danceable rhythms and the use of Moroccan instruments, such as the *oud, qamanji*, and *derbouka*, as well as Western instruments such as keyboards, guitars and drums, which result in a bombastic mosaic of sounds (Aydoun 2001: 141-141). This urban-style *shaabi* is influenced by several other Moroccan genres, and its emergence dates from the 1940s, when the cassette and gramophone encouraged new artists to tap into new commercial markets (ibid.: 141-142). *Shaabi* is sung in the Moroccan-Arabic dialect and some-times in a Berber language. In the past century, the *shaabi* song has broken through regional boundaries and has become a nationally known genre and is considered part of a national Moroccan music culture (ibid.: 143). New means of distribu-tion of music, such as cassette players and radio, instigated the dispersal of the genre throughout Morocco (ibid.) *Shaabi* music is today filled with new mixing techniques and electric instruments. Aydoun stresses that *shaabi* focuses on the festive experience of dancing, singing and being together with friends and family. The primary social context where *shaabi* plays a dominant role is "the private party" during which the audience can participate in the performance (ibid.: 143). He also emphasizes the randomness of the lyrics and the capability of its performers to improvise lyrics and keep the audience interested by constantly changing melodies, rhythms, and lyrics during a performance (ibid.: 141-142). Aydoun concludes that a successful *shaabi* performance depends on the performer's skill to captivate the audience and secure its participation (ibid.).

A quick analysis of *shaabi* lyrics reveals a set of recurrent themes. First, traditional lyrics describing family celebrations such as weddings or lyrics about harvest celebrations make up a large part of the traditional *shaabi* repertoire. Nowadays, songs dealing with immigration have also become important. For example, many *shaabi* songs that have proved to be very popular outside Morocco are songs about the loss of a loved one, the loved one in many cases being an emigrant.

Many *shaabi* artists improvise lyrics during performances, singing about all kinds of topics. Today, well-known Moroccan artists performing this urban style *shaabi* are for example, Khalid Bennani, Tahour, Daoudi, Najat Aatabou, Mustapha Bourgogne, and many, many others. In the Netherlands, several bands and little orchestras also perform *shaabi*. Most of these bands consist of Dutch-Moroccan musicians. Ismaïlia is one of the oldest and best-known Dutch-Moroccan *shaabi* bands. Other Dutch-Moroccan bands are Al Kanar and Anghaam. Note however, that most Dutch-Moroccan *shaabi* bands have a varied and mixed repertoire and specialize in more than one genre. They often play whatever genre is in demand.

Performances of famous *shaabi* artists, like Najat Aatabou, Senhaji, Daoudi, and Mustapha Bourgogne, can attract thousands of visitors. *Shaabi's* danceable beats and its festive character are elements that Dutch-Moroccan youth like about this music. *Shaabi's* popularity also relates to the fact that Dutch-Moroccan youth consider it to be part of Morocco's cultural heritage. A great number of Dutch-Moroccan musical events are aimed at providing a space in which one can identify with (other) Dutch- Moroccans. The events are often full of symbols (flags, food, dress, music, and stands selling books on Morocco, and jewelry,) referring to Morocco's traditional culture, at least traditional in the eyes of the visitors. The prevalence of *shaabi* music has to do with the fact that this music represents a link with Morocco and is perceived as Moroccan music above all. Additionally, the events enable visitors to incorporate elements from their parents' culture, of which *shaabi* music is a prominent component, into their own youth culture, without parental interference or intrusion of non-Dutch-Moroccans.

These events represent a space where young people can freely be "Moroccan", can behave, dance, sing, and interact in the way they perceive to be "Moroccan". Infused with nostalgia for Morocco, *shaabi* and its attendant events play a significant role in the assertion and preservation of "Moroccanness" among

Moroccan-Dutch youths, some of whom have never even been to Morocco. Afterwards, when playing, for instance, *shaabi* music in the privacy of one's room, one can relive the experience one had at that event, reinforcing the solidarity expressed there.

A large number of Dutch-Moroccan youth value their Moroccan background and want to give explicit expression to this feeling during these events, but they do this in their own youthful way, without interference of elders or other authority figures. These *shaabi* events are their own spaces, in tune with their specific musical preferences and their socio-cultural background. Moreover, these events have also become partly adjusted to their religious needs. A trend of Islamization of Moroccan musical events in the Netherlands is developing. This trend involves both consumers and producers of these events, who are adding Islamic elements to non-religious events. Party promoters and concert organizations try to tune into Dutch-Moroccan youth's needs.

The role of Islamic norms and Dutch-Moroccan social norms, implicitly linked to Islamic norms, thus manifests itself in the way Dutch-Moroccan youth have created a musical youth culture. In regular Dutch nightlife, drinking alcohol and the mingling of men and women are the norm. As a consequence, Dutch nightlife is not an option for those Dutch-Moroccan young women (and men) who want to spend their leisure time in a way that is Islamic, at least in their eyes. It explains the popularity of Dutch-Moroccan events that are attuned to these needs. The growing popularity of the women-only parties indicates that Dutch-Moroccan youth have a need to spend time together during their leisure time in an environment of fun, music, and entertainment. They prefer to do this in their "own" specific leisure time spaces and with activities which are tuned into their specific religious and socio-cultural tastes. As a result, a large part of the Dutch-Moroccan scene remains in a peripheral position in relation to "regular" Dutch nightlife, and is an unfamiliar and "underground" phenomenon for most Dutch people.

HIP-HOP: RECORDS OF RESISTANCE

Dutch-Moroccan youth have recently become more active and visible in the Dutch hip-hop scene. Hip-hop music is an eclectic type of music, known for its bricolage of sounds and beats, but also for its bricolage of text fragments. Thus, a distinctive feature of hip-hop music is the extensive use of sampling. Hip-hop music often incorporates bits and pieces from different sources, such as songs, films, TV, commercials and street sounds. Originally, hip-hop music, came from the United States, specifically New York. In the 1970s, young African-Americans started rapping, that is talking in a rhythmic and melodic way, over drumbeats. In general, hip-hop fans and experts refer to Kool Herc and Africa Bambaata as the founders of hip-hop. Hip-hop culture is often considered to have three focal points: music, graffiti art, and break-dancing. In daily speech, the term hip-hop often refers to hip-hop music, which is often rap music.

Music critics and hip-hop fans often make a rough distinction between two kinds of hip-hop music, based on lyrical themes. On the one hand there is the materialistic type of hip-hop. To this category belong songs about fast cars, money, and jewelry. In this kind of hip-hop, also called "brag & boast rap" in hip-hop terms, materialism, being rich, or in hip-hop terms "living large", and also being adored by many women are glorified. The message is that getting rich is an ideal way of life. On the other hand, there exists another kind of hip-hop characterized by political awareness, social engagement, and expression of social criticism. This type of hip-hop is often labelled "message rap." Minority groups worldwide have found in message rap a way to articulate their frustration about their (often difficult) position in society. The volume edited by Tony Mitchell *Global Noise. Rap and Hip-Hop outside the USA* (2001) portrays in detail how hip-hop has been appropriated by minority groups worldwide. In general, scholars and music critics agree that what attracts minority groups to hip-hop music is its ability to express dissatisfaction and social engagement.

Dutch-Moroccan youth did not randomly choose to make hip-hop. A number of underlying conditions facilitated this choice. First, hip-hop is an accessible and widely accepted genre because it has international recognition. It has become one of the most commercially successful genres in the last decade (Watkins 2005: 209). A second reason why many young people choose to make hip-hop lies in the fact that making hip-hop music does not have to be an expensive activity. It is in fact a very low-budget genre. All a rapper needs in order to make hip-hop is a voice, a feeling for rhythm, a computer with music software, and a microphone. A third element that makes hip-hop an accessible genre is the fact that nowadays the Dutch music culture and the media have accepted rap in the Dutch language wholeheartedly, whereas in the past this was not the case. To be more precise, Dutch-Moroccan rappers usually rap in street slang, which is a mix of several languages such as Moroccan-Arabic, Berber, English, Papiamento, and Sranan[4] (De Koning 2005: 36-41).

Dutch-Moroccan youths have recently become more visible on the Dutch music scene and in the media. The rapper Raymzter's 2002 hit-record *Kutmarokkanen* (*Fucking Moroccans*) put Dutch-Moroccan hip-hop on the musical map. Raymzter, a half-Dutch-half-Moroccan rapper, twenty-five at that time, wrote this song in reaction to a Dutch politician's controversial remark, a slip of the tongue referring to Dutch-Moroccan youth as "those fucking Moroccans." A microphone picked up his words and a controversy was born. In reaction to this, Raymzter rapped:

They wanna denigrate us, when they talk about us. We did not do anything wrong, but still they wanna hate us. They wanna denigrate us when they talk about us. It's time to change this, don't you realize it?[5] (Taken from the song Kutmarokkanen [Fucking Moroccans] by Raymzter, from the album *Rayalistisch*, released 2003 by Top Notch/Virgin).

Eventually, this song became a big hit and cleared the way for other Dutch-Moroccan rappers and ever since Dutch-Moroccan youth have been more active and particularly more visible, in the production of a growing hip-hop scene. Ali B. has since become the most famous Dutch-Moroccan rapper and the most famous rapper in the Netherlands. He released two albums successfully in 2004 and 2006[6].

The recurrent themes in the repertoire of Dutch-Moroccan rappers include local, national, and international themes. The songs report on the personal biographies of the rappers and their experiences in a local neighborhood and their battles with other rap crews in rival towns. By using a typical vocabulary, accent, and speech, and addressing specific local topics, the rappers are able to put forward sensibilities and affinities towards their social Dutch surroundings, concretely placing themselves in these local places, while at the same time the rappers express a connectedness to both their local Dutch hometowns and the worldwide hip-hop community.

A considerable part of the lyrics, but certainly not all, is an attempt to undermine stereotypes through presenting alternative points of view, including personal biographies of experiences with stereotypes; Dutch-Moroccan rappers aim to subvert stereotypical ideas about Dutch-Moroccans, like Raymzter's Fucking Moroccans. Stereotypes that Dutch-Moroccan youth often feel are imposed upon them are the assumption that they are criminal, radical Islamists, terrorists, un-integrated, anti-authoritarian, and homophobic. The lyrics talk of escaping these imposed labels or they create narratives that invalidate or reverse these stereotypes. At times, these lyrics are aggressive and violent, at other times they are humorous or sarcastic.

Others songs often reveal a political awareness. These lyrics deal for instance with international politics. The war in Iraq, 9/11 and especially the Israeli-Palestine conflict, the situation in the Middle East, or US foreign policy (in Afghanistan or Iraq) are popular song subjects. Like the songs about national themes, these songs indicate a considerable political consciousness among these rappers. For example, Omar and El Moro's track Palestijnse strijders (Palestinian fighters) is a song that talks about the Israeli-Palestine conflict:

Palestinian fighters, they're fighting for their country / Abbas and Sharon when will they finally shake hands? / When will there be peace / Yo, I wanna know now.

In this type of songs, one can find signs of a (pan-) Islamic identity among the rappers, since they express a sense of affiliation with Muslims worldwide. Through these songs, Omar and El Moro and DHC created a musical space connecting to Palestinian youth, transgressing their own local boundaries of hometowns and rival towns, going beyond the borders of Dutch society by affiliating themselves to their Muslim brothers in the Middle East. It clearly reveals that their frames of mind go beyond their own local situation. The rappers identify strongly with their "Palestinian brothers."

Concerning the vernacular, different languages are juxtaposed. The refrain is sung in a mix of Arabic and Dutch, and consequently creates a link between the rappers, their Dutch background, Palestine, and the rest of the Arab world. By singing in Arabic, the rappers express a link with "their Palestinian brothers" as well with the whole Arab-speaking world. Besides, by claiming that Palestine should be Arab and Islamic, they put forward a clear political statement, supporting the end of the Israeli occupation in Palestine and the domination of Islam.

With hip-hop music rappers respond to the Dutch socio-political climate and international events and the contents of their lyrics are clear signs of this. Hip-hop music functions as a channel through which rappers can air their frustrations regarding the political debate on integration, the stereotypes about Dutch-Moroccans, international political events, such as 9/11 and the war in Iraq and so on. The music reflects their way of perceiving, interpreting, and representing the world. Through hip-hop, rappers respond to processes of categorization to which they feel subjected. The stereotypes Dutch-Moroccan youth feel are imposed upon them play a significant role in many of the lyrics of Dutch-Moroccan rappers. These imposed category labels have a negative connotation (criminal, terrorist, radical) and their lyrics play on these labels and invalidate them, sometimes attacking them with an aggressive tone, at other times mocking them with humour. Dutch society's categorization of Dutch-Moroccans has a clear effect on the way rappers identify themselves, through their lyrics, with *allochtonen*, Muslims, Palestinians, Arabs, and other Dutch-Moroccans. In their repertoire, Dutch-Moroccan hip-hoppers constantly change their perspective, affiliate themselves with different musical worlds and social groups, and escape imposed labels.

CONCLUSION

Popular culture, including pop music and mass media channels, often serve as important reservoirs of images, expressions, loyalties, and discourses, from which young people draw inspiration in the way they present, represent, articulate, and express processes of identification. In this article I have shown how music is used as in instrument in the production of a youth culture and hence serves symbolises an identification processes of second-generation Dutch-Moroccans in a post-migration context. It shows that music and youth culture are inherently linked to all kinds of social, cultural, and political processes taking place within the society these young people live in. Through an investigation of youth culture and musical preferences of post-migration youth we gain insight into how they position themselves in society and how their music, leisure time, and musical activities are affected by socio-political events and their own social, religious, and cultural backgrounds.

The *shaabi* events are sites where Dutch-Moroccan youth feel free to express their Moroccan roots in their own youthful way without interference from outsiders and without feeling like they are being imposed by all kinds of negative stereotypes. Being together, dancing and interacting with "like-minded" people in a surrounding embellished with their favourite music, their favourite artists and DJs, makes these events an important site in Dutch-Moroccan youth culture. Even though these events are often not Islamic by design, it is not unusual for some Islamic norms and values to be incorporated, like the absence of alcohol and the segregation of the sexes.

Whereas for Dutch-Moroccan youth *shaabi* music symbolizes a link with their common past and shared ancestry, hip-hop music is used as a tool to express opinions and frustrations about their current position in Dutch society. Rap lyrics of Dutch-Moroccan hip-hoppers are ongoing dialogues between rappers and their audiences (including fans, and other "enemy" rap crews), but also between rappers and overall society.

Hip-hop's articulation of alternative points of view about the "true" nature of Dutch-Moroccans, which rejects the public opinion about them, is a form of criticism of the way Dutch-Moroccans are represented by some Dutch politicians and media. Rappers create a musical space in which they can safely subvert current power structures. Making rap music offers them a possibility to symbolically become more powerful, gain prestige as an artist, and escape their marginal position. In sum, the significance of Dutch-Moroccan hip-hop lies in the fact that it enables its producers and consumers to transgress the imposed, stereotypical boundaries of what it means to be Dutch-Moroccan. Through becoming involved in hip-hop, Dutch-Moroccan youth can retaliate and counter-attack the stereotypical and imposed labels, either by sheer dissociation from these stereotypes, or by articulating and prioritizing alternative identities that are significant and meaningful for them.

At times, Islam plays a prominent role in Dutch-Moroccan youth culture, although its importance and significance varies from time to time. One moment, Islamic discourse is used to assess whether one can listen to certain music or watch certain TV channels; at another time Islam is presented as a tool to connect oneself to the world of Palestinians in the Middle East or to the world-wide *ummah*, the community of Muslims worldwide. Looking at the growth of Islamized commodities, such as cell phones, toys, food, fashion, and music appearing on the Dutch and European markets and their increasing popularity, it seems that Islam is also becoming a style in itself. Being Muslim has become "cool" and expressing yourself as a "cool Muslim" can be done using these Islamized commodities in your style. So, besides choosing to become a hip-hopper, a skater, or a gothic, one can also choose to be "Muslim" (see also Buitelaar 2008: 243-244).

A number of Dutch politicians and Dutch media continue to stress the "problem of Islam and Dutch-Moroccans" and talk frequently of Islamic terrorism, the prevention of Islamic radicalism among Dutch-Moroccan youth, and fear of the Islamization of Dutch society and many other issues related to Islam and Dutch-Moroccans. Incidentally, Dutch politician Geert Wilders and his Party for freedom (PVV) particularly expresses this fear of the Islamization of Dutch culture and society. As this article has shown, how one is categorized by others affects the way one identifies and presents oneself to the outside world. Considering this constant labelling of Dutch-Moroccans as Moroccans and Muslims, rather than as Dutch, it may not be surprising that new Islamic youth cultures surface.

NOTES

1   "European Muslim youth: towards a cool Islam?" First appeared in *Yearbook of Muslims in Europe* edited by Jorgen S. Nielsen, Samim Akgonul, Ahmet Alibasic, Brigitte Marechal, Christian Moe. (2009): 305-327. Muslim youth in the Muslim world are also in the process of creating new cultural practices. See for example Marc LeVine's *Heavy Metal Islam: Rock, Resistance, and the Struggle for the Soul of Islam* (New York: Three Rivers Press 2008). My focus in this article, however, is on Muslim youth in Europe and especially on Dutch-Moroccan youth.

2   Taken from: www.fullashop.nl, d.d. 31 December 2008.

3   The Dutch term used in this context is *allochtonen*, coming from the word *allochthonous* meaning of foreign origin.

4   Papiamento and Sranan are languages spoken on the Dutch Antilles and in Surinam. Original Dutch lyrics are: "Ze willen ons zwart maken als ze over ons praten. We hebben ze niks gedaan en alsnog willen ze ons haten. Ze willen ons zwart maken als ze over ons praten. Tijd dat dit verandert, heb je dat niet in de gaten."

5   Ali B. is Ali Bouali, born in 1981 in Zaanstad, the Netherlands and currently Holland's most famous rapper.

Music Consumption
and the Navigation of Identities

Transnational Moroccan Youth in Britain

Carolyn Landau

INTRODUCTION

The process of identity construction is one of importance but also a great struggle for many young people. The adolescent period is fraught with both tension and opportunity as young men and women seek to express themselves as individuals and as a part of peer and community groups. For the offspring of migrants living in a host culture far away and very different from the homeland, this process is often further complicated with yet more issues to negotiate. Discovering and asserting "who you are" means exploring your identity which can include social, national, ethnic, religious, and cultural dimensions. For young people whose parents grew up elsewhere this can be a complex and confusing process. Music is one of many ways in which people can express these multiple identities. Tarrant et al (2002:135) have pointed out that listening to music is, for adolescents, one of the most important and preferred pastimes. It enables them to explore and express their various identities in ways that other media cannot. Indeed, Slobin has also noted the powerful ability of music to express identity, remarking that "people identify themselves strongly, even principally, through their music" (1994: 243). As adolescents undergo dramatic changes in many areas of their lives, the music that is consumed during this often turbulent period may well also change, revealing that identity is "*mobile*, a process not a thing" and that listening to music can be "an experience of this *self-in-process*" (Frith, 1996:109).

The article examines the consumption of music by some British-born Moroccans[1] living in London in relation to the construction and negotiation of various transnational cultural and religious identities. The structure of the article is influenced by the nature of my empirical and qualitative data – that is, around the narratives, experiences, and observations of a relatively small number of young Moroccans in London[2]. It is important to note, therefore, that this article is by no means representative of all Moroccan youth in London. I begin by introducing

the Moroccan community in Britain and specifically London, where the majority of my research has taken place. I situate my case studies within the context
of ongoing contemporary public debate in Britain surrounding the current crisis
of British identity, with specific reference to what it means to be a young British
Muslim today. A general introduction will be followed by the presentation and
examination of some of the narratives of British-born Moroccans in relation
to their perceptions of self-identity and belonging. Their thoughts and feelings
about the relationship between music consumption and religious and cultural
identities will be explored. More specifically, how the latter has led to significant
changes in the former. First, an effort is made to draw on some of the historic
and current debates on the place of music within Islam. This will be followed by
the exploration of specific case studies in music consumption among British-born
Moroccans. I will examine a number of singers and groups in order to investigate
their significance in terms of the construction and negotiation of multiple identities and how these may or may not connect to transnational cultural and religious
networks.

MOROCCANS IN THE UK

Diplomatic and economic links between Morocco and the UK date back to the
thirteenth century (Cherti, 2008: 73). Migration from Morocco to the UK began
as early as the nineteenth century (Halliday, 1992: 162). The earliest Moroccan
migration to the UK is documented as having occurred from around 1830, from
the Imperial city of Fez in central Morocco, to Manchester in the North of
England. These migrants were merchants who traded in silverware and textiles.
Evidence suggests that this community numbered up to 150 during the 1890s but
returned to Morocco in 1930 due to competition from Japanese traders (Hayes,
1905: 205–212). The next significant outflow from Morocco to Britain did not
take place until the 1960s. It has been divided by Myriam Cherti (2009: 1) into
four phases or decades. Cherti's research has shown that, during the 1960s, so-
called unskilled-workers from the Jbala region in northern Morocco hired by
Spanish nationals came to work in the service industries such as hotels and small
businesses. This was followed, in the 1970s, by a phase of family reunification. The
1980s saw a phase of migration of young, semi-skilled professionals and entrepreneurs mainly from large cities across Morocco and the 1990s saw a phase of
migration of highly skilled professionals from both Morocco and France (ibid.).

Despite these historical links between Morocco and Britain, Moroccans in the
UK have remained a largely invisible community officially and statistically. This
is mainly because the National Censuses carried out in the past forty years (in
2001, 1991, 1981 and 1971) have been fairly vague in terms of categorising ethnicity
thus leaving no opportunity for Moroccans to make themselves more visible in

this area[3]. Unofficial estimates of the current Moroccan population in Britain are around 65,000–70,000 (ibid.). Approximately half of the Moroccans in Britain live in London (mostly originating from the Jbala region of Morocco, centered around Larache, Tangiers and Tetouan). There is also a significant Moroccan presence in Edinburgh, Slough, St. Albans (originating mainly from Meknes), Crawley and Trowbridge (originating mainly from Oujda) (ibid)[4]. Within London, a large proportion of Moroccans live in West London, particularly centered on and near the Golborne Road,[5] which is known locally as "Little Morocco" due to its numerous Moroccan cafés, restaurants, butchers, grocers, and community centres. The Moroccan community in this area has been described as "close-knit", with "a strong and proud Moroccan identity ... even amongst the second and third generations" (ibid).

NATIONAL AND RELIGIOUS IDENTITIES

Cherti's observation of a strong and proud Moroccan identity is particularly meaningful due to the current, ongoing public debate exploring identity on a national scale. With continuing immigration to Britain as well as the "coming of age" of second and now third generations of more established migrant communities, the question of what it means to be British continues to be hotly debated by the British government, media, and academia. The debate took on an urgency following a series of suicide bomb attacks in London in July 2005[6], since all of the perpetrators were British-born Muslims. The fatal attacks, therefore, raised serious questions about the allegiance and identity of all British citizens, with their diversity of cultural, religious, ethnic, and national heritages. Immediately following the attacks, prominent British Muslims were swift to distance themselves from the acts of terrorism carried out in the name of Islam. Large-scale cultural events have been organized to demonstrate British Islam's commitment to peace. One such event is the annual "Eid in the Square", a celebratory event organised by the Mayor of London and the Muslim Council of Britain (MCB)[7], held in Trafalgar Square in central London at the end of Ramadan. During the opening speech at the 2008 celebration, Dr. Muhammad Abdul Bari, Secretary General of the MCB remarked:

> Today you Muslims here in Trafalgar Square represent diversity of our community: outside of the Hajj, the London Muslim community is perhaps the most multicultural Muslim community on earth. I urge you all to celebrate that diversity and share all the good our community has to offer with those around you (http://www.mcb.org.uk/article_detail.php?article=features-152, accessed April 2009).

Included within this diverse multicultural Muslim community of London are Moroccans, many of whom are continually exploring and celebrating the diversity that is contained within their multiple identities. In a recent interview for a BBC Radio Four documentary on Britishness, Gordon Brown, the then British Prime Minister, made the point that "everyone wants to be rooted, everyone wants to feel a sense of belonging" (d'Ancona, 2009.03.31). Achieving a sense of rootedness and belonging is often particularly challenging for the children of migrants. The first generation typically feel a strong sense of belonging to, and pride in, the homeland. It is usually very important for the first generation to pass on these emotional sentiments as well as Moroccan cultural and religious values to their children, as one respondent was keen to tell me:

At the end of the day, we belong to another culture and we have to be proud of what we are. [...] Believe me that I am one hundred percent Moroccan, one hundred percent Moroccan Arab in terms of the way I dress, the way how I eat, the way how I speak to people. I've got the principles about the way I believe. [...] If you are Moroccan you have to show people what you are, what is your civilization, what is your culture (F-G, M, 43, London, 2008-02-28).[8]

Moroccans born in Britain often feel torn between at least two cultures. First, there is the pressure from their parents to conform to Moroccan and Muslim cultural and religious norms, which are often the norms that their parents grew up with several decades previously while still in Morocco. Secondly, there is a desire to find a sense of belonging within British mainstream youth culture among their peers at school and college. Thirdly, during the annual trips back to Morocco (that usually last for at least six weeks every summer) there is often an expectation that they are returning to their roots, their homeland, or where, at least for their parents, they *really* belong. It is no surprise, therefore, that for British-born Moroccans these various, conflicting expectations and desires can cause some confusion. This was the case when speaking to some second-generation Moroccans:

When it comes to a form I usually put British. How do I feel? Mixed, Moroccan and British. Like for example, I can be here [Britain] all year round. Come the summer, the Moroccan in me starts talking and I have to go to Morocco and I'll be, like, "Oh my god, yes, I'm home, I'm home!" Four weeks will go by and I'll be, like, "Oh no, I miss fish fingers and beans. Get me to an airport!" And when I get home, I feel like "Yes, I'm home, I'm home!" It's confusing (S-G, F, 32, London, 2008-11-19).

For other second-generation Moroccans, spending periods of time in Morocco while growing up has led to a painful realization that they feel less Moroccan than they once did:

We're not Moroccans. We like to think we are, but when we go out there [Morocco] we're different, little things. We realize we're not Moroccan really. I'm talking about the ones that are born and brought up here [Britain]. Our culture is too Westernized. I used to think I was Moroccan-Moroccan, but now I feel more British. It's a different culture and mind-set. I don't fit in there [Morocco]. It's difficult (S-G, F, 29, London, 2007-08-29).

If you grow up outside of Morocco, even if you are one hundred percent Moroccan by blood, when you go to Morocco they know you're not Moroccan by the way you dress, walk, everything. This [Britain] is home now. This is where I belong (S-G, F, 34, 2007-09-20).

As British-born Moroccans have attempted to negotiate these various identities, their relationships with their parents have not always been easy, due to the inevitable clash of cultures. These intergenerational misunderstandings have at times led to anti-social behavior on the part of some British-born Moroccans. In many cases, however, these tensions have led to more positive behavior, as one second-generation male described to me:

I think Moroccan parents are struggling to help their children understand their place in society. We're in different worlds; in many ways a better world than where our parents have come from, but they want to help us find our identity. So sometimes people of my generation are getting into a lot of trouble, hanging out with junkies [drug users] and stuff because maybe they're lost and very disenfranchised from their whole background, their whole cultural heritage. So for me it's been really important to find out where I'm from, saying, "This is what's inside me". My way in was history and Islam[9]. Other people go after money and end up in prison (S-G, M, 35, London, 2007-12-06).

For this young man, along with many other British-born Moroccans, reaching the end of their teenage years coincided with a strong desire to understand Islam better as a way of discovering more about themselves:

I was twenty and I remember people would ask me about Islam and I wouldn't have a clue how to answer them. This didn't sit comfortably with me. I was also feeling a bit empty inside. I felt that there was a void or a gap in myself and I felt I wanted to find out some information about Islam, identity-wise, ethnicity-wise. I think it was more do to with finding out about Islam as a way of life, which then led to me finding out more about myself. [...] It was a case of realizing I'm not white, I'm not English, I don't have an English name, I'm not C of E [Church of England]. Erm, you know, lots of these things make you think, "Well what am I?" (ibid.)

For some British-born Moroccans, forging a religious identity, as opposed to an ethnic one, has, in many ways, been the most pertinent struggle with their parents. They have discovered the need to cultivate a unique identity distinct from their parents' that incorporates British, Moroccan, and Muslim elements, as Cherti has poignantly pointed out:

> Unlike their parents, the second and third generation do not take their status as Muslims for granted. Religion for them not only provides guidance, but is vital to their process of identity construction. [...] For many, the absence of *clear* religious guidance from their parents triggered their interest in learning more about Islam and a desire to go back to the sources of religion (*Quran* and *Sunnah*),[10] instead of basing their beliefs on mere *cultural practices* that they inherited from their parents. [...] The events of 9/11 also contributed indirectly to the eagerness of the younger generation to separate their national, ethnic, and religious identities. For many, there was a subsidiary compulsion; triggered by government responses and the media, they also felt compelled to make a choice and even prioritize which part of their identities mattered most, primarily the British or the Muslim (Cherti, 2008: 248-51).

This desire to rediscover Islam for oneself and the notion that one's upbringing as a Muslim is not adequate, have been a recurring narrative as I have spoken to some British-born Moroccans, as is illustrated in the following example:

> I mean, when I was growing up, Islam wasn't available. Let me give you an example. At the time, I was dressed as a European girl [...] My mum didn't tell me to wear *hijab*. My family around me, that's all we knew. [...] When I was fifteen, I met a revert [a convert to Islam] and she came to me and said, "Where are you from?" I said, "Morocco" and she said, "Are you a Muslim?" [I replied,] "Yes" [she said,] "So, why are you dressed like that?" [I replied,] "Because I'm from Morocco, it's ok to dress like this in Morocco," she said. "But you're a Muslim. You're meant to cover up," I said. "No, no, no. Only the Saudis dress like that." ... But now, in the past ten years, Islam is everywhere. It's on TV, there's talks, scholars talking, you get revert scholars [saying] "I'm a German Muslim", "a Jamaican Muslim", Islam is there. It's on a platter. If you're blind you'll hear it, if you're deaf, you'll see it. It's on TV, on the internet. I put on the Islam channel and learn (S-G, F, 32, London, 2008-11-19).

Discovering a version of Islam that is distinct from their parents' has enabled British-born Muslims to cultivate their own sense of identity, negotiating the Muslim, Moroccan, and British parts. Such identities can, of course, be expressed in many ways, such as through how people dress and behave, what they eat, what school they send their children to, as well as what music they choose or not, to consume. Since music has always had an ambiguous place within Islam, it is perhaps not surprising that it is being used to both divide and define some British-born Moroccans from their parents' generation as well as some of their peers.

MUSIC AND ISLAM

During one of the very first interviews I conducted, a Moroccan community leader gave me some advice as to how I should go about investigating the consumption of music by Moroccans in London. He said to me, "It's better not to ask them about music" (F-G, M, 43, London, 2008-02-28). His advice has remained at the back of my mind since then, often seeming wholly irrelevant as I have met with many Moroccans who are puzzled by the mere notion of music being problematic. But, scattered among those encounters, have been other experiences such as henna, Eid and wedding parties that have allowed me glimpses into the daily lives of Moroccans in London. These narratives about music consumption, however, stand out as evidence of the paradoxes that exist within the community.

Two years later, during a series of percussion workshops I had helped to organize for a Moroccan community oral history project, an encounter with a very young Muslim girl brought home to me, in a particularly striking manner, the problematic nature of music for some Muslims. The workshop took place on a Saturday morning in a secondary school in West London in December 2008. As it happened, the school was also being used by an Arabic supplementary school, which meant that many of the children from the school were able to attend the workshops in their break times. As the children were beginning to gather for the workshop, one young Muslim girl, who was about six years old, approached me to ask if she could join in. I told her she was very welcome. She then asked me what would happen during the workshop and I explained that the musicians would teach the children to play some traditional Moroccan rhythms. "Oh", she said, "well that's music and I'm not allowed to do music" and promptly ran back to her classroom and shut the door behind her. When I contrast this situation with my various trips to Muslim countries during which I have encountered recorded and live music at almost every turn, I am often left feeling somewhat confused. The confusion, however, is not that puzzling since the place of music in Islam has long been contested by scholars:

It is not easy to comprehend how the question [of whether listening to music is lawful or not] arose, seeing that there is not a word of direct censure against music in the *Qur'ān*, and above all, in face of the fact that music was almost an indispensable item in the social life of the Arabs (Farmer, 1929:22).

Farmer is not alone in making that claim since there is general consensus that the Qur'an does not refer explicitly to music. Some of the *ahadith*[11], however, do mention and, at times, condemn music, although, as al-Faruqi points out, "Of the many collections of *ahadīth* that can be used for documentation, not all are equally qualified to gain either Muslim or scholarly respect for accuracy" (1985: 4). Al-Faruqi's use of the word "accuracy" in this quotation is not necessarily very helpful, since the various *ahadith* have different authors, some of whom are more or less respected than others. For this reason, it is not so much a matter of accuracy, but rather of interpretation and application, since there are many different opinions as to how the *adhadith* that do refer to music should be understood and put into practice.

Despite this ambiguity, the four main Islamic legal schools[12] have all stated that music is *haram* (illegitimate), although these condemnations have not deterred many scholars from openly disagreeing and attempting to disprove the rulings (Farmer, 1929:29). Furthermore, in terms of this particular discussion on the consumption of music, it is also important to note that the listener of music "has generally been accorded no better or no worse treatment" than the performer, since "both socially and legally, there has been little differentiation between the attitude toward musicians, on the one hand, and listeners or patrons, on the other" (al Faruqi, 1985: 16). Even today, there is considerable disagreement among scholars, clerics and lay Muslims with regard to such matters.

In Britain, for example, the debate on the permissibility (or otherwise) of music became of increased concern to some Muslim scholars and communities in the mid-1990s when music became a compulsory subject in the National Curriculum. One response to this perceived "crisis" was from the Association of Muslim Researchers who organized a conference in 1993 to discuss the implications of such developments for British Muslim communities (Mayer, 1996). The heated debate has been sustained (Harris, 2006: 14–16). One scholar, who took part in the 2002 discussions and who is often quoted by the British media on issues surrounding Islam in Britain and Europe was Tariq Ramadan, Swiss-born Professor of Islamic Studies currently based at the University of Oxford (Ramadan, 2001, 2004). During the 2002 conference on music and Muslims in schools he summed up the issues surrounding music and Islam as follows:

> I have come to the opinion that there will never be a definite and common answer to this question, and what we have to deal with is the diversity within Muslim cultures (Ramadan, cited in Harris, 2006: 15).

Similarly, another scholar (Schuyler) who has worked on music in various different Muslim contexts has repeatedly pointed out that Muslims "have always been divided in their attitudes towards music" and that the debate "has never been a simple dispute between right-thinking religious notables and low-class degenerates; rather, the division runs through all levels of society" (Schuyler, 1990: 4).

These inconsistent views can be further illustrated by interposing the voices of some young British Moroccans. One second-generation Moroccan male, for example, remembers the rather ambiguous place that music had in his home as he grew up:

> It was strange, because when we were young and growing up, music per se, whether it was English, Moroccan, Arabic, anything, was seen as quite, what's the word? Erm, just not to listen to it, because it was seen as taboo, just a bit rebellious. It's hard to explain because I don't think it was ever explained to us really. You could now and again listen to very traditional classical music maybe, not too loud (S-G, M, 31, London, 2009-03-31).

A second-generation female, on the other hand, grew up with quite an opposite attitude towards music present:

> Music is not a problem in my family. On my dad's side it's probably more problematic to listen to religious music! There's never been, like, "don't listen to this, because it's bad!" (S-G, F, 26, London, 2008-11-01).

Consuming Anasheed in London

To continue this discussion, I return again to the advice I received at the beginning of my research: "It's better not to ask them about music", to which my interviewee then added, "If I were you, I'd start with *anasheed*" (F-G, M, 43, London, 2008-02-28). *Anasheed* (sing. *nasheed*, literally "to recite") are Islamic songs, which have traditionally been performed for religious ceremonies (such as for births and deaths) as well as for patriotic occasions. In the past ten years or so, the term *anasheed* has been most closely associated with a movement of new Islamic songs with a much broader lyrical content addressing many contemporary issues from an Islamic standpoint. This movement is part of the broader "Islamic Revival" or "Islamic Awakening" (*al-Sahwa al-Islamiyya*) that has swept the Muslim world since at least the 1970s (Mahmood, 2005: 3). In terms of style and presentation, many contemporary *nasheed* artists market their songs for a young Muslim audience, blending traditional *nasheed* lyrics with various elements from pop to hip-hop. For a song to be classified as *anasheed*, it is generally agreed by such artists (as well as many of the consumers of such songs that I have spoken to) that the song must either be entirely unaccompanied ("a cappella") or else employ only un-tuned percussion instruments, since the use of melodic instruments is considered by some to be prohibited (*haram*). Unravelling this second piece of advice is helpful in further understanding the complexities within the debate. At its heart, I would argue, is the ambiguity surrounding the terminology, epistemology, and ontology of the word "music".

The Arabic word *mūsīqā*, for example, is not synonymous with the English word music. The term is borrowed from the Greek and refers "to musical practices imported into Islamic societies" (Bohlman 2002:8). According to al-Faruqi, "in most instances, it [*mūsīqā*] applies only to certain secular musical genres" (1985: 6). Al-Faruqi's definition is adhered to by Nettl, who also adds to it by stating that *mūsīqī* (the equivalent term used in Iran) refers to instrumental music rather than vocal music and to "metric, composed sounds more than the non-metric and improvised" (Nettl, 2009: Section II. Part 3). Nooshin has pointed out, however, that in Iran, although instruments are considered inappropriate in religious settings, it is in fact the voice that is far more problematic, at least for women, since solo female singers are prohibited from performing to mixed audiences by the Iranian government. Female instrumentalists on the other hand are becoming increasingly more widespread and popular (Nooshin, personal correspondence: 2009). I include this point to illustrate the contradictions and diversity of opinions and experiences that exist and to highlight the importance of addressing such paradoxes.

It is clear, therefore, that the English word "music" and the European-American concept of music are not universally applicable but are, rather, culture-specific. Indeed, music's epistemology (or ability "to be part of culture as a whole" (Bohlman 2002: 5)), and ontology ("properties of being a part of a lived-in-world" (ibid.)) vary enormously from culture to culture. In this way, it is vital that music is understood within its cultural context. For, as Ian Cross has pointed out, "Music can only make sense as music if we can resonate with the histories, values, conventions, institutions, and technologies that enfold them" (2003: 19). The values that enfold music in the Muslim world are of great importance when trying to understand what does and does not constitute music, since "Each culture decides what it will and will not call music; sound patterns, as well as behavior, which fall outside these norms are either unacceptable or are simply defined as something other than music" (Merriam, 1964: 27).

Ethnomusicologists such as Merriam have, of course, long debated the nature of music and music making[13] and it is interesting to apply some of their definitions to the notion of *anasheed*. If for example, we take Blacking's definition of music as "humanly organized sound" (1973:3), or Nettl's definition of music as "human sound communication outside the scope of spoken language" (1983: 24), it is clear that *anasheed* does comply with at least some ethnomusicological understandings of music. However, due to the religious nature of *anasheed* and the lack of melodic instruments there within, some Muslims (including many British-born Moroccan Muslims I have spoken to) would not consider these to be music.

In her article on "Music, Musicians and Muslim Law", al-Faruqi refers her readers to a hierarchy of *handasah al sawt* ("sound art expression" or "literally artistic engineering of sound"), which she believes is implied within the Muslim world (1985: 7). Within this hierarchy different musical genres are ordered according to their legitimacy and "'appreciability'", with Qur'anic recitation sitting at the top of the hierarchy (ibid: 13). She states that the closer a musical genre is to Qur'anic recitation in terms of its musical, poetic, or religious inspiration, the more appreciated and legitimate (*halal*) the genre is. Furthermore, those genres that are closest to Qur'anic recitation are categorized as "non-*mūsīqā*", whereas those genres further away are considered as "*mūsīqā*" and range from controversial to illegitimate (*harām*) (ibid.). For those Muslims who adhere to this hierarchy *anasheed* is therefore considered to be *halal* since its religious (and sometimes poetic and musical) inspiration is close to Qur'anic chant. It is important to note, however, that al-Faruqi's understanding of *mūsīqā* is by no means shared by all Muslims, which will become apparent as I turn now to explore specific contemporary case studies of young British-Moroccans and their consumption of different types of *anasheed* and Islamic songs.

Music Consumption, Devotion and Religiosity amongst Young Moroccans in London
A number of second-generation Moroccans that I have met have experienced fairly dramatic changes in their listening habits over the years. Such experiences have usually occurred during their early twenties and often due to their changing perceptions of Islam and the consequent impact on their behaviour and outlook on life. One second-generation female, for example, explained to me that in the past few years she has tried to stop listening to most types of music and prefers to consume *anasheed* and Qur'anic recitation.

> Listening to *anasheed* is good. More uplifting, more calming, you know. The best thing for me is the *Qur'an* ... You don't get any bad feelings (S-G, F, 28, London, 2008-11-19).

When I asked her why she had made this change in her listening habits, she responded:

> I think it's more because of me trying to become a proper Muslim and trying to go about my religion the right way and that's why I'm going into it. [...] I like the fact of my religion and I think if I can put myself towards the right way then it'd be good for me. I'm going step by step in the right direction (ibid.).

For many respondents, music has been an important part of life while growing up in London. One second-generation female told me that, as a child and young teenager, she adored British and American bands such as the Beatles, the Bay City Rollers and the Osmonds. At school she learnt all instruments available to her and joined music ensembles and choirs. While she was in her mid teens, her older brother started playing in a band, which performed songs of contemporary and revolutionary Moroccan bands such as Nass el Ghiwane and Jil Jillala. She found herself drawn to this music in a powerful way. As a result she started listening to Moroccan music with greater interest and eagerness. At around the same time, she also grew to appreciate Moroccan *chaabi* (popular music) through attending Moroccan weddings and parties in West London as well as during her summer holidays in Morocco. She was brought up as a Muslim and, as a teenager, started wearing the *hijab* (headscarf), while dressing in modest but Western-style clothing, much like many of the other Moroccan girls she knew in London. In her early twenties she married another British-born Moroccan man and soon grew close to her new sisters-in-law, all of whom had also been born in London. Upon returning from honeymoon, she was extremely surprised to discover that they had recently decided to stop listening to music entirely and had thrown away all of their CDs and cassettes. This, they explained to her, was due to fresh insights and knowledge about Islam, which they had learned from Muslim scholars on satellite Islamic television stations. All they would now listen to was *anasheed*, since they did not consider this to be music.

This radical change in behaviour was initially shocking and incomprehensible to this young woman, who loved music and had no desire to stop listening. However, over a period of time various incidents – such as her CD player "blowing up" when she tried to listen to a recently purchased CD of Canadian pop singer Celine Dion – forced her to accept the change. Another episode was associated with a powerful dream based on one of the *sura* (chapters) of the Qur'an. Both these rather mysterious episodes were seen by her as a divine or spiritual message or reckoning. From then on, her life was rearranged. She no longer attended parties where secular music was played. She give away all her CDs and cassettes of secular music. Her change in listening habits also coincided with her decision to start wearing *niqab* and *burqa*. In her case this consisted of wearing a loose-fitting ankle-length garment over her house clothes and covering all of her face except her eyes. As she started to attend parties and weddings where *anasheed* were sung, she was pleasantly surprised at how much she enjoyed them and at how much fun everyone was having (despite the lack of secular music). Soon she started to compose some *anasheed* songs together with her sisters-in-law, which they began to perform at Muslim weddings across London, accompanied by Moroccan frame-drums and goblet-drums. These occasions were, unsurprisingly, segregated, all-female events, which were attended by Muslims not only of Moroccan, but also Algerian, Tunisian, and South Asian background. In this way, she felt she was beginning to connect with a multi-ethnic British-Muslim community, where religious commitment and belief were the binding force, rather than any ethnic, national, or cultural affiliation.

Her mother, on the other hand, whose understanding and way of practicing Islam was entirely bound up with her cultural identity as a Moroccan, was left baffled by her daughter's behaviour. She saw her own devotion to Moroccan music as part of her religious as well as her cultural heritage. This is how her daughter described her reaction to me:

Even my mum when I started listening to *anasheed*, she wanted to play her *chaabi* in the house, and I said "No Mum, don't listen to this" and she would say "ah, you're born yesterday, you're teaching me, telling me what to do. What do you know? What do you know? You're bringing me this new rubbish!" I say, "Mum this is really tranquil, it's bringing you words of Allah in your home." "All right, all right" [she said]. But then again, when she's in a bad mood and she just wants something to cheer her up, she'll just put on a Moroccan tape of *chaabi*. And I say, "Why does *chaabi* make you cheer up? Why can't you put on *anasheed* and it'll mention Allah and it'll put a calmness in your heart, tranquillity, it'll make you be forgiving, you don't need to feel this anger." She just looks and says "Ok, ok, just leave me. Whatever!" And I just let her because she's old, I can't make her (S-G, F, 34, London, 2008-11-19).

Tariq Ramadan has also commented on the intergenerational tensions that can occur between first and second generations as they define and articulate their own notion of being a Muslim in the West:

Parents who saw their children losing, or no longer recognizing themselves as part of, their Pakistani, Arab, or Turkish [*or Moroccan*] culture seemed to think that they were losing their religious identity at the same time. However, this was far from being the case: many young Muslims, by studying their religion, claimed total allegiance to Islam while distancing themselves from their cultures of origin. [...] This awareness and the birth of a new understanding of Islam marks the period of transition we are experiencing today, and it is inevitably difficult, even impossible, for parents of the first generation to cope with (Ramadan, 2004: 215, words in square brackets mine).

Another second-generation female articulated to me her desire to distance herself from her culture of origin in terms of her music consumption. She also revealed the internal struggles she has faced in so doing:

Now I'm older, I only want to listen to *anasheed*. We [her and her husband] haven't said it's wrong, we must shun all types of music, but we just haven't felt we want to [listen to music] any more. It's difficult though. I was born here, but I'm Moroccan. I'm used to listening to Moroccan music. Moroccan music gets in your blood, it flows through your body and it's very difficult to switch off and say, "Right! I'm only going to listen to *anasheed*" [...] Music can either divert you from your path or take you to your path ... Music is a powerful force (S-G, F, 32, London, 2007-09-20).

From Anasheed to Hip-Hop and Ladbroke Grove to the Transnational Ummah
The growth of satellite television and the internet as media with which to access

anasheed and other Muslims songs does not only provide easy access to indulge ones desires in such outlets. Many British-born Moroccans have discovered that what they choose to listen to can be a way of connecting them to a transnational community of Muslims or *ummah*. An effort is made in this final section to explore some of the *anasheed* and other artists that are most popular among the British-born Moroccans.

Anasheed and Transitional Networks

In October 2007, I attended an Eid party, celebrating the end of Ramadan. This was organized by one of the mosques near the Golborne Road for children, mainly of Moroccan origin, who attend one of the many Arabic supplementary schools in the area. When I arrived, the party was already in full swing. The children, aged five to eleven, were playing musical chairs with great energy and competitiveness. The music being played from the stereo and which continued for the whole afternoon was the latest children's album by Yusuf Islam, formerly and more widely known as Cat Stevens. Yusuf Islam was born in central London in 1948, of Greek Cypriot and Swedish ancestry and converted to Islam in 1977. This particular album, entitled *I look I see* (2006, Jamal Records)[14], is marketed as *anasheed* by various Islamic websites that sell *anasheed* products. This label has been confirmed to me by those who consume the songs. The reason they give is that the lyrics encourage children to be good Muslims, as well as the lack of melodic instruments. It should be noted, however, that some of the accompanying digitally produced percussion is, in fact, tuned and fairly melodic sounding, although this has not made the songs problematic in any way for my respondents. The songs are sung by Yusuf Islam and friends (both adults and children), predominantly in English with some Arabic interspersed. In between each song, there is a short educative speech given in English by a woman to the children on the album as if they are in a classroom setting. These sections teach the children about basic Islamic principles, and these lessons are then repeated during the songs. Stylistically (harmonically, melodically, and rhythmically) the majority of the songs are most closely affiliated to styles of European-American art music. These musical and stylistic choices reflect Yusuf Islam's musical background, as a European performer as well as his desire to reach an audience of Anglophone Muslims whether European or American converts or the offspring of Muslim migrants in Anglophone countries.

As I have attended various Arabic supplementary schools and children's Eid parties, visited people's homes and spoken with children and their parents, it has become evident that Yusuf Islam is one of the most popular *nasheed* artists, his children's albums[15] being eagerly and widely consumed by Moroccan families I have met across London. As young families of second- and third-generation Moroccans consume such songs, with their European-American harmonies and predominantly English lyrics sung by Anglophone *nasheed* singers, they are perhaps expressing a religious identity quite distinct from their parents, which owes far more to

European Anglophone artistic cultures than Muslim societies. In one sense, this may be understood as a way of articulating their identities in a manner that makes more sense of their everyday experiences, as Philip Lewis has also observed:

> A new generation of Muslims is [sic] searching for expressions of Islam which can connect with their lived experience as British Muslims whose first language is English. In short, Islam has had to become self-conscious and articulate in a new and bewildering culture which owes little or nothing to it (2007: xvii).

Converts to Islam, such as Yusuf Islam, Dawud Wharnsby-Ali and Hamza Robertson are playing an important role in articulating a form of Islam that is genuinely meaningful to British-born Muslims and the situations they face. Yusuf Islam is a particularly interesting example because, soon after his conversion in 1977, he made the decision to stop making and performing music:

> I have suspended my activities in music for fear that they may divert me from the true path, but I will not be dogmatic in saying that I will never make music again. You cannot say that without adding "Insha Allah" [God willing] (Islam, 2009: http://www.mountainoflight.co.uk/ , accessed 2009-10-04).

Over the years, however, Islam's objections to the use of music and songs "gradually softened" (ibid.) due to various events. One of these was the horrific genocide in Bosnia in 1992, out of which came many *nasheed* songs composed locally to inspire and motivate Bosnians during the troubles. Through this experience, Yusuf came to realize that his own musical gifts and songs could also help and inspire people and "show Muslims and non-Muslims the transcendent beauty and light of Islam" (ibid.). His children's albums have not been particularly controversial within the Muslim community due to their lack of instrumental accompaniment, despite the melodic nature of some of the percussion. Some of his other albums, however, make use of melodic instruments[16] and it has been these that have caused more controversy, which he has addressed in articles and songs. Due to the problematic nature of music within Islam, it is of course inevitable that Muslim singers who choose to use melodic instruments in their songs will face a certain amount of criticism from some Muslims. Even the most popular of contemporary Muslim singers, Sami Yusuf, is not impermeable to such attacks. His songs have perhaps done more than any other Muslim singer to change attitudes and unite Muslims worldwide as regards the permissibility of music for Muslims.

Sami Yusuf has been hailed in the Anglophone media as "The king of Islamic pop" (Al-Jazeera, 2009.02.12), "Islam's biggest rock star" (Wise, 2006.07.31), "the biggest name in Muslim music – anywhere" (Brown, 2007.10.03) and even "the voice of Islam" (ibid.). His first two albums (*Al-Mu'allim*, 2003 and *My Ummah*, 2005, both released with the Muslim label Awakening Worldwide Ltd) have sold over five million copies (Al-Jazeera, 2009.02.12). Yusuf has performed all over the world, his largest audience totaling 250,000 in Istanbul in 2007 (http://www.samiyusufofficial.com/?page_id=12, accessed April 2009). He was born in Tehran, Iran, in 1980 to Azeri parents, with whom he moved to West London at the age of three, where he grew up and was educated, including a short period at the prestigious Royal Academy of Music in London. Although he currently lives between Cairo, London, and Stockport (northern England), he has a strong sense of home: "For me, home is the UK, home is England, home is London" (Brown, 2007.10.03). He is also keen to identify himself as a British Muslim who seeks much of his inspiration from the East, as he told a British journalist in an interview in 2006: "I am proud to be Muslim and British and to be living and learning in Cairo. I see no contradiction in these identities" (Rahman, 2006.04.27). As such, Yusuf has also been described as having a good claim to be "the most famous British Muslim in the world" (Edermariam, 2007.11.05). Indeed, he was listed as one of the world's top 1000 influential Muslims in the recent study conducted by Georgetown University. He saw his sell-out charity concert at Wembley Stadium in October 2007, in aid of the crisis in Darfur (Sudan), as symbolizing "the true spirit of the British public, and among them the British Muslims" (ibid.).

Among the 10,000 strong audience at Wembley arena were some British-born Moroccan fans. Speaking to them about the event, many pointed out that his songs are popular with all generations of Muslims. The American journalist, Lindsay Wise, concurs:

His screaming fans include not just star-struck young women in head scarves, but teenage boys in blue jeans and gelled hair, old men in traditional Arab robes, and middle-aged moms bouncing toddlers on their knees (2006.07.31).

While in conversation about music and Islam with various British-born Moroccans, Sami Yusuf's songs have often been cited to me as examples of music that are not only acceptable but also well-loved, despite their controversial use of melodic instruments:

But since Sami Yusuf's come out, on the piano, everybody in the beginning was, like, "ah Sami Yusuf's really great" but he started gradually bringing in, each time, other instruments. So there's this debate: "No, don't listen to Sami Yusuf because it's got too much instruments ... oh, bla bla bla bla, oh bla bla bla bla" But I got to the stage where, you know what? If it's got really good words, it's sending a message, I don't care what he's playing. I don't care what drums, what instruments he's using. He's using very good words, he's done a song about the prophet, about love your mother, obey your mother. The words! So I've got to the stage where, I'm like, I don't care what instruments they use as long as the words are clean, nothing to do with love (S-G, F, 34, London, 2008-11-19).

Yusuf himself is clearly aware of the controversies that surround his music. For this reason he released two versions of his second album, *My Ummah*: one with melodic instruments and the other with only percussion instruments. When questioned about his views on music and Islam, Yusuf has tended to avoid the question, focusing on the positive qualities of both music and Islam: "But music is a universal language which has united people for thousands of years and will continue to keep doing so" (Brown, 2007.10.03); and "Islam is all for modernity and all that is good and beautiful in this world" (Wise, 2006.07.31). Furthermore, Yusuf himself does not wish to be seen as a religious singer, despite the fact that he is perceived and labeled as one by the media and his fans:

> "I never intended to be a clean-cut singer, a Muslim singer or a religious singer. All I ever wanted to do was make good music. I have an issue with being labelled a religious singer," he says. "I see myself as an artist who is versatile and who sings about whatever inspires him" (Brown, 2007.10.03).

So what is it exactly that has made Yusuf so popular among Muslims across the globe? The instrumentation, vocal and instrumental techniques, tonality, melody, harmony, and rhythm of his compositions draw on Arab, Persian, Turkish, Indian, and European-American musical traditions. The principal language used in his songs is English, but he also sings in many other languages, such as Arabic, Farsi, Hindi, Turkish, and Urdu.

Take, for example, his hit single, *Hasbi Rabbi* (My Lord is Sufficient), from his best-selling album, *My Ummah* (My Community of Believers). The song opens in English, and has verses in Arabic, Turkish, and Hindi, whilst the accompanying video is set in central London, around the Hagia Sofia mosque in Istanbul, the pyramids in Egypt and the Taj Mahal in India. The musical references are equally as diverse. The lyrics though are simply a song in praise of and supplication to Allah. Yusuf's other songs are equally diverse in their musical referencing and choice of languages. They also address many themes ranging from loving one's mother and celebrating Eid, to supporting oppressed Muslims around the world, and condemning acts of extremism and terrorism conducted in the name of Islam.

When British-born Moroccan Muslims choose to listen to the songs of Sami Yusuf, describing him as "absolutely superb" (S-G, F, 34, London, 2008-11-19) and his music as "phenomenal ... it moves people ... it's like a bulldozer" (S-G, F, 31, London, 2007-09-20), they are joining millions of other Muslims from all over the world. Yusuf is a British Muslim, but this is not why he is popular with many British-born Moroccans. Indeed, some of those I interviewed were not even aware that he grew up in London and is a British citizen. Yusuf is perhaps more representative of a transnational or global Islam than he is of a British Islam since he draws his musical inspiration from all over the Muslim world as well as from European traditions. The subjects of his lyrics are relevant and appealing to

Muslims the world over, to such an extent that they draw in audience members who might otherwise dismiss his songs as *haram* due to his use of melodic instruments. His use of multiple languages widens his appeal yet further. By identifying with the songs of Sami Yusuf, British-born Moroccans could be understood to be connecting with a transnational community of Muslims, or *ummah*, which defies national, ethnic, and often generational boundaries.

In response to these music consumption choices by some second- and third-generation Moroccans, a number of first-generation Moroccans have expressed concerns that the younger generations are abandoning their Moroccan cultural and religious heritage, which is also causing divisions and tensions within the community:

> When religion comes before the music, you're talking about a religious identity and not a cultural identity. Because the religion will only make you a Muslim, but the culture will make you a Moroccan and I think there's a big difference between the two. [...] In the end, the only thing about you that is Moroccan is your name. [...] They listen to Islamic music – *anasheed* and so forth – but that's religious music, it has no link to Morocco, it could be any country in the world, but you wouldn't be feeling Moroccan, you'd be feeling Muslim, it's not the same thing. [...] Morocco has its own Islam which is a mixture of local traditions with Islam and it gives it a very much more flexible character ... they may feel relaxed listening to *chaabi* in Morocco, but they wouldn't listen to it here [in Britain]. Now, with 9/11 and the war on terror, so many Moroccans are becoming more Muslim. They're going back. They believe their plight is because they're far from their religion so they're going back to what they believe to be its roots. They say Islam transcends boundaries – ethnicities and nationalities. That could be the end of Moroccan music, unless people don't become so extreme. How to get to the middle ground? (F-G, M, 34, London 2008-12-11).

> It's quite sad that we [the Moroccan community in London] have adopted an understanding of Islam that's not necessarily Moroccan. And that I find quite concerning [...] Music can unite people across many boundaries, but religious ones, no, because unfortunately, and I say quite clearly and loudly, unfortunately, some of the Muslim community generally I think has adopted a much more, it's almost like born-again approach. I don't want to use the born-again Christian syndrome, but we have it, and so you probably wouldn't have them in any gathering that has music anyway, so I think they are excluded in that sense (F-G, F, 44, London, 2008-12-04).

It is perhaps not surprising that such divisions and tensions exist within the community as its individual members try to construct and negotiate their own identities in varying and often contrasting ways. But I would also add that I have not observed any examples of total disengagement from Moroccan culture or music by the younger members of the community. Indeed, among the third generation, many of whom take their Muslim identity very seriously, certain genres of Moroccan music form an important part of the contents of their iPods. Take, for example, a henna party I attended in October 2008, organised for a six-teen-year-old bride of Algerian background on the eve of her wedding day, by a Moroccan family in their council-rented flat in West London. The majority of the guests were girls of Moroccan background (third generation) between the ages of fifteen and nineteen, as well as some of Algerian and Palestinian background. Also present were some of the girls' mothers (second generation) and grand-mothers (first generation). In charge of the music was a sixteen-year-old third-generation Moroccan girl, whose iPod was linked up to the hi-fi in the corner of the room. While the older generations were present in the room, the young DJ played a selection of Moroccan *chaabi*, Moroccan wedding music (such as the very popular *daqqa marakchya*), Moroccan hip-hop as well as some American Islamic rap. When the older women left the room to eat, she changed the music to contemporary British and American R&B and the younger girls all leapt up and started dancing with great enthusiasm. It was at this point that the host (a second-generation Moroccan woman) tried to get hold of the iPod and change the music. She told me later, "I was like 'You're in my territory now' and everybody knows what comes out of this house – my mum, you know. And then you've got all of this kind of music on and I was like 'No, don't! I've got a reputation to keep up!' I kept saying to them" (F-G, F, 43, London, 2008-11-19).

Intergenerational differences such as these are by no means unique to the Moroccan community in London. I draw attention to this example, however, in order to illustrate the differences that exist between the discourses on music and Islam and the reality of what is consumed and how this is justified in conversations. Sami Yusuf's songs, as illustrated above, have played a key role in changing attitudes towards music, due to his use of Islamic or Islamically inspired lyrics. This attitude is also evident in the popularity of rap and hip-hop music by third-generation Moroccans. Whilst in conversation with British-born Moroccan teenagers, I have discovered a general consensus that rap and hip-hop are by far the most popular genres of music with this generation, which again is not unique to this community. However, when asked which groups are the most popular with these particular young people, there are two groups that seem to continuously recur in conversation. These are the African-American group Native Deen and the Moroccan group Fnaire.

Native Deen market themselves as a *nasheed* group and only use percussion instruments, which they say is "in line with the majority Muslim opinion on the use of musical instruments" (http://www.nativedeen.com/, accessed April 2009) Their latest album, *I Am Not Afraid To Stand Alone* (2007, no label), however, makes heavy use of digitally produced tuned (melodic) percussion such as vibra-phone and steel pan, such that the overall effect of their songs is, at times, very melodic. Their lyrics address issues facing Muslims living in the United States, encouraging positive behaviour and keeping the faith despite the challenges faced. According to the teenagers I have met, Native Deen are popular due to the "good beats" (T-G, M, 16, London, 2008-11-19) they use, but they also mention the "good, clean lyrics" (ibid.), which are in English and deal with some of the same issues facing British Muslims also belonging to an ethnic minority. The fact that hip-hop as a genre has, at least in the past, been closely associated with US cultural hegemony, as well as messages of anti-establishment and often violent behaviour, does not seem of relevance or importance to the third-generation Moroccans. Some second-generation Moroccans, however, have been more aware and weary of these associations: "Native Deen – I don't like it. It's a bit fake. I dunno, it's like it wants to be hip-hop but at the same time it wants to bring an anti hip-hop message" (S-G, M, 32, London, 2009-03-31). Tariq Ramadan has also criticised such expressions of Islam due to the messages that are often implied when parts of contemporary culture are "Islamized":

> Muslims of today must not become imitators of the fashions of the day or be satisfied with the law of least resistance by contenting themselves with "Islamizing" whatever "goes" commercially. [...] in numerous Muslims gatherings, the bands, the varieties of music, and the types of presentation are pure reproductions of what one might see on television or at some young people's parties. The event has been "Islamized", that is to say, made permissible (*halal*), without any great concern for the implicit messages conveyed by this so-called substitute (*badil*) culture (2004: 222).

Interestingly, the other group that has currently caught the imagination of third-generation Moroccans in London is Fnaire, who are not part of the Islamic pop, hip-hop or *anasheed* movement. Fnaire is a Marrakech-based hip-hop group, whose latest album, *Yed El Henna* (*The hand of henna*, 2007, Platinum Music Company) fuses traditional Berber musical styles, harmonies, and instrumentation with hip-hop beats based on Moroccan rhythms. They sing in *darija* (Moroccan Arabic), Berber, Spanish, Dutch, English, and French and their lyrics aim "to educate and inform Moroccan citizens mainly", spanning "citizenship, culture, the new moudawana of Women Rights, safe driving, HIV, the sense of country belonging" (http://www.myspace.com/fnairemaroc, accessed April 2009). Although the lyrics are not specifically Islamic, they are nonetheless considered to be *halal* by the second- and third-generation Moroccans I have interviewed due to their positive and educative messages – another reason, I have been informed, that the group is so popular. Indeed, Fnaire songs were the most played and most enthusiastically received at the parties and gatherings of third-generation Moroccans I have attended. British-Moroccan teenagers at such events consider Fnaire to be the best type of hip-hop around – far better than hip-hop coming out of the US.

CONCLUSIONS

During my research I have been privy to various discussions – between and among different generations of Moroccans – on the acceptability of certain songs, artists, or groups in relation to Islamic cultural norms. Such discourses and consumption choices can be understood, in the words of Hirschkind, as ways in which consumers are honing "an ethically responsive sensorium", which enable them "to live as devout Muslims in a world increasingly ordered by secular rationalities" (Hirschkind, 2001: 624). Being an "ethical listener" can take various forms. Some choose to stop consuming all "music", preferring to listen only to *tajweed* and *anasheed*. Others choose to consume artists who market themselves as *anasheed* singers such as Native Deen and Yusuf Islam, or else Muslim pop, such as Sami Yusuf. These artists, it should be noted, are contributing to a sort of commodification of Islam, which is enabling the consumers to "identify with a set of cultural and religious practices in ways that are different from their parents – and are hip to the popular and the commercial" (Clark, 2007: 23). Others choose to consume much more widely in terms of musical genre and style and justify their consumption choices by pointing to the content of the lyrics and the positive effect of the music on their behavior. For as Gazzah has pointed out, the issue is just as much to do with where and how music is performed or consumed as it is with what is performed or consumed (2008: 155).

This article, then, has examined music consumption (and the surrounding narratives and observations) by a small number of pious British-born Moroccan Muslims and, as such, has shed light on experiences of "selves-in-process" (Frith, 1996: 109). By placing this exploration within the context of contemporary discourses on British Muslim identity, I have also tried to bring fresh insights to this ongoing and complex discussion. As a largely invisible minority ethnic group within British society, young Moroccans are choosing to express their distinctive identities in multiple ways – music consumption being one of these. The examination of four different artists/groups, as highlighted to me by British-Moroccan young people during fieldwork, has revealed trends in listening habits that point to the importance of not only the ethnic, national, and cultural, but also the religious in terms of how choices are made. By using empirical data as a way of structuring my argument, I have also focused on the interesting and fluid term *anasheed*, which has emerged as a floating signifier, being interpreted differently to fit with various discourses within the debate on music in Islam and according to the needs and wants of different artists and consumers. The debate will no doubt continue but I hope that this article has brought fresh insights to the many complexities at play as young Moroccans in London consume or choose not to consume music in its various forms. Young Muslims of Moroccan origin face many challenges as they try to construct for themselves a distinctive identity and their music consumption, as one of many indicators, points to their connections with evolving transnational communities of both Muslims and Moroccans.

NOTES

1   For purposes of analysis, it is necessary to distinguish between three generations. By first generation, I mean those Moroccans born in Morocco, who migrated to the UK. Second-generation Moroccans are the children of the first generation; the third generation are the children of the second generation. I.e. both the second and third generations are born in Britain.

2   This data was collected during fieldwork conducted between October 2006 and May 2009 for my PhD. My doctoral research (more broadly) examined the relationship between ethnomusicology sound archives and ethnic minority diasporic communities whose musical heritage is represented on the recordings held by archives in the countries where they have settled. My case studies for the research were the Moroccan music recordings held by the British Library Sound Archive and the Moroccan community in London (c.f. Landau, forthcoming).

3   For more information, see http://www.statistics.gov.uk/census2001/census2001.asp and http://www.ons.gov.uk/census/index.html, both accessed April 2009.

4   For more information on the migratory stories of Moroccans across Britain, see the Moroccan Memories in Britain project website: www.moroccanmemories.org.uk, accessed April 2009. See also Cherti (2008) and Change Institute (2009).

5   The Golborne Road is in the northern ward of the Royal Borough of Kensington and Chelsea.

6   The bombings were carried out on London transport (tubes and a bus) during the morning rush hour, killing 52 people and injuring 700.

7   According to its own website, the Muslim Council of Britain is "a national representative Muslim umbrella body with over 500 affiliated national, regional and local organizations, mosques, charities, and schools. The MCB is pledged to work for the common good of society as a whole; encouraging individual Muslims and Muslim organizations to play a full and participatory role in public life" (http://www.mcb.org.uk/aboutmcb.php, accessed April 2009).

8   I have anonymized all citations from second- and third-generation Moroccans for reasons of privacy. F-G = first-generation, S-G = second-generation, T-G = third-generation; this is followed by the gender and age of the interviewee and the location and date of the interview.

9   This interviewee did a BA in Arabic and Islamic Studies at a university in the UK, which included modules in Islamic history.

10 The Qur'an is the Muslim scriptures revealed by Allah to the Prophet Mohammed. The *Sunnah*, meaning custom, are "the habits and religious practice of the Prophet Muhammad, which were recorded for posterity by his companions and family and are regarded as the ideal Islamic norm" (Armstrong, 2000: 174).

11 *Ahadith* (singular, *hadith*): "news, reports. Documented traditions of the teachings and actions of the Prophet Muhammad, which were not in the Qur'an but which were recorded for posterity by his close companions and the members of his family" (Armstrong, 2000: 171).

12 The legal schools (*maddhabi*) are the Hanafi, the Maliki, the Shafii, and the Hanbali (Armstrong, 2000: 55).

13 See, for example, Nettl, 2009: Section II. Part 3; Wade, 2004: 3–6; Bohlman, 2002: 5–9; Cross, 2003: 19; Cook, 1998: 4–6; Blacking & Byron: 1995: 31–53; Nettl, 1983: 15–25; and Merriam, 1964: 27–28.

14 An MP3 version of the album was released in 2003.

15 Yusuf Islam's first children's album was *A is for Allah*, released in 2000 (Mountain of Light). His third children's album, *I look I see 2,* was released in 2008 (Jamal Records).

16 For example, *An Other Cup*, released in 2006 by Ya Records, which was his first solo album since his conversion to Islam using melodic instruments, aimed at non-Muslims as well as Muslims.

Scratch the Past – this is OUR Soundtrack
Hip-Hop in Lebanon

Angie Nassar

I'm throwing ink on paper, because I'm lost in my tears
I'm sticking a pen in the ground, to find my roots
I'm scratching on time, to regain my rights
I'm tearing up the nation that suppressed my childhood
(Rayess Bek, "Khartech 'al Zamann/Scratch on the Past")

Open your ears to hear with your eyes
(Kita' Beirut, "Fi 'alam/There are People")

Anchored in specific historical circumstances, the production and practice of music can reveal various "truths" reverberating from the social order. In our sonic terrain, rhythm harnesses soul, timbre attaches to emotion, and voice – the psychic prophet of infinite imagination – projects "self" across the soundscape. These "truths" are not fixed or absolute, rather, shifting intimations of consciousness that elaborate on the ways in which music can translate into cultural space and generate meaning and possibility.

With allegorical charm, the streets of Beirut profess a daily "culture of war." The noise of car horns fight sonic battles against the violent roar of oversized SUVs. Blaring radios combat the clamoring rush of motorbikes. Wayward taxis concede to courageous pedestrians clamoring for equal urban utterance. Fireworks, lit with playful intent, reignite the aural memory of moments when war rang out with unpredictable alarm in Lebanon's streets. Conflict – as the country's hip-hoppers know – comes with a soundtrack.

Every type of music describes a certain geography, a certain way of life, a certain vision ... What I like about hip hop: it reflects the real urban life, like modern poetry ... From hip hop and its lyrics you can discover secrets of life and society. (Rapper Ramcess).

Listen closely, and you'll hear the sounds of cultural production flowing from the Palestinian Bourj al-Barajneh refugee camp, gliding over the valley of the Bekaa, echoing against Tripoli's Mediterranean port and drumming through the streets of Hamra. This soundscape, constructed in music and narrated in performance, tunes into pleasure, amplifies cries of pain, and in moments of palpable desperation, draws out the silence.

> Every day they try to shut me down
> A lot of you listen to me
> But you are still asking me
> Why I'm speaking in silence
> (Rayess Bek, "'am Beheki Bil Sokout/I'm Speaking in Silence")

In Lebanon's cultural politics of music, hip-hop emerges as an instrument for contesting inherited forms of meaning. It socializes alternative discourse – with its own ideological terms, creative yearnings and lexicon of ideas – into the public sphere. Perhaps only a small interruption against the repetitive, exacting beats of the social order, but this is not about volume or even flow. It is about testing the limits and pushing the boundaries of what is considered acceptable. Hip-hop in Lebanon emerges as a space of possibility, where political bargaining and moral contestation are summoned in defense of the self, and in defense of real and imagined communities. Here, rappers situate themselves in relation to others based on their own laws of cultural capital, not the classifying norms of the dominant social arrangement. And in a country where the inclination to categorize – based on sect, family, religion, political affiliation, and social status – is instant and pervasive, this freedom to forge unique identities that defy stereotypes and promote dialogue is significant. Yet musical genres, as Adorno (1976: 69) said, carry the contradictory tendencies of society as a whole. There are a number of hip-hop "territories" in Lebanon, and they often coalesce at the juncture where youth demand a new definition of group solidarity. They disavow the sectarian-communal mechanisms of the political and social system, and they refuse conventional forms of identity branding. But amending what rappers profess with how they interact in the creation of a distinct hip-hop community, or in this case, communities, reveals that some of these young people remain caught up in redefining a system that they often loudly reject. Still, we cannot ignore the complex processes of how youth in Lebanon are working out "who" and "how" they want to be in the language of a hybrid, glocal form such as hip-hop. With alternative style and an admittedly irreverent approach to scholarship, this essay hopes to deconstruct Lebanon's hip-hop soundscape: disaffection, fragmentation, false consciousness, conflict. It is in this range of sentiments and experiences that youth can realize what they lack, but it is precisely what they lack that drives them in the search for wholeness. In perhaps small, but no less meaningful moments hip-hop seeks to challenge the parameters of the social order. In this essential respect, life for these young people might be occasionally resisted, and identity re-assembled.

HIP-HOP AND THE PRODUCTION OF MEANING

Popular music is nothing if not dialogic, the product of an ongoing historical conversation in which no one has the first or last word. The traces of the past that pervade the popular music of the present amount to more than mere chance:

> they are not simply juxtapositions of incompatible realities. They reflect a dialogic process, one embedded in collective history and nurtured by the ingenuity of artists interested in fashioning icons of opposition (Lipsitz, 1990: 99).

> The thing about hip-hop that people keep forgetting, is that it's not just one definite thing. It's a lot of things, different sounds, different styles, different feelings. You can basically do with it what you want. (Bennett interview, 2004: 188).

Debates over the substance and weight of hip-hop are now far removed from academic circles. Hip-hop matters. It connects with youth in a remarkable way and "when virtually nothing else could, hip-hop created a voice and a vehicle for the young and the dispossessed" (Watkins, 2005: 7). The substance of the original hip-hop project was bound to the socio-economic and political context of the time. In the mid-1970s, African-American and Latino youth in New York's South Bronx were part of a disadvantaged minority who faced high unemployment and a flourishing gang culture. They often lived in drug-infested ghettos marred by poverty and social neglect (see Chang, 2005; Cheney, 2005; Rose, 1994). One of hip-hop's founding figures, former gang head Afrika Bambaataa, said he launched his "Zulu Nation" to give those young people a venue for expression; a way to channel anger outside of the urban decay (Lipsitz, 1994, 26). Hip-hop handed down youth the ability to negotiate, and even demand identity in a community whose older support system was becoming increasingly impotent (Rose, 1994: 34). Take note. This was a culture generated in the context of oppression, but bent on resisting it.

The performance of rap and its critical engagement with speech and communication are powerful modes for analyzing how youth produce and practice meaning.[1] Hip-hop is, at a very basic level, a framework for relaying voice. For rapper Bolo-B, "It's freedom. I can say whatever I want." Rap is a blend of vernacular, rhyme and rhythmic speech loosely chanted over a musical soundtrack (based on Keyes' definition, 2002: 1). In its homegrown street-style and verbal slang aesthetic, rap music "speaks to real people in a real language about real things" (Light, 2004: 144). Rappers "represent." They signify. They express a self-defined duty to convey authentic, cultural commentary. In many ways the performance of rap re-defines how music should be dealt with: no longer background noise or a danceable rhythm, but something to actively construct and consciously take part in. Borrowing or "sampling" music from other songs is a key characteristic of the genre. "Hip hoppers stole the music off the air and cut it up ... the cut 'n' mix attitude was that no one owns a rhythm or a sound. You just borrow it, use it and give it back to the people in a slightly different form" (Hebdige, 1987: 141). This license to move across musical boundaries untangles fixed cultural artifacts and liberates rappers from the hegemonic into the hybrid world. Forget anxieties about reaching, grasping for a space in the cultural sphere. This is the process of constructing, transforming, borrowing, taking it all in, and releasing new meaning back into the center.

Scholars say the culture is grounded in African-American oral tradition and verbal-musical forms (Rose, 1994: 95; Keyes, 2004). But decades after it first emerged, different youth from around the world have reworked the language, fashion, and politics of hip-hop in ways that accommodate a local context (Bennett, 2000: 137). It can no longer be thought of as some pure process of cultural retrieval. As Paul Gilroy has noted, "we have to ask how a form which flaunts and glories in its own malleability as well as its transnational character becomes interpreted as an expression of some authentic African-American essence?" (Gilroy, 1995: 33–34). What is more useful, then, is to explore how the initial identification hip-hoppers make with the culture's African-American origins can be an impetus for re-identification with local musics and struggles. "Hip Hop is no longer the host culture, but ... a direct link back to traditional ways of singing, dancing, and telling stories" (Pennycook and Mitchell, 2001: 30). They found their source of power in a global force, but Lebanon's hip-hoppers have localized the form to fit their distinct circumstances.

It always existed in our traditions but we never paid attention to it. It's a modern style of poetry – hip hop ... It's not about forming a hip hop culture in Lebanon, it exists in *Zajal* and *Atabah* ... hip hop already existed in Lebanon. (MC Edd)

During a cab ride one day, MC Edd recorded the driver singing *Atabah*, a form of improvised Arabic poetry, on his cell phone. Later, he laced it into the love song *Qatshe' Ma' Kamal* for his hip-hop band Fareeq el Atrash's current album. He wanted "to remember our culture ... capture it." Palestinian rapper Yaseen, from hip-hop duo I-Voice, has created his own hybrid form of hip-hop. He calls it *Ta-rap*. It is a blend of rap and the Arabic music form *Tarab*. The term has several meanings, but the one Yaseen is looking to achieve describes *Tarab* as an emotional state induced by the "ecstasy" of the music (Racy, 2003: 6). Palestinian hip-hop group Katibe 5 is often accompanied by an oud player and spoken-word poet. Rapper Rayess Bek's latest project includes an orchestra[2]. Hip-hoppers in Lebanon fuse African drums with bombshell beats, funky vibes, and urban streets. They spit rhymes over swing-jazz sounds. Reggae joins rapping, and the traditional oud meets acoustic guitar tapping. New spaces for expression are being born all the time in this hybrid exchange of cultural sounds and forms.

Against criticism that youth are merely appropriating global trends and losing touch with local traditions, some are drawing on their rich history in order to contest and redefine it. "Rap is *for* Arabic. We are the history of poetry," rapper Bolo-B says. Apart from only a few exceptions, if you want to be taken seriously in the country's hip-hop scene, you have to rap in Arabic[3].

> We stress using Arabic because we feel in Lebanon everyone is forgetting it … we are influenced too much by western culture and that's bad for us because we are losing our culture … When I see a kid talking in perfect English, who doesn't know how to speak Arabic – that makes me sad because this is Lebanon … I see our culture fading away, and I feel like it's our responsibility to save that. (MC Edd).

Female MC Malikah rapped in English for five years before switching to Arabic. Her impetus: the July 2006 War in Lebanon. At the time, Malikah was studying at a university in Canada. While devastation was happening back home, the rapper says she felt powerless. "So I decided to write a song … I wanted to talk to my people, why would I do that in English?" Rapper Ramcess says, "it's important for hip-hop to be in the geography of the language. There's certain elements and metaphors and ways of expression." "We are talking about real social problems and substance from our culture. That's why we use our language, our accent," say Gaafar and Naserdayn, members of the rap group Touffar from Baalbek. These two young men are staunchly proud and persistent about maintaining the Baalbeki accent in their songs. It is in this way that Touffar fiercely subverts the cultural code that demands a focus on the linguistic norm of the center – on the Beiruti accent. This is the deliberate drive and texture of the sound of hip-hop in Lebanon: it is rooted in Arabic and layered with a moral geography of musical meaning[4].

POST-WAR YOUTH AS CULTURAL NOMADS

The borderline work of culture demands an encounter with "newness" that is not part of the continuum of past and present. It creates a sense of the new as an insurgent act of cultural translation. Such art does not merely recall the past as social cause or aesthetic precedent; it renews the past, refiguring it as a contingent "in-between" space, that innovates and interrupts the performance of the present. The "past-present" becomes part of the necessity, not the nostalgia, of living (Bhabha, 1994: 7).

The children of Lebanon's post-war generation are fashioning themselves as cultural nomads – transgressing the boundaries of traditional norms and parental values with new, dynamic resources. Glocal tools like hip-hop shift almost effortlessly between social territories. Cutting across difference, the "ritual of communication" guides the way: "Not toward extension of message in space but maintenance of society in time, not the act of imparting information but the representation of shared beliefs" (Carey, 2009: 18).

Lebanon's hip-hoppers converge around an "awareness of the need to speak, to give a voice to the varied dimensions of our lives" (Hooks, 1989: 13). They want to define the social world on their own terms, but also re-imagine it. And there is no single narrative, but fugitive vibrations, continually being reworked and transformed into makeshift sites for negotiation. They experiment with unique grammars and irreverent musings to develop a vocabulary capable of articulating and narrating life on their own terms. Hip-hop is a space where young people in Lebanon are trying to make sense of the ruptures and contradictions that shape their lives. It is a testing ground for alternative frameworks through which they can view the world, search for identity, and make meaning. It is, at a basic level, a struggle over representation for ideological versions and visions of the world. The vehicle for experimenting with hip-hop's musical possibilities lies in the thoughtful intersection of context, language, and local conditions as they are relayed through voices: whether of discord or harmony; this is not the point. Voice is.

Because You Know the Truth is not Written in an Article
And I speak the unspoken reality
(Rayess Bek, "'am Beheki Bil Sokout/I'm Speaking in Silence")

There is nothing more I want to do
Than vomit the contents of my mind
(Tina Fish, slam poet, "2 Minutes")

I know I don't have a voice, but I will sing for them
(Zeinedin, "Manteq/Logic")

This is a new generation. A generation who, for the most part, did not live the atrocities of the fifteen-year civil war, but are forced to live with the ugly scars inflicted by a depraved generation, and the pervasive, but tacit fear that war will return. "I have the past, and I have the past of my fathers. I'm holding this past and it's very heavy," rapper Rayess Bek intones.

In some cases, hip-hoppers in the country are not just articulating discourse, they are revenging against the absence of any. The failure on the part of the Lebanese to engage in any national debate or open dialogue about the traumas and torments of the civil war has created what Sune Haugbolle (2005) calls a "discourse of consent." "Many private memories simply never find a voice, be this because of social, political, or emotional constraints and censure, and they die unuttered."

As the debate rages on over whether the Lebanese should forget or remember, and if so, how – the country's young people are forced to live in the "now." They do not have the luxury of longing for some pre-war golden era. "Never mind about the past," rapper Bolo-B says. "We have to live in this moment." Armed with tools of rhetorical resistance, bred in the hybridized field of glocal flows, rappers refuse subordination to nostalgia and tradition. How powerful the force then, as Gramsci implicated, of the subaltern voice to recognize the importance of "knowing all the truths, even the unpleasant ones." These voices come from outside of "formally dialectical" structures, because they "need to grasp the dialectic as it is forming in the process of becoming history in itself" (as cited by Bhabha, 2001: 39–40).

Are you suffering? Who's not suffering!
From physical, mental pain – constantly
(Fareeq el Atrash, "Demoqrati/Democratic")

I might have woken up late ...
But every day I wake up, I see that you are still asleep ...
You – who saw the war, tell me what you concluded from it?
(Rayess Bek, "Baye' Manem/Dream Seller")

I'm not healed from the July (2006) War yet,
My wound is still open and you're adding to the pain
(Zeinedin featuring Ramcess, "'ifouni/Leave Me Alone")

What am I supposed to be?
And what are you supposed to see?
When you see what I can be,
I'll already be gone
Hope is impossible, it's impossible to find hope
I'm bored of the answer: "We'll see tomorrow"
(Rayess Bek, "Baye' Manem/Dream Seller")

You took all the pride and possessions
Leave us life, is that too much to ask?
(Malikah, "Ana 'am Beheke/I'm Speaking")

I learned to look down at the ground, because the sky wasn't blue
We were all packed together, Muslims, Christians, and Druze
After the civil war, we didn't learn any lessons
Then the July War came, and Lebanon was being destroyed again
(Rayess Bek, "Khartech 'al Zamann/Scratch on the Past")

Our culture is dead, for sure it's not alive
(Ramcess, "L'Kalem L'Jamil/Sweet Talk")

"We have to wake up," Rapper Zeinedin says. A 2009 viral video commercial
from director Sary Sehnaoui portrays with eerie familiarity downtown Beirut
at the center of war[5]. Gray ashes spin rapidly through the sky, while destroyed
condos tremble to the choppy tune of exploding bombs and automatic weapons.
A camera pan to Beirut nightclub "Basement" shows a young couple walking
out the exit to find the devastation that awaits them. They glance at one another,
and immediately retreat back down the steps. Booze and dancing are in order.
The club's motto – coined during the July 2006 War – "it's safer underground,"
pops onto the screen. Samir Khalaf talks about the "allure of kitsch in post-war
Lebanon: the need to forget and escape the atrocities and futility of a senseless
war; the mindless hedonism and narcissism associated with an urge to make
up for lost time ..." (Khalaf, 2001: 276–77). It is too often in the "aesthetics
of deception" that many Lebanese have learned to deal with their problems
(Khalaf, 2001: 277). But just like the effects of a drug, it is not so much the high
that keeps users coming back for more, it is the comedown: the moment when
the "distractions and deceptions" begin to wear off and an overwhelming sense
of uneasiness creeps in. You attempt to navigate your surroundings, but are
frozen by the sudden realization that nothing feels familiar. It is almost impossible to recognize what is new or what belongs to the past. The self-loathing and
fear are back. Withdrawal bites, but the truth is terrifying. The search for the
next high is already underway.

If the current trend in the country's club scene – house and trance music – is
a metaphor for society, then certainly the Lebanese lack a sense of identity and
mutual biography. House and trance music call for highly synthetic, place-less
beats that throb with rigorous repetition. It is static and undiscerning; a clear can-
didate for Reynolds' term "schizoid music." Time becomes blurred; there is no
sense of past or future; it takes us "nowhere ... no place" (Reynolds, 1990: 138-9).
As beatboxer Hisham from Saida rap group D.I. so poignantly put it: "People
in Lebanon don't want to listen, they just want to dance." "Music forgot about
revolution after the civil war" (Mohamed Hamdar, Sound Bomb festival). It went
from Marcel Khalife's rebellious soul and Ziad Rahbani's acerbic wit, to Haifa's
stylized apathy and Nancy's plasticized kitsch. Contemporary Arabic pop music
is sanitized by design, apolitical by nature and deliberately glossed with inof-
fensive shine. "Hip hop is for angry people who don't accept reality" (Rapper
Omarz). "Rappers are the people who are suffering" (MC Osloob). "The difference between me and the pop singer: I don't sell the dream, I sell reality" (Rapper
Rayess Bek). Dyson's description of hip-hoppers as "verbal shamans exorcising
the demons of cultural amnesia" resonates attractively in the Lebanese context
(Dyson, 2004: 408).

We're afraid to face it, so we choose to divert it
(Sabah Taqat, "Lebnen Wahem/Lebanon is an Illusion")

I'm not here to make you dance.
Not yet.
There are a lot of things to be sad about, before being happy.
Don't suppress sorrow and pain.
Deal with them.
(Double A the Preacherman)

With fists pounding I Call for help
Lying strew down on the floor
I belt
For someone to hear me
And the dichotomy?
Everyone's dancing
I need to speak
(Tina Fish, "2 Minutes")

I'm sick of everything called music in Lebanon
Same lyrics and rhythm
Everybody moans
They all talk about love
They don't have a point
(Rayess Bek, "Shoufo Halon/ They See Themselves" [They're Vain])

The raw energy of hip-hop in Lebanon persists in stark contrast to the sheer spectacle of decadence and decay that increasingly characterizes Lebanese music and society. "We are the complete opposite of Arabic pop," Omar from the rap group Ashekman says. Rappers are the "people trying to deal with problems seriously" (Ghazi Abdel Baki, Forward Music). "Hip hop is not a status thing. It's an in your face thing – telling you something. You can't ignore the message" (Kinda Hassan, Eka' Productions). Where music symbolizes social boundaries, Lebanon's hip -hoppers are locating themselves in opposition to those who indulge in the usual rituals of false consciousness.

DON'T DANCE, JUST LISTEN

To understand their lyrical projects, it is essential to understand what these young people feel they are up against. The pulse of hip-hop in Lebanon beats with a contemporary youth consciousness that feels at once suffocated and abandoned by society. This is a country that counts on young people to participate and contribute to the public sphere, yet largely excludes them from it. Constant electricity cuts, water shortages, unemployment, rising poverty, and unequal access to higher education fuel a strong sense of alienation, discontent, and disillusion among the youth. "This country is always in a state of crisis ... it makes us worry more about war than (fixing) roads, electricity, water" (Kinda Hassan, Eka' Productions).

The electricity is cut every day
We keep silent
We block our mouths
There is no work in this country
So it's better we empty our heads
(Bolo-B, "Laqannak Lebneni/Because You are Lebanese")

They say he who succeeds will be left without friends
Life is hard [sarcastic], just ask Rafik [Hariri] ...
Check the oil; they raise the price every minute ...
If not, don't worry, you'll suffocate from the smell of gas
(Rayess Bek, "Shoufo Halon/See Themselves" [They're Vain])

Because you are Lebanese, it's forbidden for you to live ...
Because you are Lebanese, it's forbidden for you to sleep at night
Because you are Lebanese, it's forbidden to empty what is inside you
(Bolo-B, "Laqannak Lebneni/Because You are Lebanese")

I'm living in an illusion that I can't get out of
Lebanon is being destroyed and everyone gave up on it
Each politician blames the other one
The first doesn't care and neither does the second one
Where are we going on this road we're taking?
(Sabah Taqat, "Lebnen Wahem/Lebanon is an Illusion")

"Everything is based on the dad, and what *wasta* he has,' Maroun from rap group Militia says[6]." "Without *wasta*, you're a nobody in this country, even if you're talented" (MC Malikah). *Wasta*, or connections, is a key component to finding a job in Lebanon. One study found that 68 percent of all salaried first-time employees were mainly hired because of personal or family contacts (Chaaban, 2009: 128). Another study found that non-specialized jobs are more often obtained through connections than merit (Chaaban, 2009: 128). The message this is sending to youth: it does not matter how educated or qualified you are for a position, if you do not know the right people, if your family does not have the right connections, it will be very difficult to find a job in the country.

You finish university and set your BA [degree] in a frame at home
But your job is to sell bread or collect garbage
We started taking out loans [to pay] for the price of the [cab] ride to Beirut
Perhaps we're better off dead[7]
(Bolo-B, "Laqannak Lebneni/Because You are Lebanese")

No matter how hard you work, they never let you advance
Nor is it enough to get promoted,
You get stuck in the same position
You search for other companies holding your degree
But no one is ready to employ you ...
So, no need to work in the first place
(Fareeq el Atrash, "Khabreetein/Two Stories")

To continue my studies I'm putting all the money I have
To serve my country
Even though my country never served me
Sacrifice my blood, my knowledge,
But nothing is for free
Dream seller, I'm awake from Friday to Monday
(Rayess Bek, "Baye' Manem/Dream Seller")

And if you get in trouble, wherever you run
You're going to be slapped
To remind you that your country won't help you up tomorrow
Tomorrow we'll finish university and won't find a job
Tomorrow
(Malikah, "Hek Sayra Bledna/This is what our country's become")

"We all have ideas, but we have no way of achieving them," producer and musician Zeid Hamdan says. Lebanon's young people live in a society entrenched in politics, but which offers no real outlet for their ideas or concerns. "Today they need you, tomorrow they won't need you. Most people they take advantage of us" (Rapper Rayess Bek). The legal voting age in the country remains at twenty-one, in comparison to large parts of the world where eighteen is often deemed an appropriate age for political participation (Chaaban, 2009: 121).

You're 18 and you're not allowed to vote
But you can participate in Superstar[8]
(Ramcess, "Intihabet")[9]

He stands on the podium and pretends to be a leader

But all he does is read from a paper
This one is a political party founder and this one is a militia founder
Believe me my friend this is not how you solve the situation
(Sabah Taqat, "Lebnen Wahem/Lebanon is an Illusion")

If we see an Adam [a good man]
We say: "What a stupid"
And the bad guy: He is the biggest leader
And we play the drums for him
(Bolo-B, "Laqannak Loubneni/Because You are Lebanese")

8 and 14 are the dates of two protests
And he who shall win will be called June 7
The best thing that can happen, is that they all fail
And the students with official exams pass[10]
(Ramcess, "Intihabet")

They told me: "Go vote".
I told them: "I intend to go vote ...
But I need to vote for someone who represents me, right?" ...
The politicians haven't changed ... for 40 years.
The same people. The same issues.
The same wars ...
So me, personally, who represents me?
Who should I vote for?
Anyway, could anyone explain to me what these elections are for?
How are they different from the last elections?
Or the ones before that?
Or the ones before that one?
How are they different from the next elections?
Elections? Yeah right.
(Rayess Bek, "Intikhabet/Elections")

Youth in Lebanon are expected to stay within very specific boundaries of behavior, speech and attitude. Malikah[11] pointed out to me an Arabic proverb that goes: "He who mimics his father can do no wrong" (*Man shabaha abahou fa ma zalam*). Like the proverb says, "you're supposed to listen to what your parents tell you, and do like they do." When the female MC first started rapping publicly in 2001, she covered her face during performances. At the time, her parents did not accept her rapping. In a country where "the whole family shares one's successes or failures and is held accountable to one's transgressions and sins," Malikah chose to censor her physical self for fear of risking her family's reputation (Faour, 1998: 63).

When I cross my limits and sin
Don't categorize me
I'm not waiting for society to expose me
(Kita' Beirut, "Fi 'alam/There are People")

This is a society where people monitor "how you talk, what you do, how you dress ... It's not about what is allowed versus what is not allowed, it's about being comfortable versus not being comfortable. This is a socially small country where people gossip a lot. You always feel like you're going to be seen by someone you know" (Kinda Hassan, Eka' Productions). Rapper Binelli points out that "you can't contradict yourself easily here, people will call you out." You have to "be careful of what you say and in front of whom" (DJ Stickfiggr). Ours is a "struggle between what we want to do, versus what we are supposed to do. A struggle between what we want to be, versus what we are supposed to be," rapper H2Z says.

And they may not always know exactly what it is they want to be. But that is not the point. They know what they *don't want to be*. That is to say, there is a strong *disidentification* with the overarching identities firmly ascribed to young people here. As rapper Omarz puts it, hip-hoppers in Lebanon are "so desperate to be a part of something." But they want to be a part of something not directed by the hegemonic web of kinship, religious, political, and sectarian affiliation. Resoundingly, they want to remove themselves from the institutionalized forces of classification. And this is a remarkable point: in their search to mark themselves out as different from the "other", these young people are not retreating to the kind of boundary-making strongholds and territorial rigidity that left an indelible mark on their parents' generation.

Habitus and the "sectarian hood"
My life in Lebanon is like a separating line
(Rayess Bek, "Schizophrenia")

The drawing up of communal boundaries lends provocative nuance to this study. Hip-hop culture has an "in-built element of competition" that has "traditionally been staged within geographical boundaries that demarcate turf and territory among various crews, cliques, and posses" (Forman, 2004: 203). Rappers often emphasize and organize themselves around spatial alliances in defense of themes and imagery belonging to the "hood." The spatial inheritance of hip-hop culture could proffer huge implications when invoked in a country like Lebanon.

Communal loyalties, charted geographically and mobilized by confessional sentiment, are the basic form of social support and political affiliation in the country. In an elaborate spectacle, the Lebanese have nurtured an aesthetic for partitioning neighborhoods along sectarian lines with gang-like semiotics. Flags, checkpoints, color schemes, architecture, symbols, and graffiti all serve to mediate the ways people locate, experience, and understand their place and identity in the country.

During the civil war, staggering population shifts pushed groups into self-contained spaces. Massive displacement dropped the proportion of Christians living in the southern regions of Mount Lebanon, for instance, from 55 percent in 1975 to near 5 percent by the late 1980s (Khalaf, 2002: 247). Maha Yahya (1993) explains that protracted violence and an increasingly inadequate government forced the Lebanese to create self-sufficient neighborhoods where blocks rallied together to generate electricity, gather resources, and ensure some means of safety for residents. It was the basic need to survive that in the end pushed sectarian communities into close proximal spaces.

Today, the confession-cutting logic is reinforced in the social and political system: "religious heritage, symbols, and habitus" are used to legitimize politics and draws attention to difference (Peleikis, 2001). Furthermore, "One is not heard or recognized unless confessional allegiance is first disclosed. It is only when an individual is placed within a confessional context that ideas and assertions are rendered meaningful or worthwhile" (Khalaf, 2001: 275). The result:

Most of the youth here have no voice. They are in the clan system, the community, the father, the god – always under an authority. And if you want to be accepted you have to follow the chief. If it is god or if it is the clan leader, or the father, or the big brother, you always have to follow them. Hip-hop gives a voice to the ones who want to express without following the leader's voice. (Zeid Hamdan, producer and musician).

Lebanon's historical context sets the stage for hip-hoppers to act on the sensibilities of defending the "sectarian hood". Yet overwhelmingly, the country's sectarian system and its religious fabric are the repeated victims of vehement criticism from the hip-hoppers. "Everything revolves around religion," producer and rapper Zoog says. "Religion here is racism; you use it to divide and contrast people" (Ghazi Abdel Baki, Forward Music). "We don't want religion to be in hip hop. There is no space for hate in music" (Rapper Double A the Preacherman).

They say in Lebanon the religions are married
But I was never invited to the wedding
I've seen them fighting ever since I was 15
(Rayess Bek, "Schizophrenia")

The presidents are using religion to light up smoke
The blood of Muslims and Christians is painted on walls
(Kimewe from Sabah Taqat, "El Mot Jekon/Death is Coming to You")

I'll pay with my blood to defend my people,
But I won't put up with religious segregation
So let me Live
(Zeinedin featuring Ramcess, "Leave me Alone")

Battling because of opposing political factions
Using religion to defend our physical actions
Afraid the urge to fight has become inborn
Unsure of what we're fighting against, and what we're fighting for
(Venus, "Enough Talk")

I was found between a lot of savage characters
They're using religion to get their way
(RGB, "Ya Wled Loubnen/Hey, Chlidren of Lebanon")

They all support sectarianism: Muslims, Christians
Let's keep this up, and maybe we'll repeat the civil war
(Rayess Bek, "La Min?/For Who?")

"The whole system, it puts us all in adversity, one against the other. We are born into this adversity because we are born into a sectarian system. So as an artist, our first goal, our first aim is to be beyond all this. Just give arts to anyone who can think, and never put our name on a color or sect" (Zeid Hamdan, producer and musician). Hip-hop in this country can address "issues that represent our racism: sectarianism" (Mohamed Hamdar, Sound Bomb festival). Malikah says one of the roles of her music is to "tell younger generations about the mistakes of sectarianism." Rapper Zeinedin believes "hip hop is all about tolerance, that's why we don't get involved in sectarian politics. It's music for the discriminated. How could we talk about being true to yourself, if you are obsessed with sects?" Hip -hop "reminds us that music needs to be rethought in a communal sense" (John Nasr, bass player from Fareeq el Atrash).

Let's sing together
Let's let go of sectarianism
So our goal is to join the people together
So we can harvest unity
(Sabah Taqat, "Yalla, Rkedou!/Let's go, Run!")

"We hate sectarianism when it divides us," members of the rap group Sabah Taqat from Tripoli say. These seven boys express a particularly powerful sense of solidarity with one another. They are not involved in the politics of sectarianism but "we understand how others are dragged into it ... You need to belong to a party or group just to survive; your only reason is to see your family live ... There is a tribal attitude here." As Khalaf points out, confessionalism is both emblem and armor in the country: a "viable medium for asserting presence and securing vital needs and benefits. Without it, groups are literally rootless, nameless and voiceless" (Khalaf, 2001: 275). But instead of firmly rooting themselves in the "cult of sectarianism," the guys in Sabah Taqat are their own support structure. They do not have much, but they have each other. "If someone wants to start a fight, we can defend ourselves – but that won't happen." It is in this way that members of Sabah Taqat have converted traditional confessional sentiments into their own arena of social and emotional support. This is their imagined, and in many ways real, community.

But Sabah Taqat's community is not the same as the one Fareeq el Atrash belongs to. Hip-hop duo State of Mind's scene is different from Touffar's. The same goes for Zeinedin and Bolo-B. Making dramatic the hegemonic structure that underscores the inability on the part of these young people to form a singular, cohesive community, rapper H2Z says: "We rappers are deeply connected, and somehow different." Bourdieu's notion of habitus has key explanatory power for elaborating on why hip-hop is "like everything in Lebanon, everything is divided" (Rapper Zeinedin). Habitus is an acquired set of subjective dispositions, attitudes, or habits which objectively manifest themselves in particular conditions (Bourdieu, 1977: 95). Here, agency is a given, but so is the mediation of structural restriction. Cultural practices are gripped by habitus – those unconscious preferences that explain why individual actions are not always deliberate. Oppositely, when action *is* calculated, the concept explains why the individual fails to achieve his/her desired result. And so the brutal irony is: Lebanon's hip-hoppers are in many ways loosely held together by a stiff rejection of the worldview that encourages sectarian and, by extension, communal enclaves of solidarity. And yet, in their failure to reach out across communal and, by extension sectarian, borders, they reproduce the very system they are bent on rejecting. Bourdieu's habitus helps us to explain not *what they do*, but what hip-hoppers in Lebanon *do not do* that gives credence to the behaviors of the generation before them. When asked why hip-hoppers in Lebanon have not been successful at forming a community, some responses were:

"This is the Lebanese problem ... they can't come together." (Rapper Ramcess)

"Rappers are afraid of each other ... Do they want to work together? No." (Rapper L'Fahrass)

"The vision [to work together as a community] doesn't exist. They don't see that if they joined hands they could have a bigger impact ... It is fear of the other eating you up. They are afraid to work together because they could be beat by another in competition." (Kinda Hassan, Eka' Productions)

"Between each other they have problems; they have their own agendas, own conflicts ... Here everyone has their own network and they want to keep it to themselves." (Rapper Yassen)

"They are afraid to affiliate because it's dangerous in the end." (Johnny Headbusta, Beirut Bandits)

"This is a culture of survival ... since we're physically not there [in Beirut], they don't see us, they just don't. So because we're not in the center of the event where concerts happen, we don't get that attention – we simple don't exist." (Rapper H2Z)

The great danger of habitus "is that it naturalizes itself and the cultural rules, agendas and values that make it possible" (Virkki, 2007: 278). What may have started out as a "geography of fear" (Khalaf, 2002: 247) for their parents' generation is simply now a geography of difference. Social relations have to be reproduced and reaffirmed in interactions across territorial borders if these young people are to fully realize their goals. Or else, they face the disarming paradox of their lyrics:

How are you planning on building a future if the past keeps on repeating itself? (Fareeq el Atrash, "Terikhna bi lebnen/Our History in Lebanon")

You lived the war, but I'm living the consequences (Rayess Bek, "Baye' Manem /Dream Seller")

LEBANON AS A SOUNDSCAPE

We have talked about the erection of visual boundaries to demarcate the social arena of difference in Lebanon. But the cultural politics of music in this country reminds us that markers of difference and practices of identity lie in a more complex semiotic terrain. That is to say, Lebanon is not just a landscape, it is a *soundscape*, where politicized spaces can be mapped out in an aural terrain. The larger-than-life personalities of the country's leaders and politicians come with their own soundtrack: from Lebanese Forces leader Samir Geagea's *akeed, akeed* to Free Patriotic Movement leader Michel Aoun's *halaq tnee*. Most Lebanese remember Hezbollah Secretary General Sayyed Hassan Nasrallah saying: *Ladayana sawarikh tasilou ila ba'd w ma ba'da Haifa* during the summer of 2006. And then *ela ayn?* Progressive Socialist Party leader Walid Jumblatt frequently asks[12].

When legendary singer Fairuz refused to sing in Lebanon during the country's fifteen-year civil war, she was using her voice as a political strategy, a source of power and security in an otherwise uncertain world. With willful silence, she rejected appropriation of her voice by political forces. Yet still today, various groups habitually appropriate the singer's recorded voice, playing her songs at political rallies, as they profess Fairuz as the unified voice of the nation. "Music is a tool of power," as Attali says. "It can make people forget the fear of violence ... make them believe in order and harmony ... and silence those who oppose authority" (Attali, 1985: 19–20).

The politics of sound in Lebanon reminds us that verbal props are just as prevalent as visual symbols of demarcation. Most local media outlets are privately owned, but strongly affiliate with, and are often directly funded by, political parties. Overarching divisions, then, are played out in the press.

> The clans are (invested) into communities opposing each other (so), that every artistic attempt will have to be catalogued in a certain clan. I'm saying that particularly through media. Let's say I'm a hip hop artist and I want to go on air and make it big. Well if Future TV broadcasts my music then I'll be affiliated with Future TV. Let's say LBC broadcasts my music, then I'll be affiliated with LBC. The media, those people who should promote arts, are so much divided that either way, no artist can go big. No one can be unanimous on all the media, because the media are divided. Our artists from the Lebanese Underground, most of them are nowhere because they would never give their music to any clan. So they're just nowhere. (Zeid Hamdan, producer and musician).

Just like Fairuz during the war, many youth in the country fear appropriation of their voices into the resounding spectrum of divisive semiotics. Malikah says she tries to "say a lot of stuff between the lines," and "transmit my message without anybody being able to tell exactly what I am talking about," because "I don't want people to brand me as something ... there is a big probability you will be misunderstood (in your music)." "When you write metaphors," MC Chyno says, "you weave between clarity and the abstract. You can tell a story in rap that is not so obvious." "What a rapper is allowed to do, not even a poet is allowed to do," rapper L'Fahrass says. It is about "finding a way to get your point across without using the exact words ... You can't cuss a political figure, because then you are cussing out that sect ... If I talk bad about someone, I might end up dead" (Rapper L'Fahrass). "It's not a rule, but once you do speak out (against this system), you're an enemy. It's not written, but it is a taboo" (Rapper Black Scorpion from Sabah Taqat). In the song "Inkelab", Palestinian rapper Yaseen said he did not want to explicitly name each media outlet, so he raps them in with playful exploit:

The dust of the *lighthouse* [Al-Manar]
The collapse of the *future* [Future]
Put on your clothes, because nobody's tolerant [LBC]

The Palestinian is now an *island* and he's wandering all around [Al-Jazeera]
The Arab had a dot added to her [Al-Arabiya]
Make a *new* plan [New TV]
The free voice has been *transferred* [Television du Liban]
We were *built* on a bitter dream [NBN]
Your end is *near* [Orbit]
(I-Voice, "Inkelab/Revolt")[13]

"If you cross the limit (and say something wrong), you can lose your life here," Rapper Rayess Bek notes. It is clear that alongside the very real violence many of Lebanon's young people are faced with, symbolic violence plays a significant role as well. Bourdieu used the term to describe the type of domination that takes no real intimidation or effective action to enforce. It is the population's unknowing submission, perhaps very recognition of those in power that gives symbolic violence its metaphorically lethal leverage (Bourdieu, 1991: 51). "People are afraid. And the best censorship in the world is self-censorship. When you are afraid, you censor yourself without anyone asking you to" (Rapper Rayess Bek).

We're prevented from speaking and telling a word of truth
We're afraid that our life is the cost to lose
We should have the guts to speak freely
I write on paper and turn it into a song
I want to deliver my message no matter what happens
I discuss my points of view
I make it long, not short
I explain my bars and destroy the barriers
I'm ready to lose my life if I get to deliver my word
(Sabah Taqat, "Lebnen Wahem/Lebanon is an Illusion")

Music "has a political function: that it can and should actively intervene in the production and the distribution of knowledge in ways that counter oppression and injustice" (Heble, 2000: 119). "We're shedding light on the things they want to keep hidden ... We say what's real, we say what's true" (Rapper Black Scorpion from Sabah Taqat). Rap music socializes resistant and subversive discourse into a realm where young people feel more at ease in the quest to self-assert, experiment, and imagine.

Malikah says, "I can be a completely different person" with hip-hop. "I have alter egos ... With my family and friends, I'm Lynn. Malikah, she is tough and hardcore. Then there's my feminine side, Lyxx. She is sexier, and touches on the R&B side." "You can make this character and be your character, and express and remain your character," MC Chyno says. It only "depends on whatever I want to be. I am a f***ing politician, an army general" (Rapper Omarz). "You can express yourself in so many ways with rap ... I'm not going to stand out on the street and give a speech, instead – I'll put it in a song" (Rapper H2Z).

People never remember political speeches. They remember great political speeches, you know – the great ones. But the sea of speeches and those things that should change, the ideas – they are not remembered. The songs are remembered. You look at your life and you have always a song. You listen to a song and it brings you ... you relate to it personally, the song becomes yours internally and it affects you. (Zeid Hamdan, producer and musician).

In the Fareeq el Atrash song "Demoqrati",[14] Edd takes aim at the political system, and the language of politics that endorses it.

"Where is our country going? Do you know?" he raps.
An audio clip of Lebanese Forces leader Samir Geagea responds:
"I don't deny that there is, here, somewhere, or someplace, there, something. I don't know what I am going to call it. I mean ... I mean ..."

Geagea's words flow with uncanny ease over the song's beat, as if he were actually rapping on the track. But the sycophancy only goes that far, because as the song aims to demonstrate, what politicians in the country are saying, is that they are not really saying anything at all. The sample further demonstrates how rappers can appropriate and manipulate the constructs of discourse in the public sphere in order to criticize and subvert it. This is in the tradition of hip-hop's cut 'n' mix culture: no one owns sound or voice. It is yours to take, cut, mash up, and do with as you like. It is through the reorganization and manipulation of a social reality that otherwise constricts them, that hip-hoppers can gain some control over it. Interestingly, Edd does not include the Geagea sample when he performs the "Demoqrati" song live, and because of this, he says people understand the song in different ways: some fans confuse him for being pro-March 8 alliance, others believe he is with March 14. "Always, it must be one of those sides. If they think you are criticizing this one, then it means you are with the other one" (Rapper Rayess Bek).

Hip-hop in Lebanon represents the struggle to negotiate between inherited systems of knowledge production, history and modes of behavior and the ones young people are striving to invent on their own terms. Music has the potential to shift everyday experiences of social reality; sound can muffle, moan, intone, and speak to specific contexts. But its great potential lies in its ability to constantly transform, cross boundaries, and transgress marked categories. Music is a cultural "map of meaning"; individuals can draw on it and erase themselves from it; they can locate themselves in real and imaginary geographies (Cohen citing Hall, 1998: 287). Here is a "breathing space, in which the normal categories of order and hierarchy are less than completely inevitable" (Scott, 1990: 168). This is the kind of social creativity that transcends the limits of where we are placed in the world (Stokes, 1994: 4).

FROM SOUNDSCAPE TO SOUND ESCAPE

There is a very real difference between the kind of music being produced inside Beirut, and the fabric of the sounds emanating from the periphery. No doubt, all of Lebanon's hip-hoppers are cultural entrepreneurs, producing and exchanging their ideologically charged discourses in meaningful ways. But it is the youth on the margins, in Baalbek, Tripoli, Saida and the refugee camps, who are deploying hip-hop with an often fervent zeal and angry conviction. "Hip hop is not a kind of music; it is a way of living," members of the rap group Touffar from Baalbek say. "In the coming days, we might have guns. For now we use music." "It is a real war. We are not kidding. We are not just singing." The music on the periphery grinds with rich and complex emotion; it is the sound of misery and hardship, of frustration and disillusion. You don't need to dissect the lyrics to understand what these young people are trying to say, you can simply hear it, feel it.

Songs bear meaning and allow symbolic work not just as speech acts, but also as structures of sound with unique rhythms, textures and forms. Thus, it is not always what is sung, but the *way* it is sung, within particular conventions or musical genres which gives a piece of music its communicative power and meaning (Willis, 1990: 64).

"Even without the beat, we know what we want to say ... we are doing this for the people, to get our rights," Gaafar and Naserdayn say. The young men paint a bleak picture of life in the Bekaa region: "If you go to Baalbek, you will see that it is a prison ... The way that the government deals with us in Baalbek, they deal with us like we are not welcome in Lebanon. They think we only deal drugs; that we are just killers. They put us in prison. There is no electricity, no university. People freeze to death in the winter. They go hungry." Gaafar and Naserdayn say they are not involved in Baalbek's well-known drug trade, but many people in their community are. And you have to understand why: "If we don't do that ... we will die ... we have to find a way to live, so we have to deal hash just to live." "The only way to get a good life, is to plant hash. That is the only way. We don't want to do that. But for some that is the only solution." It is clear the boys in Touffar see themselves as representatives, spokespersons, defenders of their real community. "In Baalbek you are a landowner, in Beirut you are a dog." "We are the voice of the community in Lebanon that lives with oppression daily."

If a nation's hungry, it should eat its rulers, not stones
Swindling, trickery, profiting from assassinations
To a law that's too strong for us, stamped on by Solidere

Their system deteriorated when they went into a game of death
All for the Riyal of the elections, all the bonds go to the Jews
To the Khaleejis, Americans, Europeans, and Russians
For Starbucks, Costa, Coca-Cola is our master
There's no place for the poor, among the filth of wealth
Just like you swallowed up Beirut, she'll swallow you up too
Just like you deprived us in the Bekaa, we'll deprive you too

This country, this work, this talk
It's going on
This theft, this sin, this swindling
It's going on
The center of Beirut only shines due to the darkness of the homes of the poor
The Baalbek native never goes into the dirty business
(Touffar, "Wasakh al-Tijari/Dirty Business")

Declining status, real and cultural territory threatened, Gaafar and Naserdayn use their words to defend, symbolically or otherwise, their social plight. "Nobody knows rap in Baalbek. They listen to us because they feel our lyrics ... they hear it. They believe in it." With insurgent energy and dissonance, Touffar resists the margins as a space of weakness. They may not be able to reorganize the social order, but they can challenge the value and meaning of it. As Hooks writes:

I was not speaking of a marginality one wishes to lose – to give up or surrender as part of moving into the center, but rather as a site one stays in, clings to even, because it nourishes one's capacity to resist. It offers the possibility of radical perspectives from which to see and create, to imagine alternatives, new worlds ... A message from that space in the margin that is a site of creativity and power, that inclusive space where we recover ourselves, where we move in solidarity to erase the category colonizer/colonized. Marginality is the space of resistance. Enter that space. Let us meet here. (Hooks, 1990: 149-52).

Rappers in the group Sabah Taqat, from Tripoli, took their name from the northern city's slang term for a pocket knife. "We cut people up with our lyrics," one group member explains. These boys come with a hard exterior, and are quick to explain that "unless you want to punch someone, (hip hop) is the only peaceful way to express yourself." Beneath the edge and hostility, though, are signs of some tired, worn souls lingering in Sabah Taqat. You cannot see it in their faces. No. That would be a sign of weakness.

I'm holding back a Lebanese scream with the tears of my mic
(Kimewe from Sabah Taqat, "El Mot Jekon/Death is Coming to You ")

We took a walk around the neighborhood where group member Kimewe sprays graffiti and the boys explained, "You can't be an angel between devils." Compared to Beirut, "all the trouble is more intense here – there is more poverty, more corrupt politicians ... Tripoli is the toilet of Lebanon, everybody messes it up." "We don't get the same opportunities or education as everyone else." "How can you grow up like this... without water, without electricity, without an infrastructure ... and not become aggressive?" one of the guys questioned.

> Have you ever felt scared from the sound of a belt?
> Held by a guy waiting to hit you?
> A prisoner in your own house
> Living in a state of shame
> (Sabah Taqat, "Shi Marra Hasset?/Have You Ever Felt?")

It seems apparent that Sabah Taqat's amplified sense of masculinity and aggression at peers who they perceive as homosexual, is a desperate attempt to overcome feelings of impotence. The group says emo kids are their "number one enemy" because "we hate them, they are acting out, they're gay, they're all f***ing faggots." Emo is short for "emotional music." It first emerged in the United States around the mid-1980s, and has since evolved into a global subculture with its own music and fashion. Emos are largely associated with being emotional, sensitive, shy, and introverted (Bailey, 2006: 338-339). With a posture of satisfaction, the members of Sabah Taqat recount for me an incident in which some of the guys threw a local emo kid in the trunk of a car and urinated on him, before locking him inside for several hours. They allude to the incident in a song about emos:

> We make fun of emos with tight clothes
> With waxed hair and sissy names
> Living it up, tight shirt that fits the body
> A piercing in the right ear as if he's a girl
> It's a fashion now, you see them everywhere
> If you make fun of one of them, you know what's going to happen?
> He'll get his friend to throw you a manicure party ...
>
> They all got attracted to sexual desire
> They deserve a public assassination
> And I do have the will to make you victims
> It's better for you to hide when you see us
> Because we're going to stuff the emos in the trunk
> Kimewe won't have any mercy on any emo
> And I'm set to piss on your dignity
> (Sabah Taqat, " Eh-Mos/Emos")[15]

"The idea that as culturally constituted subjects we embody the contradiction of the social relations that shape us, and that contradiction, as opposed to coherency, guides our actions and reactions, is important here" (Best, 1997: 22). And so with swift contradiction Sabah Taqat's members tell me: "Not all people can express their feelings, so they leave it for us." As one song goes:

The women in our society will always be controlled
No law or doctrine can grant her rights
All the guys act manly, threatening with divorce
And saying "no" to whatever she proposes

Her wounds took the pain off her mind
With his tongue he bred a hatred that's still going on
He keeps cavorting, getting drunk, day and night he gambles
Her character is on the verge of collapse
Five different feelings of guilt will lead you to destruction
All because of hatred and poverty
Your feelings of revenge and shame erupted
I use the ink of the pen to talk to you, show you, care for you
For the single purpose of making you stronger
It's true that our society is not on your side, protecting you
But believe me I can feel you, wherever I am, I'm encouraging you

In your eyes I've seen agony, felt it in your voice
Even though life is wide, it feels like I'm in a prison
Your ideas are not welcome, your voice is not heard
I keep wondering when this society will wake up
Everybody's mistreated you, forgotten about you
No one is feeling your pain
And no one is there to support you
Your rights are always taken
Guilty and misunderstood
Tears flow from your eyes

You have the right to blame
You do your job well and no one is ever satisfied
This case needs mediation, it needs deep thought
Have no fear, we're by your side, and we'll keep on supporting you
Helping you,
Getting you away from people who hurt you
The ones who terrify you
Those who are destroying your morals

They've dimmed your lights
And muted your voice
I feel you, so I give you this song as a gift
To support you and give you faith and believe in yourself
(Sabah Taqat, "Hases Fiki/I Feel You")

In his research on biker boys, Paul Willis argues that musical preference is not an "arbitrary or random juxtaposition" (Willis, 1977: 62). The music they actively select and listen to richly parallels characteristics valued in the biker culture: security, authenticity, and masculinity. For Sabah Taqat, hip-hop offers an acceptable, masculine venue for expressing emotion. As for Gaafar and Naserdayn, it seems impossible these two could ever look at their music as any kind of mindless diversion, because fundamentally, it is not what they are saying that matters – it is that they are *saying*, and being *heard*, at all. When Touffar performs, these young men make "noise"; they demonstrate that the margins of the country do exist, and they exist meaningfully.

"We are indignant together," Durkheim wrote (cited by Maffesoli, 1996: 12). Hip-hoppers in Lebanon may be pitted between competing knowledges and distinct circumstances, but the desire to develop a highly personalized space for making sense of the world, harmonizes their intentions. Hip-hop is a "way to express my feelings, my problems" (Emjay from Sabah Taqat). "Being emotional is being gay, you got to be a man, you can't cry. What you can't express in real life, you express in music" (Rapper L'Fahrass). MC Zeinedin says he started writing lyrics because "I was angry, pissed off; everyone else was talking about life for me." For hip-hopper Binelli, what gave rise to his desire to rap, is what captures the essence of this genre of musical experience: "It was the only thing I could do for myself." The performance of music, listening and dancing to it, even arguing and thinking about it, is a form of creative resistance. But even more powerful, when the music is embedded with a meaning and message: to expose contradictions in the social order and collectivize the experiences of people who are otherwise voiceless. "Being Palestinian, you can't be so many things. You don't have it. So you make it with hip hop" (Yaseen from I-Voice). "What we write is what we feel and what we live" (Maroun from Militia). "Hip hop is the one place I don't feel judged … where I get to explain myself, my actions; why I do what I do. And it's not weird because it's ok to be different (here). That's the point. I think you wouldn't be here unless you were different. I feel, then, like I belong" (Rapper Venus).

OUR SOUNDTRACK

Not quite the Same, not quite the Other, she stands in that undetermined threshold place where she constantly drifts in and out. Undercutting the inside/outside opposition, her intervention is necessarily that of both a deceptive insider and deceptive outsider. She is this Inappropriate Other/Same who moves about with always at least two/four gestures: that of affirming "I am like you" while persisting in her difference; and that of reminding "I am different" while unsettling every definition of otherness arrived at. (Minh-ha, 1991: 74).

Lebanon takes a hold of you. In some mysterious, yet charming way, she grabs at you; and if you resist, she retaliates in a hardy, audacious manner. You saw her beauty and you saw her destruction and you accepted it. But because you accepted her contradiction – perhaps, better to call it illusion – of wonder and plight, of elation and rage – she holds you to it.

No one knows this better than the country's hip-hoppers: squeezed and stretched, subordinates of discipline, but desperately trying to flee from it. They set out on the precarious road between becoming who they are, and staying faithful to the shrewd muse – the formidable force that is Lebanon. In resistance, hip-hoppers transform into chameleons – blending in, but fixing deviant ways to reveal the hidden; speak the unspoken; expose the secrets and enigmatic "truths." They commit blasphemy by waging a war on the myth of solidarity – and thus symbolically threaten their own existence. They oppose banal routines with emotive creativity and outright challenge. They fantasize escape from the "tyranny of the home" (Thornton, 1995: 18). They disavow rituals of categorization. They rap elegiac lament for social and political disorder. They resent the profound lack of control they have over their own lives. They "live in a world of others' words" (Bakhtin, 1986, 143). And so in creating their own words, hip-hoppers reveal the greatest obscenity of all: the systematic and repeated denial of voice, and the great deception that most people have one. "Your children are not your children," Kahlil Gibran wrote.

They are the sons and daughters of Life's longing for itself.
They come through you but not from you,
And though they are with you yet they belong not to you.
YOU may give them your love but not your thoughts,
For they have their own thoughts. (Gibran, 1938: 17).

The range of discourses recited by these young artists reveal not some singular cultural form, but a multifarious narrative which can make important statements about how youth live in Lebanon. They add terms and distract, they inject sentiment and scoff at the social order. They develop "rituals of resistance" that challenge the deeply impressed habitus of Lebanese society. "For that idea of community, togetherness – that's what we rap for" (Rapper Binelli). And with the kind of youthful wisdom that tempts you to believe in the romantic ability of music to transform the way we live – and feel – and think – in this world, they say: "Before we can fix things in Lebanon, we need to start by fixing ourselves" (Rapper Venus).

A unique speech on the mic that makes the deaf hear it
As soon as it enters your ear , it will drum on your eardrum
My vocals flow with the wind , it will get to you even if you're hiding
Like fre-fre-frequencies it will find you
It's a message for you to receive
For me to fully deliver without skipping any details[16]
So when we leave a trace, people will not clear that trace
They'll clean around it on their own free will
That means, they'll hold on to it and take care of it
Without us paying them a fee to do it
It's their respect for art that's running through my veins,
I am convinced about it and can't let go of it
So don't mind me, you simply have to listen ...
(Fareeq el Atrash, "Intro")

NOTES

1   It should be noted that hip-hop culture consists of four traditional components: rap music, graffiti, DJing and break-dancing. This study is not an all-inclusive analysis of hip-hop in Lebanon; it focuses only on rappers in the country. Furthermore, while the term "rap" is usually reserved for the genre of music, and "hip-hop" the culture, I will occasionally use the terms interchangeably.

2   Rayess Bek's orchestra includes traditional instruments like the oud (oriental luth) and nay (oriental flute), in addition to a bass player and DJ. The rapper calls this project "orchestral hip-hop."

3   MC Chyno, MC Zoog and freestyler Double A the Preacherman rap in their native English and have garnered huge respect among the hip-hoppers.

4   It is interesting to note that profanity has become somewhat of a staple trope of western, mainstream rap, but to a large extent, hip-hoppers in Lebanon do not curse in their songs. In fact, most rappers refuse to work with self-proclaimed "gangsta" rap group *Erhab* (Terrorist) *Records* because of this. *Erhab's* lyrics are saturated with common elements of the 'gangsta' genre: expressions of street violence, criminality, drug use, and profanity. As one hip-hopper said about *Erhab*, "They're not gangsters, the real gangsters are the guys in power" (John Nasr, Fareeq el Atrash). The often deliberate rejection of cursing in Lebanon's hip-hop scene is provocative: coarse language full of slang and profanity can be considered an act of defiance against authority. But for the most part, Lebanese hip-hoppers do not choose to be defiant in this way.

5   Sehnaoui, Sary, director (2009, January 30), *The Basement Beirut*. Retrieved September, 2009 from http://www.youtube.com/watch?v=0ful75l6RMY.

6   The group chose the name Militia to "express our souls in songs, and not by fights and wars – like the real militias do."

7   The original translation is: "becoming the kind of people who collect the cost of a coffin." The line was adjusted for clarity.

8   *Superstar* was a reality show that broadcast on Future News between 2003 and 2008. It is based on the British singing competition and TV show *Pop Idol*.

9   Ramcess made up the word "intihabet" as a play on the Arabic word *intikhabet*, which means "elections."

10   To explain some the numbers used in this bar, the March 14 coalition in Lebanon is named after the date of a massive rally held in 2005 to demand Syria withdraw from the country. It was held in response to a pro-Syrian rally held on March 8, which the rival coalition draws its name from. All

this was in response to the February 14, 2005 assassination of former Prime Minister Rafik Hariri. Lebanon's most recent parliamentary elections were held on June 7, 2009.

11 I first saw Malikah perform at the Fete de la Musique concert in the summer of 2009. I was instantly drawn to her natural prowess on stage, her self-assured rhythm practically bouncing off the back of her Nike high tops. Malikah's voice is grainy – and she raps with a dynamic sense of rage that often stumbles into a proud, raspy shout. Her delivery is determined, accentuated by repetitive fist pumps and arm motions that hammer towards the ground. On the one hand, everything about her – the way she dresses, the way she interacts with people, even just the fact that she is a rapper – powerfully counters model expectations for the typical Lebanese woman. But on the other hand, Malikah has in many ways melded herself to fit the patriarchal character that dominates the Lebanese social order. As the only major female rapper in the country, you have to wonder: "would she have gotten this far, if she did not feign such an air of machismo?"

12 Samir Geagea: "Sure, sure." Michel Aoun: "Now again." Sayyed Hassan Nasrallah: "We have rockets that could reach Haifa and further than Haifa." Walid Jumblatt: "To where?"

13 Al-Manar, a television station in Lebanon, translates to "lighthouse" in English.
   • Future TV is a television station in Lebanon.
   • The letters "l, b, c" sound like the string of Arabic letters "*lu-bu-suh*" which means "to wear."
   • Al-Jazeera is "the island" in English.
   • The channel Al-Arabiyya, which means "the Arab," starts with the Arabic letter "*ein.*" When you "add a dot to it" – as the lyrics go – the letter becomes "*ghein,*" which changes the word to "Al-Gharbiyya," which means "the western."
   • New TV is a television station in Lebanon.
   • The letters "t" and "l" short for "Television du Liban," sound like the Arabic word "*intiqal,*" which means "transfer."
   • The letters "n, b, n," for the television channel NBN, sound like the word "*inbanena,*" which means "we were built."
   • The name of the television channel Orbit sounds like Arabic the word "*erbit,*" which means "it has come near."

14 The title of this song, "Demoqrati," is a play on the word "democratic." In Arabic, "*qrata*" literally means "being fucked." As Edd explains, "They call it a democratic system, but it's not. It's a dictatorship. It's not going to bring order. The system is fucking us."

15 The title of this song is a play on words. In Arabic, "*eh*" means "yes" and "*mos*" means "suck." So while also saying the word emos, the group is also trying to say, "Yeah, (you) suck."

16 This phrase originally translates to "without a single hair missing," but was adjusted for clarity.

About the Contributors

MOHAMMAD ABI SAMRA is a Lebanese journalist and novelist. He earned his diploma, d'études superiures, in the Sociology of Culture from the Lebanese University (1985). Abi Samra has been a journalist, writer, and reporter since 1977 and has served as director of investigative reporting at *Al Makassed* (1980–2). He has contributed weekly to the following literary supplements: *Assafir* (1985–7), *Al Hayat* (1988–92), and *Annahar* (1994–2009). As a prolific writer, he has produced rich and intimate ethnographies of urban neighborhoods in Tripoli, the southern suburbs of Beirut, and elsewhere. His publications include: *Arrested Indivdualism in Arab Culture* (2001), *Les Habitants des Images* (2003), and *Pays de l'humiilation et de la peur: Kurdistan, Beyrouth, Casablanca* (2004).

ASEF BAYAT was Professor of Sociology and Middle Eastern studies and held the Chair of Society and Culture of the Modern Middle East at Leiden University. He served as Academic Director of the International Institute for the Study of Islam in the Modern World (ISIM) and ISIM Chair of Islam and the Modern World at Leiden University from 2003 until 2009. Bayat has published widely on issues of political sociology, social movements, urban space and politics, the everyday of politics and religiosity, contemporary Islam, and the Muslim Middle East. Additionally, he has conducted extensive studies on the Iranian Islamic Revolution, Islamist movements in comparative perspective since the 1970s, non-movements of the urban poor, Muslim youth, women, and the politics of fun.

YOUSSEF COURBAGE was born in Aleppo and spent his childhood in Beirut. After studying economics and sociology at St-Joseph and the Lebanese University, he graduated from the Sorbonne and Dauphine University in Demography and Urban Planning. Since then, his career has been mainly devoted to demographic research and training, primarily with the United Nations in Beirut, Cairo, Yaoundé (Cameroon), Port-au-Prince (Haiti), and Rabat (Morocco). In 1990 he was appointed researcher and director at the National Institute of Demographic Studies in Paris. From 2003 to 2005 he headed the department of contemporary studies at the French Near East Institute in Beirut (IFPO). His numerous publications include: *Christians and Jews Under Islam* (with Philippe Fargues, 1997), *New Demographic Scenarios in the Mediterranean Region* (1998), *The Demographic Characteristics of Immigrant Populations in Europe* (edited with P. Compton and W. Haug, 2002), and *Le Rendez-Vous des Civilizations* (with Emmanuel Todd, 2007).

LARA DEEB is Associate Professor of Anthropology at Scripps College. She is the author of *An Enchanted Modern: Gender and Public Piety in Shi'i Lebanon* (2006) as well as numerous articles and chapters on gender, public spheres, ritual, temporality, and Hizbullah. Deeb is currently working on a co-authored book project with Mona Harb on new moralities and spatialities related to leisure in the southern suburb of Beirut. She is a member of the Middle East Report editorial committee.

JENNIFER DUECK is currently a British Academy post-doctoral research fellow at Oxford. She studied Modern History at Merton College, Oxford. Her doctoral thesis on "Culture and Politics in French Mandate Syria and Lebanon" was awarded the Leigh Douglas Memorial Prize from the British Society for Middle East Studies. She has held positions in Middle Eastern History at the University of Cambridge and the London School of Economics. Dueck is the author of *The Claims of Culture at Empire's End: Syria and Lebanon under French Rule* (2009).

CHRISTIAN GAHRE earned his MA in Middle Eastern Studies from the American University of Beirut, writing his thesis on the youthful mobilization of the Spring 2005 Independence Intifada. At the time, he was affiliated with the International Peace Research Institute in Oslo. Gahre is currently a humanitarian worker based in Kabul, Afghanistan.

MIRIAM GAZZAH currently works at a Dutch provincial museum (Limburgs Museum), conducting research on the migration history of this Dutch province. Born in the Netherlands (with Tunisian roots), she received her PhD in September 2008. Her dissertation entitled "Rhythms and Rhymes of Life: Music and Identification Processes of Dutch-Moroccan Youth" is one of the first and most extensive studies on Dutch-Moroccan youth culture. Gazzah studied Mediterranean Studies at the Radboud University in Nijmegen (1996–2001) and wrote her MA thesis on the emergence of the Algerian raï music subculture. She worked as a journalist for several Dutch regional newspapers (2001–03) and was a PhD fellow at the ISIM (Institute for the Study of Islam in the Modern World) at Leiden University (2003–07). She is also a post-doctoral researcher on the emergence of new youth cultures in Europe at Amsterdam University.

MONA HARB is Associate Professor of Urban Planning and Policy at the American University of Beirut. She specializes in research and teaching on the politics of public action and urban management. Her interests focus on the urban politics and cultural geography of Shi'a groups in Lebanon. Harb is the author of *Hezbollah: de la banlieue à la ville*, (forthcoming). Her more recent research investigates the geographies of pious morality in Beirut, with Lara Deeb. Harb also conducts research on post-war reconstruction and municipal governance. She occasionally consults on urban planning and city development issues for the World Bank, the European Union, UNDP, and UNESCWA.

NICOLIEN KEGELS completed her MA in Anthropology and Sociology of Non-Western Societies at the University of Amsterdam in 2007. In 2004 she spent one year at New York University to obtain a minor in Anthropology and Africana Studies. In 2006 Kegels conducted research on the Lebanese upper class and their discourse of national identity. Currently she resides in Beirut, where she works as an independent researcher and writer.

SAMIR KHALAF is Professor of Sociology and Director of the Center for Behavioral Research at the American University of Beirut. He has held academic appointments at Princeton, Harvard, MIT, and New York University. Among his books are *Sexuality in the Arab World* (with John Gagnon), *The Heart of Beirut*, *Cultural Resistance*, and *Lebanon Adrift* (forthcoming), all by Saqi Books.

CAROLYN LANDAU is Visiting Lecturer in the Music Department at City University, London, where she teaches Ethnomusicology and Musical Traditions from North and East Africa. Landau is currently undertaking doctoral research into music consumption and identity amongst Moroccans in London. She holds a BA in Music and French (University of Birmingham) and an MA in Ethnomusicology (SOAS). Landau worked for several years in the British Library Sound Archive, World and Traditional Music Section, and in Cameroon recording and researching traditional music. Her published articles are on Moroccan and Algerian musicians in London. She has also produced an album of UK-based Moroccan musicians (entitled *Moroccan Melodies in Britain*), in addition to many educational resources on Moroccan music and musicians as part of the project "Moroccan Memories in Britain."

CRAIG LARKIN is a Research Fellow at the Politics Department of Exeter University, working on an ESRC-funded project "Conflict in Cities and the Contested State." He received his PhD in Middle East Studies from the Institute of Arab and Islamic Studies, Exeter University in April 2009. His doctoral thesis "Memory and Conflict – Remembering and Forgetting the Past in Lebanon" focused on issues of identity, collective memory, and conflict resolution models in post-war Lebanon. His research interests include: the politics of memory and identity; urban and social division and conflict; processes of reconciliation and forgiveness. He has also been involved in research work for the European Commission on monitoring and verifying a Peacekeeping force, in South Lebanon (2000) and more recently employed as a research analyst for "Conflicts Forum" (2005) reviewing Islamist websites and assessing regional trends.

PARDIS MAHDAVI is Assistant Professor of Anthropology, at Pomona College. Mahdavi obtained a joint PhD from the Departments of Sociomedical Sciences and Anthropology at Columbia University. Her research interests include sexuality, human rights, youth culture, transnational feminism, and public health in the context of changing global and political structures. She has published in the *Encyclopaedia of Women in Islamic Cultures, Culture, Health and Sexuality, Anthropology News,* and the *Institute for the Study of Islam in the Modern World Review*. She has recently published her book *Passionate Uprisings: Iran's Sexual Revolution* (Stanford University Press, 2008). She is a recipient of several research awards from the American Public Health Association, the Society for Medical Anthropology, and the Society for Applied Anthropology.

ANGIE NASSAR is a reporter and blogger at Now Lebanon, an English news website based in Beirut. She is currently completing her Master's thesis on hip-hop in Lebanon at the Center for Arab and Middle Eastern Studies at the American University of Beirut. From 2007–8 she attended the American University in Cairo where she conducted research on Egyptian bloggers. Prior to that, Nassar worked as a television news producer for a CBS-affiliate station in Rochester, New York.

JULIE PETEET is Professor of Anthropology and Director of Middle East and Islamic Studies at the University of Louisville. Her research has focused on Palestinian displacement and refugee camps in Lebanon and more recently the spatio-temporal dimensions of the policy of separation and closure in Palestine. She has authored two books: *Gender in Crisis: Women and the Palestinian Resistance Movement* (Columbia University Press, 1991) and *Landscape of Hope and Despair: Palestinian Refugee Camps* (University of Pennsylvania Press, 2005). She has published in a variety of journals including *Signs, American Ethnologist, Cultural Anthropology, Cultural Survival, International Journal of Middle East Studies, Third World Quarterly,* and *Middle East Report* as well as contributed numerous chapters in edited volumes. Her research has been funded by SSRC, Wenner-Gren, Fulbright, the Mellon Foundation, CAORC, and PARC. She serves on the Editorial Board of MERIP, is a board member of PARC, and was an associate editor of the *Encyclopedia of Women and Islamic Cultures.*

CURTIS N. RHODES, JR., is General Director of Questscope in Bromley, England.

ROSEANNE SAAD KHALAF is Associate Professor of English and Creative Writing at the American University of Beirut. She is the author and editor of five books, among them *Transit*

Beirut, a 2003 collection of literary snapshots from today's Beirut, *Hikayat: Short Stories by Lebanese Woman* (2006) and, most recently, *Arab Society and Culture* (2009), co-edited with Samir Khalaf.

FIDEL SBEITY was born in South Lebanon and became a journalist while pursuing a law degree in Beirut. Since 2000, as a writer and freelance journalist, he has contributed articles and reports to numerous Lebanese and Arab periodicals and newspapers, including *Assafir, Alhiwar, Albalad, Al Mustaqbal, NowLebanon* and the cultural supplement of *Annahar*, where he also publishes poems, essays and short stories. Among his publications are: *Touffahat Newton* (*Newton's Apples* 2005) and *Kill the Man; Lift his Skull High* (2008).

DIANE SINGERMAN is Associate Professor in the Department of Government, School of Public Affairs at American University (in Washington, DC). She received her BA, MA, and PhD from Princeton University and did graduate work at the American University in Cairo, living in Egypt for several years throughout her career. Among her publications are: *Cairo Cosmopolitan: Politics, Culture, and Urban Space in the New Globalized Middle East* (with Paul Amar, 2006), *Avenues of Participation: Family, Politics, and Networks in Urban Quarters of Cairo* (1995) and *Development, Change, and Gender in Cairo: A View from the Household* (with Homa Hoodfar, 1996). She is interested in comparative politics, gender and politics in Egypt and the Middle East, informal politics, political participation, urban studies, globalization, and social movements. Her recent research interests include Personal Status Law reform, the cost of marriage, poverty, the problems which young people face in the Middle East, and urban politics in the era of globalization.

JOHANNA WYN is Director of the Australian Youth Research Centre at the University of Melbourne. Her research focuses on young people's experiences of education and work, their health and well-being. She leads the Life-Patterns research program, a comparative longitudinal panel cohort study of young people comparing two generations of young Australians. Her books include *Rethinking Youth* (with Rob White, 1997), a classic text within youth studies, *Youth, Education and Risk: Facing the Future* (with Peter Dwyer, 2001), *Youth and Society: exploring the social dynamics of youth* (with Rob White, 2004, 2008) and most recently, *Youth Health and Welfare: the cultural politics of education and wellbeing* (2009).

MAI YAMANI is an independent academic with a PhD in Social Anthropology from Oxford University. In 2008 she was a visiting scholar at Carnegie Middle East Center and a visiting fellow at the Brookings Institute in Washington DC in 2008. Yamani was a research fellow at the Royal Institute of International Affairs (Chatham House) in London (1997–2007) and at the Centre for Middle Eastern and Islamic Law at London University (1992–2000). From 1990 to 2000 she held the position of academic adviser at the Center for Contemporary Arab Studies at Georgetown University and from 1981 to 1984 Yamani was a lecturer in anthropology and sociology at King Abdul Aziz University, Jeddah. Her publications include *Cradle of Islam: The Hijaz and the Quest for an Arabian Identity* (2004), *Changed Identities: The Challenge of the New Generation in Saudi Arabia* (2000) and *Feminism and Islam: Legal and Literary Perspectives* (1996).

Bibliography

Abaza, Mona. 2001. "Perceptions of 'Urfi Marriage in the Egyptian Press." *ISIM Newsletter* 7 (March): 20–21.

Abdel-Hay, Ahmed Tahami. 2002. "Al-Tawajjohat al-Siyasiyya Lil-Ajyal al-Jadida," *Al-Demokratiya*, no. 6, pp: 117–8.

Abdul Khabeer, S. 2007. "Rep that Islam: The Rhyme and Reason of American Islamic Hip Hop," *The Muslim World*, vol. 97 (1): pp.125–141.

Abdullah, A. 2004. *Al-Ulama' Wal 'Arsh: Thunaiyyat Al Sultah fi Al Saudiyya* (The Ulema and the Throne: The Duality of Authority in Saudi Arabia) (Paris: Maktabat Al sharq).

Abdul-Rahman, Mustafa. 2001. "Sex Urfi Marriage as Survival Strategy in Dahab," term paper Fall, p. 18.

Abu-Lughod, Lila. 1986. *Veiled Sentiments: Honor and Poetry in a Bedouin Society.* (Berkeley: University of California Press).

Adelkhah, F. 2004. *Being Modern in Iran.* (New York, NY: Columbia University Press).

Adorno, Theodor. 1976. *Introduction to the Sociology of Music.* (New York: Continuum).

Al-Ahmad, J. 1962. *Gharb-zadagi* (Weststruckness). (Tehran: Azad Press).

Al Faruqi, Lois Ibsen. 1985. "Music, Musicians and Muslim Law". *Asian Music* 17, no. 1: 3–36.

Al-Hassan, H. 2006. "The Role of Religion in Building National Identity-Case Study: Saudi Arabia." Unpublished PhD. Dissertation (London: University of Westminster).

Al-Husri, Sati'. 1946. *Ara' wa ahadith fi al-tarbiya wa al-ta'alim* (Cairo: Matbaat al-risāla, 1944), 68–75. Public Record Office, London, Foreign Office/371/52909, Young to Bevin, "Political Review of Syria and Lebanon for 1945."

Al-'Isa, A. 2009. *Islah al ta'lib fi Al Saudia: Bain Ghiab al Ru'ya al Siasiyya wa Tawajjus Al Thaqafah al Diniyya* (Beirut: Dar Al-Saqi): 78–80.

Al-Jazeera. 2009. "Riz Khan Interviews Sami Yusuf."

Al-Riyadh. 2005. "Prince Sultan: 'We Will Select Members for the Shura from all Parts of the Kingdom.'"

Allam, Abeer. 2000. "Urfi Delivers the Goods, at Half Price." *Middle East Times* (February 18).

Altorki, Soraya. 1986. *Women in Saudi Arabia: Ideology and Behavior among the Elite.* (New York: Columbia University Press).

Amer, Mona. 2006. "The Egyptian Youth Labor Market, School-to-Work Transition, 1998–2006." Dissemination Conference. Cairo. The Population Council. October 30.

Amin, H. 2001. "Mass Media in Arab States Between Diversification and Stagnation: An Overview." In Kai Hafez (ed.) *Mass Media, Politics, and Society in the Middle East.* (Cresskill, NJ: Hampton Press).

Aminzade, Ronald R. & Doug McAdam. 2001. "Emotions and Contentious Politics". in Aminzade, Ronald R., Jack A. Goldstone, Doug McAdam, Elizabeth J. Perry, William H. Sewell, Jr., Sidney Tarrow & Charles Tilly (eds.), *Silence and Voice in the Study of Contentious Politics.* New York: Cambridge University Press.

Ammar, Hamid. 1954. *Growing Up in an Egyptian Village.* (London: Routedge & Kegan Paul).

Amnesty International. "Israel and the Occupied Territories." 1991. *The Military Justice System in the Occupied Territories: Detention, Interrogation and Trial Procedures.* (New York: Amnesty International).

Amuzegar, J. 2004. "Iran's Unemployment Crisis". *Middle East Economic Survey* vol. XLVII, No. 41. October 11, 2004.

d'Ancona, Matthew. 2009. "Britishness." BBC Radio.

Anderson, Benedict. [1983] 1991. *Imagined Communities*, New York: Verso.

Andres, A., & Wyn, J. 2010. *The Making of a Generation: Young Adults in Canada and Australia*, (Toronto University Press: Toronto) (forthcoming).

Armstrong, D. 2004. "A Risky Business? Research, Policy, Governmentality and Youth Offending." *Youth Justice*, 4 (2), 100–7.

Armstrong, Karen. 2000. *Islam: A Short History, Universal History*. (London: Weidenfeld & Nicolson).

Aronoff, Myron. 1982. "Culture and Political Change." *Political Anthropology Series*, 2. (New Brunswick, NJ: Transaction Books).

Aronson, Geoffrey. 1987. *Creating Facts: Israel, Palestinians, and the West Bank*. (Washington, DC: Institute for Palestine Studies).

Asad, Talal. 1993. *Genealogies of Religion: Discipline and Reasons of Power in Christianity and Islam*. (Baltimore, MD: Johns Hopkins University Press).

Ash, Timothy Gorton. 2005. "Soldiers of Hidden Imam," *New York Review Books* 52, no.17 (November 3).

Ashraf, Ahmad & Banuazizi, Ali. 1985. "The State, Classes and Modes of Mobilization in the Iranian Revolution." *State, Culture and Society*, Vol. 1, no. 3.

Assaad, Ragui. 2006. "The Egypt Labor Market Panel Survey, 2006: Employment and Unemployment Dynamics." Dissemination Conference. Cairo. The Population Council. October 30.

Assaad, Ragui and Malik Rouchdy. 1998. "Poverty and Poverty Alleviation Strategies in Egypt." A Report Submitted to the Ford Foundation. Cairo. January.

Assaad, Ragui and Roudi-Fahimi, Farzaneh. 2007. "Youth in the Middle East and North Africa: Demographic Opportunity or Challenge?" Population Reference Bureau. Washington, DC.

Attali, Jacques. 1985. *Noise: The Political Economy of Music*. (Minneapolis: University of Minnesota Press).

Attenhoffer, Jonas. 2007. "Youth Bulge Violence", *The Jerusalem Post*.

Australian Bureau of Statistics. 2005a. *Australian Social Trends 2005, Catalogue No. 4102.0* (Canberra, Commonwealth of Australia).

Australian Bureau of Statistics. 2005b. *Information Paper: Key Issues Relating to Children and Youth*, Australia, (Canberra: Australian Bureau of Statistics).

Aydoun, A. 2001. *Musique du Maroc*, Casablcanca: Editions EDDIF/ Autres Temps.

Baden-Powell, Robert. 2004. *Scouting for Boys: A Handbook for Instruction in Good Citizenship*, ed. Elleke Boehmer (Oxford: Oxford University Press,): 282–4, 299–301.

Bailey, Brian. 2006. "Emo Music and Youth Culture." In Shirley Steinberg, Priya Parmar and Birgit Richard. Eds. *Contemporary youth culture: an international encyclopedia*. Volume 2. (Greenwood Publishing Group).

Baily, J. and Collyer, M. 2006. 'Introduction: Music and Migration', *Journal of Ethnic and Migration Studies*, vol. 32(2): pp. 167–182.

Bakhtin, M. M. 1986. *Speech Genres and Other Late Essays*. Trans. by Vern W. McGee. (Austin: University of Texas Press.)

Balasescu, Alexandru. 2007. "Haute Couture in Tehran: Two Faces of an Emerging Fashion Scene." *Fashion Theory*, 11(2/3): 299–318.

Barendregt, B. 2006. "The Art of No-Seduction: Muslim Boy-Band Music in Southeast Asia and the Fear of the Female Voice," *IIAS Newsletter*, vol. 40 (Spring): p. 10.

Bashshur, Munir. 2003. "The Deepening of Social and Communal Cleavages in the Lebanese Educational System." In Theodor Hanf & Nawaf Salam (eds.) *Lebanon in Limbo: Postwar Society and State in an Uncertain Regional Environment*. (Baden-Baden: Nomos): 159–179.

Basmanji, K. 2006. *Tehran Blues: Youth Culture in Iran*. (Tehran: Saqi Books).

Bauman, Z. 2001. *The Community: Seeking Safety in an Insecure World (Themes for the 21st. Century)*, (London: Polity Press).

Bayat, Asef. 1997. *Street Politics: Poor Peoples Movements in Iran* (New York: Columbia University Press) Chapter 1.

— 2002. "Islamism and the Politics of Fun". *Public Culture* vol. 19 no. 3.

— 2007. "Islamism and the Politics of Fun." *Public Culture*, 19 (3): 433–45.

— 2010. *Life as Politics* (Stanford University Press): 43–65.

Beattie, Meriel. 1999. "Why Emirati Weddings are Getting Less Lavish." BBC Online. 16 December. http://www.zawaj.com/weddingways/emirati99.html. (November 3, 2006).

Beck, U. and Beck-Gernsheim, E. 2002. *Individualization* (London: Sage).

Beck, U., & Lau, C. 2005. "Second Modernity as a Research Agenda: Theoretical and Empirical Explorations in the 'Meta-Change' of Modern Society," *The British Journal of Sociology*, 56(4) pp. 525–57.

Beehner, Lionel. 2007. "The Effects of Youth Bulge on Civil Conflicts", *Council of Foreign Relations*.

Ben-Ari, Eyal. 1989. "Masks and Soldiering: The Israeli Army and the Palestinian Uprising." *Cultural Anthropology* 4: 372–389

Bennett, A. 2000. *Popular Music and Youth Culture. Music, Identity and Place*, (London: MacMillan Press).

— 2001. *Cultures of Popular Music*, (Buckingham: Open University Press).

— 2004. "Hip-Hop am Main, Rappin' on the Tyne: Hip-Hop Culture as a Local Construct in Two European Cities." In Murray Forman and Mark Anthony Neal. Eds. *That's the Joint!: The Hip-Hop Studies Reader*. (New York: Routledge).

Bennett, A. & Kahn-Harris, K. (eds) . 2004. *After Subculture. Critical Studies in Contemporary Youth Culture* (Houndmill: Palgrave MacMillan).

Best, Beverly. 1997. "Over-the-counter-culture: retheorizing resistance in popular culture." In Steve Redhead, Derek Wynne and Justine O'Connor. Eds. *The Clubcultures Reader: readings in popular cultural studies*. (Malden: Blackwell Publishers).

Beutell, N. J., & Wittig-Berman, U. 2008. "Work-Family Conflict and Work-Family Synergy for Generation X, Baby Boomers, and Matures." *Journal of Managerial Psychology*, 23(5) 507–23.

Bevan, Robert. 2006. *The Destruction of Memory: Architecture at War.* (London: Reaktion).

Bhabha, Homi K. 1994. *The Location of Culture*. (New York: Routledge).

— 2001. "Unsatisfied: Notes on Vernacular Cosmopolitanism." In Gregory Castle, ed. *Postcolonial discourses: an anthology*. (Oxford: Blackwell Publishers Ltd).

Bilu, Yoram. 1991. "The Other as Nightmare: The Articulation of Aggression in Children's Dreams in Israel and the West Bank." Paper presented at the 90th Annual Meeting of the American Anthropological Association, Chicago.

Bin Baz, A. 1993. *Collection of Fatwas.* (Riyadh: Dar Uli al-Nahi): 302.

Birth & Childhood Among the Arabs: 1947. *Studies in a Muhammadan Village in Palestine.* (Helsingfors, Finland: Soderstrom & Co.)

Blacking, John. 1973. *How Musical Is Man*: (University Washington Press).

Blacking, John, & Reginald Byron. 1995. *Music, Culture, & Experience: Selected Papers of John Blacking*. (Chicago; London: University of Chicago Press).

Bohlman, Philip V. 2002. *World Music: A Very Short Introduction*. (Oxford: Oxford University Press).

Borneman, John. 1992. *Belonging in the Two Berlins: Kin, State, Nation.* (Cambridge: Cambridge University Press).

Boubekeur, A. 2005. "Cool and Competitive. Muslim Culture in the West," *ISIM Review*, vol.16: pp. 12–3.

Bourdieu, Pierre. 1977. *Outline of a Theory of Practice.* (Cambridge: Cambridge University Press).

— 1989. "Social Space and Symbolic Power," *Sociological Theory*, 7 (1):14–25.

— 1991. *Language and Symbolic Power.* (Cambridge: Harvard University Press).

— 1993. "'Youth' Is Just a Word," in Bourdieu, *Sociology in Question* (London: Sage).

Bousetta, H. 1996. "Kunst, Cultuur en Literatuur in de Marokkaanse Gemeenschap in Nederland," *Migrantenstudies*, vol. 12 (4): pp.182–94.

Braudel, Fernand. 1979. *The Perspective of the World*. Vol. 3 (New York: Harper & Raw): 621.

Brenneis, Donald. 1987. "Performing Passions: Aesthetics and Politics in an Occasionally Egalitarian Community." *American Ethnologist* 14:236–250.

Brookings Institution. 2009. "Middle East Youth Bulge: Challenge or Opportunity?"

Brown, Jonathon. 2007. "Holy Rock Star: The Voice of Islam." *The Independent*.

Buitelaar, M. 2008. "De islamisering van Identiteit onder Jongeren van Marokkaanse afkomst," in

Ter Borg, M., Borgman, E. Buitelaar, M., et al (eds) *Handboek Religie in Nederland*, Zoetermeer: Meinema, pp 239–52.

Bundy, Colin. 1987. "Street Sociology and Pavement Politics: Aspects of Youth and Student Resistance in Cape Town, 1985." *Journal of Southern African Studies* 13, no. 3: 303–30.

"By a Margin of 2 Million... Egyptian Young Men are Ahead of Young Women in 'Onoussa" [Spinsterhood]. 2006. *Al-Arabeyya*. 25 June. http://www.alarabiya.net/Articles/2006/06/25/25066.htm. (November 25, 2006). (In Arabic).

Bynner, J. 2005. Rethinking the Youth Phase of the Life-Course: The Case for Emerging Adulthood?, *Journal of Youth Studies*, 8(4) 367–84.

Cadiot, Jean-Michel, 2001. *AP Report*, at Iran Mania.com, August 20.

Çağlar, A. 1998. "Popular Culture, Marginality and Institutional Incorporation: German-Turkish Rap and Turkish Pop in Berlin," *Cultural Dynamics*, vol. 10 (3): pp. 243–61.

Caincar, L., & Abunimah, A. 1998. *Poverty and Social Exclusion*. (Chapin Hall Center for Children at the University of Chicago Report).

Carey, James W. 2009. *Communication as Culture: Essays on Media and Society*. (New York: Routledge).

Carrington, B., & Wilson, B. 2004. "Dance nations: Rethinking Youth Subcultural Theory" in Bennet, A., Kahn-Harris, K (ed.) (2004) *After Subculture. Critical Studies in Contemporary Youth Culture*, (Houndmill: Palgrave MacMillan) pp. 65–78.

Caton, Steven. 1985. "The Poetic Construction of Self." *Anthropological Quarterly* 58:141–51.

Central Agency for Public Mobilization and Statistics. 1996. *The Statistical Year Book* (Cairo: CAPMAS).

Chaaban, Jad. 2009. "The Impact of Instability and Migration on Lebanon's Human Capital." In Navtej Dhillon and Tarik Yousef. eds. *Generation in Waiting: the unfulfilled promise of young people in the Middle East*. (Washington, DC.: Brookings Institution Press).

Chang, Jeff. 2005. *Can't Stop, Won't Stop: a history of the hip-hop generation*. (New York: St. Martin's Press).

Change-Institute. 2009. "The Moroccan Muslim Community in England: Understanding Muslim Ethnic Communities." London: Communities and Local Government.

Cheney, Charise L. 2005. *Brothers Gonna Work it Out: Sexual Politics in the Golden Age of Rap Nationalism*. (New York: NYU Press).

Cherti, Myriam. 2008. *Paradoxes of Social Capital : A Multi-Generational Study of Moroccans in London, Imiscoe Dissertations*. (Amsterdam: Amsterdam University Press).

— 2009. "British Moroccans: Citizenship in Action – a Runnymede Community Study." In *A Runnymede Community Study*. (London: Runnymede).

Christiansen, Catrine, Mats Utas & Henrik E. Vigh. 2006. "Introduction: Navigating Youth, Generating Adulthood." In *Navigating Youth, Generating Adulthood: Social Becoming in an African Context*, 9–30. (Stockholm: Nordiska Afrikainstitutet, Uppsala).

City Skype conference, 2009, 12 January.

Clark, Lynn Schofield. 2007. "Introduction: Identity, Belonging, and Religious Lifestyle Branding (Fashion Bibles, Bhangra Parties, and Muslim Pop)." In *Religion, Media, and the Marketplace*, edited by Lynn Schofield Clark, 1–36. Piscataway, (NJ.: Rutgers University Press).

Cockburn, Alexander & Blackburn, Robin (eds.) 1969. *Student Power: Problem, Diagnosis, Action* (London: Penguin Books).

Cohen, P. & Ainley, P. 2000. "In the country of the blind?: Youth Studies and Cultural Studies in Britain." *Journal of Youth Studies*, 3(1), pp. 79–95.

Cohen, Sarah. 1998. "Sounding out the City: Music and the Sensuous Production of Place." In Andrew Leyshon, David Matless and George Revill. Eds. *The Place of Music*. (New York: Guilford Press).

Cole, Jennifer. 2007. "Fresh Contact in Tamatave, Madagascar: Sex, Money, and Intergenerational Transformation." In *Generations and Globalization: Youth, Age and Family in the New World Economy*, 74–101, ed. J. Cole and D. Durham. (Bloomington: Indiana University Press).

Cole, Jennifer and Durham, Deborah. 2007. "Introduction: Age, Regeneration and the Intimate Politics of Globalization." In *Generations and Globalization: Youth, Age, and Family in the New World Economy*, 1–28. (Bloomington: Indiana University Press)

Comaroff, Jean. 1985. *Body of Power, Spirit of Resistance: The Culture and History of a South African People*. (Chicago and London: University of Chicago Press).

Comaroff, Jean and Comaroff, John L. 1987. "The Madman and the Migrant: Work and Labor in the Historical Consciousness of a South African People." *American Ethnologist* 14:191–209.

Combs-Schilling, Elaine. 1991. "Etching Patriarchal Rule: Ritual Dye, Erotic Potency, and the Moroccan Monarchy." *Journal of the History of Sexuality* 1:658–81.

Cook, Nicholas. 1998. *Music: A Very Short Introduction*. (Oxford: Oxford University Press).

Cook, M. 2003. *Forbidding Wrong in Islam: An Introduction*. (Cambridge University Press).

Courbage, Youssef. 1997. "The Demographic Factor in Ireland's Movement Towards Partition, (1607–1921)", *Population an English Selection*.

— 2003. *New Demographic Scenarios in the Mediterranean*, (INED, Paris).

Courbage, Youssef & Todd, Emmanuel. 2007. *Le rendez-vous des civilisations*, (Paris).

Cross, Ian. 2003. "Music and Bio-cultural Evolution." In *The Cultural Study of Music: A Critical Introduction*, edited by Martin Clayton, Trevor Herbert and Richard Middleton, 19–30. (London: Routledge).

Dandashi, Ali. 1996. *The Man Who Spread the Arab Scout Renaissance* (Beirut: Dār al-Sirāj li- l-tibā'a wa-l-nashr):11–12.

Daoudi, B. and Miliani, H. 1996. *L'aventure du raï. Musique et société*, (Paris: Editions du Seuil).

— 2002. *Beurs' Melodies. Cent ans de Chansons Immigrés du Blues Berbère au Rap Beur*, (Paris: Editions Séguier).

Davis, Susan. & Davis, Douglas. 1989. *Adolescence in a Moroccan Town*. (New Brunswick and London: Rutgers University Press).

Deeb, Lara. 2006. *An Enchanted Modern: Gender and Public Piety in Shi'i Lebanon*. (Princeton: Princeton University Press).

— 2008. "Exhibiting the 'Just-Lived Past': Hizbullah's Nationalist Narratives in Transnational Political Context." *Contemporary Studies in Society and History*, 50 (2): 369–99.

Deeb, Lara & Harb, Mona. 2007. "Sanctioned Pleasures: Youth, Piety and Leisure in Lebanon." *Middle East Report* 245 (winter): 12–9.

— 2010. "Politics, Culture, Religion: How Hizbullah is Constructing an Islamic Milieu in Lebanon." *Review of Middle East Studies*. Winter, 2009.

Denis, Eric & Bayat, Asef. 2001. "Egypt: Twenty Years of Urban Transformation, 1980–2000." Report for the International Institute of Development and Urbanization (London).

Diani, Mario. 2000. "Simmel to Rokkan and Beyond: Towards a Network Theory of (New) Social Movements". *European Journal of Social Theory* 3(4): 387–406.

Dusseldorp Skills Forum, 1999. *Australia's Young Adults: The Deepening Divide*, (Dusseldorp Skills Forum: Sydney).

— 2006. *How Young People are Faring 2006 Key Indicators*, (Dusseldorp Skills Forum: Sydney).

Dwyer, P., Smith, G., Tyler, D. & Wyn, J., 2005. *Immigrants in Time: Life-Patterns 2004*, Research Report 27, (Youth Research Centre: Melbourne).

Dyson, Michael Eric. 2004. *The Michael Eric Dyson Reader*. (New York: Basic Civitas Books).

Edermariam, Aida. 2007. "Muslim Superstar." *The Guardian*.

Eickelman, Dale F. & Anderson, Jon W. (eds.) 1999. *New Media in the Muslim World: The Emerging Public Sphere*. (Bloomington, IN: University of Indiana Press).

El-Khazen, Farid. 2000. *The Breakdown of the State in Lebanon, 1967–1976*, Cambridge, Massachusetts: Harvard University Press.

El-Solh, Raghid. 2004. *Lebanon and Arabism: National Identity and State Formation* (London: I.B. Tauris,): 243–5.

El-Tawila, Saher and Khadr, Zeinab. 2004. "Patterns of Marriage and Family Formation among Youth in Egypt, 2004." Cairo: National Population Council, Center for Information and Computer Systems, Faculty of Economics and Political Science, Cairo University.

El-Taybeb, F. 2004. "Kanak Attak! Hip-hop und (anti-)Identitätsmodelle der Zweiten Generation," in: Sökefeld, M. (ed.) (2004) *Jenseits des Paradigmas kultureller Differenz. Neue Perspektiven auf Einwanderer aus der Türkei*, (Bielefeld: Transscript Verlag) pp. 95–110.

El-Zanaty, Fatma. 2000. "Behavioral Research among Egyptian University Students," NEDTECG,

FHI, Behavioral Research Unit, Cairo, 1996; reported in Barbara Ibrahim and Hind Wassef, "Caught between Two Worlds: Youth in the Egyptian Hinterland," in *Alienation or Integration of Arab Youth*, Roel Meijer (ed.) (London: Curzon Press).

Emirbayer, Mustafa & Jeff Goodwin. 1995. "Network Analysis, Culture, and the Problem of Agency". *The American Journal of Sociology* 99 (6): 1411-1454.

Esposito, J. L., & R. K. Ramazani. 2001. *Iran at the Cossroads*, 1st edition. (New York: Palgrave).

Soueif, M.I. et al, 1990. "Use of Psychoactive Substances among Male Secondary School Pupils in Egypt: A Study of a Nationwide Representative Sample," *Drug and Alcohol Dependence* 26, pp. 71–2.

Ewick, P. & S. Silbey. 1995. "Subversive Stories and Hegemonic Tales: Towards a Sociology of Narrative." *Law and Society Review*, 2, 197–226.

Ezzat, Dina. 2000. "Sacred Knots and Unholy Deals: The Road Towards Pro-Women Legal Reform in Egypt." In *No Paradise Yet*, eds. Judith Mirsky and Marty Radlett, 39–60. (London: Panos/ Zed Press).

Fanon, Frantz. 1969. *The Wretched of the Earth*. (Harmondsworth: Penguin Book Ltd).

Faour, M. 1998. *The Silent Revolution in Lebanon: Changing Values of the Youth*. (Beirut: American University of Beirut).

Farmer, Henry George. 1929. *A History of Arabian Music to the Xiiith Century*. (New Delhi: Goodword Books).

Faust, D. G. 2004. "'We Should Grow Too Fond of It': Why We Love the Civil War," *Civil War History* L (4): 368–83.

Feldman, Allen. 1991. *Formations of Violence: The Narrative of the Body and Political Terror in Northern Ireland*. (Chicago: University of Chicago Press).

Flynn, Donna. 1997. "'We are the Border': Identity, Exchange and the State along the Benin- Nigeria Border." In *American Ethnologist* 24: 311–30.

Flyvbjerg, Bent. 2001. *Making Social Science Matter: Why Social Inquiry Fails and How it Can Succeed Again*. (Cambridge: Cambridge University Press).

Forman, Murray. 2004. "Represent: Race, Space, and Place in Rap Music." In Murray Forman and Mark Anthony Neal. Eds. *That's the Joint!: The Hip-Hop Studies Reader*. (New York: Routledge).

Foster, Angel. 2006. "Reproductive and Sexual Health: Knowledge, Attitudes and Behaviors of Female University Students in Tunisia and Jordan." Unpublished paper delivered at Second World Congress of Middle Eastern Studies (WOCMES), 14 June, Amman, Jordan.

— 2002. "Young Women's Sexuality in Tunisia: The Health Consequences of Misinformation among University Students." In *Everyday Life in the Muslim Middle East*, Donna Lee Bowen and Evelyn A. Early, eds., 98–110. (Bloomington, IN: Indiana University Press).

Foucault, Michel 1979. *Discipline and Punish: The Birth of the Prison*. (New York: Vintage Books).

—(1988) 'Technologies of the Self', in *Technologies of the Self: A Seminar* with Foucault, Michel, L. H. Martin, H. Gutman, and P. Hutton (eds), (London: Tavistock Publications).

Foundation for Young Australians (FYA). 2008. *How Young People are Faring 08*, Foundation for Young Australians: Melbourne.

France, A. 2008. Risk Factor Analysis and the Youth Question. *Journal of Youth Studies* 11(1): 1–15.

France, A. & Homel, R. 2006. "Societal Access Routes and Developmental Pathways: Putting Social Structure and Young People's Voice into the Analysis Pathways Into and Out of Crime." *Australian and New Zealand of Criminology*, 39 (3), 287–94.

Frith, Simon. 1996. "Music and Identity." In *Questions of Cultural Identity*, edited by Stuart Hall and Paul du Gay, 108–27. (London: SAGE).

Fuller, Graham. 1995. *The Demographic Backdrop to Ethnic Conflict: a Geographical Overview*, (Washington).

— *The Youth Factor: the New Demographics of the Middle East and the implications for U.S. policy*, The Brooking Project on US policy towards the Islamic World, n.d.

Garbarino, J. 1995. *Raising Children in a Socially Toxic Environment*. (San Francisco: Jossey-Bass).

Gazzah, Miriam. *Rhythms and Rhymes of Life : Music and Identification Processes of Dutch-Moroccan Youth*. (Leiden).

— 2005. "Maroc-Hop: Music and Youth Identities", *ISIM Review*, vol. 16 (autumn): pp. 6–7.

— 2007a. "Het Nederlands-Marokkaanse Uitgaanscircuit: een mix Van Popcultuur en religie?", *Al Nisa, Islamitisch Maandblad voor Vrouwen*, vol. 7 (July): pp. 18–22.

Gender in Crisis. 1991. *Women and the Palestinian Resistance Movement*. (New York: Columbia University Press).

Gerlach, Luther. & Hines, Virginia. 1970. *People, Power and Change: Movements of Social Transformation*. (Indianapolis: Bobbs-Merrill Educational Publications).

Gibran, Kahlil. 1938. *The Prophet*. (London: Heinemann). (Original work published 1926).

Giddens, A. 1990. *The Consequences of Modernity* (Stanford, CA: Stanford University Press).

— 1991. *Modernity and Self-Identity: Self and Society in the Late Modern Age*. (Stanford, Calif.: Stanford University Press).

Gilmore, David. 1990. *Manhood in the Making: Cultural Concepts of Masculinity*. (New Haven and London: Yale University Press).

Gilroy, Paul. 1995. *The Black Atlantic: modernity and double consciousness*. (Cambridge: Harvard University Press).

Gilsenan, Michael. 1982. *Recognizing Islam: Religion and Society in the Modern Arab World*. (New York: Pantheon Books).

Goffman, E. 1971. *The Presentation of Self in Everyday Life*. (New York: Doubleday).

Golzari's, Mahmoud. 2004. "Young Girls and the Challenges of Life," cited in *ISNA News Agency*, 22 Ordibehest 1383.

Goodwin, Jeff & James M. Jasper (eds.). 2004. *Rethinking Social Movements: Structure, Meaning, and Emotion*. Lanham: Rowman & Littlefield Publishers, Inc.

Goodwin, Jeff, James M. Jasper & Francesca Polletta. 2001. *Passionate Politics: Emotions and Social Movements*. Chicago: The University of Chicago Press.

— 2004. "Emotional Dimensions of Social Movements". in Snow, David A., Sarah A. Soule & Hanspeter Kriesi (eds.), *The Blackwell Companion to Social Movements*. Oxford: Blackwell Publishing Ltd.

Grandjouan, M. 936. *Le scoutisme chez les musulmans', Entretiens sur l'évolution des pays de civilisation arabe*, vol. 1 (Paris: Paul Hartmann,): 111.

Granqvist, Hilma. 1931 & 1935. *Marriage Conditions in a Palestinian Village*. 2 vols. (Helsingfors, Finland: Societas Scientiarum Fennica).

Griffith, R. Marie. 2000. *God's Daughters: Evangelical Women and the Power of Submission*. (Berkeley: University of California Press).

Gross, J., McMurray, D., Swedenburg, T. 1992. "Raï, Rap and Ramadan Nights. Franco- Maghrebi Cultural Identities," *Middle Eastern Report*, vol. 178 (September-October): pp. 11–6.

Gupta, Akhil & James Ferguson. Reprint 1997. *Culture, Power, Place*. Durham, N.C.: Duke University Press.

Haeri, Shahla. 2004. "Mut'a: Regulating Sexuality and Gender Relations in Postrevolutionary Iran." In *Islamic Legal Interpretation: Muftis and their Fatwas*, (eds.) M. K. Masud, B, Messick, & D. S. Powers, 251–61.

Hage, Ghassan. 2000. *White Nation: Fantasies of the White supremacy in a multicultural society*. Annandale: Pluto Press Australia.

Hajjar, Lisa, & Beinin, Joel. 1988. "Palestine for Beginners." *Middle East Report* 154:17–20.

Hall, Stuart, & Jefferson, Tony, (eds.) 1975. *Resistance through Rituals: Youth Subcultures in Post-war Britain*. (London: Hutchinson).

Halliday, Fred. 1992. "The Millet of Manchester: Arab Merchants and Cotton Trade." *British Journal of Middle Eastern Studies* 19, no. 2: 159–76.

Hammond, Andrew, 1998. "Campuses Stay Clear of Politics," *Cairo Times*, October 15–28, p. 7

Hanf, Theodor. 1993. *Coexistence in Wartime Lebanon* (London: I.B. Tauris).

— 2003. "The Sceptical Nation: Opinions and Attitudes Twelve Years after the End of the War. In Theodor Hanf & Nawaf Salam (eds.) *Lebanon in Limbo* (Baden-Baden): 197–228.

Harb, Mona. 2005. "Islamizing Entertainment and Tourism Activities in Lebanon." Paper Presented at the conference: In *Visible Histories: The Politics of Placing the Past*, Amsterdam, Institute for the Study of Islam in the Modern World.

— *Hezbollah: De la Banlieue á la Ville*. (Paris: Karthala-IFPO) in press.

Harb, Mona & Deeb, Lara. 2009. "Claiming Rights to the City? Pious Youth's Leisure Geographies in Beirut's Southern Peripheries." Paper presented at the conference "Peripheries: Decentering Urban Theory," (University of California: Berkeley).

Hargreaves, I., 2003. *Journalism: Truth or Dare*. (London: Oxford University Press).

Harlow, Barbara. 1989. *Narrative in Prison: Stories from the Palestinian Intifada*. Modern Fiction Studies 35:29–46.

Harris, Diana. 2006. *Music Education and Muslims*. (Stoke-on-Trent: Trentham Books).

Harris, A., Wyn, J., & Younes, S. 2007. Young People and Citizenship: An Everyday Perspective, *Youth Studies Australia*, 26(3) 18–26.

Harvey, David. 1989. *The Conditions of Postmodernity* (Oxford: Blackwell).

Hasan, M. 1997. *Children and Youth: A Situational Analysis*. (Study commissioned by the General Union of Voluntary Societies, Amman, Jordan).

Haugbolle, S. 2005. "Public and Private Memory of the Lebanese Civil War," *Comparative Studies of South Asia, Africa and the Middle East*, 25 (1):191–203.

— 2007. "Memory as Representation and Memory as Idiom". In Youssef Choueiri (ed.) *Breaking the Cycle: Civil Wars in Lebanon* (London: Stacey International): 121–33.

Hayes, Louis M. 1905. *Reminiscences of Manchester and Some of Its Local Surroundings from the Year 1840*: pp. 349. (Sherratt & Hughes: London: Manchester).

Hays, S. 1999. "Generation X and the Art of the Reward," *Workforce*, November. 45–8.

Hebdige, D. 1979. *Subculture. The Meaning of Style*, (London: Methuen).

— 1987. *Cut 'N' Mix: Culture, Identity and Caribbean Music*. (London: Methuen).

Heble, Ajay. 2000. *Landing on the Wrong Note: jazz, dissonance, and critical perspective*. (New York: Routledge).

Hegland, Mary. 1983. "Ritual & Revolution in Iran." In *Culture and Political Change*, Political Anthropology Series, 2. Myron J. Aronoff, ed. pp. 75–100. (New Brunswick, NJ: Transaction Books).

Heiman, R. 2001. *Childhood*, (Sage: London).

Heinsohn, Gunnar. 2006. "Demography and War", A City Defense Forum Round Table.

— 2007. "Islamism and War: The Demographics of Rage", *Open Democracy*.

Henderson, S., Holland, J., McGrellis, S., Sharpe, S., Thomson, R with Grigoriou, T. 2007. *Inventing Adulthoods, A Biographical Approach to Youth Transitions*, (Sage: London).

Henfling, M. 2007. "'Moslims Hoeven Niet te Beledigen'. Drie Amerikaanse Stand-up Comedians doen met 'Allah made me funny'- tournee Nederland aan," *de Volkskrant*, November 12, 2007.

Herzfeld, Michael. 1985. *The Poetics of Manhood: Contest and Identity in a Cretan Mountain Village*. (Princeton, NJ: Princeton University Press).

Hiltermann, Joost. 1991. *Behind the Uprising*. (Princeton, NJ: Princeton University Press).

Hirsch, J. S. 2003. *A Courtship after Marriage: Sexuality and Love in Mexican Transnational Families*. (Berkeley: University of California Press).

Hirsch, Marianne. 1997. *Family Frames: Photography, Narrative and Postmemory*. (Cambridge: Harvard University Press).

— 1998. "Past Lives: Postmemories in Exile." In S. R. Suliman (ed.) *Exile and Creativity: Signposts, Travellers, Outsiders, Backward Glances* (Durham, NC & London: Duke University Press): 418–46.

— 2008. "The Generation of Postmemory." *Poetics Today*, 29, pp: 103–28.

Hirschkind, Charles. 2001. "The Ethics of Listening: Cassette-Sermon Audition in Contemporary Egypt." *American Ethnologist*, 28, 3, 623–49.

Hirszowicz, Lukasz. 1966. *The Third Reich and the Arab East* (Toronto:): 14, 18–9.

Holland, Dorothy & Jean Lave (eds.). 2001. *History in Person: Enduring Struggles, Contentious Practice, Intimate Identities*. Santa Fe, New Mexico: School of American Research Press.

Holland, Dorothy, William Lachicotte Jr., Debra Skinner & Carole Cain (eds.). 1998. *Identity and Agency in Cultural Worlds*. Cambridge, Massachusetts: Harvard University Press.

Hoodfar, Homa. 1997. *Between Marriage and the Market: Intimate Politics and Survival in Cairo*. (Berkeley: University of California Press).

Hooks, B. 1989. *Talking back: Thinking feminist, Thinking Black*. (Boston: South End press).

— 1990. *Yearning: Race, Gender and Cultural Politics*. (Boston: South End Press).

— 2009. *Belonging: A Culture of Place*. (New York: Routledge).

Hourani, Albert. 1988. "Visions of Lebanon", in Barakat, Halim (ed.), *Toward a Viable Lebanon*. London, Croom Helm.

Hourcade, B. & S.M. Habibi. 2007. *Atlas of Tehran Metropolis*. (Tehran Geographic Information Center).

Howe, N. and Strauss, W. 2000. *Millennials Rising : The Next Great Generation*. (New York: Vintage Books).

Huntington, Samuel. 1996. *The Clash of Civilizations and the Remaking of World Order*. (New York).

Huq, R. 2006. *Beyond Subculture: Pop, Youth and Identity in a Postcolonial World*, (London: Routledge).

Ibrahim, Barbara et. al. 2000. *Transitions to Adulthood: A National Survey of Egyptian Adolescents*. 2nd Edition. (The Population Council, New York).

"Iran Sets up 'Love Fund' with Huge Oil Revenues." 2005. *IranMania*: September 01. http://www.iranmania.com/News/ArticleView/Default.asp?NewsCode=35049&NewsKind=Current+Affairs

Jaafar, A. 2004. "Film: Domestic Battlefields: Danielle Arbid on Maarek Hob," *Bidoun* (online edition), 2 (fall), www.bidoun.com.

Jameson, Frederic. 1998. *The Cultures of Globalization* (Durham: Duke University Press).

Jankowski, James. 1975. *Egypt's Young Rebels: "Young Egypt": 1933–1952* (Stanford: Hoover Institution Press): 58–60.

Jasper, James M. 1997. *The Art of Moral Protest, Culture, Biography, and Creativity in Social Movements*. Chicago: The University of Chicago Press.

Jeal, Timothy. 1991. *Baden-Powell* (London): 543–53.

Joseph, S. and A. Najmabadi. 2005. *Encyclopedia of Women and Islamic Cultures*. (Brill Academic Publishers).

Jurkiewicz, C. 2000. "Generation X and the public employee," *Public Personnel Management*, 29(1), 5574.

Kabbani, Nader and Kothari, Ekta. 2005. "Youth Employment in the MENA Region: A Situational Assessment." Social Protection Discussion Paper. No. 0534. September. The World Bank. Washington, D. C.

Kamler, B. 2001. *Relocating the Personal* (Albany: State University of New York).

Karam, E. G, Mneimneh, H. Dimassi, J. A. Fayyad, A. N. Karam et al., 2008. "Lifetime Prevalence of Mental Disorders in Lebanon: First onset, Treatment, and Exposure to war." In *PLOS Med* 5: e61.

Kasmir, S. 2002. "'More Basque Than You': Class, Youth and Identity in an Industrial Basque Town," *Identities: Global Studies in Culture and Power, 9*: 39–68.

Kassir, Samir. 2003. *Histoire de Beyrouth*. Beirut: Fayard.

Kater, Michael H. 2004. *Hitler Youth* (Cambridge MA: Harvard University Press).

Kaya, A. 2002. "Aesthetics of Diaspora: Contemporary Minstrels in Turkish Berlin," *Journal of Ethnic and Migration Studies*, vol. 28 (1): pp. 43–62.

Keddie, N. 2008. Personal communication.

Keesing, Roger. 1985. "Kwaio Women Speak: The Micropolitics of Autobiography in a Solomon Island Society." *American Anthropologist* 87: 27–39.

Keith, Michael & Steve Pile (eds.) 1993. *Place and the Politics of Identity*. London: Routledge.

Kelly, P. 2006. "The Entrepreneurial Self and 'Youth at-Risk': Exploring the Horizons of Identity in the Twenty-first Century," *Journal of Youth Studies*, 9(1) 17–32.

Kertzer, David. 1988. *Ritual, Politics, and Power*. (New Haven, CT: Yale University Press).

Keyes, Cheryl L. 2002. *Rap Music and Street Consciousness*. (Chicago: University of Illinois Press).

Khalaf, Roseanne Saad. 2009. "Youthful Voices in Post-War Lebanon." *The Middle East Journal* Winter, no. 1, 63: 49–68.

Khalaf, S. 1982. "On the Demoralization of Public Life in Lebanon: Some Impassioned Reflections," *Studies in Comparative International Development*, spring: 49–72.

— 1993b. "Culture, Collective Memory & the Rehabilitation of Civility," in D. Collines (ed). *Peace for Lebanon* (Boulder, Co.: Lynne Rienner).

— 2001. *Cultural Resistance: global and local encounters in the Middle East*. (London: Saqi).

— 2002. *Civil and Uncivil Violence in Lebanon*. (New York: Columbia University Press).

— 2006. *Heart of Beirut: Reclaiming the Bourj* (London: Saqi Books).

Khalaf, Samir & Philip S. Khoury (eds.). 1993. *Recovering Beirut: Urban Design and Post-War Reconstruction.* Leiden: E.J. Brill.

Khalifa, Ayman. 1995. "The Withering Youths of Egypt," *Ru'ya*, no. 7. pp. 6–10.

Khosravi, Shahram. 2008. *Young and Defiant in Tehran.* (Philadelphia: University of Pennsylvania Press).

Khoury, Philip. 1983. *Urban Notables and Arab Nationalism: The Politics of Damascus, 1860–1920* (Cambridge: Cambridge University Press): 31–2.

Kian-Thiebaut, Azadeh. 2002. "Political Impacts of Iranian Youth's Individuation: How Family Matters," paper presented at MESA, Washington, D.C.

Koning, M. De. 2005. "'Dit is Geen Poep Wat ik Praat'. De Hirsi Ali Diss Nader Belicht," *ZemZem: Tijdschrift over het Midden-Oosten, Noord Afrika en Islam*, vol.1: pp. 36–41.

— 2008. *Zoeken naar een "zuivere" Islam. Geloofsbeleving en identiteitsvorming van jonge Marokkaans Nederlandse moslims,* (Amsterdam: Bert Bakker).

Koon, Tracy H. 1985. *Believe, Obey, Fight: Political Socialization of Youth in Fascist Italy, 1922–1943* (London: Chapel Hill,): 87–100.

Landau, Carolyn. "Moroccans, Music and Identity: Exploring the Relationship between Ethnomusicology Sound Archives and Diaspora Communities." PhD thesis. Music Department, City University, London, forthcoming.

Laqueur, Walter. 1962. *Young Germany: A History of the German Youth Movement* (New York: Transaction, 1962/1984).

Lateef, N. 1997. *Women of Lebanon: Interviews with Champions for Peace.* (Jefferson and London: McFarland & Co. Inc., Publishers).

Leccardi, C. and Ruspini, E., (Eds), (2006), *New Youth? Young People, Generations and Family Life* (Aldershot: Ashgate).

Lesko, N. 1996. "Denaturalizing Adolescence, the Politics of Contemporary Representations," *Youth & Society*, 28(2), pp. 139–61.

Lewis, Bernard. 1990. "The Roots of Muslim Rage", *The Atlantic Monthly*.

Lewis, Brenda Ralph. 2000. *Hitler Youth: The Hitlerjugend in War and Peace* (Staplehurst: Spellmount)

Lewis, Mark. 1990. *Beyond Innocence and Redemption: Confronting the Holocaust and Israeli Power.* (San Francisco: Harper & Row Publishers).

Lewis, Philip. 2007. *Young, British and Muslim.* (London: Continuum).

Light, Alan. 2004. "About a Salary or Reality? Rap's Recurrent Conflict." In Murray Forman and Mark Anthony Neal. Eds. *That's the Joint!: The Hip-Hop Studies Reader.* (New York: Routledge).

Lipsitz, George. 1990. *Time Passages: collective memory and American popular culture.* (Minneapolis: University of Minnesota Press).

— 1994. *Dangerous Crossroads: Popular Music, Postmodernism and the Poetics of Race.* (London: Verso).

Maffesoli, Michael. 1996. *The Time of the Tribes: the decline of individualism in mass society.* (London: Sage).

Mahdavi, Pardis. 2008. *Passionate Uprising: Iran's Sexual Revolution* (Palo Alto, California: Stanford University Press).

— 2009. "Who Will Catch Me If I Fall? Health and the Infrastructure of Risk in Post Revolution Iran" in Gheissari, A. (ed) *Contemporary Iran.* (Oxford University Press).

Mahmood, Saba. 2005. *Politics of Piety: The Islamic Revival and the Feminist Subject.* (Princeton: Princeton University Press).

Makdisi, Saree. 2006. "Beirut, a City without History? In Ussama Makdisi & Paul A. Silverstein (eds.) *Memory and Violence in the Middle East and North Africa* (Bloomington: Indiana University Press): 201–14.

Manesh-Erfan, Jalil. 1996. *Iran*, 19 Aban 1375.

Mannheim, Karl. 1952. "The Problem of Generations." In *Essays on the Sociology of Knowledge, 276–320.* Paul Kecskemeti (ed.) (New York: Oxford University Press).

Manning, B. and R. Ryan. 2004. *Youth and Citizenship Final Report.* (Hobart: National Youth Affairs Research Scheme).

Marcuse, Herbert. 1969. "On Revolution," in *Student Power: Problems, Diagnoses, Action,* (ed.) Alexander Cockburn and Robin Blackburn (London: Penguin Books): 367–72.

Mardam Bey, Salma. 1994. *La Syrie et la France: Bilan d'une équivoque* (1939–1945) (Paris: L'Harmattan).

Marranci, G. 2000. "Le raï aujourd'hui. Entre métissage musical et world music moderne" *Cahiers de Musiques Traditionelles*, vol. 13: pp. 139–49.

— 2000a. "A Complex Identity and its Musical Representation: Beurs and raï Music in Paris," *Journal of Musical Anthropology of the Mediterranean*, vol. 5.

— 2003. "Pop-raï: from a 'Local' Tradition to Globalization," in Plastino, G (ed) *Mediterranean Mosaic: Popular Music and Global Sounds*, (New York: Routledge), pp: 101–21.

Martin, Emily. 1987. *The Woman in the Body: A Cultural Analysis of Reproduction*. (Boston: Beacon Press.

Martin, P. 2004. "Culture, Subculture and Social Organization," in Bennett, A. and Kahn-Harris, K. (eds), *After Subculture. Critial Studies in Contemporary Youth Culture*, (Houndmills: Palgrave Macmillan).

Mayer, Farhana Ed. 1996. *Much Ado About Music*: Association of Muslim Researchers.

McDonald, K. 2006. *Global Movements: Action and Culture*, (Blackwell, Malden).

McDowell, David. 1989. *Palestine and Israel: The Uprising and Beyond*. (Berkeley: University of California Press).

Mcmurray, D. & Swedenburg, T. (1991) "Raï Tide Rising," *Middle East Report*, vol. 169 (March–April): pp. 39–42.

McRobbie, A. 1999. *In the Culture Society. Art, Fashion and Popular Music*, (London: Routledge).

"Measuring Up 2008: The National Report Card on Higher Education." www.highereducation.org (Visited 11 December 2008).

Mensik, J. 2007. "A view on Generational Differences from a Generation X Leader," *JONA*, 37(11), 483–84.

Merriam, Alan P. 1968. *The Anthropology of Music*: [S.l.] : Northwestern U.Pr.

Midhat, Fuad. 2001. "Youth Centers without Youths," *Sawt ul-Azhar*: pp. 2.

Milbourne, L., Macrae, S. and Maguire, M. 2003. "Collaborative Solutions of New Policy Problems: Exploring Multi-agency Partnerships in Education and Health Work," *Journal of Education Policy*, vol. 18, no.1. pp. 19–35.

Mills, C.W. 1959. *The Sociological Imagination* (Oxford University Press).

Minh-ha, Trinh T. 1991. *When the Moon Waxes Red: representation, gender and cultural politics.* (New York: Routledge).

Minio-Paluello, L. 1964. *Education in Fascist Italy* (London: Oxford University Press,): 37.

Ministry of Economy and Statistics-Census Data, 1999. Available from: http://www.cdsi [Accessed 3 August 2008].

Mir-Hosseini, Ziba. 1999. *Islam and Gender: The Religious Debate in Contemporary Iran*. (Princeton: Princeton University Press).

— 1993. *Marriage on Trial: A Study of Islamic Family Law Iran and Morocco Compared*. (London: I.B. Tauris).

Mische, Ann. 2003. "Cross-talk in Movements: Reconceiving the Culture-Network Link", in Diani, Mario & Doug McAdam (eds.), *Social Movements and Networks: Relational Approaches to Collective Action*. Oxford: Oxford University Press.

Mitchell, T. (ed) 2001. *Global Noise. Rap and Hiphop Outside the USA*, (Middletown: Wesleyan University Press).

Mitterauer, M. 1993. *A History of Youth*, transl. Graeme Dunphy, (Oxford: Blackwell).

Mizen, P. 2004. *The Changing State of Youth*, (New York: Palgrave).

Moller, Herbert. 1968. "Youth as a Force in the Modern World", *Comparative Studies in Society and History*.

Moors, Annelies & Tarlo, Emma. 2007. "Introduction". *Fashion Theory*, 11 (2/3): 133–42.

Muawwad, J. 2008. Saudi Arabia's Bold Bet on New Riches. *International Herald Tribune*, 20, January.

Nabawi, Morteza. 2001. *Resalat*, October 27.

Naficy, H. 1995. "Iranian Cinema Under the Islamic Republic" in *American Anthropologist*, vol. 97 no. 3.

Naguib, Rime. 2002. "Egyptian Youth: A Tentative Study," term paper, American University of Cairo.

Nantet, Jacques. 1986. *Pierre Gemayel* (Paris: J. C. Lattes,): 33–5.

Naqqāsh & Khalīfa, 1927. *Al-Ḥaraka*, 37; *Al-Kashshāf (The Scout)* 1.2: 110.

Nasrawi, Seif. 2002. "An Ethnography of Cairo's Metro," (American University in Cairo).

National Archives and Records Administration, Washington DC, PF84/Lebanon/6, illegible (Aleppo) to Theodore Marriner (Beriut), 14 Oct., 1936.

Neimark, Marilyn. 1992. American Jews and Palestine: The Impact of the Gulf War. *Middle East Report* 175:19–23.

Nettl, Bruno. 1983. *Study of Ethnomusicology : Twenty-Nine Issues and Concepts.* (Urbana: Illinois U.P).

— 2009. "Music: Ii. The Concept in a Variety of Cultures: 3. Iran and the Middle East." In *Grove Music Online.* (Oxford: Oxford Music Online).

Newman, David. 2007. *Sociology Exploring the architecture of Everyday Life* (Los Angeles: Pine forge Press).

Nicosia, Francis. 1980. "Arab Nationalism and National Socialist Germany, 1933–1939: Ideological and Strategic Incompatibility," *International Journal of Middle East Studies*, 12, 3: 356–67.

Nooshin, Laudan. 2009-05-05.

Nordbruch, Goetz. 2009. *Nazism in Syria and Lebanon: The Ambivalence of the German Option, 1933–1945* (London: Routledge).

Norton, Augustus Richard. 1987. *Amal and the Shi'a: Struggle for the Soul of Lebanon.* (Austin: University of Texas Press).

— 2007. *Hezbollah.* (Princeton: Princeton University Press).

Nuwayed Al-Hout, Bayan. 2004. *Sabra and Shatila, September 1982.* (London: Pluto Press).

Okaz, 2009. January 25.

Ortner, S. 1998. "Generation X: Anthropology in a Media-Saturated World," *Cultural Anthropology*, 13(3) 414–440.

Outram, Dorinda. 1989. *The Body and the French Revolution: Sex, Class and Political Culture.* (New Haven, CT: Yale University Press).

O'Zoux, M. 1948. "Les insignes et saluts de la jeunesse en Syrie et au Liban," *Entretiens sur l'évolution des pays de civilisation arabe*, vol. 2 (Paris, 1938): 96–104.

Palestine Human Rights & Information Campaign. 1990. Palestine Human Rights and Information Campaign 3:1 3. Human Rights Update.

Peleikis, A. 2001. "Shifting Identities, Reconstructing Boundaries. The Case of a Multi-Confessional Locality in Post-war Lebanon," *Die Welt des Islams*, 41 (3):400–29.

Pennycook, Alistair and Mitchell, Tony. 2009. "Hip Hop as Dusty Foot Philosophy: Engaging Locality." In H. Samy Alim, Awad Ibrahim and Alastair Pennycook. Eds. *Global Linguistic Flows: hip hop cultures, youth identities and the politics of language.* (New York: Routledge).

Peretz, Don. 1990. *Intifada: The Palestinian Uprising.* (Boulder, CO: Westview Press).

Peteet, Julie. 1987. "Socio-Political Integration and Conflict Resolution in a Palestinian Refugee Camp." *Journal of Palestine Studies* 16(2): 29–44.

— 1991. *Gender in Crisis: Women and the Palestinian Resistance Movement.* (New York: Columbia University Press).

Peterson, Scott. 1997. "Ecstasy in Iran, Agony for its Clerics," in *Christian Science Monitor*, December 5.

Phalet, K. & Ter Wal, J. (eds) 2004. *Moslim in Nederland (2004) Een onderzoek naar de religieuze betrokkenheid van Turken en Marokkanen* (samenvatting onderzoeksrapport 2004/9), (Den Haag: Sociaal en Cultureel Planbureau).

— 2004a. *Moslim in Nederland. De publieke Discussie over de Islam in Nederland: Een Analyse van artikelen in de Volkskrant 1998–2002*, (Den Haag: Sociaal en Cultureel Planbureau/ ERCOMER – ICS/ University of Utrecht).

Picard, Elizabeth. 2002. *Lebanon. A Shattered Country: Myths and Realities of the Wars in Lebanon*, revised ed., tr. Franklin Philip. New York, Holmes & Meier.

Pinto, P., 2007. "Pilgrimage, Commodities, & Religious Objectification: The Making of Transnational Shiism between Iran and Syria." *Comparative Studies of South Asia Africa and the Middle East*, 27 (1): 109–25.

Popp, M. 2004. *Hip-hop, Islam and Islamic Rap: Hip-Hop as a Tool in Identity Politics for Muslims*, (Amsterdam: Amsterdam University) (unpublished paper).

— 1987. "Power, Persuasion, and Language: A Critique of the Segmentary Model in the Middle East." *International journal of Middle East Studies* 19: 77–102.

Qotbi, Mansour. 2000. "Causeless Rebellion in the Land of Iran." *Iran Javan,* no. 166, Mehr 1379.

Questscope. 1995. "Urban Community Development with a Focus on the Status of Children in Exceptionally Difficult Circumstance. Phase One. Community Results and Program Directions." (unpublished report to UNICEF JORDAN).

Racy, A. J. 2003. *Making Music in the Arab World: The Culture and Artistry of Tarab.* (Cambridge: Cambridge University Press).

Rahman, Samia. 2006. "The Biggest Star in the Middle East Is a Brit." *The Guardian.*

Ramadan, Tariq. 2001. *Islam, the West and the Challenges of Modernity.* (Leicester: Islamic Foundation).

— 2004. *Western Muslims and the Future of Islam.* (New York ; Oxford: Oxford University Press).

Rashad, Hoda, Osman, Magued, and Roudi-Fahimi, Farzaneh. 2005 "Marriage in the Arab World" Population Reference Bureau. Washington, D.C. December. http://www.prb.org/pdfo5/MarriageInArabWorld_Eng.pdf. (January 13, 2007)

Reynolds, Simon. 1990. *Blissed Out: The Raptures of Rock.* (London: Serpents Tail).

Rose, N. 1999. "Inventiveness in politics," *Economy and Society,* vol. 28, no. 3, pp. 467–93.

Rose, Tricia. 1994. *Black Noise: rap music and black culture in contemporary America.* (Middletown: Wesleyan University Press).

Rosen, Lawrence. 1984. *Bargaining for Reality: The Construction of Social Relations in a Muslim Community.* (Chicago: University of Chicago Press).

Rosenthal, Michael. 1986. *The Character Factory: Baden-Powell and the Origins of the Boy Scout* (London: Collins), Ch.7.

Rowe, Peter & Hashim Sarkis. 1998. Projecting Beirut: Episodes in the Construction and Reconstruction of a Modern City. Munich: Prestel.

Rudolph, Suzanne Hueber. 2005. "The Imperialism of Categories: Situating Knowledge in a Globalizing World." *Perspectives on Politics,* 3: 5–14.

Rugh, Andrea. 1984. *Family in Contemporary Egypt.* (New York: Syracuse University Press).

Rushdie, Salman. 2006. *Shalimar the clown,* (London).

Safa, Ousama. 2006. "Lebanon Springs Forward." *Journal of Democracy,* 17 pp: 22–37.

Saghiyeh, Hazem. 1995. *Thaqafat al Khoumeinieh: Mowqef min al-Istishraq 'am Harb Ala Tayf.* "Khomeinist Cultures: A Form of Orientalism or a War against a Ghost?" (Beirut: Dar Al-Jadid).

Sahlins, Marshall. 1981. *Historical Metaphors and Mythical Realities: Structure in the Early History of the Sandwich Islands Kingdom.* (Ann Arbor: University of Michigan Press).

Salehi-Isfahani, Djavad. 2005. "Human Resources in Iran: Potentials and Challenges," *Iranian Studies* 38 (March): 117–47.

Salibi, Kamal S. 1988. *A House of Many Mansions: The History of Lebanon Reconsidered.* London: I.B. Tauris.

Salvatore, Armando & Le Vine, Mark. 2005. *Religion, Social Practice & Contested Hegemonies: Reconstructing the Public Sphere in Muslim Majority Societies.* (New York: Palgrave Macmillan).

Samii, Bill. 2005. "Iran Youth Movements Has Untapped Potential," in *Radio Free Europe,* (April 13).

Scarry, E. 1985. *The Body in Pain.* (New York: Oxford University Press).

Schiefellin, Edward. 1985. "Performance and the Cultural Construction of Reality." *American Ethnologist* 12: 707–24.

Schielke, S. 2006. "Snacks and Saints: Mawlid Festivals and the Politics of Festivity, Piety and Modernity in Contemporary Egypt," unpublished PhD thesis, (University of Amsterdam).

— 2009. "Being good in Ramadan: Ambivalence, Fragmentation and the Moral Self in the Lives of Young Egyptians." *Journal of the Royal Anthropological Institute.* Special Issue 2009: S24–S40.

Schneider, B. and Stevenson, D. 1999. *The Ambitious Generation: America's Teenagers: Motivated but Directionless.* (New Haven: Yale University Press).

Schram, Sanford F. 2004. "Beyond Paradigm: Resisting the Assimilation of Phronetic Social Science." *Politics and Society,* vol. 32, no. 3, September (417–33).

Schuyler, P. D. 1974. "Al-Milhun: The Fusion of Folk and Art Traditions in a Moroccan Song Form." MA Thesis, (University of Washington).

— 1979a. "A Repertory of Ideas: The Music of the 'Rwais,' Berber Professional Musicians from Southwestern Morocco." PhD Thesis, (University of Washington).

— 1979b. "Rwais and Ahwash: Opposing Tendencies in Moroccan Berber Music and Society." *World of Music* 11, no. 1: 65–80 [http://www.azawan.com/tachelhit/schuyler/art.htm]

— 1981. "Music and Meaning among the Gnawa Religious Brotherhood in Morocco." *World of Music* 23, no. 1: 3–13.

— 1984. "Berber Professional Musicians in Performance." In *Performance Practice: Ethnomusicological Perspectives*, edited by G. Behague, 91–148. (Westport, CT: Greenwood Press).

— 1985. "Rwais and the Zawia: Professional Musicians and the Rural Religious Elite in Southwestern Morocco." *Asian Music* 17, no. 1 : 114–31.

— 1990. "Hearts and Minds: Three Attitudes toward Performance Practice and Music Theory in the Yemen Arab Republic." *Ethnomusicology* 31, no. 1: 1–18.

— 1993. "A Folk Revival in Morocco." In *Everyday Life in the Muslim Middle East* edited by Donna Lee Bowen and Evelyn A. Early, 287–93. (Bloomington: Indiana UP).

— 1997. "Review of Gnawa Leila, 5 Cds " *Music and Anthropology online* 2: http://www.fondazionel-evi.org/ma/index/ma_ind.htm.

— 2000. "Joujouka/Jajouka/Zahjoukah: Moroccan Music and Euro-American Imagination." In *Mass Mediations : New Approaches to Popular Culture in the Middle East and Beyond*, edited by Walter Armbrust, 146–60. (Berkeley ; London: University of California Press).

— 2002. "Malhun: Colloquial Song in Morocco." In *Garland Encyclopedia of Music: The Middle East*, edited by V. Danielson, S. Marcus and D. Reynolds. (New York: Garland Publishing Inc.).

— 2009. "Moroccan Andalusian Music." *The World of Music* 10, no. 1 (1978): 33–46.

— "Morocco." In *Grove Music Online*: Oxford Music Online.

Scott, James. 1990. *Domination and the Arts of Resistance: Hidden Transcripts*. (New Haven, CT: Yale University Press).

Seidman, S. 2009. "Streets of Beirut: Self and the Encounter with the Other." (Unpublished paper).

Serajzadeh, Hossein Seyed. 1999. "Non-Attending Believers: Religiosity of Iranian Youth and its Implications for Secularization Theory," a paper presented at the World Congress of Sociology, Montreal.

Shahine, Gihan. 1998. "The Double Bind" *Al Ahram Weekly* 397 (1–7 October).

Shalabi, Muhammad. 2003. "Egypt's Youth Centers: Between Ideals and Reality," (American University in Cairo).

Shammas, Anton. 1988. "A Stone's Throw." *New York Review of Books*, March 31:10.

Shapiro, Samantha. 2009. "Revolution, Facebook-Style." *New York Times* (January 25).

Sharara, W. 2007. *The Days of Ordinary Killing. 'Ayyan al Qatl al' Adi* (Beirut: Dar an-Nahar).

Sheahan, P. 2005. *Generation Y: Thriving and Surviving with Generation Y at Work*, (Melbourne: Hardie Grant).

Sibai, T., Tome, R.A., Beydoun, H.A., Kanaan, N., & Sibai, A.M. 2009. "Violent Behavior among Adolescents in Post-war Lebanon: The Role of Personal Factors and Correlation with other Problem Behaivors." *Journal of Public Health Medicine*, 31: 39–46.

Silver, Hilary and Miller, S. M. 2003. "Social Exclusion: The European Approach to Social Disadvantage." *Indicators* 2 (Spring): 5–21. http://www.brown.edu/Departments/Sociology/faculty/hsilver/documents/silver_and_miller-european_approach_to_social_disadvantage.pdf. (February 12, 2007).

Singerman, Diane. 1995. *Avenues of Participation: Family, Politics, and Networks in Urban Quarters of Cairo*. (Princeton: Princeton University Press).

Singerman, Diane and Ibrahim, Barbara. 2001. "The Cost of Marriage in Egypt: A Hidden Variable in the New Arab Demography and Poverty Research." Special Edition on "The New Arab Family," Nick Hopkins. ed., *Cairo Papers in the Social Sciences*, 24 (Spring): 80–116.

Slobin, Mark. 1994. "Music in Diaspora: The View from Euro-America." *Diaspora* 3, no. 3 : 243–51.

Solomon, T. 2005. "'Living Underground is Tough': Authenticity and Locality in the Hip-Hop Community in Istanbul, Turkey," *Popular Music*, vol. 24 (1): pp.1–20.

Sonbol, Amira El Azhary, ed. 1996. *Women, the Family, and Divorce Laws in Islamic History*. (Syracuse: Syracuse University Press).

Sontag, Susan. 2003. *Regarding the Pain of Others* (N.Y.: Farrar, Straus & Giroux).

Soja, Edward W. 1989. *Postmodern Geographies: The Reassertion of Space in Critical Social Theory.* London: Verso.

— 1996. *Thirdspace.* Oxford, Blackwell Publishing.

Soysal, L. 2001. "Diversity of Experience, Experience of Diversity. Turkish Migrant Youth Culture in Berlin," *Cultural Dynamics*, vol. 13 (1): pp. 5–28.

Starrett, G. 1995. "The Political Economy of Religious Commodities in Cairo." *American Anthropologist,* 97 (1): 51–68.

Stein, R. L. 2002. "Israeli Leisure, 'Palestinian Terror,' and The Question of Palestine (Again)," *Theory & Event*, 6 (3).

Stokes, Martin, ed. 1994. *Ethnicity, Identity and Music: The Musical Construction of Place.* (Oxford: Berg Publishers).

Swedenburg, T. 2001. "Arab 'World music' in the US," *Middle East Report*, vol. 31 (2): pp. 34–7.

— 2001a. "Islamic Hip-Hop Versus Islamophobia: Aki Nawaz, Natacha Atlas, Akhenaton," in: Mitchell, T. (ed), *Global Noise: Rap and Hip-Hop Outside the USA*, (Middletown: Wesleyan University Press).

— 2002. "The Post-September 11 Arab Wave in World Music," *Middle East Report*, vol. 32 (3): pp. 44–7.

— 2003. "Raï's Travels," *Middle East Association Bulletin*, vol. 36 (2): pp. 190–3.

— 2007. "Imagined Youths." *Middle East Report* 245 (winter): 4–11.

Szanton Blanc, C. 1994. *Urban Children in Distress: Global Predicaments and Innovative Strategies.* (Yverdon, Switzerland: Gordon and Breach Science Publishers).

Tapper, Nancy. 1991. *Bartered Brides: Politics, Gender, and Marriage in an Afghan Tribal Society.* (London: Cambridge University Press).

Tarrant, Mark, North, Adrian C., & Hargreaves, David J. 2002. "Youth Identity and Music." In *Musical Identities*, edited by Raymond A. R. MacDonald, David J. Hargreaves and Dorothy Miell, 134–50. (Oxford: Oxford University Press).

Taussig, Michael. 1987. *Shamanism, Colonialism, and the Wild Man: A Study in Terror and Healing.* (Chicago: University of Chicago Press).

Te Riele, K. 2006. "Youth 'At Risk': Further Marginalising the Marginalised?" *Journal of Education Policy*, 21(2) pp. 129–45.

Te Riele, K., and Wyn, J. 2005. "Transformations in Youth Transitions in Australia," Chapter 7 in N. Bagnall (Ed)., *Youth Transitions in a Globalised Marketplace*, (New York: Nova Science Publishers).

Theodoulou, Michael. 2001. "Iran's Culture War Intensifies," *Christian Science Monitor,* August 21.

Thompson, Edward P. 1978. *The Poverty of Theory and Other Essays.* (New York: Monthly Review Press).

Thornton, S. 1995. *Club Cultures. Music, Media and Subcultural Capital*, (Cambridge: Blackwell).

Tourné, Karine. 2003. "Getting Married in Egypt: Forms of Social Control and New Familial Architectures in Egypt." Unpublished paper delivered at the First Meeting on Youth and Societies in Europe and Around the Mediterranean, 22–4 October, Marseille: Centre Population et Développement. (In French).

Tse-tung, Mao. 1967. "The Orientation of the Youth Movement," in *Selected Works of Mao Tse-tung* (Peking: Foreign Languages Press, 1967), vol. 2 pp. 241–9.

Turner, Victor. 1977. *The Ritual Process: Structure and Anti-Structure.* (Ithaca, NY: Cornell University Press).

Twenge, J. M. 2006. *Generation Me.* (New York: Free Press).

Tyler, F. B. 1997. *Urban Settings, Youth Violence and Prosocial Communities.* Paper presented at Urban Childhood Conference, Trondheim, Norway, June 1997. (College Park: University of Maryland, Department of Psychology).

UNDP, 2003. Human Development Report: Kingdom of Saudi Arabia, http://hdr.undp.org/en/reports/ (Accessed 20 August 2008).

"United Arab Emirates." 2006. Forum on Countries and their Cultures. http://www.everyoneculture.com/To-Z/United-Arab-Emirates.html (14 February 2007).

Van de Port, M. 1998. *Gypsies, Wars and Other Instances of the Wild: Civilisation and its Discontents in a Serbian Town*. (Amsterdam: Amsterdam University Press).

Van Gennep, Arnold. 1961. *The Rites of Passage*. (Chicago: University of Chicago Press).

Varzi, Roxanne. 2006. *Warring Souls: Youth, Media and Martyrdom in Post-Revolution Iran*. (Durham, NC: Duke University Press).

Vigh, Henrik E. 2006. "Social Death and Violent Life Chances." In *Navigating Youth, Generating Adulthood: Social Becoming in an African Context*, 31–60. (eds.) C. Christiansen, M. Utas and H.E. Vigh. (Stockholm: Nordiska Afrikainstitutet, Uppsala).

— "Violence and Resistance in the Americas: 1990. The Legacy of Conquest." *Journal of Historical Sociology* 3: 209–24.

Virkki, Tuija. 2007. "Emotional Capital in Caring Work." In Hartel Charmine, Neal Ashkanasy and Wilfred Zerbe. Eds. *Functionality, Intentionality and Morality*. (Cambridge: Emerald Group Publishing).

Wade, Bonnie C. 2004. *Thinking Musically : Experiencing Music, Expressing Culture, Global Music Series*. (New York, N.Y.; Oxford: Oxford University Press).

Watenpaugh, Keith. 2002. "Steel Shirts, White Badges and the Last Qabaday: Fascism, Urban Violence and Civic Identity in Aleppo under French Rule," in Méouchy, Nadine (ed.), *France, Syrie et Liban*, 1918–1946 (French Institute).

— 2006. *Being Middle Class in the Modern Middle East: Revolution, Nationalism, Colonialism, and the Arab Middle Class* (Princeton).

Watkins, S. C. 2005. *Hip Hop Matters. Politics, Pop Culture, and the Struggle for the Soul of a Movement*, (Boston: Beacon Press).

White, Harrison. 1992. *Identity and Control*. Princeton, N.J.: Princeton University Press.

Wild, Stefan. 1985. "National Socialism in the Arab Near East between 1933 and 1939," *Die Welt des Islams*, 25: 131–7.

Williams, A, Coupland, J., Folwell, A., Sparks, L. 1997. "Talking about Generation X: Defining them as they define themselves," *Journal of Language and Social Psychology*, 16(3) 251–77.

Willis, Paul. 1977. *Learning to Labour: how working class kids get working class jobs*. (Farnborough Hampshire: Saxon House).

— 1990. *Common Culture: symbolic work at play in the everyday cultures of the young*. (Boulder: Westview Press).

Wise, Lindsay. 2006. "Meet Islam's Biggest Rock Star." *Time Magazine*.

Wooden, M. 1998. "The labour market for young Australians." In: Dusseldorp Skills Forum (Ed.). *Australia's youth: reality and risk*. (Sydney: Dusseldorp Skills Forum).

World Bank. 2002. "World Development Indicators." (Online, Washington, DC.)

Wright, J. & Burrows, L. 2004. "Being Healthy: The Discursive Construction of Health in New Zealand Children's Responses to the National Education Monitoring Project," *Discourse: Studies in the Cultural Politics of Education*, 25(2), pp. 11–30.

Wyn, J. 2007a. "Generation and Class: Young People's New, Diverse Patterns of Life and their Implications for Participation in Civic Society," *International Journal of Children's Rights*, 15: 1 – 16.

— 2007b. Learning to become somebody well: challenges for educational policy, *Australian Educational Researcher*, 34(3) 35-52.

— 2008. "New Youth Transitions in Education," in R. Bendit and M. Hahn-Bleibtreu (Eds.), *Youth and the Future. Processes of Social Inclusion and Patterns of Vulnerability in a Globalised World*. (Opladen & Barbara Budrich Publishers, Farmington Hills, USA).

— 2009. "Educating for Modernity," in A. Furlong (Ed), *Handbook on Youth and Young Adulthood: New Perspectives and Agendas*, (Routledge: London).

— 2009. *Youth Health and Welfare: the Cultural Politics of Education and Wellbeing*, (Oxford University Press: Melbourne).

Wyn, J. & Dwyer, P. 2000. "New Patterns of Youth Transition in Education." *International Social Science Journal*. 164: pp. 147–59.

Wyn, J., Smith, G., Stokes, H., Tyler, D., and Woodman, D. 2008. *Generations and Social Change: Negotiating Adulthood in the 21st Century*, Research Report 29, (Australian Youth Research Centre: Melbourne).

Wyn, J. & White, R. D. 1997. *Rethinking Youth* (London: Sage Publication).

Wyn, J. and Woodman, D. 2006. "Generation, Youth and Social Change in Australia." *Journal of Youth Studies,* 9(4), 495–514.

Yaghmaian, Behzad. 2002. *Social Change in Iran* (Stony Brook: State University of New York Press): 61–5.

Yahya, Maha. 1993. "Reconstituting Space: the aberration of the urban in Beirut." In Samir Khalaf and Philip Khoury. Eds. *Recovering Beirut: Urban Design and Post-War Reconstruction.* (Leiden: E.J Brill).

Yamani, Mai. 1996. *Feminism and Islam: Legal and Literary Perspectives.* (New York: New York University Press).

— 2000. *Changed Identities: The Challenge of the New Generation in Saudi Arabia* (London: Royal Institute of International Affairs)

— 2004. *Cradle of Islam: The Hijaz and the Quest for an Arabian Identity.* (London: I. B. Tauris).

— 2005. "The Limits of Political Reform in Saudi Arabia." In Birgitte Rahbek, ed. *Democratisation and the Middle East.* (Aarhus: Aarhus University Press).

— 2008. "Saudi Arabia's Media Mask." In Madawi Al-Rasheed, ed. *Kingdom Without Borders: Saudi Arabia's Political, Religious, and Media Frontiers.* (New York: Columbia University Press).

— 2008. "The Two Faces of Saudi Arabia." *Survival.* Vol. 50, no. 1. February–March, 144.

— 2009. "Saudi Shi'a Stand Up." *Project Syndicate.* March.

Zittrain, J. and Edelman, B. Documentation of Internet Filtering in Saudi Arabia. Berkman Center for Internet and Society. Harvard Law School. Available from: http://cyber.law.harvard.edu/filtering/saudiarabia/ (Accessed 18 July 2009).

al-Zubaydi, Umar. 2001. "Saudi Women To Attend Shura Council Debate on High Marriage Costs." *Arab News,* 31 December. [World Connection].

Acknowledgments

Editing a meaningful, coherent volume of disparate papers and conference proceedings can be a demanding, thankless task, particularly when it comes to safeguarding the distinctive quality of individual contributions. It is our hope that *Arab Youth* will prove well worth the effort.

As we were preparing the volume for publication, the startling events of the "Arab Spring" uprisings serendipitously started to unfold. The outrage, incited by the self-immolation of Muhammad Bouazizi in Tunisia (December 17, 2010), spread like wildfire to other parts of the region. Similar to Lebanon's 2005 Cedar Revolution, the uprisings have been largely homegrown and spontaneous, the participants fearless. But unlike the bloodless Cedar Revolution, the unarmed protesters continue to pay dearly, and in mounting numbers. In this respect, some chapters in *Arab Youth* are especially relevant because they provide timely evidence of non-belligerent forms of civil and popular mass mobilization employed by disgruntled youth.

Another key feature of the volume deserves noting: the comparatively young age of the authors and the "freshness" of their contributions. Overall, the texts are the outcome of recent ethnographic studies and field research by pre- and post-doctoral colleagues. Together they offer a relevant and engaging synthesis of grounded narratives and intuitive conceptual analysis.

Since these papers were originally delivered at a conference hosted by the Center for Behavioral Research at the American University of Beirut (April, 2009), we wish to extend our gratitude to the presenters and their subsequent efforts to comply with our editorial demands. Special thanks are due to Asef Bayat and Curtis N. Rhodes for allowing us to include articles we solicited from them.

We are also indebted to numerous colleagues and friends who kindly offered useful feedback. Special thanks to Yussef el-Khoury and Ghassan Moussawi for coordinating conference sessions and helping to locate bibliographical sources. We are grateful to Leila Jbara for her resourcefulness in organizing the conference, attending to the demands of participants, and preparing the final version for publication. And, as always, Saqi Books' André and Lynn Gaspard provided valuable insight and encouragement. Working with one's spouse can often be taxing but, thankfully, we managed to transform the experience into a creative, engaging venture. Now, we even look forward to other such prospects.

Both the conference and *Arab Youth* would not have been possible without the generous support of George Khoury & Co. Leila Khoury Tabet, Habib, Adib, and all AUB graduates made the gift in memory of their younger brother, Albert Khoury (BA, 1970). Albert, a gifted philosophy major and committed student activist was pursuing a PhD at Oxford University when his untimely death occurred at the age of twenty-two. In many ways, his courageous convictions, alongside the leadership necessary for mobilizing student protests in the late 1960s, made him a precursor to what we are witnessing today. Our book is dedicated to the enduring legacy Albert left behind.

Samir Khalaf and Roseanne Saad Khalaf

Index